LIVING
THEATER
A HISTORY

LIVING
THEATER
A HISTORY

Second Edition

Edwin Wilson
Graduate School and University Center
The City University of New York

Alvin Goldfarb
Dean of the College of Fine Arts
and Professor of Theater
Illinois State University

McGraw-Hill, Inc.
New York   St. Louis   San Francisco   Auckland
Bogotá   Caracas   Lisbon   London   Madrid   Mexico City   Milan
Montreal   New Delhi   San Juan   Singapore   Sydney   Tokyo   Toronto

LIVING THEATER: A HISTORY

This book is printed on acid-free paper.

1 2 3 4 5 6 7 8 9 0   AGM   AGM   9 0 9 8 7 6 5 4

ISBN 0-07-070733-2

This book was set in Caslon by Black Dot, Inc.
The editors were Judith R. Cornwell and Susan Gamer;
the designer was Joan E. O'Connor;
the production supervisor was Louise Karam.
The photo editor was Inge King.
New drawings were done by Fine Line Illustrations, Inc.
Arcata Graphics/Martinsburg was printer and binder.

Cover Photo
Engraving by Giacomo Franco (1566-1630?)
Victoria & Albert Museum, London

Library of Congress Cataloging-in-Publication Data

Wilson, Edwin.
    Living theater: a history / Edwin Wilson, Alvin Goldfarb.—2nd ed.
      p.   cm.
    Includes bibliographical references and index.
    ISBN 0-07-070733-2
    1. Theater—History.   I. Goldfarb, Alvin.   II. Title.
PN2101.W54   1994
792'.09—dc20   93-43475

ABOUT
THE
AUTHORS

Edwin Wilson, as teacher, author, and critic, has worked in many aspects of theater. Educated at Vanderbilt University, the University of Edinburgh, and Yale University, he received a Master of Fine Arts degree from the Yale Drama School, as well as the first Doctor of Fine Arts degree awarded by Yale. He has taught at Yale, Hofstra, Vanderbilt, Hunter College, and the CUNY Graduate Center. At Hunter he served as chair of the Department of Theater and Film and head of the graduate theater program. At CUNY he directs The Center for Advanced Study in Theater Arts (CASTA).

Since 1972 he has been the theater critic of the Wall Street Journal. He is the author of *The Theater Experience* and a coauthor, again with Alvin Goldfarb, of *Theater: The Lively Art,* also published by McGraw-Hill. He edited and wrote the introduction for *Shaw on Shakespeare.* He is a member of the New York Drama Critics' Circle, of which he served as president, and has been on the selection committees of the Pulitzer Prize in drama, the Tony Awards, and the Susan Smith Blackburn Prize. He has been president of the Theater Development Fund, and he is on the board of the John Golden Fund.

Alvin Goldfarb is Dean of the College of Fine Arts and Professor of Theater at Illinois State University. Dr. Goldfarb has been at Illinois State since 1977 and served as department chair of Theater from 1981 through 1988. He has published articles, notes, and reviews in many journals and scholarly anthologies, including *Theatre Journal, Performing Arts Journal, Journal of Popular Culture, Theatre Survey, Southern Theatre, Exchange, Tennessee Williams: A Tribute,* and *American Playwrights since 1945: A Guide to Scholarship, Criticism, and Performance.* Dr. Goldfarb provided the annotated bibliography of Holocaust dramatic literature for the anthology *Plays of the Holocaust.* He is coauthor of *Theater: The Lively Art* with Edwin Wilson. Dr. Goldfarb holds a Ph.D. in Theater History from the Graduate Center of the City University of New York.

To the Memory of Our Parents

CONTENTS

PREFACE

Anyone writing a theater history faces a daunting task. By definition, a *history* is a chronicle, a recapitulation of events from the past. It cannot, therefore, be a contemporary, spontaneous event. And yet, that is precisely what theater is. Theater exists not in the past but in the present. In fact, it exists *only* at the moment when it occurs. The essence of theater is an immediate exchange between the audience and what unfolds onstage: performances, words of a text, and visual effects of sets, lights, and costumes.

The first challenge of writing a theater history, therefore, is to bring theater from the past to life today. In *Living Theater* we have taken a number of steps to achieve this. First, the opening of each chapter is a vignette: a reenactment of what it was like to attend a performance of a particular play on a particular day. We try to take the reader back to the past and recreate the atmosphere and the experience of going to the theater in a different time and place.

We have also set each theatrical era in a broad social, political, and economic context. In each chapter, the section following the opening scene establishes the background which formed a framework for theater practitioners: playwrights, performers, managers, architects, and designers.

In describing the various aspects of theater, we have striven to give flesh and blood to each activity. As we discuss the artists who created theater, we provide details of their personal histories: interesting information that makes them come alive. To focus on these people as individuals, we have often highlighted them in the text—with their names, their dates, and photographs or drawings. Rather than being set apart in separate boxes, however, as was the case in the first edition, in this edition these biographical sections are an integral part of the text, so that the flow of *Living Theater* is not interrupted. There are also a number of additional profiles with a special emphasis on women and members of ethnic and racial minorities.

The teaching of theater history—like the teaching of most history—has undergone a radical transformation in recent years. For one thing, there are now varying approaches to how history should be viewed and taught—revisionism, feminism, deconstructionism, multiculturism, semiotics. We take account of these approaches in the Introduction and deal with them where appropriate elsewhere in the text.

A second way in which theater history has changed is that it is no longer seen as a monolithic, *ex cathedra* body of facts. New evidence is constantly being gathered, new discoveries are being made, and new insights are being offered. In the text, we provide the most recent discoveries and theories in every era; in addition, we include a section in each chapter called "Debates in Theater History," in which we focus on some point of disagreement among scholars and historians. This feature underscores for students the fact that no single view of history should be taken as immutable.

This edition of *Living Theater* can be considered a revision of our first edition, published over a decade ago. But it represents much more than a revision.

The latest information and scholarship have been incorporated. We have included discussions, for instance, of the excavations of the Globe and the Rose in London, and the important work of Prof. John J. Allen regarding the Corral del Principe in Madrid. Beyond this, however, we have reorganized the book to include such features as the "Debates" sections described above. Moreover, the entire text has been reworked, and we have added a significant amount of new material. Though the book is now more comprehensive than the first edition, it remains entirely appropriate for all undergraduate history courses.

As before, we have deliberately avoided an approach too frequently taken by theater historians—lengthy, undifferentiated lists of plays, playwrights, or performers, sometimes known as the *catalogue* approach. Instead, we separate the foreground from the background to give the student a clear perspective on the material covered. At the same time, we believe that most of the significant figures, trends, and developments have been covered, not only fully but, we hope, excitingly.

The important features that were well received in the first edition have been retained. One is an accessible writing style. We have attempted to present material clearly, completely, and simply, but in language that will engage and hold the reader. Also, the illustration program—interesting and informative photographs and drawings—is once again a key feature, with every illustration tied closely to the text. We have included—in a more attractive format than in the first edition—a series of "time lines" that relates important dates in theater to significant events in politics, economics, and the other arts. As appendixes, we have an informative glossary of theatrical terms and an up-to-date bibliography.

ACKNOWLEDGMENTS

Retained from the first edition is the excellent material provided by Prof. James V. Hatch on African American theater and by Prof. J. Thomas Rimer on Asian theater. Much of the original biographical information was developed by Dr. Rita Plotnicki; for African American figures, the original material was furnished by George C. Wolfe. Prof. J. K. Curry and Thom Thomas provided information on the many additional figures who have been given biographies in this edition, and Edward Dee compiled a comprehensive list of plays and playwrights for each period.

At Illinois State University, a number of people provided computer assistance, including scanning and software conversion. We would particularly like to thank Georgia Bennett, David Kuntz, Lorraine Loving, David Williams, and Owen Williams. Steve Meckstroth, Humanities Librarian at Illinois State, helped with many emergencies; and Dawn Flood, a theater graduate assistant, provided much help with research, the bibliography, and the glossary.

Prof. Alan Woods was especially helpful in offering advice on this edition; and we are grateful as well for the important contributions of the following people, who read and commented on the manuscript while it was being prepared: Stephen M. Archer, University of Missouri–Columbia; William Cameron, Washington and Jefferson College; Barbara Clayton, University of Wisconsin–Madison; James Coakley, Northwestern University; Timothy D. Connors, Central Michigan University; Glorianne Engel, Arizona State University; Peter Ferran, University of Michigan; Laurilyn J. Harris, Washington State University; Jack Hrkach, Ithaca College; William Lacey, Boston University; Dale Luciano, Southern Oregon State College; Annette McGregor, Purdue University; Charles Neel, West Virginia University; James Norwood, University of Minnesota; Susan E. Sanders, Northern Essex Community College; Michael Swanson, Franklin College; and Randy Wonzong, California State University–Chico.

Two people have worked with one or both of the authors on a total of ten books through the years. They are Joan O'Connor, our truly amazing and always talented designer; and Inge King, our unbelievable, enormously resourceful photo editor. For this edition a special word of thanks is due to Susan Gamer, our editing supervisor; her patience, skill, and commitment to the project far exceeded any limits the authors could expect. We also appreciate the helpful support of our other editors at McGraw-Hill: Niels Aaboe and Judith R. Cornwell.

Edwin Wilson
Alvin Goldfarb

LIVING
THEATER
A HISTORY

INTRODUCTION

Throughout the United States on any given day, audiences attend literally hundreds of theater events. They may see an outdoor production in a large open space such as the Shakespeare festival in Ashland, Oregon; or they may see an indoor production in a small theater like the Sullivan Street Playhouse in New York, where the musical *The Fantasticks* has been playing for many years. They may see a new play at one of the many regional professional theaters scattered across the country; or they may see a classic—a tragedy by Shakespeare or a comedy by Molière—at one of the hundreds of college or university theaters in the United States and Canada. They may see a lavish Broadway musical or a simple play set on a bare stage; they may see a formal, stylized kabuki production by a visiting Japanese troupe, or a modern American play set in a family kitchen.

The experiences audiences have at these events are almost as diverse as the events themselves. A young woman sees a production of Shakespeare's *Romeo*

BASIC ELEMENTS OF THEATER. Whenever and wherever theater occurs, certain elements are always present. Three of the most important are a performance space, an audience, and performers—the actual presence of the performers sets theater apart from films and television. These three elements are shown here at the Oregon Shakespeare Festival in Ashland, Oregon. The idea of a theater festival is as old as ancient Greece and continues in our own world today. *(Christopher Briscoe/Oregon Shakespeare Festival)*

and Juliet and is amazed at how this 400-year-old play illustrates the problems she is having with her parents, who are trying to prevent her from going out with a young man from a different background. A young man sees *The Miser* by Molière and identifies with the son in the play, whose father disinherits him and also tries to steal his girlfriend. An older couple see a revival of a musical comedy—filled with melodies they know—and are thrilled not only with the music but with the lavish scenery and costumes. Someone who works hard at a job sees a farce or a family comedy, presented just for fun, and enjoys escaping from problems at the end of the day. Someone who relishes mental puzzles and clever language sees a play by a writer like the British dramatist Tom Stoppard or the Italian Luigi Pirandello and takes pleasure in being challenged intellectually. A young African American sees a production of *A Raisin in the Sun* by Lorraine Hansberry and is caught up in the plight of its hero, who is struggling with his own identity and with the prejudice his black family must face. Many people who identify with specific groups see plays about problems of race, gender, or politics and feel a kinship with the characters portrayed onstage and the challenges those characters face.

The myriad of theatrical events and experiences open to us have their roots in the theater we have inherited—2,500 years of western theater and nearly 2,000 years of Asian theater. What are these many kinds of theater, and where did they come from? These are questions that *Living Theater* will address.

THEATER IN EVERYDAY LIFE

Before we begin our study of theater history, we should note that theater has a number of first cousins or near relations in everyday life. A wide range of human activities—both personal and communal—have a theatrical component. Among these are imitation, role playing, storytelling, many forms of popular entertainment, and numerous ceremonies and rituals.

Imitation, Role Playing, and Storytelling

Imitation is universal among children. A child sees an older person walking upstairs or opening a door, and learns to do the same by imitation. Role playing is universal among young and old alike, and it too has a theatrical component. People assume family roles—father, mother, grandfather, sister, brother—and also social roles, such as doctor, lawyer, salesperson, and social worker. In playing these roles, individuals adopt behaviors required by their society. Both imitation and role playing involve aspects of acting.

Another everyday activity with a theatrical element is storytelling, found in cultures throughout the world. Experienced storytellers are able to build suspense, evoke laughter or tears, and keep alive traditions of their culture. They often adopt the voices of characters in their stories; they take on the personalities of old men, young warriors, innocent maidens, or ghosts and other supernatural creatures. At these moments, storytellers become actors or actresses not unlike those we see onstage.

Thus, a child who imitates the gestures and voice patterns of older people, a judge who fills a prescribed role by acting a certain way toward people appearing in a courtroom, and a tribal elder who relates a story to a group gathered around a campfire—all of these are, in some sense, engaging in a form of acting.

Popular Entertainment

Certain types of group activities with a strong theatrical component are referred to as *popular entertainment.* They include singing, dancing, pantomime, juggling, magic, acrobatics, dramatic sketches, and even some kinds of storytelling. In almost every culture and every age, individuals or small groups with acrobatic, musical, or other skills have entertained others.

At times and in places where there is no organized theater, popular entertainment is frequently the chief means of perpetuating theatrical activity. A good illustration is the long period in European history from the end of the Roman empire in the fifth century after Christ until medieval theater took form almost 1,000 years later. There was no formal theater during these centuries; but groups of troubadours, jugglers, dancers, and mimes criss-crossed parts of Europe, entertaining at large manor houses—often during banquets and on other special occasions—and at public locations where people congregated, such as markets and religious centers.

Ceremonies and Rituals

THEATRICAL ASPECTS OF CEREMONIES AND RITUALS

Ceremonies and rituals are found in every human society, and they invariably have important theatrical elements. A *ceremony* is a formal religious or social occasion, usually led by a designated authority figure such as a priest or chief; examples would include a graduation, an inauguration, and a marriage ceremony. A *ritual* is the acting out of an established, prescribed procedure; rituals can range from a family event such as Thanksgiving or Christmas dinner to elaborate religious events—such as the Roman Catholic mass and the Jewish Yom Kippur service during the High Holy Days. Both ceremonies and rituals are observances that follow a prescribed course; thus they are closely related to each other.

People in the west are most familiar with the kinds of ceremonies and rituals just mentioned, but important examples are also found in nonwestern cultures, and these too have theatrical elements. Throughout central and western Africa, for instance, striking and imaginative costumes and masks are used in a variety of ceremonies. In a ceremony performed by the Guro tribe in the Ivory Coast, a dancer depicting an animal figure wears a large mask that combines antelope

THEATER AND RELIGION. Religious celebrations, such as this Greek Orthodox Good Friday procession, have many things in common with theater: music, ritual, a form of costumes, exchanges of dialogue. In fact, religious processions were actually a part of theater in ancient Greece. But a religious ceremony, which is intended for worship of a deity, is essentially different from theater, which is an end in itself—an art form that focuses on human concerns.

horns, an abstracted human face, and a large toothed beak. The costume consists of orange netting on the arms and bamboo reeds on the body. Other dancers wear masks and costumes appropriate to their roles.

The costumes and masks used for ceremonies in Africa are among the most beautiful to be found anywhere in the world, but theatrical elements are also found in the actions of the celebrants. Frequently, participants enact someone or something—a bird, an animal, or a spirit. In many cases, people who take part in these rituals believe that a performer is actually inhabited by the animal or spirit being portrayed, that the performer is transformed during the ceremony and *becomes* the figure represented. In addition, leaders and their assistants, as well as other celebrants who play key roles in a ceremony, have definite, assigned tasks and perform in a prescribed manner. Their actions thus bear a certain similarity to those of actresses or actors in dramatic presentations, who learn specific movements and repeat dialogue from a script. Also, rituals and ceremonies generally follow a set sequence of events: the same words and actions are repeated each time, often exactly reproducing previous presentations. This sequence of events corresponds to the "script" and dramatic structure of a theatrical production.

RITUAL THEATER OF AFRICA. All tribal ceremonies—whether in Africa, among North American Indians, or in southeast Asia—have a strong theatrical component. This includes masks, costumes, repeated phrases, music, and dancing. Shown here is a Kuba initiation rite in Africa.

An example: The Abydos ritual in ancient Egypt One ritual with theatrical elements was enacted in ancient Egypt for nearly 2,000 years, from around 2500 B.C. to around 550 B.C., at a holy place called Abydos. The evidence suggests that every year thousands of Egyptians made their way to Abydos to see this ceremony. The ritual drama performed at Abydos deals with the Egyptian god Osiris, who became the ruler of Egypt and married his sister Isis. Osiris's brother later became jealous of him and killed him, scattering the parts of his body throughout the Egyptian kingdom. Isis recovered the pieces and, helped by another god, brought Osiris back to life. Because his body had been mutilated, Osiris could not stay in this world, and so he was buried at Abydos. His spirit then ruled the dead in the underworld, where he became the most human of the Egyptian gods. The tale of Osiris is a virtually universal religious story, recurring in societies throughout the world: a story of betrayal, death, and life after death. We do not have an exact script of the Abydos ritual, but we do have a partial account by a performer named Ikhernofret, dating from about 1868 B.C. It is clear from his description that the ceremony had unmistakable theatrical elements: people played the roles of characters in the story and acted out episodes from the life of Osiris.

DANCE AND THEATER. These Native American dancers are performing in an intertribal ceremony in New Mexico. Many historians believe that theater orginated out of such dance performances, which have many theatrical elements. A primary difference, however, is that these dances were believed to be effacacious—to affect the environment and even the gods.

NONTHEATRICAL ASPECTS OF CEREMONIES AND RITUALS

Efficaciousness One noteworthy aspect of religious ceremonies and rituals sets them apart from dramatic presentations: religious ceremonies and rituals are *efficacious;* that is, they are intended to achieve direct results. Some of the best-known dances of Native Americans, for example, are carried out in the hope of bringing rain to water the crops. Throughout the world, ceremonies have been used to entreat the gods to provide a plentiful harvest, to alleviate suffering, or to bring victory in battle. Formal religions—Catholicism, Protestantism, Judaism, Islam, and others—also have ceremonies intended to serve some purpose: to ask forgiveness, to plead for help, to request a better life in this world and beyond it.

The efficacious nature of a religious ceremony—whether it is a ritual in Africa or a service in a church, synagogue, or mosque—reminds us that an essential difference between theater and religion lies in their purpose and focus. Religion centers on the worship of a deity or deities; and the intent of a religious ceremony is to pray to the deity: to ask forgiveness, seek help, or offer praise. The focus of theater, by contrast, is not worship. Theater acts as a mirror or a celebration of life here on earth. Theater can serve a number of purposes: it can challenge people to think, transport them to the past, entertain them, take them outside themselves, make them cry, and make them laugh. But its focus is always on human beings—their suffering, their pain, their frustrations, their hopes, their joys, their laughter. Even when theater deals with a religious subject, it concerns itself with how religion affects human lives.

Methexis: Group sharing Religious ceremonies often have another quality which distinguishes them from theatrical performances. In the theater with which we are familiar, there is a clear separation between performers and audience. A space is set aside—the stage—where the performance takes place, and audience members observe the action as spectators. Audiences may become engrossed in what happens onstage and may be emotionally involved, but their involvement is always vicarious. Audience members experience the emotions—the heartaches and joys—of characters onstage *empathically,* by identifying in their own imaginations with the characters. Spectators may cry real tears and give way to uncontrollable laughter; but this participation occurs at a distance: in the minds and hearts of the spectators, who remain in their seats.

The experience of many tribal ceremonies is different from this kind of theatrical experience, as we can see in certain ceremonies in Africa. To understand the difference, we should consider for a moment how earlier African societies viewed themselves in the world. They did not see the universe as a series of dichotomies such as good versus evil or spiritual versus material; rather, they saw it as a vast, intricate harmony of people, nature, and gods, each having some element of spiritual as well as material existence. Human beings, because they have consciousness and the invocative power of the spoken word, were responsible for maintaining a balance with nature. If this balance was violated through stupidity, greed, or folly, both people and nature suffered. One very important means of maintaining the balance was religious ritual, which embraced song, dance, and drama.

Partly as a result of this philosophy, rituals in many African societies had an aesthetic or artistic principle different from that of the theater which originated in Europe and was adopted in North and South America and elsewhere. European theater is based primarily on *mimesis:* imitation or representation of an action. It also stresses the importance of individual creativity by performers, playwrights, and others, and a set text from which little variation is permitted. And, as we have just seen, audience members in European theater are spectators rather than participants.

The African tradition, on the other hand, is generally based on *methexis: group sharing.* It emphasizes audience participation, group creativity, and improvisation. As a result, whereas European theater is meant to affect the audience—to entertain or to teach—the purpose of the African tradition is to embody or to *be.* African ceremonies, although set, offer opportunities for improvisation, and not only the leader or priest but everyone participates, entering into the action and also into transformations of body and spirit.

A new world version of such an African ritual can be found in the Caribbean, where the African gods were integrated with the practices of the Catholic church through religious rituals such as *vodum* in Haiti and *santería* in Trinidad, Puerto Rico, and Cuba. For instance, the Afro-Cuban ritual drama *Shango de Ima,* a mystery play, is a re-creation of the life of the Yorub god Shango, who is known in Cuba as Saint Barbara. This drama, still performed today, contains many Yoruba words and chants; its power sometimes "possesses" the "performers" so that they "become" *orishas* (gods), thus bringing both worshipers and performers into a community of gods and nature.

"Participatory" Theater

In addition to imitation, role playing, storytelling, popular entertainments, and ceremonies and rituals, theatrical elements can be found in many contemporary educational and therapeutic activities that stress active participation by the people involved. Good examples are psychodrama, sociodrama, and classroom exercises or therapy groups using dramatic improvisations. Psychodrama focuses on individuals and sociodrama on groups. In both cases, the aim is for participants to engage in deliberate "role playing" as a means of understanding the dynamics and emotional tensions in a situation.

Interestingly, in the United States in recent years there are also examples of "participatory theater" in theater itself—attempts to remove the barrier between performers and spectators. During the 1960s a number of avant-garde organizations invited spectators to move from their seats in the auditorium and become part of the action. Before a presentation began, audience members might be "initiated" or "indoctrinated" by being led to their seats by performers, or engaged by performers in conversation. During a performance they would be invited to come to the playing area to take part in the action, or perhaps to participate in the aisles of the auditorium.

Prohibition of Theater

We now consider one additional—and paradoxical—aspect of theater in our lives: prohibitions against it. Wherever complex social organizations and population centers develop, theater is likely to emerge. When it does not, the explanation may be that a society stresses other forms of communal activity—religion or art, say—rather than theater. But sometimes a society specifically forbids theater.

One of the strongest deterrents to the emergence of theater in an advanced society is religious opposition. We have noted the close relationship between theater and religion: religion has theatrical elements, and theater has at times evolved from religious ceremonies. The connection between the two, however, has often taken the form of a love-hate relationship, and there have been times when religion has bitterly opposed theater.

The early Christians, for example, repeatedly denounced Roman theater and at one point issued an edict that any Christian attending the theater on a holy day would be excommunicated. In England, when the Puritans came to power under Oliver Cromwell and took control of Parliament in 1642, one of the first things they did was to close all the theaters in London. Two other important examples are found in ancient Judaism and Islam.

Considering the contributions of Jewish people to theater in later times, it may seem puzzling that the ancient Hebrew nation did not produce theater. There is evidence of poetic and narrative skills in the Old Testament, and we know from the psalms and other sources that there was singing and dancing; but no separate theater developed. However, there were both social and political reasons for this. The ancient Jews were a nomadic people, moving from place to place, who did not at first develop permanent centers of population like those in Greece and elsewhere. And even after they had established a kingdom and settled in urban centers such as Jerusalem, they did not develop theater, apparently because of their religious beliefs. David S. Lifson, in a book on Yiddish theater in the United States, has noted that during the biblical period Jews were forbidden to attend the pagan theater. A prayer from the period underlines this fact: "I thank thee, my Lord, that I spend my time in the temples of prayer instead of in the theaters."[1] Some commentators believe that this injunction against theater stems from the Second Commandment in the Bible: "You shall not make a graven image, or any likeness of anything that is in heaven above or in the earth beneath." According to this theory, "any likeness" was interpreted to include a performer impersonating a character onstage.

In Islam, the prohibition of theater is even more explicit. Islam, founded by the prophet Mohammed in A.D. 610, became the dominant religion in regions stretching from beyond Persia (now Iran) in the east to Spain in the west. It included all of the middle east, the eastern Mediterranean, North Africa, and southern Spain. Islam forbids the personification of God, that is, showing a person who might embody God; and this rule has remained steadfast from its earliest days to the present.

No permanent theater as such has emerged in Islamic countries; however, it is significant that despite this strong deterrent, theater has crept into Islamic societies. There is archaeological evidence of circuses and other entertainments, and there are indications of popular plays in the eastern part of the Persian empire. Even more noteworthy is the Taziya "passion play," a religious drama performed each year as part of the festival of Muhurran in areas where the Shiite sect of Islam prevails. The play recounts the survival of Zain, a grandson of Mohammed, after the other members of his branch of the family were slaughtered. The Shiites consider Zain the legitimate successor of Mohammed. There are many versions of the Taziya passion play; an Englishman living in Persia in the 1860s found fifty-two versions and in 1878 had thirty-seven of them published. The Taziya has been performed regularly in Baghdad (Iraq) and Teheran and Isfahan (Iran), as well as in smaller towns and villages. This is because the Taziya, though a drama, was considered part of a religious festival through all of its early history. But theater was not allowed to develop independently in Islamic countries. The Taziya is an exception; the firm rule in most Islamic countries is no theater whatsoever.

[1] David S. Lifson, *The Yiddish Theater in America,* Thomas Yoseloff, New York, 1965, p. 18.

The subject of theater in daily life—including "role playing" in all its aspects, as well as the whole range of religious, educational, and celebratory rituals and ceremonies—is clearly important and worthy of detailed study. Prohibition of theater, of course, is also significant. The subject of this book, however, is the history of theater where it has evolved, free from outside strictures, as a separate art form, not as a component of other practices. We must examine, therefore, how theater operates as a distinct activity with its own principles, functions, and aesthetics and review its various elements through the course of its history.

ELEMENTS OF THEATER

No one knows exactly how theater originated. We know *where* it emerged: in Greece in the fifth century B.C.; in India in the fourth century after Christ, and—after being dormant in western civilization—again in Europe in the Middle Ages. But precisely how it evolved in each case has been hotly debated by scholars. Some scholars argue that theater emerges from religious ceremonies; as we have pointed out, there are significant similarities between such ceremonies and theater. Others have suggested that theater evolves from storytelling. Still others argue that in certain instances theater—especially comedy and farce—has come from various forms of popular entertainment or from secular pagan celebrations. Our purpose here is not to attempt to settle this argument, or even to take one position against another. We are concerned not with the origins of theater but with the art form once it becomes established.

When theater does emerge as a separate art form, it has certain distinguishing features which it will be helpful to review now. These elements are a playing space, an audience, the performers, visual elements, human subject matter, a dramatic structure, and coodination of all these. There are also certain social requirements.

A Playing Space

One essential element of theater is a *playing space* where people can come together to watch a performance. Whether it is outdoors in an amphitheater or indoors in a college playhouse, whether it is a permanent space such as Broadway theater or a temporary theater set up in a town hall or a church, a place must be set aside where actresses and actors can perform and spectators can observe.

As we try to reconstruct historic playing spaces, we will be exploring a number of key issues. What was the relationship between performers and audiences in these spaces? How large were the spaces? What was the configuration of the stage? Where was the audience? Were the spaces permanent or temporary? What building materials were used? Were there areas for selling tickets, changing costumes, storing scenery, and so on?

The Audience

A second element of theater is the *audience*. Unlike some arts—literature or painting, for instance—theater requires more than a single spectator. One person can read a book or look at a painting, but theater calls for a collection of people as observers. It is a communal experience for the audience, and this coming together is one of its essential elements.

In order to understand the makeup of audiences of past historic eras, we will need to answer a number of questions. What was the social, economic, political, and gender configuration of the audience? Were any people excluded from the theater because of gender, race, or economics? Why did audiences attend the theater? What function did theater serve in the lives of audience members? How did audiences behave during the course of a production?

The Performers

Equally important are the *performers:* the other half of the actor-audience equation. Performance is the essence of theater. A man or woman stands onstage and impersonates another man or woman, and this feature—people playing other people—makes theater unique. Actresses and actors are always playing roles: young women, old women, murderers, saints, heroes, cowards, larger-than-life figures like kings and queens, ordinary people like carpenters, clerks, and hairdressers. Acting also requires special skills: the precision of a Shakespearean actor delivering the soliloquies from *Hamlet;* the graceful, intricate dance steps in a musical; the swift, sure movements of two opponents in a sword fight in a swashbuckling drama like *Cyrano de Bergerac.*

Many of the questions we will ask about acting will be similar to those we ask about audiences. Who were the actors? What was their social and economic standing within their society? Were people excluded from performing because of gender, race, or economics? How did a person become an actor? How were productions rehearsed, and what was expected of performers during rehearsals?

Possibly the most difficult question we will try to answer is, What was the style of acting in a given historical period? This question is nearly impossible to answer because acting is the most ephemeral of the theater arts: it disappears as soon as a performance is over. In addition, we consider performance in terms of our own contemporary biases. As we discuss acting throughout this text, we will try to describe the unique conventions and techniques of various historical periods in order to create a flavor of what acting was like in the past.

Visual Elements

Another requirement of theater is the *visual elements:* scenery, lighting, and costumes. The *scenery* may be simple—little more than the architecture of the theater space itself—or it may be elaborate, as in an expensive Broadway musical; but there is always some visual environment in which the drama occurs. This environment contributes immeasurably to the total experience.

Lighting not only illuminates the performers and the playing space; it also provides moods, color changes, shifts in visual focus, and a host of other qualities that enhance a performance. *Costumes* not only make performers resemble the persons they are portraying but also include decorative and symbolic elements, such as masks and elaborate headdresses.

In reconstructing how visual elements were used in the past, we will confront a number of key issues. What materials were used to create the visual elements? Who was responsible for designing and providing the visual elements? How unified were these elements? What functions did they serve? What kinds of machinery were used to create scenic and lighting effects?

The Subject Matter: Human Beings

Another element of theater is its *human subject matter*. In contrasting theater and religious ceremonies, we pointed out that theater is always human-centered. It can deal with a famous person (such as Joan of Arc or Abraham Lincoln), or with a family and family conflicts, or even with a parable where animals or fantasy creatures are stand-ins for people; but the focus of theater is invariably human beings: their problems, joys, fears, foolishness, and aspirations.

A Dramatic Structure

A further requirement of theater is that the material must have a *dramatic structure*. Dramatic structure might take any of several forms that have evolved through the years. It might be a direct reenactment of scenes from everyday life, as in Henrik Ibsen's *A Doll's House* or Eugene O'Neill's *Long Day's Journey into Night*. It might be a structure like that in Greek tragedies, in which confrontations between characters alternate with choral sections that are sung and danced. It might be a series of episodes, as in Shakespeare: scenes that move rapidly from one place to another and one time to another, almost as movies do. Whatever the structure, it will be a recognized pattern, a framework for some story of human adventures.

As we consider subject matter and structure in past eras, we will need to answer several questions. Who created the dramatic materials? How were the materials structured? What was their dominant subject?

Coordination of the Elements

Finally, these various elements must be combined. In today's theater, the director is responsible for bringing the elements together; but even before the time when someone was actually designated as a director, the aspects of a theatrical production had to be coordinated to make a meaningful whole—to create a production onstage during which performers and audience would interact.

As we discuss the history of directing, we will ask if there was an individual who served the function of director, and—if so—whether this person also had other production duties. What were the responsibilities of that person? How unified and coordinated were productions during each of the historical periods?

Social Requirements

Even if the elements outlined above are in place, theater has still other requirements. For one thing, it is a communal art calling for the collaboration of many individuals and groups, and those involved must be highly trained and highly skilled. This requires a theater *tradition* in which training can take place. It also calls for *organization* of a kind that can be found only in societies that have developed a complex social structure. Usually this requires a *population center*—a place where a number of people have gathered together. A population center such as a village, town, or city is important, too, in providing an audience. Without a population center, there would be no audience to attend an event.

Absence of population centers may partly explain why theater did not develop in certain cultures—among Native Americans, for example, or societies in Africa. These people were nomadic; they developed religious rituals and other ceremonies, but it would have been difficult for them to create a structured theater.

As we noted earlier, theater tends to emerge wherever complex social organization develops and population centers exist; societies that prohibit theater, such as ancient Judaism and Islam, are exceptions to this rule. The subject of this study will be those places where theater has evolved. We will focus mainly on the western tradition, because it is out of that tradition that modern American and European theater primarily comes. But we will also look at Asian theater, and at African and Caribbean influences on modern African American theater.

THE STUDY OF THEATER HISTORY

A Positivist Approach

In *Living Theater*, we will look at theater as it has unfolded through the ages. In western history, theater began in Europe and later spread to North and South America. We will also trace theater as it emerged. We will note how one country built on the experience of another or appropriated from another: seventeenth-century French theater, for example, was greatly influenced by the Italian theater that immediately preceded it.

We will point out threads that seem to be woven through several periods and several countries. For instance, domestic comedies began with Greek New Comedy in the third century B.C., were perfected by Roman writers in the centuries that followed, were picked up by playwrights in Europe in the Renaissance, and have persisted to the present time on the stage, in films, and as situation comedies on television.

In presenting theater history, we are taking what is sometimes called a *positivist* approach. Positivism suggests that history can be explained logically and chronicled objectively. In *Living Theater*, we attempt to describe what has happened; to relate the present to the past and show how it anticipates the future; to look in depth at the people who have created theater by perfecting older forms or developing new ones; and to look at the full range of theatrical activity—not just dramatic literature, but every aspect of theatrical production, including performance, scene design, and theater architecture.

Before moving into our own chronicle, however, we will note some recent developments and departures in the way theater history is studied and taught, since in the course of this book we will occasionally find it appropriate to call attention to these trends.

Recent Historical Approaches

How theater history is studied and analyzed, a discipline known as *theater historiography,* has become a particular concern of some scholars in recent years. Many contemporary historians argue that there have been fallacies in the traditional representation of history which need to be rectified. They argue that such historical errors are a result of flawed methodologies or flawed approaches. They particularly disagree with attempts to create a linear presentation which focuses on cause and effect. (An example of linear development would be church drama in the Middle Ages leading directly to medieval theater and medieval theater in turn leading directly to the Renaissance theater of England and Spain.) To clarify many of the scholarly debates which we will focus on later in this text, we need to point out some of the new approaches to studying theater history.

Revisionist historians stress that history has usually been told from the point of view of a social elite; they also suggest that significant "mainstream" phenomena have been ignored because historians focus on what is revolutionary. For example, in theater history, popular entertainments are frequently disregarded as unworthy of study; only in the last quarter-century has there been significant scholarly examination of the popular arts. Revisionists also force us to revise our usual analysis of historical documents and sources, frequently pointing out misreadings resulting from cultural and social biases.

Feminist historians argue that the place of women in theater history has not been carefully explored. They assert that women have been "invisible" in male-centered history and that a reevaluation of history, with a primary focus on the role of women, is needed.

Deconstructionists argue that history is written and taught by people in power and therefore needs to be analyzed in terms of who is empowered by history and who is not. Deconstructionists have greatly influenced feminist historians, who argue that in western culture, history has been written from the dominant male perspective of a given society and thus ignores the accomplishments of women. The deconstructionists oppose the concept of linear development; instead, they often see history as a series of ruptures. They argue against the traditional evolutionary or cause-and-effect approach to historical events.

Multicultural historians focus on groups which have been underrepresented in the course of history. For example, in theater history they emphasize the contributions of African Americans and Hispanic Americans to contemporary American theater.

Semioticians argue that theater historians should focus on the response of audiences to the various elements of a production which function as *signs* and thus have inherent meaning for the viewer. They believe that performance has been undervalued in the study of theater history and that there has been too much emphasis on the literary text and on descriptions of individual elements of theater—descriptions which fail to take audiences' reactions into account. Semioticians are primarily interested in audiences' responses to the elements of theatrical events—much as contemporary literary analysts have become interested in the multiplicity of readers' responses to literary texts. All audience members react to scenery, costumes, and acting; however, few historians have discussed the impact of these elements on audiences during important historical periods. Semioticians also ask what various elements *signify* to the audience. For example, when discussing theater architecture, historians have almost never described lobby spaces. Yet a lobby often reveals characteristics of an audience and the nature of a theatrical event. Contrasting the rough, tiny lobbies of off-off-Broadway theater spaces in New York with the spacious, luxurious lobbies of new, large arts complexes in some other American cities underlines differences in their productions and audiences.

There are, of course, still other recent approaches to theater history. We should also note that the approaches just described are not mutually exclusive. Feminist historians, for instance, frequently acknowledge the influence of the deconstructionists and the semioticians.

In this text, we will try to point out areas in which theater historians disagree. We will attempt to illustrate some of the current debates which have been engendered by these new approaches to the study of theater history. We will also spend time in each chapter reviewing issues connected to either multiculturalism or gender, in order to highlight some contemporary views of theater history. In this process, we hope to convey the complexity of theater history and the way our understanding of the past is still evolving.

Why Study Theater History?

Why should we study theater history? In most universities, theater history is a requirement for students who intend to become theater practitioners. In some schools it is part of the general education requirement for all students. Yet few students ask why this requirement is appropriate or what purpose it serves.

Theater history is a discipline that serves a multitude of functions. To begin with, it can help future professionals understand their artistic heritage. Theater history also presents techniques, conventions, and ideas which can be borrowed by contemporary practitioners. We will see, in our discussion of modern theater, how often contemporary artists adapt historic conventions to create productions which speak to their own audiences. We should note that this is different from re-creating historically accurate productions—another common use of theater history.

If theater is a reflection of its society, then theater history can also give us insights into societies of the past. We can learn significant information about the major issues and concerns of a historical period by studying its theater; we can learn about the conventions and norms of a society by analyzing its theatrical presentations.

Theater history is also an exciting and unique discipline worthy of study purely for the sake of scholarly exploration. Because theater is an ephemeral art, theater history is immensely difficult to reconstruct. But this difficulty leads to exciting debates and constant reevaluation. Like the art form it tries to reconstruct, theater history itself—as we noted when discussing the various approaches to theater historiography—is constantly being reconstructed.

Theater in History: Points to Remember

Living Theater is a journey, an exploration of the theaters of the past that form a rich heritage—the many kinds of theater experience open to us today. As we begin this adventure, we should make a few additional observations.

First, anyone studying theater history tends to focus on periods when theater reached a high point: the Renaissance in Europe, for example, when theater architecture and scene design were revolutionized in Italy and a form of improvisatory theater—commedia dell'arte—was perfected; and when there was an outpouring of inspired drama in Spain and England. It is important to remember, though, that there are significant accomplishments in the years that precede and follow such achievements, and also that a great deal of other theater activity surrounds them. In the Renaissance, other playwrights were active and countless productions were taking place which we do not have time or space to describe. Also, there are frequently lengthy periods between high points when few new developments occur in scene design, playwriting, or acting; but theatrical activity does not cease at these times—it may, in fact, be vigorous. We tend not to focus on periods between high points, because we place such a premium on the innovative and the new. Similarly, what of those countries where there is a lively theater but no playwright who enters the history books as a pioneer? Those countries should not be ignored, but again, because of limited time and space, they are not always given their full due. The key point to remember is that when historians highlight certain countries during certain periods, this does not mean that theater did not exist before or after those periods, or in other places at the same time.

Second, it is important to keep in mind that the achievements we discuss in *Living Theater* are only a part of what actually happened in theater. For instance, during the fifth century B.C. in Greece, approximately 900 tragedies were produced at the City Dionysia Festival held each spring in Athens—three tragedies by each of three dramatists each year. But today we have only a small sampling: 7 plays by Aeschylus, who we believe wrote about 90 plays; 7 out of perhaps 125 plays by Sophocles; and 18 out of about 90 plays by Euripides. That is a total of 32 plays out of 900; thus the sample we have is far from offering a complete picture. The same would be true of any other historical period, such as English, Spanish, and French theaters during the Renaissance: we have only a small percentage of the plays that were written.

Moreover, we often have little or no idea of the acting styles of earlier periods. We do not know, for instance, what the singing or dancing of Greek choruses was like. Nor do we know what acting styles were characteristic when Sanskrit drama in India was in its golden age. For that matter, we are not at all certain about performance styles in the theater of Shakespeare or Molière.

It should be remembered, too, that although we present theater as if it were a constantly unfolding activity, there are times and places where little formal theater exists. There are also periods when theater appears to have remained somewhat the same over an extended number of years. The first comedies of the Roman playwright Plautus were presented in the third century B.C., and Roman comedy was altered by Terence half a century later; but after that, we assume that a similar type of comedy was the mainstay of Roman theater for the next 500 years. What happened during that time? Did comic acting change? Did playwriting change? Were there major alterations in acting styles and dramatic composition, or only minor shifts? We do not know. But if we assume 500 years of a fairly stable form of theater, we have a situation drastically different from the 500 years from A.D. 1500 to 2000, during which a constant series of shifts, innovations, and mutations have occurred.

Third, we should keep in mind that commentators designate specific achievements from the past—in playwriting, acting, stage design, or some other aspect of theater—as outstanding. But we must pause on the word *outstanding.* These judgments are made by observers today, at the end of the twentieth century. Plays and performers we now consider exceptional may not have been considered so in their own day, or in some subsequent period. To take one example, Georg Büchner, a young playwright in Germany in the early nineteenth century, wrote two plays and fragments of a third which were not considered particularly noteworthy when they first appeared and were not even performed until after 1900. In this century, though, Büchner's works have been rediscovered and are produced frequently; people in the twentieth century feel that these plays—*Danton's Death, Leonce and Lena,* and *Woyzeck*—speak to the alienation and pessimism of the modern world. We say of Büchner that he was "ahead of his time," that he anticipated the future. But which judgment is correct—the judgment of the early nineteenth century, when the plays were written but never produced; or that of the late twentieth century, when they are applauded? And what will be the judgment at the end of the twenty-first century? In contrast, of course, theater history is replete with examples of plays which were praised in their own day but later came to be considered dated or shallow: certain nineteenth-century melodramas such as *Uncle Tom's Cabin* are examples.

Not only plays but styles of acting as well are viewed quite differently in different periods. Approaches to acting that are praised in one period may be damned in another. Even in this century, we have seen notions of what constitutes outstanding acting move from a more formal approach early in the century, to emphasis on earthy psychological realism in mid-century, and back to an appreciation of eloquent speech and graceful stage movements toward the end of the century.

The point here is that no judgment is final. Each age has its own standards of excellence and its own yardstick for measuring theater. When we point out that certain plays or playwrights are superior, or that specific performers in the past were exemplary, we are presenting the consensus of today's scholars and commentators. We are looking at events and accomplishments through the prism of the end of the twentieth century. The assessment half a century from now may be different.

Fourth, a key factor to be considered is the audience for which theater is intended. Once again, there is no uniformity from one period to another. In some ages and places, theater has been strictly or primarily for royalty or the upper classes. This was true of the theaters that emerged in ancient India and China and of theater in England during the Restoration of the late sixteenth century. At other times, however, theater has been for mass audiences. Two examples are the medieval period, when plays depicting scenes from the Bible would be presented to everyone in a town and the surrounding countryside; and the nineteenth century in England and the United States, when theater was embraced by a broad spectrum of the middle class.

Fifth and finally, it is important to realize that in different places and at different times, different aspects of theater have been treasured. In some eras comedy has been the most highly valued form; in other eras, tragedy. There have also been periods when neither form was valued as highly as melodrama. Equally significant is whether written drama—the script itself—was of paramount importance rather than acting or scenic spectacle. During certain ages, the emphasis is not on playwriting or new drama, but on how plays are interpreted. At other times, neither text nor performance is paramount, but rather the visual splendor of the scenery, lighting, and costumes.

Now that we have called attention to some key perspectives on theater history, we are ready to begin the journey: to strike out and look at the numerous manifestations of theater which have surfaced through the ages and of which we are the fortunate inheritors today.

SUMMARY

Today's vast variety of theater experiences have their roots in 2,500 years of western theater and nearly 2,000 years of Asian theater.

Many everyday personal and communal human activities—imitation, role playing, storytelling, popular entertainments, ceremonies and rituals, and "participatory theater" such as psychodrama and sociodrama—have a theatrical component. Though religious ceremonies and rituals have striking theatrical aspects, they differ from theater in at least two important ways: they are meant to be efficacious, and they emphasize group sharing—audience participation and collective creativity. One significant aspect of theater is prohibitions against it, as in ancient Judaism and Islam.

The subject of this text is theater where it has evolved as a separate art form. Elements of theater—characteristics by which we identify it—are a playing space, an audience, performers, visual elements (scenery, lighting, and costumes), human subject matter, dramatic structure, and coordination of these elements. In addition, there are social requirements for theater: tradition, social structure, and population centers.

While much of this text takes a positivist approach to theater history, references will be made to other approaches such as revisionism, feminism, deconstructionism, and multiculturalism. Theater history as a discipline serves a number of functions but is also intrinsically valuable.

In beginning a study of theater history, it is important to bear several considerations in mind. Although theater history focuses on "high points," this does not mean that theater did not exist between high points; and what theater history takes up is only a part of what actually happened. Also, there are differences between cultures with regard to judgments of what is "superior" in theater, the intended audience for theater, and which aspects of theater are most highly valued.

PART ONE

EARLY THEATER

The theaters we refer to as *early theaters*—Greek, Roman, medieval, and Asian—actually cover a period of nearly 2,000 years: from Greek theater in the fifth century B.C. through medieval theater, which began 1,500 years later; and from Indian and Chinese theaters, which came to flower, respectively, in the fourth and seventh centuries after Christ.

In western theater—that is, in Greece, Rome, and medieval Europe—this is a long time span to encompass the beginnings of theater. But it is important to remember that for nearly 1,000 years—from the declining years of the Roman empire until the emergence of medieval theater—there was no formal theater: in the Middle Ages, theater had to begin all over again. It was also during this thousand-year period that Indian and Chinese theater began.

The Greek, Roman, and medieval theaters can legitimately be called *early theaters* because they established the foundations on which all subsequent western theater was built. Not only in theater, but in virtually every area of life, these cultures formed the basis of western civilization. The list of their accomplishments is monumental: the classical Greeks developed democracy, philosophy, the study of science and mathematics, and architecture; the Romans were great conquerors, architects, and lawmakers; the medieval Europeans organized methods of farming and established trade guilds.

We do not want to oversimplify the relationship among the theaters of these three societies, but there are important common elements. One is the significant connection in all three between the theater and religious and civic celebrations. It is often argued that the roots of theater lie in religious rituals, and this seems to be substantiated by the Greek theater's initial connection to rites honoring the god Dionysus, the Roman theater's relation

20

to the festival of Jupiter (Zeus), and the medieval theater's close tie with the Roman Catholic church. At the same time, a strong secular element permeated all three theaters; there was a desire to treat human as well as religious subjects. This is the natural evolution of theater in any society; when theater becomes an art form on its own, it concentrates on human problems and aspirations.

Another common element is that in each of these cultures, theater was a significant civic and social event. This is reflected in the huge open-air theaters of Greece and Rome as well as the spectacular outdoor medieval stage settings. We have large outdoor theaters today—for summer Shakespeare festivals and rock concerts, among other events—but in these earlier societies a large proportion of the population became involved in theater to a degree that will never be equaled in modern times.

In Asia, the theaters of India, China, and Japan reached a high point of artistic achievement when religion and philosophy were also central in each culture. This level of excellence kept traditional theater allied to religion and philosophy even when society changed and became more secular. Like culture in the west, the great Asian civilizations we will be considering served as foundations for later societies.

As we begin to survey these early theaters, we should remember how much of their drama has survived and is still performed in our own day. Greek tragedies and comedies are still produced; plays of the Roman dramatist Plautus have been adapted as Broadway musicals; and there are modern versions of the medieval morality play *Everyman*. In Japan, the traditional theaters, such as noh, bunraku, and kabuki, are kept alive even today; and there is an almost unbroken line from past to present.

In Part One, as we explore the theater from its origins to a time several centuries later, we should not view it as a remote activity; rather, we should search for elements that continue to be part of our theater today.

CHAPTER 1

GREEK THEATER

The year is 441 B.C., and the place is Athens, Greece. It is a morning in late March, and we are up early—along with about 15,000 other citizens of Athens. We have dressed in our best robes and are making our way to the Theater of Dionysus, an open-air theater on the south side of the Acropolis, the highest hill in Athens. Atop the Acropolis are several temples; the Parthenon, a magnificent new temple dedicated to the goddess Athena, is under construction at this very time.

The Theater of Dionysus has a semicircular seating space built into the slope of the hill on the side of the Acropolis. At the foot of the seating area is a flat, circular space, called the *orchestra,* where the actors will perform. Behind the orchestra a temporary stage house has been built from which the performers will make entrances and exits.

We arrive early, and because we will be here a good part of the day, we have brought food and wine. Priests of various religious orders sit in special seats at the edge of the circle opposite the stage house. Other dignitaries, such as civic and military officials, range around them in the first few rows; above them sit both citizens and slaves. Since the seaport near Athens has recently been

DRAMA OF ANCIENT GREECE.   Dramas written during the classical era of Greece are still being produced as part of our modern repertoire. One unique element of Greek drama is the chorus; seen here is the chorus from Euripides' *Iphigenia at Aulis.*
(Michal Daniel/Guthrie Theater)

reopened after being closed for the winter months, a number of foreign visitors are also present. Even those sitting in the top row will have no trouble hearing the performers; the acoustics are so good that a whisper by an actor in the orchestra will carry to the upper reaches of the amphitheater.

The plays we will see today are part of the City Dionysia festival, an annual series of events lasting several days. During this festival, all business in Athens—both commercial and governmental—comes to a halt, and all attention is focused on the festival itself. On a day before the plays there was a parade through the city; it ended near the theater with a religious observance at the altar of the temple dedicated to the god Dionysus, for whom the festival is named.

Today is one of three days of the festival devoted to presenting tragedies. On these days, one playwright will offer three tragedies and a satyr play, and another will offer a comedy. (The *satyr play* is a short comic piece burlesquing tragic subjects, with actors dressed as satyrs, mythological creatures that were half-man and half-goat.) The three tragedies might be linked to form one long play, called a *trilogy*, or, as is the case today, they can be three separate pieces.

Sophocles, the author of today's plays, announced a few days ago that one of them will deal with the story of Antigone, and this is the play which we are eagerly anticipating. The subject comes from a myth familiar to the playgoers. Antigone was the daughter of King Oedipus. After her father's death, her two brothers, Eteocles and Polynices, became involved in a war against each other to see who would be king of Thebes, and they killed each other. Antigone's uncle, Creon, then became king of Thebes. Creon blamed one brother, Polynices, for the conflict, and he issued an edict that Polynices was not to be given an honorable burial. Antigone decided to defy Creon's order and bury her brother Polynices.

We and other members of the audience, who know the myth well, are curious to see how Sophocles, one of our favorite dramatists, will deal with the story. As the play begins, two actors, each wearing the mask and costume of a woman, appear in the playing area. We realize immediately that they represent Antigone and her sister, Ismene. As the scene begins, Antigone tells Ismene that she means to defy their uncle, the king, and give their brother Polynices an honorable burial. Ismene, unlike her sister, is timid and frightened, and argues that women are too weak to stand up to a king. Besides, Ismene points out, Antigone will be put to death if she is caught. Antigone argues, however, that she will not be subservient to men, even the king.

When the two women leave, a chorus of fifteen men enters. These men represent the elders of the city, and throughout the play—in passages that are sung and danced—they will fulfill several functions: providing background information, raising philosophical questions, and urging the principal figures to show restraint. The choral sections alternate with scenes of confrontation between Antigone, Creon, and the other main characters.

In the play, Antigone does attempt to bury her dead brother, is caught, and is brought before the king. When the showdown between Antigone and Creon comes, Antigone defies him, and as punishment is put into a cave to die. In the end, not only is she dead, but so too are Creon's wife and son, who have killed themselves. In the final scene, we see Creon standing alone, wearing his tragic mask, bereft of all those he held dear.

After *Antigone* and the other two tragedies we have seen, we watch a short satyr play—a comic comment on the previous material—and a full-length comedy. But our minds return again and again to *Antigone,* and we recall highlights of the drama: the scene in which Antigone argues vehemently with Creon, standing up to him as his equal; and the final, dreadful tableau of Creon left alone.

BACKGROUND: THE GOLDEN AGE OF GREECE

There are times in history when many elements come together to create a remarkable age. Such a time was the fifth century B.C. in Athens, Greece, when there were outstanding achievements in politics, philosophy, science, and the arts. It was at this time, too, that western theater was born.

A number of events had prepared the way. Long before 500 B.C., impressive civilizations had developed around the eastern part of the Mediterranean Sea: in Egypt, in Persia (which included present-day Iran, Iraq, Turkey, and other countries), and in Greece. Advances had been made in art—in pottery, for example, and in the performance of elaborate ceremonies such as the one at Abydos in Egypt—as well as in science, astronomy, and mathematics. Athens carried this tradition forward.

Greece at this time was not an empire or even a united country but a series of independent city-states occupying parts of the Greek peninsula and nearby islands: at the start of the fifth century B.C., the most important city-state was Athens. Early in the century the Persians had attempted to conquer the Greeks, but the Greeks had defeated them. Later in the century—from 431 to 404 B.C.—there was a costly conflict between Athens and Sparta known as the Peloponnesian War. Between these two events, however, Athens enjoyed a period of remarkable achievements—a time known as the *classical period* and also as the *golden age* of Greece. There are good reasons for calling it a "golden age," because there were important accomplishments in so many fields.

Athens is credited, for example, with being the birthplace of democracy. In 510 B.C., the rulers of Athens established a democracy of free citizens, which means that all male citizens—men who were not slaves or of non-Athenian origin—were given a voice in politics and government. Though there were slaves in Athens, and women were subservient, it should be remembered that the United States, also founded on democratic ideals, once suffered from similar limitations: slavery was not abolished until 1865, and women could not vote until 1920. Despite these drawbacks in ancient Athens, it was an admirable achievement to establish democracy for such a large portion of the population.

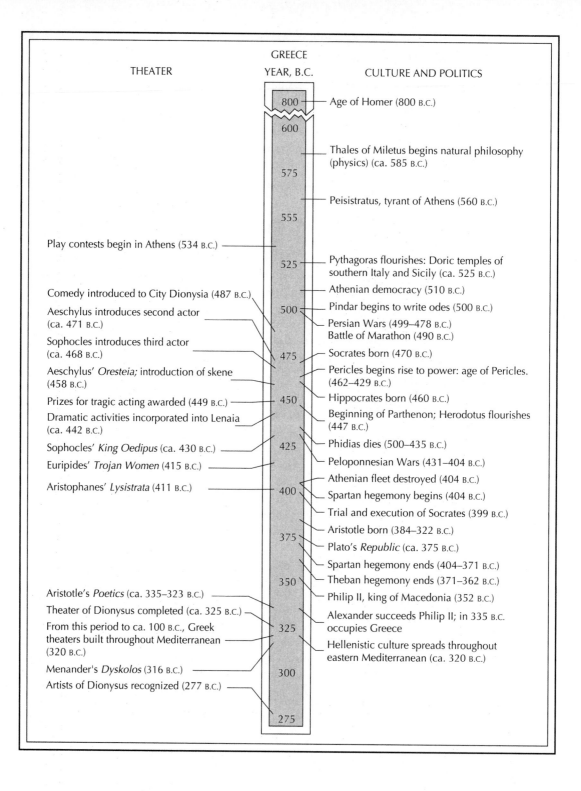

GREECE
YEAR, B.C.

THEATER

CULTURE AND POLITICS

800 — Age of Homer (800 B.C.)

600

Thales of Miletus begins natural philosophy (physics) (ca. 585 B.C.)

575

Peisistratus, tyrant of Athens (560 B.C.)

555

Play contests begin in Athens (534 B.C.)

525 — Pythagoras flourishes: Doric temples of southern Italy and Sicily (ca. 525 B.C.)

Athenian democracy (510 B.C.)

Comedy introduced to City Dionysia (487 B.C.)

Pindar begins to write odes (500 B.C.)

500

Aeschylus introduces second actor (ca. 471 B.C.)

Persian Wars (499–478 B.C.)
Battle of Marathon (490 B.C.)

Sophocles introduces third actor (ca. 468 B.C.)

475 — Socrates born (470 B.C.)

Aeschylus' Oresteia; introduction of skene (458 B.C.)

Pericles begins rise to power: age of Pericles. (462–429 B.C.)

Prizes for tragic acting awarded (449 B.C.)

450 — Hippocrates born (460 B.C.)

Dramatic activities incorporated into Lenaia (ca. 442 B.C.)

Beginning of Parthenon; Herodotus flourishes (447 B.C.)

Sophocles' King Oedipus (ca. 430 B.C.)

425 — Phidias dies (500–435 B.C.)

Euripides' Trojan Women (415 B.C.)

Peloponnesian Wars (431–404 B.C.)

Athenian fleet destroyed (404 B.C.)

Aristophanes' Lysistrata (411 B.C.)

400

Spartan hegemony begins (404 B.C.)

Trial and execution of Socrates (399 B.C.)

375 — Aristotle born (384–322 B.C.)

Plato's Republic (ca. 375 B.C.)

Spartan hegemony ends (404–371 B.C.)

350 — Theban hegemony ends (371–362 B.C.)

Philip II, king of Macedonia (352 B.C.)

Aristotle's Poetics (ca. 335–323 B.C.)

Theater of Dionysus completed (ca. 325 B.C.)

Alexander succeeds Philip II; in 335 B.C. occupies Greece

From this period to ca. 100 B.C., Greek theaters built throughout Mediterranean (320 B.C.)

325

Hellenistic culture spreads throughout eastern Mediterranean (ca. 320 B.C.)

Menander's Dyskolos (316 B.C.)

300

Artists of Dionysus recognized (277 B.C.)

275

(From R. Sullivan et al., A Short History of Western Civilization, 8th ed., McGraw-Hill, New York, 1994.)

THE WORLD OF CLASSICAL GREECE.   Greece was divided into a number of city-states. During the fifth century B.C., Athens (near the center of the map) was the most powerful of these. It was during this period that Greek drama was first performed at the City Dionysia and other festivals and reached a high point of development. Other cities important to Greek drama are Thebes (northwest of Athens), where the mythical events surrounding Oedipus and his family took place; and Delphi (northwest of Thebes), the site of an oracle visited by the Greeks and referred to in several plays. On the Hellespont (to the northeast) is the legendary city of Troy; the Trojan war figures prominently in plays about Agamemnon and others. Sparta (southwest of Athens, on the Peleponnesus) is the city that finally conquered Athens, at the end of the Peleponnesian war in 404 B.C.

There were advances in other areas as well. Greek philosophers, such as Socrates and Plato, tried to explain the world around them; and Herodotus transformed history into a social science. A number of important scientific discoveries were made: the Greek mathematician Pythagoras formulated a theory that remains one of the cornerstones of geometry, and the physician's oath written by Hippocrates is the one still taken by doctors. The classical Greeks were also remarkable artists and architects: Greek sculpture from this period is found in museums around the world, and the Parthenon, the temple on the Acropolis, has withstood time and natural catastrophes—its columns and proportions remain models for architects even today. Obviously, this was a time conducive to developments in many fields, and one of the most significant was theater.

ORIGINS: GREEK THEATER EMERGES

As we noted in the Introduction, theater is a complex art, which requires the coming together of many elements: a story to be told, a dramatization of the story (the script by the playwright), a meeting place for performances, performers to enact the drama, costumes for the performers, some form of stage, perhaps scenery, and an audience for the performance.

In different ways, these elements had been developing in Athens before the fifth century B.C. Important forerunners of theater in Greece were religious ceremonies, which were a prominent feature of Greek society: funeral services, festivals celebrating the seasons, and ceremonies honoring the gods.

Of particular significance to theater were the ceremonies honoring Dionysus, the god of wine, fertility, and revelry. Later Greek drama was presented in honor of Dionysus, and most historians, though not all, believe that Greek drama originated in the dithyrambic choruses presented to honor Dionysus. The *dithyramb* was a lengthy hymn, sung and danced by a group of fifty men. Its format may have been similar to a modern-day choral presentation: the leader of the chorus recited or sang an improvised story while the other members sang a popular refrain. By about 600 B.C., the dithyramb became a literary form, detailing heroic stories.

Arion, a talented harpist and poet who had been born in Lesbos but lived in Corinth at the end of the seventh century and the beginning of the sixth century B.C., was an influential figure in the development of the dithyramb. According to the historian Herodotus, Arion made significant changes in the dithyramb and moved it toward a dramatic form by interspersing spoken sections with the musical portions; these spoken segments were supposedly more dramatic than the songs.

Even more than Arion, a performer named Thespis is customarily credited with transforming the dithyramb into tragedy, in the sixth century B.C., by stepping out of the dithyrambic chorus and becoming an actor. Thespis delivered a prologue and presented dialogue that required him to impersonate a character: thus a purely narrative, storytelling form became a dramatic form in which characters exchanged lines. Thespis is said to have been the first writer of tragedy as well as the first actor; his decisive contribution is reflected in the modern term *thespian,* a synonym for "actor." The ancient Greek word for "actor" was *hypokrite*—literally, "answerer"—underscoring the fact that drama required the verbal give-and-take of dialogue and interaction between actor and chorus.

We should note that there are other theories about the origin of Greek theater. The Greek philosopher Aristotle suggested that theater developed out of human beings' natural desire to imitate, as we discussed in the Introduction. Some contemporary historians have suggested that because of the popularity of storytellers before the classical period, a storyteller was added to the dithyrambic presentation, creating dramatic interaction. However, these theories are not necessarily mutually exclusive; in fact, they all point to the strong relationship between Greek theater and religion, which we discuss below.

THEATER IN THE FIFTH CENTURY B.C.

Greek Theater and Greek Religion

It is important to understand the part religion played in the life of the people of Athens, because Greek theater is intimately bound up with Greek religion. Through the centuries, the Greeks had developed a religion based on the worship of a group of gods, of whom Zeus was the leader along with his wife, Hera. The Greeks did not regard the gods as all-powerful, but they did believe that the gods could protect them and reveal the future. In the cities, annual festivals were held in honor of those gods who the people felt would guide and protect them.

Theater became a central feature of certain religious festivals. Theatrical presentations were both religious events and entertainment. Partly because of these religious connections, people of all social classes attended theatrical performances. We know that the lower as well as the upper classes participated because Pericles, the great ruler of Athens in the middle of the fifth century B.C., established the Theoric Fund in 450 B.C. to assist those who were too poor to afford admission to the theater.

FESTIVALS AND THE CITY DIONYSIA

The significance of the "religious-theatrical" event in Greek society gave theater a far more important place than it occupies in our society. Business came to a standstill during dramatic festivals; wars ceased; political concerns were ignored. Today, certain televised events—such as the Super Bowl and the election returns after a presidential race—attract the attention of millions of Americans. But the total cessation of a society's activities for religious purposes, as practiced by the Greeks, has no present-day equivalent; moreover, the Greeks obviously attended their festivals in person.

One festival in particular became important for theater in Athens. This was the *City Dionysia*, a festival honoring the god Dionysus. The City Dionysia was a signal event in Athens; it was held toward the end of March, when spring had arrived and the port near Athens, which was closed for the winter, had reopened and visitors began pouring into the city. This was also the season when trees and flowers began to come to life again. In 534 B.C., tragedy was incorporated into the City Dionysia, and by 486 B.C., two other forms of drama—comedy and the satyr play—had been added. (The satyr play, a brief comic parody, discussed below, was added in 501 B.C.)

The City Dionysia in Athens lasted for several days. Before the opening of the festival, all the major theatrical participants paraded and appeared in the *proagon*, a preliminary presentation designed to advertise and provide information about the coming plays. On one or two other days, there were parades and sacrifices honoring Dionysus. Five days were then assigned to dithyrambs and plays. On two of these days, ten dithyrambic choruses were presented: probably, one day was assigned to choruses made up of men and one day to choruses of boys. Three days were allotted to tragedies and satyr plays, with three tragedies and one satyr play by a single playwright being presented each day; these four plays by one dramatist were called a *tetralogy*.

There has been considerable debate over when the comedies, which were added to the City Dionysia in 486 B.C., were staged. At one time, historians believed that a separate day of the festival was devoted to five comedies, each by a different playwright. Some scholars now suggest that a comedy was added on the five days in which dithyrambs and tragedies were performed.

A few days after the festival, awards were given, the festival operation was reviewed by a representative body, and people who had behaved improperly or disrespectfully were judged and penalized. We are told, for example, that punishment would be meted out to a festival-goer who used violence to prevent someone else from taking a seat in the theater or who carried a whip and struck an enemy with it while intoxicated. (Like most accounts passed down through the ages about misconduct in the theater, these are difficult to date or prove, but they provide a flavor of the event.)

The Greeks were great proponents of competition; the Olympic Games, for example, originated during the classical era. At the end of the City Dionysia, the best tragic and comic playwrights were awarded prizes; in 449 B.C., the best tragic acting in the festival was also recognized with an award. (Modern counterparts are the Tony awards in theater and the Oscars in film.)

Since theater was both a religious and a civic event, the organization of the dramatic presentations was undertaken by the city-state. The *archon*, an appointed government official, chose the plays 11 months before the next festival.

The archon appointed a *choregus*, the equivalent of a modern-day producer, for each of the selected playwrights. In commercial theater today, the producer raises funds for a production. In the fifth century B.C., the choregus, a wealthy individual, provided the money himself and paid all major expenses connected with the chorus: rehearsals, costumes, and musicians. The city provided the theater space, the awards, and the playwrights' and actors' salaries. While it is true that a stingy choregus could hurt a playwright's chances of winning the contest, usually the choregus would strive to produce a winner. When their productions won, some of them erected monuments in their own honor.

During the classical era, theater became part of other festivals, though not to so great an extent as with the City Dionysia. Before the end of the fifth century B.C., theatrical activities were added to the Lenaia, a festival celebrated at the end of January in the city of Athens; and to the Rural Dionysia, celebrated in December by the rural areas of the Athenian city-state.

The concept of the Dionysian theater festival still inspires contemporary theater producers and directors. A month-long international theater festival, for instance, is a biannual event in Chicago. The many Shakespeare festivals held throughout the United States each year are also in the tradition of these ancient events. These modern versions are not religious festivals or contests, but the idea of regularly scheduled festivals, highlighting significant playwriting and theatrical accomplishments, is an attempt to remind audiences of the centrality of theater in our lives and of its ability to establish a sense of community.

DID WOMEN ATTEND DRAMATIC FESTIVALS?

The likelihood is that women attended the Athenian dramatic festivals in the fifth century B.C., but this is a question that has been debated by historians, since it is known that women did not participate fully in the Greek democracy of the golden age and did not act in tragedies or comedies.

One historian of classical Greek theater, Peter Arnott, notes in *Public and Performance in the Greek Theater*, "It is still not certain . . . whether or not women were admitted (though it is a reasonable surmise that they were)."[1] J. Michael Walton, in *Greek Theater Practice*, lists sources which argue that women were present at classical Greek performances. He cites an account by a contemporary choregus indicating that men and women were impressed by his dress for the theater and an often-repeated tale that some women in attendance at Aeschylus's *Oresteia* suffered miscarriages.[2] In Aristophanes' comedy *The Frogs*, the character of Aeschylus states, satirically, that all decent women committed suicide after seeing one of Euripides' plays; although this comical remark is obviously not to be taken literally, it does indicate that women attended the theater. Walton suggests that women were probably segregated into separate blocks in the theater, a seating process which would have been facilitated if (as some scholars believe) tribes were also seated in distinct areas.

The question whether or not women were part of the classical Greek audience reminds us, of course, that women did not have equal status with men.

[1] Routledge, London and New York, 1991, p. 5.
[2] Greenwood, Westport, Conn., 1980.

Some contributions to this debate also remind us that scholars themselves have sometimes made "sexist" generalizations. For example, Victorian historians believed that Greek women could not have attended comedies because these were bawdy and sexual, but that they could attend tragedies. In many of his plays, however, Aristophanes jokes about women in attendance at performances, demonstrating the fallacy of this belief. Moreover, if women were present at tragedies, then they would also have been present for the satyr plays—which, as we will see, were as sexual as the early comedies.

Greek Theater and Greek Myths

Let's now consider the plays that were written for the festivals. What kind of stories did they tell, and where did the writers find these stories? In most cases, the source was Greek myths.

Along with festivals and the move from dithyrambic choruses to drama, other aspects of theater had been developing before the fifth century B.C. One was the accumulation of a group of stories on which much of Greek drama, particularly tragedy, was based. In the centuries before the golden age, a number of myths had become an important part of the Greek heritage.

A *myth* is a story or legend—sometimes invented, sometimes based loosely on fact—that is handed down from generation to generation. Frequently, a myth is an attempt to explain natural and human events: the changing of the seasons, for example, or a cataclysmic occurrence like an earthquake or a civil war. Myths may also deal with extreme family situations: one branch of a family opposing another, or a difficult relationship between a husband and wife or between parents and children. In each culture, certain myths are seized on because they seem to sum up its view of human relationships and of the problems and opportunities life presents to individuals.

In Greece, there were a multitude of myths. Good examples are the poet Homer's accounts of the Greek war with the Trojans in the *Iliad* and the hero Odysseus's return from the Trojan War in the *Odyssey*. These and other myths furnished many of the stories for Greek drama, but before they could be performed at the theater festivals, they had to be transformed by a playwright into dramatic form.

Greek Tragedy

TRAGIC PLAYWRIGHTS

The first Greek writers of whom we are aware who attempted to create dramatic pieces appeared in the sixth century B.C. Though their works have not survived, we know the names of a few writers, including Arion and Thespis. It was in the fifth century B.C. that the drama which we still read and perform took shape. The three best-known writers of Greek tragedy in this period were Aeschylus, Sophocles, and Euripides.

Aeschylus

(525–456 B.C.)

Of writers whose works still exist, Aeschylus is the first to develop drama into a form separate from singing, dancing, or storytelling. For this reason he is often considered the founder of Greek drama and therefore of all western drama.

Aeschylus's plays dealt with noble families and lofty themes and were praised for their superb lyric poetry as well as their dramatic structure and intellectual content. They won a number of first prizes in the drama contests, and Aeschylus was the acknowledged master of the tetralogy—four plays which can stand separately but are united by a single story or theme.

Before Aeschylus, a drama would have only one actor, who interacted with the chorus. Aeschylus added a second actor; this was an important development in theater practice, since it allowed for a true exchange of dialogue. He also reduced the size of the chorus, making it more manageable. Later, a third actor was introduced by Sophocles, and Aeschylus then incorporated this new feature into his own plays. Aeschylus's theatrical work included directing and acting as well as playwriting. He was fond of theatrical spectacle and is sometimes credited with having developed new forms of stage scenery, painted scenery, and elaborate costumes.

In Aristophanes' comedy *The Frogs,* Aeschylus was caricatured as pompous and rhetorical. In the same play, however, he was also judged as a dramatist superior to Euripides.

Aeschylus was born of a noble family in Eleusis, near Athens, and was highly regarded as a soldier and prominent citizen as well as a playwright and poet. Among his other military exploits, he fought for Athens against the Persians at the battle of Marathon in 490 B.C. Ten years later he served with the Athenian fleet during a second Persian invasion and was present at the important victory at Salamis. He died in 456 B.C. at the age of 69.

Aeschylus is believed to have written ninety plays. The titles of seventy-nine are known, indicating a diversity of subject matter. Only seven of his plays still exist, however (the dates given here indicate when the plays are known or thought to have been first produced): *The Suppliants* (ca. 490 B.C., but possibly considerably later); *The Persians* (ca. 472 B.C.); *Seven Against Thebes* (ca. 469 B.C.); *Prometheus Bound* (ca. 460 B.C.); and *The Oresteia* (458 B.C.), a trilogy consisting of *Agamemnon, The Choephori (Libation Bearers),* and *The Eumenides.* Aeschylus competed in the City Dionysia drama contest for the first time in 499 B.C.; he won first prize for the first time in 484 B.C.

Sophocles

(ca. 496 B.C.–406 B.C.)

Sophocles developed Aeschylus's dramatic techniques even further. He was particularly noted for his superb plot construction: he introduces characters and information skillfully and then builds swiftly to a climax. The Greek philosopher Aristotle used Sophocles' *King Oedipus* as the model for his analysis of tragedy. Exploration of character and a focus on the individual are also characteristic of Sophocles' plays. In addition, his poetry is widely admired for both its beauty and its lucidity.

As a boy, Sophocles performed in a public celebration of the victory of the Athenians over the Persians at the Battle of Salamis. As an adult, in addition to being a playwright, he acted in his own early dramas. His first victory as a dramatist came when he defeated Aeschylus in the contest of 468 B.C. From his very first play, Sophocles was a popular success. Over the years he evidently wrote over a hundred plays, winning first prize eighteen times and never finishing lower than second.

Aristotle credits Sophocles with realistic innovations in scene painting. Sophocles also increased the tragic chorus from twelve to fifteen members and is credited (as noted above) with introducing a third actor to Greek tragedy—a development which, by increasing the number of characters in a play, enlarged the possibilities for conflict and interaction.

Sophocles told his stories as single dramas instead of extending them into the traditional trilogy of three connected plays; this change added more action to the plot. Today, three of Sophocles' surviving plays—*King Oedipus, Antigone,* and *Oedipus at Colonus*—are sometimes grouped as a trilogy because they all concern the fate of the same family; but they were originally written and performed as parts of different trilogies.

As a general, a civic leader, an ambassador, and a priest, Sophocles participated fully in Athenian life during the Greek golden age. He was born near Athens at Colonus (where Oedipus received sanctuary in his final years), the son of a wealthy Athenian factory owner. He was devoted to his native city-state, Athens, and refused many invitations to live at the courts of foreign kings. He died, age 90, in 406 B.C. and thus was spared the sight of the defeat of his beloved Athens by Sparta. Throughout his long life, he was known for his good nature, a fact noted by Aristophanes in *The Frogs*.

Though Sophocles wrote over 120 plays, only seven complete tragedies have survived: *Ajax* (ca. 450 to 440 B.C.); *Antigone* (ca. 441 B.C.); *King Oedipus* (ca. 430 to 425 B.C.); *Electra* (ca. 418 to 410 B.C.); *Trachiniae* (ca. 413 B.C.); *Philoctetes* (409 B.C.); and *Oedipus at Colonus* (ca. 406 B.C.). Fragments of some of his satyr plays also survive, including a large portion of *The Trackers*.

Euripides

(ca. 480–406 B.C.)

Of the three great tragic playwrights of ancient Greece, Euripides is considered the most "modern." This description is particularly telling because Euripides actually was a contemporary of Sophocles and died a few months before him. There are several reasons why Euripides is often thought of as a more modern writer: his sympathetic portrayal of women, the greater realism of his plays, his mixture of tragedy with melodrama and comedy, and his skeptical treatment of the gods.

In fact, Euripides was often criticized for "modernism" during his own time: his characters behaved as people do in everyday life, and such realism was not considered appropriate for tragedy. His plays were also criticized for other reasons, such as their plots (which were held to be weak), their diminished use of the chorus, and their sensational subject matter. His mixing of comedy and tragedy was derided (though it became a model for the tragicomedy and melodrama of later periods). The most controversial element of Euripides' plays was his portrayal of the gods as human and fallible, a treatment that was said to undermine the traditional moral order.

Unlike Aeschylus and Sophocles, Euripides took no active part in the political or social life of Athens. He was probably born on the Athenian island of Salamis and was the son of a wealthy citizen. But though his family background and education prepared him for public life, he was by temperament reclusive and moody, interested in observing society and examining the philosophical and scientific movements of the day. It was often said that he had marital problems and disliked women; these reports about his personal life may have developed because many of his plays focus on strong-willed, passionate women. As a dramatist, Euripides created believable female characters and showed a greater understanding of women than his contemporaries.

Aristophanes frequently parodied scenes from Euripides, ridiculing both his philosophy and his dramatic methods. Only five of Euripides' ninety-two plays received prizes during his lifetime, but his reputation grew rapidly after his death. He came to be much admired for his originality and independence of thought, and many of his dramatic methods were copied by both ancient and modern playwrights.

Eighteen plays by Euripides still exist: among the best-known are *Alcestis* (438 B.C.); *Medea* (431 B.C.); *Hippolytus* (428 B.C.); *Andromache* (ca. 424 B.C.); *The Suppliants* (ca. 420 B.C.); *The Trojan Women* (415 B.C.); *Electra* (ca. 412 B.C.); *Iphigenia in Tauris* (ca. 410 B.C.); *Helen* (412 B.C.); *Orestes* (408 B.C.); *The Bacchae* (ca. 406 B.C.); and *Iphigenia in Aulis* (ca. 406 B.C.), as well as *The Cyclops,* a satyr play whose date is unknown.

A TRAGIC FIGURE. Greek playwrights perfected tragedy, which is described by Aristotle in *The Poetics*. One of the best-known tragic heroines is Medea, played here by Brenda Wade at the Guthrie Theater in Minneapolis; her unfaithful husband, Jason, is played by Stephen Yoakam.

ARISTOTLE AND THE TRAGIC FORM

The first critic who tried to pinpoint the characteristics of the Greek tragedies written by the great dramatists of the fifth century B.C. was the philosopher Aristotle. Aristotle wrote nearly a hundred years after the golden age and thus was describing a type of drama that had flourished long before his own lifetime, but his work on the subject—*The Poetics* (ca. 335 B.C.)—is still the best starting point for a discussion of tragedy.

In addition to being a philosopher, Aristotle was a scientist who described and catalogued the world he saw around him. In analyzing tragedy, he followed the same careful, sensible approach that he brought to other fields; and though *The Poetics* is loosely organized and incomplete—it may have been based on a series of lecture notes—it is so intelligent and penetrating that it remains today the single most important piece of dramatic criticism we have.

According to Aristotle, there are six elements of drama, which he ranked in order of priority:

1 Plot—the arrangement of dramatic incidents
2 Characters—the people represented in the play
3 Thought or theme—the ideas explored

4 Language—the dialogue and poetry
5 Music
6 Spectacle—scenery and other visual elements

The implication in *The Poetics* is that tragedy deals with the reversals in fortune and eventual downfall of a royal figure. In "complex" tragedies, which Aristotle feels are the best type, the suffering hero or heroine makes a discovery and recognizes what has led to his or her downfall. There are also a number of what Aristotle calls "simple" tragedies, in which there is no such scene of recognition.

Though there are variations in the structures of the thirty-one Greek tragedies that still exist, many follow the same pattern in the unfolding of their scenes. First comes the *prologos*, the opening scene, which sets the action and provides background information. Next comes the *parodos*, in which the chorus enters. This is followed by the first *episode*, a scene in which the characters confront each other and the plot starts to develop. Next there is a *choral ode* performed by the chorus. Through the body of the play, episodes alternate with choral odes until the *exodos*, the final scene, in which all the characters exit from the stage. Aristotle suggests that Greek tragedy usually focuses on one major plot without bringing in subplots or unrelated secondary concerns, though some plays do have subplots.

Several points raised by Aristotle have been subject to different interpretations because his language is sometimes ambiguous; it is difficult to know exactly what he meant. Below, for instance, are two translations of his definition of *tragedy*, neither of which gives a fully satisfactory explanation of his meaning:

> Tragedy, then, is an imitation of an action that is serious, complete, and of a certain magnitude; in language embellished with each kind of artistic ornament, the several kinds being found in separate parts of the play; in the form of action, not of narrative; through pity and fear effecting the proper purgation of these emotions.[3]

> Tragedy, then, is an imitation of an action which is serious, complete, and has bulk, in speech that has been made attractive, using each of its species separately in the parts of the play; with persons performing the action rather than through narrative carrying to completion, through a course of events involving pity and fear, the purification of those painful or fatal acts which have that quality.[4]

Parts of this definition are clear enough: tragedy presents a complete story (an action) that is serious and important (has magnitude and bulk) and is dramatized for presentation on the stage rather than recounted by a narrator. When we come to the last part of the definition, though, there is disagreement. Aristotle says that tragedy produces the emotions of pity and fear but that there is a *katharsis* of these emotions. One of the translators above calls katharsis a "purgation" of emotions and the other a "purification."

---

[3] S. H. Butcher, *Aristotle's Theory of Poetry and Fine Art*, 3d ed., Macmillan, London, 1902, p. 23.
[4] Gerald F. Else, *Aristotle's Poetics: The Argument*, Harvard University Press, Cambridge, Mass., 1957, p. 221.

The most widely accepted explanation of katharsis is the one suggested by the first translation: members of the audience feel pity for the suffering tragic hero and fear that a similar fate could befall them. If a king or queen suffers so greatly, how much more probable it would be for an ordinary person to confront similar circumstances. These emotions, however, are purged by the drama because the audience acknowledges them, and by doing so cleanses itself of their evil effects. Some critics, however, would not define *katharsis* in this way. They suggest that the tragic character, rather than the audience, is purged of pity and fear by discovering the reason for his or her suffering and downfall; this is the implication of the second translation above. Still others suggest that katharsis occurs in the chorus, as it is confronted with the tragic details of the plot, and that the audience is meant to identify with the emotional impact on the chorus. What Aristotle does make clear, however, is that changes occur as a result of the strong emotions associated with tragedy.

There is another debate, concerning Aristotle's discussion of the tragic hero, often called the *protagonist,* who is usually a royal figure. Why does the tragic hero suffer? The traditional interpretation of Aristotle's commentary suggests that the hero suffers because of a tragic flaw, or *hamartia,* in his or her character. Scholars see the flaw of *hubris,* or excessive pride, in many of the Greek tragic figures. There is, however, a great deal of disagreement over what Aristotle actually means by *hamartia.* The literal translation is "missing the mark," which has suggested to some scholars that hamartia is not so much a character flaw as an error of judgment made by the protagonist. Some recent critics have suggested that the "flaw" is often not in the leading character but in the tragic world represented by the play, a world that is temporarily disordered or "out of joint." The characters themselves may act nobly but are damned by circumstances or fate.

Despite the debates about the meaning of certain passages in *The Poetics,* Aristotle's analysis of tragedy is still considered one of the most important documents ever written on the subject.

(The Bettmann Archive)

Aristotle

(384–322 B.C.)

Born at Stagira in northern Greece, Aristotle was the son of a doctor who became court physician to the king of Macedon. Aristotle's lifelong interest in the sciences, especially biology, may be a reflection of his upbringing. As a young man he went to Athens to study with Plato at his Academy, where he remained for 20 years. There he began to develop his own philosophic system, at first by suggesting improvements in Plato's ideas. After Plato died in 347 B.C., Aristotle left the Academy and spent 13 years away from Athens, including 3 years as tutor to the young Alexander the Great in Macedon.

Aristotle returned to Athens in 335 B.C. and opened his own school, the Lyceum. He remained in Athens until a wave of hostility against Macedon— the region where he was born— swept Athens following Alexander's death in 323 B.C. Aristotle left Athens and died the following year on a nearby island.

Aristotle's *Poetics,* the work in which he outlines his views on literature, is incomplete and (as we noted above) may have originally been written as notes for a series of lectures. Most of the treatise is on tragedy; comedy, epic poetry, and other forms of literature are mentioned only briefly. Aristotle's discussion of tragedy, however, is of supreme importance. Plato had charged that drama, especially tragedy, is a danger to society because it encourages irrationality. As if answering Plato, Aristotle argues in *The Poetics* that tragedy is positive and helpful because it not only arouses pity and fear but also purges these emotions, restoring harmony to the soul.

Logic, metaphysics, psychology, physics, theology, ethics, politics, biology, and literary theory are among the topics covered by Aristotle in his 170 works. In his writings he stressed the importance of detailed observation and description of a phenomenon before attempting to form a theory—a process that still forms the basis of scientific method. Aristotle employed the same technique when examining drama. In *The Poetics,* rather than formulating rules, he carefully observed classical Greek tragedy and described it in detail. Aristotle, Socrates, and Plato are recognized as the most influential Greek philosophers, but Aristotle was the only one of the three to include an analysis of drama in his philosophic writings.

The Poetics was little studied by the Greeks and Romans, but it became the basis of dramatic criticism when it was rediscovered by Renaissance scholars. During this period, Aristotle's descriptions and suggestions were misinterpreted as inflexible rules for the writing of tragedies; Aristotle never intended that, but the distortion has unfortunately persisted to modern times.

CRISIS DRAMA

Aristotle's analysis of tragedy emphasizes plot. The Greeks developed an approach to dramatic structure that became the prototype—in an altered and more rigid form—for plays written in the Renaissance (in Italy and France) and the modern period (the well-made plays of Ibsen, Strindberg, and others). We will refer to this structure as *crisis drama.* Though not every Greek play conformed to it, its elements were first developed in Greece and are evident in a number of dramas, particularly those by Aeschylus and Sophocles.

In crisis drama the action begins near the climax, or high point, of the story, with the characters already in the midst of their struggles. There are very few characters, and there is only one main action; the play occurs within a short span of time (frequently 24 hours or less) and takes place in one locale. Dramatic tension is increased because calamities befall the characters in a very short time. Since the play begins in the midst of the crisis, the audience must be provided with a great deal of background information, which is known as *exposition.* Thus the plot of a crisis drama often unravels like a mystery.

To understand the structure of Greek tragedy, it will be helpful to examine a single play, Sophocles' *King Oedipus,* which was first presented around 430 B.C. There are structural similarities among all extant Greek tragedies, but it should be noted that *King Oedipus* is the only one that conforms exactly to Aristotle's description.

Like most Greek tragedies, *King Oedipus* is based on a myth. In this case, the myth tells how the infant Oedipus, son of the king and queen of Thebes, is left on a mountaintop to die because of a prophecy that he will murder his father and marry his mother. However, he is rescued and taken to be raised by the king and queen of Corinth. When he grows up, Oedipus hears about the prophecy and, not knowing that he is adopted, leaves home so that he will not kill the king of Corinth, the man he thinks of as his father. On the road he encounters a stranger, argues with him, and subsequently kills him, unaware that it is actually his own father whom he has slain. Later, Oedipus becomes king of Thebes and, still in ignorance, marries the woman who is really his mother, Jocasta. When a plague strikes Thebes, Oedipus sets out to find the cause.

Following the pattern of crisis drama, Sophocles begins his play near the major crisis in the story. He also structures his plot by using the basic elements of classical Greek tragedy. The play opens with a prologue in which Oedipus learns about the plague and also learns from his brother-in-law, Creon, that an oracle has said that the plague will end when the murderer of the former king is found and punished. Next comes the parodos: the appearance of a chorus of elderly men, who pray to the gods to end the plague. Then begins the first episode. Oedipus proclaims that he will find and punish the guilty person. The blind prophet Teiresias arrives and professes ignorance of past events, but when accused by Oedipus of conspiring with Creon against him, Teiresias hints that the guilty person is Oedipus himself. Oedipus is incensed at the suggestion. Following this, in the first choral song, the chorus asks who the murderer can be and expresses doubt that it is Oedipus.

In the second episode, Creon defends himself against an angry Oedipus, who accuses him of a conspiracy with Teiresias. Jocasta, Oedipus's wife, enters to tell her husband to ignore the oracle; it had predicted that her first husband would be killed by his son, but according to all reports he was killed by thieves at a crossroads. Oedipus, remembering that he has killed a man at a crossroads, begins to fear that he is the murderer; but he is reassured by Jocasta, who urges him to ignore his fears. (Notice how skillfully Sophocles alternates good news and bad news for Oedipus, carrying him from the heights to the depths and back again time after time.)

In the next choral song, the chorus—beginning to have doubts about Oedipus's innocence—says that reverence for the gods is best; prosperity leads to pride, which will be punished. In the third scene, or episode, a messenger from Corinth announces that the king there is dead. Jocasta is jubilant, for this means that the oracle cannot be trusted: it had said that Oedipus would kill his

A SCENE FROM KING OEDIPUS. In Sophocles's *King Oedipus*—one of the most famous Greek tragedies—Oedipus becomes king of Thebes after unknowingly killing his father and marrying his mother. Here, Jocasta, Oedipus's wife and mother, begs him to stop seeking the king's murderer because she has figured out the horrible truth.

father, but the father has died of natural causes. The messenger then reveals that Oedipus is not the son of the king of Corinth. Fearing the worst, Jocasta tries to persuade Oedipus to cease his search. When he will not, she rushes into the palace. Oedipus sends for a shepherd who knows the full story of his origins and forces the shepherd to tell it. Learning the truth, Oedipus then goes into the palace himself.

In the following choral song, the chorus says that all life is sorrowful and bemoans the fall of Oedipus. In the exodos, or final scene, a messenger from the palace describes how Jocasta has killed herself and Oedipus has put out his own eyes. The blind Oedipus reappears to recite his sad story, courageously accepts his fate, and goes into in exile.

King Oedipus is admired for several reasons. One is the masterful way in which Sophocles unfolds the plot; it is like a detective story in which Oedipus is the detective tracking down a murderer. Another is the beauty of Sophocles' language. Though most modern readers do not understand ancient Greek, even in translation we can often appreciate the effectiveness of Sophocles' poetic expressions. For example, here are the words of the chorus just after Oedipus has discovered his fate; the chorus is saying that life is only a shadow and happiness often an illusion.

Alas, you generations of men, I count your life as nothing more than a shadow. Where, where is the mortal who wins more of happiness than just the appearance, and, after the appearance, a falling away? Yours is a fate that warns me—unhappy Oedipus—to call no earthly creature blest.

King Oedipus is also admired because of the religious and philosophical questions it raises. Why does a man like Oedipus suffer? Is it because of some flaw in his character—his pride, for example—or because of an error in judgment? Is it, perhaps, to test Oedipus, as Job is tested by God in the Bible? Or is it because the world is a place where life is sometimes cruel and unjust and the innocent must suffer?

King Oedipus also affects audiences because of the tragic fall of the protagonist. Oedipus not only loses his kingdom; equally affecting is his loss of his family—dramatized by his separation from his children at the close of the play—and of his community as he goes into exile. We should note that in the great classical tragedies, the playwrights frequently dramatized the political, familial, and social suffering of their protagonists, possibly to heighten katharsis.

People have been studying *King Oedipus* for over 2,000 years, and they continue to find profound and complex meanings in what its characters say and do. The psychoanalyst Sigmund Freud, for instance, developed a theory that men subconsciously wish to murder their fathers and marry their mothers, and he called this desire the *Oedipus complex*.

Satyr Plays and Old Comedy

As was mentioned earlier, on the days devoted to tragedy at the dramatic festival, three tragedies by a single playwright were presented. (*King Oedipus* would have been performed as one of three tragedies by Sophocles.) When the three tragedies presented in one day were linked to form a connected dramatic whole—for example, *The Oresteia* of Aeschylus—they were called a *trilogy*. Following the presentation of the three plays, whether they formed a trilogy or were independent, a short play by the same author, called a *satyr play*, was given as an afterpiece.

A satyr play was a comical play involving a chorus of satyrs, mythological creatures who were half-goat and half-man. It was structured like a Greek tragedy but parodied the mythological and heroic tales that were treated seriously in tragedies. Satyr plays poked fun at honored Greek institutions, including religion and folk heroes, and often had elements of vulgarity. The only complete satyr play still in existence is *The Cyclops* by Euripides.

The third type of drama presented at Greek festivals was comedy. The comedies of this period are called *Old Comedies;* the only ones that survive are all by Aristophanes and have certain recurring characteristics. Most Old Comedies do not follow the pattern of crisis drama: they do not take place in a short span of time, are not restricted to one locale, and have large casts of characters. Old Comedy always makes fun of society, politics, or culture, and frequently its characters are recognizable contemporary personalities. In *The Clouds*, for instance, the philosopher Socrates is shown as a character suspended in midair in a basket—in other words, his head is always in the clouds. A present-day equivalent might be the kind of television variety-show sketch that caricatures political figures, such as the president of the United States.

SATYRS. Because we have few visual records of Greek theater itself, we rely on evidence from artifacts such as vases. This vase painting depicts satyrs—the mythical half-man, half-goat creatures who appeared in short plays presented after a set of three tragedies. The satyrs in the painting are playing harplike instruments called *lyres*.

Old Comedy uses fantastical and improbable plots to underline its satire. In *The Birds*, two characters who are unhappy with their earthly existence leave for Cloudcuckooland to observe the lives of the birds and discover ludicrous parallels between bird society and human society. In *Lysistrata*, Aristophanes condemns the Peloponnesian War, which was then raging in Greece. The Greek women in this comedy go on a sex strike, refusing to sleep with their husbands until the men cease warring. Miraculously, the scheme works.

Old Comedies do have sections similar to those in tragedy: prologos, episodes alternating with choral odes, and the exodos. There are, however, certain unique episodes in Old Comedy. One is the *agon,* a scene with a debate between the two opposing forces in a play—each representing one side of a social or political issue. Another is the *parabasis,* a scene in which the chorus speaks directly to the audience, makes fun of the spectators and specific audience members, or satirizes other subjects. Religious and political officials attended dramatic festivals and were seated in the front row of the theater; during the parabasis, the chorus would single them out for ridicule. (A counterpart today would be television or standup comics who attack their audiences.)

Aristophanes

(ca. 448–380 B.C.)

The best-known comic playwright of the Greek golden age was Aristophanes. In his play *The Clouds*, Aristophanes complains that other playwrights are copying his plots and ideas; if this was true, it suggests that his comedies were very popular. Written in the style of Old Comedy, Aristophanes' plays reflect the social and political climate in Athens as it declined in power toward the end of the fifth century B.C.

The son of a wealthy citizen, Aristophanes was a member of the prosperous, conservative Athenian middle class. His plays indicate that he came from a cultured, old-fashioned home. Life in Athens was changing rapidly during his lifetime—greed for an empire was undermining the traditional simplicity, stability, and moral order—and he used his plays to ridicule the ideas and people that he felt were leading Athens to ruin. One of his targets was the Peloponnesian War with Sparta, a conflict that drained Athens of wealth and destroyed its social order. His death came after the Peloponnesian War had reduced Athens to poverty and disarray.

In spite of his conservative outlook, Aristophanes' plays are full of bawdy wit—a reflection of the open attitude toward sex in Athenian society. Since Old Comedy did not emphasize plot or character, Aristophanes' plays are distinguished for their inventive comic scenes, witty dialogue, and pointed satire. Because of their many references to contemporary people and events, his plays are difficult to translate into playable modern versions.

Besides what we know about him from his plays, an incident recorded in Plato's *Symposium* reveals that Aristophanes was very much involved in the daily life of Athens, including attending parties with friends. Plato reports that after outdrinking and outtalking all the guests at an all-night party, Aristophanes left with the philosopher Socrates, debating whether one man could write both comedy and tragedy.

Though he wrote about forty plays, Aristophanes did not feel competent to stage his own works and usually turned his plays over to a producer-director. Eleven of the plays survive. Among the best-known are *The Clouds* (423 B.C.), *The Wasps* (422 B.C.), *Peace* (421 B.C.), *The Birds* (414 B.C.), *Lysistrata* (411 B.C.), and *The Frogs* (405 B.C.). Aristophanes' last plays—in particular, *Plutus* (388 B.C.)—are often categorized as *Middle Comedies,* transitional works which led to the development of the nonpolitical New Comedy. (New Comedy is described later in this chapter.)

The Chorus

The chorus is an integral and unique feature of classical Greek drama. Its importance is seen in the fact that a *chorodidaskalos*—a choral trainer—was employed for all festival productions. The chorus in tragedy probably consisted of twelve male members when Aeschylus began writing and then was increased to fifteen by Sophocles. In comedy, there were twenty-four men in the chorus. Greek comedy often employed a double chorus, with the twenty-four members divided into two groups of twelve. In *Lysistrata,* there are choruses of old men and old women. Chorus members probably intoned their lines in unison; on occasion, the choral leader delivered his lines independently.

The Greek chorus performed a number of dramatic functions. It provided expository information, commented on the action, interacted with other characters, and described offstage action. In tragedy, the chorus often represented the common people of the city-state ruled by the tragic hero or heroine;

(Michal Daniel/Guthrie Theater)

THE GREEK CHORUS. The chorus in classical Greek theater served many functions. It provided exposition, interacted with the other actors, and added spectacle. In this production of *Iphigenia at Aulis* at the Guthrie Theater in 1992, the chorus adds a visual component to the drama: dance and unique costuming.

audience members could identify with the feelings and ideas of these people. Since choruses sang and danced, they also provided spectacle, as choruses do today in musical comedies. In Old Comedy, the chorus was frequently fantastical; for example, chorus members appear as birds in *The Birds* and as frogs in *The Frogs*.

Of the various Greek dramatic conventions, it is the chorus that is probably most difficult for modern audiences to envision; a group of performers speaking in unison, chanting, and dancing is hard for modern spectators to imagine.

Greek Theater Production

THE THEATER BUILDING

An important element of Greek theater was the kind of space in which plays were presented. Since tragedies, comedies, and satyr plays were offered at religious festivals, huge theaters were necessary: the classical Greek theater probably accommodated 15,000 to 17,000 spectators. The most noted of these theaters was the Theater of Dionysus in Athens.

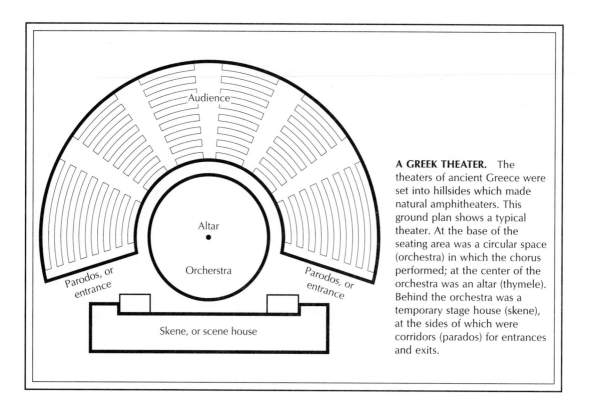

A GREEK THEATER. The theaters of ancient Greece were set into hillsides which made natural amphitheaters. This ground plan shows a typical theater. At the base of the seating area was a circular space (orchestra) in which the chorus performed; at the center of the orchestra was an altar (thymele). Behind the orchestra was a temporary stage house (skene), at the sides of which were corridors (parados) for entrances and exits.

Greek theaters were outdoor amphitheaters with light provided by the sun, and the Greeks were often resourceful in the use of natural lighting in their dramas; if a play required a "sunrise effect," for example, it would be presented as the first drama of the day, at dawn.

There were three separate parts in a Greek theater: the *theatron* (literally, "viewing place"), which was the seating area for the audience; the *orchestra,* or playing area for the actors; and the *skene,* or scene building. These three units were adjacent but unconnected architectural entities.

The audience sat in the theatron. The Greeks ingeniously built their theaters into hillsides which provided naturally sloped seating and excellent acoustics. During the classical period the hillside theatron probably had temporary wooden bleachers, but these were replaced by stone seats during the later Hellenistic period (336–146 B.C.). Some historians believe that a specific seating plan was followed in the Greek theatron; they suggest that the various Greek tribes were segregated and that men and women sat separately. Front-row seats, known as the *proedria,* were reserved for political and religious dignitaries. The theaters, though huge, could not accommodate everyone, and therefore in the fifth century B.C. entrance fees were charged. It is important to remember, though, that (unlike a theater event today) each play was seen by a substantial portion of the population. (Today, it would be as if virtually the entire population of a small town took part in a single event—truly a communal occasion.)

In commercial American theaters, the orchestra is the audience seating area on the ground floor. In the classical Greek theater, the orchestra was the playing area. The orchestra was the first permanent structural element in the Greek theater; it was a circle about 66 feet in diameter, paved with stone. Here again, there had been an evolution from earlier practices. In ceremonies of earlier days, it is believed, a circle was beaten down in a field of grain to serve as an area for presentations, and this circle was the forerunner of the orchestra. (We should note that some historians, on the basis of recent studies of excavations of the Theater of Dionysus, suggest that the first orchestra may have been a rectangle.)

The acting area was surrounded on three sides by audience members—a configuration similar to the modern thrust theater or three-quarter-round theater. In this type of theater, the stage juts out into the auditorium and the audience sits around the stage in a semicircle or on three sides. In the center of the orchestra there was probably a *thymele,* an altar; this is a reminder that Greek drama was a part of religious rituals. Some scholars believe that the thymele may have been used as a scenic element. (For example, in *King Oedipus* Jocasta makes an offering, suggesting one possible use of the thymele.) Other commentators, however, argue that the altar was too holy to have been used in dramas; and still others doubt that the altar was included in the orchestra at all.

The third element in the classical Greek theater building was the skene, or scene building, located behind the orchestra. Our knowledge of the skene is sketchy, but we do know that it contained dressing space for actors who needed to change costumes and was used to store properties. (A *property,* or *prop,* in the theater is any object used by the actors during a play, such as a sword or shield in a battle scene.) It is also believed that the skene building was used as the basic setting for all plays after 458 B.C.

What the skene looked like is another major point of contention among theater historians: how tall was it, for example, and how many doors did it have? At first it was a temporary wooden structure; after the classical period, it became a permanent stone edifice. In the classical period, the building was probably one story high, but it later became a two-story structure. The skene also had side wings *(paraskenia)*. Since the most common setting for Greek tragedies is a palace, the skene had to be patterned after such an edifice. There were doorways—probably three, although some historians think there was only one—for entrances and exits.

There is another controversy surrounding the architectural configuration of the playing area. Some scholars believe that there was a raised stage area in front of the skene and directly behind the orchestra; others strongly reject the idea of a raised stage. We know that after the classical period, huge raised stages were constructed in Greek theaters. A possible compromise is the suggestion that there was a slightly raised platform in front of the skene.

Debates in Theater History:
THE GREEK STAGE

The difficulty of reconstructing the classical Greek theater building can be easily seen in the debate among historians over whether there was an elevated stage in front of the skene. Many of the arguments have to do with the appearance of the scene building because no skenes from the classical era survive.

Margarete Bieber, a renowned historian of the Greek and Roman theaters, states categorically, "The most important thing to bear in mind when reading Greek plays is that in the classical age there was no such thing as a raised stage."[*] The Roman architect Vitruvius, on the other hand, argued that there was a stage, 10 to 12 feet high—although this was probably not true of the classical era but is more accurately a description of the Hellenistic

[*] Margarete Bieber, *The History of the Greek and Roman Theater*, 2d ed., Princeton University Press, Princeton, N.J., 1961, p. 73.

stage. Other historians argue that there was a slightly raised platform (or possibly a flight of stairs) in front of the skene, which would spatially separate the actors from the chorus. These scholars base their argument on needs implied by texts of plays, on contemporary references to staging, and on analysis of excavations of the Theater of Dionysus.

These differing views lead historians to form different ideas about how the Greek tragedies and comedies were originally staged and about how the skene was used. Ultimately, this argument (like the argument about how many doors there were in the scene building) demonstrates how little we actually know about the configuration of this key element in classical Greek theater architecture. It also indicates that most of our theories are based on later historical commentaries rather than on primary sources from the classical era itself.

SCENERY AND SPECIAL EFFECTS

The standard setting for Greek tragedy, with its royal heroes and heroines, was a palace; but there are some tragedies with other scenic requirements, and the comedies require a wide variety of locales. How, then, did the Greeks transform the facade of the skene so that it might appear to be a different setting for different plays?

We have no definite knowledge about the methods used during the classical period, but some scholars believe that the scene-changing techniques of the later Hellenistic period were adopted from classical theater. One device was the *pinake,* a type of flat—a wooden frame covered with stretched fabric. Another was the *periaktoi:* these consisted of three painted flats hinged together, each showing a different scene; rotating these flats would reveal a new scene to the audience.

What should be kept in mind is that scene changes in classical Greek theater were not realistic. Modern audiences expect the environments of different plays to be markedly distinct; but in Greek theater there were only hints that the setting had changed—and frequently these hints were provided only by the dialogue. Because of the vast size of the theaters and the limitations imposed by an outdoor space, it was impossible to create a unique environment for every tragedy, comedy, and satyr play. Also, many historians argue that such devices as the pinakes and periaktoi were not used at all in the classical era but appeared much later in Greek theater. (Part of the debate revolves around the interpretation of Aristotle's statement that Sophocles introduced scene painting to Greek theater.)

The skene also masked the mechanisms for special effects. If modern audiences are hypnotized by technological wonders in theater, the classical Greeks were no different. The two most popular special-effects devices were the *mechane,* or "machine," and the *ekkyklema.*

Greek dramas often reached a climax with the sudden appearance of a deity who resolved all the dramatic problems. The mechane, a crane hidden behind the upper level of the skene, was used to effect the entrance of the actor playing the god or goddess in such a way as to suggest a descent from the heavens; hence the term *deus ex machina,* which means "god from a machine." (In subsequent usage, of course, this term has been broadened; today, any unjustified or arbitrary dramatic device employed to unravel a plot is still referred to as a *deus ex machina.)*

Since the Greeks did not present violence onstage, stage machinery was needed to reveal climactic offstage deaths. One such machine was the ekkyklema, a wagon that would be wheeled from behind the skene.

MECHANE AND EKKYKLEMA. This conjectural reconstruction of Greek stage machinery shows, on the left, a crane used for flying in characters located on a side wing (paraskenia) of the scene building; and, on the right, a mechane higher up on the roof of the skene. The ekkyklema, shown at bottom, was a platform on wheels used to bring characters out from inside the building.

(Adapted from Margarete Bieber, The History of the Greek and Roman Theater, 2d ed., Princeton University Press, Princeton, N.J., 1961)

Mechane

Mechane

Skene

Skene

Paraskenion

Ekkyklema

ACTING IN GREEK THEATER

Actors may or may not have been paid for their participation in festivals during the classical period; but even if they were paid, there were not enough of these events for them to make a living by acting, and so they could not have been full-time professionals. At first, when tragedy had only one actor, the role was usually performed by the playwright; both Thespis and Aeschylus wrote plays and performed in them. Sophocles was the first playwright to give up acting.

As we have seen, Aeschylus is credited with introducing a second actor, and Sophocles supposedly introduced a third actor. Sophocles also introduced a "three-actor rule" in tragedy, calling for no more than three actors, excluding the chorus; this rule seems to have been followed by other Greek dramatists. (Comedy was not restricted by the three-actor rule.) The rule was bent to allow additional performers to portray mute roles, that is, minor characters who did not speak lines. Since one actor could *double*—play more than one part in a play—there could be more than three characters in a play, though never more than three onstage at one time. Sophocles' *King Oedipus,* for instance, has seven speaking parts, and the same actor might play several minor parts.

At first, playwrights chose their own performers and also oversaw the production of their own plays. The tragic playwrights, in particular, functioned as directors; they worked with the chorus and also assisted the actors, conferring with them about roles and scripts. After acting contests were introduced in 449 B.C., to ensure fairness the state conducted a lottery that determined which star performers would appear in which plays. Greek dramatists—like today's playwrights, directors, and producers—were aware that it is difficult to discern the quality of a play when the acting is poor.

To imagine the acting style of the fifth century B.C. is almost impossible. It could not have been very realistic—that is, it could not have conformed to everyday speech and gestures—because many of the conventions of classical theater seem to argue against such realism. For example, in many plays (such as *Lysistrata)*, it is important for the audience to believe that the female characters are sexually alluring; but women were not allowed to perform, and men played the female roles. Furthermore, all forms of Greek drama required dancelike movement and chanting.

COSTUMES AND MASKS

The major element in Greek costuming was the mask. All Greek performers wore masks, which covered the whole head and included hair, beards, and other distinctive facial features. These helped the audience identify characters and allowed the actors to perform multiple roles. During the classical period, the facial coverings were not highly exaggerated, and in tragedies, the masks for all the chorus members were probably the same. Comic choruses, on the other hand, often required unusual masks; in two of Aristophanes' plays, as we've seen, chorus members represented frogs and birds.

Greek costuming, for the most part, was fairly conventional. Our knowledge of costumes comes mostly from scenes painted on Greek vases. Tragic characters of Greek origin, regardless of historical period, probably wore a very ornate tunic and a short or long cloak. Illustrations often depict Greek performers wearing a thick-soled boot known as a *kothornos,* but this was not used until the later Hellenistic period; in the classical period, soft-soled footwear was used. (There is, however, much debate over the validity of drawing conclusions from vase paintings about costuming during the classical era.)

Comic costumes, which were based on everyday clothing, were often cut tight to create a humorous effect by emphasizing certain physical features. A unique element in comic costuming was the phallus, an exaggerated penis which all male characters wore around the waist. It has been suggested that this use of the phallus originated in the fertility rites out of which comedy possibly originated. Some historians believe that the phallus was a foot long, made of leather, and stuffed. At times, it was probably rolled up and concealed; at other times, it hung loose for a comic effect.

THEATER IN THE HELLENISTIC AGE

The Hellenistic period in Greece—which followed the classical period—is dated from the beginning of the reign of Alexander the Great in 336 B.C. to the conquering of the Greeks by the expanding Roman civilization in 146 B.C. Significant changes took place in theater during the Hellenistic age: New Comedy was developed; construction of new theaters was emphasized; and the focus appears to have shifted from the playwright to the actor.

New Comedy

For 75 years after the end of the fifth century B.C., Greek theater continued to follow classical conventions. The major change in Greek drama in the fourth century B.C. occurred in comedy.

By 336 B.C., Old Comedy had given way to a form called *New Comedy.* The only extant example of New Comedy is *The Grouch* by Menander (342–291 B.C.), though there are fragments of a number of others. New Comedy is an extremely important form because most modern comedy continues to use its dramatic techniques. Instead of the political, social, and cultural satire of Old Comedy, the plots of New Comedy deal with romantic and domestic problems. A typical romantic plot line can be summarized as "boy meets girl, boy loses girl, boy gets girl." A domineering parent usually comes between the young lovers, and the romantic complications are resolved by sudden dramatic coincidences and discoveries.

The characters in New Comedy are recognizable stock types, such as domineering parents, romantic young lovers, and comic servants. The chorus is relegated to a minor position. (In tragedy the chorus had also become less important toward the close of the classical period, particularly in the works of Euripides.) Strong parallels can be drawn between New Comedy and today's television comedies, which also focus on domestic and romantic complications.

THE THEATER AT EPIDAUROS. One Hellenistic theater still standing is at Epidauros. Note the semicircular seating area in the hillside and the circular orchestra. However, only remains of the skene's foundation have survived.

Hellenistic Theaters

Numerous theaters were built throughout the Greek world in the Hellenistic period. We know of at least forty Hellenistic theaters—doubtless there were more—in places from Asia Minor in the east to Italy in the west. The remains of some of these are still standing; their sizes range from 3,000 seats to over 20,000.

Hellenistic theaters, which had become permanent stone structures, contained huge raised stages—part of the remodeled skene. The scene house was now two stories high, with the wings removed, and the stage was supported by the lower level of the skene. The upper level provided the background for the stage. In some theaters, ramps led up to the stage, and doorways—12 feet wide and almost as high as the skene's second story—led onto the stage. In some Hellenistic theaters, there were as many as seven of these doorways, known as *thyromata;* other theaters, however, continued to have a single portal.

The stages were between 8 and 13 feet high, 6 to 14 feet deep, and in some theaters 140 feet long; thus both their height and their length were considerably greater than in most modern theaters. The relationship between the stage and the circular orchestra has been debated; some historians believe that the orchestra gradually fell out of use as a playing area and others that the stage was used for new plays and the orchestra for revivals of classical dramas.

The remodeled skene, the huge raised stage, and other changes in theater structures all indicate a sharp shift of visual focus to the actor—a development we'll consider next.

Hellenistic Acting

THE RISE OF THE ACTOR

Throughout theater history, there are shifts in focus from one theatrical element to another: from script, for instance, to performers to visual effects. Such a shift occurred during the Hellenistic period as new scripts—which had been a prominent feature of the classical era—became less important and the work of performers became more prominent. This is similar to the focus of much of contemporary film and television, which, like Hellenistic theater, is actor-centered: scripts take second place to star performers.

In the Hellenistic era, there was a general increase in both number and kind of theatrical activities. Worship of Dionysus was no longer the sole reason for staging drama, and plays were therefore included in other festivals, such as those honoring military victories. With more productions, there developed a need for professional actors.

The ascendancy of the actor led to the establishment, by 277 B.C., of a guild known as the Artists of Dionysus. Actors, chorus members, playwrights, and various other theater personnel belonged to it; and if a local government wanted to stage a play, local members of the Artists of Dionysus had to be hired. (Wealthy individuals were no longer expected to produce plays, probably because there was a decrease in personal wealth in Greece at this time. Instead, the government became the producing agency, with a government official, the *agonthetes,* in charge of production details.) The Artists of Dionysus—an early ancestor of Actor's Equity, the union of American professional actors—provided actors with professional security.

During times of war, actors, who were not expected to take part in military service, could travel unhindered, and performers were called on to serve as ambassadors and messengers.

Developments in costumes also indicate the ascendancy of the actor. Masks exaggerated facial features and were larger than life; this had not been the case in classical Greece. Tragic characters wore large, exaggerated headdresses known as the *onkos,* and according to some scholars, the shoes *(kothornoi)* worn by tragic characters were extremely elevated. Because the actor was costumed to look bigger than life and performed on a raised stage, he became the clear focus of the audience's attention.

Though the actor was the center of the Hellenistic theater, this should not obscure the fact that he was viewed as less than socially acceptable. In the classical period, the actor had been a semiprofessional involved in religious activity. Yet even in the early fourth century B.C., the philosopher Plato, in *The Republic*, expressed his disapproval of theatrical performers, concluding that they should not be allowed to enter the ideal state. Plato's distrust was rooted in his fear that actors would employ their chameleon-like personalities to harm society. In the Hellenistic era, this distrust intensified, and even Aristotle, a great admirer of drama, considered actors disreputable. (The belief that actors are "less moral" than the average citizen still persists; today's gossip columnists feed the public's obsession with "immorality" in Hollywood and on Broadway.) It was because Hellenistic performers wanted to avert public hostility and remind audiences of their ties with religion that they named their guild the Artists of Dionysus.

The disrepute of actors was reinforced by the lifestyle of the *mimes*, who were probably the earliest professional performers in Greece. The mimes were not originally involved in religious festivals; they were traveling players who presented a variety of entertainments, including juggling, acrobatics, wordless dances dramatizing fables, and sketches with dialogue. (Greek mimes, who spoke and engaged in varied entertainment activities, were not the equivalent of modern mimes, such as Marcel Marceau, who perform without words.) Many of the mime troupes originated in southern Italy, and their most popular dramatic pieces were satires of the great tragedies. Their lifestyle seems to have earned them general condemnation. These performers were nomads who entertained at banquets and probably in the streets on temporary stages. After 300 B.C., they were allowed to perform at festivals, but they were never given recognition in the Artists of Dionysus. The traveling mime troupes were also criticized because they included women. The Greeks—and many succeeding civilizations—considered theater an unsuitable profession for women, and women involved in theatrical endeavors were castigated as licentious and immoral.

While theater continued to flourish in Greece long after 146 B.C., it was no longer purely Greek but, rather, theatrical art influenced by the omnipresent Roman civilization. Therefore, we turn next to Rome in our study of the evolution of the dramatic arts.

SUMMARY

Greek theater set the stage for all western theater to follow. A dramatic form known as *crisis structure* evolved during the classical era; and the tragedies of Aeschylus, Sophocles, and Euripides—which dramatize the downfall of a royal figure caught in a difficult or impossible situation—set a standard for all subsequent tragedy. Aristotle's *Poetics* began the development of serious critical consideration of drama and theater. The Greeks were leaders in comedy as well: Aristophanes' Old Comedies, which poked fun at contemporary political, social, and cultural events as well as personalities, are forerunners of later satire.

Classical Greek theater buildings were huge outdoor spaces built into hillsides; they accommodated audiences attending religious festivals in honor of the god Dionysus. Behind the orchestra, which was a circular playing space, the scene building served as the basic scenic unit. The performers, all of whom were males, almost certainly acted in a style that did not conform to everyday life. The chorus was an integral element of all classical Greek drama and theater.

Major changes took place during the Hellenistic period. New Comedy, which was concerned with domestic and romantic situations, prepared the way for almost all popular comedy to follow and continues to influence contemporary playwrights. The drama of the Hellenistic period was not as noteworthy as that of the classical era, but the ascendancy of the actor was an important development, prefiguring today's star system. The huge raised stage in theaters, distinctive footwear and large headdress in costuming, and the founding of the Artists of Dionysus—a theater guild for actors—all indicate a new focus on the performer. The permanent stone theater structures suggest the permanent hold theater was to have in western civilization.

CHAPTER 2

. . . .

ROMAN THEATER

I t is 184 B.C. and we, along with many of the inhabitants of the city of Rome, are on our way to attend performances at a spring festival in honor of Jupiter. Our mood today is happy and ebullient, partly because it is spring, but even more because we are on our way to see a comedy by Plautus, whose plot twists and comic invention make his works favorites with everyone.

The theater we are about to enter is a large temporary wooden building, seating several thousand people, that has been erected next to a temple honoring Jupiter. All theater productions in Rome at this time take place during religious festivals, and all theaters are near temples. The Roman theater— unlike the Greek theaters in the lands Rome has conquered—is a single unit, with the stage house attached to the ends of a semicircular audience area. In front of the stage house is a long platform stage; and in front of that, surrounded by the audience, is a half-circle which is a holdover from Greek theaters. But whereas Greek theaters were carved out of hillsides, this theater is a freestanding structure, built on level ground.

A FUNNY THING HAPPENED ON THE WAY TO THE FORUM.   This popular musical is testimony to the enduring qualities of Roman farce: written by Bert Shevelove and Larry Gelbart, with words and music by Stephen Sondheim, it is based on several plays by Plautus, particularly *Miles Gloriosus, Mostellaria,* and *Pseudolus.* The production here is by the Williamstown Theater Festival. *(Richard Feldman)*

The group we join today, converging on the theater, consists of people from all walks of life. Plautus himself has remarked in his writings that the Roman audience is a genuine mixture. In addition to well-to-do middle- and upper-class citizens, it includes government officials and their wives, children with nurses, prostitutes, and slaves—in short, members of virtually every social group. Because this is a state festival, admission is free. As we enter the theater, people are jostling to get good seats and to be near their friends. Since we are to see comedies today, a festive, carefree atmosphere prevails.

Magistrates of the state have received a grant to produce today's plays; they have engaged acting troupes to present the individual plays, each troupe under the direction of a manager. One of these managers has purchased from Plautus a play called *The Menaechmi* and has arranged for the costumes, music, and other production elements.

As we enter the theater, we see two doors on the stage: one opens on the house of Menaechmus of Epidamnus (the Greek city in which Plautus has set his play); the other is the door to the house of Erotium, a woman with whom Menaechmus is having a love affair that he is trying to keep secret from his wife. The stage represents the street in front of the two houses; at one end is an exit to the port, and at the other end is an exit to the center of town.

As the play begins, an actor comes onstage to deliver a prologue, spoken directly to the audience. He asks us to pay careful attention to what Plautus has to say, and then he outlines the background of the story: how the Menaechmi twins were separated when they were infants and how the twin from Syracuse is just now returning to try to find his long-lost brother. As is true with most of Plautus's plays, most of the dialogue is sung, somewhat like the musical numbers in twentieth-century musical comedies.

When the action of the play begins, we first meet Menaechmus of Epidamnus and a friend, a hanger-on known as "Sponge." In their conversation these two establish a number of plot threads. For example, under his outer clothes Menaechmus is wearing one of his wife's prettiest dresses, which he is going to give to his mistress, Erotium. Later, Erotium sends the dress out to be altered, and when Menaechmus's wife looks for the dress and cannot find it, all kinds of complications develop. A bit later Menaechmus's twin from Syracuse comes on the scene and is mistaken for his brother by both the wife and the mistress, at which point Menaechmus of Syracuse becomes hopelessly confused and the audience is highly amused.

All through the play, both the befuddled characters and the complicated plot evoke boisterous laughter. Roman audiences are quick to express their approval or disapproval of everything about a play; today, we make it clear to Plautus and the acting troupe that *The Menaechmi* is a success.

BACKGROUND: THE REPUBLIC AND THE EMPIRE

As Greece declined in power and importance, another civilization began to emerge in Europe, on the Italian peninsula. Its center was the city of Rome, from which it took its name.

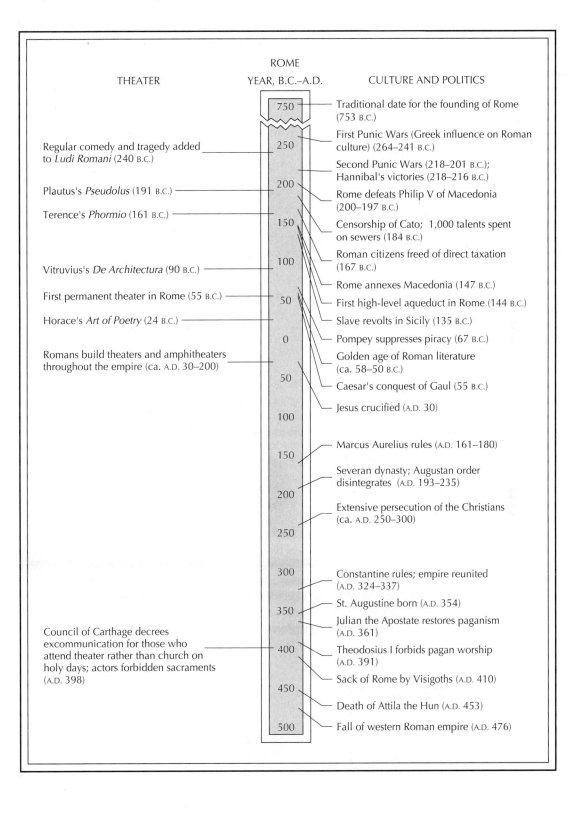

ROME
YEAR, B.C.–A.D.

THEATER

CULTURE AND POLITICS

750 — Traditional date for the founding of Rome (753 B.C.)

Regular comedy and tragedy added to *Ludi Romani* (240 B.C.)

250 — First Punic Wars (Greek influence on Roman culture) (264–241 B.C.)

Second Punic Wars (218–201 B.C.); Hannibal's victories (218–216 B.C.)

200

Plautus's *Pseudolus* (191 B.C.) — Rome defeats Philip V of Macedonia (200–197 B.C.)

Terence's *Phormio* (161 B.C.) —

150 — Censorship of Cato; 1,000 talents spent on sewers (184 B.C.)

Roman citizens freed of direct taxation (167 B.C.)

100

Vitruvius's *De Architectura* (90 B.C.) — Rome annexes Macedonia (147 B.C.)

First permanent theater in Rome (55 B.C.) —

50 — First high-level aqueduct in Rome (144 B.C.)

Horace's *Art of Poetry* (24 B.C.) — Slave revolts in Sicily (135 B.C.)

0 — Pompey suppresses piracy (67 B.C.)

Romans build theaters and amphitheaters throughout the empire (ca. A.D. 30–200) — Golden age of Roman literature (ca. 58–50 B.C.)

50 — Caesar's conquest of Gaul (55 B.C.)

Jesus crucified (A.D. 30)

100

Marcus Aurelius rules (A.D. 161–180)

150

Severan dynasty; Augustan order disintegrates (A.D. 193–235)

200

Extensive persecution of the Christians (ca. A.D. 250–300)

250

300 — Constantine rules; empire reunited (A.D. 324–337)

St. Augustine born (A.D. 354)

350 — Julian the Apostate restores paganism (A.D. 361)

Council of Carthage decrees excommunication for those who attend theater rather than church on holy days; actors forbidden sacraments (A.D. 398)

400 — Theodosius I forbids pagan worship (A.D. 391)

Sack of Rome by Visigoths (A.D. 410)

450 — Death of Attila the Hun (A.D. 453)

500 — Fall of western Roman empire (A.D. 476)

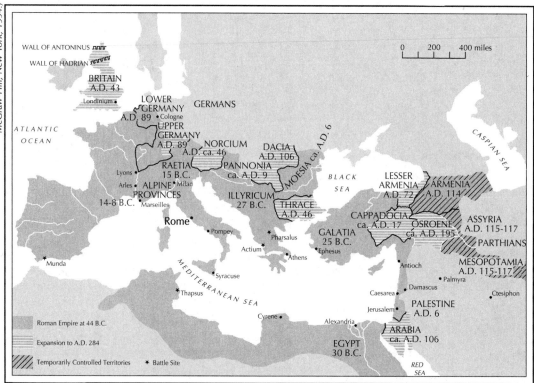

THE ROMAN EMPIRE. Note how extensive the Roman conquests were: the Romans conquered much of the eastern and western worlds. The centers of the empire were the cities of Rome and Constantinople, known today as Istanbul.

Rome was founded, according to legend, around 750 B.C. and for over 200 years was ruled by a series of kings from its northern neighbor, Etruria. Around 500 B.C. the kings were overthrown and a republic was established which was to last nearly 500 years. During the early years of the republic, there were three main classes in Rome: patricians, the rich upper class who ruled the country through the Senate; plebeians, ordinary citizens who gradually gained an equal voice in government through a people's assembly; and slaves, who made up roughly half the population. For those who were free, the republic offered a representative form of government.

After the republic was established and had extended its control over much of Italy, it was challenged by Carthage, a nation based in a seaport in North Africa. During the third and second centuries B.C. (from roughly 264 to 146 B.C.), Rome and Carthage engaged in a lengthy conflict, the Punic Wars, from which Rome finally emerged victorious. As a result, Rome controlled large parts of the central and western Mediterranean, including Spain, Sicily, Sardinia, and some of North Africa. At this time, Rome came into contact with Greece and saw Greek art and culture, including theater, firsthand.

During the first century B.C., the Roman republic began to show signs of strain. By this time, Rome had control of far-flung territories, and the problems of governing so vast an area—along with the difficulties of maintaining the checks and balances of its own political system—led to upheavals and wars. In the midst of this turmoil, Julius Caesar made himself dictator; he was subsequently assassinated by a group led by Brutus, who in turn was defeated in battle by Mark Antony and Octavian. (These events are the basis of Shakespeare's play *Julius Caesar.)*

The republic could not survive these shocks; in 27 B.C., Rome became an empire with one supreme ruler. This form of government continued for several centuries, during which most of the civilized western world was unified under Roman rule. The Roman empire included most of the lands bordering on the Mediterranean Sea and all of Europe through what is now Spain, France, Britain, and the Balkans.

Throughout their long history, the Romans were always practical. Their laws dealing with property, marriage, and inheritance still continue to influence western civilization. The Romans were also great engineers and architects, developing aqueducts and roadways. Today—2,000 years later—modern highways throughout Europe are built on the foundations of roads laid by the Romans; and a number of Roman aqueducts, though no longer in use, are still standing.

Religion was of the utmost importance in Roman history. The Romans worshiped gods who were counterparts of the Greek deities, and also a large number of other divinities: to their own pantheon, they continually added the gods worshiped by peoples they conquered. The Romans also staged religious festivals which incorporated elements of theater.

The emergence of Christianity had a profound influence on the Roman world. The Romans persecuted the early Christians, but in the fourth century after Christ the emperor Constantine (founder of Constantinople, the capital of the eastern empire) was converted to the new belief; thus began the eventual conversion of much of the Roman world to Christianity. The original religions of Greece and Rome had condoned theater, but the early Christians considered it pagan and therefore evil; the church was to be a contributing factor in the decline of theater during the later years of the Roman empire.

THE DEVELOPMENT OF ROMAN THEATER

Let's now look at the theater that flourished in Rome and note why it is significant for us today.

Where Greece had been noted for its creativity and imagination—in art, architecture, and philosophy—Rome came to be known for its mastery of more practical arts: law, engineering, and military conquest. And just as the achievements of Rome as a civilization were more down-to-earth than those of Greece, so too was its theater.

THE BOYS FROM SYRACUSE.   Roman comedies have often been adapted by later playwrights. Plautus's *The Menaechmi*—about lost twin brothers who are mistaken for each other—was transformed by Shakespeare into *The Comedy of Errors* and by Rogers and Hart into the musical *The Boys from Syracuse* (1938).

Instead of concentrating on high-minded tragedy, Roman theater focused on comedy and other popular entertainments, comparable to our own movies, television, and rock concerts. Taking off from Greek New Comedy, the Romans developed a form of domestic farce that has remained the prototype of this kind of entertainment—straight through to today's situation comedies on television.

Several threads were woven together to create Roman theater. Its first source was the Etruscans. Etruria—from which the term *Etruscan* comes—was a civilization north of Rome that flourished from about 650 to 450 B.C. The Etruscans introduced many of the popular entertainments—chariot races and gladiator battles, for example—for which Rome was later noted. They also incorporated performance elements in their religious festivals. The Roman critic Horace (whom we will discuss later in this chapter) held that Roman comedy had developed out of comic improvisations which the Etruscans included in their fertility and marriage rites. Other Roman sources suggest that the first professional actors to come to Rome were from Etruria.

Another contributor to Roman theater was a form of farce developed south of Rome and known as *Atellan farces*. These entertainments were probably developed from contact with Greek mimes who had traveled into southern

Italy. Atellan farces were improvised comedic pieces dealing with exaggerated family problems; they also made fun of historical or mythological figures. At first they were presented by touring mimes, but in the first century B.C., Roman authors began to write down these comic pieces, turning them into a literary genre. The plays featured recurring stereotyped characters who wore stock costumes and satirized people from the Roman countryside who were motivated by base instincts, such as lust and greed. (This type of humor also occurs in modern comedies, which frequently poke fun at "country bumpkins.")

The most important influence on Roman theater, however, was Greek theater. Between 250 and 150 B.C., Roman civilization came into close contact with Greek culture. In sculpture, architecture, art, and virtually all other forms of culture, the Romans were strongly affected by the Greeks and borrowed freely from them. The Romans were aware of Greek theater practices and Greek forms such as tragedy, though—as we will see—it was Greek New Comedy with which Roman writers felt a special affinity.

The Romans are not known for innovations in theater or for fostering theater as a high art. Rather, they adapted theatrical practices derived from the Greeks, the Etruscans, and Atellan farces and used them for their own purposes. The Romans are significant, then, because of their development of theater as popular entertainment.

This entertainment was designed in large measure to meet the demands of Roman audiences. Rome's many conquests led to prosperity for its citizens, who, because of their wealth and slave labor, had an abundance of leisure time. To help fill leisure time, theater was offered not just at a few festivals, but many times during the year.

The first major Roman festival to incorporate theater was called the *Ludi Romani;* it was dedicated to Jupiter, the Roman equivalent of Zeus. (We should note that this festival was first established by an Etruscan king who incorporated popular entertainments into its ceremonies.) The Ludi Romani, although it dated back to the sixth century B.C., did not include drama until 240 B.C., which was just about when the Romans came into contact with Greek culture. Additional festivals eventually incorporated theater, and more days were set aside for minor festivities and theatrical activities during the republic and the empire. Historians estimate that after A.D. 250, theatrical presentations were staged on 100 days of the year.

Despite this extensive theatrical activity—and despite the fact that Roman theater flourished for nearly seven centuries—the works of only three Roman playwrights have survived: Plautus, Terence, and Seneca. We have only scant, inconsistent bits of information about the playwrights who preceded them. The first known dramatist to write in Latin—the language of Rome—was Livius Andronicus (fl. 240–204 B.C.), who created both tragedies and comedies; but he may have been born in one of the Greek territories rather than in Rome itself. It is believed that the first playwright who was born a Roman citizen was Gnaeus Naevius (ca. 270–ca. 201 B.C.). Gnaeus was especially noted for his comedies, which dramatized Roman subject matter.

ROMAN COMEDY

As we noted above, Roman playwrights had a special affinity for Greek New Comedy. They took this Greek form and perfected their own brand of comedy, which became immensely popular with the masses. Interestingly, Roman New Comedy is the direct ancestor of all western situation comedy; these Roman comedies set a pattern that continued through many centuries and reappeared in Hollywood "screwball" comedies of the 1930s, in Broadway comedies of the same period, and in the situation comedies we see on television today.

Plautus and Terence—two of the three Roman playwrights whose works have survived—are both noted for comedy and are key figures in its history.

(New York Public Library, Picture Collection)

Plautus (Titus Maccius Plautus)

(ca. 254–184 B.C.)

Plautus, who wrote in the last part of the third century and the first part of the second century B.C., was the most popular of all Roman comic writers. According to the Roman critic Cicero, Plautus was "choice, urbane, talented, and witty." His plays were written to entertain, and they delighted Romans for a long time. During the empire, mime became the favorite form of entertainment; but even when Plautus's plays were no longer being produced, they were still read and admired for their farcical situations and mastery of colloquial Latin. In modern times, adaptations of plays by Plautus have continued to be extremely popular.

Born in Umbria, Plautus went to Rome at an early age and became an actor. When he began writing his own plays, Plautus took his familiarity with song, dance, and native Italian farce and combined it with characters and plots from the New Comedy of Hellenistic Greece. His comedies, like Greek New Comedy, did not have a chorus and did not deal with contemporary political or social issues. Instead, they depict the trials and tribulations of romance. In performance, Plautus's plays may have resembled modern musical comedies, because it is believed that a good portion of the dialogue was sung.

By concentrating on domestic situations and romance, Plautus gave new life to an old plot formula: boy meets girl, boy loses girl, boy gets girl. The many theatrically effective twists and turns of the plots—caused by some character's scheming and tricks or simply through accidental misunderstandings—are happily straightened out in the end. Often, a clever slave drives the plot, taking charge of events for a young master who is too overwhelmed with love to accomplish much on his own.

Plautus did not create original plots; but though his plays are adapted from Greek comedies, he made them thoroughly Roman by using colloquial language, local allusions, vulgarity, alliteration, comic word play, and parody, especially parody of the Roman legal and military system. He used comic repetition and digression, humorous monologues, and a variety of character types, known as *stock characters*—especially parasites and slaves—to amuse his audience.

The Menaechmi—the play about mistaken identity involving two sets of twins described at the beginning of this chapter—is a typical comedy by Plautus. Many stock Roman characters can be found in *The Menaechmi*. Peniculus or "Sponge" is a parasite; Erotium is a comic courtesan; Messenio is a comic servant. The minor characters include a domineering wife, a doddering father-in-law, and a quack doctor.

Because of his reputation as the master of comedy, over 100 plays were attributed to Plautus, but no more than 45 are now considered authentic. Twenty of his plays and fragments of one more have survived and have been used as models by playwrights from the Renaissance to the present day, including Shakespeare, Ben Jonson, and Molière. Shakespeare's *Comedy of Errors* and Rodgers and Hart's musical *The Boys from Syracuse* are based on *The Menaechmi*. In his *Miles Gloriosus*, Plautus established the braggart soldier as a type—a blustering, pompous soldier who is secretly a coward. Material from *Miles Gloriosus* and another of his plays, *Pseudolus*, is included in the musical comedy *A Funny Thing Happened on the Way to the Forum*. His *Amphitryon* was the basis of comic versions of that myth by numerous later writers, including Molière and Jean Giradoux. Some of Plautus's other well-known plays are *The Rope, Casina, The Pot of Gold, The Captives, The Haunted House,* and *The Girl from Persia*. (The dates of individual plays by Plautus are unknown, but they are all presumed to have been written between 205 and 184 B.C.)

Terence (Publius Terentius Afer)

(ca. 185–159 B.C.)

After Plautus, the most important Roman comic writer was Terence. Where Plautus's plays were robust and broadly entertaining, Terence stressed characterization, subtlety of expression, and elegant language.

Like Plautus, Terence based most of his work on Greek models. Accused of plagiarizing materials from Greek comedies, Terence wrote that he did "not deny having done so," and added that he "meant to do it again." Actually, reworking Greek comedies was a common practice among other Roman authors (including Plautus, as we have seen), so it is likely that this criticism of Terence was motivated by other reasons—perhaps by envy of his talent and his rapid rise in social status.

Debates in Theater History:
WAS TERENCE THE FIRST BLACK PLAYWRIGHT?

There are many scholarly debates about Roman theater, one of the more intriguing being the ethnic background of the playwright Terence.

Most of the biographical details about this comic playwright come from *The Life of Terence,* written after his death by the Roman author Suetonius. Suetonius states that Terence, whose full name was Publius Terentius Afer, was born in Carthage and brought to Rome as a slave. Suetonius also remarks that Terence was "dark-complected," and some scholars have suggested that this indicates that he was a black African. The use of "Afer" as part of his name was a reference to North Africa; in a Latin name, it frequently denoted a person from Libya.

This interpretation has become more prominent in recent years, as historians try to identify Afrocentric rather than Eurocentric origins of cultural achievements. (An Afrocentric approach to history suggests that scholars explore the African origins of many accomplishments usually credited to European cultures.)

However, Walter E. Forehand, in *Terence,* notes that there is little evidence that Terence was a black slave from Africa.* He argues that many biographers of the time embellished their subjects' life stories to make them more interesting literary figures. In addition, he argues that while Terence may have been from Carthage or Libya, it is unlikely that he was from an area south and east of them, and it is those areas which had black populations.

The debate over whether Terence was a black African slave—and therefore the first black playwright in western theater—is not easily resolved. As Forehand states, "As interesting as the question may be, nothing in our biographical sources suggests an answer."†

*Twayne, Boston, Mass., 1985.
†Ibid., p. 6.

It was Terence's practice to combine plot elements from two Greek plays to create one new work. Terence provided his defense of his work in his spoken prologues. In this, he broke with the tradition of using the prologue to provide background information or to summarize the plot.

Terence's life was itself dramatic. He was born in Carthage and brought to Rome as a slave. The *Afer* in his name may indicate that he was an African, and therefore he may have been the first major black playwright in western theater. His owner, a senator, educated the young playwright, freed him, and may have introduced him to a literary circle that included a group of prominent writers and philosophers.

Terence's association with high society is reflected in his comedies, which are noted for their subtle humor and cultivated Latin. His plots are more carefully constructed than those of Plautus; and he often used a double plot, placing two characters in similar romantic situations and examining their differing reactions. Though his plays were admired by his learned friends, the populace preferred more lively entertainments. Terence had to present his play *The Mother-in-Law* three times before he could get an audience to sit through the whole performance. On the first two tries, audience members were distracted by nearby circus-type entertainments, which they left the theater to attend.

While Terence's plots are as complicated as Plautus's, Terence's style is different: more literary and less exaggerated. Terence's *Phormio* dramatizes the attempts of two cousins, Antipho and Phaedria, to overcome their fathers' objections to their lovers. Both young men are aided by Phormio—a tricky parasite—and by dramatic coincidences. The plot complications and stock characters are similar to those in Plautus's *The Menaechmi,* but *Phormio* is less farcical and less slapstick. Much of its humor is verbal; there is less physical comic action but more sparring with words—which makes Terence's work less theatrical than Plautus's. It should also be noted that while much of Plautus's dialogue was meant to be sung, Terence's dialogue was spoken.

Subsequent periods, such as the Middle Ages and the Renaissance, held the plays of Terence in great esteem. His plays—more than those of any other Roman dramatist or any Greek dramatist—were used as literary models in medieval convents and monasteries and in Renaissance schools. Hrosvitha of Gandersheim, for example, was called a "Christian Terence." (Hrosvitha is discussed in Chapter 3.) The simple style of Terence's Latin and the high moral tone of his plays made them popular with teachers and scholars.

Terence wrote six plays, all of which have survived: *Andria* (166 B.C.); *The Mother-in-Law* (165 B.C.); *The Self-Tormentor* (163 B.C.); *The Eunuch* (161 B.C.); *Phormio* (161 B.C.); and *The Brothers* (160 B.C.).

We have no idea what happened to comedy following Terence's death; no works survive from that period. We assume, however, that because no plays have been preserved, there was a decline in the quality of comedies written after Terence.

ROMAN TRAGEDY

References to only a few Roman tragic playwrights survive. Many scholars believe that tragedies written after the first century B.C. were not meant for large public performances because Roman society became much more interested in spectacular popular entertainments. The only tragic playwright of note in the Roman period was Seneca.

Seneca (Lucius Annaeus Seneca)

(ca. 4 B.C.–A.D. 65)

The chief Roman tragic writer whose plays have survived is Seneca. Though there is no absolute proof of his identity, it is generally believed that he is the Roman writer by that name who served as tutor to the emperor Nero.

Seneca's life was somewhat contradictory. As a writer, he espoused stoicism, a philosophy of moderation and calm acceptance of whatever happens. In his personal life, though, he was an epicure and something of a voluptuary, enjoying the pleasures of the flesh which stoics were supposed to forgo. These extremes reflect the contradictory forces that characterized Roman life during his time.

Seneca was born in Cordoba, Spain, and was sent to Rome at an early age. He explored a number of philosophies, including one based on a vegetarian diet, before beginning to write his essays on stoicism and launching his career in politics. By A.D. 32, he was a noted orator. Caligula, the mad Roman emperor, was so envious of Seneca's oratorical skills that he considered executing him and actually did exile him for 2 years, hoping that he would die abroad. Seneca was later exiled again, for 7 years, by Messalina, wife of the emperor Claudius, probably for political reasons, though the charge was adultery with the emperor's niece.

In A.D. 49, Seneca was recalled to Rome by Agrippina, Claudius's new wife, to be tutor to her son, Nero. When Nero became emperor in 54, Seneca became one of his chief advisers, running the government for 5 years and amassing a fortune. He fell from power in A.D. 62, and in A.D. 65 the emperor ordered him to commit suicide (being ordered by a ruler or a court to take one's own life was a common practice in Greece and Rome). Seneca the stoic obeyed calmly, discussing philosophy to the end.

Nine plays by Seneca—*The Trojan Women, Medea, Oedipus, Phaedra, Thyestes, Hercules on Oeta, The Mad Hercules, The Phoenician Women,* and *Agamemnon*—are the only surviving examples of Roman tragedy based on Greek myths. (Individual dates for his plays are not known.) Scholars continue to debate whether Seneca's dramas were staged during his lifetime or whether he wrote them as "closet dramas" intended not for production but rather for recitation at banquets or other special events attended by royalty and the nobility.

On the surface, Seneca's plays appear to be similar to Greek tragedies. His plots are reworkings of Greek tales and, like the Greeks, he employs a chorus. But his tragedy is quite distinct. His choruses are not integral to the dramatic action, and unlike Greek dramatists, he emphasizes violent spectacle. Scenes which the Greeks would have banished from the stage—stabbings, murders, suicides—are often the climactic onstage moments in Seneca's works. In his *Thyestes,* for example, Thyestes eats the flesh of his children and drinks their blood in full view of the audience; and in his *Oedipus,* Jocasta cuts out her womb and Oedipus blinds himself onstage. This interest in violent spectacle has later historical parallels, of course. Today, there are numerous examples of suspense films that emphasize brutally realistic moments of violence. Some of these—such as the films of Alfred Hitchcock (like *Psycho* and *The Birds)*—are artistically interesting. The majority, however, exploit sensational violence: hatchet murders, animals and insects that prey on humans, demonic forces let loose. Seneca, by contrast, does not exploit violence; he relates it to his themes and to the tragic circumstances of his characters.

Seneca's plays also differ from Greek tragedy is that his characters do not have a tragic flaw; instead, they are obsessed by an overwhelming emotion. In *Thyestes,* for instance, Atreus is obsessed with revenge.

Because Seneca's characters are consumed by one motive, his plays seem highly melodramatic. Supernatural beings often appear in the dramatic action, adding to this melodramatic quality. Seneca's scripts include long, detailed monologues, and his characters frequently spout moralistic axioms.

While Seneca's popularity has never matched that of the Greek tragic dramatists, his influence on later periods is noteworthy. Seneca's tragedies, written in Latin—and therefore more accessible than the works of the Greek golden age—had a tremendous influence on Renaissance playwrights. His structure of five episodes separated by choral odes became the basis for five-act tragedy. Other elements of Senecan tragedy admired in the Renaissance included the use of supernatural characters, such as ghosts and witches, the depiction of violence onstage, and the use of soliloquies and asides. Shakespeare, for example, was greatly influenced by Seneca's dramatic style; *Hamlet*—which presents much onstage violence, includes soliloquies, and has a supernatural character, the ghost of Hamlet's father—is often described as a Senecan revenge tragedy.

POPULAR ENTERTAINMENT IN ROME

Because most of the works of Plautus and Terence were based on Greek models and the plays of Seneca are not outstanding examples of tragedy, the Romans are not considered creators of great drama. However, they did develop a variety of popular entertainments, many of them adopted from Etruscan and Greek culture. Popular entertainments appeal to all levels of society, and no educational, social, or cultural sophistication is required to appreciate them. Some historians say that twentieth-century American culture, with its highly developed popular entertainments—television, film, rock concerts, and other less sophisticated dramatic arts—is much like Roman culture.

Many Roman entertainments correspond to the modern circus. Chariot racing (today's equivalent would be automobile and stock car races) was popular from the seventh century B.C. through the sixth century after Christ. Equestrian performances, gymnastics, and various forms of hand-to-hand combat were also popular.

Gladiatorial combats were included in festivals at the close of the second century B.C. These were not necessarily make-believe fights; in some cases they were actual battles to the death. The *naumachiae* were sea battles staged on lakes, artificial bodies of water, or flooded arenas; the first one was organized by Julius Caesar in 46 B.C. Trained animals were often used in popular entertainments; they were also put on display and used in combat with unarmed humans. This interest in blood sports also has modern counterparts: in parts of the United States, illegal cockfights still take place, and in Spain and Mexico bullfighting continues to attract large numbers of spectators.

THE COLOSSEUM IN ROME.   The Romans were engineers and architects who built roads, aqueducts, temples, and theaters. They were also fond of popular entertainment. These two interests were combined in the construction of colosseums. The one in Rome—seating 50,000 spectators—was completed in A.D. 80 and is still standing; it is infamous as the site where the Romans fed Christians to the lions.

In ancient Rome, special buildings were constructed to house sporting and other spectacles. The Circus Maximus, constructed in 600 B.C. for chariot races and frequently remodeled thereafter, seated over 60,000 people. The most renowned Roman amphitheater was the Colosseum, built in A.D. 80. The caverns beneath the Colosseum may have held Christians waiting to be sacrificed to wild beasts; the slaughter of early Christians by lions was viewed by the Roman populace as a spectacular diversion. Again, this interest in human executions is not confined to the Romans; throughout the eighteenth and nineteenth centuries in England and elsewhere, public hangings drew huge crowds.

The Romans also developed popular entertainments which were more truly theatrical. Roman mime, like Greek mime, included gymnastics, juggling, songs, and dances and became popular in the third century B.C. The variety of entertainments referred to as *mime* during Roman times make this form difficult to define. Short dramatic and risqué (that is, sexually suggestive) comedic skits were frequently part of mime performances. (The Romans enjoyed sexually provocative dramatic material, and the emperor Heliogabalus, in the first part of the third century after Christ, is said to have forced mimes to perform actual sexual acts.)

The mimes performed in *found spaces,* that is, spaces in town squares or open courtyards that could be used for performances even though not specifically designed for them. Mimes provided the primary theatrical entertainment at the Roman fertility festival, the Ludi Florales, starting about 238 B.C. But even though mime troupes were allowed to entertain at festivals, they, like the Greek mimes, were castigated for being transients and for including women in their ranks.

A unique Roman stage presentation was the pantomime, which some scholars believe may have developed during the first century B.C. It required a single dancer, a chorus, and musical accompanists and might be compared to ballet. The major performer in Roman pantomime danced a mythological, historical, or occasionally comical story; the chorus chanted the narrative and explained the action. Pantomime performers were often supported by emperors and wealthy individuals.

DRAMATIC CRITICISM IN ROME

Like Roman drama, Roman dramatic criticism was also based on the work of others, especially Aristotle. The best known writer of dramatic theory and criticism in the Roman period was Horace, who is sometimes referred to as the "Roman Aristotle." Horace's *Ars Poetica* (*The Art of Poetry;* 24–20 B.C.) is the only Latin treatise on dramatic criticism still in existence. Horace's work, known to Renaissance scholars and writers before the rediscovery of Aristotle, had tremendous impact on Renaissance dramatic theory and on the structure of Renaissance plays.

(Culver Pictures)

Horace (Quintus Horatius Flaccus)
(65–8 B.C.)

Son of a freed slave, Horace was a poet who became the friend of Virgil and other leading literary figures of the early Roman empire. He was famous for his lyric poetry—the *Satires* and the *Epodes*—as well as *The Art of Poetry.*

Horace was born in Venusia, an Italian town that had once been a Greek colony. His father, a government collector of market dues, sent the young writer to study in both Athens and Rome so that he might qualify for a high government post. During the civil war that followed the assassination of Julius Caesar, Horace fought with Brutus's army at Philippi. Pardoned by Augustus, the new emperor, Horace went to Rome, obtained a government post, and began writing.

At that time, wealthy Romans, following the lead of the emperor, supported literature and the arts; Horace's literary patron gave him a farm which freed him from financial worries so that he could concentrate on writing. His careful craftsmanship, humor, and use of language attracted the attention of the emperor, who commissioned him to write a fourth book of odes. When he died, Horace was the leading lyric poet of his time.

In his essay on poetic form, Horace surveys the history and theory of dramatic poetry. Less detailed and profound than Aristotle, Horace stressed rules, such as his rule that comedy and tragedy must never be combined. He held that a play should have five acts, that only three speaking characters should appear at the same time, and that gods should not be brought in unless absolutely necessary to resolve a plot. The chorus should be used to forward the action, set a high moral tone, and give "good and sage counsel." Horace felt that the purpose of drama was "to profit and to please"; in other words, writers should both entertain and instruct their audience. This opinion was not found in Aristotle, but Renaissance critics made it a rule of drama.

Another of Horace's concerns emphasized during the Renaissance was *decorum.* Basically, decorum meant that the language and actions of characters must fit traditional ideas of suitable behavior for their age, gender, social status, and emotional state. Horace wanted writers to avoid extremes of emotion and to attempt to be truthful. Anything overly offensive or overly marvelous (fantastical) should be kept offstage.

THEATER PRODUCTION IN ROME

Actors and Acting Companies

Roman production practices differed slightly from those of Greece. Festivals were under the jurisdiction of a local government official who hired an acting troupe. The *dominus,* or head, of a troupe—who was usually the leading actor—made financial arrangements, bought dramas from playwrights, hired musicians, and obtained costumes. Since several companies were hired for each festival, there was an atmosphere of "unofficial" competition, with popular performers vying for rewards from prestigious audience members. Popular entertainments, however, frequently overshadowed the traditional dramatic presentations.

Acting companies hired to stage drama consisted of at least six male members; the Romans ignored the Greek "three-actor rule" even though it was endorsed by Horace. Roman acting technique emphasized detailed pantomime

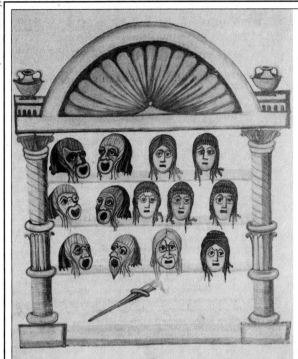

MASKS FOR A COMEDY BY TERENCE. The two most famous Roman dramatists were the comic writers Plautus and Terence. In their plays the characters were all stereotypes, and the actors wore masks that depicted specific characteristics. Shown here is a shelf of masks—from a ninth-century manuscript—for characters in Terence's *Andria*.

and broad physical gestures, which were necessitated by the size of the Roman theaters; it also stressed beautiful vocal delivery. As noted earlier, probably about two-thirds of the lines in Plautus's comedies were sung.

In today's theater, actors who play the same kinds of roles over and over again are less esteemed than those who perform a variety of roles. The Romans, however, admired performers who specialized in playing one type of role and refined a stock characterization. Facial expression was unimportant, since full linen head masks were worn; only mimes performed without masks.

The position of actors in Roman society continues to be debated by theater historians. Some believe that actors were usually slaves and that the dominus who organized a troupe was a free man who purchased his performers. Other historians note that "stars" in Roman theater were highly respected, well rewarded financially, and accepted socially. Aesopus and Roscius were two such stars. Claudius Aesop (known as Aesopus), who died in 54 B.C., left an estate estimated to have been worth the equivalent of $500,000. Quintus Roscius Gallus (Roscius) was so well connected socially that his friends included the statesman and orator Cicero; when Roscius died in 62 B.C., his estate was evidently worth about $1 million. Still, the majority of actors were probably slaves or unesteemed members of Roman society, barely able to survive financially.

THE ROMAN THEATER AT ORANGE. The Romans built theaters throughout their empire, which circled the Mediterranean Sea. One of the best-preserved is at Orange in France, near the center of town; it was built in the first or second century after Christ. Note the semicircular orchestra, the large stage area, and the stagehouse at the back, which has an ornate facade with niches for statues and other adornments.

Theater Buildings and Scenic Elements

To make theater available to large numbers of people, the Romans built many impressive theaters throughout the empire. They redesigned the Greek amphitheater but, ironically, did not construct a permanent theater until 55 B.C.; thus there were no permanent spaces for presenting the works of Plautus and Terence—the best playwrights Rome produced—during their own lifetime. Temporary wooden structures, probably similar to the later permanent theaters, were originally erected for theatrical presentations.

Roman theaters had the same three units found in the Greek buildings: the *cavea* (the Roman version of the theatron, or audience seating area), the *orchestra*, and the *scaena* (the Roman version of the skene, or scene house).

The Roman structures, however, were different from those of classical

Greece. The Romans had developed the arch and other engineering techniques that allowed flexibility in construction, and they put this knowledge to good use in building theaters. Roman theaters were usually not built into hillsides but were freestanding structures with a tiered audience section connected to the scene house. The cavea, the audience seating area, was often larger than the Greek theatron; some Roman theaters could hold up to 25,000 spectators. (The seating capacity of Roman theaters varied, however; for example, one of the three permanent theaters constructed in Rome accommodated only 8,000 spectators.) Roman planners also attempted to make audiences comfortable: to protect the spectators from intense heat, awnings were set up and fans blew air over cooled water—a primitive form of air conditioning.

The orchestra was semicircular rather than circular. It was rarely used for staging; it was used instead for seating government officials and for the flooding required for sea battles. In front of the scaena was a large raised stage about 5 feet high called the *pulpitum;* its dimensions varied from 100 feet by 20 feet to 300 feet (the length of a football field) by 40 feet. Few of today's performers will have an opportunity to act on a stage that huge.

The scaena itself was a unique feature of the Roman theater. Two or three stories high, it was used for storage and dressing space, and a roof extended out from the scene building over the stage to protect the actors from the elements. Two side wings enclosed the pulpitum and connected the scaena to the cavea. The *scaena frons*—the facade of the scaena—was elaborate and ornate, with statuary, columns, recesses, and three to five entrances; the central entrance

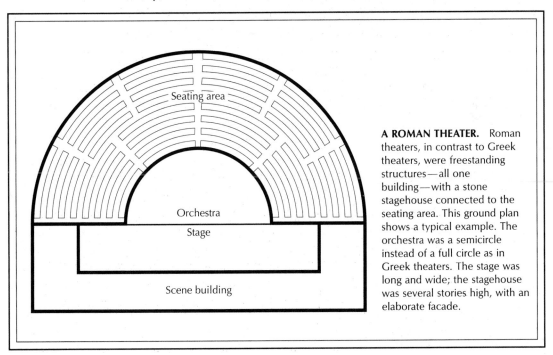

A ROMAN THEATER. Roman theaters, in contrast to Greek theaters, were freestanding structures—all one building—with a stone stagehouse connected to the seating area. This ground plan shows a typical example. The orchestra was a semicircle instead of a full circle as in Greek theaters. The stage was long and wide; the stagehouse was several stories high, with an elaborate facade.

was the largest and had stairs leading up to it. The facade was meant to represent a typical Roman street scene, the basic scenic requirement of Roman comedy; it could also represent a palace, the customary tragic setting.

The scaena frons could serve as the basic setting because the Romans, following the Greek tradition, did not require a unique environment for each play. (At the beginning of *The Menaechmi,* for example, the actor who speaks the prologue points out that it is up to the audience's imagination to turn the playing space into the town of Epidamnus.) The Romans, however, did try to alter the scaena frons slightly by employing periaktoi, three-sided scenic units described in Chapter 1. Where the periaktoi were located on the high pulpitum or scene house is a matter of conjecture; possibly one was placed in each of the doorways on the sides of the large central portal.

The Romans also used curtains to alter the scenic environment. There were two types of curtains: the *auleum* and the *siparium.* The auleum was a front curtain which was raised and lowered on expandable poles from a trench in front of the stage. Given the size of the scaena, the auleum could not mask the entire facade; instead, its function was to conceal actors before they were revealed to the audience, much as front curtains in theaters are still used. The siparium, a painted backdrop placed against the scaena frons, slightly altered the appearance of the facade. Because of the size of the scaena frons, the siparium could never completely mask the permanent three-dimensional background.

Much of what we know about Roman theater architecture comes from Marcus Vitruvius, who lived in the first century B.C. and whose ten-volume work *De Architectura* shows how much of Roman architecture was based on Hellenistic models. Vitruvius's massive treatise, which includes a discussion of theater buildings, became particularly influential when it was rediscovered in the Italian Renaissance. We can also reconstruct the characteristics of Roman theater buildings by examining those which have survived the ravages of time, in such diverse locations as France, Libya, and Israel.

THE DECLINE OF ROMAN THEATER

In the fourth century after Christ, it was clear that the Roman empire was beginning to fall apart. In 330, the emperor Constantine established two capitals: Rome in the west and Constantinople in the east. From that point on, the center of gravity moved from the west to the east, toward Constantinople, and Rome became less and less of a factor.

The downfall of Rome, marked by the unseating of the western Roman emperor by a barbarian ruler in A.D. 476, was caused by the disintegration of the Roman administrative structure and the sacking of Roman cities by northern barbarians. Not all of Rome, however, fell. The eastern part, known as the Byzantine empire, continued to exist until 1453, when it was conquered by the Islamic Turks.

The decline of Roman theater coincided with the downfall of the western empire. Yet the fall of Rome is not the only explanation for the deterioration of its theater. Theater itself had become less of an art form and more of an entertainment, to the point where it often became difficult to distinguish between theatrical offerings and circuses, or between gladiatorial contests and pantomimes.

Another important factor in the decline of Roman theater is the rise of Christianity. From the outset, the Christian church was opposed to theater. Early Christians saw a connection between theater and pagan religions, and the church fathers argued that the evil characters portrayed onstage taught immorality. Church leaders were offended by the sexual content of Roman entertainments and by their frequent satirical attacks on Christianity. As a result, the church issued various edicts condemning theater and its participants. In 398, a church council decreed that anyone who went to the theater rather than to church on holy days would be excommunicated, and performers were not allowed to take part in holy rites. These attacks had far-reaching historical ramifications. As late as the seventeenth century, the French playwright Molière was refused Christian burial because he had been an actor and dramatist. Ironically, the institution that condemned theater to perdition was to revive it five centuries later: the Roman Catholic church was the catalyst in the rebirth of western theater. But this was later; the early Christian church opposed theater, and that was one reason why theater as an organized institution disappeared for the time being.

Still another important reason was the disintegration of Roman civilization. The invaders from the north plundered the cities of the Roman empire, and after a time no large centers of culture remained. People scattered, and in many places the buildings that had housed government offices, schools, and performing spaces were abandoned. The plays of the Greek and Roman dramatists and the writings of Aristotle and Horace were lost or forgotten. The tradition of theater that had stretched virtually unbroken for nearly a thousand years, from the Greeks in the fifth century B.C. through the early centuries of the Christian era, was at an end.

The dispersal and destruction of educational, political, and cultural institutions led later historians to call the period after the fall of the Roman empire the *dark ages.* Many present-day historians, however, believe that this term is simplistic and too negative. The fall of the Roman empire did not occur overnight; the empire had been deteriorating from within for many years. Meanwhile, by the seventh and eighth centuries the medieval system of self-contained, church-centered communities had begun to emerge—though it would be some time before theater was again a full-fledged institution in Europe.

Ironically, the Roman Catholic church, which attacked theater during the first centuries of the Roman empire, would become involved in its rebirth during the Middle Ages. We turn to this rebirth in Chapter 3.

SUMMARY

The Romans borrowed many Greek conventions, including the introduction of drama and theater into religious and civic festivals, but modified them so that they became uniquely Roman. The Romans did not produce great plays, but the New Comedies of Plautus and Terence, as well as the tragedies of Seneca, are noteworthy because of their influence on later playwrights. Instead of significant drama, Roman civilization developed sophisticated forms of popular entertainment.

Horace's *Ars Poetica* was an attempt to establish dramatic rules for Roman dramatists.

Roman theaters were usually huge outdoor buildings. In Roman playhouses (unlike Greek theaters) all elements were connected. The most significant elements were the ornate facade of the scene house and the huge raised stage. The Romans were the first to use curtains for scenic variety. The male actors who performed in these playhouses, unlike the Greeks, were professionals.

CHAPTER 3
MEDIEVAL THEATER

CHAPTER 3

MEDIEVAL THEATER

The time is 1501, and we are in a large town square in Mons—in present-day Belgium—where a series of small stage houses, called *mansions*, have been erected. They serve as the setting for a series, or cycle, of plays based on the Old and New Testaments—dramatized Bible stories that move from the creation to the crucifixion. In the biblical plays at Mons this year, about 150 actors will perform 350 roles. They have held 48 rehearsals, and it will take 4 days to present all the plays in the cycle.

The mansions set up across the stage area are changed to suit whatever play is being performed. We have heard that 67 different mansions—representing the garden of Eden, the manger in Bethlehem, the temple where Christ drove out the money changers, and so forth—will be used during these 4 days. At each end of the stage area are two permanent mansions, symbolic of the opposing sides in this giant religious drama: one is heaven and the other hell. Hell is represented by the large mouth of a monster, out of which devils and smoke pour at appropriate moments.

A MYSTERY CYCLE. Interest in medieval mystery plays is still strong: the Court Theater in Chicago presented this very successful staging of a cycle in 1992. As can be seen here, contemporary directors build on anachronisms already present in medieval drama to make references to modern society. *(Matthew Gilson/Court Theatre)*

A good percentage of the people who live in Mons and the surrounding areas are here. This is one occasion when we see a cross-section of the community. The members of the audience either sit in temporary wooden bleachers or stand in the town square, trying to get the best possible view of the acting area.

We have already seen dramas about Adam and Eve and about Cain slaying his brother Abel; now we are waiting for a play about Noah, who is commanded by God to build an ark to save his family and the animals when the flood comes. In the play, Noah is warned by God that it will rain for 40 days and 40 nights, and that he must build an ark into which he will take his family and two animals of every kind. As Noah begins building, his neighbors make fun of him, and his shrewish wife argues with him. We enjoy this byplay, but the moment we are waiting for is the deluge of rain, which is expected to be spectacular.

At last the moment arrives, and we are not disappointed. On the roofs of houses behind the "Noah" stage area, water has been stored in wine barrels and men are standing by, waiting for a signal to open the barrels. Now the signal is given, and the deluge begins: torrents of water fall onto the stage. The audience is completely in awe; enough water has been stored to provide a steady rain for 5 minutes. Water rises all around, but Noah, his family, and his animals are safe in the ark. Soon after, a dove comes, indicating that Noah can leave the ark.

When the play about Noah is over, the next play begins, but the sensational flood remains in our minds. What an effect—what a deluge! It was a wonder to behold.

BACKGROUND: THE MIDDLE AGES

As we begin to examine the Middle Ages—or the *medieval* period, as it is also called—it is important to remember that divisions of history are artificial and are used primarily so that historical developments will be easier to discuss. In western culture, the period from A.D. 500 through 1400 is referred to as the *Middle Ages,* and the years between 1400 and 1650 are known as the *Renaissance*—the era when the classics of Greece and Rome were rediscovered. But these dates are arbitrary: in some cases the Middle Ages are extended to 1450 or 1500; and in some cases the Renaissance is said to have begun by 1350. This is often a matter of which country or which form of art is being studied; developments vary from one country and one branch of art to another. Thus, the Renaissance came to Italy before it came to France and England, and Renaissance painting had emerged while theater was still in its medieval phase: the greatest medieval drama was created between 1350 and 1550, a period when Renaissance painting and sculpture were already established. Medieval theater, therefore, extends through 1550—well past the time when most cultural historians would say that the Renaissance had begun.

This overlap between the Middle Ages and the Renaissance points up the fact that developments in theater often seem to lag behind other cultural developments. This suggestion, of course, is not meant to demean theater.

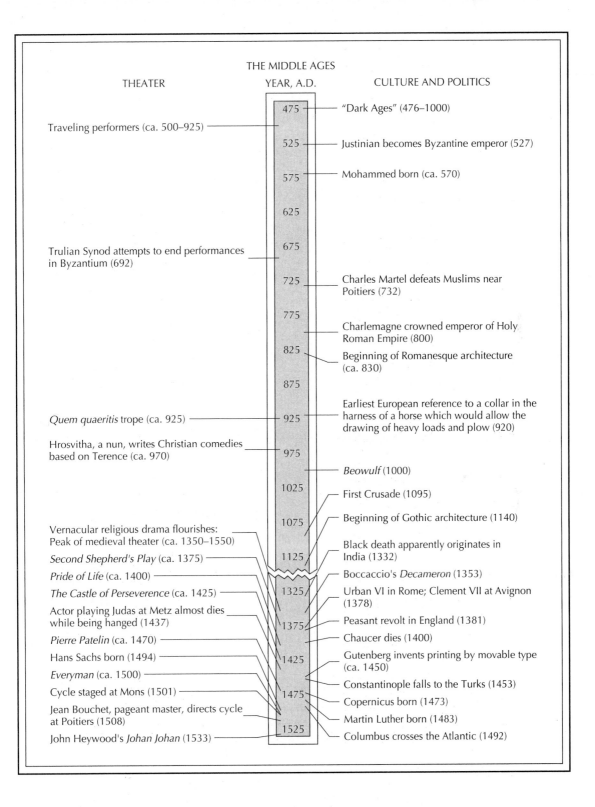

THE MIDDLE AGES

THEATER	YEAR, A.D.	CULTURE AND POLITICS

475 — "Dark Ages" (476–1000)

Traveling performers (ca. 500–925) ——— 525 — Justinian becomes Byzantine emperor (527)

575 — Mohammed born (ca. 570)

625

Trulian Synod attempts to end performances ——— 675
in Byzantium (692)

725 — Charles Martel defeats Muslims near
Poitiers (732)

775

Charlemagne crowned emperor of Holy
Roman Empire (800)
825 — Beginning of Romanesque architecture
(ca. 830)

875

Earliest European reference to a collar in the
harness of a horse which would allow the
Quem quaeritis trope (ca. 925) ——— 925 — drawing of heavy loads and plow (920)

Hrosvitha, a nun, writes Christian comedies ———
based on Terence (ca. 970) 975

— *Beowulf* (1000)

1025
— First Crusade (1095)

— Beginning of Gothic architecture (1140)
1075

Vernacular religious drama flourishes:
Peak of medieval theater (ca. 1350–1550)
— Black death apparently originates in
Second Shepherd's Play (ca. 1375) ——— 1125 India (1332)

Pride of Life (ca. 1400) ——— — Boccaccio's *Decameron* (1353)

The Castle of Perseverence (ca. 1425) ——— 1325 — Urban VI in Rome; Clement VII at Avignon
(1378)
Actor playing Judas at Metz almost dies ———
while being hanged (1437) — Peasant revolt in England (1381)
1375
Pierre Patelin (ca. 1470) ——— — Chaucer dies (1400)

Hans Sachs born (1494) ——— — Gutenberg invents printing by movable type
1425 (ca. 1450)
Everyman (ca. 1500) ———
— Constantinople falls to the Turks (1453)
Cycle staged at Mons (1501) ——— 1475 — Copernicus born (1473)

Jean Bouchet, pageant master, directs cycle ——— — Martin Luther born (1483)
at Poitiers (1508) 1525
John Heywood's *Johan Johan* (1533) ——— — Columbus crosses the Atlantic (1492)

(From R. Sullivan et al., A Short History of Western Civilization, 8th ed., McGraw-Hill, New York, 1994.)

SCOTLAND

IRELAND

WALES

ENGLAND

Durham •

York • ★ STAMFORD BRIDGE 1066

Cambridge •
Oxford •
• London
Clarendon • Winchester • Canterbury
HASTINGS 1066 ★

DENMARK

Elbe R.
• Libick
Holstein
Bremen •

POMERANIA

Oder R.

POLAND

FRISIA

SAXONY

Brandenburg

MARCH OF
LUSATTA

Meissen

THURINGIA

Prague •

BOHEMIA

MORAVIA

Antwerp
Bruges •
Ghent •
FLANDERS
BOUVINES 1274 ★

RHINE R.
LOWER
LORRAINE
Cologne •
Aachen •

FRANCONIA
• Mainz
• Worms

NORMANDY

Reins •

CHAMPAGNE

Trier •
Verdun •

UPPER
LORRAINE
• Toul

Rennes •
BRITTANY
MAINE

Chartres •
Orléans •

BLOIS

Danube R.

Augsburg •

LECHFELD ★

Passau •

AUSTRIA

Vienna •

Nantes •
ANJOU
Tours •
Loire R.

SWABIA
Freiburg •

BAVARIA

Salzburg •

Styria

DUNAINE
• Portsers

Dijon •
BURGUNDY
Autun •
Cluny •
Lyons •

• Bensancon

Constance •

Carinthia

Saintes •

AQUITAINE

PERIGORD

Bordeaux •

AUVERGNE

KINGDOM
OF
BURGUNDY
ARLES

LOMBARDY
LEGNANO 1776 ★ • Milan
Po R.
• Pavia
Roncagila

Venice •

REPUBLIC OF VENICE

GASCONY

TOULOUSE

• Toulouse
LANGUEDOC

Avignon •
Arles •
PROVENCE
Montpelier • • Marseilles

Canossa •

• Bologna

Florence •
Pisa •
TUSCANY

PATRIMONY
OF
ST. PETER

NAVARRE

ARAGON

Barcelona •

SPAIN

Suirl •
Rome •

KINGDOM
OF
TWO
SICILIES

Naplea •
Salerno •

French royal domain

987

987-1180

1180-1328

Boundary of English holdings
in France 1180

English holdings in France 1328

Holy Roman Empire ca. 1200

★ Battle site

HUNGARY

0   100   200 miles

MEDIEVAL EUROPE.   European society was highly fragmented, and only late in Middle Ages did the rise of monarchies lead to national unification. Major urban areas that developed during this period were London and Paris.

Theater is a reflection of society and is particularly concerned with people and their relationships to each other and to society. It takes time for shifts in these relationships to be absorbed, and therefore it is not surprising that theater needs time to take in and mirror societal transformations. Another reason why theater sometimes reflects cultural changes more slowly than other art forms is that in order to survive it must usually have wide appeal: it must attract a cross section of society. A single patron can commission a painting or a sculpture; but a theater performance needs an audience. *They did.*

Byzantium: The Eastern Empire

Before examining western society and theater during the Middle Ages, we should turn our attention briefly eastward. When Rome fell in A.D. 476, only the western Roman empire collapsed. The eastern empire, centralized in A.D. 330 by Constantine in Constantinople (today Istanbul, Turkey), continued to function until 1453. Withstanding expansion by Islamic peoples, Byzantium, as the eastern empire was known, synthesized three important influences: ancient Greece, Rome, and Christianity. The western world came into contact with Byzantium during the Crusades—the religious wars of the twelfth and thirteenth centuries undertaken to prevent the expansion of Islam. The western world, however, had always looked on the eastern empire as a secondary civilization, and a sharp split between east and west occurred in 1054, when eastern Christianity broke from western Christianity, refusing to acknowledge the supremacy of the papacy.

The theater of Byzantium was reminiscent of theater during the Roman empire. The Hippodrome, a huge arena in Constantinople, was the Byzantine equivalent of the Circus Maximus or the Colosseum, and popular entertainments like those of Rome flourished in the east. However, the contribution of the Byzantine empire to the continuity of theater is not these popular presentations. Rather, it is the fact that eastern scholars copied manuscripts of classical Greek drama: the plays of Aeschylus, Sophocles, and Euripides and the criticism of Aristotle. These scholars recognized the importance of classical texts and made certain that they were not destroyed. When the eastern empire fell in 1453, these manuscripts were transferred to the western world and became part of the rediscovery of the past that influenced the Renaissance.

The Middle Ages in Western Europe

Most discussions of medieval society are concerned with western developments from the Early Middle Ages (A.D. 500 to 1000), through the High Middle Ages (about 1000 to 1400). The years from 500 to 1000 were traditionally called the *dark ages,* because historians originally viewed this period as one in which few cultural or historical advances were made. Most historians now argue that this era actually laid the groundwork for the advances of the High Middle Ages, and we will therefore refer to it as the Early Middle Ages.

During the Early Middle Ages, the vestiges of the Roman empire were overrun by barbarians, primarily from the north, and institutions established by the Romans were toppled; Roman towns and roadways fell into disuse. The institution that stepped in to provide a semblance of order to the chaotic society was the Roman Catholic church. As noted in Chapter 2, the Roman empire had been Christianized before its fall, and when the pagan barbarians invaded, many of them were converted to the new belief. The church's power was centralized in Rome under the pope; when Charlemagne became the most powerful secular ruler in Europe, during the early part of the ninth century, he was crowned emperor of the Holy Roman Empire. Secular rulers were always subject to the church's influence.

By about 1000, medieval society had begun to establish its own patterns of organization, and between the years 1000 and 1400 major advances were made in most areas of human endeavor. During this period, the powerful church, though frequently questioned and threatened, was ever-present.

Medieval society was primarily agrarian; people everywhere were close to the land. For financial reasons and because of the way society was organized, most people rarely strayed far from the area where they were born and brought up. During the Middle Ages, the development of mechanical inventions—heavier plows, better harnesses, and windmills—made agricultural work more efficient. Production was increased and soil depletion was prevented by the "three-field" system: agricultural land holdings were divided into three parts so that crops could be rotated, and each plot remained unplanted once every 3 years.

Medieval society developed feudalism as a means of political organization. Under this system there were three major categories or classifications of people. At the top of the hierarchy were *lords* or *counts*—who controlled large areas of land and protected less wealthy landholders. In return for a lord's protection, his subjects—the second level, *vassals* or lesser lords, who controlled smaller areas of land—agreed to provide military service, consult with him, and pay him occasional fees. Under the vassals were the *peasants,* or *serfs,* who were attached to their lord's land and required to work it. In return they received protection and a very small financial reward. Serfs, though bound to the land, had a higher status than slaves; unlike slaves, serfs had some recognized rights and at times could move to other areas. Medieval society became the first western culture that did not practice slavery on a large scale.

In France, the chief figure among the lords came to be the monarch. Some historians argue that the growth of national monarchies at the end of the Middle Ages developed directly out of feudalism.

During the High Middle Ages, there was a rebirth of towns as a result of expansion of commerce and trade. The towns were self-governing units, independent of the feudal system, and their growth led to a liberalizing of feudalism and possibly to the eradication of serfdom in the fifteenth century. Within the towns, merchants and artisans, such as butchers, weavers, and goldsmiths, organized themselves into guilds to protect their interests and privileges. (A rough parallel might be drawn to our trade associations.) Under the guilds, vocational training was organized: to become a master craftsman, for instance, one would have to serve first as an apprentice and then as a journeyman. The guilds controlled the number of people entering various professions.

An important aspect of the medieval period was the spread of knowledge. By the year 1500—after the end of the High Middle Ages—there were over 100 universities in Europe. Earlier, in the twelfth century, the writings of Aristotle and other classic texts were rediscovered by scholarly monks. (However, despite a new awareness of ancient philosophy and the arts in the High Middle Ages, the most esteemed discipline remained theology—the study of religion —which had been the main intellectual pursuit of the Early Middle Ages.) Monks copied influential manuscripts, and as a result the monasteries were centers of learning. As early as the tenth century, a nun in a convent in Germany, Hrosvitha of Gandersheim, wrote plays patterned on those of the Roman dramatist Terence.

Hrosvitha

(ca. 935–1001)

Hrosvitha, the earliest known female dramatist, flourished during the tenth century in northern Germany. During this phase of the Middle Ages, religious communities served as centers of scholarship and intellectual life. Hrosvitha was a nun who lived and worked in one of these—Gandersheim, a Benedictine abbey in Saxony led by women of noble families. Gandersheim was an influential center.

There are indications that Hrosvitha was of noble birth and had more access to the world than the other nuns at Gandersheim. One of the scholars who have written about Hrosvitha, Sister Mary Marguerite of Mercy College, finds evidence that Hrosvitha was a "canoness" and therefore was not completely cloistered.

Hrosvitha read and wrote in Latin, which was the language of the Roman Catholic church and of western scholarship during the Middle Ages. Like other medieval scholars, she studied classical Roman texts for their form and style. During the Middle Ages, one Roman writer admired for his style was the playwright Terence; Hrosvitha particularly admired Terence's plays, but she feared that his subject matter was not suitable for Christian readers. To provide dramas that students could read without risk of corruption, Hrosvitha wrote six plays in the Terentian manner but using Christian stories. In the preface to her collected plays, she noted that her purpose was to glorify Christian virgins.

Debates in Theater History:

WHY HAS HROSVITHA BEEN IGNORED?

Hrosvitha is considered the first female playwright in the history of theater and is at least the first female playwright of whom we have any record. However, she has received very little attention from theater historians. Why?

The feminist critic Sue-Ellen Case, in her essay "Re-Viewing Hrotsvit,"* tries to explain why Hrosvitha has been ignored by scholars and why her plays have rarely been produced. Case argues that Hrosvitha is too often depicted as a poor imitator of the Roman playwright Terence, whose plays she adapted. Furthermore, it is frequently assumed that if she was cloistered, Hrosvitha must have created these dramas only as a monastic exercise. Case suggests that these ideas come from a male-oriented view of dramatic technique and

*Theatre Journal, vol. 35, no. 2, December 1983, pp. 533–542.

history. She reinterprets Hrosvitha's scripts: according to Case, Terence presents female characters who are manipulated by men, are controlled by the institution of marriage, and have little on-stage presence; but Hrosvitha represents women as controlling dramatic action and as responding to male aggression. In addition, Case argues that Hrosvitha used a variety of uniquely feminist dramatic techniques and for that reason has never been well received critically. Case also asserts that Hrosvitha created her plays for the community of women who lived with her in the convent.

Case's analysis of Hrosvitha's work forces us to consider that, because of the biases of historians, key figures and their works may be ignored; it also leads us to ask whether the traditional list of great dramatists and their works—known as the canon—needs revision. In addition, it forces us to reevaluate traditional ideas that we have come to accept as historic reality.

Martyrdom of devout Christians, hard-won conversions of nonbelievers, renunciations of sinful pasts, and strict penance for the past are the recurring dramatic actions in Hrosvitha's plays. Her plays *Paphnutius* and *Abraham* both concern a woman's redemption from sexual sins. Another of her plays, *Dulcitius*, depicts the martyrdom of three Christian virgins, Agape, Chionia, and Irena. This play has a surprisingly comic scene, in which the captor Dulcitius visits the sisters in the middle of the night and mistakenly makes love to some dirty pots and pans. Other plays written by Hrosvitha are *Gallicanus*, *Callimachus*, and *Sapienta*.

There is no evidence that Hrosvitha's plays were intended for performance or ever received performances in her own time. Without an active theater tradition, it is unlikely that Hrosvitha had much knowledge of dramatic performance. On the other hand, it is possible that the plays were read aloud at Gandersheim.

In addition to her plays, Hrosvitha wrote poetry, biographies of saints, and history. Her work was not widely known until it was rediscovered and published in 1501. In retrospect, Hrosvitha's plays are of interest because of their connection to both the formal composition of classical drama and the themes and subject matter of medieval mystery and morality plays.

LITURGICAL DRAMA

Development of Medieval Liturgical Drama

During the Middle Ages, with the church omnipresent, it is not surprising that medieval drama was mostly religious. Not only was much of this drama religious; it was actually presented in churches and cathedrals. How could the church, which had attacked theater so vehemently in the late Roman empire and the Early Middle Ages, become the instrument of its rebirth?

There are several possible explanations for the development of church, or liturgical, drama. We noted in the Introduction that religious rites have theatrical elements, and the rituals of Roman Catholicism are no exception. Roman Catholic rituals had many elements that contained the seeds of the rebirth of theater. The mass and the Hours, the vestments worn by the clergy, the church space, the musical accompaniment, and the annual symbolic events (such as the burial of the cross on Good Friday and its resurrection on Easter Sunday) are all inherently theatrical.

Church drama seems to have developed along with changes in liturgical music. By the ninth century, extended musical passages, called *tropes,* had been added to services; later, lyrics were written for these passages. The mass was the most rigid of the numerous daily services; for that reason, tropes were most often incorporated into other services, such as the Hours, which changed daily and also had special texts for occasions like Christmas and Easter. These tropes, which were sung or chanted in Latin to musical accompaniment, were in most cases performed in monasteries.

Medieval records indicate that in some places a trope called *Quem quaeritis* was added to the introductory section of the Easter service around the year 925. The Latin words *Quem quaeritis*—"Whom do you seek?"—are the first words in this trope: they are the question asked by an angel when the three Marys visit the tomb of Christ. When the women reply that they are seeking Christ, the angel announces that Christ has risen. We do not know whether the trope of 925 was acted out by performers playing the Marys and the angel, but between 965 and 975 it definitely became a tiny play. We know this because those are the dates of *Regularis Concordia,* a book by Ethelwold, bishop of Winchester in England. *Regularis* was intended to establish goals and rules of conduct and procedure for monasteries. Among other things, it described how the *Quem quaeritis* trope was to be performed.

It is a reasonable assumption that around 965—and certainly soon after—tropes on other parts of the Bible had also begun to be staged; and more than 400 plays dealing with the visit of the Marys to the tomb have been found in various places in Europe. By the year 1000, then, liturgical dramas—short plays on this story of the visit to the tomb as well as other biblical events—had been incorporated into the services of churches in England and on the European continent. At first, as we noted above, these were presented primarily in monasteries; but as urban centers began to emerge in the eleventh and twelfth centuries and larger churches were built, services incorporating the small dramas of the tropes were produced in churches and cathedrals.

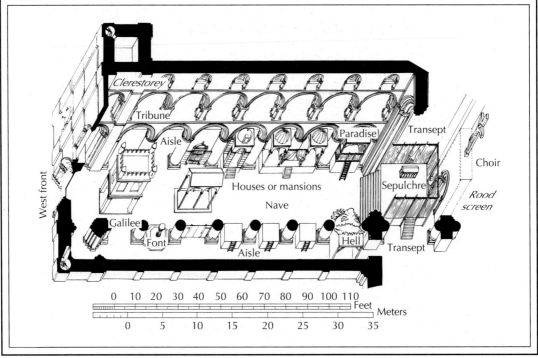

(Richard Leacroft, The Development of the English Playhouse, Cornell University Press, Ithaca, N.Y., 1973. By permission of Reed Book Services/Methuen London.)

Within the figure: Clerestorey, Tribune, Aisle, Paradise, Transept, Choir, Rood screen, West front, Houses or mansions, Nave, Sepulchre, Galilee, Font, Aisle, Hell, Transept

Scale: 0 10 20 30 40 50 60 70 80 90 100 110 Feet / Meters 0 5 10 15 20 25 30 35

STAGING LITURGICAL DRAMA. This reconstruction shows how the interior of a medieval church was used for staging liturgical plays. In addition to the specially created mansions, existing areas within the church were used; note the open space used for the platea.

Producing Liturgical Drama

Liturgical dramas were written in Latin and presented by clergymen and choirboys. At first, the presentations were staged in monasteries; the general public did not attend. Between 1000 and 1300, however, several significant changes took place. Urban centers developed where large groups of people congregated and where sizable churches began to be built. It was during this period that church architecture changed from Romanesque to Gothic; the Gothic style, with its pointed arches and buttressed walls, allowed for larger, more sweeping interior spaces. With the development of centers of population and the construction of Gothic churches and cathedrals, the production of liturgical plays was no longer confined to monasteries but became widely available.

Two spatial elements were employed for staging liturgical dramas within a church: the *mansion* and the *platea*. The mansion was a scenic building depicting some locale needed for a biblical tale. Such a scenic unit could be specially constructed—sometimes elaborately—or it could be an existing area within the church, such as an altar or the crypt. Mansions were set up around the larger central playing area, the platea. Since the mansions were too confined for actual performances, they were used only to indicate locale. Once an action had been initiated at a mansion, it would move to the platea; the entire platea then became associated with the originating mansion for the duration of the scene.

The mansions in a church (and, later, in an outdoor space) were all on view at the same time. This convention of multiple, simultaneous settings is difficult for modern audiences to visualize. We are accustomed to seeing only one locale at a time; if various locales are set up on a modern stage, lighting will be used to focus our attention on a particular area of the stage. In the medieval church, since the various mansions were visible simultaneously, the audience had to focus on one at a time and ignore the others. Interestingly, some twentieth-century avant-garde theater companies have designed theater spaces where several playing areas are used simultaneously. In today's theater, however, this technique has most often been meant to shatter the theatrical illusion of realistic drama and force audiences to become aware of the fact that they are watching a play. Medieval theater, which was highly conventional, did not use, or need, its simultaneous settings for this purpose. In early English liturgical dramas, for example, males performed all roles and church vestments served as costumes. Acceptance of multiple settings was in keeping with these conventions; it was also in keeping with the medieval worldview: the concept that all times and places were tied together in God's scheme of things.

As we have said, liturgical drama was written and performed in Latin, the language of scholarship and the church. When people attended a church service, there were many Latin words they understood—phrases from the mass, for example, such as *In nomine Patris, et Filii, et Spiritus Sancti*, which means "In the name of the Father, the Son, and the Holy Spirit." Still, Latin was not the language they spoke every day, and therefore most of the dialogue of liturgical plays would not have been understood by the audience. In the thirteenth century, however, dramas began to be written and presented in the languages spoken by ordinary people: Italian, French, Spanish, English, and so forth. The language of these plays could be understood by everyone; thus the plays became more meaningful and immediate. The term for everyday speech is *vernacular,* and so this new form of drama—to which we now turn—is called *religious vernacular drama.*

THE DEVELOPMENT OF RELIGIOUS VERNACULAR DRAMA

Historians continue to debate how medieval vernacular drama originated. Some suggest that church dramas performed in Latin simply metamorphosed—were transformed—into the vernacular. Scholars who hold this evolutionary theory also believe that in addition to changing from Latin to the vernacular, religious plays moved from inside church buildings to stages erected outside.

THE YORK CYCLE. Medieval religious drama usually took the form of a cycle of short plays based on events in the Old and New Testaments. Seen here is an outdoor staging of the York mystery plays outside Saint Mary's Abbey in that English city.

Among the reasons suggested for this move are the following: (1) Productions were becoming increasingly elaborate and were therefore difficult to stage in churches. (2) The cost of staging these dramas was becoming burdensome to the church. (3) Church officials were opposed to using holy spaces for theater. One play that supports the notion of a move from inside the church building to outside it is *The Mystery of Adam* (ca. 1150), whose stage directions clearly indicate that it was performed outdoors, alongside the church.

Other contemporary scholars believe that later vernacular drama developed independently from the liturgical plays—that there is no evolutionary relationship, though there are similarities in dramatic style and subject matter. Whatever its origin, between 1350 and 1550 religious vernacular drama presented outside church buildings flourished in a number of European countries, including England, France, Spain, Germany, Switzerland, and the Netherlands.

In describing religious vernacular drama, it is important to remember that attempts to categorize various types have been made only long after these plays were actually performed. However, to help us understand what kinds of plays were produced, scholars have separated religious vernacular dramas into two general categories: *mystery* or *cycle* plays and *miracle* plays. A third type of vernacular drama is *morality* plays, which are difficult to categorize as religious or secular. The following sections examine these three forms.

MYSTERY OR CYCLE PLAYS

The term *mystery* comes from *ministerium,* meaning a religious service or office; this suggests the religious origin of mystery dramas. Mystery plays dramatized a series of biblical events, from the creation to the last judgment. They were distinct from the brief liturgical plays: first, they were not presented as part of a religious ceremony but were staged independently as drama; second, they were not small, individual scenes, but short dramas presented as part of a sequence. When a number of plays were presented in sequence, they constituted a "cycle"—which is how the term *cycle plays* originated.

Spring and summer were the most popular seasons for the presentation of vernacular drama, primarily because of the weather. A favorite occasion for cycle plays was Corpus Christi, a religious festival which took place sometime between the last week in May and the last week in June. This festival was intended to remind laypeople of the doctrine that the bread and wine of the mass become the body and blood of Christ; but it went further than that—it presented a principal tenet of Roman Catholicism: the presence of the earthly and godly in Christ and the possibility of eternal life promised by his death and resurrection. It was because of this breadth of meaning, and because the festival took place in late spring, that Corpus Christi became a favorite occasion for cycle plays. But cycle plays were also presented at other times and in conjunction with other festivals. Though no exact parallel can be drawn, it is interesting to note that Greek and Roman drama was also presented in conjunction with religious observances or festivals. They appear to be natural times—times when people are gathered together and are in a celebratory mood—for dramatic presentations.

Since mystery plays were written in the vernacular and staged outdoors, they were meant to appeal to large audiences and to popular tastes. The mysteries are set in biblical times, but the characters are medieval in nature; Abraham and Isaac, for example, are dramatized not as Old Testament Jews but as medieval Christian serfs. Old Testament characters in the cycle plays speak of saints who have not yet been born. Such a displacement in time is called an *anachronism,* and mystery plays are filled with anachronisms. Presenting characters and events outside their proper historical sequence made biblical characters more identifiable to audiences and also drew parallels between biblical and medieval times. Abraham and Isaac, Noah, Joseph, and the Virgin Mary were depicted as ordinary men and women just like the friends and neighbors of medieval audiences. The charm and directness of these characterizations is still evident when we read the plays today.

To popularize these biblical adaptations, medieval dramatists also highlighted the spectacular. Even today, audiences can be mesmerized by biblical spectacle, as is evidenced by the popularity of biblical epic films. Comedy was also introduced to make the mystery plays more appealing; Noah's wife, as we saw at the opening of this chapter, was caricatured as a shrew, always nagging her husband.

The Second Shepherds' Play

One way to understand the themes and dramatic structure of mystery plays is to consider a specific example: *The Second Shepherds' Play* (ca. 1375) from England's Wakefield cycle. (The English mystery plays are grouped in a series of cycles, named for the places where they were performed: York, Chester, Wakefield, and "N." The last has only an initial; we do not know which of the 125 towns in England where cycle plays were performed is designated by it.)

The Second Shepherds' Play tells the biblical story of the shepherds who were told by an angel of the birth of Christ and instructed to visit the manger where he was born. Its first section comically depicts the stealing of a sheep from three shepherds by a rogue, Mak. When the three shepherds search for the missing sheep in Mak's home, Gil, his wife, pretends that it is her newborn child. The shepherds return a second time to offer gifts to Mak's "child" and discover that the infant is the stolen sheep. Though thievery was a capital offense in medieval law, the lenient shepherds merely toss Mak in the air in a blanket.

The humble and just shepherds are then called by the angel to visit the newborn Christ child, to whom they bring gifts in the second section of the play. The farcical "birth" of the first section, therefore, sets the stage for the holy nativity. Parallels are drawn between these two plots: the "child" in the first section is a sheep, just as Christ is the lamb of God; and in both sections there are scenes of adoration and gift-giving.

The Second Shepherds' Play uses most of the standard dramatic techniques of medieval cycle plays. It is written in the vernacular and in verse and is filled with anachronisms. The shepherds are characters out of the Middle Ages, not the Bible: they complain about their lords and feudal conditions, and even though Christ is not born until the close of the play, they pray to him and to various saints throughout the first section. Though the play dramatizes the birth of the Christian savior, this event is preceded by an extended comic section which reflects the influence of secular farce. The mixture of comic and serious elements itself indicates the two strains of medieval theater—religious and secular.

The Emergence of Episodic Form

In Chapter 1, we examined the first important dramatic form that emerged in western theater, the crisis drama developed in Greece and Rome. The second major dramatic form to develop in the western tradition is the *episodic* structure found in medieval religious drama.

Episodic drama stands in marked contrast to crisis drama. The "crisis" structure of Greek drama is formal and somewhat rigid. In a typical Greek play, the plot begins near the climax of the story, there are very few major characters, the locale of the action is limited (often to one place), and comedy and tragedy are not mixed. In the religious drama that emerged in the Middle Ages, the structure is quite different.

In *The Second Shepherds' Play,* as we have seen, the action shifts abruptly from a field to Mak's hut and then to Christ's manger some distance away; and comic and serious elements are freely intermingled. Obviously, a play about the birth of Christ should be serious; but the taste for earthy farce was irrepressible in English drama of this period, and so comedy also became a part of the drama.

Moreover, *The Second Shepherds' Play*—unlike crisis drama—does not have a single plot; it has two separate, though related, stories: Mak and the theft of the sheep, and the visit to the Christ child. The fact that two stories are followed at once suggests how these plays achieved unity and advanced a theme. The method is to juxtapose two stories, two plot threads, and two sets of characters so that they reverberate and thus reinforce one another. A theme is looked at from two or more points of view so that the whole becomes greater than its separate parts. In *The Second Shepherds' Play,* Mak steals a lamb, and we recall that Christ is often called the *lamb of God.* As we move from the story of Mak to the story of Christ's birth, we are aware of two babies and two lambs; and the echoes and resonances of these two ideas bring the parts of the drama together to create a forceful image.

Frequent changes in time and place occur in *The Second Shepherds' Play;* but this did not bother medieval audiences, who were not concerned with a realistic or literal rendition of a story. In a series of cycle plays, the story would unfold from beginning to end and would often involve a great many characters.

In the cycle plays, then, instead of the economy and compression of Greek drama, we find expansiveness and a juxtaposition of elements. We switch from one element to another: from one group of characters to a different group; from one historical period to another; from one story line to another; from comedy to serious drama. Tension and excitement, as well as meaning, often come from this shifting back and forth.

This episodic structure was logical for the cycle plays, given the medieval worldview—the concept of all time as part of God's continuum. The biblical past was considered part of the medieval present; therefore, anachronisms and sudden changes in time and place were not seen as incongruous. A parallel can be drawn with medieval triptych paintings: many of these paintings were designed as altarpieces and show three separate religious scenes side by side.

Episodic drama was in its infancy in the medieval period, but in later years it became the foundation for highly complex plays, such as those of English playwrights like Shakespeare and Spanish dramatists like Lope de Vega. The episodic approach entered the mainstream of western drama; it and the Greek crisis form became the two predominant dramatic structures from the sixteenth to the twentieth century.

Producing the Cycle Plays

Liturgical drama, as we noted earlier, was produced within the church building. For the mystery plays—and this is also true of the miracle plays—production techniques varied throughout Europe.

On the continent, mystery plays were most often produced by religious charitable organizations called *confraternities*. In northern England, they were produced by the trade guilds. In England, plays were often assigned to the trade guild that seemed "appropriate." The last supper, for example, might have been presented by the bakers' guild because of the bread served by Christ; the Noah play by the shipbuilders' guild; and the visit of the magi (in which the three wise men bring gold, frankincense, and myrrh to the Christ child) by the goldsmiths' guild. Because of the guilds' participation, the presentations were often civic and commercial events; the cycle plays provided an opportunity for tradespeople and artisans to display their abilities. Frequently, town councils assisted in financing and scheduling, although the church continued to oversee outdoor religious theatrical events.

Cycle plays were usually produced once every 2 to 10 years, and some were extremely elaborate. A passion play at Valenciennes in France in 1547 lasted 25 days; and *The Acts of the Apostles*, given in 1536 at Bourges (also in France), lasted for 40 days and had a cast of 300 performers. Probably, these were exceptions and most productions took place over a shorter time; nevertheless, productions were often complex to mount. Performances often began early in the day and, after a break for lunch, continued until late afternoon. Depending on the locale, this would go on for 2, 3, or more days.

Most people knew about forthcoming performances because so many members of a community were involved, but those who were not aware would be informed by announcements and processions a few days beforehand.

Practices on charging spectators varied. In England most productions were free; for certain productions on the continent, a fee was charged.

PERFORMERS

Both on the continent and in England, the performers in cycle plays were amateurs. As the productions became more complex, however, professionals may have supplemented the amateur casts. Customs regarding women performers varied: women performed in France, for instance, but were excluded in England. Because of the extensive scope of the cycle plays, doubling—having performers play two or more different parts—was not unusual. Rehearsal time was minimal; typically, there were fewer than five rehearsals for a single mystery play. Amateur actors agreed under oath to perform and were fined for being absent or disrupting a rehearsal. Since nonprofessionals were used, they were usually type-cast and were requested to repeat their roles when a cycle was restaged. *Type-casting* means choosing people who have certain qualities in real life to play characters with similar qualities. A tough-looking man with a strong voice, for instance, would be cast as Cain, who kills his brother Abel; an innocent-looking young woman would play the Virgin Mary.

The financial burden on the performer could be great, but the task was undertaken as a religious duty. If an actor could not attend work because of his obligations in the production, he had to hire a replacement at his job.

COSTUMES

Actors in the cycle plays provided their own costumes. They would be assisted, however, if they needed unusual costumes: God, for example, would be costumed as a pope (the pope being God's earthly representative), and angels wore church vestments with attached wings.

The assumption has usually been that the common characters in medieval mystery plays wore contemporary clothing: such costuming would be in keeping with the anachronistic nature of these plays and with the desire to let audience members identify with biblical characters.

Some recent scholarship, however, questions this traditionally accepted view. A few historians point out that in medieval visual art there is considerable interest in representing clothing from earlier periods, although most of these representations are historically inaccurate. In addition, lists of props and costumes which survive from certain pageants, as well as stage directions in some of the plays, suggest that costuming was not contemporary. For example, the "N Town" passion play requires one character to be costumed as a Jewish high priest.

What is most likely is that the approach to costuming in medieval theater was not uniform—just as there was no single approach to staging. In fact, this uncertainty about costumes again reminds us that to try to establish a single, uniform concept of "medieval theater" is to diminish a vital, robust art form which flourished in many parts of Europe in a number of unique configurations.

PAGEANT MASTERS

Because of the complexity of cycle plays, there developed, both on the continent and in England, a practice of having one person organize and oversee a production. In England, there are records of someone referred to as a *pageant master,* who supervised the mounting of plays on wagons. This might include advance preparation—both of the wagons and of the rehearsals of plays to be presented on them—and the logistics of seeing that the plays unfolded on schedule.

In the 1500s on the continent—in France, Spain, Belgium, Switzerland, and Austria—men were hired to oversee the elaborate production of cycle plays, and some of their names are known. One of them, a Frenchman named Jean Bouchet, outlined the duties of the manager or director. These responsibilities, according to Bouchet, included finding people to construct scenery as well as seating for the audience; supervising the building of the stage (or stages); positioning machines and scenery; selecting and rehearsing performers; disciplining performers and fining those who violated the rules; assigning people to collect money at the entrances; and serving as a narrator between plays—describing what had happened before and arousing interest in what was to come.

The duties and responsibilities of managers or pageant masters varied a great deal from place to place. As we have mentioned, in some areas the plays were organized by guilds and in other places by committees. But in many instances there was a single person who oversaw and managed the production. These people did not perform the same duties as modern directors—they did not, for instance, develop an interpretation of the text or an overall concept to guide the production. But in terms of organization and management, the pageant masters anticipated the director, who was to come very much to the forefront several centuries later.

STAGING

Processional and stationary staging Two traditions developed for staging the cycle plays: processional and stationary. The English, Spanish, and Dutch seem to have used primarily processional staging for their mystery plays; the rest of Europe used mainly stationary staging. Recent research suggests, however, that both forms of staging were probably used in most countries.

In *processional staging,* audiences would assemble in various places and the cycle play would be set up on a wagon which moved from locale to locale, so that the play could be presented separately for each audience area along its route. Numerous questions remain unanswered regarding processional staging in England.

For example, what did a pageant wagon look like? One theory is that the wagon was a two-story structure on four to six wheels, with the bottom level serving as a curtained dressing area, and the second level containing scenery and acting space. This theory has been challenged, though, because such wagons might have been too large and unwieldy to move through the narrow streets of medieval English towns and would not have provided a large enough area for acting. A second theory is that one-story wagons carrying scenery were used in conjunction with bare scaffold carts for acting; costume changes would take place in a curtained-off back area of the scenery cart. This theory is based on the Spanish practice of pulling scenery wagons up to a platform for performances; however, the Spaniards used two, three, or four scenery carts for each play. The most radical theory is that true processional staging was too complicated: a town that had set aside only one day for a religious theatrical event could not have staged a complete cycle at a series of locales; also, since the plays were not uniform in length, it would have been difficult to coordinate a processional production. Therefore, some scholars believe that the pageant wagons, carrying scenery and possibly actors in a mute tableau, were paraded through a town (much like floats in a modern parade) and then pulled up to a stationary stage for the actual performance.

Though there is debate among historians about precisely what form processional staging took, there is no question that it was a major type of theater presentation in the Middle Ages, particularly in England, Spain, and the Netherlands.

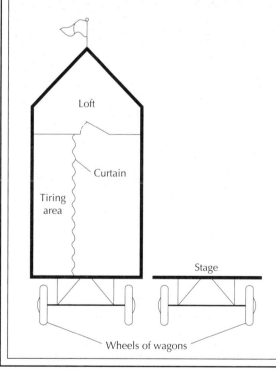

Loft

Curtain

Tiring area

Stage

Wheels of wagons

PAGEANT WAGONS. One form of staging medieval religious plays was the pageant wagon, which could be rolled into a town or a nearby field. A wagon or wagons would be set up to serve as a stage, with a backstage area for costume changes. We do not know exactly how these pageant wagons worked, but two possibilities are shown here. At the top is a model of a pageant wagon in a town square: the wagon has a platform with a cloth covering its lower part (from which devils could emerge). At bottom is a drawing of two wagons side by side, one serving as a stage platform and the other as a place for changing costumes and hiding special effects.

OUTDOOR STAGES AT VALENCIENNES. A popular form of medieval staging, especially on the European continent, was a series of areas alongside each other. This model is of such an arrangement in Valenciennes in France. At the far left is heaven, or paradise; at the right is hell; in between are other "mansions" representing various biblical scenes and locales. The action would move from one area to the next.

The second major form of production for cycle plays was *stationary staging.* In this form—which predominated throughout Europe—a series of small scenic mansions stood side by side. Usually, a huge platform stage was erected in an open courtyard of a town or in a town square, but smaller indoor stages were sometimes used. In certain places, existing sites provided a setting for performances. In Rome, Italy, and Bourges, France, there were amphitheaters remaining from Roman days; and in Cornwall, England, there was a circular structure, known as the *Cornish round,* with earthen embankments approximately 10 feet in diameter surrounding various stage areas.

Scenic units—the mansions—were placed side by side on the stage or, in some instances, directly on the ground. At times, a cycle would be divided into sections by intermissions, some of them as long as 24 hours, during which the mansions could be changed or rearranged. The most popular and most spectacular mansions, representing heaven and hell, were placed at opposite ends of the platform. Heaven was elevated and frequently contained flying machinery—that is, equipment to lift performers aloft. The entrance to hell was most often depicted as the head of a monster which spewed forth fire and smoke. Between heaven and hell were less intricate mansions representing various earthly locales.

Special effects, called *secrets,* were enormously popular and ingeniously worked out. They were so important that sometimes a *secrets master* was hired to oversee them. In Belgium, the flood for the play about Noah described at the beginning of this chapter was staged by storing barrels of water on the roof above the platform stage and releasing the water at the appropriate time. On stationary stages, actors impersonating heavenly beings could be "flown in" on lines or ropes from the roofs of adjoining buildings. On movable stages, characters could be flown in from the tops of the wagons; trapdoors also allowed actors and props to be raised and lowered. Shiny surfaces were used to reflect light and create "halo" effects; the halo was quite common in medieval religious painting and also popular in religious theater. Between 1350 and 1550, religious drama devised many innovations for special effects.

The relationship between the audience and the stage varied; occasionally, spectators viewed the action from all sides, in what was almost theater-in-the-round, but sometimes they were on three sides or only one side. Seating was temporary: people closest to the stage stood, and farther back scaffolding and box seats were erected. Rooms in nearby houses and on adjoining roofs held additional spectators; in some instances, these choice locations were no doubt sold to people who wanted the best possible view.

The neutral platform stage   One aspect of medieval staging that was to have important ramifications for the theaters of England and Spain in years to come was the concept of a neutral, nonlocalized platform stage. A pageant wagon might have a specific scenic background, and stationary settings might have mansions for individual scenes, but in both cases the most important playing area was a stage platform in front of these settings. (It will be recalled that dramas presented inside churches also used a generalized area where most of the performance took place—the central platea.)

We know from the texts of many cycle plays that action would often move instantaneously from one locale to another. In *The Second Shepherds' Play*, for instance, at one moment the shepherds are in a field, at the next moment they are at Mak's house, and a few minutes later they are at Christ's manger. In *Abraham and Isaac*, at one point the characters are preparing to go on a journey to a mountaintop; after a few steps across the stage, they have arrived there. To accept such abrupt, sudden transitions, the audience had to regard the platform itself as a neutral area, not a specific locale. In the audience's imagination, the stage could be transformed instantaneously into whatever the play indicated it was: a field, a room in a house, a mountaintop.

As with dramatic structure, this concept of stage space differs from Greek and Roman practice. Instead of a specific locale, such as the palace of Oedipus or Agamemnon, the medieval stage was like a slate from which writing can be erased. A place could be designated, and then the slate could be "wiped clean" so that another locale could be assigned to it. Shifts of locale could be created in the imagination of the spectators rather than by changes of scenery—an arrangement that we sometimes find in today's theater.

MIRACLE PLAYS

Miracle plays—another popular form of religious drama—were similar to mystery plays in dramatic technique. Instead of biblical tales, though, miracle plays were based on the lives of saints. Though mystery plays deal with biblical tales and miracle plays do not, the two are so similar that some scholars do not distinguish between them. In fact, the term *miracle* was originally used to describe all medieval drama; only in the 1700s did it come to denote a play staged on the feast-day of a saint and honoring his or her legendary feats. The most popular subjects of miracle plays were the Virgin Mary and Saint Nicholas. In England, the legends of Saint George were also frequently dramatized.

MORALITY PLAYS

Thus far in this chapter we have focused on religious drama, and particularly on the cycle plays. We now turn to another important form of medieval drama, the *morality play*. A morality play attempts to teach a moral lesson through allegorical characters. In allegory, people represent ideas: one character stands for charity, another for integrity, another for greed, and so forth. In morality plays, characters often undertake a journey through which they learn the moral lesson. Some scholars describe morality plays as *station dramas* because during the journey the protagonist is confronted by a series of crises that can be seen as analogous to Christ's journey through the "stations of the cross."

Scholars debate whether to categorize morality plays as religious or secular. It is true that the main characters in morality plays are ordinary men and women, rather than the saints or biblical figures of the miracle and cycle plays. However, the morality plays dealt with moral issues and were deeply rooted in Christianity—and this is the important thing to remember about them.

One important aspect of the morality play reappears in plays of the Renaissance, particularly in England. Frequently, the basis of these dramas is a struggle between two forces, one good and the other evil, for the soul of the main character. This struggle could be between God and Satan, or between a good angel and a bad angel; the crucial element was a battle between two sides for a person's soul. In the English Renaissance, we will see this idea refined by the playwright Christopher Marlowe and developed still further by Shakespeare in several of his plays.

Everyman

Everyman remains the most popular example of a morality play. In this drama, the character Everyman—who represents humanity—is suddenly and unexpectedly told by Death, a messenger of God, that his earthly life is over. Unprepared for death and afraid to journey to the next world alone, Everyman

EVERYMAN. The best-known medieval morality play—shown here in a German adaptation staged annually outside the cathedral at Salzburg in Austria—is the story of Everyman, who is summoned to die. In the play, whose main object is to teach a lesson, abstract ideas become characters: Death, Good Deeds, and so on. Everyman tries to forestall dying, and then tries to get others to come with him, but all refuse except Good Deeds.

seeks a companion to accompany him. He speaks to a number of characters, each representing an abstract idea—Worldly Goods, Kin, Beauty, and others—but none of them except Good Deeds will accompany him to the afterlife. The lesson that Everyman, and the audience, learns is that only Good Deeds can be of any assistance when one is summoned by Death.

Producing the Morality Plays

Though the subject matter of medieval morality plays was religious, by the early sixteenth century they were probably staged by professional performers —unlike mystery or miracle plays. The introduction of professional actors was in keeping with a transition from religious to secular theater which is reflected in the morality plays of the late Middle Ages. The text of *Everyman*, however, suggests that staging techniques for moralities were similar to those for the cycle plays and were based on the same concept of a neutral platform stage.

SECULAR THEATER IN THE MIDDLE AGES

A battle between secular and religious studies unfolded slowly during the High Middle Ages, leading to an explosion in the Renaissance. One reflection of this struggle is found in medieval theater: during the centuries in which liturgical drama and—later—mystery and morality plays were developing, nonreligious or *secular* drama was also emerging. Secular theater, which could be classified as popular entertainment, was often comic and sometimes irreverent.

Throughout the Early Middle Ages and into the High Middle Ages, the tradition of professional theater was kept alive by wandering minstrels, mimes, jugglers, and rope dancers. These performers, who were attacked by the church as pagan and sacrilegious, continued a tradition of touring players that can be traced back to ancient Greece. Other secular entertainments inspired by festivals, such as May Day games, were enjoyed by the conquering barbarians. Many of these festivals, which featured phallic maypoles and the like, celebrated fertility and sensual freedom. The church was unable to coerce the pagans into renouncing these activities even after they were converted to Christianity.

These minor forms—indicative of a desire to keep the theatrical impulse alive—came to fruition in the High Middle Ages. Out of the festival celebrations came two forms of secular drama: folk plays, dramatizing the heroic exploits of folk heroes; and farce, which comically depicts universal human weaknesses. Secular farce seems also to have been influenced by such church-related events as the Feast of Fools and the festival of the Boy Bishop. During the Feast of Fools, young clergymen selected a mock "bishop" or "pope of fools" who was allowed to misuse his religious power; they also sang and danced indecently, burlesqued sermons and services, and staged plays satirizing the church. The Festival of the Boy Bishop was similar, though tamer.

Such popular festivities, which were criticized by the church hierarchy, contained the seeds of farce. There was something earthy and basic about these comic pieces; as a result, they had an appeal that continued for many years and eventually found their way into the plays of Shakespeare and other writers of his time.

Nonreligious comic pieces of the Middle Ages contrast sharply with religious drama. Religious drama, obviously, focuses on the significance of religion—the importance of the Bible, the rewards of virtue, the punishment of vice. Comic drama emphasizes the imperfections and scandals of everyday human behavior; adultery, hypocrisy, and other kinds of misbehavior form its subject matter. Also, this subject matter is presented in a strongly satirical or comic light.

We have records of secular drama and farces dating from the thirteenth century. One extant drama, *The Play of Greenwood* by Adam de la Halle of Arras in France, dates from about 1276. This play combines folk material about fairies and supernatural events with satirical material about people living in Arras. There is even more native material in *The Play of Robin and Marion*, written about 1283 by the same author. The popularity of brief secular comedies and farces grew steadily during the fourteenth century.

TOURING MINSTRELS AND WANDERING PLAYERS. One of the traditions influencing the secular theater that developed in the Middle Ages was the touring minstrel, who performed in makeshift spaces—often on the street or in a booth. This drawing was done after the Middle Ages, in 1598, and shows that the tradition of the strolling players continued.

Among surviving plays from the fifteenth century is *Pierre Patelin*, a French farce which dates from around 1470 and was so popular that it went through thirty editions in the next 130 years. It is about a lawyer—Patelin—who cheats a merchant out of a roll of cloth and then, proud of this, tells a peasant how to get out of paying his debts, whereupon the peasant turns the tables on the lawyer and cheats him out of the fee the peasant owes him.

A German writer of farce who emerged in the sixteenth century was Hans Sachs (1494–1576). A shoemaker and also a singer, Sachs learned a great deal about drama in his wide travels. A prolific author, he wrote nearly 200 plays. A good example of his work is *The Wandering Scholar from Paradise*. The play is about a woman who, because her second husband is a brute, dreams fondly of her deceased first husband. When a traveling student tells her that he is from Paris, she thinks he has said *Paradise*. She assumes that he can contact her dead husband and asks him to take clothes and money to the dead husband when he returns to "Paradise." The student readily agrees and goes on his way with his spoils. When the second husband returns and hears the story, he chases after the student to recover the money; but when he overtakes the student, he too is fooled and the student escapes not only with the woman's money but also with the second husband's horse.

In England, farce also developed in the sixteenth century. John Heywood (ca. 1497–1580) wrote a play called *Johan Johan* in which a henpecked husband's wife is having a love affair with a priest. When the husband is ridiculed by his wife and her lover, he sends them both away from home but then realizes that he has made a mistake—he has actually thrown them into each other's arms.

In France, a first cousin to native farce was the *sottie*. In French *sot* means "stupid," "foolish," or "absurd," and *sottise* means "foolishness" or "nonsense." These short sketches, which frequently had the figure of a fool as a central character, were often critical of the church or religious figures. A sense of native fun as well as satire predominated in the *sottie*.

At the same time that farce was developing, vagabond players began organizing into troupes and finding wealthy patrons among monarchs, lords, and merchants. They found that this was the best way to develop some continuity and stability in their transient, unreliable profession. The type of entertainment they often presented to their patrons was the *interlude,* a short dramatic piece staged between the courses of a banquet. For their performances, a large banquet hall was used rather than a theater space. European professional players, who toured a great deal, were accustomed to performing in such improvised spaces.

With the rise of the monarchy in parts of Europe, nonreligious court entertainments became more popular. An intriguing medieval dramatic form staged for royalty was the *street pageant.* By the fifteenth century, allegorical, biblical, and mythological dramatizations, honoring visiting monarchs, were staged along town routes. These were pantomimed tableaux with occasional narration.

It is important to remember that nonreligious drama was being performed at the same time as mystery and miracle plays. These satiric pieces, farces, and folk plays in which ordinary people were heroes no doubt had some influence on religious drama, and vice versa: the way in which religious plays were written and performed must have affected secular drama, and the down-to-earth comic quality of nonreligious plays affected the cycle plays. Much of what is popular in the medieval mysteries is reminiscent of folk plays and farces. The fact that so many of the cycle plays contain farcical characters and scenes is an indication of the interaction between religious and secular drama.

THE DECLINE OF RELIGIOUS THEATER

The weakening of the church in the sixteenth century, culminating in the widespread Protestant Reformation, was one reason for the demise of religious theater. Roman Catholicism withdrew its support from religious theater, which it accused of having weakened the church; for example, it outlawed religious drama in Paris in 1548. Protestantism considered religious drama a tool of Catholicism; thus Elizabeth I, as head of the Anglican church, banned religious drama in England in 1559.

Another reason for the decline of religious drama was that its secular qualities finally overwhelmed the religious material. The farce within *The Second Shepherds' Play* and the focus on the human struggle in *Everyman* were steps in the development of the great secular drama of the Renaissance.

Medieval religious theater—in the form of drama it developed and in its staging practices—was to be a major influence on later theater and drama, particularly in Elizabethan England and the Spanish golden age. In Spain, religious drama continued to flourish alongside secular drama until well into the Renaissance. Furthermore, religious theater continues to thrive in many parts of the world today. A significant example is the controversial community-staged Oberammergau Passion Play in Germany. (Debate rages over whether the play's portrayal of Jewish characters is anti-Semitic. In medieval cycle plays dealing with the life of Christ, Jews were often presented negatively.) Still, although religious theatrical works remain important spiritual experiences for some audiences, after the Middle Ages religion was no longer the central concern of most theater.

In Part Two, we will begin to see how western theater developed after the Middle Ages, as we take up the theaters of the Renaissance. Before this, however, we turn in Chapter 4 to early Asian theater, which was developing half a world away from Europe.

SUMMARY

During the Early Middle Ages, touring minstrels kept the theatrical tradition alive. Later in the Middle Ages, theater was reborn in the Roman Catholic church. Musical and dramatic interpolations added to religious services grew into liturgical dramas; these plays, written in Latin and dramatizing biblical events, were staged in churches by the clergy.

In the fourteenth century, plays in the language of the people—religious vernacular drama—developed. Mystery or cycle plays, which depicted a series of biblical tales, were staged and acted outdoors by guilds in northern England and by confraternities on the continent. In England, Spain, and the Netherlands, mystery plays were usually presented on pageant wagons which probably traveled through towns. In other parts of the continent, a large open playing space with a series of scenic mansions set side by side was common. Miracle plays, another form of religious vernacular drama, presented legends of the saints. A medieval dramatic form difficult to categorize is the morality play, which presents allegorical characters and moral lessons and was staged by professional performers.

Medieval plays employed simple, direct dramatic techniques that called on the imagination of the spectators. They frequently used symbols and exercised great freedom in shifts in time and space.

Secular theater also flourished in the Middle Ages. During the High Middle Ages, folk drama and farce developed, and professional performers were employed at the courts of the emerging monarchs. The influence of secular theater can be seen in the farcical and folk elements of the cycle plays.

CHAPTER 4

EARLY ASIAN THEATER

The year is 1413, and we are at the Kitano Temple in Japan. A platform stage, with a floor of polished wood, has been set up; there is also a wooden walkway or bridge on which actors can move to the stage from a dressing room set up in one of the temple buildings. The spectators are on three sides of the stage.

The actor performing today is Zeami, a 50-year-old man who has been under the patronage of the shogun—the ruler of this area—since the age of 11. Zeami's father, Kwanami, was a renowned actor before him, and Zeami has carried Kwanami's art to even greater heights. He has studied different acting styles, perfected his own technique, trained other actors, and written plays for them to perform. The theater he has fashioned from all this, called *noh,* has elements of opera, pantomime, and formal, stylized dance. The main character in noh, who wears a beautifully carved and painted wooden mask, recites his or her adventures to a constant accompaniment by several onstage musicians. Toward the end of the play, the chief actor will perform a ritualistic dance with symbolic head and hand gestures and stomps of the feet on the wooden floor.

The crowd is gathered today for a special reason. Usually, Zeami performs only in a restricted environment—for the shogun and the members of his court

KABUKI. Most Asian theaters, in contrast to western theater, are highly stylized: some use masks, and many incorporate dance. Actors in Japanese kabuki use exaggerated movements, and all the parts are played by men. In this scene, a traveling silk merchant comes upon a girl from a teahouse and is struck by her beauty. Notice the detailed makeup and costumes, and the highly theatrical style of the scene as a whole. *(AP/Wide World Photos)*

or at a temple for a select audience. But here at the Kitano Temple performances will go on for 7 days and will be open to everyone; as one commentator will later explain: "All were admitted, rich and poor, old and young alike." We feel ourselves privileged to be a part of this group.

As with all noh performances, several plays will be presented each day. The play we are awaiting now—*Sotoba Komachi*—is one in which Zeami plays a woman; as in ancient Greek theater, all the noh performers are men. *Sotoba Komachi* was written by Zeami's father and is based on a legend well-known to the audience. In this legend, Komachi, a beautiful but cruel woman, is pursued by a man named Shii no Shosho. She tells him that he must call on her for 100 nights in a row, and for 99 nights he comes, in all kinds of weather. But on the hundredth night he dies.

As the play begins, we see two priests enter, discussing the virtues of following Buddha. They then come upon an old woman—Zeami in the mask and wig of Komachi in old age. She says that she was once beautiful:

Long ago I was full of pride;
Crowned with nodding tresses, halcyon locks,
I walked like a young willow delicately wafted
By the winds of Spring.
I spoke with the voice of a nightingale that has sipped the dew.
I was lovelier than the petals of the wild-rose open-stretched
in the hour before its fall.[1]

But now Komachi has grown old and lost her beauty. She argues with the priests about religion and then reveals who she is. She recounts the story of what she did to Shosho.

As the play progresses, the audience watches Zeami's performance with rapt attention. At one point his character becomes possessed: the spirit of Shosho takes over Komachi's body, and Zeami acts this out in pantomime to musical accompaniment. At other times he enacts Komachi's part while a chorus—ten or twelve men sitting at the side of the stage—chants her lines. At another time, Komachi is dressed as Shosho and actually becomes him, feeling his death agony. Zeami performs this episode as a mesmerizing, frightening dance. At the end of the play, the spirit of Shosho leaves Komachi, and she prays to Buddha for guidance and for a peaceful life in the hereafter.

We in the audience, who have heard much about Zeami but have never seen him perform, watch in awe. Throughout, he plays the various parts with astounding grace, subtlety, and understatement, developed through years of training and performance. When he lets go—as in Shosho's death agony—he is all the more effective because of the contrast with his usual stately, measured style. For the audience, the play is a revelation of how moving a theatrical performance can be; it is an experience unlike any we have had before.

[1] Arthur Waley, *The No Plays of Japan*, 1957, p. 151. Reprinted by permission of Grove Press, Inc. All rights reserved.

BACKGROUND: THE THEATERS OF ASIA

For 1,000 years, from approximately A.D. 350 to 1350, there was no organized theater in the west. During that time, however, theater was beginning in another part of the world, thousands of miles away: on the continent of Asia. The traditions of Asian theater, established centuries ago, were to continue to the present day.

The people who created theater in Asia knew nothing of the theater of Greece or Rome. In the Introduction, we discussed the universal tendency toward theater and observed that except where theater is expressly forbidden by religious or other laws, it is likely to emerge in any civilization. This was true in India, China, and Japan—the countries we will focus on in this chapter—and also in other Asian countries, such as Indonesia.

Each of the Asian theaters is unique, but these theaters also have aspects in common that set them apart from western theater. To mention two: they rely much more on dance than western theater does (in many instances, Asian theatrical presentations could be called *dance dramas*), and they emphasize symbolism. All of the three great Asian traditions—Indian, Chinese, and Japanese—have created and sustained one form or another of what has been described as *total theater*. In this type of theater there is a synthesis or integration of elements—acting, mime, dancing, music, and text—more complete than in traditional western theater. Though each of the three theatrical traditions is unique and self-contained, all of them have qualities that may seem familiar to westerners who have been exposed to opera, in which a colorful blending of ideas, art, and technique is crucial.

One reason why this kind of synthesis developed in Asia and found continued support lies in the fact that the religious roots of theater are still kept alive there. Each of the three Asian traditions reached a high point of artistic excellence at a time when religion and philosophy were central in its culture. This level of excellence has kept the focus of traditional theater at least allied to religion and philosophy, even when society itself changed and became modernized. The development of theater in India, China, or Japan often remains rather obscure before the high point, which occurred when writers of poetic and intellectual ability began to create a dramatic tradition in which the text assumed a central place. (Some scholars suggest a connection among the three traditions, noting that Chinese theater may have been influenced by Indian theater, which in turn may have influenced Japanese theater.)

What remained in later years was usually the words rather than the production style; this is, of course, partially explained by the fact that anything written, such as a script, has some permanence, whereas a performance is ephemeral. Thus little is known of early performance practices in China or India; Japan is unique in having preserved many of its ancient techniques of acting, dancing, and singing. Still, in all three theaters the ancient traditions—interpreted and reinterpreted as these cultures developed and changed—have continued to color and shape many later experiments.

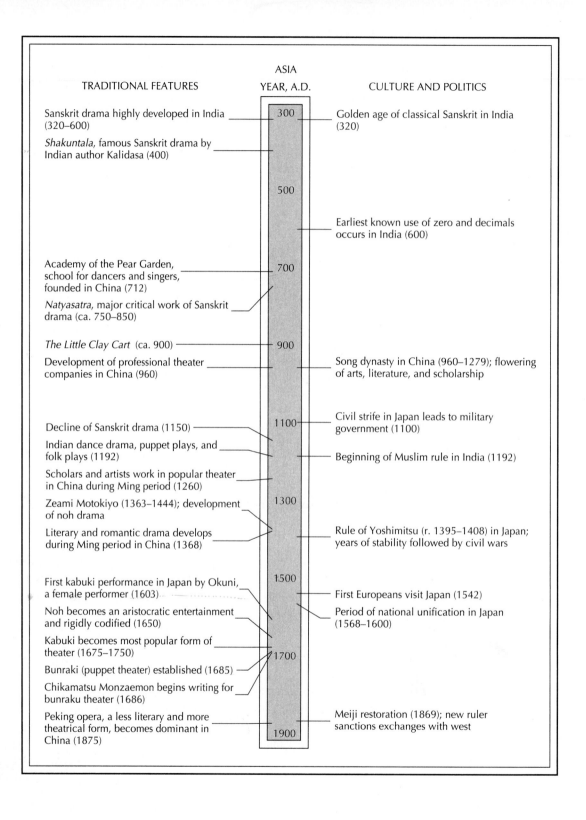

ASIA
YEAR, A.D.

TRADITIONAL FEATURES

CULTURE AND POLITICS

Sanskrit drama highly developed in India (320–600) — 300 — Golden age of classical Sanskrit in India (320)

Shakuntala, famous Sanskrit drama by Indian author Kalidasa (400)

500

Earliest known use of zero and decimals occurs in India (600)

Academy of the Pear Garden, school for dancers and singers, founded in China (712) — 700

Natyasatra, major critical work of Sanskrit drama (ca. 750–850)

The Little Clay Cart (ca. 900) — 900

Development of professional theater companies in China (960) — Song dynasty in China (960–1279); flowering of arts, literature, and scholarship

Decline of Sanskrit drama (1150) — 1100 — Civil strife in Japan leads to military government (1100)

Indian dance drama, puppet plays, and folk plays (1192) — Beginning of Muslim rule in India (1192)

Scholars and artists work in popular theater in China during Ming period (1260)

Zeami Motokiyo (1363–1444); development of noh drama — 1300

Literary and romantic drama develops during Ming period in China (1368) — Rule of Yoshimitsu (r. 1395–1408) in Japan; years of stability followed by civil wars

First kabuki performance in Japan by Okuni, a female performer (1603) — 1500

First Europeans visit Japan (1542)

Noh becomes an aristocratic entertainment and rigidly codified (1650) — Period of national unification in Japan (1568–1600)

Kabuki becomes most popular form of theater (1675–1750)

Bunraki (puppet theater) established (1685) — 1700

Chikamatsu Monzaemon begins writing for bunraku theater (1686)

Peking opera, a less literary and more theatrical form, becomes dominant in China (1875) — Meiji restoration (1869); new ruler sanctions exchanges with west

1900

INDIAN THEATER

Indian history has been characterized as a succession of immigrations into the Indian subcontinent. Early traces of civilization there go back to 3000 B.C. The Aryans, who came into southern India 1,000 years later, left behind works in Sanskrit that constitute the basis of the great Indian literary traditions. Scholars believe that by 1000 B.C., certain fundamental aspects of Indian civilization were already established; one of these is the caste system, under which people are classified by heredity: a person must remain in the caste to which he or she is born, and people are forbidden to change occupations.

Around 400 B.C., Buddhism, the religion of eastern and central Asia, reached a peak of development. Buddhism, based on the ideas of Gautama Buddha (ca. 563–483 B.C.), teaches that suffering is inherent in life but that human beings can be liberated from suffering by mental and moral self-purification. King Asoka, who ruled about 240 B.C., managed to unite the whole nation under Buddhist rule, but a period of disorder and confusion followed until the Guppy dynasty began to unite the nation again around A.D. 320.

It was at this time that Hindu culture entered its golden age, and it was during the following centuries that the great Sanskrit dramas were written and performed. Hinduism stresses the belief that soul or spirit is the essence of life; that the goal of all people is to achieve oneness with the supreme world-soul, known as *Brahman;* and that the things of this life do not exist in the same way as Brahman, which is eternal, infinite, and indescribable.

Sanskrit Drama

What remains from the tradition of the Indian golden age is a group of plays that were written in Sanskrit, the language of the noble classes, to be performed in various court circles. There are between fifty and sixty plays that can be reliably assigned to this period, and the greatest of them are among the finest works of classical Indian literature.

Although their texts have been preserved, no information remains on how these plays were acted. However, we do have descriptions of a typical theater in which they were performed. It was 96 feet long and 48 feet wide, divided equally into stage and auditorium, and its seating capacity was probably about 400. There were four pillars in the auditorium—each colored white, yellow, red, or blue—indicating where members of different castes were to sit. A curtain divided the stage into two parts: one part for the action, and the other for dressing rooms and a behind-the-scenes area. The few records available from the later period of Sanskrit drama indicate that most performances were given by troupes invited to the courts of the nobility, and performing spaces were arranged in courtyards and similar areas.

Scenery was evidently not used, although elaborate costumes probably were. Dance, symbolic gestures, and music were important in the productions; but again, we have no specific information about performance practices. The plays often use fixed characters, such as a narrator and a clown; once again, there are no details about how these performers appeared onstage.

As we have noted, these plays were written in Sanskrit, the classical language of the nobility, though some of the "lower" characters in the later plays speak a hybrid of Sanskrit and local dialect. Thus they had little following among the general public, who could not understand them. The plays usually draw on themes from Indian epic literature.

Among the best-known of these plays is *The Little Clay Cart*, written about 900 (its authorship is uncertain). *The Little Clay Cart* concerns the love between a ruined merchant and a courtesan; its style is enlivened and enriched by politics and humor. The most famous Sanskrit play, however, comes from the fourth or fifth century: this is *Shakuntula*, which is usually considered the finest classical Indian drama and whose author, Kalidasa, is the greatest of the playwrights from the classic period.

Kalidasa

(A.D. 373?–415)

Though *Shakuntala* is an acknowledged masterpiece of Indian drama, almost nothing is known about its author, Kalidasa. Many scholars have attempted to establish his date of birth and to learn some details of his life, but they have had little success. At one point, it was thought that he lived in the ninth century after Christ, but recent studies have placed his writings in the late fourth or early fifth century. It is possible that he lived at the court of King Chandragupta II, in the city of Uj Jain.

There is no doubt that *Shakuntala* is a masterwork of Sanskrit drama. In seven acts, the play recounts the romance of King Dushyanta and Shakuntala, the foster daughter of a hermit, who secretly marry and are then subjected to a long separation brought about by the curse of an irate sage. After many trials, the lovers are reunited and the king finally meets his son and heir.

Shakuntala, which is subtitled *The Recovered Ring*, has story elements similar to Wagner's *Ring of the Nibelung:* a secret marriage, forgetfulness caused by a curse, and a magic ring. It also has ideas from Indian philosophy, religion, aesthetics, and psychology. Like all Sanskrit drama, it has both serious and comic elements and includes a large number of locations and characters. It also includes supernatural elements. In addition, *Shakuntala* has a recognition scene, where the lovers confirm their identity through signs; this recognition through signs bears some resemblance to scenes in classic Greek tragedy.

Kalidasa's power as a lyric poet is shown in his description of the king's journey in a chariot and in his account of Shakuntala caring for her plants and a pet fawn. In fact, while *Shakuntala* follows traditional patterns of Sanskrit drama, it is set apart by Kalidasa's delicate lyricism. Kalidasa also wrote several poems which mingle love, nature imagery, and religion; and two other plays: *Malavike and Agnimitra,* a courtly comedy about a king's love for one of the palace servingwomen; and *Vikrama and Urvashi,* a heroic mythological drama focusing on the love of a king and a nymph.

Shakuntala is known in the west through many translations—beginning in the eighteenth century, when the German playwright Goethe found himself profoundly inspired by it. It was first translated into English in 1798 by William Jones and became well-known to the literary elite throughout western Europe. It has been widely performed as a play, an opera, and a ballet.

Indian Dramatic Criticism

Along with playwriting, dramatic criticism also reached a peak during the era of Sanskrit theater. The fact that the ideas and ideals of this period were written down in a definitive form established an important link with later traditions.

The greatest work of dramatic criticism of the Sanskrit period is doubtless the *Natyasastra,* often attributed to the early dramatist Bharata but actually of a later date, probably the eighth or ninth century. Many Indian critics have said that the *Natyasastra* represents a perfect philosophical description of Kalidasa's dramas. In the course of this complex treatise, the author defines a quality called *rasa,* or "flavor," which permits spectators to surrender themselves to a dramatic situation corresponding to some powerful feeling that they themselves possess. Theater can thus serve as a means toward enlightenment; art becomes a way to move toward metaphysics and the divine.

The *Natyasastra* also serves as a kind of encyclopedia of theatrical practice. In an abstract way, every element of the complex ancient theater is treated, from gesture and posture to music, dance, voice, and so forth. Types of characters and categories of plays are discussed, and all this specific information is related in turn to a series of metaphysical principles which, although perhaps difficult for the modern reader to grasp, are nevertheless challenging, even humbling, to read. The *Natyasastra* is one of the finest works of theatrical theory and criticism ever written.

Later Indian Drama

Sanskrit drama—both the plays themselves and dramatic criticism—had faded by the end of the ninth century. By the twelfth century, the Arabs had begun to invade India, and in 1206 they established the sultanate of Delhi. With this series of invasions, the Hindu Sanskrit tradition disappeared. Under Islamic rule, theatrical activities were not encouraged and the old ways of performing were no longer maintained among educated people.

However, folk dramas in the many vernacular languages of India had always been popular, and the continued performance of such works, while they may not have achieved a very high artistic level, helped to keep certain traditions alive. Many of these folk plays have continued to the present day. They used the same traditional epic materials as Sanskrit dramas, but most of them were created by dramatists whose names are now unknown, and the scripts— assuming that these dramas were written down—have not been preserved. Folk plays were eclectic and emphasized spectacle rather than profundity.

KATHAKALI. Much Asian drama has a large element of dance. A prime example is kathakali, a dramatic form found in southwestern India. In kathakali, stories of strong passions, the furies of gods, and the loves and hatreds of extraordinary human beings are told in mime and dance. Notice the heavy makeup and the stylized headdresses and costumes.

Also popular with the public were dance dramas that took up aspects of Indian myths. In the performance of such dramas, movement, rather than the spoken word, was strongly emphasized. An interesting form of dance drama prominent in southwestern India during the past three centuries is *kathakali*. It is presented at night, by torchlight, on a stage approximately 16 feet square covered with a canopy of flowers. It heightens elements of Sanskrit drama: violence and death are shown onstage in dance and pantomime. The stories revolve around clashes between good and evil, with good always winning. The passions of demons and gods, as well as extraordinary human beings, are featured.

Aside from the folk traditions, Indian theater was not to reemerge in a meaningful way until several centuries later—a development we will look at in later chapters.

CHINESE THEATER

The civilization of China can be traced back to at least 2000 B.C., when a unified culture spread over large parts of the area that is now the People's Republic of China. The Shang dynasty (ca. 1500–1000 B.C.) represents the first period that can be authenticated through artifacts and documents. During the succeeding, turbulent Zhou dynasty (ca. 1000–250 B.C.), Confucius, Laozi, and Mencius—three of the greatest Chinese philosophers—lived and wrote. By 200 B.C., the centralized imperial system had been developed, and China was provided with a central government that continued to remain effective through many long periods of stability down to modern times.

Early Theater in China

The early development of theater in China—as with many other forms of Chinese art—was linked to the patronage of the imperial court. Popular forms of theater may also have flourished, of course, though no records of early folk performances survive. Records of court entertainments, however, go back as far as the fifth century B.C., and such diverse activities as skits, pantomimes, juggling, singing, and dancing are frequently mentioned in ancient chronicles. The court of the emperors during the Tang period (A.D. 618–906) was one of the high points of human culture. At this time there was a kind of actors' training institute in the capital; it was called the "Pear Garden." Details of activities and performances at the Pear Garden have not been preserved, but it firmly established a tradition of training theatrical performers.

In the Sông dynasty (960–1279), which preceded the coming of the Mongols, various court entertainments contributed to the development of what are known as *variety plays*. In addition to court records, there are other documents recording the existence of traveling theatrical troupes, some permanent playhouses, and theatrical activity that involved not only actors, dancers, and singers but also shadow puppets and marionettes. Low comedy was popular; its effect must have been something like our vaudeville. The synthesis of art and the popular tradition was to come in the dramas of the Yuan period, which followed the Sông.

Theater in the Yuan Dynasty

The Yuan dynasty (1280–1368), was well-known in the west through the writings of the Italian explorer Marco Polo. The ruler at this time was not a Chinese emperor but a Mongol, Kublai Khan, whose grandfather Genghis Khan had conquered China.

The Mongols, although they tolerated many Chinese customs, nevertheless dismantled much of the traditional bureaucracy. Ironically, this turned out to be an important impetus for the development of Chinese theater. Earlier, the highly educated literati—literary intellectuals—had composed essays and poetry of the highest quality but had disdained plays as beneath their dignity. With the coming of the Mongols, many of the literati were no longer employed by the government and took up literary and theatrical work to make a living. In this way, high art and the popular theatrical tradition met. Because the complex mixture of cultural influences produced such a rich outpouring during the Yuan dynasty, scholars have compared its theater to that of Greece in the fifth century B.C. and Elizabethan England.

The form of drama perfected in the Yuan dynasty usually had four acts or—perhaps more accurately, since these plays used a great deal of music—four song sequences. Rather than writing specifically for the dramas, playwrights composed their texts to suit the rhythms and meters of popular music already known to the audience. Usually the protagonist sang all the music in any act. Unfortunately, none of this music has survived.

The poetic content of these plays was considered the central factor in their success. Because of their lyrical nature, these dramas had only a few characters and avoided subplots and other complications. Accounts from the Yuan period tell us that topics chosen by the playwrights ranged from love and romance to religion and history, domestic and social themes, crimes and lawsuits, and bandit heroes like the western Robin Hood.

IMPORTANT PLAYS FROM THE YUAN PERIOD

Though we do not know exactly how many plays were produced during the Yuan period, there are records indicating that over 500 dramatists were writing at this time, and we know the titles of some 700 plays of which about 170 survive.

Perhaps the most famous of the surviving plays from this period is *The Romance of the Western Chamber*, actually a cycle of plays, by Wang Shifu (fl. late thirteenth century). These dramas chronicle the trials of two lovers—a handsome young student and a lovely girl of good family—who have been models for thousands of imitations down to the present century. The plays contain a certain amount of adventure and also a good deal of superlative poetry.

Another popular play that has survived is *The Orphan of Chao,* which deals with vengeance, sacrifice, and loyalty. *The Orphan of Chao* was one of the first Chinese plays known in the west, as a version of it was translated into French in 1735 and was adapted for the French stage by Voltaire.

Another popular Yuan drama, *The Story of the Lime Pen,* is an excellent example of the lawsuit-and-trial genre in which a clever, Solomon-like judge frees an innocent person accused of a crime. When the twentieth-century German playwright Bertolt Brecht saw a version of this play (it had been freely adapted and translated into German), he was so intrigued with the theme that he created his own version: *The Caucasian Chalk Circle.*

Debates in Theater History:

DID PLAYWRIGHTS IN THE YUAN PERIOD CREATE TRAGEDIES?

In his book *A History of Chinese Drama,* William Dolby writes, about certain serious plays of the Yuan period: "Such plays as *Dream of Two on a Journey, Autumn in the Han Palace* and *Rain of the Paulownia Tree* raise the perennial question of whether early Chinese drama ever contained tragedy."*

The question arises because, though most Yuan plays end happily, a few of them are predominantly serious. These serious works are considered by some scholars and commentators to be the equivalent of tragedies in the west such as those of the Greeks, the Elizabethans, and the French neoclassical playwrights. The serious Yuan plays have a perfunctory or formal "happy" ending, but many scholars are not convinced that this is the ultimate outcome intended by the playwright.

As Dolby points out, *Rain on the Paulownia Tree* ends on a "purely sad note." *Dream of Two on a Journey* is, in Dolby's words, "consistently gloomy." It ends on a note of revenge, which could be considered "happy," but Dolby feels that there are circumstances which might have led the audience to feel otherwise. Knowing the history and background behind the story of *Dream of Two on a Journey,* they would realize that the revenge called for in the play actually occurred and resulted in a national disaster.[†]

In other words, it is argued—with some strength—that when we consider both the content and the context of several key plays, they embody many of the characteristics of dramas which in the west have long been classified as tragedy.

At the same time, there are arguments against considering these Yuan dramas as tragedies. One argument is the presence of the "happy" endings. It may be said that these endings merely conform to custom and do not indicate the true intentions of the dramatist; nevertheless, the endings are there. There is another argument which fascinates linguists and other scholars of language: the Chinese of the Yuan period had no character or symbol for *tragedy.* If there was not even a "word" to denote tragedy, how could anyone have written a play containing the tragic spirit or the tragic point of view? This question is posed by scholars who oppose considering these plays as an Asian version of tragedy.

Thus, whether we can justifiably think of these plays as tragedies remains undecided.

*Harper and Row, New York, 1976, p. 47.

[†]Ibid., pp. 47–48.

THEATER PRODUCTION IN THE YUAN PERIOD

Despite the fact that many Yuan texts survive and have been admired down to the present day, relatively little is known about how they were performed. Contemporary spectators left few records of their reactions, perhaps because theatergoing was regarded as beneath the notice of highly educated people. Nevertheless, in recent years careful scholarship has managed to piece together a certain amount of information on theater presentations.

Professional actors and actresses performed in Yuan dramas, and both would on occasion play male and female roles. Some of the actresses performed for private entertainments at the palace, and stories of their affairs in high society were as eagerly sought out as stories about the activities of today's film and television stars. The performers were organized into troupes, some of which were run by women.

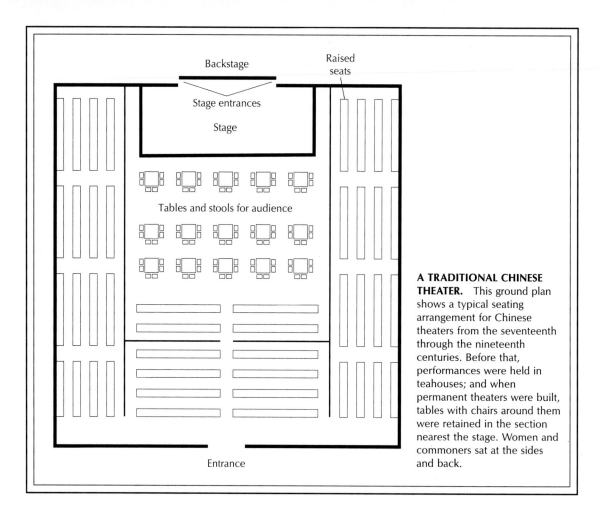

Backstage

Raised seats

Stage entrances

Stage

Tables and stools for audience

A TRADITIONAL CHINESE THEATER. This ground plan shows a typical seating arrangement for Chinese theaters from the seventeenth through the nineteenth centuries. Before that, performances were held in teahouses; and when permanent theaters were built, tables with chairs around them were retained in the section nearest the stage. Women and commoners sat at the sides and back.

Entrance

Only meager information remains about the theaters used for these performances. Evidently, there was a bare stage with two doors on each side at the rear, and a painted hanging between the doors; such an arrangement is shown in a wall hanging from northwestern China painted about 1324. Most stages seem to have been built for outdoor use and were not roofed over. (Later, performances were given in teahouses; and still later, when permanent theaters were built, tables and chairs continued to be included near the stage.) Curtains and such properties as swords and fans were used, but there is no evidence of any scenery. Much of the color in performances came from elaborate costumes. Some of the stylized robes, which are illustrated in art works of the time, resemble those in modern Peking opera. Makeup was also important and was evidently applied in a heavily stylized manner.

Theater in the Ming Dynasty

By the end of the Yuan period, the level of accomplishment in theater was very high and drama had become firmly established as a respectable art form. With the overthrow of the Mongols, however, and with the establishment of the Ming dynasty (1368–1644), a Chinese emperor was restored to the throne. At this point, the traditional patterns of social behavior were restored; highly educated scholars were still able to write plays, but they tended to confine their efforts more and more to dramas that would please the elite. The theater, because of its very legitimacy, tended to become ornate and artificial; and it therefore lost contact with the broad mass of the public, which had originally supported it.

What had been an active theater in the Yuan dynasty, responsive to general audiences, now became a kind of "literary drama" which emphasized poetry and was averse to sustained or powerful dramatic action. The structure of Ming plays often became far more complex than that of Yuan plays. Also, only one actor had sung in each act of a Yuan play, but several actors were now permitted to sing during an act, and the instrumental accompaniments became very elaborate.

One of the earliest and best plays written in this expanded form is *Lute Song* by Gao Ming (ca. 1301–1370), dealing with questions of family loyalty in a woman whose husband has abandoned her for political reasons. *Lute Song* contains strong characterizations and beautiful poetry and has been popular ever since its composition; this story of a faithful wife even reached Broadway in a musical comedy version, also called *Lute Song,* written for Mary Martin in 1946.

Attempts to create drama of distinction during the Ming dynasty culminated in the works of Li Yu, a scholar who failed his examinations and became instead a playwright, theater critic, and impresario.

Li Yu

(1611–ca. 1680)

Li Yu, China's first important drama critic, believed that a playwright should write clearly, with a mass audience in mind, and should be well versed in practical stage knowledge. These conclusions were based on his own experience as a popular playwright. His writings on theater—in which he dealt with such matters as plot construction, dialogue, music, and versification—are among the most important in the history of Chinese dramatic criticism.

Li Yu turned to the theater to earn a living after he had failed several times to pass the provincial examinations for government service. To support his forty wives and his numerous concubines and children, he and his company of singing girl actresses traveled around the country, seeking the patronage of local mandarins. Because of the beauty and skills of his young actresses, his troupe was often charged with corrupting the morals of young men. Though he had many influential friends, he was forced to sell his home, and he also worked from time to time as a landscape gardener in order to pay his debts.

As a playwright, Li Yu was criticized by contemporary Chinese literary figures for his dramatic style. He wrote his plays for entertainment and placed little emphasis on the poetic songs that other playwrights favored. Instead, he developed well-made situation comedies with intricate plots and sophisticated dialogue. Rather than borrow his material from standard literary sources, Li Yu created original plots that were based on the lives of common people. He was particularly skilled at writing strong female characters for his girl actresses. Most of his notable plays, including *Ordained by Heaven, Be Circumspect in Conjugal Relationships,* and *The Error of the Kite,* revolve around romantic themes.

In his dramatic criticism, Li championed the methods and knowledge he had gained as a practicing playwright; but he had little influence on other dramatists. He is said to have been an expert on painting, music, poetry, architecture, the sexual arts, travel, recreation, diet, hygiene, and furniture. Li Yu's plays and his extensive knowledge made him a popular author in both China and Japan.

Chinese Theater after the Ming Dynasty

The Ming period in China had been important in many ways. In addition to theater, excellent paintings, porcelains, and carpets were produced. Also, the Ming emperors built numerous tombs and palaces, the most famous being the Imperial Palace in Peking (Beijing). However, at the end of the Ming dynasty, theater, which was heavily patronized by the rich, began to lose all real contact with the larger public, and its vitality seeped away.

By the middle of the sixteenth century, Manchu peoples had begun to advance southward into northern China, and in the middle of the seventeenth century—like the Mongols before them—they conquered the country. The Manchus set up a period of foreign rule that lasted until the dissolution of the empire in 1912. The Manchu rulers enjoyed Chinese culture, including theater, and they continued to support the sort of lavish literary productions that had become the tradition among the elite. On the other hand, popular theater was often suppressed, and its scripts were destroyed, for political or moral reasons.

JAPANESE THEATER

Although the civilization of Japan is younger than that of China, the Japanese heritage is long and complex. The origins of the Japanese people are obscure, but anthropologists have found artifacts suggesting migrations from such diverse areas as Siberia, Korea, south China, and southeast Asia. We know that by the fifth century after Christ the southern portions of Japan were consolidated and a series of capitals were established in the vicinity of present-day Kyoto. At the time, the Japanese followed a religion called Shinto, or the Way of the Gods, closely allied to nature and spirit worship.

With the growing influence of the Tang dynasty in China (A.D. 618–906) on the Japanese aristocracy, Buddhism, a religion that was more sophisticated than Shinto in both ritual and doctrine, became a prevailing influence, first in court circles and then in the country as a whole. Influences from both Shinto and Buddhism were strong in the development of theater in Japan.

Early Theater in Japan

The earliest recorded theatrical activities in Japan are the court entertainments of the Heian period (A.D. 794–1195). These entertainments were influenced by Chinese models; but this is the only link—a very remote one—between the two traditions. Later, similar kinds of performances formed part of annual Shinto and Buddhist ceremonies. These were usually of a popular nature and included juggling, skits, dancing, and the like.

The first great period in Japanese theater occurred in the fourteenth century, not long after similar developments in China. The sudden and remarkable development of noh (the term is also written as *no* or *nō*)—one of the three important forms of traditional Japanese theater—came about when popular stage traditions were combined with serious scholarly pursuits. Despite similarities in theatrical developments, however, there was no direct connection between Japan and China at this time; and there are significant differences in how theater emerged in the two cultures. In the Yuan period the Chinese upper classes often disdained theater; but well-known, powerful people—in both politics and the arts—shaped Japanese noh. For this reason, the development of noh is far better documented than the development of Yuan drama.

Noh

In the fourteenth century in Japan, there were a number of roving troupes of actors who performed in a variety of styles; some of their presentations were simply popular entertainment, but some aspired to art. One of the more artistic troupes was directed by the actor Kwanami (1333–1384), whose son Zeami's performance was described at the beginning of this chapter. A presentation by Kwanami's troupe was seen by the shogun Ashikaga Yoshimitsu (1358–1408), a man of wealth, prestige, and enormous enthusiasm for the arts. Fascinated by what he saw, he arranged for the young Zeami to have a court education in order to improve the quality of his art.

When Zeami succeeded his father as head of the troupe, it remained attached to the shogun's court in Kyoto. With a patron of this caliber, Zeami was freed from financial problems and could devote himself to all aspects of theater: writing plays, training actors, and constantly refining his own acting style, whose outlines had been inherited from his gifted father.

Zeami Motokiyo
(1363–1443)

Over 500 years after his death, Zeami Motokiyo is still considered the most important figure in the history of Japanese noh theater, a complex form of classical dance drama favored by the aristocracy. A gifted actor, Zeami brought new prestige to noh, and his plays remain an important part of the noh repertory. He was most influential, however, as a theorist; in his writings, he established the aesthetic and philosophical basis of noh.

Zeami's father, Kwanami, was a talented noh actor and manager, known for his plays and his improvements in production methods. Zeami began training to be an actor while he was still a child, and as we have seen, when he was 11 he attracted the attention of the shogun. Thereafter, he enjoyed the shogun's patronage and protection.

Zeami became the director of his father's troupe when Kwanami died in 1384. He continued to improve noh, borrowing elements of other, earlier, forms of dance drama. His 200 plays, 124 of which remain in the noh repertory, incorporated his innovations.

He also began writing on the theory and philosophy of noh, presenting ideas that were heavily influenced by his study of Zen. In his several volumes of theoretical works, Zeami developed the concept of *yugen*, the mysterious, inner heart or spirit behind outward form. Yugen is the aim of a noh performance; another definition of it might be philosophical and physical gracefulness. Zeami's theoretical writings remained secret, however; they were written to instruct his own son and pupil, Motomasa.

Though Zeami was at the height of his acting powers in 1408, he and his troupe lost the patronage of the court when his friend the shogun Yoshimitsu died. Zeami continued to perform and to write until 1422, when he gave the troupe to his son and became a Buddhist monk.

A new shogun made Zeami chief court musician in 1424, but he lost that post to his nephew in 1429 when another shogun took office. Motomasa died young, leaving Zeami with no direct heir to his theoretical writings on noh. At the age of 72, he was exiled to the island of Sado for political reasons, but 3 years later he returned to Kyoto, where he died in 1443.

NOH PERFORMANCE TODAY. Traditional noh theater is still performed in Japan and other parts of the world, and its stylized acting, minimalist settings, ornate costumes, and distinctive makeup continue to be used. Shown here is a recent noh-like performance staged in San Francisco.

CHARACTERISTICS OF NOH THEATER

Under Zeami's direction, noh became the dominant form of serious theater in his generation, and it remained dominant well past 1600, until it was supplanted in the popular taste by bunraku and then kabuki.

Noh, as perfected by Zeami, was and is a remarkably successful synthesis of various theatrical forms into a single, total experience. Noh actors (there were no actresses in Zeami's theater) trained from childhood and became adept at singing, acting, dancing, and mime. The plays they performed were sophisticated in language and content and were all constructed around a definite series of organizational principles based on musical, psychological, and mimetic—or imitative—movements which change gradually from a slow to a fast tempo. Many of the greatest noh plays were written by Zeami himself, and a number of these are still in the active repertory.

The stories considered appropriate for noh plays were often from literary or historical sources. One important source was a famous novel of Heian court life, Lady Murasaki's *The Tale of Genji*, written around 1220. Another important source was *The Tale of the Heike*, a chronicle of the devastating civil wars that destroyed the power of the aristocracy in Japan at the end of the Heian period in 1185. Noh characters were generally based on figures already familiar to the audience. A noh play reveals some working-out of passions felt by a character, who often appears as a ghost or spirit.

The major roles in noh are the *shite,* or main character, who is often masked; the *waki,* or explainer; and the *tsure,* an accompanying role. There are various smaller roles as well, including a *kyōgen,* or comic character.

A typical noh play is divided into two parts. In the first part, for example, a Buddhist priest on a pilgrimage might visit a famous site, such as a tree or a gravestone, related to the life of the main character. The priest may find there an old person who will say something about the legend of the chief character and then disappear. In the second part of the play, the chief character will appear, revealing to the priest that the old person in the first part was actually himself or herself in disguise, and then describing some profound experience in his or her life. Usually, this recitation will end with a dance or in some other powerful way. Generally, the second half of the finest noh plays provides an unusual combination of fine poetry with stirring movements and music.

PRODUCING NOH THEATER

The elegance, mystery, and beauty of noh have fascinated the Japanese since the time of Zeami; and the noh tradition, passed on from teacher to disciple, has been carried on to this day. In most of the larger Japanese cities, noh can be seen in excellent performances by troupes whose traditions go back to the fourteenth century—a remarkable legacy. There have been some changes in performance practice since Zeami's time; for one thing, scholars have established that today's performances are much more stately and take a good deal more time than those of Zeami's day. Still, the general effect of a modern performance is certainly in consonance with Zeami's intentions.

Even the noh stage has remained roughly the same since the time of Zeami and his immediate successors. There is a bridge, the *hashigakari,* which leads from the actors' room offstage to the stage. The bridge is anywhere from 20 to over 40 feet long, depending on the size of the theater; the main playing space to which it leads is about 18 feet square, is roofed, and has a ceremonial pine tree painted on the rear wall. At the back of the playing space is a narrow section for four or five musicians who accompany the play. Noh theaters were originally outdoors, but the modern noh theater is built inside a larger shell, as though it were a giant stage set itself.

Noh actors move in a highly stylized fashion that involves important elements of both dance and pantomime. During the performance of a noh text, the actors alternate sections of chanting with a kind of heightened speech that might best be compared to recitative in western opera. The costumes made for noh are usually of great elegance, and the masks worn by the shite are among the most beautiful, subtle, and effective created for any theater.

There are occasional comic elements in noh, and these elements eventually developed as a form called *kyōgen.* Originally, kyōgen plays were short farcical

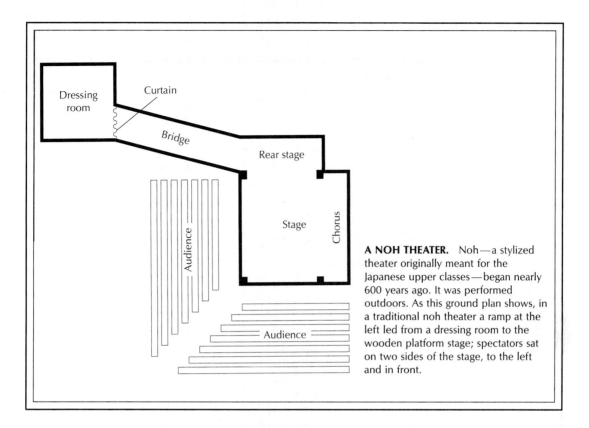

A NOH THEATER. Noh—a stylized theater originally meant for the Japanese upper classes—began nearly 600 years ago. It was performed outdoors. As this ground plan shows, in a traditional noh theater a ramp at the left led from a dressing room to the wooden platform stage; spectators sat on two sides of the stage, to the left and in front.

interludes performed between the acts of noh plays; later, they became an independent genre. Kyōgen plays, which use a good deal of folk humor and slapstick, are still performed and appreciated today.

Bunraku

Noh remained the most popular form of theater during Japan's medieval period. At this time, civil wars and other disturbances caused political disarray of increasing gravity, until in 1600 a general, Tokugawa Ieyasu, unified the country. All through the long Tokugawa period (1600–1868), which bears his family name, Japan was unified and at peace, but this calm was purchased at a price. Alarmed at the political maneuvering of Japan's growing number of Christians, who had been converted by European missionaries, the Tokugawa family outlawed Christianity and cut Japan off from any extensive contact with either China or Europe until the middle of the nineteenth century.

Peace did bring a rapid development of commerce and trade that led to increasingly sophisticated urban life. As the merchant class grew, its members' wealth and their increasing leisure time allowed them to patronize various entertainments. The aristocracy and the Tokugawa family continued to support noh as a kind of private state theater, but the merchants supported theatrical arts that more closely mirrored their own world. These entertainments flourished in large cities, particularly Osaka.

Puppet theater, now usually called *bunraku,* was the first of the new popular forms. It developed in a most unusual way. One widespread form of entertainment in the medieval period was the art of the chanter who, with his *biwa* (a kind of large lute), would travel around the countryside intoning chronicles of wars and tales of romantic heroes and heroines, much like medieval troubadours in the west. By around 1600, it became customary to add to these performances, as a kind of extra attraction, companies of puppeteers who would act out the stories, "illustrating" the chanter's music.

The chanted texts are called *joruri,* and the chanters, down to the present day, have been regarded with the kind of awe reserved for opera singers in the west. The chanters perform all the voices in a play, as well as the narration, and set the general mood. Originally, they also wrote their own scripts. Eventually, however, it became customary to ask someone else to write the text.

In bunraku, handlers dressed in black (and thus presumed to be invisible) manipulate puppets which today are approximately two-thirds life-size but were originally smaller. The first and undoubtedly the best of the bunraku writers, Chikamatsu Monzaemon, contributed enormously to the transformation of this popular form into a vehicle for great art.

BUNRAKU: PUPPET THEATER. Shown here is a performance of one of the most famous bunraku puppet plays, *The Love Suicides at Amijima.* Bunraku—which is still popular in Japan today—has many more uniquely theatrical conventions than western puppet theater. For example, the handlers, dressed in black, are in full view of the audience; part of the excitement of bunraku comes from watching their great skill.

Chikamatsu Monzaemon

(1653–1725)

Chikamatsu Monzaemon was born to a provincial samurai family in 1653 and became the first important Japanese dramatist since the great period of noh drama 300 years earlier. His family apparently had literary interests; in 1671, they published a collection of haiku poetry which included some pieces by the future dramatist.

Chikamatsu wrote of his early life: "I was born into a hereditary family of samurai but left the martial profession. I served in personal attendance on the nobility but never attained the least court rank. I drifted in the marketplace but learned nothing of trade." Though he did not succeed at these early occupations, he gained valuable insights into all classes of Japanese society that he would later use in his plays.

Chikamatsu did not begin to write plays until the age of 30, but thereafter he was a prolific writer. Most of his dramas were written for the puppet theater, bunraku, the favorite form of theater in Japan during that period. He is the world's only major dramatist to write primarily for that form. He also wrote for kabuki theater (discussed below), and many of his puppet plays were later adapted for kabuki.

As a playwright, Chikamatsu used his knowledge of Japanese life to create vivid, detailed, and accurate pictures of his society. His history or heroic plays are loosely constructed stories about the nobility; they feature military pageantry and supernatural apparitions. In his domestic dramas he explored the problems of the middle and lower classes; several of these plays are based on actual events. Often, his domestic plays deal with unhappy lovers, who may even be driven to suicide by the problems they face. Both Chikamatsu's history plays and his domestic plays are known for the beauty of his poetry, which elevates the incidents and the characters. He was a firm believer in the ancient Japanese code of honor; he often incorporated it in his plays, and this sometimes makes them appear unconvincing and moralistic to western audiences. In Chikamatsu's drama, the text remained central; the puppets were less elaborate at this time than the magnificent ones that are now used, and the scenery remained subservient to the art of the chanter.

Western critics have compared Chikamatsu to both Shakespeare and Marlowe because of the quality of his verse and his knowledge of society. His most famous history play is *The Battles of Coxinga* (1715). His notable domestic dramas include *The Love Suicides at Sonezaki* (1703), *The Uprooted Pine* (1718), *The Courier for Hell* (1711), *The Woman Killer and the Hell of Oil* (1721), and *The Love Suicides at Amijima* (1721). Though his history plays, originally highly esteemed, have not kept their popularity, the domestic plays—including *The Love Suicides at Amijima,* which is considered his masterpiece—are still staged regularly.

Chikamatsu spoke of maintaining in his dramas "what lies in the slender margin between the real and the unreal," and this quality, plus his remarkable ability as a poet, have kept his plays popular. His emphasis on ordinary people, too, not only was new to the Japanese stage but foreshadowed later developments in European theater.

Kabuki

By the beginning of the eighteenth century, a new form of Japanese theater, *kabuki,* had emerged. Combining elements of noh, bunraku, and folk theater, kabuki soon became the most popular of all and has remained a favorite with Japanese audiences to the present day.

ORIGINS OF KABUKI

Kabuki is generally considered to date from about 1603, when a dancer named Okuni began to give public performances at Kyoto. The kabuki Okuni developed became so popular that in 1616—only a few years after she had begun her performances—there were seven licensed kabuki theaters in Tokyo.

Okuni of Izumo

(ca. 1596)

According to Japanese legend, credit for developing kabuki, the most popular form of traditional Japanese theater, belongs to a Shinto priestess, Okuni of Izumo. Though little is known of her life or of the circumstances that led to the development of kabuki, tradition holds that in 1596 this priestess began kabuki by dancing on a temporary stage set up in the dry bed of the Kamogawa River in Kyoto.

Probably, Okuni's early dances were of Buddhist origin and had been secularized by being intermingled with folk dances. It is said that Nagoya Sanzaemon, a samurai warrior who is believed to have been Okuni's lover, taught her adaptations of dances from noh, the court drama of the period. She might have used noh dances as well as elements of popular dances, but no detailed descriptions of her performances survive.

That her dances were popular, however, is shown by the fact that she and her troupe toured Japan in 1603—a tour which culminated with a performance at the imperial palace in Kyoto. The following year, Okuni built a semipermanent theater in Kyoto similar in structure to the noh stage of the period. Her theater opened on October 23, 1604, with a 5-day performance to raise money for a shrine in her honor in Uzumo.

KABUKI PERFORMANCE TODAY.   According to legend, kabuki theater in Japan was developed around 1600 by a woman named Okuni. Today, all roles in kabuki are performed by men; most of the actors are descended from generations of kabuki actors and train for years. Kabuki plays are often spectacular and melodramatic. Shown here is a scene from *The Forty-Seven Ronin,* which is based on a true story of samurai loyalty.

DEVELOPMENT OF KABUKI

Dance was the basis of early kabuki performances, and the musical dance-dramas that developed revolved around stories that were romantic and often erotic. As a composite entertainment appealing to townspeople, kabuki was seen by some authorities as an unsettling influence on the rigid social and artistic structure.

A fascinating gender-related development occurred in the early days of kabuki. Originally, most of the performers were women, but when prostitution became common among these women, the shogun was irritated, and in 1629 he banned women's kabuki. Thereafter, young boys performed kabuki; but eventually it was felt that they, too, were becoming sexual targets for older men in the audience, and so in 1652 the shogun also banned boys' troupes. Men's troupes then became the rule—a custom that remains to the present day. Though the men's troupes were heavily regulated, kabuki flourished in the following centuries.

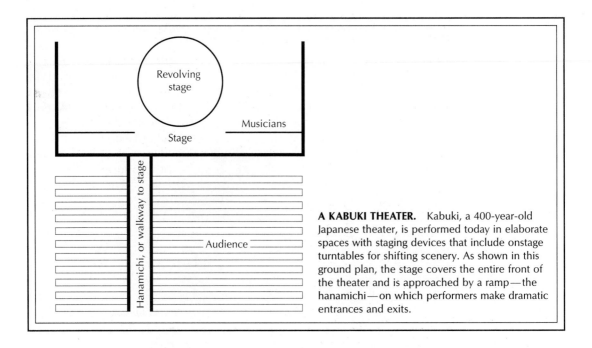

A KABUKI THEATER. Kabuki, a 400-year-old Japanese theater, is performed today in elaborate spaces with staging devices that include onstage turntables for shifting scenery. As shown in this ground plan, the stage covers the entire front of the theater and is approached by a ramp—the hanamichi—on which performers make dramatic entrances and exits.

When kabuki began, bunraku was already so popular that actors found themselves competing with puppets. Often, actors and puppets performed the same repertory, and the exaggerated gestures of kabuki are often attributed to the fact that in its early phases a conscious attempt was made to imitate puppets. Despite its exaggerated and stylized gestures, kabuki was less formal and distant than noh, which remained largely the theater of the court and nobility.

As kabuki itself became popular, the playwright Chikamatsu tried writing for troupes of kabuki actors; but he soon abandoned the attempt, because these performers, unlike chanters, tended to change his lines. Many of the plays performed by kabuki actors were taken over from the puppet repertory. Probably the most famous of these is *Chushingura,* or *The Forty-Seven Ronin* (1748), which is perhaps Japan's most popular traditional play and still draws tremendous crowds today. It is based on an actual historical incident in which a provincial lord was falsely accused and forced to commit ritual suicide. The play traces the vendetta or revenge of the forty-seven retainers who are left behind and is a remarkable blend of adventure, pathos, and romance. Ghost stories, too, were popular dramas in the kabuki repertory.

PRODUCING KABUKI

Kabuki actors are trained from childhood in singing, dancing, acting, and physical dexterity. The male actors who play women's parts (these parts are called *onnagata)* are particularly skillful at imitating the essence of a feminine personality through stylized gestures and attitudes. Costumes and makeup in kabuki are elegant and gorgeous. The effect of an actor's performance is always highly theatrical and a bit larger than life.

The stage used for kabuki underwent various changes during the history of this art, but the same principles were observed after the middle of the eighteenth century. The stage is long and has a relatively low proscenium. Musicians generally accompany the stage action, sometimes onstage, sometimes offstage. Kabuki features elaborate and beautiful scenic effects, including the revolving stage, which was developed in Japan before it was used in the west. Another device used in kabuki is the *hanamichi,* or "flower way," a raised narrow platform connecting the rear of the auditorium with the stage. Actors often make entrances on the hanamichi and occasionally perform short scenes there.

SOUTHEAST ASIA: SHADOW PLAYS

Though we have focused on theater in India, China, and Japan, it is important to remember that considerable theater activity has occurred in other parts of Asia. A good example is a unique form that came to prominence in southeast Asia in the eleventh century after Christ. This was the *shadow play,* which is widely performed in Thailand, Malaysia, and Indonesia. It appears to have been developed most fully in Java, an Indonesian island.

A shadow play uses flat puppets made of leather. These figures are intricately carved to create patterns of light and shadow when their image is projected on a screen. The puppets are manipulated by sticks attached to the head, the arms, and other parts of the body. The person manipulating the puppets also narrates the drama and speaks the dialogue of the characters. Shadow plays usually take place at night—sometimes they last all night long—and are accompanied by music and sound effects.

In various places, other theatrical forms have been developed from shadow puppets. One variation uses doll-like puppets; another uses human performers wearing masks.

In this chapter we have looked at the early development of theater in India, China, and Japan. These theaters were formed independently of theater in the west; in some cases, they emerged when formal theater in Europe was dormant. We have covered a period that goes up to approximately 1700. Though this is several centuries beyond the time when theater reemerged in the west, there was little or no contact between the two theater traditions until considerably later.

In Parts Three and Four, we will look at later developments in Asian theater: for example, Peking opera in China. We will also note the significant exchanges between Asian and western theater that began at the end of the nineteenth century and continued through the twentieth century. Modern theater artists such as Bertolt Brecht and Antonin Artaud were strongly influenced by Asian theater; and playwrights and directors in India, China, Japan, and other Asian nations have been affected by western theater.

In the meantime, however, we return to the theater of the west in the time of the Renaissance—the subject of Part Two.

SUMMARY

The traditional theaters of Asia originated from religious ceremonies and concepts. Most of these theaters are highly theatrical and stylized and fuse acting, mime, dance, music, and text.

In India in the fourth and fifth centuries after Christ, theater of a very high order—Sanskrit drama—was developed. Dramatic criticism also reached a high point in India with the *Natyasastra*.

In China, an acting school called the "Pear Garden" flourished in the early eighth century, and professional theater companies flourished in the tenth century. The first significant Chinese theater from which we have surviving manuscripts emerged during the Yuan Dynasty from 1280 to 1386. During the succeeding Ming Dynasty, from 1368 to 1644, theater became more "literary" and less in touch with ordinary people.

In Japan, the first important theater form was noh, which emerged in the fourteenth and fifteenth centuries and is still performed today. Bunraku—puppet theater—came on the scene in Japan in the seventeenth century, followed closely by kabuki. Both bunraku and kabuki are still performed in Japan. Like most Asian theater, noh, kabuki, and bunraku are complex; to understand them, audiences need to be aware of their intricate conventions.

Considerable theater activity has also taken place elsewhere in Asia; one example is the shadow play performed in Thailand, Malaysia, and Indonesia.

PART TWO

··

THEATERS
OF THE
RENAISSANCE

PART TWO

....

THEATERS
OF THE
RENAISSANCE

The Renaissance was an age of humanism, discovery, and exceptional art. *Renaissance* is a French word meaning "rebirth," and during this historical period—from roughly 1400 to 1650—European culture is said to have been reborn. Its rebirth included a rediscovery of earlier cultures, but equally important was a new view of human possibilities. In the Middle Ages, human beings had been seen as small, insignificant figures on the lower rungs of a sort of universal ladder, with the deity and other divinities at the top. In the Renaissance, people began to regard the individual as important and as having enormous potential.

A significant aspect of the Renaissance was, of course, the rediscovery of the civilizations of Greece and Rome. For the first time in several centuries, the heritage of these civilizations—their art, literature, and philosophy—became available, largely through the rediscovery of ancient manuscripts. The achievements and ideas of Greece and Rome struck a sympathetic chord in men and women of fourteenth-century Italy and France, who hoped to create a new classical civilization that would equal the old.

Other things were happening in addition to this rediscovery of the past. The major distinction between the Middle Ages and the Renaissance was a secularization of society—that is, a move away from religion. The dominance of the Roman Catholic church was eroded as Renaissance society became more concerned with "this world" than with the "next world," the afterlife in heaven.

There was a great sense of experimentation and discovery during the Renaissance, and several parallels with our own time are striking. The exploration of the new world in the Renaissance created the same kind of excitement as our own first attempts to open the frontier of space:

136

Columbus's voyage across the Atlantic to the Americas was like the astronauts' first landing on the moon. The discovery of gunpowder in the Renaissance transformed military strategy, as the development of the atomic bomb did in our own day. Gutenberg's printing press opened up the world to the masses, as film, television, telecommunication, and microcomputers do today. There is also a parallel in economics: at the end of the Renaissance in the seventeenth century, societies suffered from severe inflation, just as many countries have done in the twentieth century. And the questions which shook the Renaissance world—questions about God, rulers, and the place of humanity in the universe—continue to reverberate in our own time.

Throughout Europe, the Renaissance brought a burst of theatrical activity. Italian innovations such as opera, commedia dell'arte, the proscenium stage, painted-perspective scenery, and the neoclassical rules for playwriting would affect theater for the next 200 years. *Neo* means a new or different form of something from the past; thus *neoclassical* refers to the revival or adaptation in the Renaissance period of practices of Greece and Rome. French drama in the late seventeenth century was greatly influenced by Italian neoclassicism. The theaters of the English Renaissance and the Spanish golden age were distinctly different from those of Italy and France but were no less active and innovative.

The impact of the Renaissance is still apparent in theater today. When we sit in a proscenium-arch theater or enjoy a Shakespearean play produced at a festival, we are taking part in the rich theatrical heritage of the Renaissance.

CASTIGAT   MORES

RIDENDO

LE DOCTEUR   COLOMBINE   SCARAMOUCHE
ISABELLE   MEZZETIN   PASQUAREL

CHAPTER 5

THE THEATER OF THE ITALIAN RENAISSANCE

T he time is the late 1500s; the place is a town square in Rome. Set up in the square is a wooden platform stage with a backdrop at the rear from which performers can make their entrances and exits. A crowd is beginning to gather; we join it and try to get the best position to see the performance that is about to begin. If we want to face the stage directly, we will have to stand several rows back; if we move to the side, we will not face the stage directly but we can be closer to the action. As we find a place, we note that the audience represents a cross-section of Roman citizens.

There is great anticipation in the air, because the performers are members of a troupe called I Gelosi, one of the best-known theater companies in Italy. Led by Francesco and Isabella Andreini, the ten members of the company have perfected commedia dell'arte, a form of improvisational comedy which has become the most popular in this part of the world.

Soon the performance is underway and the fun begins. The story is about a woman performer who is pursued by both the married and the unmarried men

CHARACTERS FROM COMMEDIA DELL'ARTE. The most important development in acting in the Italian Renaissance was the emergence of commedia dell'arte, in which the performers improvised dialogue around a fixed scenario. Commedia had stock characters, wearing set costumes and masks. This form also became popular outside Italy, particularly in France. Shown here is an engraving of a French commedia troupe.
(*Bibliothèque Nationale, Paris*)

of the town where she lives; another part of the story concerns the adulterous intrigues of these men's wives. We and the other audience members who crowd around the platform know that the performers are improvising—playing from a script that outlines the action but does not include dialogue. We are amazed at how quick on their feet the performers are and how readily they respond to the dialogue thrown at them.

The characters are stock figures: an old Venetian merchant, a foolish pedant, a cowardly braggart soldier, comic servants, and young lovers. All the characters except the lovers wear masks, most of which are half-masks covering the upper part of the face. Each character wears a costume which makes him or her easily recognizable; the pedant wears academic robes; the captain wears a uniform; the young lovers are fashionably dressed. One of the comic servants wears a patchwork costume of many-colored cloth and a black mask which comes down to his nose.

The interaction of the performers is very physical. In one scene, a master beats a servant with a stick, which is hinged with a flap to make an exaggerated sound when it hits the servant's backside. In another scene, a soldier challenges a lover to a duel and becomes hopelessly entangled with his own sword; at times his sword sticks out from between his legs, taking on a sexual connotation. The more entangled he becomes, the louder the audience laughs.

At the end of the play, we talk to others who have seen it, sometimes laughing out loud when we recall special moments and highlights of the performance.

The performance we have just been watching, known in Italy as *commedia dell'arte,* is a farcical theater that looks back to the comedy of ancient Greece and Rome and ahead to the comedy of the twentieth century. We are now in the Italian Renaissance, where professional theater is being brought back to life by people who are trying to re-create techniques established in Greece and Rome.

BACKGROUND: THE RENAISSANCE IN ITALY

During the Renaissance, European culture advanced dramatically, and the center of cultural activity was Italy. At that time, Italy (like classical Greece) was not a unified nation but a group of independent city-states.

European politics changed markedly during the Renaissance, as the autocratic rule of kings and princes superseded the decentralized feudal system and the dominance of the church. The methods by which a ruler maintains control were outlined by Machiavelli, an Italian author, statesman, and political philosopher. Machiavelli looked on politics as a science and argued in his book *The Prince* (1513) that to protect their subjects rulers must do whatever is necessary and practical—even if it borders on the unethical.

Because of the extensive growth in trade in Italy, the entrepreneur, or enterprising merchant, became the key economic figure. The merchant class grew in strength and power, and as the merchants' wealth increased, they had

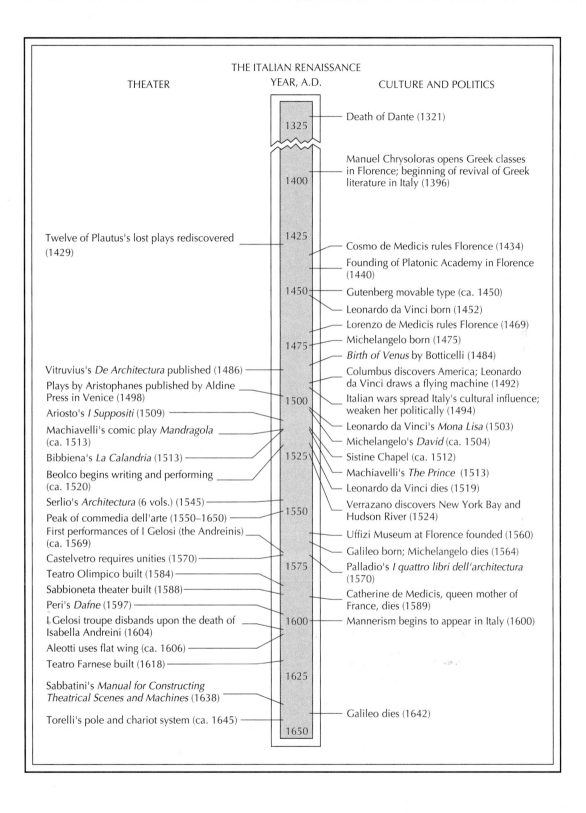

THE ITALIAN RENAISSANCE

THEATER | YEAR, A.D. | CULTURE AND POLITICS

Death of Dante (1321)

1325

Manuel Chrysoloras opens Greek classes in Florence; beginning of revival of Greek literature in Italy (1396)

1400

Twelve of Plautus's lost plays rediscovered (1429)

1425

Cosmo de Medicis rules Florence (1434)

Founding of Platonic Academy in Florence (1440)

1450

Gutenberg movable type (ca. 1450)

Leonardo da Vinci born (1452)

Lorenzo de Medicis rules Florence (1469)

Michelangelo born (1475)

1475

Birth of Venus by Botticelli (1484)

Vitruvius's *De Architectura* published (1486)

Plays by Aristophanes published by Aldine Press in Venice (1498)

Columbus discovers America; Leonardo da Vinci draws a flying machine (1492)

Italian wars spread Italy's cultural influence; weaken her politically (1494)

Ariosto's *I Suppositi* (1509)

1500

Leonardo da Vinci's *Mona Lisa* (1503)

Machiavelli's comic play *Mandragola* (ca. 1513)

Michelangelo's *David* (ca. 1504)

Bibbiena's *La Calandria* (1513)

1525

Sistine Chapel (ca. 1512)

Beolco begins writing and performing (ca. 1520)

Machiavelli's *The Prince* (1513)

Leonardo da Vinci dies (1519)

Serlio's *Architectura* (6 vols.) (1545)

Verrazano discovers New York Bay and Hudson River (1524)

Peak of commedia dell'arte (1550–1650)

1550

First performances of I Gelosi (the Andreinis) (ca. 1569)

Uffizi Museum at Florence founded (1560)

Galileo born; Michelangelo dies (1564)

Castelvetro requires unities (1570)

1575

Palladio's *I quattro libri dell'architectura* (1570)

Teatro Olimpico built (1584)

Sabbioneta theater built (1588)

Peri's *Dafne* (1597)

Catherine de Medicis, queen mother of France, dies (1589)

I Gelosi troupe disbands upon the death of Isabella Andreini (1604)

1600

Mannerism begins to appear in Italy (1600)

Aleotti uses flat wing (ca. 1606)

Teatro Farnese built (1618)

1625

Sabbatini's *Manual for Constructing Theatrical Scenes and Machines* (1638)

Galileo dies (1642)

Torelli's pole and chariot system (ca. 1645)

1650

RENAISSANCE EUROPE. The countries whose theater shaped western stage practices were Italy, England, Spain, and France.

leisure time to fill; they were also eager to display their fortunes. As a result, a patronage system developed, in which wealthy merchant-princes, such as the Medici family in Florence, gave financial support to artists.

Renaissance art is quite different from the art of the Middle Ages, as can be seen when paintings by Renaissance artists such as Michelangelo and Leonardo da Vinci are compared with medieval art. During the Middle Ages, paintings—such as Giotto's *Madonna Enthroned* (ca. 1310)—had religious subjects. Many Renaissance artists also took inspiration from religion: good examples are Michelangelo's *David* and *Moses* and his ceiling in the Sistine Chapel; and Leonardo's *Last Supper*. Renaissance artists, however, treat religious subjects secularly: no longer are the religious figures idealized;

instead, they are human beings with whom we can identify. Artistic techniques also changed drastically during the Renaissance. Through the use of new materials and skills, paintings became more "natural"; what they reflected on canvas was closer to what people saw in life as they looked about them. The introduction of oil paints made portraits more lifelike, and perspective was introduced and refined. *Perspective* is a convention for representing depth on a flat surface, that is, for approximating the way a scene looks to the human eye: objects in the distance are smaller than those in the foreground, and parallel lines—such as the sides of a long alleyway—converge in the distance. Perspective gives an illusion of depth because the eye is attracted to a vanishing point; with perspective, the human subjects in Renaissance art were placed in realistic backgrounds.

In Renaissance literature, the major movement was humanism. The humanists focused on people rather than gods; they were preoccupied with describing humanity and human powers, and they studied and imitated the Greeks and Romans. The printing press, invented in the mid-fifteenth century by the German Johannes Gutenberg, made literature available to great numbers of people; this, like humanism, aided the spread of literature rediscovered from the past.

The Renaissance was a period of invention and exploration. People moved away from the otherworldly concerns of the Middle Ages and became anxious to explore and conquer the world around them. Sailing expeditions brought discoveries in many parts of North and South America and contributed new wealth to the old world. However, although the Renaissance had begun in Italy, other European countries initiated the exploration and exploitation of the new world. Columbus, who reached America in 1492, was sponsored by the monarchy of Spain; Portugal led in the circumnavigation of Africa and the development of a sea route to India; and the English, the Dutch, and the French were also successful explorers.

Scientific advances revolutionized the perception of humanity's place in the universe. The Italian astronomer Galileo, the Polish scientist Copernicus, and the German mathematician Kepler proved that the sun, not the earth, is the center of the solar system. These men demystified the cosmos by developing mathematical formulas for astronomical phenomena. (The invention of the telescope, of course, was a factor in these scientific breakthroughs.) Though Galileo was condemned by many philosophers and theologians because his theories questioned long-held beliefs—and he was forced by the church to recant—his ideas eventually won out. In 1992, the Roman Catholic church revoked the charges which had been brought against Galileo during the Renaissance.

As a part of this general cultural and social revolution, theater in Italy was transformed radically between 1550 and 1650. The Italian Renaissance witnessed major innovations in four areas of theater arts—acting, in commedia dell'arte; dramatic criticism; theater architecture; and scene design.

ITALIAN DRAMA

Plays

As was pointed out in the Introduction, different aspects of theater come to the forefront in different historical periods. Neither Roman theater nor medieval theater, for example, is noted for great playwriting, and the same is true of the Italian Renaissance. Most of the plays written during the Italian Renaissance were staged, or sometimes just read aloud, at academies—formal institutions of learning—or for wealthy patrons. These plays left no lasting mark except for their influence on writers who were to follow: some Renaissance playwrights in England, Spain, and France did draw on Italian plays.

COMEDIES AND TRAGEDIES

In the 1300s and 1400s, Italian playwrights continued to write religious dramas in the medieval style; these were known as *sacra rappresentazioni* ("sacred representations") and were based on biblical stories and the lives of saints. At the same time, a few early Renaissance playwrights in Italy wrote comedies and tragedies based on those of antiquity—in fact, the earliest secular dramas were actually written in Latin—but their adaptations were, for the most part, staid and dry and never equaled the Greek and Roman originals. *Eccerinus* (ca. 1315), by Albertino Mussato (1261–1329), is often cited as the first tragedy of the Renaissance; it presents the story of a tyrannical contemporary ruler of Padua. The comedy *Paulus* (1350) by Pier Paolo Vergerio (1370–1445), subtitled *To Correct the Behavior of Youth,* dramatizes, in a style reminiscent of Terence, the plight of a student torn between the influences of two servants: one moral, the other immoral. Comic theatrical sketches were presented at the graduation exercises of Italian academies, and this tradition probably influenced some of the early comic playwrights of the Renaissance.

The renewal of interest in classical dramatic traditions was inspired by several developments, including a revival of the teaching of Greek by such noted scholars as Manuel Chrysolaras at the close of the 1300s; a transfer of surviving Greek and Roman manuscripts to Italy after the fall of Constantinople—which had been the center of the eastern Roman empire—in 1453; the publication of all the extant plays attributed to Aeschylus, Sophocles, Euripides, Aristophanes, Plautus, Terence, and Seneca; and the dissemination of the writings of Aristotle and Horace. The publication of some influential works was made possible by Gutenberg's printing press; early examples include the printing of Aristophanes' works in Venice in 1498, Sophocles' in 1502, Euripides' in 1503, and Aeschylus's in 1518.

Beginning in the early 1500s, Italian plays were no longer written in Latin but in Italian; they were still, however, based on classical models. For example, *La Cassaria (The Chest,* 1508) and *I Suppositi (The Counterfeits,* 1509) by Lodovico Ariosto (1474–1533) and *La Calandria (The Follies of Calandro,*

1513), by Cardinal Bernardo Dovizi da Bibbiena (1470–1520) are clearly indebted to plots and techniques popularized in Roman New Comedy. Two Renaissance tragedies of the early sixteenth century were *Sofonisba,* which was written in 1515 by Giangiorgio Trissino (1478–1550) and published in 1518 but not produced until 1562 at the Olympic Academy in Vicenza; and *Orbecche* (1541) by Giambattista Giraldi Cinthio (1504–1574). Trissino's play borrowed many structural elements from classical Greek tragedy; Cinthio's was modeled on Seneca's more melodramatic tragic style. Trissino also wrote an adaptation of Plautus's comedy *The Menaechmi,* entitled *I Simillimi* (1547).

INTERMEZZI AND PASTORALS

Two other popular dramatic forms developed in the Renaissance which were influenced by classical subject matter and dramatic techniques were inter-mezzi and pastorals. (Another form—opera—also reflects classical influences; it is discussed below.)

Intermezzi were short pieces depicting mythological tales; they were presented between the acts of full-length plays and were often thematically related to the full-length works they accompanied. These short works had developed out of the popular court entertainments. Intermezzi often required spectacular scenic effects. Although popular in the sixteenth century, this form disappeared in the 1600s.

The Italians also imitated Greek satyr plays—short, ribald comic pieces that had been presented as a follow-up to Greek trilogies—in a form they called a *pastoral.* The subject matter of a Renaissance pastoral is romance; the characters are usually shepherds and mythological creatures who inhabit the forest and countryside. Unlike the Greek satyr plays, the Italian pastorals were not overtly bawdy or sexual in style or subject matter. These pastorals usually deal with lovers who are threatened and often at odds with each other; while the action is serious, the endings are happy, with the lovers being reunited.

The most famous example of a pastoral play is *Aminta* (1573) by Torquato Tasso (1544–1595). Aminta, a shepherd, is passionately in love with Sylvia, who does not love him. Even after Aminta saves her from an evil satyr, she refuses to return his affection. When Aminta hears a false report that Sylvia has been killed by a lion, he throws himself off a hillside. Sylvia's heart is finally moved when she is told of Aminta's suicide, and she sets off to give him an appropriate burial, hinting that she too will commit suicide. However, in the final act it is reported that Aminta was saved when his fall was broken by bushes and has been revived by a kiss from his beloved Sylvia. The classical influences on Tasso's pastoral are quite clear. Its characters are reminiscent of those in satyr plays. Also, a chorus is used to reflect on the action and interact with the characters. All the violent action—including Sylvia's being threatened by the villainous satyr and Aminta's jumping off the hill—occurs offstage and is described.

THE MANDRAKE. One of the few Italian Renaissance plays still produced today is *Mandragola—The Mandrake*—by the political philosopher Niccolò Machiavelli. It is very reminiscent of Roman New Comedy and reflects the influence of the classical era on the Renaissance. Shown here is a recent production at the Public Theater in New York.

Because Italian Renaissance authors were usually more interested in copying Greek and Roman dramatic forms and plot lines than in imaginatively adapting or building on these earlier traditions, their dramas are of little interest to contemporary theater practitioners and are rarely revived. *Mandragola (The Mandrake,* ca. 1513–1520), a bawdy comedy by the Italian political theorist Niccolo Machiavelli (1469–1527), is the one most often produced today. This raises the general questions of adaptations as sources of theater, which we consider briefly next.

A NOTE ON ADAPTATIONS AS SOURCES OF DRAMA

The dramatists of the Italian Renaissance were not the first or the last to turn to other sources for stylistic inspiration or content. As we noted in Chapter 1, the great Greek tragedies were based on myths and other fictionalized accounts of Greek history. The Roman playwright Seneca turned to Greek drama for the plot lines of many of his more melodramatic tragedies; Plautus and Terence borrowed a great deal of their comic technique and subject matter from Menander. During the Middle Ages, amateur playwrights turned to the Bible as a source of stories.

In later eras, dramatists often borrowed from playwrights who had preceded them or adapted materials from other literary forms. Shakespeare appropriated many of his plot lines from popular stories of the Italian Renaissance, from English history, and from classical sources; his *Comedy of Errors,* for example, is a reworking of Plautus's *The Menaechmi.* The French comic dramatist Molière used techniques of commedia dell'arte. Jean Racine turned to the Greek tragedies; his *Phaedra* is a retelling of Euripides' *Hippolytus.* In the eighteenth century, many authors rewrote Shakespeare in an attempt to make his plays adhere to the neoclassical ideals or to expand certain roles for leading performers; the actor David Garrick, for example, adapted *Macbeth* for his own performances. In the nineteenth century, many dramatists turned to popular novels—as many screenwriters do today—and adapted the story lines. The novels of Charles Dickens were often staged, and the most successful play of the nineteenth-century American theater was an adaptation of Harriet Beecher Stowe's novel *Uncle Tom's Cabin.*

In the twentieth century, in the period between the two world wars there were numerous attempts to imitate and adapt techniques and story lines of Greek and Shakespearean drama. Like Italian Renaissance playwrights, some twentieth-century authors believed that copying the style and subject matter of earlier periods would enhance the artistic worth of their works. The American playwright Maxwell Anderson (1888–1959), in *Elizabeth the Queen* (1930), *Mary Queen of Scotland* (1933), and *Winterset* (1935), used verse reminiscent of Shakespeare's, trying to create a modern equivalent of Shakespearean history plays; but Anderson's plays do not have the unique linguistic brilliance of Shakespeare's, nor does Anderson dramatize historic events as imaginatively as Shakespeare did. Among other playwrights who were contemporaries of Anderson and used classical story lines or techniques were Jean Cocteau, Jean Giraudoux, and Eugene O'Neill.

American and British musical theater has a long history of borrowing from popular dramas and novels. Two famous examples are Leonard Bernstein's *West Side Story,* which is an adaptation of Shakespeare's *Romeo and Juliet;* and Andrew Lloyd Webber's *Phantom of the Opera,* based on a nineteenth-century novel which had already been dramatized and filmed in several other versions.

Some critics have argued that the frequent reliance on adaptation by playwrights reflects the fact that there are only a limited number of plot lines, which must therefore be used and reused throughout theater history. In addition, of course, playwrights who must work quickly to create new drama for popular theater will have to turn to other sources for inspiration. What is most intriguing is to try to identify the differences between authors who copy unimaginatively and those who use sources creatively, building on the originals to produce great works of drama.

Opera

Opera was the only theatrical form of the Italian Renaissance to survive. It was developed at a Florentine academy at the end of the sixteenth century; its inventors, in keeping with the Renaissance desire to revive classical forms, believed that they were recreating the Greek tragic style, which had fused music with drama. The earliest operas were based on Greek mythology and ancient history. *Euridice* (1600) by Jacopo Peri (1561–1633) and *Orfeo* (1605) by Claudio Monteverdi (1567–1643), for example, dealt with the Greek myth of Orpheus, who went to the underworld—Hades—to try to bring back his wife, Euridice. By the mid-seventeenth century, several public opera houses had been built in Venice, indicating the popularity of the new form.

Opera is quite dramatic and could be considered part of drama; but it is usually studied as a part of music because most operas are completely sung, and dramatic action, mood, and characters are created through song and music. The text of an opera, called the *libretto,* is often secondary to the music. The two basic elements of opera are the aria and the recitative. An *aria* is a solo song accompanied by the orchestra; duets, trios, and quartets are songs by two, three, and four persons respectively. A *recitative* is sung dialogue. Understandably, opera stars must be both actors and singers. Because opera is generally considered a part of music, we will not focus on it here; we will, though, look briefly at how it unfolded.

After its creation in Italy, opera was further developed in other countries. In the middle of the seventeenth century, the French created operas, modifying Italian opera to suit their own tastes. French opera insisted on textual clarity and incorporated ballet. The first master of French opera was the Italian-born composer Jean-Baptiste Lully (1632–1687). The subject matter of most seventeenth-century opera was historical or mythological.

One of the great composers of eighteenth-century opera was Wolfgang Amadeus Mozart (1756–1791), who was born in Salzburg, Austria, but lived much of his short life in Vienna.

The nineteenth century was the era of grand opera: major works with powerful, melodic arias and full choral and orchestral elements. Two of the best-known composers in this form are the Italian Giuseppe Verdi (1813–1901) and the German Richard Wagner (1813–1883).

In the modern period, in addition to such works as *Wozzeck* (1921) and *Lulu* (1934) by Alban Berg (1885–1935), contemporary American and British musical theater includes works that might be categorized as opera. George Gershwin's *Porgy and Bess* (1935), Stephen Sondheim and Hugh Wheeler's *Sweeney Todd* (1978), Andrew Lloyd Webber and Tim Rice's *Jesus Christ Superstar* (1971) and *Evita* (1978), and Webber's *Phantom of the Opera* (1987) are operatic, using recitative instead of dialogue to move the dramatic action along. Hit songs in operatic-style musical comedies are the modern-day equivalent of arias. Because their music has popular appeal, these shows are more accessible to contemporary audiences than the grand opera of earlier centuries.

Debates in Theater History:

WOMEN PERFORMERS IN COMMEDIA DELL'ARTE

In their textbook *A History of the Theater,* George Freedley and John A. Reeves remark: "One of the most important achievements of the commedia dell'arte was the introduction of women onto the stage on equal (frequently even more favorable) terms with men. Occasionally they appeared as themselves in the Middle Ages but the widespread use of them in female parts sprang out of Italian comedy."* It is clear that women were significant members of Italian commedia troupes at a time when they were excluded from the English stage. (The exclusion of women from English acting troupes during the Shakespearean period will be discussed in Chapter 6.) But why women were accepted as performers in commedia companies is still debated, as is their actual status in these companies.

Some historians point to the fact that theatrical forms which may have been forerunners of commedia dell'arte—such as Greek and Roman mime presented by traveling troupes—included women. Others note that many noteworthy women in commedia dell'arte were married to male performers; this meant that there was less likelihood that their morality would be called into question. The status of women in commedia, therefore, would have been similar to that of actresses in companies

of the Spanish golden age, who were required to be married or otherwise related to a male member. (We will discuss this in Chapter 7.) Some commedia actresses were greatly admired; Isabella Andreini, as we have seen, was idolized during her lifetime and greatly mourned when she died. Nevertheless, the female characters she played were often stereotypical, and most of the praise she received from poets focused not on her acting but on her beauty and her high sense of morality. For that matter, Pierre Louis Ducharte notes that the roles played by all the women in commedia dell'arte were recurrent types: "innamoratas, servants, *ingenues,* mistresses, wantons, and matrons."[†]

Thus while Freedley and Reeves are correct in pointing out that women were significant figures in commedia dell'arte, research still needs to be done on several key points: why women were initially employed in commedia troupes, what their financial status was in these companies, what their social status was, and how female characters were represented in the scenarios of commedia dell'arte. The question whether, as Freedley and Reeves argue, women were "on equal (frequently even more favorable) terms with men" needs much more analysis.

*Crown, New York, 1941, p. 81.

[†]*The Italian Comedy*, Randolph T. Weaver (trans.), Dover, New York, 1966, p. 20.

Commedia dell'Arte

Commedia dell'arte—a form as popular as opera in Renaissance Italy—was pure theater: this is the theater described at the opening of the chapter.

Commedia dell'arte is Italian for "play of professional artists." Commedia companies usually consisted of ten performers—seven men and three women, though sometimes the numbers varied. They were traveling troupes, possibly the successors of Greek and Roman mimes. Although there were instances when commedia performers staged serious forms of drama, they usually staged comedies, and through the years the term *commedia dell'arte* has come to be associated primarily with comedy.

TWO FAMOUS COMMEDIA CHARACTERS.
Commedia dell'arte was noted for stock characters who reappeared in its popular scenarios. These characters can usually be categorized as *zanni,* or comic servants; lecherous old men; and young lovers. The two seen here are (right) Pantalone, a miserly old Venetian merchant who chases after younger women; and (left) Pulcinella, a Neapolitan servant.

Commedia thrived in Italy over a considerable period of time, from 1550 to 1750. It was not a written, literary form, but rather consisted of improvised presentations: that is, the performers had no set text but invented the words and actions as they went along. Scenarios—short scripts without dialogue—were written by members of a company, and these scripts provided plot outlines; well over 1,000 scenarios survive from the Italian Renaissance. Using these outlines, actors would create dialogue and would be expected to move the action along through improvisation.

CONVENTIONS OF COMMEDIA DELL'ARTE

The conventions of commedia dell'arte made the actors' task simpler than its improvisatory nature would suggest. For one thing, commedia actors played the same stock characters throughout most of their careers. Among the popular comic figures were a lecherous, miserly old Venetian, *Pantalone;* a foolish academic type who was always involved in his neighbor's affairs, *Dottore;* a cowardly, braggart soldier, *Capitano;* and sometimes foolish, sometimes sly servants known as *zanni. Arlecchino,* or *Harlequin,* was the most popular of the comic servants. Commedia scenarios also included serious young lovers whose romances were often blocked by Pantalone and Dottore. Since the performers fused their own personalities with those of their characters, improvisation was easier. And since the performers worked together, playing the same characters, for extended periods of time, they became adept at creating comic interaction on the spur of the moment.

Improvisation was also made easier because all the commedia characters employed standard *lazzi*—repeated bits of physical comic business (the singular form is *lazzo)*. Capitano, for example, would get entangled with his sword so that it often became a ludicrous phallic symbol. A lazzo from Florence—dating from 1612—shows how bawdy these comic physicalizations could be: "Hearing about the physical perfection of a certain woman, Pantalone's (or the Captain's) dagger begins to rise between his legs."[1] (Twentieth-century film and television comics have their own lazzi; the great film clowns—such as Laurel and Hardy, the Marx Brothers, and the Three Stooges—had pieces of physical business that they repeated in all their performances.) In addition, commedia actors used conventional entrance and exit speeches as well as prepared musical duets. Surviving from the Renaissance are manuscripts put together by commedia actors which contain jokes, comic business, and repeated scenes and speeches. (These books were referred to by many different names, but the most common term for them was *zibaldoni.)*

Costuming also facilitated improvisation. Commedia characters all wore traditional costumes, such as Harlequin's patchwork jacket and Dottore's academic robe, so that audiences could recognize them immediately. Usually, each character would always wear the same outfit, and its exaggerated details reflected his or her comic personality. A significant addition to Harlequin's costume was the *slapstick,* a wooden sword used in comic fight scenes. Sometimes the slapstick consisted of two thin slats of wood, one on top of the other; when a performer was thwacked with it, the effect was greatly exaggerated by the sound of the two pieces of wood smacking together. Today we use the term *slapstick* for comedies emphasizing physical horseplay. Masks, covering either the whole face or part of the face, were an essential element of commedia costumes. Pantalone's mask, for example, always had a huge hooked nose. The young lovers, however, did not wear masks.

COMMEDIA COMPANIES

Commedia dell'arte was enormously popular with audiences. One measure of its success is its popularity outside Italy, particularly in France.

The most successful commedia companies were often organized by families and chose names which were meant to characterize them: *I Gelosi* (The Zealous), *I Fideli* (The Faithful), *I Confidenti* (The Confident), and *I Accesi* (The Inspired). Most companies were based on a profit-sharing plan: a company's members shared in its profits as well as its expenses and losses. Commedia performers were flexible: they could perform in town squares, in unused theater spaces, in the homes of wealthy merchants, or at court.

[1] *Lazzi: The Comic Routines of the Commedia dell'Arte,* Mel Gordon (ed. and trans.), Performing Arts Journal, New York, 1992, p. 32.

I Gelosi (ca. 1569–1604)

Isabella Andreini (1564–1604)

Francesco Andreini (1548–1624)

I Gelosi (The Zealous) became the most acclaimed commedia dell'arte acting troupe in Europe through the talents of two performers, Francesco and Isabella Andreini. I Gelosi was formed about 1569 from the remnants of another noted company; after 1578, when Francesco Andreini became one of the group's leaders and married Isabella, it reached its greatest renown.

Francesco Andreini had acted with the troupe for several seasons before his marriage. Originally, he played the *innamorato,* or male lover, but then he switched to his most famous role, the military figure Captain Spavento. As a young man he had been a professional soldier, and it is likely that this experience helped to shape his performance. Francesco was also a poet, musician, and linguist.

At the age of sixteen Isabella Canali married Francesco Andreini and began her stage career as the company's *innamorata,* or female lover. The leading poets of Italy and France wrote verses praising Isabella's beauty and charm, but she was equally renowned for her wit, intelligence, and virtue. A Latin scholar, she also wrote her own sonnets, songs, and pastorals.

Friends of the Andreinis included members of the Italian and French nobility and even royalty—the prince of Mantua was godfather to one of their seven children. In 1600, Henry IV of France invited the troupe to Paris for his wedding to Marie de Medici. They stayed in Paris for 4 years, winning the esteem of both Henry and Marie. On the journey back to Italy, Isabella had a miscarriage, and she died at Lyons in France; the entire city turned out for her funeral.

After Isabella's death, Francesco disbanded the troupe and retired from the stage. One of their sons, Giambattista (c.1578–1654), became a renowned commedia actor and an author. Around 1605, he organized a company known as *Comici Fedeli* (Faithful Players) with several actors who had been members of I Gelosi. The Comici Fedeli troupe survived until 1652, though it never quite matched the fame and high reputation of I Gelosi. Giambattista Andreini usually assumed the role of Harlequin or that of Lelio, an innamorato. He married twice, both times to women who played the innamorata in his company.

The historical significance of commedia dell'arte is seen in its influence on later theater practitioners. Its stock characters—who seem to have evolved from figures in ancient mime, from the plays of Plautus and Terence, and from medieval farces—were further refined by later playwrights. The miserly merchant Pantalone, for instance, is the ancestor of the avaricious Harpagon in the late-seventeenth-century French play *The Miser* by Molière, and the comic servant Pulcinello evolved into Punch in the English Punch and Judy puppet shows. The improvisatory nature of commedia has influenced many twentieth-century avant-garde theater companies, including the politically oriented San Francisco Mime Troupe, popular in the 1960s and 1970s and still performing today; and contemporary performers like Bill Irwin and David Shiner, who brought their commedia clowning to Broadway in 1993 in a show called *Fool Moon*, described in Chapter 15.

As noted earlier, comparisons can also be drawn between commedia performers and many of the classic film comics—including Charlie Chaplin, Laurel and Hardy, the Marx Brothers, Abbott and Costello, and the Three

(Joan Marcus)

A MODERN COMMEDIA PERFORMER. Commedia dell'arte continues to have a strong influence—in comic business, in stereotypical characters, and in costuming. Shown here is the performance artist Bill Irwin in his 1993 Broadway production *Fool Moon*. Irwin performed this piece with another clown and created one segment specifically based on commedia. Irwin's physical vaudevillian style has been compared to that of the great commedia performers.

Stooges. The zany films of the Marx Brothers, for example, used many techniques reminiscent of commedia. Groucho, Harpo, and Chico portrayed the same kinds of characters, with only slight deviations, in all their movies; that is, they created stock characters. Groucho was an unsuccessful, pedantic gigolo; Harpo was a lecherous, musically inclined mute; Chico was a scheming immigrant. Much of their action and dialogue—to the chagrin of their screenwriters—was improvised. Also, the Marx Brothers employed standard lazzi and stock costumes. Groucho walked with a stoop and toyed with a cigar; Harpo always wore a long trench coat, carried a horn, and mimed messages. Audiences enjoyed seeing repetitions of these characters' wildly comic business as they became involved in different complicated situations.

ITALIAN DRAMATIC CRITICISM

The Neoclassical Ideals

If the written drama of Renaissance Italy was of limited historical significance, the same cannot be said of its dramatic criticism. The rules formulated by Italian critics, known as the *neoclassical ideals,* dominated dramatic theory in Europe for nearly 200 years.

The neoclassicists believed that they were formulating rules which would force dramatists to imitate the Greeks and Romans; and they said that their ideals were derived from their examination of Greek and Roman models and from their interpretations of—and on occasion their deviations from—Aristotle and Horace. These claims need to be looked at with a certain skepticism, however, because the neoclassicists were far more rigid than Aristotle; they had many more rules and applied these rules with greater strictness. In fact, Aristotle did not prescribe rules; he analyzed what Greek dramatists had actually done. The neoclassicists, by contrast, wanted to establish mandates for playwrights. (Thus some historians have argued that the Italian neoclassicists were really more influenced by the Roman critic Horace than by Aristotle.) Three of the major neoclassical critics were Julius Caesar Scaliger (1484–1558), Lodovico Castelvetro (1505–1571), and Antonio Minturno (d. 1574).

DECORUM AND VERISIMILITUDE

One of the neoclassical ideals was *decorum,* a term which meant that all dramatic characters should behave in ways based on their age, profession, sex, rank, and the like. Each character, in other words, was expected to follow this set behavior.

An even more important ideal of the neoclassicists, however, was *verisimilitude:* all drama was to be "true to life." Thus, because they were not observed in everyday life, such things as ghosts, apparitions, and supernatural events were forbidden. At the same time, the neoclassicists' concept of verisimilitude was not the kind of "realism" we find in modern drama, in which characters and situations are individualized—a real family shown in a real living room or kitchen, for example. The neoclassicists had in mind what we would now consider stock dramatic situations and stock characters, but they insisted that these be recognizable and verifiable from real life.

THE UNITIES: TIME, PLACE, AND ACTION

The most famous mandate of the neoclassicists grew out of their desire for verisimilitude: this was their insistence on observance of three unities—time, place, and action. The critic who was most responsible for codifying the unities was Castelvetro.

Unity of time required that the dramatic action in a play should not exceed 24 hours. A few radical neoclassicists argued that time should be limited to 12 hours; the most radical wanted the dramatic action to match the time provided for the presentation: if, for instance, a play lasted 2 hours, its action should cover 2 hours. Most neoclassicists, however, insisted only on the 24-hour rule. Their argument for unity of time was based on their belief that audiences could not accept a long passage of time as "truthful."

Unity of place restricted the action of a play to one locale. Again, there were varying interpretations of this rule; liberal neoclassicists argued that "one locale" would permit a dramatist to present scenes within the same general location—for example, it would be allowable to dramatize various scenes within one city. The rationale for this rule was that audiences could not accept as "truthful" a representation of more than one place within the confines of a theater.

Unity of action (which was the only unity suggested by Aristotle) required one central story, involving a relatively small group of characters. This meant there could be no subplots, such as the one we find in Shakespeare's *King Lear:* the main plot is the story of King Lear and his three daughters, and the story of the Duke of Gloucester and his two sons is a subplot.

GENRE AND OTHER RULES

The neoclassicists also defined *genre*—a French word meaning "type" or "category"—very narrowly. Tragedy dealt with royalty, comedy dealt with common people; tragedy must be resolved calamitously, comedy must be resolved happily. The two genres must never be mixed, and the function of all drama was to teach a moral lesson. In short, all drama must be didactic.

There were numerous minor rules. Characters must act decorously, and their actions must be morally acceptable to the audience. Onstage violence was forbidden. Since the neoclassicists were obsessed with verisimilitude, they condemned several Greek and Roman dramatic conventions as untrue to life. For instance, the neoclassicists banished the chorus and the *deus ex machina*, and for the same reason they opposed the soliloquy—a monologue through which a character reveals thoughts by speaking them aloud. Playwrights who ignored these precepts were vigorously attacked by the neoclassicists.

The Neoclassicists' Influence

As noted earlier, the Renaissance was a time when there was a widespread desire to analyze and explain the world. Just as the great advances in science and exploration grew out of a desire to map the universe, so too the neoclassical ideals came from a desire to map the workings of classical drama. The neoclassicists considered themselves proper authorities to develop rules and regulations for theater through their analysis of rediscovered ancient drama.

It should be noted that the neoclassicists were exceedingly literal-minded in applying their ideas to drama. Despite the extreme rigidity of the neoclassical ideals, however, they were closely adhered to in many European countries. In France, for example (as we will see in Chapter 8), Cardinal Richelieu—the power behind the throne of Louis XIII—in 1636 gave his blessing to the French Academy, which strictly enforced the neoclassical principles, censuring playwrights who deviated from them.

There were, of course, countries in which the neoclassicists were largely ignored—Elizabethan England and Spain in its golden age—but the ideals were an important influence during the Renaissance; and beyond that, they established dramaturgic rules which would be sharply debated for several centuries to come.

Issues of Dramatic Criticism

We have now looked at several important figures in dramatic theory and criticism: Aristotle, Horace, and the neoclassicists of the Italian Renaissance. When we study the history of western theater, we find three key issues which divide theoreticians, and all three had emerged by the time of the Renaissance, in the works of these critics. These issues continue to influence western criticism.

THE NATURE OF CRITICISM:
DESCRIPTIVE AND PRESCRIPTIVE CRITICISM

The first issue is that some criticism is *descriptive,* or analytical, while other criticism is *prescriptive.* Descriptive criticism analyzes what has gone before. Thus Aristotle in the fourth century B.C. wrote about the Greek drama of the previous century. Modern critics who examine the works of a dramatist like Eugene O'Neill or a period like the American theater of the 1920s and 1930s are usually writing descriptive criticism. They attempt to tell us what type of drama was written, how it was put together, what it means, and so forth.

Prescriptive criticism, on the other hand, argues for a certain point of view, sets down rules, and prescribes formulas. This approach is often referred to as *didactic,* that is, intended for instruction. Most neoclassic critics of the Italian Renaissance were didactic, telling playwrights what they could and could not write. So, too, were the writers and theoreticians of the French Academy in the seventeenth century. In the nineteenth century, the French writer Émile Zola set forth a program for naturalism in theater. Zola argued that drama must adhere closely to the laws of nature as they were understood at that time. In the twentieth century, the German playwright and critic Bertolt Brecht argued that theater should instruct its audience, especially in political matters. In the late twentieth century there are several types of critics who could be considered prescriptive or didactic; good examples are Marxist critics and politically oriented feminist critics.

It is important to note that both kinds of critics—descriptive and prescriptive—make important contributions.

THE NATURE OF DRAMA: SHOULD THEATER BE DIDACTIC?

A second issue that has divided critics through the centuries has to do not with the nature of criticism but rather with the nature of the art work being criticized. This issue is whether or not drama should be didactic. The question here is not whether critics should instruct their readers but whether a play itself should teach a lesson and be morally uplifting.

Many critics feel that art need not—indeed, should not—be didactic; they hold that art is its own excuse for being. These critics would argue that in distilling life and presenting its essence, art provides a unique mirror in which we can see ourselves. If we learn from that—as we may very well do—so much the better, but it is not incumbent on art to teach a lesson; teaching is the job of people like educators and the clergy. Critics who take this position would argue that in some cases making art didactic might distort it beyond recognition. How, for example, could you make a simple landscape painting or an abstract design morally instructive?

On the other side are critics who say that art should be didactic. The Roman writer Horace, who first raised this issue, did not insist on instruction in drama, but he did say that entertainment joined with instruction was the best kind of drama. In certain periods—in seventeenth-century England and France— theater was attacked as immoral; writers like Molière in France and Ben Jonson in England defended it on the basis that it taught a lesson.

This controversy has continued into the twentieth century. We have already mentioned Bertolt Brecht, and in the 1950s there was a famous debate on this question between the absurdist playwright Eugène Ionesco and the critic Kenneth Tynan (1927–1980). Ionesco took the view that didacticism is not a primary function of art; Tynan argued that it is.

THE FORM OF DRAMA: NEOCLASSICAL STRUCTURE

A third issue that engaged critics for several centuries concerns dramatic structure. This debate was set in motion by the Italian neoclassical critics and carried forward by the French Academy; it concerns the neoclassicists' strict rules of structure: verisimilitude and the unities of time, place, and action.

As we will see in Chapters 6 and 7, the plays of Shakespeare and other Elizabethan playwrights and those of Spanish playwrights like Lope de Vega have a very different structure—the episodic form. Lope de Vega wrote a spirited defense of his approach to structure, and in the eighteenth century the German critic Gotthold Lessing questioned the neoclassical rules and praised the dramaturgy of Shakespeare. This issue of neoclassical structure raged for several hundred years, but unlike the debate over didacticism, it had subsided by the nineteenth century.

A great deal of debate stemmed from the dramaturgic rules set down by Italian Renaissance critics, but such rules were not the only theatrical concern of the period. Theater architecture—to which we turn next—was also very much on people's minds.

ITALIAN THEATERS

Theater Buildings

The architects of the Italian Renaissance revolutionized theater construction and design. Since much of the drama written during the Renaissance was staged at academies, changes in theater architecture frequently developed within these institutions. Three buildings in particular showed a move toward a new kind of theater architecture, and fortunately all three are still standing.

TEATRO OLIMPICO

The oldest surviving theater constructed during the Italian Renaissance, the Teatro Olimpico in Vicenza, was initially designed by the architect Andrea Palladio (1518–1580) for the Olympic Academy in that city. When Palladio died, Vincenzo Scamozzi (1552–1616) completed the building in 1584. The premiere production in the Olimpico was Sophocles' *King Oedipus* in 1585.
   Palladio was influenced by the writings of the Roman architect Vitruvius, and therefore the Olimpico was designed as a miniature indoor Roman theater. Its auditorium, accommodating 3,000 spectators, consisted of curved benches connected to the scaena, or stage house; this arrangement created a semicircular orchestra. There was a raised stage, about 70 feet wide by 18 feet deep, in front of the scaena. The ornate facade of the scene house, patterned after the Roman scaena frons, was designed to look like a street. There were five openings in the facade—three in the back wall and one on each side. Behind each opening was an alleyway or street scene that seemed to disappear in the distance. To achieve the effect of depth, in each alleyway there were three-dimensional buildings—houses and shops—which decreased in size as they were positioned farther and farther away from the opening onstage.

TEATRO OLYMPICO. The Olympico, a 3,000-seat theater in Vicenza, Italy, was completed in 1584 and is the oldest theater surviving from the Renaissance. Its stage, shown here in a model, was an attempt to duplicate the facade of a Roman scene house. Five alleyways led offstage: the model shows three of them in the back wall, and there was also one in each side wall.

THE THEATER AT SABBIONETA

In 1588, Scamozzi constructed a tiny 250-seat theater in Sabbioneta, Italy. This theater, paid for by the duke of Mantua, was erected for the Academia dei Confidenti. It had only one background vista, which extended from one side of the stage to the other. The vista was a perspective scenic view painted on the sides and back of the stage area.

TEATRO FARNESE AND THE PROSCENIUM STAGE

Some historians believe that the single-vista design at Sabbioneta influenced the architect Giovan Battista Aleotti (1546–1636), who was responsible for the most famous theater building of the Italian Renaissance, the Teatro Farnese in Parma. The Farnese was completed in 1618. It had a typical court and academic theater auditorium, with raised horseshoe seating accommodating 3,500 spectators and a semicircular orchestra in front of the stage. The orchestra could be used for additional seating, or it could be flooded for nautical scenes—a spectacular practice adopted from the Romans.

(Alinari/Art Resource)

TEATRO FARNESE.   The Farnese, completed in 1618, was the first theater with a proscenium arch—the opening behind which scenery and stage machinery are concealed. Its horseshoe-shaped auditorium held 3,500 spectators; there was a semicircular orchestra between the audience and the stage.

(Based on a drawing in Theater Design, George C. Izenour, McGraw-Hill, New York, 1977.)

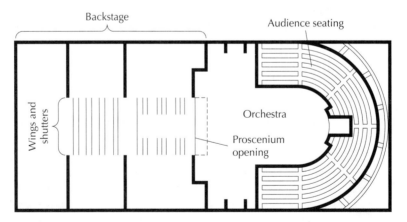

Backstage

Audience seating

Wings and shutters

Orchestra

Proscenium opening

GROUND PLAN OF THE FARNESE.   Note, in this plan, the large backstage area of the Farnese.

Debates in Theater History:
WHAT IS THE EXACT ORIGIN OF THE PROSCENIUM ARCH?

Why did the Italians develop the proscenium arch? There is continuing debate over *when* the proscenium-arch space was first used; but *what* influences led to this design may be an even more significant question, because of all Renaissance innovations, the proscenium arch has had the most lasting impact. The roots of the proscenium-arch stage have been traced to several sources, and there is no universal agreement among Renaissance scholars about its origin.

Given the significant influence of classical theorists and the desire to revive classical theatrical traditions, some historians have argued that the *thyromata*—the large openings in the stage house of Greek Hellenistic theaters and the large central portals of Roman theaters—may have been the inspiration for the Italian theater designers who introduced the proscenium arch.

Other historians have pointed to medieval traditions which were popular at court. These scholars suggest that triumphal arches, which were used for medieval pageantry and were frequently set up in the streets of medieval cities for the grand entry of a visiting dignitary, were the ancestors of the proscenium arch. Since there were an immense number of theatrical presentations at courts in the Italian Renaissance—and since the first proscenium arch may have been used in a temporary space at an Italian court—this medieval influence seems logical.

Another theory is that the frames in which perspective paintings were placed in the Italian Renaissance were copied by designers who introduced painted-perspective scene designs; thus the proscenium would be the theatrical equivalent of the frame of a painting.

The final explanation of the origin of the proscenium arch therefore remains unresolved. Though its origins are debatable, however, there is no question that the development of the proscenium arch has been of immense importance in western theater.

What was revolutionary in the Teatro Farnese was its proscenium-arch stage. The Farnese was probably not the first theater space in Italy with a proscenium; it is believed that temporary arches were used earlier at court performances and that another permanent proscenium stage may have been constructed earlier. But the Farnese is the most famous because it is still standing—though it required extensive renovation after 90 percent of it was damaged during World War II. Actually, very few performances took place in the Farnese; it is significant because it is the prototype of the proscenium-arch theater.

The *proscenium-arch stage*—also known as the *picture-frame, peephole,* or *conventional* stage—is still the best-known type of theater space. The audience, facing in one direction, views the action through the arch, which frames the stage picture. (In most modern theaters, the "arch" is not rounded but rectangular.) The proscenium hides the stage mechanisms for scene changes and special effects from the audience, increasing theatrical illusion. The proscenium arch, along with Renaissance innovations in scene design (discussed below), was an impetus for the development of greater realism in theater.

Audience Seating

Along with developments in the stage arrangement, there were also changes in the auditorium where the spectators sat. The Italian revolution in auditorium design occurred in the public opera houses of Venice, four of which had been constructed by 1641. These were proscenium-arch houses, and, as commercial ventures, they needed as many paying customers as possible; thus they required a larger audience area than the academy theaters. The opera houses were therefore designed with "pit, boxes, and galleries," an auditorium style that had already been used in France, England, and Spain. Combining a "pit, box, and gallery" auditorium with a proscenium-arch stage made the Venice opera houses innovative.

The *pit,* in which audience members stood, was an open area on the house floor extending to the side and back walls. Built into the walls were tiers of seating. The lower tiers were usually the most expensive; they were divided into separate private *boxes* frequented by the upper classes. The upper tiers, called *galleries,* had open bench seating. The pit—a raucous area where the spectators ate, talked, and moved around—and the galleries were the least expensive accommodations. The proscenium-arch theater with pit, box, and gallery seating was to become the standard theater space throughout the western world for over 200 years.

Scene Design

Advances in scene design during the Italian Renaissance were no less impressive than those in theater architecture. Again, the initial impetus came from the rediscovery, in 1414, of a classical source—Vitruvius's *De Architectura,* a Roman text on architecture which deals extensively with theater design. Historians believe that the earliest designs in Italy during the late 1400s were attempts to create a Roman stage and to replicate Vitruvius's suggestions for comic, tragic, and satyr settings.

PERSPECTIVE IN SCENE DESIGN

The most significant innovation in scenic design was perspective drawing, which had become such an important part of Renaissance painting. With the use of perspective, scenes onstage, although painted on flat surfaces (such as backdrops), could achieve an illusion of depth—a three-dimensional quality. While there is debate over when perspective painting was first used to create a theatrical setting, most historians believe that it was employed as early as 1508, for a court performance of Ariosto's *La Cassaria.*

Many artists wrote treatises about perspective in drawing and painting in the first half of the fifteenth century. The person who detailed many of the early methods for creating perspective settings was Sebastiano Serlio, in his book *Architettura* (1545).

SERLIO'S TRAGIC SETTING. The Italian architect and designer Sebastiano Serlio developed the use of perspective—a convention for representing three-dimensionality—in scene design. In a book on architecture, he set forth three basic settings: tragic, comic, and pastoral. This model shows his tragic setting, with the scene disappearing into the distance.

Sebastiano Serlio
(1475–1554)

The Italian architect, painter, and designer Sebastiano Serlio is an important figure in the history of scene design. In the second book of his work on architecture, published in 1545, Serlio devoted only a small portion to theater, but that section was to influence European theater for the next 100 years.

Serlio helped introduce perspective—with its sense of visual realism—into scene design. He also believed that there should be three basic settings for drama: a tragic setting, showing a street of stately houses; a comic setting, showing a common street scene; and a pastoral setting, showing trees, hills, and cottages.

To create these settings Serlio recommended using a series of *angled wings*—flats hinged in a fixed position and painted in perspective—placed one behind another on both sides of the stage. Each wing would give the appearance of a house and would have some three-dimensional ornamentation. To increase the illusion of depth, the tops of these painted houses were constructed so that they slanted downward. The set was enclosed in the back by either a painted *backdrop* or two painted *shutters*.

The back area of the stage, according to Serlio, was to be *raked*—that is, slightly inclined or slanted—so that the bottoms of the wings slanted upward; this too would enhance the illusion of depth. Later in the Italian Renaissance, theaters were designed with permanently raked stages. Today, in describing stage areas, we still refer to the area farthest from the audience as *upstage*. In Renaissance theaters, this area was literally "up," or higher; the front of the stage was "down." In modern theaters, stages are usually not raked; instead, the seating for the audience is.

Before writing his treatise on architecture, Serlio—who was the son of an Italian ornament painter—had studied extensively and had worked as both a painter and an architect. He went to Rome to work with Baldassare Peruzzi (1481–1537), the first designer to apply principles of perspective to the stage. In Rome, Serlio also studied the many examples of classical architecture in the city. He eventually settled in Venice. In 1537, the year of Peruzzi's death, Serlio published a section of a proposed seven-volume work on architecture. Serlio used ideas from Vitruvius, the Roman architect who was the source for classical architectural theory, and from Peruzzi's unpublished notes and designs, but he combined these sources in a new way. He fused architectural theory with detailed, practical instructions on building.

Serlio's method can be seen in his passages on theater, in which he tells how to construct a theater building and also how to light the stage, color the lights, create mobile heavenly bodies, and produce thunder and lightning.

Serlio became a court architect, and his knowledge in that capacity came from practical experience; he served many princes, most notably Francis I of France at the palace of Fontainebleau. His books were translated and circulated throughout Europe, where they became basic texts for architecture and stage design.

SCENE SHIFTING

The angled-wing settings advocated by Serlio were difficult to change. Another designer, Nicola Sabbattini (1574–1654), in his *Manual for Constructing Theatrical Scenes and Machines* (1638), described some primitive methods for scene changing, including the Greek periaktoi, the three-sided scenic devices mentioned in Chapter 1. And by the early 1600s, angled wings were replaced by flat wings.

Flat wings were a series of individual wings on each side of the stage, parallel to the audience, placed in a progression from the front to the back of the stage

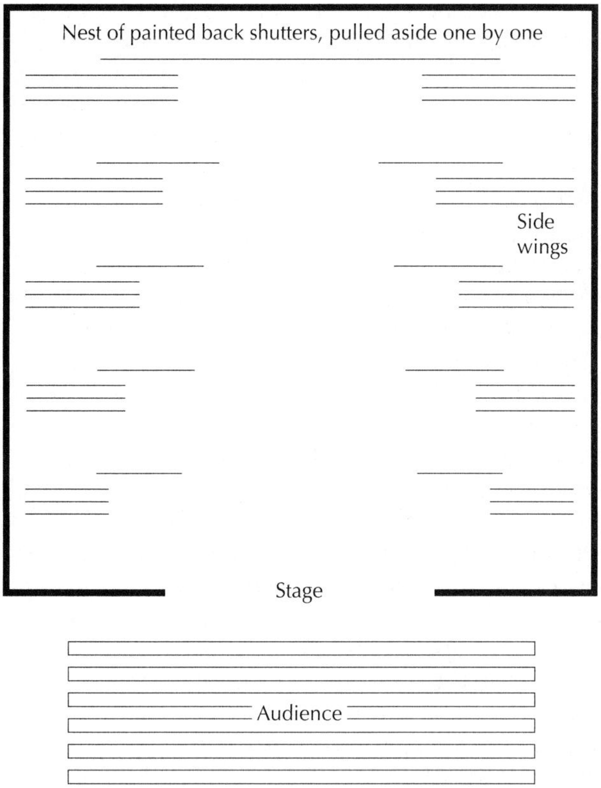

Nest of painted back shutters, pulled aside one by one

Side wings

Stage

Audience

THE GROOVE SYSTEM. During the Italian Renaissance, the groove system for shifting scenery was perfected. This drawing shows a Renaissance stage with side wings and back shutters. Along the sides of the stage, in parallel lines, scenery was set in sections. At the back, two shutters met in the middle. Together, these pieces formed a complete stage picture. When one set of side wings and back shutters was pulled aside, a new stage picture was revealed.

and enclosed at the very back by two shutters that met in the middle. The final element in these perspective settings was an overhead border—a strip across the top of the stage—that completed the picture. The first use of flat wings is usually credited to Giovan Battista Aleotti in 1606; Aleotti was also the designer of the Teatro Farnese, the famous proscenium-arch theater described earlier in this chapter.

The earliest method of scene shifting for flat-wing settings is often referred to as the *groove system*. Wings and shutters were placed in grooves on and above the stage floor; the grooves allowed these elements to be slid offstage easily and quickly so that a new series of wings and shutters—in place behind the original set—would be suddenly revealed to the audience. In this fashion, a number of sets were positioned one behind the other, allowing for rapid scene changes. The major problem with this system was coordinating the removal of the flat wings by scene shifters at each groove position. (Renaissance theaters had curtains, but since they were used only at the beginning and end of a presentation, scene changes were not hidden.)

A later innovation facilitated scene changing: between 1641 and 1645, Giacomo Torelli developed the *pole-and-chariot* system.

A DESIGN BY TORELLI. Giacomo Torelli, a master scene designer of the Italian Renaissance, continued the use of painted-perspective scenery; he also improved scene shifting by inventing the pole-and-chariot system for wings and shutters. The setting shown here would have been created from wings and shutters, with some three-dimensional ornamentation, and shifted by the pole-and-chariot method. Torelli's work was so highly esteemed that he was invited to France to design for the court.

Giacomo Torelli
(1608–1678)

For his many spectacular stage settings and scene changes Giacomo Torelli was nicknamed the "great wizard." His elaborate stage machinery and designs were influential in both Italy and France, and his method of shifting scenery became standard throughout continental Europe.

Torelli came to the stage from an unlikely background. Born to a noble family of Fano in Italy, he was given an education befitting his rank. It is possible (though not certain) that he also studied design in Pesaro and Ferrara, two theatrical centers near his home. At some point, Torelli must have offended his family, because he was disinherited in his father's will. By 1640, he was designing in Venice, which was developing into a center of opera, and it was at the Teatro Novissimo in Venice that he developed the staging methods which were to make him famous.

At the Teatro Novissimo, Torelli perfected the pole-and-chariot method of scene shifting, which allowed an entire set of flat wings to be changed mechanically. In Torelli's system, poles were attached to scene flats; these poles went below the stage floor, where they were connected to wheels—the "chariots"—that ran in tracks. In this way, flats could be moved offstage smoothly; with a series of connected ropes and pulleys, an entire set could be removed by turning the handle of a crank on a winch.

The pole-and-chariot system was adopted widely throughout the western world (the only exceptions were in England, the Netherlands, and later the United States). Audiences were astounded by the many variations of scene changes Torelli explored with the new system. Another of his innovations was occasional use of cutout flats that produced an effect of three-dimensional trees and shrubs.

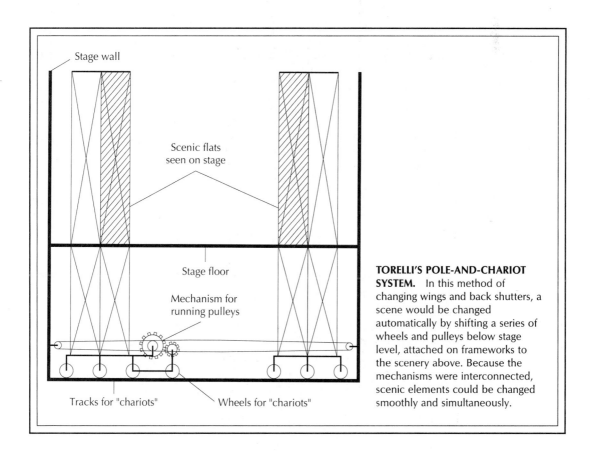

Stage wall

Scenic flats
seen on stage

Stage floor

Mechanism for
running pulleys

Tracks for "chariots"

Wheels for "chariots"

TORELLI'S POLE-AND-CHARIOT SYSTEM. In this method of changing wings and back shutters, a scene would be changed automatically by shifting a series of wheels and pulleys below stage level, attached on frameworks to the scenery above. Because the mechanisms were interconnected, scenic elements could be changed smoothly and simultaneously.

In 1645, Torelli, now internationally renowned, was invited to Paris to stage an opera sponsored by the royal family. When he found that he was expected to work on this opera with an Italian commedia dell'arte troupe, he considered it an indignity and protested—unavailingly—to the queen. Ironically, the opera, *La Finta Pazzo,* was a great success at court and hastened the adoption of Torelli's scenic inventions in Paris.

Though he married a French noblewoman and staged many successful productions for the French court—notably, Corneille's *Andromède*—Torelli was disliked in France because of his Italian background and his association with Cardinal Mazarin, the king's Italian minister. When Mazarin died in 1661, Torelli was ordered to leave France; and most of his French designs were destroyed by Gaspare Vigarani, a rival Italian designer at court. Torelli returned to Fano, his birthplace, where in 1677 he staged his last production at the theater he had designed there.

SPECIAL EFFECTS AND LIGHTING

Italian Renaissance theater, which emphasized spectacle, developed many ingenious special effects. For example, there were flying machines, called *glories;* trapdoors; and primitive sound-effects devices to create thunder and wind.

There were also some primitive attempts to deal with stage lighting. Since Italian Renaissance theaters were indoors, artificial lighting was needed; candles and oil lamps were used, but these produced a smoky, hazy environment. Candles—the primary means of illumination—were placed at the front of the stage as well as in chandeliers and on poles above and along the sides of the stage. There were also some attempts to control the intensity of onstage lighting; for example, open canisters would be used to cover some of the candles, to diminish the amount of light. Because it was difficult to provide sufficient illumination, the auditorium as well as the stage was always lit.

THE LEGACY OF THE ITALIAN RENAISSANCE

Almost all of western theater was eventually influenced by the advances in theater architecture and scenic design initiated during the Italian Renaissance. This influence was felt first in France and later in other countries such as England, Spain, and Germany. With regard to performance, commedia dell'arte similarly influenced theater in France in a very direct way and other nations less directly. The long-range effect of commedia continues, in some respects, to the present.

We turn next, however, to two countries which did not look immediately to developments in Italy, but rather looked to their own roots in medieval theater and to the effect of rediscovering Greek and Roman classics. These countries are England and Spain.

SUMMARY

The innovations of the Italian Renaissance in theater architecture and scene design have been unparalleled in theater history. For the next 200 years, anyone attending a theater anywhere in Europe would be in a proscenium-arch playhouse watching the stage action from either the pit, a box, or a gallery. The scenery would consist of painted-flat wings and shutters which could be shifted either by Torelli's mechanized pole-and-chariot system or—as in England, the Netherlands, and the United States—by stagehands who pulled them off in grooves.

The Italian Renaissance also produced opera, commedia dell'arte, and the neoclassical rules of dramatic structure. Although this period left us few significant plays, the rigid neoclassical rules shaped much of the world's drama through the eighteenth century. The improvisatory actors' theater known as *commedia dell'arte* remained popular into the 1700s and has influenced many contemporary theatrical experimenters.

The Italian Renaissance was more than a rebirth of theater; in many respects, it was a period that witnessed the restructuring of theater.

CHAPTER 6

THE THEATER OF THE ENGLISH RENAISSANCE

I t is early afternoon around the year 1600 in London, England. We join people from many parts of the city who are gathering along the north bank of the Thames River to be carried across to its south bank. A number of boatmen make a living by ferrying people across the river in small vessels, and today business is brisk. There is a special excitement in the air because most of those crossing the Thames are headed for the Globe Theater, to see the first public performance of a new play by William Shakespeare called *Hamlet.*

The Globe is one of the newest and finest playhouses serving London; the reason we must cross the Thames to get to it is that officials in London censor theatrical performances, and putting on plays is easier outside city limits. The first permanent theaters in England have been built to the north of London or across the Thames to the south, outside the jurisdiction of city officials.

Despite this political opposition, however, theater is enormously popular with the people of London; it is a favorite entertainment of Queen Elizabeth, the members of her court, and the nobility, as well as ordinary citizens like us from all walks of life. These are the men and women now making their way

KING LEAR. One of the great tragedies of the English Renaissance is Shakespeare's *King Lear.* In this play, Lear divides his kingdom between his two dishonest daughters and banishes his third daughter, who truly loves him but will not proclaim her love. As in many Elizabethan tragedies, there is an important subplot, violence is presented onstage, and comic and serious elements are mixed. Shown here is a scene from a production at the Shakepeare Theatre in Washington, D.C. *(Joan Marcus/The Shakespeare Theatre)*

across the Thames: lords and ladies, dukes and duchesses, merchants, coachmakers, upholsterers—and a few low-lifes such as pickpockets and prostitutes.

When we arrive at the theater—well over 2,000 people all together—we can pay a penny at the main door to get in or we can use another entrance for the more expensive accommodations. Those who use the main door move into a central courtyard, open to the sky, where they will stand during the performance around three sides of a platform stage at one end of the courtyard. We are among those who can afford more, and so we will pay to enter one of three levels of covered gallery seats surrounding the stage and courtyard on three sides. By paying even more, the nobility can sit on cushioned seats in boxes next to the stage. The two separate entrances are a recent innovation; in earlier playhouses, everyone would use the main entrance to enter the yard and then those who wanted to go up to the galleries or boxes would pay more.

Food and drink—apples, nuts, water, ale—are being sold throughout the playhouse. We decide not to eat or drink much, since the only toilet facilities are buckets or a walk to the river. Many men are smoking, and the theater smells of tobacco. As we find seats, we try to avoid sitting behind anyone wearing a large hat, which would obstruct our view of the stage.

As the audience gathers, there is a great deal of conversation and anticipation. Some audience members have advance knowledge about *Hamlet;* they are familiar with earlier versions of the story that have appeared in books or on the stage. They know that *Hamlet* will be a revenge play, one of their favorite types of drama: another revenge play, *The Spanish Tragedy* by Thomas Kyd, first appeared about 12 years ago and has been the most popular play of its time. There is keen interest, too, because *Hamlet* is by William Shakespeare, a favorite playwright; and its star is Richard Burbage, considered by many the finest actor in England.

At two o'clock the play is about to start. The people in the *yard,* as the floor of the courtyard is called, jockey for a good view of the stage; and an air of expectancy envelopes the entire audience.

As the play begins, two sentinels standing watch on the parapet of a castle appear onstage, soon to be joined by Horatio, a friend of Hamlet's. The three men discuss a ghost that has been appearing every night, and all of a sudden, there is the ghost itself: it is the ghost of Hamlet's father, played by Shakespeare, who is not only the playwright but also an actor with the company. The men are frightened; the ghost stays briefly and then disappears.

The scene shifts to the interior of the castle: King Claudius enters. He is the brother of Hamlet's father, the dead king, and he has married Hamlet's mother, Queen Gertrude. Onstage, too, are the other principals of the play, including Hamlet, who is dressed in black and standing apart from the others. The action of the play is full of twists and turns. In the next scene, Hamlet himself sees the ghost of his father, who says that Hamlet must avenge his murder at the hands of his brother, Claudius. Hamlet later has a group of strolling players present a drama which proves that Claudius did murder the older Hamlet. In a later scene, Hamlet thrusts his sword through a curtain in his mother's bedroom, thinking that Claudius is hiding behind it, but the person concealed there turns out to be someone else. As the plot continues to unfold, the audience is enthralled—all the way to the end, when almost everyone is killed: Hamlet and Laertes in a duel, Gertrude by poisoning, and Claudius by stabbing.

Throughout the play we enjoy not only the action and suspense but also the memorable lines and speeches. Several times Hamlet stands alone onstage delivering a soliloquy. In one of them—which begins "To be or not to be, that is the question"—he weighs the advantages and disadvantages of suicide. In these speeches, as well as in the action of the play, important questions are raised about life and death, corruption and innocence, appearance and reality. We and other audience members are set to thinking about Hamlet's words at the same time that we follow the plot.

When the play is over, the audience's reaction is enthusiastic: we have enjoyed the ghost, the swordplay, and the intrigues of the plot; and we have relished the language and the ideas. On the way back across the Thames, and all evening, we will continue to discuss *Hamlet*. We would like to see it again because we feel that there is more to it than we were able to take in at one viewing; and we want the experience of living through it once more to feel the thrill of the action and to sort out our thoughts about what it means.

BACKGROUND: THE RENAISSANCE IN ENGLAND

The English Renaissance, though it began later than the Renaissance in Italy, was equally explosive and led to major developments in English society and culture, especially theater.

The English Renaissance is frequently called the *Elizabethan* period, because the major political figure during this time was Queen Elizabeth I, who reigned for 45 years, from 1558 to 1603. Actually, the English Renaissance began during the reign of Henry VII, who became king in 1485, and ended with the Puritan takeover of England and the subsequent removal of Charles I in 1649; during this 165-year period, English culture rose to unequaled heights.

A secularization of English society which had begun at the end of the Middle Ages was reinforced when Henry VIII broke with the Roman Catholic church. Henry wanted to have his marriage to Catherine of Aragon annulled so that he could marry Anne Boleyn; in 1534, when the pope refused, Henry declared that the papacy no longer had any authority in his kingdom, establishing the Church of England (also known as the Anglican church) as an independent entity with himself as its head. The establishment of Anglicanism was part of the Protestant Reformation that was sweeping through Europe and cutting away the power of Roman Catholicism.

After Henry VIII's death and the brief reign of his only son Edward VI, his daughter Mary became queen. Mary attempted to reinstate Catholicism in England; because of the numerous executions during her 5-year reign, she was nicknamed Bloody Mary. After her death, however, Henry's daughter by Anne Boleyn became Elizabeth I. As queen, Elizabeth strengthened the Anglican

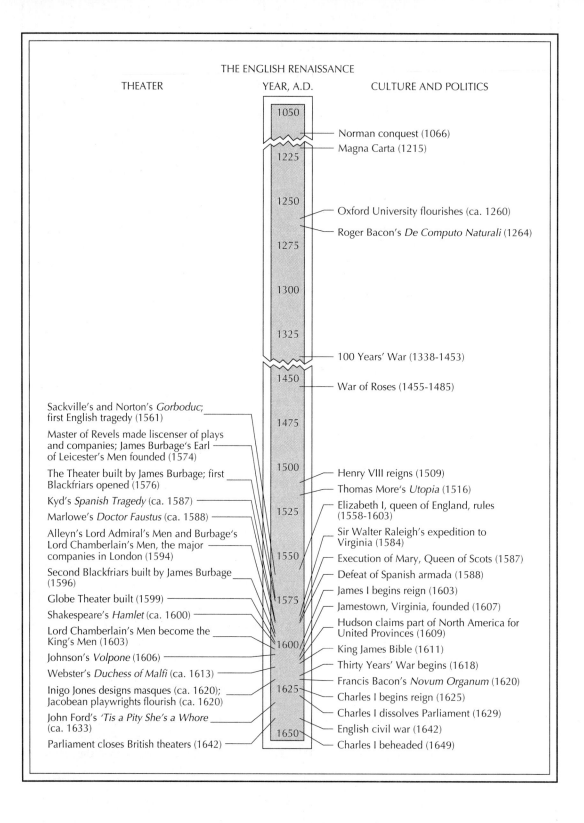

THE ENGLISH RENAISSANCE

THEATER   YEAR, A.D.   CULTURE AND POLITICS

1050

Norman conquest (1066)

Magna Carta (1215)

1225

1250

Oxford University flourishes (ca. 1260)

Roger Bacon's *De Computo Naturali* (1264)

1275

1300

1325

100 Years' War (1338-1453)

1450

War of Roses (1455-1485)

Sackville's and Norton's *Gorboduc*;
first English tragedy (1561)

1475

Master of Revels made liscenser of plays
and companies; James Burbage's Earl
of Leicester's Men founded (1574)

1500

Henry VIII reigns (1509)

The Theater built by James Burbage; first
Blackfriars opened (1576)

Thomas More's *Utopia* (1516)

Kyd's *Spanish Tragedy* (ca. 1587)

Elizabeth I, queen of England, rules
(1558-1603)

Marlowe's *Doctor Faustus* (ca. 1588)

1525

Alleyn's Lord Admiral's Men and Burbage's
Lord Chamberlain's Men, the major
companies in London (1594)

Sir Walter Raleigh's expedition to
Virginia (1584)

1550

Execution of Mary, Queen of Scots (1587)

Second Blackfriars built by James Burbage
(1596)

Defeat of Spanish armada (1588)

Globe Theater built (1599)

1575

James I begins reign (1603)

Shakespeare's *Hamlet* (ca. 1600)

Jamestown, Virginia, founded (1607)

Lord Chamberlain's Men become the
King's Men (1603)

1600

Hudson claims part of North America for
United Provinces (1609)

Johnson's *Volpone* (1606)

King James Bible (1611)

Webster's *Duchess of Malfi* (ca. 1613)

Thirty Years' War begins (1618)

Inigo Jones designs masques (ca. 1620);
Jacobean playwrights flourish (ca. 1620)

1625

Francis Bacon's *Novum Organum* (1620)

Charles I begins reign (1625)

John Ford's *'Tis a Pity She's a Whore*
(ca. 1633)

Charles I dissolves Parliament (1629)

1650

English civil war (1642)

Parliament closes British theaters (1642)

Charles I beheaded (1649)

church; and with the execution of another Mary—her cousin Mary Stuart (known as Mary, Queen of Scots)—she ended the Catholic claim to the English throne. It was during the reign of Elizabeth I that the English Renaissance reached its peak. One reason was Elizabeth's ability to unite the English people, in both internal affairs and the rejection of Catholicism.

Another step in England's break with Catholicism came in 1588, with the defeat of the Spanish armada; with this victory England proved that it was not to be ruled by Spanish Catholics. The defeat of the armada also brought England to ascendancy on the seas, and this naval superiority allowed England to take full advantage of the age of discovery—the period of intense exploration of new lands, especially in the Americas.

Throughout the English Renaissance, language and literature flourished. The Renaissance in English literature was inaugurated in 1516 with the publication of Thomas More's *Utopia*, a political romance describing an ideal country. The English were intrigued by language, and Queen Elizabeth herself was an amateur linguist. But at the heart of the English Renaissance in literature and arts was theater.

THE EARLY DRAMA OF THE ENGLISH RENAISSANCE

During the first three-quarters of the sixteenth century, a number of developments prepared the way for an explosion of theatrical activity in the Elizabethan era. Under Henry VII and Henry VIII, *interludes*—brief dramatic entertainments written and staged by professionals—were presented at court and in the homes of the nobility. From the early 1500s through about 1580, English *school drama* became increasingly popular. These plays, written at the universities and presented at schools rather than for the general public, usually reflected some Greek and Roman influence, but they also used many medieval dramaturgical techniques. Two of the best-known school dramas were *Ralph Roister Doister* by Nicholas Udall (1505–1566), written in the late 1530s; and *Gammer Gurton's Needle* (author uncertain), written in the late 1550s. Both were rollicking comedies which, though based on Roman models, were written in English and incorporated medieval elements.

The popularity of drama in the schools is frequently cited as a reason for the later development of boys' acting companies. These companies were first established by Elizabeth I for court entertainments. In 1575, one of the boys' masters, Richard Farrant, persuaded the queen to allow his company to give plays to the public. For these public presentations, the boys' companies used Blackfriars Hall (a private theater space), and many major playwrights provided them with dramas.

Among the playwrights who provided boys' companies with scripts were members of a group known as the *university wits*. The "wits," almost all of whom were university graduates and professional dramatists, wrote plays based on Roman models and also introduced medieval elements into them. These full-length dramas paved the way for Shakespeare and his contemporaries.

A MEDIEVAL UNIVERSITY STAGE.   This is a model of a stage set up at a university for a production of Terence's *Andria* in the late Middle Ages. Medieval universities had a profound impact on early writers of the English Renaissance: many early Elizabethan dramatists were known as *university wits* because they were trained at the universities and had contact with drama there.

ELIZABETHAN DRAMA

We noted in Chapter 1 that there are certain times in history when a number of elements come together to make important achievements possible. In Greece, the fifth century B.C. was such a period; another was Elizabethan England. During the Elizabethan age, many elements—politics, exploration, literature, learning—converged to produce a favorable climate for England and for English playwrights, who included not only William Shakespeare but Christopher Marlowe, Ben Jonson, and a number of others.

Many influences contributed to the art of Shakespeare and his contemporaries. For example, we can see important Roman influences on Elizabethan drama. Seneca's revenge-obsessed characters, his presentation of violence onstage, and his use of supernatural beings were freely imitated by Elizabethan playwrights. Plautus's and Terence's comic plots and techniques were also adapted by the English; Shakespeare's *Comedy of Errors,* for instance, was an adaptation of Plautus's *The Menaechmi.* In some instances, Elizabethan dramatists took stories from Roman and English history and also borrowed plot lines from Italian Renaissance literature. (Shakespeare reworked Italian novellas in several of his plays.)

In Chapter 3, we discussed medieval plays in which episodic structure began to emerge. This structure involves many characters and many scenes ranging through time and shifting from place to place. Drama of the English Renaissance followed this pattern: thus it was almost totally counter to the Italian neoclassical ideals described in Chapter 5. The Italians attempted to resurrect Greek crisis drama; the Elizabethans used an episodic form growing out of medieval drama.

Few English dramatists observed the neoclassical unities of time, place, and action; and rather than tell only one story, they often had parallel plots or subplots related to the main dramatic action. They presented violence onstage and filled their plays with supernatural characters. The soliloquy, attacked by the Italians, was a popular dramatic convention in England. Like the Italians, the Elizabethans featured royal or noble characters in tragedies and lower-class characters in comedies; but the English were not as rigid as the Italians about such distinctions: they often mixed higher and lower characters and included comic scenes in serious plays. A good example is Thomas Preston's *Cambyses,* written about 1569; part of its subtitle is *A Lamentable Tragedy Mixed Full of Pleasant Mirth.*

As written drama was taking shape, there were also significant developments in theater production. The stage that had been developing in England was well suited to Elizabethan episodic plays. In Chapter 3, we noted that a neutral platform stage was used for medieval mystery plays: this could become any place the dramatist designated. In the English Renaissance, the neutral platform stage had evolved to a point where it was ideal for plays in which scenes moved freely from one place to another and from one time to another. Thomas Kyd's *The Spanish Tragedy,* written around 1587, is an example: in Acts I and II, we move from the court of Spain to the court of Portugal, then back to the court of Spain, then to the palace of a nobleman, then to a garden, and so forth.

In fact, *The Spanish Tragedy* was an important forerunner of later plays in more ways than one; it skillfully incorporated a number of devices that had come to the forefront during the sixteenth century, such as episodic structure, ghosts, soliloquies, and the theme of revenge. Stories chosen by Kyd and his contemporaries established material that would be used shortly thereafter by Shakespeare and his colleagues.

From accounts of the professional performances that gave life to these plays, we can assume that acting had also been progressing during the sixteenth century: that performers were becoming increasingly accomplished at creating both comic and serious characters, at speaking verse effectively, and at mastering such physical activities as sword fighting. Moreover, the organization of the acting companies that would mount the plays of Marlowe, Shakespeare, and Jonson was beginning to take shape.

In short, the ground had been prepared for both playwrights and performers. Let us now look at the two most important Elizabethan playwrights; we'll then consider theaters and acting companies.

DOCTOR FAUSTUS. The most important Elizabethan playwright before Shakespeare was Christopher Marlowe, whose best-known play is *Doctor Faustus*. Faustus—a man who sells his soul to the devil—is shown here in a production by the CSC Repertory in New York City.

ELIZABETHAN PLAYWRIGHTS

Marlowe and the Mighty Line

The most famous of the "university wits" was Christopher Marlowe, who advanced the art of dramatic structure and contributed a gallery of interesting characters to English theater.

Marlowe also perfected another element that was to be central in later Elizabethan plays—dramatic poetry. Critics speak of Marlowe's "mighty line," the power of the dramatic verse he developed. As an example, the title character in his *Doctor Faustus* makes a pact with the devil—Mephistopheles—to give up his soul if the devil will grant him a number of wishes, one of which is to be with the beauteous Helen of Troy. When Faustus meets Helen, Marlowe gives him these lines:

Was this the face that launched a thousand ships,
And burnt the topless towers of Ilium?
Sweet Helen, make me immortal with a kiss.

This verse is *iambic pentameter;* that is, it has five beats to a line, with two syllables to each beat and the accent on the second beat. In Marlowe's hands, dramatic verse in iambic pentameter developed strength, subtlety, and suppleness, as well as great lyric beauty.

Another element which Marlowe developed had originated in medieval morality plays. In *Everyman,* as we saw in Chapter 3, good and bad forces vie for the soul of the main character. This struggle became an accepted theme in English drama, and Marlowe used it in *Doctor Faustus:* a good angel and a bad angel attempt to influence Faustus. Thus an abstract notion from the morality plays was incorporated into a full-length Elizabethan drama.

Christopher Marlowe

(1564–1593)

The plays of Christopher Marlowe, the first significant dramatist to emerge in the Elizabethan period, include *Tamburlaine,* Parts I and II (ca. 1587), *The Tragical History of Doctor Faustus* (ca. 1588), *The Jew of Malta* (ca.1588), *The Massacre at Paris* (ca. 1592), and *Edward II* (ca. 1592). Among his other accomplishments, Marlowe perfected the chronicle play, a history play that emphasizes important public issues.

As was usual in his day, Marlowe wrote for production rather than for publication. His *Doctor Faustus,* for example, was not published until 1604, more than 10 years after his death. Though it is a serious play, it includes many comic scenes, some apparently not written by Marlowe but added later by actors; thus there has been some dispute over how the text should be edited to reflect Marlowe's intentions.

Marlowe's verse and subject matter, as well as some of his dramatic techniques, influenced Shakespeare. *The Massacre at Paris* and *The Jew of Malta* show Marlowe's interest in Machiavellian characters. *Edward II* explores the personal tragedy of a king; *Doctor Faustus* explores the damnation of a soul. All his plays are noted for the beauty of their dramatic verse.

The son of a Canterbury shoemaker, Marlowe attended Corpus Christi College, Cambridge, on a scholarship. He received his B.A. in 1584 and continued studying for his M.A., although he had become a secret government agent. A letter from the queen's privy council, submitted to explain his frequent absences, thanked him for his service to the country and requested that he be granted his degree, which he received in 1587.

Marlowe's writing career began at Cambridge, and when he moved to London, he became one of the "university wits," a circle of young writers who had studied at Oxford or Cambridge. With Thomas Nashe, another member of the group, he wrote *Dido, Queen of Carthage.* The first drama he wrote alone, *Tamburlaine the Great,* Part I, was performed in 1587; Part II was produced the following year. Marlowe continued working as a government agent; in 1589, he spent 2 weeks in Newgate Prison for killing a man in a street fight.

Little is known about Marlowe's personal life, but it was said that he held unorthodox religious views and had difficulties with the law. In May of 1593, the queen's privy council ordered his arrest on a charge of atheism. Before he could be arrested, however, Marlowe was stabbed to death in a tavern brawl by a man named Ingram Friser. Two government agents were accessories to the killing, and Friser was acquitted on the grounds that he had acted in self-defense; it is possible that Marlowe's stabbing was a planned assassination related to his government activities. In any case, it cut short the life of one of Elizabethan England's most talented playwrights.

Shakespeare and Hamlet

When Shakespeare appeared on the theater scene around 1590, the stage for great drama was set. As we have seen, he took established elements—Senecan devices; episodic plot structure; the platform stage; powerful dramatic verse; and stories from English history, Roman history, Roman drama, and Italian literature—and fused them into one of the most impressive bodies of plays ever created.

(Victoria and Albert Museum, London)

William Shakespeare

(1564–1616)

William Shakespeare was born in Stratford-on-Avon, a town about 85 miles northwest of London. Though he spent many years in London as a member of an acting company, he never cut his ties to Stratford. Most of his land investments were in or around his birthplace; they included New Place, one of the largest houses in the town, which he bought in 1597. He also used his money to pay his father's debts and restore his family to prosperity and honor.

When Shakespeare was born, in 1564, his father—John Shakespeare—was a prosperous glovemaker and town alderman; his mother, Mary Arden, was the daughter of a yeoman farmer and landowner. As the son of a burgess—a town official—young William was entitled to a free education at the King's New School in Stratford, an institution that prepared students for the university. When he was 13, however, his father suffered business losses, and so he was probably withdrawn from school and apprenticed to a trade. Town records mention William Shakespeare in November 1582, when he married Anne Hathaway, who was several years older. Their daughter Susanna was born in March of 1583; Hamnet and Judith, twins, were born in 1585. Shakespeare's actions and whereabouts between 1585 and 1590 are not recorded, but by 1590 he was in London working as an actor and playwright.

For the next 23 years—except for 1593–1594, when the theaters were closed because of a plague and he wrote his narrative poems—Shakespeare was a working member of a London acting company. From 1595 until his retirement, he was associated with the Lord Chamberlain's Company, London's leading troupe. As an actor, he preferred small but significant roles like the Ghost in Hamlet. His duties as a playwright probably took up most of his time; besides writing plays for the company, he was also expected to help stage them. As a shareholder in the company and a part owner of the theater, he was also involved with the management of the troupe.

The following are some of Shakespeare's best-known plays, together with the approximate dates when they were first presented. Tragedies: *Romeo and Juliet* (1595), *Julius Caesar* (1599), *Hamlet* (1601), *Othello* (1604), *Macbeth* (1605–1606), *King Lear* (1605–1606). Comedies: *Comedy of Errors* (1592), *A Midsummer Night's Dream* (1595), *Much Ado about Nothing* (1598), *As You Like It* (1599), *Twelfth Night* (1601). Histories: *Henry IV*, Parts I and II (1597–1598), *Henry V* (1599).

After the Globe Theater, where his plays were produced, burned in 1613, Shakespeare retired to Stratford and became one of its leading citizens. He died 3 years later.

Shakespeare excelled in many aspects of theater. As an actor and member of a dramatic company, he understood the technical elements of theater. His plots, in episodic form, are exemplary; his verse—especially in the power of his metaphors and the music of his language—is extraordinary; his characters are so well-rounded and so carefully detailed that they often seem like living people. To understand Shakespeare's accomplishments, it will be helpful to look closely at one of his plays, *Hamlet,* which was written about 1600 or 1601; this is the play whose production is described at the opening of the chapter.

Before the events of the play begin, Hamlet's father, the king of Denmark, has died. He has been succeeded on the throne by his brother Claudius, who has married Gertrude—the dead king's widow and Hamlet's mother. Hamlet believes that his father has died of natural causes; but as the play opens, his father's ghost reveals to him that he was murdered by Claudius and Gertrude and urges Hamlet to avenge his death.

During the course of the play, conspiracies and intrigues swirl about the Danish court. To confound his enemies, Hamlet feigns madness. His fiancée, Ophelia, is part of a plan to unmask him: her father, Polonius, sets up a supposedly accidental meeting between Hamlet and Ophelia, convinced that Hamlet's behavior when he thinks he is alone with Ophelia will prove that his "madness" is no more than a lover's unhappiness. Polonius and Claudius watch from behind a screen, but when Hamlet comes in, he still pretends to be insane. Ophelia, confused by Hamlet's rejection and by other disorienting factors, later goes mad and commits suicide.

HAMLET. The continuing popularity of Shakespeare is illustrated in the many productions of his plays around the world. Ever since it was written, Shakespeare's *Hamlet* has been staged by great actors and directors—for one reason, because of the intriguing and complex questions it raises. Here, Tom Hulce plays Hamlet in a production at the Shakespeare Theatre.

Not certain whether Claudius really killed his father, Hamlet stages a play that proves his guilt; but when Hamlet first tries to kill Claudius, he finds Claudius at prayer and does not go through with his revenge. He then confronts Gertrude and accidentally kills Polonius, mistaking him for Claudius. Meanwhile, Claudius has arranged with two supposed friends of Hamlet's —Rosencrantz and Guildenstern—to take Hamlet to England, where he is to be executed. Hamlet turns the tables on them and returns to Denmark. In the last scene, Hamlet duels with Ophelia's brother, Laertes; the Queen takes poison that was intended for Hamlet; and Hamlet finally kills Claudius just before dying himself. In the final moments, Fortinbras—a prince of Norway who has marched against Poland to avenge his own father's wrongs—appears and orders that Hamlet be buried with full honors.

Hamlet illustrates how influences from earlier drama came together during the English Renaissance and how complex these influences were. Shakespeare's tragedy is reminiscent of Seneca's plays, particularly in its use of the revenge theme (Hamlet, Laertes, and Fortinbras are all seeking vengeance), onstage violence, a supernatural apparition (the ghost of Hamlet's father), feigned and real madness, and soliloquies in which Hamlet reveals his inner thoughts. Because Elizabethan playwrights were expected to turn out dramas quickly for the popular theater, they often adapted other dramas, literary pieces, and history. Many scholars believe that Shakespeare's tragedy is a reworking of an earlier *Hamlet*, perhaps written by Thomas Kyd; this earlier version was itself based on thirteenth-century Danish history and a French adaptation from 1576.

Following a tradition that had developed in Elizabethan drama, Shakespeare made no attempt to observe the structural rules of the Italian neoclassicists. His episodic structure derives from medieval drama rather than from the neoclassical unities. The action frequently shifts from one locale to another, and much time passes as Hamlet plots against Claudius. Comic relief is provided by a pair of gravediggers: while preparing for Ophelia's burial, they joke about corpses and skulls and are generally irreverent.

Shakespeare, like other Elizabethan dramatists, was not simply reacting against the neoclassical rules. He and others were developing a new and powerful dramatic form based on different rules. In *Hamlet*, Shakespeare uses episodic structure to create a forceful, imaginative play that has its own dynamics. As the scene shifts from one locale to another, we also move from private to public episodes: from scenes where Hamlet is alone giving a soliloquy or is in conference with a friend to scenes of pageantry in the throne room. Shakespeare skillfully alternates scenes so that each episode illuminates or forms a counterpoint to the one just before it and just after it. Also, there is a subplot: Fortinbras, the prince of Norway, attempts to avenge his own father's death by fighting the Poles, who he believes have wronged his father.

Shakespeare shows tremendous skill in creating this rich tapestry, pulling many diverse elements together to form a unified picture. One unifying element is thematic: the theme of a web of corruption and conspiracy permeates the play; and the subplot of Fortinbras' revenge parallels the main plot of Hamlet's revenge.

Another accomplishment in this play is Shakespeare's creation of a fascinating group of characters. Probably no character in literature has been analyzed or written about more than Hamlet, and actors and audiences continue to debate interpretations of this role. Why does Hamlet behave as he does? Is he simply unable to act? Is he too melancholic? Too calculating? Does he suffer from an Oedipus complex? Is some combination of these factors responsible? So subtle and complex is Shakespeare's creation that the play offers no clear answer.

Another important aspect of *Hamlet* is its consummate dramatic poetry. Hamlet's speeches—such as "To be, or not to be" and "Oh, what a rogue and peasant slave am I"—are still quoted today, and many phrases from this play have become part of our everyday language. Hamlet's description of human beings at their best is an excellent example of Shakespeare's language:

> What a piece of work is a man! how noble in reason! how infinite in faculties! in form, and moving, how express and admirable! in action how like an angel! in apprehension how like a god! the beauty of the world, the paragon of animals.

Shakespeare has been rightly praised, not only for the individual aspects of *Hamlet*—its plot, characters, language, and so forth—but for the way he put the parts together; as has been proved time and time again, the play works brilliantly on the stage.

How were plays like *Hamlet* staged in Shakespeare's day? This brings us to the subjects of theaters and acting in the English Renaissance.

ELIZABETHAN THEATERS

Theaters and Production Practices: Problems of Research

There is considerable confusion—and controversy—surrounding the appearance of Elizabethan playhouses. At this point, therefore, it is appropriate to pause in our examination of the English Renaissance theater and discuss the reasons for this uncertainty. To understand the situation, we need to become familiar with certain problems of theater research.

In order to reconstruct earlier theatrical events and production techniques, historians consult *primary sources*—that is, materials surviving from the period under study. Imagine, for example, what kinds of materials might help scholars of the twenty-first century reconstruct the theater of the 1990s. These materials might include surviving playhouses, scripts, sketches of costumes, models of sets, reviews, promptbooks, contracts, autobiographies, and photographs. Of course, all such sources would have to be carefully examined and interpreted; future historians would have to ask, for example, whether the people who reviewed a Broadway opening of the 1990s had any biases that colored their opinions; and whether or not to take at face value the autobiography of an actor who represented himself as having been of crucial importance in certain productions. Evaluating the reliability of sources is an essential aspect of the theater historian's job. History is not simply accumulating information but analyzing its validity and significance.

Only a few sources have survived that can help us reconstruct the theaters of ancient Greece or Rome, the Middle Ages, or most early Asian cultures. Vase drawings are visual sources for classical Greek drama. Ruins like those at Epidauros and Delphi are sources for Hellenistic theater; the theater at Orange in France is a well-preserved Roman playhouse. From the tenth century after Christ, there is a description by Bishop Ethelwold of Winchester of the staging of the *Quem quaeritis* trope. Medieval town documents are sources for some of the arrangements for producing cycle plays. Drawings by Serlio are sources for developments in scene design during the early Italian Renaissance.

Of course, conclusions about theatrical practices drawn from these materials vary, because the sources do not tell us everything and are open to various interpretations. To take just one example, no skenes have survived from Hellenistic playhouses. In many eras, no special care was taken to preserve theatrical artifacts, because theater was considered popular and impermanent. The ephemeral nature of live theater implies that once an event is completed, it disappears; thus the art work itself will not survive to be studied.

The problem of recreating the Elizabethan playhouse is an example of the difficulties of theater research. Few documents survive, and controversy

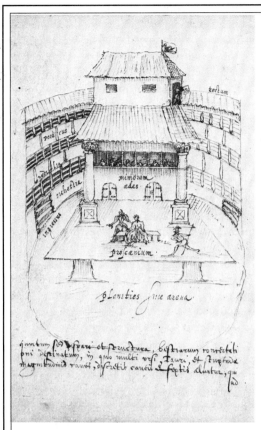

SOURCES OF THEATER HISTORY. These illustrations are often used as a basis for conjectural reconstructions of the Elizabethan public playhouse. All three also illustrate problems faced by theater historians. The drawing (upper left) of the Swan Theater is a copy of a sketch made by a Dutch visitor in 1596. Though it shows the platform stage, tiring house, yard, and galleries, it is controversial. Is the sketch complete? If so, where is the "reveal" space? Who are the people in the gallery? Is this a rehearsal or a performance? The illustration (lower left) from William Alabaster's *Roxana* (1630) seems to show a performance in the late Renaissance. The curtained space could be an "inner below" for "reveal" scenes. But again, who are the people in the gallery above the stage? Also, is this a public playhouse or a converted court hall? The third drawing (upper right) is from Francis Kirkman's *The Wits; or Sport upon Sport* (1672). It was drawn after the English Renaissance and is therefore questionable. Does it show a real playhouse, an imaginary one, or perhaps one from the commonwealth period or the early Restoration? Given such questions, it is understandable that there is no definitive reconstruction of the English public theater.

surrounds most of them. A principal visual source, for example, is a copy of a drawing of one of the London theaters, the Swan; the original was made in 1596 by a visiting Dutchman, Johannes de Witt. Because what we have is not the original, and because even the original was done by someone not completely familiar with English stage practices, there are questions about the validity and accuracy of this source. There are also questions about how it should be interpreted. For example, historians debate what is depicted as going on in the playhouse. If you believe that a performance is shown, you will draw conclusions quite different from those you will draw if you think that what is shown is a rehearsal. Another unanswered question is: Are the people shown in the second level of the tiring house—that is, the stage house—spectators or actors?

In addition to de Witt's drawing, two other important documents also survive: contracts for the construction of two theaters, the Fortune in 1600 and the Hope in 1613. These give dimensions and some additional facts about the theaters; yet they too can be frustrating. The Fortune contract, for example, takes for granted a familiarity with other Elizabethan playhouses; often, it calls for some feature of the Globe Theater of 1599 to be copied. Unfortunately, we do not know exactly what the Globe looked like. And the Hope Theater is not a representative example; since it doubled as an arena for bear-baiting—a popular recreation of the time—its platform stage and tiring house could be removed to clear the space.

Legal documents concerning the Red Lion Theater—which was possibly the first public playhouse—have also been discovered; and in addition there have been some recent excavations of the Rose and the Globe. But these new sources have led to theories about the Elizabethan playhouse which are in conflict with generally accepted ideas. Finally, there are some drawings relating to indoor theaters converted from cockpits; but there is debate over their authorship.

It is clear, then, why so much disagreement exists over the physical appearance of the Elizabethan playhouses. What these sources might tell us, however, is that historians (including the authors of this textbook) too often try to create a homogeneous point of view; in reality, history is not that easily homogenized. In this case, what is most likely is that there was no "standard" Elizabethan playhouse; rather, many different versions of theater spaces existed.

A similar situation is found with Elizabethan scenery. Debate over how much scenery was used and how complex it was often revolves around interpretations of Philip Henslowe's diary. Henslowe—along with his son-in-law, the actor Edward Alleyn—managed a theater company called the Lord Admiral's Men; and his diary contains lists of scenic pieces and props. Many of them, however, are not fully or clearly described.

Given the paucity of primary sources and their frequent lack of clarity, it is no wonder that so much debate rages over Elizabethan staging practices. This should be kept in mind as we turn our attention to Elizabethan theaters, scenery, and costumes.

EXCAVATION OF THE GLOBE. Two of the most exciting discoveries for theater historians were excavations of the foundations of the Rose and the Globe in 1989, which led to significant reassessments of how public playhouses looked. Shown here are archeologists working at the site of the Globe.

As we have seen, Elizabethan drama was distinctly different in structure from Italian Renaissance drama; and Elizabethan playhouses and staging practices also developed differently from those in Italy: in English theaters, the proscenium arch and painted-perspective scenery had not been introduced. There were two types of theaters available to Elizabethan audiences: public and private.

Public Theaters

Public theaters were the primary playing spaces for professional adult companies until 1610. Between the 1560s and 1642, at least nine open-air public theaters were built outside of London. There is disagreement among historians over which was the first public theater to be built during the English Renaissance. Recent discoveries suggest that the Red Lion was first, sometime in the late 1560s; but earlier research suggested that a theater constructed in 1576 by James Burbage—the brother-in-law of the man who built the Red Lion and the father of Richard Burbage, the great actor of Shakespeare's plays—was the first public theater. There is no question, however, that the most famous public theater was the Globe, constructed in 1599 by Richard and Cuthbart Burbage, James's sons, for the Lord Chamberlain's Men.

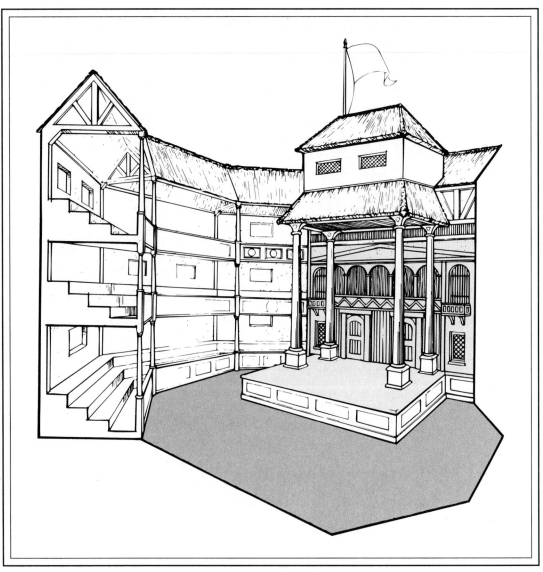

AN ELIZABETHAN PLAYHOUSE. This drawing shows the kind of stage on which the plays of Shakespeare and his contemporaries may have been presented. A platform stage juts out into an open courtyard, with spectators standing on three sides. Three levels of enclosed seats rise above the courtyard. There are doors at the rear of the stage for entrances and exits, and there is an upper level for balcony scenes.

Estimates of the audience capacity of Elizabethan public theaters range from 1,500 to 3,000; the larger number, however, is more widely accepted. The shape of these buildings varied: some buildings are said to have been circular and others octagonal; and at least one, the Fortune, was square. In 1989, when the foundations of the Rose Theater, on the south bank of the Thames, were found, an unusual discovery was made: the excavations revealed that this public theater had thirteen or fourteen sides. The excavation of part of the Globe's foundation indicates that Shakespeare's playhouse had twenty sides.

AUDIENCE SEATING IN PUBLIC THEATERS

Audiences at public theaters were accommodated in the pit, boxes, and galleries. Usually, there were three tiers of seating around the sides of the theater. Part of one tier—most likely the bottom one—was divided into boxes, which were known as *lords' rooms* because they were frequented by wealthy people. According to the Puritans—who, however, were opposed to theater and are therefore not entirely reliable—prostitutes sometimes rented the lords' rooms, giving public theaters a bad reputation. The other tiers, or galleries, were undivided and had bench seating. On the house floor, in front of and on the sides of the stage, was a standing area known as the *yard;* the lower-class spectators who stood there were known as *groundlings.* All strata of society, then, attended productions at the public theaters.

THE STAGE IN PUBLIC THEATERS

The stage in an Elizabethan public theater was a raised platform surrounded on three sides by the audience; thus it was closer to a contemporary thrust stage than to a proscenium arch. (Some historians have theorized that the public theaters were arena spaces, with a gallery divided into additional lords' rooms encircling the back of the stage; but most scholars would not agree with this.) Spectators were never very far away from the stage; however, there is a great deal of debate over how far into the yard the platform stage extended. While documents dealing with the Fortune theater suggest that its stage extended 27½ feet—or halfway—into the yard (see the drawing on page 190), analysis of the excavations of the Globe and the Rose suggest that stages did not usually extend this far. The excavations at the Rose, for instance, show that when it was built in 1587 its stage was only 16 feet 5 inches deep by 39 feet 9 inches wide at the rear and 36 feet 10 inches wide downstage; and when it was altered 5 years later, the stage (though somewhat more rectangular) was still only 17 feet deep.

There were trapdoors leading below the platform; the gravediggers' scene in *Hamlet,* for instance, was staged with a trap in the Globe Theater.

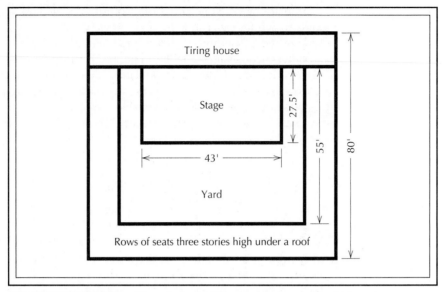

THE FORTUNE THEATER. The only English Renaissance theater for which we have a number of specific dimensions is the Fortune; from the builder's contract we know the size of the building itself and of the stage, standing pit, and audience seating area. As this ground plan shows, the building was square, the backstage area ran along one side, the stage was rectangular, and the audience—both standing and sitting—was on three sides of the stage.

THE TIRING HOUSE

Behind the raised platform was a stage house, known as a *tiring house,* which functioned much like a Greek skene. The tiring house was probably a three-story building that served as a place for changing costumes as well as storing properties and set pieces. Its facade was the basic scenic element in the Elizabethan public theaters. Exits into the tiring house and entrances from it indicated scene changes.

There is a great deal of controversy regarding the exterior appearance of the tiring house. To begin with, some historians debate whether the tiring house was built into the back wall of the playhouse or set up as a separate unit on the stage, extending out from the rear wall. The excavation at the Rose suggests that the stage went right up to the rear wall. This back wall was made up of three sides of the polygonal playhouse and served as the facade of the tiring house, which would have been angled—not flat as shown in de Witt's drawing of the Swan Theater.

The first level of the tiring house had doorways, but the number is debated; that there were at least two—one on each side—is shown by the drawing of the

Swan. Many historians have maintained, though there is little pictorial evidence, that Elizabethan drama requires a "discovery space" or "reveal space" on the first level; this space, it is argued, is necessitated by the spectacular Elizabethan "reveal" scenes (in such a scene, for instance, a body might be revealed to the audience). The most famous example of a "reveal" scene occurs in Shakespeare's *Hamlet*. Polonius hides behind a curtain in Queen Gertrude's bedroom to eavesdrop on her conversation with Hamlet. Believing the figure behind the curtain to be Claudius, Hamlet stabs it through the curtain. When the curtain is drawn, Polonius's body is revealed to the audience. Where did the actor playing Polonius hide?

Three major theories have been formulated. The least complicated, and the one which has gained the most acceptance in recent times, suggests that Polonius stood behind one of the doors. The problem with this theory is that a highly climactic scene would have been invisible to many of the spectators. A second theory is that there was a curtained area between the two doors leading into the tiring house; this "inner" area would serve as a hiding space. The third theory is that an "inner" space would require a climactic scene to be staged upstage from the audience and that this would have been highly unpopular, since Elizabethans expected intimate contact with the dramatic action. Instead, it is theorized, a pavilion-like structure, extending out from the tiring house, was erected between the two doors; this pavilion had a curtained lower level for staging "reveals." A variation of this third theory is that there were also stairs leading up to the lower level of the pavilion.

An upper playing area—that is, a sort of second-story platform at the back of the stage—is also required in many Elizabethan dramas. This too has created controversy over the appearance of the tiring house. The best-known example of a scene requiring an upper playing area is the balcony scene in Shakespeare's *Romeo and Juliet*. Some scholars suggest that there were windows or a gallery above the doors. Historians who believe that there was an "inner below" for reveal scenes also believe that there was a similar "inner above" space between the two windows in the tiring house. Historians who think that a pavilion was used for "reveals" argue that the roof of this tentlike element would have provided an upper playing space.

The third level of the tiring house, called the *musicians' gallery*, probably (as the term implies) housed the musicians who provided accompaniment for the plays.

A roof, extending out from the tiring house, protected the stage. This roof, called the *heavens* or the *shadows*, was supported by pillars in some theaters and was suspended from the back in others. The underside of the roof was often painted to represent the heavens literally (in fact, some scholars believe that much of the interior of public playhouses was painted in highly decorative ways). A flag was flown from the top of the tiring house to advertise that a performance was taking place.

Debates in Theater History:
THE CAMPAIGN TO SAVE THE ROSE

In January 1989, at an excavation site for a new high-rise office building in London, archeologists from the Museum of London made a key discovery: the foundation of the Rose Theater, one of the two most significant playhouses of the Elizabethan era (the other, of course, was the Globe). Analysis of the Rose's foundation has led historians to reevaluate much of what they once believed about the Rose. Earlier ideas had been based on all the sources then available, but those sources were insubstantial; the new discovery generated fresh scholarly debate over what the Elizabethan playhouse really looked like.

For example, the excavation suggests that the Rose was a thirteen- or fourteen-sided building, smaller than had previously been thought, and that its stage extended much less than halfway into the yard, even after the theater was enlarged in 1592. In addition, the archeologists suggest that the first Rose, built in 1587, did not have a "heavens" over the stage, but that the remodeled Rose included a "heavens" which extended to the front edge of the stage. The archeologists also argue that the Rose's tiring house was not a separate unit like the one shown in de Witt's drawing of the Swan Theater but was built into the theater structure.

However, an even greater controversy arose over the excavation itself—a public debate over whether the site should be preserved or the new high-rise should be allowed to be built over it. Some people argued that the discovery was, historically, priceless and that covering the Rose over would be a desecration of a national treasure. The developers argued that forbidding construction would impede the modernization of London and that throughout English history each civilization had built on top of its predecessors. Christine Eccles, who chronicles the debate in *The Rose Theatre,* even suggests that

"Philip Henslowe would have been taken considerably aback if told he could not have planning permission for the Rose Theatre because it might disturb some Roman revetments beneath."*

This debate was reminiscent of one that arose in New York City in the 1980s, when developers tore down two famous Broadway Theaters—the Helen Hayes and the Morosco—that had been the home of many historic productions. These developers argued that their project, a new hotel and theater complex, was needed to revitalize the deteriorating Broadway district. People who wanted to save the theaters—including the founding director of the Public Theater, Joseph Papp; and the American actress Colleen Dewhurst—argued that these theaters were cultural landmarks. Papp and Dewhurst actually chained themselves to buildings at the demolition site and were arrested.

For a few months, the Rose site in London was given a reprieve so that the archeologists could study it. However, many people continued to maintain that the excavation should be preserved permanently. The Campaign to Save the Rose, as the preservationist movement was called, was supported by many noted performers, including Peggy Ashcroft, Ian McKellan, and Timothy Dalton. The developers, after proposing a revised version of their high-rise which they claimed would not damage the foundation of the Rose and would preserve it for future excavations, were victorious in court. The excavation was covered over with sand and concrete and the new office building, called Rose Court, was constructed over it. Ironically, the same debate immediately reappeared when a smaller section of Shakespeare's playhouse, the Globe, was unearthed in October of 1989.

*New York, Routledge, 1990, p. 150.

When we consider what influences shaped these outdoor public theaters, we again see how numerous elements came together in the English Renaissance. As noted earlier, the neutral platform stage came from medieval theater; but the influence of the Roman theater building can also be seen in the facade of the tiring house. Another influence is a tradition of earlier sixteenth-century English performers, who used a platform stage with a scenic structure erected as a background at one end of an inn yard. These early, temporary public theaters had standing room in the open courtyard and galleries in the walls of the surrounding building. Still another influence may have been the bear-baiting arenas. Bear-baiting was a popular English entertainment in which chained bears were attacked by trained dogs; a temporary stage and tiring house could turn a bear-baiting arena into a public theater.

Private Theaters

Elizabethan private theaters were indoor spaces, lit by candles and high windows. The term *private* in this context often causes confusion, because it seems to imply that certain classes of people would have been excluded. In England at this time, however, private theaters were open to the general populace, though they were more expensive to attend than the outdoor public theaters. (In any case, the terms *private* and *public* came into use only about 1600.)

From the opening of the first private theater, Blackfriars, in 1576 until about 1608, private theaters were used exclusively by the popular boys' companies. A second Blackfriars theater was built by James Burbage in 1596 for his adult company; but complaints by wealthy neighbors, who were worried about what kind of people the playhouse would attract, prevented him from moving that company into it. He, and later his sons, leased the space to boys' companies until 1608, when Richard Burbage's King's Men began to use it regularly. From then on, private theaters were used for most of the year by London's adult companies and became more popular.

Historians believe that the indoor theaters were similar to the outdoor public theaters, but there were some differences. Private theaters were usually smaller than public theaters, seating only about 600 to 750 spectators; it is for this reason that they were more expensive than the public theaters. The cheapest entrance fee at a private playhouse was sixpence; admission to the yard of a public theater cost only a penny. The pit of a private theater faced the stage in only one direction and had backless benches. The platform stage extended to the side walls. Galleries and boxes faced the stage on three sides. During the reigns of James I (1603–1625) and Charles I (1625–1642), known respectively as the *Jacobean* period and the *Caroline* period, wealthy audience members could sit on the stage itself. (A few historians believe that stools may also have been set up on the stage of outdoor public theaters, but most surviving accounts of theatergoing suggest that stage seats were available only in indoor theaters.)

The price structure in Elizabethan private theaters also differed from that in public theaters. The benches and boxes closest to the stage were most expensive; those in the upper back wall, farther away from the stage, were cheapest. This pricing system is closer to the way theatergoers are charged for seats today.

There are, again, many recent controversies regarding the configuration of Elizabethan private spaces. These controversies were set off by the discovery of drawings of two converted cockpits, one at Drury Lane and the other at court. *Cockpits* (as the term implies) were arenas for cockfighting—like bear-baiting, a popular entertainment. The drawings were supposedly made by the renowned English designer Inigo Jones (who is discussed later in this chapter), and they seem to indicate that the stage in a private theater did not extend very far into the pit area. They also suggest that the tiring house—at least in the cockpit at court—looked like the scaena of the Teatro Olimpico, with one large central doorway, smaller doors on each side, and one central window-like opening above the larger entrance.

Scenery and Costumes

Scenery in Elizabethan theaters was quite distinct from that in theaters of the Italian Renaissance. The Elizabethans did not use painted-perspective scenery in public or private theaters, and the Elizabethan stage space did not represent a specific locale. The episodic nature of English drama required an ability to suggest rapid scene changes. This was accomplished in various ways. "Spoken decor" was used: characters in the plays would describe the settings, indicating that they were in, for instance, a castle, a forest, or a bedroom. (This is a practical reason for the lengthy poetic descriptions of locales in Shakespeare's dramas.) The departure of all onstage characters and the entrance of a new group would also signal a scene change; and actors would sometimes bring out minimal properties to suggest a locale—for example, a throne could indicate the interior of a palace. The facade of the tiring house provided a constant scenic background.

The most striking element of an Elizabethan production was probably the costuming. Costuming followed the conventions and traditions of medieval English theater. While Elizabethan dramas exhibit a great deal of historical and geographical variety, the Elizabethans were not overly concerned with accuracy; most costuming was in contemporary English fashion. Even though *Hamlet* takes place in medieval Denmark, for example, actors in the original production would have worn Elizabethan clothing. However, certain traditional costumes were worn to indicate antiquity, folk heroes, supernatural creatures, and racial groups. Some historians believe, for instance, that ancient Greek and Roman characters wore a toga over Elizabethan clothing. Acting companies owned large stocks of costumes, either purchased or sometimes provided by their patrons.

ELIZABETHAN ACTING COMPANIES

Throughout the English Renaissance, the monarchy increasingly tightened its legal control over the theater. By a decree of Queen Elizabeth in 1574, all plays and companies had to be licensed by the Master of Revels, a royal official. The number of acting companies was restricted by law, and according to a 1572 ordinance, all troupes had to be sponsored by a nobleman whose rank was no lower than baron. (Later, under James I, only members of the royal family were allowed to sponsor companies.)

An acting company needed a patron not only in order to receive permission to perform but also for financial backing, legal protection, and other types of support. In return for performing for their patrons, the companies received small financial subsidies and occasional allowances for costumes (and sometimes clothing from their patrons' wardrobes). The companies were named after their patrons: for instance, the company of which Shakespeare was a member was known as the Lord Chamberlain's Men.

The Lord Chamberlain's Men (ca. 1594–1642)

The Lord Admiral's Men (1594–1621)

"Hee adds grace to the Poet's labours: . . . He entertains us in the best leasure of our life," wrote one Elizabethan in praise of the actor. Elizabethan dramatists were matched by excellent actors and acting companies. The company that was most famous—for both its actors and its dramatist—was the Lord Chamberlain's Men; Shakespeare acted in this company and wrote most of his plays for it.

The Lord Chamberlain's Men was founded in 1594. The theaters had been closed for a full season because of a plague; when they reopened, several actors who had been with other companies formed this new troupe under the protection of Henry Carey, Lord Hunsdon, the lord chamberlain. The group included Richard and Cuthbert Burbage, the clown Will Kempe, and William Shakespeare. At first the new troupe played at the Rose, but it soon moved to a playhouse called The Theater, owned by the Burbages' father. It also performed at court and for special groups, like the lawyers of Grey's Inn.

When the government again closed the London theaters in 1597—this time because of an offensive satire—it is likely that the Lord Chamberlain's Men toured the provinces until the theaters reopened. When on tour, the company had to secure a license in each town, and this placed the troupe at the mercy of local magistrates. In spite of such problems, the group probably toured towns outside of London for part of each season.

In 1599, when the lease on the land for The Theater expired, some members of the company built the Globe Theater as a permanent home. The ensemble had by then become the best in London; its repertory included plays by Shakespeare, Jonson, Thomas Dekker (ca. 1572–1632), Beaumont and Fletcher, and Cyril Tourneur (1575–1626).

In 1603, the troupe was taken under the protection of the new king, James I, and became the King's Men. Kempe left the company to perform on the continent (at this time, many English actors and companies toured in Germany, the Netherlands, and Sweden); he was replaced by Robert Armin, another noted clown. Though the Blackfriars Theater became its winter home in 1608, the company still played at the Globe during the summer. Although the Globe burned in 1613, it was rebuilt and was used by the company until 1642, when the theaters were closed by the Puritans and the group disbanded.

The only real rival of the Lord Chamberlain's Men was the Lord Admiral's Men, managed by Philip Henslowe and Edward Alleyn. The Lord Admiral's Men played at the Rose from 1594 to 1600 and at the Fortune from 1600 to 1621. Alleyn, their leading tragic actor, was considered nearly as fine a performer as Richard Burbage. Henslowe's detailed business diaries provide one of the most significant sources on Elizabethan theater.

Organization of Acting Companies

Elizabethan acting companies—each of which had no more than about twenty-five members—were organized on a sharing plan. Under this system, there were three categories of personnel in a company: *shareholders, hired men* or *hirelings,* and *apprentices.* Shareholders, the elite members of the company, bought a percentage ownership of the troupe and received a corresponding percentage of its profits as payment for their services. Their fortunes, therefore, would fluctuate with those of the company. Hirelings were actors contracted for a specific period of time and for a specific salary; they usually played minor roles. Apprentices—young performers training for the profession—were assigned to shareholders. Apprentices received room, board, training, and experience, and had hopes of eventually becoming shareholders. (Female roles were performed by boys—a fact which suggests that apprentices in a company may have been more significant than its hired men.) Since the King's Men owned the theater in which they performed, star members were given part-ownership in the theater as an inducement to remain with the company; these actors were known as *householders,* a term which was also used for people who owned theater buildings and rented them to acting companies. (Most acting companies leased their playhouses from such landlords.)

Since acting companies needed many plays, they paid playwrights for each new work. Sometimes a writer was under contract to a company, and some authors also received all the profits of the second performance of a play. However, plays did not have long runs; a play was usually performed once and then added to the repertoire, to be revived later in the season.

Debates in Theater History:
ELIZABETHAN ACTING STYLE

The debate over Elizabethan acting style illustrates how difficult it is to discuss the ephemeral art of performance. As we have noted, scholars who argue that the acting style of the English Renaissance was realistic point to Hamlet's "advice to the players"—his coaching of the actors who are to perform the play-within-a-play. In this famous passage, Shakespeare seems to call for a natural performance style. However, there are many other references to acting in Shakespeare's plays, and many of these seem to indicate a highly conventional style. For example, in *A Midsummer Night's Dream,* a comic group of Athenian commoners, led by Peter Quince and Bottom the weaver, attempt to stage a play; and Shakespeare uses them to poke fun at the bombastic style of the leading actor, the convention of doubling of roles, the lack of scenic reality, and the need for a prompter.

There are other inconsistencies as well. Most contemporary accounts of Richard Burbage's acting, for example, praise his natural approach; how are we to reconcile this with the highly theatrical qualities that are thought to have been a part of Elizabethan performances?

Possibly, we need to realize that in any period of theater history, audiences will perceive the acting of their contemporaries as "natural," because it is rooted in—and reflects—the concerns of their own society. Earlier audiences accepted many theatrical conventions. Therefore, Shakespeare's audiences could willingly believe in men playing women, actors playing more than one role, and characters conversing in verse: they readily accepted these and other highly theatrical conventions. J. L. Styan argues persuasively that in Shakespeare's theater there was considerable intimacy between actors and audiences, and that the spectators were always aware of being in a playhouse and watching performers.* Because of this, they were able to see the honesty of performances and to view these performances as natural.

When we take all this into consideration, it is interesting to wonder whether the realistic acting we praise today will be considered "natural" by future scholars and students.

*"In Search of the Real Shakespeare; or, Shakespeare's Shows and Shadows," in *New Issues in the Reconstruction of Shakespeare's Theatre*, Lang, New York, 1990, pp. 185–206.

Acting Practices

The style of acting in Elizabethan theaters continues to be debated. Some historians point to Hamlet's famous "advice to the players" as evidence of realistic acting. (For example, Hamlet says to the actors, "Nor saw the air too much with your hand, thus, but use all gently.") Others suggest that the speech indicates a lack of realism in Elizabethan acting and that Shakespeare, speaking through Hamlet, is protesting its absence.

Most Elizabethan acting conventions seem to be evidence *against* realism. For one thing, there were no actresses; young boys performed the female roles. (Today, it may be difficult for us even to imagine that the sensuous Cleopatra and the romantic Juliet were first performed by males.) Second, since the plays required huge casts, doubling or tripling of roles was not uncommon. Third, to some extent type-casting was necessary, particularly for comic roles. Fourth, the rigorous performance schedule also seems to argue against performances that could resemble behavior encountered in daily life. An acting company

RICHARD BURBAGE. Burbage—one of the Lord Chamberlain's Men and probably the most famous Elizabethan performer— played the lead in many of Shakespeare's plays.

would rarely produce the same play on two consecutive days, and the company had to be able to revive any play in its repertoire on very short notice. Thus, the primary concern would be, not a carefully realized production, but simply the delivery of lines; some actors seem to have learned their lines roughly and poorly. Actors were provided with *sides,* which contained their own lines and cues rather than the full script. *Plots,* outlines of the dramatic action of the various plays, were posted backstage so that performers could refresh their memory during a performance. Fifth, rehearsals were run by playwrights or leading actors, and rehearsal time was minimal; the prompter, or bookholder, therefore became an integral figure during presentations. For all these reasons, gestures, movements, and speech were probably stylized. Also, improvisation must have been employed frequently. (Hamlet's speech to the players suggests that comic actors, at least, often deviated from the script.)

Today, Elizabethan plays are sometimes considered too long to be produced unedited, and an uncut production can last as long as 4 hours. But performances during the English Renaissance lasted only 2 to 3 hours; a play would usually begin at 2 in the afternoon and would be presented with no intermissions (though in a public playhouse it was sometimes followed by a jig). We assume that the playing time was shorter not only because there were no intermissions but also because the performers spoke more quickly; and this too may be evidence against a realistic acting style.

Richard Burbage (ca. 1567–1619), the leading actor in the Lord Chamberlain's Men, was probably the most famous Elizabethan performer. He first came into prominence in the role of Richard III, and he played the lead in many of Shakespeare's plays, including *Hamlet, King Lear,* and *Othello.* Shakespeare, as we have said, was also an actor with the company. Edward Alleyn

(1566–1626) was Burbage's counterpart in the Lord Admiral's Men. Will Kempe (?–1603), also of the Lord Chamberlain's Men, was a leading comic actor. Shakespeare's attack on comic improvisation, found in Hamlet's "advice to the players," was probably directed at Kempe.

Female Roles in Elizabethan Theater

Historians continue to debate why women were not part of the Elizabethan acting companies. At about the same time, as we saw in Chapter 5, women were significant members of Italian commedia dell'arte troupes. Most historians believe that the absence of female performers was a continuation of a medieval English tradition and also a result of the religious attitude toward actresses: it was contended that actresses were no better than whores.

The fact that women were not members of the Elizabethan companies has led to interesting discussions about representation of female characters. Cross-dressing (dressing as the opposite sex)—which in today's drama is a popular way to point out sexual stereotyping—had many reverberations in Shakespeare's plays. For example, Rosalind, in the comedy *As You Like It*, dresses as a man to escape from her evil uncle. In modern theater, this requires an actress to dress as a male; in Shakespeare's time, it meant that a male actor would be playing a female character impersonating a male.

Feminist critics have considered the implications of this complex sexual impersonation, arguing that representation of females by males would have reinforced stereotypes of women found in many Elizabethan plays, such as Shakespeare's *Taming of the Shrew*. We should note that cross-dressing in Elizabethan drama usually did dramatize negative ideas about women; for example, the nurse in *Romeo and Juliet* would have been played by an older man who would have poked fun at her "masculine" qualities.

Some contemporary directors have used this complex subject to shed light on current feminist issues. Tracy C. Davis, in her essay "A Feminist Methodology in Theater History," summarizes questions about the absence of women from the Elizabethan stage and about the performance by women in today's modern theater of female characters who were meant to be played by men:

> Therefore, feminist historians may wonder: when women were excluded from the public forum of the stage and males played female roles, was this necessarily an act of obliteration of women, usurpation of womanhood, misogyny, silencing or ridiculing? Were women's gestures, words, and gowns taken over by men to ridicule what the gowns, words, gestures, and women stood for? . . . What could it mean when women were subsequently permitted on the stage and performed the same texts that were written for males to play? . . . When do the words, gowns, gestures, and gender become those of the women characters and performers? Do they always remain male, even when spoken by women?[1]

These same questions would also be relevant for classical Greek and medieval English drama and theater.

[1]In *Interpreting the Theatrical Past,* Thomas Postlewait and Bruce A. McConachie (eds.), University of Iowa Press, Iowa City, 1989, p. 74.

Jonson: Neoclassical Comedy

Elizabeth I died in 1603 and was succeeded by James I, whose reign—from 1603 to 1625—is called the *Jacobean* period. Some important Elizabethan dramatists were still active in the Jacobean period; one was Ben Jonson.

Jonson's comic masterpiece *Volpone*, for example, was staged in 1606. In this comedy, the schemer Volpone dupes old men out of their riches by pretending that he himself is old and dying. Volpone's servant, Mosca, promises each of these victims that when Volpone dies, the victim will inherit his fortune. Volpone's desire for the wife of one of the old men and Mosca's greed eventually lead to their undoing.

(National Portrait Gallery, London)

Ben Jonson

(1572–1637)

As a playwright, literary critic, and poet, Ben Jonson was one of the first writers in England to champion the neoclassical principles, and in his own work he wanted to prove that one could please the public by following these rules. Known for his sharp wit and imperious manner, he became an arbiter of literary taste, presiding over a group of younger poets who met regularly at the Mermaid Tavern in London.

In such plays as *Every Man in His Humour* (1598), *The Alchemist* (1610), and particularly *Volpone* (1606), Jonson developed a "comedy of humours" in which the principal characters had an excess of one trait, or "humour." Unlike many of his contemporaries, who did not think of drama as literature, he considered his plays to be important works, and he personally supervised their printing in 1616. He was also unlike other English writers of his time in championing neoclassical structure for drama, though his own plays did not always adhere strictly to the neoclassical rules. His other writings include volumes of poetry, an English grammar, and—despite his preference for neoclassical form—a laudatory introduction to the collected plays of his friend William Shakespeare.

Jonson acquired his learning and social stature through his own efforts. Raised in a poor section of London, he was a scholarship student at the Westminster School; and though he wanted to attend college, his stepfather, a bricklayer, apprenticed him to another bricklayer. To escape that trade he joined the army and served in the Netherlands, where he killed a man in single combat. He married after his return to London in 1582, but he and his wife were incompatible and lived apart after 1603.

In the 1580s, Jonson continued his studies on his own and worked as a strolling player; at this time he also began writing for Henslowe's theater. In collaboration with Thomas Nashe, he wrote *The Isle of Dogs,* a satire which proved so offensive that the authorities imprisoned everyone involved with the production, including Jonson, and closed all the London theaters. Jonson was imprisoned again the next year, this time for killing an actor in a duel.

When he was released, he became involved in the "war of the theaters," using his satiric comedies to ridicule his rivals. He had made many friends among the nobility, and when James I inherited the throne in 1603, Jonson became prominent at court. His collaboration on the satire *Eastward Ho!* landed him in prison again, but later he was restored to royal favor and became the court poet.

From 1605 to 1625, he composed court masques, expanding the form to include an "anti-masque," a burlesque of the main theme. He often quarreled with the designer Inigo Jones over the use of spectacular settings; Jonson felt that such settings detracted from his poetic allegories. Eventually Jonson retired, though he wrote several plays for public theaters before his death in 1637.

Webster: Later Tragedy

During the Jacobean period and then in the reign of Charles I from 1625 to 1649—the *Caroline* period—drama in England began to change. Plays became increasingly sensational, violent, contrived, cynical, and melodramatic. One example is *The Duchess of Malfi* by John Webster, probably the most renowned tragedy of the Jacobean era.

John Webster

(ca. 1580–1630)

In his preface to his play *The White Devil,* John Webster shows a thorough knowledge of Latin and a thorough understanding of drama. He also reviles most playgoers as "ignorant asses," makes frequent use of Latin proverbs and quotations, relates an anecdote about Euripides, and praises his fellow playwrights.

But aside from the fact that he was a man of wit and learning, little is known about John Webster's life. An actor of that name toured with an English company in Germany in 1596, and a man named John Webster was admitted to the Middle Temple to study law in 1598; it is possible that one of these was the playwright, or that both were.

THE DUCHESS OF MALFI. The most important writer of the Jacobean period was John Webster. His drama *The Duchess of Malfi* is a passionate study of love, incest, and political intrigue in the Renaissance which contains violence, horror, grotesque comedy, and lyrical poetry. In this scene, from a production at the Guthrie Theater in Minneapolis, the duchess is threatened by the villainous Bosola, her evil brothers' henchman.

Webster's early plays, written in collaboration with Thomas Dekker, included two popular comedies, *Westward Ho!* (1604) and *Northward Ho!* (1605). *The White Devil* (1612) and *The Duchess of Malfi* (1613–1614), two tragedies, are considered his masterpieces. Webster also wrote a tragicomedy, *The Devil's Law Case* (1623), and collaborated with several playwrights on other works. The playwright Thomas Heywood refers to Webster in the past tense in 1634, so it is assumed that he was dead by then.

Though his life is shrouded in uncertainty, and though his dramatic output was small in comparison with that of other Jacobean playwrights, Webster is considered a major playwright because of his two tragedies, which are regarded, after Shakespeare's, as the finest tragedies of the time. Both plays are passionate studies of love and political intrigue in Renaissance Italy. They contain violence and horror, grotesque comedy and satire, and lyrical poetry. Throughout these plays there is a brooding, ominous sense of pervasive evil and corruption. It is partly because of their spectacular elements and melodrama that Webster's plays are ranked below Shakespeare's.

The Duchess of Malfi is a terrifying study of the extent and destructiveness of human evil. After the death of her first husband, the duchess of Malfi is forbidden to remarry by her scheming brothers—Duke Ferdinand and the cardinal—who want to acquire her duchy. She defies them by secretly marrying her steward, Antonio, but is betrayed to them by the servant Bosola. The evil brothers bide their time and then torment, torture, and finally murder the duchess and her children. Bosola, the main agent of these deeds, repents and warns Antonio that his life is in danger. In an attempt to murder the cardinal, Bosola mistakenly kills Antonio. Bosola then attacks the cardinal, and the fight is joined by the duke, who by this point has been driven to insanity. In the struggle all three die.

Webster's pessimism, similar to the mood of some present-day dramas—such as "black comedies"—is one reason why his tragedies are often revived.

Beaumont and Fletcher: Tragicomedy

A significant development in English drama during the early 1600s was the mixing of serious and comic elements. Plays reflecting this development generally had many qualities of tragedy, but with a happy ending. Francis Beaumont and John Fletcher, two playwrights who often collaborated with each other, excelled at this form. (Coauthorship was not unusual in the English Renaissance. Since playwrights were paid by the script, they needed to produce dramas quickly; coauthorship could speed up the process. Some of Shakespeare's lesser-known plays, such as *Pericles* and *Two Noble Kinsmen,* are believed to have been written by Shakespeare and other playwrights.)

Francis Beaumont (ca. 1584–1616)

John Fletcher (1579–1625)

During the English Renaissance, there were many well-known teams of writers; the most famous of these collaborators were Francis Beaumont and John Fletcher. At one time, fifty-two plays were attributed to Beaumont and Fletcher jointly, although later scholarship has shown that they actually collaborated on no more than nine plays. The other plays were written by one or the other individually or with another playwright, but these plays are so similar in style and subject that the names of Beaumont and Fletcher are still linked to them.

In plays like *Philaster* (ca. 1610) and *A King and No King* (ca. 1611), Beaumont and Fletcher accelerated the development of tragicomedy—a genre that focused on serious themes but called for a happy ending. Jacobean theater audiences were becoming increasingly aristocratic and demanded romance and witty satire. The two men wrote plays in an ornate, superficial, and somewhat artificial style that had become popular and was later to be influential, especially during the Restoration.

Francis Beaumont (left) and John Fletcher (right).

Beaumont and Fletcher came from similar upper-class backgrounds. Beaumont's father was a justice of common pleas; Fletcher's father was president of a college at Cambridge and later bishop of Bristol and of London. Both playwrights attended college, though neither completed his degree. Beaumont also entered the Inner Temple in 1600 to study law. The names of the two men are first linked in 1607, in the introductory remarks to Jonson's *Volpone*. During their partnership, they are said to have roomed together in Bankside, where they shared everything, including clothes and women.

Beaumont's marriage in 1613 ended the partnership. His most famous solo play is *The Knight of the Burning Pestle,* a comedy and literary burlesque. He died in 1616. Fletcher, after the partnership broke up, collaborated with several other playwrights, chiefly Philip Massinger. Shakespeare and Fletcher worked together on *Two Noble Kinsmen* (1613) and *Henry VIII* (1613). When Shakespeare retired, Fletcher became the chief dramatist for the King's Men until his death in 1625.

Court Entertainment: The Masque

A form of drama not found in either public or private theaters was the *masque,* an elaborate entertainment presented at court. The masque flourished in the early seventeenth century during the reign of James I. Masques were elaborate, professionally staged mythological allegories intended to praise the monarch. They were embellished by music and dance; and they frequently used amateur performers from the court.

Ben Jonson was the major playwright of this form, but he stopped writing masques in 1631 because he believed that his literary contribution was being overshadowed by the elaborate scenic trappings. Many other dramatists continued to provide scripts for masques; but in this form the most important creative artist—as Jonson had correctly pointed out—was the designer. The most famous designer was Inigo Jones.

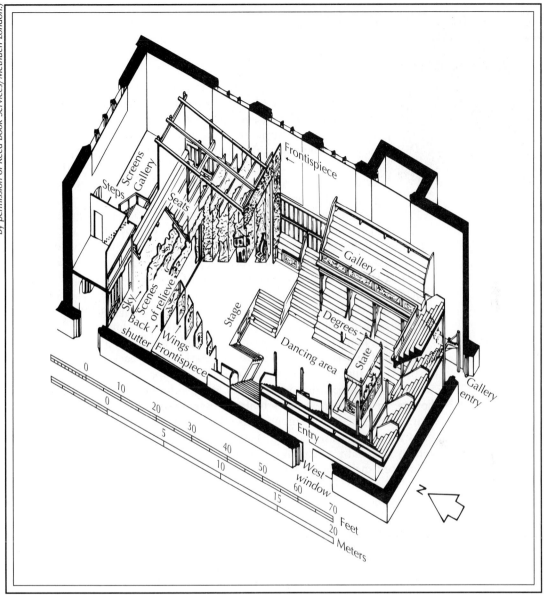

Steps

Screens
Gallery

Seats

Frontispiece

Gallery

Sky

Scenes
of relieve

Stage

Degrees

Back
shutter

Wings

Frontispiece

Dancing area

State

Gallery
entry

Entry

West
window

N

0
10
0
20
5
30
40
5
50
10
60
15
70 Feet
20 Meters

A DESIGN BY INIGO JONES. This conjectural reconstruction of Jones's design for the pastoral *Florimene* (1635) shows a large hall in Whitehall palace arranged for a court masque. Italianate scenic devices were introduced into these spectacles: painted angled wings and back shutters shifted in grooves were used to give an illusion of depth.

Inigo Jones

(1573–1652)

In the Elizabethan and Jacobean periods, English theater followed scenic practices that had evolved from medieval theater. It was Inigo Jones, court architect and designer for both James I and Charles I, who brought Italian innovations in scene design to England. These included temporary proscenium (picture-frame) arches, systems for changing scenery, and painted-perspective stage sets. In his settings for court masques, Jones introduced methods of staging that were to become standard after the Restoration.

Jones's designs were influenced by the work of Giulio Parigi (ca. 1570–1635) and Palladio, which he had studied on visits to Italy. Jones was the son of a London cloth worker and therefore not wealthy, but he had traveled to Italy by 1603 to learn painting and design. He became a portrait painter for Christian IV of Denmark; a commission from Christian's sister, Queen Anne of England, brought him to the court of James I. His first stage designs were the scenery and costumes for *The Masque of Blackness* (1605), which also began his long and stormy collaboration with the court poet Ben Jonson.

By 1610, Jones had become surveyor of works to Henry, prince of Wales; but Henry died in 1612, and Jones lost his job. He went back to Italy to study in 1613–1614 and on his return to England was appointed surveyor of works to James I, a position that involved building, rebuilding, and improving royal houses. In 1619–1622 Jones built the Banqueting House at Whitehall. The Banqueting House was intended as a home for court masques, but it was not used for this purpose because James's successor, Charles I, did not want its ceiling ruined by torch smoke. Jones's restoration of Saint Paul's Cathedral influenced the architect Christopher Wren and initiated the English classical school of architecture.

Jones was vain and dictatorial, though an able administrator. His famous quarrel with Jonson resulted in Jonson's loss of favor at court; thereafter, scenic splendor became the chief purpose of the masque, culminating in the wonders of *Salmacida Spolia* in 1640. Jones delighted his court audiences with new machinery, such as revolving platforms, that he used to make seemingly magical scene changes. All the elaborately fanciful costumes for the masques were also designed by Jones.

Political troubles caused a suspension of masques after 1640, and Jones then served the king as a designer of field arms and armor during the civil war. Captured in 1645, Jones was stripped of his estate and imprisoned, but later he was released and his property was restored. He died in 1652.

Though Charles I was not deposed—and beheaded—until 1649, the English Renaissance ended in 1642, for by then the civil war between supporters of Charles I and the Puritan-backed Parliament had begun. From 1649 through 1660, England was ruled not by a monarch but by Oliver Cromwell and his Puritan followers. When Cromwell died in 1658, his son took control of the government.

The Puritans were violently opposed to theater; they believed—to put it mildly—that playgoing was an inappropriate way to spend leisure time and that the theater was a den of iniquity and taught immorality. Not surprisingly, then, in 1642 the Puritans outlawed all theatrical activities. Although surreptitious entertainments were staged between 1642 and 1660, the vital theater of the English Renaissance came to an end. Not until the restoration of the monarchy was the English theater to flourish again.

SUMMARY

The English Renaissance was as theatrically rich as the Italian Renaissance. The greatness of this era was based on the development of brilliant drama: some critics believe that the plays of Christopher Marlowe, William Shakespeare, and Ben Jonson have been unequaled in the history of theater. English drama did not follow neoclassical principles but refined the episodic structure which had originated in the Middle Ages.

The imaginative staging techniques of the English Renaissance were also a refinement of medieval conventions. The Elizabethan theater, with its open platform stage and tiring house, allowed for rapid scenic transformations through the use of language, properties, entrances, and exits. There were two types of playhouses: larger outdoor public theaters; and smaller, more expensive indoor private theaters. Many of the performers—all of whom were male—were greatly renowned; they included Edward Alleyn of the Lord Admiral's Men, and Richard Burbage of the Lord Chamberlain's Men.

English theaters open to the public did not employ Italian staging practices such as the proscenium arch or painted-perspective wing-and-shutter scenery. These scenic innovations were introduced into court entertainments— masques—designed by Inigo Jones for James I and Charles I.

CHAPTER 7

....

THE THEATER
OF THE SPANISH
GOLDEN AGE

It is four o'clock on a lovely spring afternoon in 1620. We are in Spain, attending a new full-length play by the Spanish playwright Lope de Vega at one of the two public theaters in Madrid: the Corral del Principe. We have paid two entrance fees, one to the company presenting the play and the other to a charity supporting the city's hospital. This second fee to the charity is one reason why government and church officials allow theater performances in Madrid.

Spanish public theaters are called *corrales*, after the square or rectangular courtyards around which they are created. Once inside the courtyard we find ourselves standing in the pit area—called the *patio*—of an open-air theater, with a platform stage at one end. The windows of the surrounding houses serve as the boxes for the theater. At the front of the courtyard, near the stage, are a few benches, known as *taburetes*, which allow for minimal seating in the pit area. Along the side walls are slanted, raised seats called *gradas*. At the back of

THE SHEEP WELL. The Spanish playwright Lope de Vega was one of the most prolific dramatists of all time: he wrote religious plays, history plays, and swashbuckling adventure plays. One of his best-known works, *Fuente Ovejuna—The Sheep Well*—is about a village which turns, as a whole, against an evil government official. The scene here is a from a production at the Court Theatre in Chicago. *(Lisa Ebright/Court Theatre)*

the patio, alongside the entranceway and across from the stage, is the *alojero,* an area where refreshments are sold—nuts, fruit, spiced honey, and water. On the floors above the alojero are a series of boxes and galleries, divided into sections for women, government officials, and the clergy. Above the gradas, on the sides, are windows (protected by grills), third-floor boxes, and low-ceilinged fourth-floor galleries called *desvánes.*

As we gather, there is great excitement about the performance that will soon begin. Some years ago, in 1609, Lope de Vega remarked in an essay titled "The New Art of Writing Plays in This Age" that the most important measure of success in the theater is the audience's enjoyment. He has certainly passed his own test, for he is the most popular playwright of the day. The play we are to see, *The King, The Greatest Alcalde,* promises to be filled with thrilling episodes. People in the pit are jostling for the best vantage point; people in the galleries are exchanging pleasantries, speaking to friends, and looking around the theater to see who is here this afternoon.

Now the performance begins. First, before the actual play, there is an amusing comic prologue. Then comes the play itself. It is a *comedia:* in Spain, this is the term for any full-length nonreligious play, serious or comic. *The King, The Greatest Alcalde* is serious, but it also has comic elements. It concerns a farmer who promises his daughter Elvira to a peasant, Sancho. Sancho seeks approval for the marriage from his lord, Don Tello. Don Tello agrees, but when he sees Elvira, he wants her for himself. He postpones the wedding and later kidnaps Elvira. As the play unfolds, it seems to have all the ingredients of sparkling drama: a clash between peasants and the nobility, a wronged peasant, a kidnapping, a beautiful maiden in distress. The boisterous spectators in the pit are especially vocal in responding to each twist and turn of the plot and to the mixture of comedy and suspense, but we all find ourselves caught up in the story.

As the play continues, Sancho appeals to the king to help him regain Elvira from Don Tello; after several complications, the king arrives in disguise. When the king discovers that Don Tello has forcibly seduced Elvira, he orders Don Tello to marry her and then has him executed so that Elvira will be honorably widowed and can marry Sancho. At the conclusion of the play, everyone in the audience—in the galleries as well as the pit—is pleased that justice has been done.

The actors and actresses in the theater company play fifteen speaking roles and some nonspeaking parts, and we in the audience respond enthusiastically to their performances. Though the play has thirteen scenes in different locations, all of its action takes place on the platform stage. It is easy for us to follow the action, because—through a combination of dialogue and use of properties such as a throne—the playwright and the actors let us know each time we change locations; they indicate exactly where we are in every scene. We are also entertained by short comic pieces and musical interludes performed during intermissions between the three acts of the play.

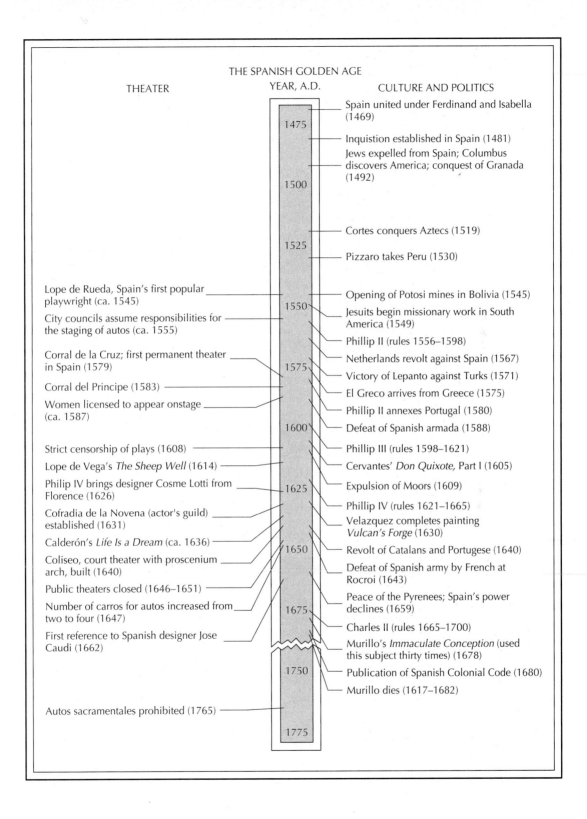

THE SPANISH GOLDEN AGE

THEATER

YEAR, A.D.

CULTURE AND POLITICS

Spain united under Ferdinand and Isabella (1469)

1475

Inquistion established in Spain (1481)

Jews expelled from Spain; Columbus discovers America; conquest of Granada (1492)

1500

Cortes conquers Aztecs (1519)

1525

Pizzaro takes Peru (1530)

Lope de Rueda, Spain's first popular playwright (ca. 1545)

Opening of Potosi mines in Bolivia (1545)

1550

City councils assume responsibilities for the staging of autos (ca. 1555)

Jesuits begin missionary work in South America (1549)

Phillip II (rules 1556–1598)

Corral de la Cruz; first permanent theater in Spain (1579)

Netherlands revolt against Spain (1567)

1575

Victory of Lepanto against Turks (1571)

Corral del Principe (1583)

El Greco arrives from Greece (1575)

Women licensed to appear onstage (ca. 1587)

Phillip II annexes Portugal (1580)

Defeat of Spanish armada (1588)

1600

Strict censorship of plays (1608)

Phillip III (rules 1598–1621)

Lope de Vega's *The Sheep Well* (1614)

Cervantes' *Don Quixote*, Part I (1605)

Philip IV brings designer Cosme Lotti from Florence (1626)

Expulsion of Moors (1609)

1625

Phillip IV (rules 1621–1665)

Cofradia de la Novena (actor's guild) established (1631)

Velazquez completes painting *Vulcan's Forge* (1630)

Calderón's *Life Is a Dream* (ca. 1636)

1650

Revolt of Catalans and Portugese (1640)

Coliseo, court theater with proscenium arch, built (1640)

Defeat of Spanish army by French at Rocroi (1643)

Public theaters closed (1646–1651)

Peace of the Pyrenees; Spain's power declines (1659)

Number of carros for autos increased from two to four (1647)

1675

First reference to Spanish designer Jose Caudi (1662)

Charles II (rules 1665–1700)

Murillo's *Immaculate Conception* (used this subject thirty times) (1678)

1750

Publication of Spanish Colonial Code (1680)

Murillo dies (1617–1682)

Autos sacramentales prohibited (1765)

1775

BACKGROUND: THE SPANISH GOLDEN AGE

Spain has had a history unlike that of any other country on the European continent. Located on the Iberian peninsula at the western end of the Mediterranean Sea, it is bounded on the east by the Mediterranean, on the west by Portugal and the Atlantic Ocean, and on the north by the Pyrenees—the mountains which separate it from France. In the second century B.C., Spain (like many other regions) was conquered by the Romans and became part of the Roman empire. In A.D. 711, however, the Moors invaded from North Africa and soon controlled all of Spain except for certain areas in the extreme north. The Moors, with their Islamic culture and religion, were to rule Spain for the next 700 years. This Moorish domination had a lasting effect, even after Spain was retaken by Roman Catholic monarchies; Moorish influences appear later in architecture and the arts, including theater. In Spanish Renaissance drama, for example, issues of honor and love—which are central to many plays—and the attitude toward women can be traced back to the Moorish occupation.

In the eleventh and twelfth centuries, northern rulers in Spain began a reconquest of the south. It was not until the fifteenth century, though, that the entire peninsula was retaken from the Moors. This came during the reign of King Ferdinand and Queen Isabella. Ferdinand was king of Aragon; Isabella, after a struggle with other heirs, became the monarch of Castile and Leon. These two married in 1469 and thereafter consolidated their control of Spain.

For several reasons, 1492 was a significant year in their reign. The best-known event is, of course, Columbus's voyage and his discovery of the western hemisphere. But 1492 was also the year when Ferdinand and Isabella finally drove the Moors out of Spain permanently; and it was the year when they undertook a religious purge of their kingdom—along with the Moors, they banished Jews. Spanish Jews were culturally and ethnically no different from Spanish Christians, but since they were not Catholics, they interfered with the goal of religious unanimity. A few years earlier, in 1480, Ferdinand and Isabella had established the Spanish Inquisition, a religious tribunal which arbitrarily decided cases of heresy. Those found guilty, whether Jews or Christians, had no court of appeal and were often banished, imprisoned, or burnt at the stake. Because of its expulsion of Moors and Jews, Spain lost some of its most notable doctors, philosophers, merchants, and scholars.

The Spain of Ferdinand and Isabella was, then, marked by religious intolerance; however, it was also becoming a world power. Beginning with Columbus's discoveries and conquests in the Americas, Spain came to dominate Europe in the early part of the sixteenth century; it conquered other European lands and continued to control the seas. Spain was also successful in commerce and trade. By 1550, it was the leading power in western Europe and was poised for what has come to be known as its "golden age," not only in conquest and commerce but also in the arts.

The year 1588, when its armada was defeated by England, marked the end of the unquestioned superiority of Spain as a sea power, but it continued to be a major factor in Europe for much of the sixteenth century. During this period, Spanish drama and theater flourished.

THE MYSTERY OF ELCHE. In the town of Elche in southern Spain, a medieval religious play has been produced continually since the fifteenth century. It is put on by the townspeople, who play all the parts, handing them down from one generation to the next. In this recent production, the boy on the right is playing the part of the Virgin Mary.

RELIGIOUS THEATER IN SPAIN

Because after 711 many parts of Spain were occupied by the Moors, the religious drama that thrived throughout much of Europe and England during the late Middle Ages and the early Renaissance did not take hold in Spain until the country was united at the end of the fifteenth century. Once religious drama did establish itself, however, it became an important theatrical activity; and it remained important in Spain long after it had ended in other countries.

Religious Dramas: Autos Sacramentales

Religious dramas in Spain were originally produced inside churches and cathedrals as part of the service, just as they were elsewhere in Europe and England. In some parts of Spain, this practice—of performing short religious dramas inside the sanctuary of a church—continued for many years. In Elche, a town in southern Spain, a mystery play telling the story of the death and assumption of the Virgin Mary, first performed in the fifteenth century, has since been presented continually and is still performed by the townspeople in the basilica of the cathedral during a festival each August.

Until roughly 1550, religious plays in Spain were similar to those produced elsewhere in medieval Europe; but after that time, in the last half of the sixteenth century, they took on distinctive characteristics that set them apart. The performance of these religious plays came to be closely associated with Corpus Christi, a festival held in late May or early June—approximately 2 months after Easter—which celebrates the power of the sacraments. (Corpus Christi is also described in Chapter 3.) The plays presented at this festival came to be known as *autos sacramentales: auto* meant a one-act play, and *sacramentale* referred to the sacraments. In time, *auto sacramentale* was the name given to any play presented at Corpus Christi, whether or not it was directly related to the sacraments.

Autos sacramentales combined elements of medieval morality and mystery plays and could be based on secular as well as religious sources; they included supernatural, human, and allegorical characters. The one requirement was that they underscore the validity of the church's teachings.

The finest dramatists of the Spanish golden age, including Calderón (who is discussed on page 223), wrote autos—a fact which highlights the close relationship between religious and secular theater in Spain. From 1647 until 1681, all the autos presented in Madrid were written by a single author—Calderón. After his death in 1681, there was a falling off in the quality of new autos; but they continued to be produced at Corpus Christi until 1765, when they were specifically prohibited because it was felt that they had come to reflect a carnival atmosphere more than a religious atmosphere—there had been a growing emphasis on the farces and dances that were interspersed between autos. For over 200 years, though, autos sacramentales, written by Spain's greatest dramatists, were an active, vital part of Spanish theater.

Producing the Autos Sacramentales

In discussing the production of the autos sacramentales, we will focus on the city of Madrid, since its practices were similar to those of other localities.

In Madrid, religious plays were staged under the auspices of trade guilds until 1550. Sometime in the decade of the 1550s, however, the city council took over this responsibility and employed professional troupes to produce these plays. From about 1560 to 1592, a single professional company would present three autos at each festival. Beginning in 1592, four plays were produced in Madrid each year and two professional companies were employed. This continued until 1647, after which only two plays were given annually.

Before the Corpus Christi festival, the troupe employed to perform the autos would be required to give one preview performance for the king and another for the city council. The public performances would then be given at sites within Madrid specifically designated by the city government.

Troupes that performed at Corpus Christi would later tour neighboring villages and would also perform in public theaters. The companies chosen to present the autos were paid a handsome fee and, in addition, obtained funds from other public performances for which they were given exclusive rights.

Religious plays were mounted on wagons, called *carros,* which could be moved into place for the festival and moved elsewhere at other times (they were pulled by young bulls). Before 1647, two carros were used for each play, to serve as a place for storing any scenic elements, housing special effects such as "flying," changing costumes, and making entrances and exits. A third wagon was joined to these two carros to serve as a platform stage. After 1647, a fixed platform was used at each playing space and four carros were used: two drawn up at the rear of the platform stage and one at each side. By the 1690s, the platform stage was 36 feet deep and nearly 50 feet long. Each of the four carros was approximately 16 feet long and 36 feet high. Since the presentations were financed and administered by the local government, carros were built and stored in a city workshop.

SECULAR THEATER IN SPAIN

An unusual feature of theater in the Spanish golden age is that religious and secular professional theater flourished side by side for such a long time. We have already pointed out that Spanish playwrights created dramatic works for both theaters; and the two were equally professional with regard to other aspects, such as acting and production.

Secular theater emerged in Spain at much the same time as its professional religious theater—during the sixteenth century. One way to trace this parallel development is through the career of Lope de Rueda (ca. 1510–1565). We first hear of Rueda in 1542, when he appeared as an actor in religious plays in Seville and was probably managing his own company. Nine years later, in 1551, he was summoned to what was then the capital of Spain, Valladolid, to perform before King Philip II. He continued to live and perform there and to write and direct plays for the Corpus Christi festivals—receiving a large annual salary—until 1558. At the same time, he began writing popular, secular plays which became part of the lively theatrical activity that was growing throughout Spain. Rueda wrote five full-length plays and about a dozen short comic pieces. He toured extensively throughout Spain, building his reputation as a performer and manager.

In the period just after Rueda, Miguel de Cervantes (1547–1616), best known for his novel *Don Quixote*, also wrote plays, though not of the quality of those that would come later from the playwrights of the golden age.

It is worth noting that as a theatrical tradition began to emerge in Spain, it was geographically dispersed. It developed not only in Madrid, which became the capital beginning in 1560, but in Seville, Granada, Cordova, Barcelona, Valencia, and elsewhere.

We should also note that touring Italian commedia dell'arte performers were extremely popular in Spain in the 1570s and 1580s and significantly influenced the later golden age Spanish dramatists.

Secular Dramas: Comedias

By the end of the sixteenth century, the different forms of Spanish secular drama that would flourish throughout the seventeenth century had taken shape. The full-length plays of the Spanish golden age were originally known as *comedias nuevas*, and then simply as *comedias*. As we have noted, they were given this name whether they were serious, comic, or some mixture of the two; in fact, there was great freedom and flexibility in mixing serious and comic elements. Comedias usually dealt with themes of love and honor, and the leading characters were often minor noblemen and noblewomen.

Like English plays of the same period, comedias were episodic in form and did not adhere to the neoclassical rules. The three unities of time, place, and action were for the most part ignored, though the unity of time was frequently observed within each act of a comedia; the supernatural was often employed; and comedias were written in three acts rather than five. A comedia was usually about 3,000 lines long.

At the beginning of this chapter, we saw that the action in Lope de Vega's *The King, the Greatest Alcalde* moves from place to place through thirteen scenes. This typical episodic form can also be seen in another play by Lope, *Fuente Ovejuna*, written about 1614. (Lope himself is discussed on page 222.)

Fuente Ovejuna—the title is often translated as "The Sheep Well"—is unusual in that its hero is not a single person but an entire village. The commander of the area is a womanizer who is attempting to seduce a village maiden when he is thwarted by a peasant. Enraged, the commander beats the peasant and the girl's father and carries her off. The villagers are upset, but inclined to be cautious. However, when the young woman returns, nearly having been ravished by the commander, she shames them into killing him. They know they will not go unpunished by the authorities, but they decide to be steadfast in maintaining that the commander was slain not by any one person but by the whole village. Despite torture, they stick by their story, and in the end the king intercedes on their behalf. In true episodic fashion, *Fuente Ovejuna* moves over a wide range of locations: it takes us from the commander's headquarters in the district, to a public square in the village, to a chamber in the offices of the rulers (Ferdinand and Isabella), to the open countryside, to the town square, to the house of the commander. The play also has a large cast of characters.

In form, therefore, plays of the Spanish golden age are very close to Elizabethan drama. There are differences in subject, however: conflicts of love and honor, daring adventures, melodramatic confrontations, and rescues are the essence of the Spanish plays. Also, there is a mixture of the serious and the comic, as mentioned above. Unlike a tragedy such as Shakespeare's *King Lear* or a light comedy such as his *Twelfth Night*, a Spanish play of this period would seem closer to the popular melodramatic entertainments of our own day: swashbuckling films of the 1940s, romantic novels, and soap operas.

Comedias were of two major types. One was known as *capa y espada*, "cape and sword." The name comes from the outfits usually worn by the minor nobility which the plays featured; it also suggests the daredevil, romantic quality of these plays. The other type of comedias featured saints, rulers, nobles, historic figures, legendary heroes, and mythological figures; this type was set in places and periods far removed from contemporary Spain. Dramas of the second type went by various names: *teatro, cuerpo* ("corpse"), and *ruido* ("noise").

Before 1615, performances of comedias were preceded by a prologue, which was either a monologue or a short sketch; the intermissions between acts featured interludes, known as *entremeses,* some of which were spoken and others sung. Besides full-length plays, the Spaniards developed many popular, short, farcical forms which were presented on the same program with comedias.

Producing the Comedias

THE CORRALES

The nonreligious plays of writers like Lope de Vega and Calderón were staged in public theaters known as *corrales.* Corrales were constructed in existing courtyards; like Elizabethan public theaters, they were open-air spaces with galleries and boxes protected by a roof. These courtyard theaters were temporary at first but later became permanent spaces. The two most famous were in Madrid: the Corral de la Cruz (1579) and—as described at the opening of this chapter—the Corral del Principe (1583).

The stage in a corral was a platform erected opposite the entrance to the yard. Access to the yard was usually through a street building; there were also several entranceways for other seating areas. The yard floor, or patio, was primarily an area for standing, like the pit of an Elizabethan public theater; in Spanish corrales, the noisy groundlings were known as *mosqueteros* ("musketeers"). At the front of the patio, near the stage, a row of stools—later, a small number of benches called *taburetes*—were set up, separated from the rest of the yard by a railing. In the late 1600s or early 1700s, the straight benches may have been replaced by semicircular benches called *luñetas*—literally, "small moons."

In the back wall opposite the stage, above the main entranceway in the yard, was a gallery known as the *cazuela,* or "stew pot." This was an area for unaccompanied women; it had its own separate entrance and was carefully guarded to prevent men from entering. Above the cazuela, there was a row of boxes for local government officials; above these boxes was a larger gallery for the clergy which may also have been divided to provide another section for unescorted women. At the back of the patio, on one side of the main entrance, was a refreshments box, the *alojero,* from which food and drinks were sold.

Along the side walls of the yard were *gradas*—elevated benches. Above the gradas were *rejas*—windows protected by grills from which a play could be viewed. On the next level were boxes *(aposentos)* which extended out from the buildings around the courtyard. A fourth floor contained *desvánes* ("attics"), which were cramped boxes with low ceilings.

A corral held about 2,000 spectators: 1,000 places for men, 350 for women, and the rest reserved boxes and other accommodations for government officials and the clergy. Special arrangements had to be made for renting boxes; individual agreements would be negotiated between the owners and inhabitants of the buildings and the people who were leasing the corral.

Corrales, clearly, were quite different from the proscenium-arch theaters that were developing in Italy and were much closer to Elizabethan public theaters.

Debates in Theater History:

WHAT WAS THE APPEARANCE OF THE CORRAL DEL PRINCIPE?

The appearance of the Corral del Principe in Madrid, possibly the most famous theater building of the Spanish golden age, continues to be debated, because there are so many questions about the few surviving contemporary illustrations.

A major problem has arisen in reconstructing the Corral del Principe because one frequently reprinted sketch was misidentified. This drawing, done for a historical study published in 1888, has often been wrongly described as dating from the seventeenth century. Actually, the sketch was made by a nineteenth-century artist, J. Comba, and it is loosely based on surviving visual sources from the Spanish golden age and on theories developed in the book for which he drew it. A carefully detailed reconstruction of the Corral del Principe by John J. Allen clearly shows that little in Comba's sketch is accurate.*

It is, therefore, surprising and unfortunate that, as Ronald Vince points out in his *Renaissance Theatre:* A *Historiographical Handbook,* "the drawing continues to illustrate books on theater history. In fact, of half a dozen popular and readily accessible introductory texts in the field—each of which was published or revised after 1967—only one notes that the sketch was done in 1888. This same volume also adds, 'that it is inaccurate in many details.'"[†]

As we noted in Chapter 6 with regard to Elizabethan theater, there are many controversies among historians over pictorial sources. What is particularly interesting about this one is that although Comba's drawing is unquestionably inaccurate, it continues to be used as a source for reconstructing the most famous public theater of the Spanish golden age. We have reproduced Comba's sketch here, of course, for the purposes of this discussion; but as far as reconstructive purposes are concerned, the issue—as Vince notes—is, "Why print the picture at all?"

*John J. Allen, *The Reconstruction of a Spanish Golden Age Playhouse: El Corral del Principe, 1593–1744,* University of Florida Press, Gainesville, 1983.

[†]Greenwood, Westport, Conn., 1984, p. 68.

COMBA'S VERSION OF THE CORRAL DEL PRINCIPE. *Opposite page, top:* This nineteenth-century drawing is speculative and incorrect in almost all details, but it has been used frequently by theater historians and thus has misled scholars attempting to reconstruct the Corral del Principe. The differences between Comba's version and the reconstruction based on Allen's research are obvious. For example, Comba's drawing gives no clear sense of the facade or the building behind the stage, and the stage itself is made to appear too much like a proscenium arch. In addition, there are sharp distinctions between Comba's and Allen's reconstructions of the audience areas, including the *gradas* (the bleacher-like seats along the side walls) and the *desvánes* (the cramped upper-level galleries along the side walls). It is evident that Comba's drawing reflects too many of the changes made in the Corral del Principe after the golden age.

A SPANISH CORRAL. *Opposite page, bottom:* This drawing is based on the John J. Allen's research on the Corral del Principe in Madrid. Note the various elements of the corral: the yard (patio), the seating areas (boxes and galleries), and the platform stage with the tiring house behind it. Note also that in front of the yard there were benches or stools and that seats were also set up at the side of the stage. In addition, notice how similar the face of the building behind the stage was to the facade of the Elizabethan tiring house.

SCENERY, THE STAGE, AND COSTUMES

Scenic conventions in Spain were also similar to those in England. In Spain, the basic scenic element was a two- or three-story stage house constructed behind the platform stage. A curtain, props, and flats might be used in conjunction with the facade of the stage house. There were three openings for entrances, exits, and "reveals" and one or two upper playing areas. The facade, therefore, served the same function as the Elizabethan tiring house. "Spoken decor"— that is, dialogue indicating locale—was also used.

The stage in a corral was a platform raised 6 feet (although some scholars believe it was as high as 9 feet) above the patio. An area under the stage served as the men's dressing room and as a storeroom for costumes. (The women's dressing room was behind the central doorway that led into the stage house.) Trapdoors on the stage were used for special effects. The stage had a semicircular apron. At each side of the platform was a railed area used for additional bench seating unless a production required the entire stage.

As we have noted, this kind of stage was much closer to the stage of an English public theater than it was to the proscenium-arch stage in use in Italy. During the Spanish Renaissance, the proscenium arch was introduced only at court; again, this parallels developments in English theater. The first proscenium-arch theater in Spain was probably the Coliseo, a court theater at the king's palace, the Buen Retiro, in Madrid; it was designed by an Italian, Cosme Lotti (?–1643), and completed in 1640. Throughout most of the seventeenth century, Spanish monarchs, like English monarchs, had lavish spectacles staged for them at court. A unique Spanish court entertainment, influenced by Italian opera and intermezzi, was the *zarzuela,* a short, stylized musical drama with a story based on mythology and ornate scenic effects.

Costuming practices in Spain were also similar to those of Renaissance England. In most instances, contemporary clothing was worn. At times, historical or mythical figures would be dressed more elaborately; Moors were almost always portrayed as villains, and any Moorish character would be dressed in some distinctive way. Where budgets permitted, costumes were extremely lavish, and individual performers often owned expensive, elaborate outfits.

ACTING COMPANIES

In Spain during the golden age, acting troupes consisted of sixteen to twenty performers and—as will be discussed below—included women. Acting companies were regulated by local government; all plays and troupes had to be licensed. Some Spanish troupes were *compañias de partes,* that is, "sharing companies" like those of Elizabethan England. Other Spanish companies, however, were organized by a manager, the *autor,* who contracted performers for a specific period of time and oversaw all artistic and business decisions. Plays were purchased from dramatists, who were paid a set fee for their work.

As in Elizabethan companies, actors played multiple roles. Type-casting was common, since the comedias had stock characters such as the *gracioso* (a clown) and the *barba* (an old man).

THE STATUS OF ACTRESSES

As we noted above, Spanish acting troupes, unlike Elizabethan companies, included women. During the Middle Ages, in many places on the European continent—in contrast to England—women had been allowed to act in religious dramas; and the inclusion of actresses in Spanish Renaissance companies was an outgrowth of this custom.

The status of the actress in theaters of the Spanish golden age is an intriguing subject. It should be noted that the Catholic church in Spain was generally opposed to theater and considered performers untrustworthy and licentious; because of this, local governments frequently intervened in theatrical matters and closely monitored the plays presented in public theaters. Given the church's opposition to acting in general, it should not be surprising that the clergy were particularly wary of women performers.

Numerous laws were passed during the late 1500s in an attempt to restrict the employment of women in theater. In 1587, however, women were legally permitted to work as performers. (Before this, women had sometimes performed, but more often the Spanish theater had followed the Elizabethan convention of using young men for female roles.) The church's dissatisfaction with women performers in public theaters led to a ban in 1596, but this was ineffective. After a great deal of debate, a new law was passed in 1599 which allowed only actresses who were the wives or daughters of company members and banned cross-dressing (that is, dressing in the clothing of the opposite sex). In addition, throughout the late sixteenth and early seventeenth century, numerous laws restricted the kinds of dances women were allowed to perform in theaters, since the church considered many of these dances too sexual.

What is extremely interesting about all these laws is the evident discomfort of Spanish society with women performers. This is understandable in light of the fact that the society was male-dominated and in general took the male perspective. But it is perhaps less easy to understand why at one point cross-dressing was considered more acceptable than the appearance of women onstage when later it was not. An attempt to control women and concern for clearly defining sexual identity are obvious motivations for the laws; thus these laws reflect gender issues that transcended theater.

SPANISH DRAMATISTS

The amount of dramatic activity during the Spanish golden age was remarkable. Among dramatists, two minor writers should be mentioned. One is Guillén de Castro (1569–1631), whose play about a Spanish hero, *The Cid,* was the source for a famous French play on the same subject by Corneille. The other is Tirso de Molina (ca. 1584–1648), who is said to have written 400 plays and who wrote the first known play about Don Juan. However, by far the two most outstanding dramatists of this era were Lope de Vega and Calderón de la Barca.

Lope Félix de Vega Carpio

(1562–1635)

Lope de Vega, one of the most prolific dramatists of all time, was said to have written 1,500 plays (although scholars now believe that 800 is a more realistic estimate); of these, 470 still survive. Lope established a distinctive episodic structure for Spanish drama, and it is one of history's fascinating coincidences that he lived at exactly the same time as Shakespeare and wrote in a similar form. Lope's plays, like Shakespeare's, have many scenes and large casts of characters, and range widely over both time and space. Besides his plays, Lope wrote twenty-one volumes of prose and poetry.

As a dramatist, Lope had one aim: to please the audience. As we have seen, he made this point clear in a treatise called "The New Art of Playwriting" (ca. 1609), in which he also defended his episodic style. Lope established the popularity of the three-act verse comedia in Spain, but he wrote plays in every genre, covering almost every possible topic and using characters from all parts of Spanish society. Several of his plays, including *The Sheep Well (Fuente Ovejuna)* (ca. 1614), deal with attempts by peasants to secure justice; others, like *The Dog in the Manger* (ca. 1615), are "cape and sword" plays revolving around the intrigues of the minor nobility. Though Lope preferred happy endings, he wrote several tragedies, including *The Knight from Olmedo* (ca. 1620–1625), one of his finest works. Lope's other well-known plays include *The Idiot Lady* (ca. 1613), *The Flowers of Don Juan* (ca. 1615), *The King, The Greatest Alcalde* (ca. 1620), and *Punishment without Revenge* (ca. 1631), to name just a few. Translations of his works were circulated throughout Europe and were influential in the development of French theater.

It is difficult to imagine when Lope found time for writing, for he led a most active life. Born in 1562 to a working-class family in Madrid, he attended several Jesuit universities and at one point studied for the priesthood. Abandoning school, he joined the navy, took part in an expedition to the Azores, and became embroiled in the first of his many love affairs. He was banished from Madrid for 8 years because of one of his intrigues but immediately broke the ban to kidnap and marry a young noblewoman. He then sailed with the Spanish armada; on his return to Spain, he served several noblemen. After the death of his first wife, he had an affair with the actress Micaela de Luján that provided further stimulus to his writing career and also provided him with several children. However, when Lope was married again, it was not to Micaela but to a wealthy woman.

A growing interest in religion led Lope de Vega to join a lay confraternity; and in 1614, when he was widowed for the second time, he became a priest. Neither his playwriting nor his womanizing was affected by his priesthood. Philip III appointed Lope director of the court theater, a post he held until his death in 1635.

Pedro Calderón de la Barca
(1600–1681)

After Lope de Vega died, Pedro Calderón de la Barca became Spain's most popular playwright. Calderón's plays are written in a variety of styles, but they all reflect the authoritarian religious atmosphere of Spain. Many revolve around the favorite Spanish concerns of love and honor, and some examine violent family situations—a reflection of Calderón's own authoritarian father and of Spanish social patterns. In *Life Is a Dream* (ca. 1636), he develops the idea that human beings are responsible for their own actions and must choose a path from a maze of possibilities.

For court entertainments, Calderón wrote and produced poetic musical dramas like *Love, the Great Enchanter* (1637). His religious plays (autos sacramentales), like *Baltassar's Feast* (1634) and *The Great World Theater* (1649), combine image-filled poetry with philosophy. Among his popular secular plays written for the public theater are *The Constant Prince* (1629), *A House with Two Doors Is Difficult to Guard* (1629), *The Physician of His Own Honor* (1635), *Secret Vengeance for Secret Insult* (1635), *The Mayor of Zalamea* (1642), and *Beware of Still Water* (1649). Many of his plays, translated first into French and then into English, influenced the playwrights of neoclassical France and Restoration England.

A year before his death, Calderón drew up a list of the plays he had written. It contained 111 secular plays and 70 autos sacramentales, a remarkable total for a man who had combined playwriting with several other careers.

As a young man, Calderón's first choice of a career was the priesthood. The son of a wealthy government official, he entered the Jesuit University of Alcala in 1614, the year he wrote his first play. After a few years of study, he left school in 1620 to enter government service. In 1623, he began to write plays for the court, becoming a leader among the court poets. His plays were also successful in the public theaters; and when Lope de Vega died in 1635, Calderón became director of the court theater. The following year, Philip IV knighted him for his services.

Calderón changed careers again in 1640, joining the army to help suppress a Catalan rebellion. He proved to be a good soldier but was discharged 2 years later for medical reasons. With both the court theaters and the public theaters closed because of wars in Catalon and Portugal and two deaths in the royal family (including the queen's), he was forced to find other work, and he became secretary to the duke of Alba. After the death of his brothers and his mistress, Calderón returned to religion and was ordained a priest in 1651. Though he stopped writing for the public stage, he continued to write autos for Corpus Christi. He was reappointed to his court post as director of theater in 1663 and held that position until his death in 1681. Calderón's death is said to mark the end of the Spanish golden age.

THE MAYOR OF ZALAMEA. Calderón de la Barca, the great Spanish playwright of the second half of the seventeenth century, was known for both religious plays—autos sacramentales—and secular plays. *The Mayor of Zalamea* is his adaptation of a play by Lope de Vega; it is about a mayor who avenges the rape of his daughter by a military captain. Seen here is a scene between the mayor (Ricardo Barber) and his daughter (Adriana Sananes) in a production at Repertorio Español in New York in 1991.

Between 1650 and 1700, Spain experienced a military, political, economic, and cultural decline, and its golden age came to an end. No significant drama was written after the death of Calderón de la Barca in 1681. During the golden age, however, the theater of Spain was as vital as that of Elizabethan England.

SUMMARY

During their golden age, the Spaniards developed dramatic and theatrical practices quite similar to those of Elizabethan England: the structure of Spanish comedias was episodic; Spanish corrales were reminiscent of English public theaters; and staging practices in the two countries were almost identical. But Spanish drama had features characteristically its own. Its two greatest playwrights, Lope de Vega and Calderón de la Barca, and their contemporaries dealt with Spanish heroes and heroines: both common people and the nobility. Also, during the golden age Spain—unlike other European countries—continued to produce religious drama, and women were employed as performers.

CHAPTER 8

FRENCH NEOCLASSICAL THEATER

CHAPTER 8

FRENCH NEOCLASSICAL THEATER

The date is February 9, 1669, and we are in the audience at the Palais Royal theater in Paris, France. We are eagerly awaiting a performance of *Tartuffe,* written by France's best-known comic playwright and actor, Molière.

Tartuffe has already been the cause of an enormous controversy. Molière first read it 4½ years ago to King Louis XIV at his palace at Versailles; the king liked it, but before it could be presented publicly, it had provoked an uproar. The reason for all this furor is its subject matter. We have already heard that the title character, Tartuffe, is a religious hypocrite. He pretends to be very pious and wears clothing that looks like a religious habit, but he is actually interested in acquiring money and seducing women. He has come to live in the house of Orgon, a wealthy man who has been completely taken in by his false piety.

THE SCHOOL FOR HUSBANDS.   The most famous comic playwright of the French Renaissance—and one of the best comic playwrights of all time—was Molière. He was particularly masterful at creating characters who become obsessed or carry an idea to extremes. *The School for Husbands* is a good example, dealing with men who are obsessed with their wives' fidelity. The production here, which shows the influence of commedia dell'arte, was by the Old Globe Theatre in San Diego. *(Ken Howard/Old Globe Theatre)*

Those who oppose this play include a number of religious figures (one of them is the Archbishop of Paris) who say that *Tartuffe* is an attack on religion. Molière insists that his play is an attack, not on religion, but on people who hide behind religion and exploit it. We are aware that the opposition has until now been successful in keeping the play out of theaters; the king did not dare authorize its presentation as long as the forces against it were so strong. The play has been presented only once before, in the summer of 1667, and then for only one night. The king was out of the country at that time, and in his absence the religious authorities had it closed down. Now, however, *Tartuffe* has finally been given royal approval, and today's performance is to be its official public unveiling.

The Palais Royal theater, where Molière's troupe performs and where we now find ourselves, is a rectangular space with a stage at one end and galleries on three sides around it. It accommodates almost 1,500 people: 300 stand in a "pit" in front of the stage, about 700 sit in a raised amphitheater behind the pit, about 330 sit in the galleries, 70 stand at the very back, and 50 wealthy nobles sit on the sides of the stage itself. Having spectators onstage is customary in French theaters but makes things very difficult for the actors.

The stage is fitted with wings and shutters, like Italian Renaissance theaters, and scenery can be changed with a pole-and-chariot system. For *Tartuffe,* however, we understand that there will be no scene change; the entire action takes place in the drawing room of Orgon's house.

After so much scandal and such prolonged disagreement about its subject matter, we feel a rush of anticipation as the performance of *Tartuffe* begins. Once the play is underway, we realize that the controversial figure of Tartuffe will not even make an appearance for two full acts. Rather, it is the figure of Orgon, played by Molière himself, on whom we first concentrate. We see that Orgon is thoroughly duped and pays no attention to the members of his family when they tell him how dishonest and disreputable Tartuffe is.

Finally, in the third act, Tartuffe makes his entrance; and though he is challenged by Orgon's family, Orgon remains loyal to him. Only when Orgon learns for himself the awful truth about Tartuffe does he realize his error. This occurs in a scene in which Orgon, hiding under a table, hears Tartuffe try to seduce his wife. As we watch the scene, we think it is one of the funniest we have ever seen.

Orgon's discovery about Tartuffe's true nature seems to come too late: at this point, Orgon has already handed his house and his fortune over to Tartuffe, disinheriting his own children. At the end of the play, though, the king intervenes. This is the same Louis XIV who in real life has intervened on Molière's behalf so that the play can be presented. A few weeks from now, both king and playwright will be vindicated: the play will be performed twenty-eight times in a row—an unprecedented number—and will show every sign of becoming a classic comedy.

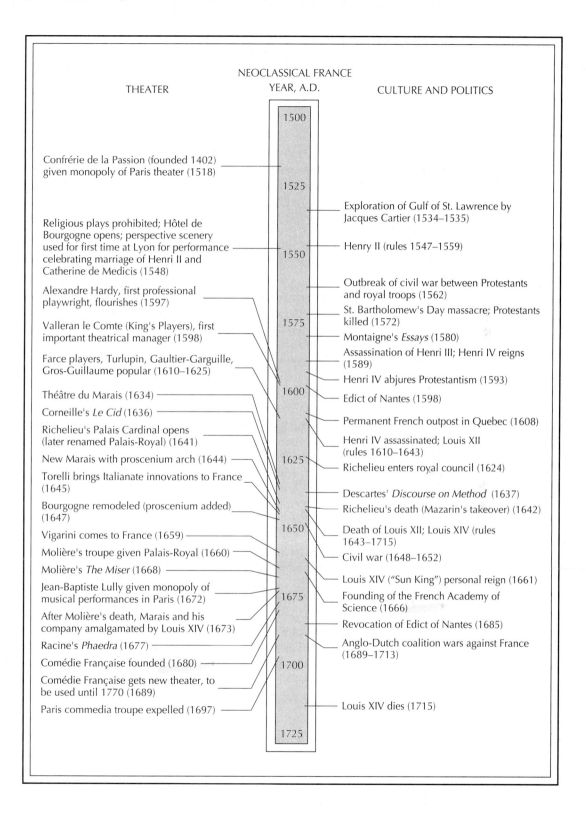

NEOCLASSICAL FRANCE
YEAR, A.D.

THEATER

CULTURE AND POLITICS

1500

Confrérie de la Passion (founded 1402) given monopoly of Paris theater (1518)

1525

Exploration of Gulf of St. Lawrence by Jacques Cartier (1534–1535)

Religious plays prohibited; Hôtel de Bourgogne opens; perspective scenery used for first time at Lyon for performance celebrating marriage of Henri II and Catherine de Medicis (1548)

1550

Henry II (rules 1547–1559)

Alexandre Hardy, first professional playwright, flourishes (1597)

Outbreak of civil war between Protestants and royal troops (1562)

St. Bartholomew's Day massacre; Protestants killed (1572)

Valleran le Comte (King's Players), first important theatrical manager (1598)

1575

Montaigne's *Essays* (1580)

Farce players, Turlupin, Gaultier-Garguille, Gros-Guillaume popular (1610–1625)

Assassination of Henri III; Henri IV reigns (1589)

Henri IV abjures Protestantism (1593)

Théâtre du Marais (1634)

1600

Edict of Nantes (1598)

Corneille's *Le Cid* (1636)

Permanent French outpost in Quebec (1608)

Richelieu's Palais Cardinal opens (later renamed Palais-Royal) (1641)

Henri IV assassinated; Louis XII (rules 1610–1643)

New Marais with proscenium arch (1644)

1625

Richelieu enters royal council (1624)

Torelli brings Italianate innovations to France (1645)

Descartes' *Discourse on Method* (1637)

Bourgogne remodeled (proscenium added) (1647)

Richelieu's death (Mazarin's takeover) (1642)

Vigarini comes to France (1659)

1650

Death of Louis XII; Louis XIV (rules 1643–1715)

Molière's troupe given Palais-Royal (1660)

Civil war (1648–1652)

Molière's *The Miser* (1668)

Louis XIV ("Sun King") personal reign (1661)

Jean-Baptiste Lully given monopoly of musical performances in Paris (1672)

1675

Founding of the French Academy of Science (1666)

After Molière's death, Marais and his company amalgamated by Louis XIV (1673)

Revocation of Edict of Nantes (1685)

Racine's *Phaedra* (1677)

Anglo-Dutch coalition wars against France (1689–1713)

Comédie Française founded (1680)

1700

Comédie Française gets new theater, to be used until 1770 (1689)

Paris commedia troupe expelled (1697)

Louis XIV dies (1715)

1725

BACKGROUND: FRANCE IN THE
SIXTEENTH AND SEVENTEENTH CENTURIES

France in the sixteenth century had a political history significantly different from that of England or Spain. In Spain, the political situation began to stabilize in the late fifteenth century under Ferdinand and Isabella, and during the sixteenth century the country prospered. With the succession of Elizabeth I to the throne in 1558, England too achieved unity and stability. In France, however, the 1500s were a time of unrest. This was partly due to a religious civil war between Protestants, who were known as Huguenots, and Catholics. The civil war was finally brought to an end in 1594, when the king of France, Henry IV—a Protestant who had ascended to the throne in 1589—converted to Catholicism. Although Henry had renounced Protestantism, he resolved the religious strife by issuing the Edict of Nantes. This revolutionary proclamation offered non-Catholics, especially Huguenots, equality and tolerance under French law.

In the seventeenth century, therefore, French society could finally stabilize and flourish—particularly under Louis XIV, who reigned from 1643 to 1715. Like England, the Netherlands, Spain, and Portugal, France profited from exploration of the new world. Among the important areas the French explored and colonized were Canada and the Louisiana Territory.

A particularly strong influence on both politics and culture in France was Italy. Many reasons can be cited for the Italianization of French society. This was a development that had begun in the sixteenth century when members of the Medici family—the renowned merchant-princes and patrons of the arts who ruled the prosperous Italian city of Florence during the Renaissance—married into the French royal family. Henry II, who ruled France from 1547 to 1559, married Catherine de Medici; after Henry's death, the three succeeding monarchs were all sons of Catherine, and she continued to wield a strong influence on the French court. In 1610, when Louis XIII inherited the throne, he was only 9 years old, and his mother—Marie de Medici—controlled the French government.

Another major political force during the reign of Louis XIII was Cardinal Richelieu, who also advanced Italian culture in France. In 1643, the year after Richelieu's death, Louis XIII died. His son, Louis XIV, was also a child (Louis XIV was only 5 when he became king), and the Italian-born Cardinal Mazarin, who had replaced Richelieu, wielded the real power. Thus French government and—in turn—French culture were strongly influenced by the Italians. This was especially true in theater, both in the types of plays that were written and in theater architecture, scenery, and production. In contrast to the English and Spanish theaters, which were characterized by episodic drama performed on platform stages, French theater adhered to neoclassical models and to Italian scene design.

FRENCH DRAMA

The Early Years

Although French theater did not come to full flower until a third of the way into the seventeenth century, there were various kinds of theatrical activity before then.

In 1402, a religious group, the Confrérie de la Passion (Confraternity of the Passion), was organized in Paris to present religious plays. For over a century it presented dramas sporadically. In the first part of the sixteenth century, the Confrérie used various locations in Paris for its presentations; then, in 1548, it built a theater—called the Hôtel de Bourgogne—which may well have been the first permanent theater constructed in Europe since Roman times. *(Hôtel* is the French term for "town house," and the Bourgogne was called a *hôtel* because a duke's town house had once stood on its site and because the neighboring buildings were town houses.) Before the Hôtel de Bourgogne was even completed, religious plays were banned in Paris, and so the Confrérie was never able to use the theater for its own productions. However, because the Confrérie had been given a monopoly on theater production in Paris, other groups were forced either to rent the Hôtel de Bourgogne or to pay a fee to the Confrérie.

During the sixteenth century, professional troupes began to spring up in other parts of France, and Italian commedia dell'arte companies performed in Paris and many other French cities. These commedia companies were another Italian influence on French theater. Most of the drama offered by both the French and the Italian troupes was popular farce; it often included song and dance as well as dramatic material.

In the middle 1500s in Paris, a literary group called the Pléiade was formed to further writing and culture; out of this group came French plays based on neoclassical models. These plays were derivative and aimed almost exclusively at an upper-class, scholarly audience.

One other form of theatrical activity worth noting in the last half of the sixteenth century is court entertainment. We have already mentioned Catherine de Medici, whose husband and three sons ruled as kings of France over a period stretching from 1547 to 1589. Catherine enjoyed royal events: festivals, court spectacles, and triumphal entries into towns. In the 1560s, she made a 2-year tour of France, and each city she entered prepared an elaborate celebration in her honor. Out of such spectacles developed various kinds of court entertainments in France that were the equivalent of intermezzi in Italy and masques in England.

In the public theaters, the man generally considered the first fully professional playwright in France appeared at the end of the sixteenth century: Alexandre Hardy (ca. 1572–1632). For 35 years, beginning in 1597, Hardy wrote several hundred plays, melodramatic in style, of which thirty-four survive.

Hardy was a popular dramatist, who used neoclassical devices such as messengers and the five-act structure. But he paid little or no attention to the unities (time, place, and action), he used supernatural characters, and he showed all the action—even the most violent—onstage. Most of Hardy's plays were probably produced at the Hôtel de Bourgogne, since that was the only permanent theater in Paris at the time. Hardy not only achieved great success with the public; he also set the stage for the great era of French theater that was soon to begin.

Most theater in France in the first quarter of the seventeenth century probably consisted of popular farces; still, acting and production appear to have become more professional at the same time that writers like Hardy were making advances in playwriting.

Neoclassical Drama

CORNEILLE: ESTABLISHING THE NEOCLASSICAL IDEALS

An important thread in the story of French theater is the triumph of the Italian neoclassical ideals. These include both dramaturgy (the way plays are written) and stagecraft (the way productions are designed and mounted). We have observed how strong the Italian influence was on politics and society. In the seventeenth century, we can trace the emergence of a marked Italian influence on theater.

At the beginning of the seventeenth century, French theater was not notably Italian. Commedia dell'arte troupes traveled in France; but in both playwriting and production, the influence of native medieval theater remained very much in evidence. Hardy's plays did not observe the neoclassical unities—time, place, and action—and there were no proscenium-arch theaters with an emphasis on scenic effects.

As noted above, however, there was an unmistakable impetus toward adoption of Italian practices. Beginning around 1620, during the reign of Louis XIII (which had begun in 1610), the most powerful man in France was Cardinal Richelieu, who ruled the country in the name of the king. After a series of new civil wars, Richelieu took power away from the nobles and the Protestants and consolidated it in the hands of the monarch.

Richelieu was particularly interested in establishing standards in French literature and the arts, and in giving them a strong Italian stamp. When he learned that some French intellectuals had organized a literary group, he urged them to form an academy along the lines of Italian academies. They did so in 1636 and the following year were given a royal charter establishing the French Academy, an organization that still exists. It was to the French Academy that Richelieu turned when a serious question of dramatic rules arose. This came about because of *The Cid*, a play by Pierre Corneille.

Pierre Corneille

(1606–1684)

A native of Rouen, Pierre Corneille was the son of a wealthy lawyer. Following his father's career, he obtained an appointment in the department of waterways and forests. He wrote a comedy, *Mélite,* in his spare time; and after an acting troupe played it successfully in Paris in 1629, he began to spend much of his leisure time writing plays. His early comedies attracted the attention of Cardinal Richelieu, who induced him to join the "Society of the Five Authors," commissioned to write plays for the cardinal's entertainment. Corneille found it difficult to write to order and incurred the cardinal's wrath for altering a part of the plot assigned to him.

Though Corneille's first dramatic works were comedies, in 1636–1637 he wrote a serious play, *The Cid,* based on an earlier Spanish play by Guillén de Castro. In Corneille's drama, a medieval Spanish hero, the Cid, kills the father of Chimena, the woman he loves, in a duel of honor. He goes on to conquer the Moors, win another duel, and persuade Chimena to marry him; all this occurs within 24 hours. Corneille's hero is an invincible superman who fights to uphold justice, morality, personal honor, and national honor.

The play was a huge success (in fact, it remains immensely popular in France to this day), but it was virulently attacked by the French Academy. The Academy held that *The Cid* violated the neoclassical rules; they argued, for example, that though it observed the unity of time, it stretched credibility by cramming too much action into 24 hours. Also, Corneille had apparently mixed dramatic genres, because this serious play has a happy ending. In addition, Chimena's agreeing to marry her father's murderer was said to be inappropriate behavior for a character of her stature. Corneille vigorously defended the dramaturgy of *The Cid,* but the controversy continued. To settle the matter, Richelieu asked the newly formed French Academy for a judgment.

When the Academy published its opinion, in 1638, it praised certain parts of the play but insisted that Corneille should have adhered more closely to the neoclassical ideals. Corneille was stung by the verdict and for several years refused to write any more dramas. In 1640, however, he began writing again; and from then on all his plays conformed to the unities of time, place, and action; to verisimilitude; and to the other restrictions of neoclassicism.

Corneille's famous tragedies *Horace* (1640), *Cinna* (1641), *Polyeucte* (1643), and *Rodogune* (1645) are models of adherence to neoclassical theory, and they established him as the most renowned playwright in France. He was elected to the French Academy in 1647 and continued to write until 1652, when a poorly received tragedy and uncertain political conditions led him to retire. The minister of finance was able to persuade him to return to playwriting in 1659, and he then continued to write for the rest of his life.

THE ILLUSION. The French neoclassical playwright Pierre Corneille is best-known for his tragedies, and for his battle with the French Academy over *The Cid*. However, his comedy *The Illusion* has recently received many productions, especially in a new adaptation by Tony Kushner, the author of *Angels in America*. Seen here are Ashley Gardner, Marco St. John, J. Grant Albrecht, and Philip Goodwin in a production of Kushner's adaptation by the Hartford Stage Company.

As a dramatist, Corneille considered theater a spectacular art. He wrote plays with heroic characters in suspenseful and surprising situations which force them to act. Long before his death in 1684, he was known as the "great Corneille," and *The Cid* had been translated and produced all over Europe, ensuring his lasting fame.

RACINE: THE TRIUMPH OF THE NEOCLASSICAL IDEALS

After the French Academy had spoken on *The Cid*, the neoclassical standards of the Italian Renaissance critics prevailed in French dramaturgy. No one was better able to create works incorporating these ideals than the tragic playwright who succeeded Corneille, Jean Racine.

(Bibliothèque Nationale, Paris)

Jean Racine
(1639–1699)

In his tragedies—especially *Andromache* (1667), *Bérénice* (1670), and *Phaedra* (1677)—Racine showed an extraordinary ability to create dramatic tension through concentration and characterization. By compressing dramatic action, Racine increases the pressure on the chief character, who is usually trying to reconcile some driving passion with honor and devotion to duty. The tension builds rapidly; the pressure becomes too much; and the character, tragically, begins to come apart.

The strictness of neoclassical form in Racine's plays parallels the strictness of his own upbringing. Orphaned at the age of 4, he was raised first by his grandparents and then by his aunt, who was in a convent at Port-Royal. She enrolled the boy in the convent school, where he received an excellent but strict and austere education. In 1658 he went to Paris to continue his studies; he became a lawyer, but he spent much of his time with literary groups. In 1660 he published an ode on the marriage of Louis XIV and left school to concentrate on a literary career.

Racine was determined to succeed as a playwright and was constantly plotting and intriguing; not surprisingly, he made many enemies. Though Molière had given the first performances of Racine's works and had given him advice and encouragement, Racine transferred one of his plays from Molière's troupe to a rival company. He also persuaded Madame du Parc—his own mistress—to leave Molière and join the rival group, an action for which he was severely criticized. Racine, however, had the support of several prominent writers, the court, and the king's mistress, and he did not hesitate to use their influence to thwart anyone who opposed him. In 1677, Racine's enemies brought about the failure of his play *Phaedra* by having another play open on the same night as its premiere. After this, Racine forsook theater, married, and obtained an appointment as royal historiographer.

When Racine retired from playwriting, he returned to the strict religious beliefs of his youth. He remained in King Louis's favor for many years and, at the request of the king's second wife, wrote two pageants for her. Eventually, though, Racine's rigid religious ideas caused him to lose the king's favor. He returned to Port-Royal and died in 1699 after a long illness.

It is ironic that Racine's *Phaedra*, which was a failure when it opened, has become one of the most famous French tragedies of all time. *Phaedra* is based on a Greek play—Euripides' *Hippolytus*—and is a perfect example of neoclassicism. The heroine, Phaedra, who is the second wife of King Theseus, falls in love with her stepson, Hippolytus. The play is arranged so that all the events occur in one place—outside Theseus's palace—and cover only a few hours. Its action is also unified, being confined to Phaedra's love for Hippolytus.

PHAEDRA. Racine's *Phaedra*, the most famous of the neoclassical tragedies, deals with a queen who falls in love with her stepson. It has always been popular with great actresses because of the heightened emotions which torment the protagonist. This scene is from an Old Vic production in England, starring Glenda Jackson.

Having heard that Theseus is dead, Phaedra confesses her love for Hippolytus, first to her maid and then to Hippolytus himself. Hippolytus reacts with disgust when he hears her declaration; shortly thereafter, Phaedra discovers that Theseus is alive and will soon be returning to the palace. To avoid the shame of having openly declared her love for her stepson, Phaedra allows her maid to spread a false story—that it was Hippolytus who made advances to Phaedra, not vice versa. Theseus, believing this false report, invokes a god to punish Hippolytus, and the young man is slain. Phaedra is grief-stricken and confesses her guilt to Theseus; she then takes poison.

Because *Phaedra* begins near its final crisis and occurs in a short span of time, information about earlier events—the background material that the audience needs to understand the play—must be reported in exposition. Racine manages this element well; he also masterfully articulates Phaedra's emotional conflict. Racine's language, especially his beautifully balanced phrases (in a line of poetry known as the *alexandrine)*, established a model that was to be followed in France for the next three centuries. To this day, French playwrights put a premium on the verbal skills and intellectual arguments of their characters.

Of all the French neoclassical playwrights, the one who exerts the most influence on modern theater is Molière, whose play *Tartuffe* was described at the opening of this chapter.

Molière

(Jean-Baptiste Poquelin; 1622–1673)

"If it be the aim of comedy to correct man's vices, then I do not see for what reason there should be a privileged class," wrote Molière in defense of *Tartuffe*. Several of his other comedies also shocked audiences, not because of their subject matter, but because he insisted on truthfully depicting vices and follies. His plays nevertheless earned the respect and patronage of enlightened theatergoers, and he remains one of the most popular dramatists of all time.

Molière wrote in the same restrictive neoclassical form as Corneille and Racine; the dialogue in many of his plays consists of rhymed couplets. In plays such as *The School for Wives* (1662), *The Doctor in Spite of Himself* (1666), and *The Would-Be Gentleman* (1670), he combined farcical humor with a gift for witty dialogue and a keen eye for human foibles. The misers, misanthropes, and hypochondriacs in his plays are still recognizable to twentieth-century audiences.

Many critics note the influence of commedia dell'arte on Molière: in particular, the characters in his plays resemble the stock types in commedia. In *The Miser,* for example, Harpagon is an avaricious old man reminiscent of Pantalone. Harpagon courts a young woman whom his son, Cléante, loves; and he betroths his daughter to an old man who does not require a dowry, even though she loves the younger Valère. His exaggerated miserliness is the basic obstacle to his children's happiness.

Molière's contrived plots, which adhere to the neoclassical rules, are frequently resolved by a deus ex machina. In *The Miser,* for example, Anselme, the old man to whom Harpagon's daughter is promised, coincidentally turns out to be the lost father of both Valère and the girl Cléante loves. Anselme allows his rediscovered son and daughter to marry Harpagon's children so that everyone can live happily ever after. Molière's plots, characters, and slapstick elements make his comedies especially popular with modern audiences.

Had he wanted financial stability, Jean-Baptiste Poquelin—Molière's original name—could have had either of two other careers. As the son of an upholsterer in the service of the king, he could have followed his father's profession; he could also have become a lawyer. In 1643, however, he left school, changed his name to Molière, and founded the Théâtre Illustre with the Béjart family of actors.

Molière's theater went bankrupt in 1645, and he was imprisoned for debt. Forced out of Paris by poor economic conditions, the troupe played in the provinces until 1658. During this time, Molière became an accomplished comic actor, noted for the subtlety of his performances. As a leader in the company, along with his mistress, Madeleine Béjart, Molière was able to coach the performers in his method, developing a disciplined ensemble.

In 1558, an influential patron secured a royal audience for the troupe. Louis XIV was much impressed by Molière's work, and the group was allowed to share a theater in Paris with an Italian commedia troupe, a situation that left the two companies constantly competing for funds. Besides being the company manager and an actor, Molière wrote about one-third of his troupe's plays. Although many of his plays were successful with the public and at court, others, like *Tartuffe,* were banned.

The king made Molière's troupe the King's Men in 1665, and Molière then wrote many court pageants and plays. By 1672, however, Louis's favor had gone to the composer Jean-Baptiste Lully, and Molière had to work harder for financial stability. Molière's home life was also unhappy. His wife, Armande Béjart, who was much younger, became notorious for her flirtations. Exhausted and suffering from a lung ailment, Molière collapsed during a performance of *The Imaginary Invalid* (1673) and died a few hours later. Because he was an actor and France at that time had laws preventing actors from receiving Christian burial, his funeral had to be held at night.

THEATER PRODUCTION IN FRANCE

Theaters and Scene Design

We have already noted that in Europe, the French were the first after the Romans to construct a permanent theater building. The Hôtel de Bourgogne, constructed by the Confraternity of the Passion, was completed in 1548 and for nearly a century was the sole permanent indoor theater building in Paris. The Bourgogne was not a proscenium-arch theater. It was a long, narrow building with a platform stage at one end. In front of the stage was a pit (the *parterre)* for standing spectators, and around the side and back walls were boxes *(loges)* and undivided galleries. The third tier of galleries along the side walls was known as the *paradis,* or "heavens." Until the seventeenth century, scenic practices at the Bourgogne were basically medieval.

When the Théâtre du Marais opened in 1634, the Hôtel de Bourgogne had its first competition. The Marais was a converted indoor tennis court. Court tennis (a game dating from the Middle Ages, played with a short-handled racket, usually in a roofed hall) was a popular Parisian diversion at the time; and before the Marais opened, if the Bourgogne was already leased to a theatrical company, other companies could perform in Paris in temporarily converted tennis courts. Since indoor tennis courts were long, narrow buildings like the

A FRENCH TENNIS COURT. This illustration, from the early seventeenth century, shows a French tennis court of the kind that was suitable for conversion to a theater space. A platform stage would be set up at one end, and seating would be added on the floor; to create a permanent playhouse, additional galleries could be added. The Théâtre du Marais in Paris is a famous example of a playing space that was converted from such a tennis court.

Bourgogne and had galleries for spectators, they were easily transformed into theaters: erecting a platform stage at one end of the building and installing additional temporary galleries would produce a theater space nearly identical to the Bourgogne. It is not surprising, then, that the second major Parisian theater building, the Marais, was a permanently converted tennis court.

Italian influences on French theater architecture became evident in 1641, when Cardinal Richelieu erected the Palais Cardinal, renamed the Palais Royal after his death. The Palais Cardinal was the first proscenium-arch theater in France; it also had Italianate scene-shifting machinery.

In the mid-1640s, the Italian scenic wizard Giacomo Torelli was brought to France to design scenery and install scene-changing equipment. Among his first undertakings was the transformation of a royal palace, the Petit Bourbon, into an Italian-style theater. He built a platform stage 6 feet high, 49 feet wide, and 48 feet deep and installed his pole-and-chariot system for scene shifting. He also installed the same system in the Palais Royal theater. With the arrival of Torelli, Italian design and scene-shifting techniques became firmly established in France; thus by the 1640s, Italian models for both playwriting and production were completely accepted.

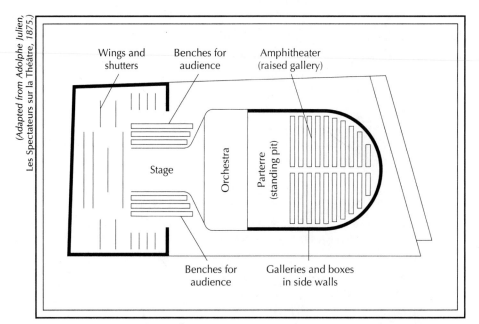

(Adapted from Adolphe Julien, Les Spectateurs sur la Théâtre, 1875.)

Wings and shutters

Benches for audience

Amphitheater (raised gallery)

Stage

Orchestra

Parterre (standing pit)

Benches for audience

Galleries and boxes in side walls

GROUND PLAN OF THE COMÉDIE FRANÇAISE. The French national theater performed in this playhouse for over 80 years, beginning in 1689. It had a proscenium-arch stage with machinery for scene changes, and a horseshoe-shaped auditorium that provided better sight lines. Spectators in the parterre stood, but the amphitheater—a raised gallery—had bleacher-like seating.

To keep up to date, both the Théâtre du Marais and the Hôtel de Bourgogne were remodeled into proscenium-arch theaters in the 1640s. Painted-perspective, wing-and-shutter scenery—shifted by the pole-and-chariot system—was used in the two remodeled theaters.

French proscenium-arch theater buildings differed slightly from those of the Italian Renaissance: in the back wall opposite the stage was an *amphithéâtre,* an undivided gallery that contained inexpensive bleacher-like seating. In both the Marais and the Bougogne, there was probably a small upper stage, raised 13 feet above the main stage, which was used for special effects such as flying. Also, at the close of the seventeenth century, upper-class audience members were frequently seated on the stage.

In the 1650s, Louis XIV's interest in ballet brought this form of entertainment back into prominence at court. Ballet productions were scenically quite spectacular. To satisfy the royal taste for elaborate effects, and to prepare for Louis's forthcoming marriage (which was to take place in 1660), Cardinal Mazarin, who had succeeded Richelieu, sent to Italy for another stage wizard, Gaspare Vigarani (1586–1663). To accommodate Vigarani's ambitious productions, the Petit Bourbon was torn down and a new theater was built in a wing added to the Tuileries Palace. This theater was known as the *Salle des Machines* ("Hall of Machines").

The Salle des Machines, completed in 1660, was the largest theater in Europe; it was 52 feet wide and 232 feet long. The auditorium took up only 92 of the 232 feet, leaving 140 feet for the stage and its machinery. The backstage equipment included one piece of machinery on which the entire royal family and all their attendants—well over 100 people—could be "flown" into the space above the stage. Because of its unsatisfactory acoustics, its size—especially backstage—and the expense of producing spectacles, the Salle des Machines was rarely used after 1670.

A major theater building of the French neoclassical period was the Comédie Française. This space housed the French national theater, which had been founded by Louis XIV in 1680 and moved into its own building in 1689. This theater was another converted tennis court; but its sight lines were significantly better than those of similar French spaces of the time because its interior had a horseshoe-shape construction. Such a shape places spectators not in back corners, but in a rounded area at the rear and sides with a better view of the stage.

Acting

ACTING COMPANIES

In seventeenth-century France, acting developed along with playwriting, stagecraft, and scenic effects.

The French acting companies of the seventeenth century were organized under a sharing plan, with *sociétaires* as shareholders and *pensionnaires* contracted to perform minor roles. Before 1650, there were generally eight to twelve performers in a company; after that, the number was larger: when the Comédie Française was formed in 1680, it had twenty-seven shareholders. Women were members of French theater companies and could become societaires.

Troupes spent little time on rehearsals, which were supervised by the playwright, by a leading actor of the company, or by both. At any given time, a company would have a repertory of up to seventy plays; and once a play had been introduced, the troupe was expected to be able to revive it on very short notice. The bill at a theater was changed daily.

Shareholders provided their own costumes, which consisted of either contemporary clothing or conventional historical outfits. Since this was an expensive practice, actors often received a subsidy for the costumes they wore in court productions—which could then be reused in public performances.

The history of acting companies in Paris is complex. In about 1629, a permanent company was organized at the Hôtel de Bourgogne. A competing company at the Théâtre du Marais was probably established a year or so later, although it did not perform in its permanent playhouse until about 1635. Throughout the century, commedia dell'arte enjoyed great success in Paris; and in 1661, one commedia troupe, under the management of Tiberio Fiorillo (1608–1694)—who was renowned for playing the role of Scaramouche—took up permanent residence in the city. As noted earlier, Molière's troupe, housed at the Palais Royal, was immensely popular between 1658 and 1673.

In 1673, then, there were five government-supported companies in Paris: these were the Opera, the Italian commedia dell'arte troupe, the Hôtel de Bourgogne company, the Théâtre du Marais company, and the troupe led by Molière. After Molière's death in 1673, Louis XIV ordered his troupe to merge with the Marais company, which thereafter performed as the Molière-Marais troupe.

In 1680, Louis consolidated the Bourgogne troupe with the Molière-Marais company. He gave the combined company a monopoly on the performance of spoken drama in French, making it the first national theater in the world. (The term *national theater* indicates a theater that is supposed to represent an entire nation. Great Britain, for example, has a Royal National Theater in London.) To distinguish it from the Comédie Italienne, which was also based in Paris, the new company was called the Comédie Française.

The Comédie Française

The establishment in 1680 of the Comédie Française, the government-supported French national theater, was a milestone in the history of western theater.

The new company—which was formed when Louis XIV merged two earlier troupes—had a number of distinguished players, and excellence in acting became one of its hallmarks. Through the years, its members have included many of France's leading actors, such as Adrienne Lecouvreur, Clairon (Claire Leyris de la Tudi), Henri Louis Lekain, François Joseph Talma, Rachel (Élisa Félix), Benoît Constant Coquelin, Sarah Bernhardt, and Jean-Louis Barrault.

To keep order among so many talented people, the Comédie Française was organized under the sharing plan of Molière's troupe; with some modifications, it still follows that plan today. Shares in the company were granted to its leading members—the *sociétaires*—according to each actor's status; some received less than a full share. The sociétaires were responsible for all company policy, including the selection of plays. Vacancies caused by retirement, resignation, or death were filled from the *pensionnaires,* actors hired by the troupe on a fixed salary. To become a pensionnaire, a performer had to audition successfully in both comedy and tragedy. The head of the company—the *doyen*—was the actor with the longest service in the troupe.

For its first 9 years, the Comédie Française used the Théâtre de Guénégaud. In 1689, the company moved into its own building; like many other French theaters of the time, this was a converted tennis court, but it had a horseshoe-shaped interior which provided better sight lines. (Today, the Comédie Française is housed in a different, later building.)

THE COMÉDIE FRANÇAISE. The establishment of the French national theater was a milestone in theater history. Shown here is its present home, in Paris.

The Comédie Française survived both the French Revolution and problems created by its own organization. For one thing, a secure appointment as a sociétaire sometimes led to complacency and arrogance. Also, since the Comédie Française had been granted a monopoly, the lack of outlets for plays had a stifling effect on French drama; this problem was worsened by the sociétaires' preference for imitative rather than innovative plays. In the nineteenth century, with the popularity of melodrama and the boulevard theaters, the Comédie Française suffered financially. Throughout its long history, however, it has preserved the best of French classical drama—Corneille, Racine, and Molière—as well as a distinguished tradition of classical acting.

PERFORMERS

There were many popular performers in Parisian acting companies of the seventeenth century. From the 1620s until his retirement in 1647, the leading actor with the company at the Hôtel de Bourgogne—called the King's Players—was Bellerose (Pierre le Messier, ca. 1592–1670), who excelled at both comedy and serious drama. (It was a common practice at this time for performers to use stage names, which were typically single names like Bellerose; another example, of course, is Molière.)

Debates in Theater History:

SHOULD THE UNITED STATES ENVY EUROPE'S NATIONAL THEATERS?

Louis XIV's creation of the Comédie Française as the French national theater in 1680 continues to have significant implications today. While theater companies in the United States can receive government support through the National Endowment for the Arts and state arts agencies, no theater has been designated as our national theater; and the concept of government-funded theater dedicated to a national drama is greatly envied by many American theater artists. Should we envy nations with a national theater?

People who say yes point to the long and illustrious history of the Comédie Française, and to the important playwrights whose works were produced there (the nineteenth-century romantic Victor Hugo is just one example). They argue that the Comédie Française keeps alive the classic plays of French theater—it is, after all, called the "home" of Molière. They also ask where in our own country we could find a theater dedicated to American drama and able to afford elaborate revivals of our great plays.

However, the issue is not that clear-cut. For one thing, the Comédie Française has frequently been criticized for being overly conservative. Many revolutionary and avant-garde playwrights, including the realists of the late nineteenth century, could not get their works produced there. In addition, its acting school—the Conservatoire, founded at the close of the eighteenth century—did not accept many of the performers who went on to significant careers and was often out of step with contemporary trends in performance. Often, the security represented by the Comédie Française has led to complacency and laziness among its tenured members. Critics of national theaters argue that rarely has the artistic director of the Comédie Française been innovative or daring. The historian Peter D. Arnott notes: "For the French, the Comédie Française has always been a mixed blessing. As a governmentally-supported institution, it has come to exemplify both the good and the ill of state intervention in the arts. . . . At times it has seemed that the main function of the Comédie Française has been to inspire experiment and creativity, out of sheer exasperation, in others."*

Furthermore, some commentators note that although government support is a financial boon to artists, it can also have insidious—even dangerous—implications. Governments can control content and political point of view through financial manipulation. Also, overreliance on government support can undermine a theater company; and such support may suddenly decrease or vanish when there are changes in the economic or political climate.

Many other countries, of course, have established national theaters along the lines of the Comédie Française. In England, for instance, the National Theater and the Royal Shakespeare Company receive significant government subsidies. Both have been criticized for becoming too commercially oriented and for being more interested in constructing new buildings than in presenting artistically innovative work, though their defenders point out that many intriguing productions have been given at these theaters during the past decade.

In the United States, many critics have argued that a national theater is not possible because our large country does not have a natural artistic center. But even if a national theater were to be founded in the United States, the question remains: Can a government-supported theater be innovative, revolutionary, and thought-provoking?

*Peter D. Arnott, *An Introduction to the French Theatre*, Rowman and Littlefield, Totowa, N.J., 1977.

MICHEL BARON. The leading tragic actor of the French neoclassical era was Michel Baron, who was noted for a less stilted, more natural acting style. Baron worked with Molière and later with the Comédie Française, the French national theater. When the Comédie Française had difficulties in the eighteenth century, Baron came out of retirement to help.

At the Théâtre du Marais, the outstanding actor was Montdory (Guillaume des Gilleberts, 1594–1654). Montdory was a favorite of Cardinal Richelieu, who granted him a subsidy. Among Montdory's roles was the title character in Corneille's *The Cid.* When Montdory retired from the Marais, he was replaced by Floridor (Josias de Soulas, 1608–1672). Because of Montdory and Floridor, the Marais troupe was regarded as the leading company in Paris until 1647; after that, however, the Hôtel de Bourgogne once more became the leading theater.

In the last half of the seventeenth century, many of the leading performers in France were associated with Molière, who was a superb comic actor himself and performed in most of his own plays. A highly acclaimed actress in Molière's troupe was Madeleine Béjart (1618–1672), who played tragic heroines in the early stages of her career but later performed comic roles for Molière.

DuParc (Marquise-Thérèse de Gorla, 1633–1668), an outstanding tragic actress, began with Molière's company but was persuaded by Racine to act at the Hôtel de Bourgogne. Another leading tragic actress—near the end of the century—was Champmeslé (Marie-Desmares Champmeslé, 1642–1698), who created such roles as Phaedra. The most noted tragic actor of his day was Michel Baron (1653–1729). Armande Béjart—who had been raised by Madeleine Béjart and eventually became Molière's wife—was the leading actress in his troupe in its later years. After its formation in 1680, Champmeslé, Baron, and Armande Béjart all joined the Comédie Française.

Armande Béjart

(1642–1700)

The young wife of Molière, Armande Béjart, created roles in many of his plays. She had been trained for the stage by Molière and also inspired some of his writing.

The youngest child of Joseph Béjart and Marie Hervé, Armande Grésinde Claire Elisabeth Béjart was born in 1642, some months after the death of her father, into a large, poor Parisian family. Armande's oldest sister, Madeleine Béjart, gave birth to an illegitimate daughter at about the same time as Armande was born, and in later years Armande was widely believed to be Madeleine's daughter. There was even speculation that Molière was Armande's father.

By the time of Armande's birth, Madeleine and her brother Joseph had begun their acting careers; and in 1643 they joined with other actors, including Molière, to found the Théâtre Illustre. Madeleine Béjart was Molière's lover and a driving force in the company, holding many responsibilities such as overseeing its finances. By 1653, Armande Béjart was apparently traveling with the company, and her education was supervised by Molière.

Given her theatrical family and her prolonged exposure to the stage, it is not surprising that Armande Béjart became an actress. In addition to a lively and charming stage manner, which suited her to roles in comedy, Armande was a talented singer and dancer. Molière had directed Armande's theatrical training, and he married his pupil on February 20, 1662; but he did not let her make her debut until more than a year later, when he was convinced that she was thoroughly prepared.

Armande's first, small role was Élise in Molière's *Critique of the School for Wives*. In May of 1644, during entertainments held at Versailles for Louis XIV, Armande moved into major roles, creating the role of Elmire in the first presentation of *Tartuffe* and the Princess in the comedy ballet *Princess d'Elide*. Other roles in Molière's plays premiered by Armande include Lucinde in *The Doctor in Spite of Himself*, Angélique in *George Dandin*, Célimène in *The Misanthrope*, Lucille in *The Would-Be Gentleman*, Henriette in *The Learned Ladies*, and Angélique in *The Imaginary Invalid*.

Although they worked together successfully, Molière and Armande Béjart did not have a happy marriage. Armande was flirtatious and attracted many men, provoking the jealousy of her husband. In fact, the couple separated after the birth of their second child in 1665, though they were reconciled 5 years later. After Molière's death, Armande led his company in cooperation with the actor LaGrange. In 1677, she married another actor, Guerin d'Estriche. In 1680, along with the remainder of Molière's company, Armande became an original member of the Comédie Française. She acted with the Comédie Française until her retirement in 1694.

Audiences

Before the founding of the Comédie Française, most French theater companies performed only about three times a week for the public; in 1672–1673, for example, Molière's troupe gave only 131 performances. These public performances did not, apparently, attract very large audiences. In the year before his death, Molière's company averaged only 400 spectators per performance. Even the Comédie Française, which had a monopoly, played to only 425 to 450 spectators per performance during the 1680s and 1690s. These figures mean that large public theaters were usually filled to only 20 to 25 percent of capacity. Some plays were popular enough to attract near-capacity audiences—and to run for 15 to 30 performances—but they were rare.

In Paris, performance time was early afternoon until 1680, when the Comédie Française began its plays at 5 P.M. Audiences at Parisian theaters included all strata of society. However, the theater probably became less and less affordable for working-class people because admission to the parterre was priced significantly higher throughout the 1600s. The parterre was only for men; women sat in boxes or in the amphitheater, depending on their social and economic status.

As in Shakespeare's time, there are some contemporary accounts of audience members as being noisy and misbehaving in other ways. However, scholars warn that these complaints must be taken with a grain of salt, since they were sometimes made by disgruntled playwrights or commentators who were unhappy with the state of French theater.

By 1700, both the French nation and its theater had settled into conservatism. In 1685, Louis XIV revoked the Edict of Nantes, which had ensured freedom of conscience; about 200,000 Huguenots were forced to leave the country, depriving France of wealth, intelligence, and talent—as had been the case in Spain 200 years earlier, when its Jews and Moors were expelled. Louis himself became more and more puritanical and no longer attended the theater. As of 1697, when Louis expelled the Comédie Italienne after its performance of a political satire, the Comédie Française and the Opera monopolized theater in Paris; and the popularity of opera put a premium on elaborate scenery. The days of new dramas by playwrights like Corneille, Racine, and Molière were over.

SUMMARY

French neoclassical theater expanded and refined Italian Renaissance practices. Most French drama, including the tragedies of Corneille and Racine and the comedies of Molière, followed the neoclassical rules. The plays of seventeenth-century France, however, achieved a quality and distinction far exceeding those produced in the Italian Renaissance.

By the mid-seventeenth century, French theaters were proscenium-arch spaces with painted-perspective, wing-and-shutter scenery.

A milestone in theater history was the establishment of the Comédie Française, the government-supported French national theater, in 1680.

PART THREE

THEATER FROM 1660 TO 1875

Between 1660 and 1875, people in Europe and America undertook to change the world—to transform politics, industry, and education.

In England, the monarchy was restored in 1660; but in the years to come, the power of kings and queens would be diminished and in many cases abolished. The end of the eighteenth century saw the American and French revolutions. France returned to authoritarian rule in the early nineteenth century, with Napoleon, but kingship there was never to be the same again. Socially, during this period, there was a significant increase in the size and importance of the middle class.

The eighteenth century was known as the *age of enlightenment*. People believed that the mind was all-powerful, and that all problems could be solved through the intellect. The nineteenth century was called the *century of progress*. It was the era of the industrial revolution—the development of machines for manufacturing and transportation. In the eighteenth century, ideas were supposed to solve problems; in the nineteenth century, industrialization was supposed to solve them. Workers in factories would get wages that would allow them to buy goods; the factories would supply goods for everyone. Things did not work out exactly as planned, but this expectation indicates the optimism of the time.

Social and political changes were reflected in the arts. Music moved from the baroque world of Bach and Handel to the classicism of Mozart and Beethoven, and then to the romanticism of Schubert, Chopin, and Liszt. Similarly, theater during this era was in transition. The roots of modern theater can be found in transformations which took place in drama of the English Restoration and the eighteenth and early nineteenth centuries.

The theatrical innovations of this period are too numerous to list. A modern version of the proscenium-arch theater—the version we still have on Broadway and across the country—was developed. Technology was introduced into scene design, and more realistic stage effects became popular. Primitive candle lighting gave way to more controllable gas lighting. (In 1881, electricity was to be introduced.) Historically accurate costumes became more commonplace, and costumes were designed in terms of characterization.

The business of theater as we know it today evolved during these years, including the rise of the theatrical entrepreneur, the decline of the repertory company, the establishment of the long run, and the appearance of the star system. The art of acting gradually became more concerned with portraying everyday life, and the director became the controlling artist in theater.

The dramatic forms of these two centuries—such as comedy of manners, romanticism, melodrama, and the well-made play—are still used by today's writers. Melodramatic films and television shows are direct descendants of nineteenth-century popular drama; the American dramatist Arthur Miller has written well-made plays; and *Private Lives* (1930) and *Blithe Spirit* (1941) by the English playwright Nöel Coward (1899–1973) are comedies of manners. If we look closely at our own theater, we can see how indebted we are to the dramatic arts of these years of change.

CHAPTER 9

THE THEATER OF THE ENGLISH RESTORATION

I t is a raw, overcast day in January 1675, and we have been invited by two young men—students at Cambridge—to join them at a theater in London. Our two friends are members of the nobility: one is the son of a duke and the other the son of an earl. Together, we are making our way to the new Drury Lane Theater. Another theater once stood at the site of the Drury Lane, but it burned in 1672; the new theater, designed by the architect Christopher Wren and erected on the same spot, opened only a year ago, in 1674.

Our friends, the two young noblemen, assure us that this will be an exhilarating afternoon. The play we will see is a new one by William Wycherley called *The Country Wife*. For several days, bills announcing this new play have been thrown into our friends' carriages and even left with the servants who answer the door at their homes. They tell us that the story is based loosely on a play by the Roman writer Terence, and on scenes from two plays by the French

RESTORATION COMEDY. Style, gossip, intrigue, and plot complications are the hallmarks of English Restoration comedy. A good example is *Love for Love* by William Congreve, which deals with the romantic intrigues of two young lovers, Angelica and Valentine. In this scene, Angelica is played by Goldie Semple, and her uncle Sir Sampson Legend by Douglas Rain; the production is by the Stratford Shakespeare Festival in Canada. *(David Cooper/Stratford Festival)* writer Molière. They know people who have recently returned from France, where Molière's plays are all the rage. They are sure, however, that Wycherley will make of this material something thoroughly English. For one thing, the language—and what language!—will be completely his. They assure us that we will hear witty, rapier-like exchanges between the characters, and doubtless many *double-entendres:* clever lines which operate on two levels, one rather ordinary and the other decidedly sexual.

It is just after two o'clock in the afternoon. The play will not begin until 3:30, but our friends want to arrive at the theater early—to talk to their acquaintances, to flirt with the attractive young women who sell oranges and other things to eat, and even to go backstage to try to see the actresses. They are not worried about finding seats; they have sent a servant ahead to reserve seats in one of the boxes, for which they have paid extra. Ordinarily a ticket is in the form of brass check, but for special performances like this new play, printed paper tickets are issued.

As we arrive at the playhouse, we join a carefree, pleasure-loving crowd. Many of the audience members, like our friends, belong to noble families. Others are part of the literary or artistic world. Still others are young gallants hoping to find a wife from a wealthy family, and men and women who have large country houses outside London but come to town for special occasions such as parties, balls, and festivities at court. With all this, there are also people who serve the others: coachmen, footmen, vendors, and prostitutes; the prostitutes consider the theater an excellent place to find customers among the gallants.

When we enter the theater—a building 58 feet wide by 140 feet long—our friends, who have been here before, are impressed once again with the new structure and its simple, classical, but elegant appearance. The new Drury Lane seats 650 people, some in a pit facing the stage, others in boxes and galleries along the sides and back. Its stage is a platform about 34 feet deep; the front half of the stage is open and the back half is framed by a proscenium and contains the scenic elements.

After socializing and other preliminaries—hearing the latest gossip about politics and the court, flirting, and making plans for future social engagements—we take our seats in our box, anxious for *The Country Wife* to begin.

The first person we see onstage is an actor named Charles Hart, who delivers a prologue; then the play itself begins. Hart is the male lead; he plays a character called Horner, who spreads the rumor that he is impotent because of a venereal disease he contracted while abroad. Horner's doctor, Quack, substantiates the rumor, and Horner uses this "cover story" to gain access to his acquaintances' wives. The one he most desires is Margery Pinchwife, a naive woman whose husband usually keeps her locked away in the country and tries to disguise her as a boy when they are in town. Coming on Pinchwife and the disguised Margery in the street, Horner realizes that the "boy" is a woman in a man's clothing and takes advantage of the situation to make amorous advances, hugging and kissing her in front of her husband, who can do nothing. During the course of the dramatic action, a subplot develops: Horner's friend Harcourt steals Pinchwife's sister Alithea away from her intended husband, Sparkish.

In our box, we are all particularly taken with Elizabeth Bowtell, who plays Margery. In France and Spain, actresses have appeared on the stage for some time; but England forbade actresses until 1660—only a few years ago—and so seeing women onstage is a novelty that strongly appeals to the men in the audience. Moreover, ever since women have been allowed to perform onstage in England, a favorite dramatic device is to have a woman dress as a man; parts that require this kind of cross-dressing are called *breeches roles.* Seeing a woman's buttocks outlined in tight trousers, and getting a good idea of the shape of her legs—which are usually hidden under wide skirts—has a strong sexual fascination. Watching Bowtell—an attractive actress—play Margery disguised as a man has a special appeal to our friends, and to us.

There is another element of the play which delights us: the characters' names. As is typical of plays written in this period, these names indicate the characters' desires and personalities. The chief character, Horner, wants to cuckold his acquaintances—that is, seduce their wives. His name, therefore, comes from a well-known image: a husband with an adulterous wife is traditionally depicted as wearing horns. Quack, obviously, is a disreputable doctor; Harcourt courts Alithea diligently. Two other characters, Fidget and Squeamish, are nervous about their reputations; Pinchwife does not want his wife pinched by other men. Sparkish, a fop, thinks he is a great wit, a social "spark"; in reality, he is dimwitted.

We are also titillated by the sexual references—especially by a scene which is to become famous, the "china closet" scene. In this scene, Horner and Lady Fidget are in a room offstage while Lady Fidget's husband is onstage listening to their conversation. Horner and Lady Fidget are supposed to be examining Horner's collection of china, but the audience soon realizes that Horner is actually making love to Lady Fidget while her husband stands by in ignorance. Then another woman, Mrs. Squeamish, arrives, and she too asks to see Horner's china. When Horner tells Mrs. Squeamish he has no more, the audience knows that *china* has become a code word for *sex* and that Horner is unable at that moment to make love.

At the conclusion of the play, Horner's scheme has been successful: he has made love not only to Margery but to the other wives as well.

We and our friends—and the rest of the audience—have enjoyed ourselves tremendously. *The Country Wife* has been titillating and highly amusing. Our aristocratic friends have responded especially to the wit, the style, and the social intrigue. We suddenly realize that, after the play was over, one of our two companions disappeared. The other explains that our vanished friend has made an assignation with one of the young actresses—which he hopes will lead to the same results offstage that Horner achieved onstage.

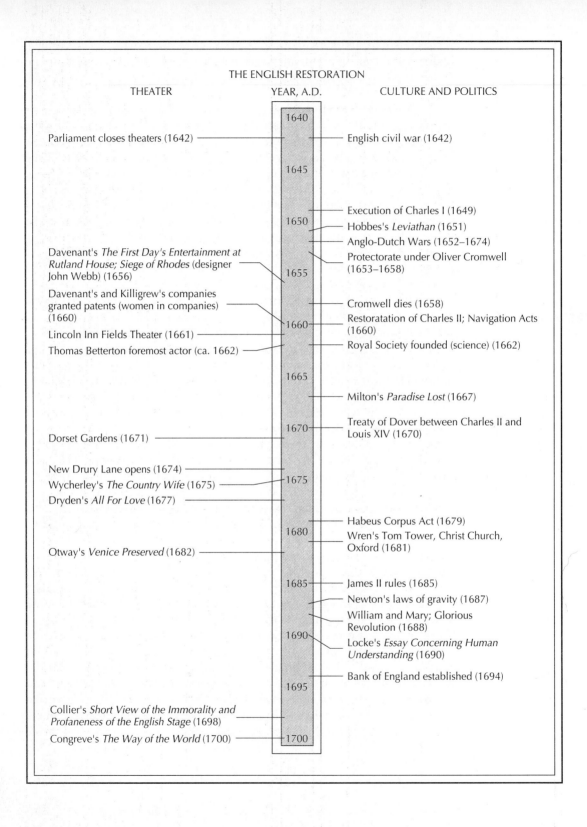

THE ENGLISH RESTORATION

THEATER	YEAR, A.D.	CULTURE AND POLITICS

1640

Parliament closes theaters (1642) ——————— English civil war (1642)

1645

——— Execution of Charles I (1649)

1650 ——— Hobbes's *Leviathan* (1651)

——— Anglo-Dutch Wars (1652–1674)

Davenant's *The First Day's Entertainment at Rutland House; Siege of Rhodes* (designer John Webb) (1656) ——— Protectorate under Oliver Cromwell (1653–1658)

1655

Davenant's and Killigrew's companies granted patents (women in companies) (1660) ——— Cromwell dies (1658)

——— Restoratation of Charles II; Navigation Acts (1660)

1660

Lincoln Inn Fields Theater (1661) ——— Royal Society founded (science) (1662)

Thomas Betterton foremost actor (ca. 1662) ———

1665

——— Milton's *Paradise Lost* (1667)

1670 ——— Treaty of Dover between Charles II and Louis XIV (1670)

Dorset Gardens (1671) ———

New Drury Lane opens (1674) ———

1675

Wycherley's *The Country Wife* (1675) ———

Dryden's *All For Love* (1677) ———

——— Habeus Corpus Act (1679)

1680 ——— Wren's Tom Tower, Christ Church, Oxford (1681)

Otway's *Venice Preserved* (1682) ———

1685 ——— James II rules (1685)

——— Newton's laws of gravity (1687)

——— William and Mary; Glorious Revolution (1688)

1690 ——— Locke's *Essay Concerning Human Understanding* (1690)

——— Bank of England established (1694)

1695

Collier's *Short View of the Immorality and Profaneness of the English Stage* (1698) ———

Congreve's *The Way of the World* (1700) ——— 1700

BACKGROUND: THE RESTORATION

Charles I of England was removed from the throne by Oliver Cromwell and the Puritans after a bitter civil war lasting from 1642 to 1649; in 1649, Charles was beheaded. For the next 11 years, England was governed by Cromwell, along with a Parliament that had been purged of his opponents: this is known as the period of the *commonwealth*. Cromwell died in 1658, and his son was unable to keep control of the English government; in 1660, Charles II, who had been living in France, was invited by a newly elected Parliament to return from exile to rule England. In other words, the monarchy was restored, and this gave the name *Restoration* to the period that followed.

The reinstatement of the monarchy also meant a restoration of other institutions: Parliament, the legislative body; the Anglican church (its counterpart in the United States is the Episcopal church), the official church formed by Henry VIII when he broke with Roman Catholicism; and the cavalier gentry, the titled nobles who owned land and were next in rank to the royal family.

Though Parliament was restored, Charles II refused to give it much power; in the final years of his reign, he ruled without it. When Charles died in 1685, he was succeeded by his brother, James II, who had been converted to Catholicism. James's reign was turbulent; when his wife gave birth to a son, a Catholic line threatened Protestant England. For this reason, Parliament invited James's Protestant daughter Mary and her husband William of Orange (the royal house of the Netherlands) to rule England. William and Mary deposed James II in the bloodless Glorious Revolution in 1688.

Many historians consider that England entered a new phase with the accession of William and Mary in 1688, and therefore that this date marks the end of the Restoration period. In theater, though, the developments of the Restoration that had begun in 1660 continued until the turn of the century; that is, Restoration drama continued beyond 1688 to 1700. Mary died in 1694; when William died in 1702 and her sister Anne became queen, both the political and the theatrical Restoration had come to an end.

During the Restoration, political thought in England was transformed by the philosophers Thomas Hobbes (1588–1679) and John Locke (1632–1704), who propounded the concept of natural law. According to both Hobbes and Locke, certain laws in the world are naturally right and should not be violated; any ruler who does violate them should be removed from power. Since human beings are rational, Hobbes and Locke believed that these natural rights could be discerned by reason. Hobbes and Locke, however, had different ideas about what form of government would best protect natural rights. Hobbes theorized, in *Leviathan* (1651), that people give up freedom of action to absolute rulers in order to secure civil order and peace. Hobbes compared the structure of government to Leviathan, a biblical monster. Absolutism is meant to ensure individual welfare and uphold natural rights. (For this reason, Hobbes's ideal absolute ruler is the antithesis of such twentieth-century totalitarian dictators as Adolf Hitler and Josef Stalin.) Locke, on the other hand, preferred a representative government with a constitution, arguing that rulers are responsible to the people and serve as their representatives. According to Locke, government is created to protect life, liberty, and property; rebellion against a government which violates these rights is more acceptable than allowing such violations to continue.

The views of Hobbes and Locke became highly influential in the eighteenth century. Enlightened despots—monarchs who believed that they ruled for the good of their people—modeled themselves after Hobbes's ideal absolutist. The leaders of the American and French revolutions were clearly influenced by the writings of Locke.

In England, the transformations that took place during the reigns of Charles II, James II, and William and Mary were not only political or religious. Immediately after the Restoration, England expanded rapidly into the new world across the Atlantic; English colonies spread from New England to the Carolinas. The East India Company established trading posts in Surat, Madras, Calcutta, and Bombay. Cultural and scientific advances were also made. In 1662, the Royal Society of London for Improving Natural Knowledge was established; Isaac Newton, renowned for his experiments with gravity, was an original member. During the Restoration the great architect Christopher Wren rebuilt Saint Paul's Cathedral, which had been destroyed by the fire of London in 1666. Thus, the restoration of the monarchy was followed by a restoration of trade, science, and culture.

THEATER DURING THE COMMONWEALTH

The Puritans closed the theaters in 1642, and from then until 1660 theatrical activity was severely curtailed. Elizabethan playhouses were dismantled, and actors were persecuted. Nevertheless, the laws forbidding theater were not completely effective, and some entertainments were organized secretly. *Drolls*—short versions of full-length plays, usually comedies—were the form of drama most often staged. One such droll was *Bottom the Weaver,* adapted from Shakespeare's *A Midsummer Night's Dream.*

An important theatrical producer during the commonwealth period was William Davenant, who had been a court playwright before the closing of the theaters. Davenant was able to circumvent the ordinances against theater by describing his presentations as musical entertainments and by originally staging them at his home. By the mid-1650s, however, opposition to the Puritans was increasing and subterfuge was not all that necessary. In 1656, Davenant presented *The First Day's Entertainment at Rutland House* and *The Siege of Rhodes.*

The Siege of Rhodes was particularly significant because the production had a proscenium arch and wing-and-shutter setting—a stage arrangement that represented a clear departure from the platform stage of Shakespeare's day. Davenant's theater was designed by John Webb (1611-1672), a student of Inigo Jones. Webb's use of Italianate devices was not surprising, since Jones had introduced such devices in court entertainments before Cromwell's abolition of the monarchy and Webb had assisted him in executing the designs.

Another figure in returning theater to England was Thomas Killigrew.

Davenant.

Killigrew.

William Davenant

(1606–1668)

Thomas Killigrew

(1612–1683)

The revival of English theater in the second half of the seventeenth century came about through the efforts of William Davenant and Thomas Killigrew. Both men were familiar with English theatrical tradition, since they had been active in theater before the commonwealth, but their leadership was to take English theater in a new direction.

Davenant's theatrical experience went back to Shakespeare, who was said to have been a frequent visitor at his father's inn in Oxford and also to have been Davenant's godfather. After briefly attending Lincoln College at Oxford, Davenant began writing plays and collaborated with Inigo Jones on several court masques. In 1638, he succeeded Ben Jonson as poet laureate. He was knighted in 1643 for his service to the royalist cause; and he was imprisoned for a year by the Parliamentary forces.

Killigrew was also a supporter of the royalist cause and had stayed with the royal family throughout its exile in France. Before the closing of the theaters, he had written a number of tragicomedies. According to the diarist Samuel Pepys, Killigrew was a "merry droll" and a favorite of Charles I.

Davenant's *The Siege of Rhodes* is considered the first English opera. It was also the first production in which actresses appeared on the English stage and the first public performance in which changeable scenery was used. In 1660, Davenant went to France to persuade Charles II to grant him a license for a theater. That year, Charles granted Davenant and Killigrew a patent that gave them a monopoly on theatrical productions in London.

After they had suppressed several unlicensed troupes, the two managers divided their own company. Killigrew formed the King's Company with the older, more experienced actors; Davenant's Duke's Company had several of the promising young actors, including Thomas Betterton, who was to become the best actor of the Restoration. Davenant's company proved to be the stronger and better managed of the two, even after his death in 1668. Killigrew—who had been made Master of the Revels in 1673, with authority over all theater in England—was often in financial difficulties. In 1682, a year before Killigrew's death, the two companies were reunited to prevent his troupe from going bankrupt.

RESTORATION DRAMA

With the restoration of the English monarchy, English theater came to life again.

During the English Renaissance, drama and theater had not followed Italian Renaissance practices. Italian practices had been introduced, however, in Jacobean and Caroline court entertainments and in Davenant's presentations, and during the Restoration they truly took hold.

This Italian influence was reinforced by contact between England and neoclassical France in the late seventeenth century. French culture was especially influential in Restoration society because Charles II had spent his exile in France and because his successor, James II, a convert to Catholicism, had ties with Catholic Europe.

As we will see, the illusionistic—almost magical—devices of the proscenium-arch theater, in which painted-perspective wing-and-shutter sets could be changed before the audience's eyes, would now become part of the English stage. On the other hand, however, much of the Elizabethan theatrical tradition would remain. The unique flavor of Restoration theater is, in fact, its fusion of Elizabethan stage conventions with those of the Italian and French theaters in drama, theater architecture, and set design.

(In this section, we'll consider Restoration drama; other aspects of Restoration theater—audiences, performers, regulation of theaters, theater architecture, and visual elements—will be discussed later in the chapter.)

Serious Drama

The serious drama of the Restoration is rarely produced, or even read, today. One type of serious drama was *heroic tragedy*, popular between 1660 and 1675. Heroic tragedies dealt with extraordinary characters who undertook extraordinary deeds. These contrived plays, which deal with the themes of love and honor, are reminiscent of the dramas of the Spanish golden age and the French neoclassical era.

Another type of serious drama, usually referred to as *Restoration tragedy*, became popular during the last quarter of the seventeenth century. The Italianate influence is immediately apparent in Restoration tragedies because of their adherence to the neoclassical rules.

John Dryden (1631–1700) is the most noted author of Restoration tragedy; his *All for Love* (1677) transformed Shakespeare's *Antony and Cleopatra* into a neoclassical tragedy. It was not unusual for Restoration playwrights to rework Shakespeare. *Romeo and Juliet,* for example, was provided with a happy ending by a writer named James Howard. Nahum Tate (1652–1715), who altered the ending of *King Lear* so that Lear is restored to his throne and Cordelia does not die, was among the best-known of the writers who adapted Shakespearean plays.

Restoration Comedy

COMEDIES OF INTRIGUE

The great plays of the English Restoration were its comedies. Several types of comedy were popular. Comedies of "humour" followed the tradition of Ben Jonson, in which characters have one trait overshadowing all others. There were also farces; comedies of manners; and comedies of intrigue, which featured daring exploits of romance and adventure and had complicated plots. One of the most successful writers of comedies of intrigue was Aphra Behn.

Aphra Behn

(1640–1689)

During the Restoration, when actresses were first appearing on the English stage, the first woman English playwright also appeared. Aphra Behn is not only the first known English woman dramatist; she is the first to have earned a living by writing. In addition to being a dramatist, she was also a poet and novelist.

Her early life was both colorful and difficult. She was brought up in the West Indies, and her novel *Oroonoko* (1688) incorporates her memories of her early life there. She returned to England in 1658, when she was 18, and married a Dutch merchant but was soon widowed. She went to the Netherlands as a spy during the war with the Dutch and was apparently successful in her work. She does not seem to have been paid, however, because she was briefly imprisoned for debt.

Friends helped her get out of prison, and she began writing. Beginning in 1670—when her first play, *The Forced Marriage,* was produced—she wrote at least twenty plays. Several of them proved successful, and some remained an active part of the theater repertoire until well into the eighteenth century.

Behn wrote at the height of the Restoration, when licentiousness in drama was the rule rather than the exception, and her plays did not shy away from bawdiness. In such plays as *The Town Fop* and *The Rover,* both written in 1677, she even went so far as to show scenes in brothels. Defending her play *Sir Patient Fancy* (1678), she wrote, "It was bawdy, the least and most excusable fault in the men writers, to whose plays they all crowd, as if they came to no other end than to hear what they condemn in this, but from a woman it was unnatural."

Though there was some prejudice against her because of her gender, she overcame it with her successes. In fact, she and her friend John Dryden were the two most successful playwrights of the period. Dryden spoke of her as "writeing loosely, and giveing, if I may have leave to say so, some scandall to the modest of her sex. I confess, I am the last man who ought, in justice, to arraign her, who have been myself too much a libertine in most of my poems."

Behn is best known for her tragicomedies of intrigue, which are skillfully contrived; some of them are influenced by Spanish theater and Italian commedia dell'arte. She also wrote tragedies, comedies, and plays concerned with moral problems; and her later work was primarily farce, which appealed to the taste of her audiences. Among her plays of intrigue are *The Dutch Lover* (1673), *Abdelazar* (1677), and *Patient Fancy* (1678). Her popular comedies include *The Amorous Prince* (1671), *The Feigned Courtesans* (1679), *The False Count* (1681), and *The City Heiress* (1682). One of her most successful farces was *The Emperor of the Moon* (1687). Thomas Betterton, one of the best-known actors of the time, performed in her first play, *The Forced Marriage,* and in her first success, *The Rover.* A lively, inventive writer, Behn was nicknamed the "divine Astrea," after a goddess in classical mythology.

Following Behn, there were a significant number of other female playwrights in Restoration and eighteenth-century England.

COMEDIES OF MANNERS

It is not for tragedy or comedy of intrigue that Restoration drama has become famous but rather for comedy of manners.

Comedy of manners, which was influenced by the works of the French dramatist Molière, focuses on the fashions and foibles of the upper class—gossip, adultery, sexual escapades. These comedies poke fun at the social conventions and norms of the time and satirize the preoccupation of the upper class with reputation: most of the upper-class characters in the plays are disreputable. Language—witty exchanges, repartee, and sexually suggestive references—is at a premium.

The dramatic structure of Restoration comedy of manners combines features of Elizabethan theater with features of French and Italian neoclassical theater. For instance, William Wycherley's *The Country Wife*—described at the opening of this chapter—has elements of both crisis form and episodic form. Its action is far more unified than the action in a Shakespearean play; it has only eight scene shifts and takes place in less than 36 hours. At the same time, unlike the plays of Racine or Molière, it moves from place to place, has a rather large number of characters, and includes a subplot. The characters in Restoration comedy are stock types; their names usually describe their distinctive personality traits. A common character is the fop who mistakenly believes himself to be witty and fashionable.

One of the first dramatists to perfect comedy of manners was George Etherege (ca. 1634–1691), in plays such as *She Would If She Could* (1668) and *The Man of Mode* (1676). By far the two most renowned playwrights of this type of Restoration comedy, however, were William Wycherley and William Congreve.

William Wycherley

(1640–1716)

In his plays, William Wycherley satirized the elegant, dissolute society of Restoration England. In his life, however, he was a member of that society, participating fully in all the vices and follies that he ridiculed as a dramatist.

Like many Restoration dramatists, Wycherley wrote only a few plays; playwriting for him was a way to display cleverness and wit rather than a serious profession. Unlike his contemporaries, he showed the faults of all members of his glittering society rather than just making fun of the usual butts. A well-read man, he borrowed characters and situations from several sources, especially Molière and Terence. He was a master of the sexual humor of his time (such as words with double meanings); his works shocked the more prudish audiences of later centuries. Congreve wrote that Wycherley's purpose was "to lash this crying age" with satire.

As the son of a landowner, Wycherley had the requisite family background for entrance into society. He was educated first in France and then, briefly, at Oxford. He began studying law at the Inner Temple in London but was soon practicing not law but pleasure. His first comedy, *Love in a Wood; or, St. James Park,* produced in 1671, brought him to the attention of the duchess of Cleveland, the king's mistress, who did not hesitate to share her favors.

Wycherley soon became one of London's leading wits and was sponsored at court by the duke of Buckingham, a favorite of Charles II. Three more of his comedies were successfully produced: *The Gentleman Dancing-Master* in 1672, *The Country Wife* in 1675, and *The Plain Dealer* in 1676.

Wycherley's most famous play is *The Country Wife.* As we have seen, it concerns a man named Pinchwife, who has recently married Margery, a girl from the country. Pinchwife tries to hide Margery away so that she will not be corrupted by the wicked ways of the fashionable set in London, but his precautions are undermined by a man named Horner. Horner is pretending to be a eunuch in order to lull the suspicions of the men whose wives he intends to seduce. *The Country Wife* was revised by David Garrick in the eighteenth century as *The Country Girl;* stripped of some of the sexual innuendo of the original, this was a popular version.

After writing *The Plain Dealer,* Wycherley went to sea and fought in the Dutch wars. When he fell ill, Charles II gave him money to recuperate in France and promised to make him the tutor of one of the princes. Instead, Wycherley married a wealthy, jealous countess in 1681 and lost Charles's favor. Wycherley's wife died the next year; he became involved in litigation over her estate, lost the case, and spent 7 years in debtors' prison before James II paid his bills and gave him a small pension. Eleven days before his death in 1716, Wycherley married a young woman, apparently to provoke his nephew.

William Congreve

(1670–1729)

Commenting on the fate of dramatists, William Congreve wrote in a prologue to his play *The Way of the World:*

> Of those few fools who with ill stars are cursed,
> Sure scribbling fools called poets, fare the worst.

His words proved to be prophetic, for *The Way of the World* ended his own brief career as a playwright. With his four comedies, however, Congreve had established his reputation as one of the Restoration's finest dramatists.

Congreve, the son of an English army officer, was raised and educated in Dublin, where the writer Jonathan Swift was one of his schoolmates. He returned to England to study law at the Middle Temple but instead became involved in the literary and social life of Restoration London. Congreve's first literary venture was an undistinguished novel; he turned next to playwriting with *The Old Bachelor,* produced in 1693 to great acclaim.

With his first success as a playwright came financial stability; this led to a series of government appointments secured for him by influential friends. Always careful with his money, Congreve acquired a reputation for miserliness in later life. His second comedy, *The Double Dealer* (1694), was less successful; but *Love for Love,* produced the following year by the actor Thomas Betterton, was Congreve's greatest stage triumph. A tragedy, *The Mourning Bride* (1697), was also well received. *The Way of the World,* however—which would later be considered the best Restoration comedy—was a failure when it was first produced in 1700, and Congreve stopped writing for the stage. One of the reasons for the failure of *The Way of the World* was a changed moral climate in England.

His four comedies gave Congreve an assured place in the best literary and social circles of London—for the rest of his life he was a friend of Pope, Swift, Steele, and Gray. Congreve died in 1729 and was buried in Westminster Abbey.

THE DECLINE OF RESTORATION COMEDY

In the satirical universe of Restoration comedy, marital infidelity abounds yet goes unpunished. It is no wonder, then, that the Puritans attacked Restoration theater. In 1698, Jeremy Collier, a minister, wrote *A Short View of the Immorality and Profaneness of the English Stage.* Some historians suggest that Collier's treatise marks the end of the theatrical Restoration: after his attack,

THE WAY OF THE WORLD. The most famous of the Restoration comedies is *The Way of the World* by William Congreve, which is sometimes described as a bridge between Restoration comedy and eighteenth-century sentimental comedy. In the scene shown here, Lady Wishfort meets with her servant Waitwell, who—as part of a scheme—is disguised a nobleman.

the sexual content of plays was toned down; and in eighteenth-century English comedy, morality was stressed.

Congreve's *The Way of the World* (1700) is often considered a bridge between Restoration comedy and eighteenth-century English sentimental comedy, which stresses traditional morality, punishes the sinful, and rewards the virtuous. Like Restoration comedy, *The Way of the World* has a number of characters involved in adulterous affairs, and some traditional stock characters; it is also marked by brilliant wit and a dazzling prose style. But as in sentimental comedy, its two young lovers (Mirabell and Millamant) are united, while the wicked characters (Fainall and Mrs. Marwood) are punished. In one famous scene, Mirabell and Millamant "bargain" with each other over the prerogatives and conditions they will agree to once they are married.

Other transitional plays include *The Gamester* (1705) by Susannah Centlivre (1667–1723) and *The Beaux' Strategem* (1707) by George Farquhar (1678–1707).

RESTORATION AUDIENCES

Many Restoration comedies, including *The Country Wife,* indicate that audiences of that era, unlike modern-day spectators, were quite spirited in their behavior during performances. The fop Sparkish in *The Country Wife* describes how audience members purchased fruit from the "orange wenches" (many of these "wenches" were prostitutes), spoke back to the actors, arranged assignations with each other, and attended the theater to be seen rather than to see the play. Activities like these provoked attacks by religious leaders who were opposed to theater.

Restoration audiences were primarily, but probably not exclusively, members of the upper class—the same group that was being satirized in the plays. Audiences who attend theater vary significantly in different periods and different places. Sometimes, audiences encompass everyone, rich and poor; at other times, audiences include only one social class. (For instance, in ancient Greece, in medieval theater, and in Elizabethan public theaters, audiences included virtually all strata of society; by contrast, productions at European courts—such as masques—were seen only by royalty and the nobility.) It is usually assumed that in the first decades of the English Restoration, only a small portion of society—the upper class—attended the theater. When theater is aimed at a narrow group, this generally means that playwrights tailor their works specifically for the audience they know will be watching. As a result, the plays are not likely to have the universality of drama written for a wider audience. Restoration comedy, however, deals with subjects—social pretention and sex—that are familiar to sophisticated society in any age.

PERFORMERS

Actresses

One of the most obvious changes from English Renaissance theater to Restoration theater was the appearance of actresses on the English stage.

As we have noted, the presence of women was exploited in some Restoration comedies: actresses were forced by plot complications to disguise themselves as men. In *The Country Wife,* Margery Pinchwife's husband has her dress as a boy to prevent his acquaintances from flirting with her when he takes her to London. Dressing actresses in tight breeches would not seem very provocative to modern audiences, but eighteenth-century religious leaders considered the practice highly licentious.

Many theater historians have asked what the actual status of actresses was during this period. Financial success was possible for actresses, but they were often seen as no better than prostitutes and were frequently seduced into sexual liaisons with other company members or with wealthy audience members. In addition, their roles—particularly the "breeches roles"—focused on their sexuality. The question arises, therefore, whether the fact that women were admitted to the acting profession was in itself a sign of any kind of equality or equitable treatment; for some historians, the answer is that it was not. In many areas of society and life, women had an inferior status, and this may have carried through to the position of actresses.

Nevertheless, a number of actresses became extremely popular during the Restoration. Elizabeth Barry (1658–1713) was the leading actress with the famous tragedian Thomas Betterton (ca. 1635–1710); Betterton was noted for his performances in Shakespeare's plays and Barry for her performances of the major female roles in these plays. Anne Bracegirdle (ca. 1663–1748), who had studied performing with Betterton, was a distinguished actress in Restoration comedies until her retirement in 1707. The best-known theater personality of the era, however, was probably Nell Gwynn, famous for her comic performances, her dancing, and her liaison with Charles II.

(The Bettmann Archive)

Eleanor (Nell) Gwynn

(1650–1687)

Nell Gwynn's remarkable career—which took her from the slums of London to the king's palace—can be attributed to her own beauty and high spirits and to the unique conditions of Restoration society. After over 20 years of Puritan rule, the main preoccupation of English society after 1660 was the pursuit of pleasure. Theater was a fashionable entertainment, and one of its attractions was the introduction of actresses to the English stage.

The daughter of the keeper of a bawdy house and an unknown father, Nell Gwynn grew up in the London slums. She was said to have begun her theatrical career as a girl selling oranges at the Theater Royal in Drury Lane. There she attracted the attention of Charles Hart, the leading actor; she became his mistress and protégé and made her stage debut in December 1664. As an actress, she relied on her natural wit and charm; she excelled in singing and dancing but was a failure in tragedy. Her specialties were "breeches roles," in which she wore men's clothing, and the delivery of prologues and epilogues.

Nell Gwynn was not typical of Restoration actresses, but in some ways she is representative. Actresses were still a novelty, and many of them were assiduously pursued by Restoration gallants. It was no disgrace to have a mistress, or to be one; because the theater was prestigious, actresses were favored as mistresses, and there were probably as many affairs within acting companies as with outsiders. Some actresses, however—such as Anne Bracegirdle—were as celebrated for their virtue as Nell Gwynn was for her impropriety.

When she delivered the epilogue to John Dryden's *Tyrannick Love* in 1669, Nell Gwynn drew the attention of Charles II. She became his mistress and left the stage, settling in a house in Pall Mall—though in 1670 she returned to the theater to play in Dryden's *The Conquest of Granada*. She had two sons by Charles; the older one became the duke of Saint Albans, but the younger died in childhood.

It seems that Nell Gwynn's rise in social status did little to change her, except to make her more extravagant. She never denied her origins or claimed to be more than the king's mistress, and unlike his other favorites, she never meddled in politics. Her chief concerns were the king's amusement, her children, and entertaining his friends. Recognizing her faithfulness, Charles, on his deathbed, told his brother, "Let not poor Nelly starve." James II rescued her from her creditors and gave her a pension that enabled her to live comfortably until her death in 1687.

Acting Companies

Restoration acting companies were larger than those of the English Renaissance; and the addition of women performers was, of course, a significant change. There were also less visible transformations, especially in organization.

The sharing plan of companies like the Lord Chamberlain's Men—Shakespeare's company—almost disappeared in London during the Restoration. Rather than sharing in the profits and losses of their companies, London actors in the Restoration were hired for a specific period of time at a set salary. The new practice was called the *contract system,* and the move from the sharing plan to the contract system marked a decline of actors' control over theater in London. (Outside London, provincial companies—as well as companies established in the thirteen colonies of North America—continued to use the sharing plan, and their actors were still the controlling force.)

At the same time, the Restoration saw the emergence of theatrical entrepreneurs who were often part-owners of theater buildings and companies. The most successful theatrical businessman of the late Restoration and early eighteenth century, the lawyer Christopher Rich (?–1714), was also the most notorious. At the turn of the century, Rich controlled the patents Charles II had issued to both Davenant and Killigrew; his insufferable financial practices—he failed to provide reasonable salaries and did not always pay his performers—drove some actors in his group to rebel and establish their own company. (The rise of the entrepreneur as a powerful force in theater was, of course, a step in the development of modern theater business. A good example of an entrepreneur in today's commercial theater is the British producer Cameron Mackintosh, who is responsible for such musicals as *Cats, Les Misérables, The Phantom of the Opera,* and *Miss Saigon.)*

THOMAS BETTERTON. The leading actor of the Restoration, Betterton was famous for his vocal prowess. He also led a revolt against Christopher Rich, an exploitative theatrical entrepreneur.

In order to increase their set wages under the contract system, actors (and other company personnel) were provided with yearly "benefits." For each major performer in a company, one "benefit performance" was designated—a performance from which he or she would keep all the profits. Frequently, ticket prices for these benefit performances were increased so that the performer's earnings would be greater. A few minor performers might share the profits from one benefit performance. The benefit system was used in England from the Restoration through the nineteenth century.

Playwrights were rarely members of Restoration troupes. Instead, they were paid a fixed sum or by the benefit system: a playwright would receive the profits from the third night of the premiere run of the play. By the turn of the century, the playwright might also receive the profits from the sixth consecutive night of the opening run. It should be remembered, however, that Restoration theater was not like modern theater, in which long runs are common; many Restoration plays never succeeded in running three nights in a row.

Actors learned their craft through apprenticeships and usually played a specific range of roles: for instance, one man would play serious heroes and another low-comedy types. Because (as in Elizabethan theater) long runs were unusual, companies changed their bills frequently, and actors had to develop skills of quick study and retention.

Rehearsals for a new play would rarely extend past 2 weeks; a revival would merit little more than a run-through on the day of the performance. For a new play, the playwright would assist in the first rehearsal, but most of the rehearsal process was the responsibility of the company's manager, who was often one of its leading actors. The function of rehearsals was usually simply to ascertain whether or not the performers knew their lines; firsthand accounts tell us that on opening night they often did not. Given these rehearsal procedures, Restoration actor-managers were never able to assume the functions of the modern director, telling performers where to move onstage or how to interpret their roles.

Many historians suggest that the acting style of the Restoration, particularly for tragedy, featured broad gestures and powerful declamatory delivery. Thomas Betterton, the leading actor of the Restoration—he was also a leader of the revolt against the entrepreneur Christopher Rich—was noted for his vocal prowess. The voice of his leading lady, Elizabeth Barry, was described as "full, clear, and strong so that no Violence of Passion could be too much for her." Because rehearsals were sketchy, out of necessity actors fell back on conventional patterns of stage movement; for example, much of the dialogue was delivered directly to the audience from the front of the stage. Some scholars argue, however, that the mechanical style of Restoration acting has been overstated; and some also believe that comic acting may have been less flamboyant than tragic acting.

RESTORATION THEATERS

Government and the Theaters

Government regulations were an important aspect of theater production in the Restoration. When theater was revived in 1660, the rules established during the reign of Elizabeth to oversee theaters were reinstituted. The Master of Revels took control and issued licenses to three theatrical entrepreneurs. Charles II, however—as we noted earlier—issued patents to William Davenant and Thomas Killigrew that superseded those issued by the Master of Revels; as a result, Davenant and Killigrew had a monopoly on theater in London.

By the early eighteenth century, this monopoly seemed unenforceable; the monarchs who succeeded Charles II had made exceptions to it, and some companies simply operated in defiance of it. In 1737, Parliament, questioning Charles's right to have issued patents without its approval, passed the Licensing Act—a new attempt to regulate London theater. Under the Licensing Act, only two theaters were authorized to present "tragedy, comedy, opera, play, farce, or other entertainment for the stage for gain, hire, or reward," and the lord chamberlain became responsible for licensing plays; thus the tradition of government regulation established by Elizabeth I continued into the Restoration and, beyond that, into the eighteenth century. The two theaters authorized by the Licensing Act were Covent Garden and Drury Lane.

DRURY LANE. The Drury Lane Theater began during the English Restoration and has continued to the present day. This illustration is from 1840. By that time, the Drury Lane no longer had an extended forestage or proscenium doors and boxes; it was still a "pit, box, and gallery" playhouse, but it had been greatly enlarged in the nineteenth century.

The Drury Lane Theater

The origins of the Drury Lane Theater—the London playhouse described at the opening of this chapter and a theater that still exists today—go back to a patent that Charles II granted to Thomas Killigrew in 1662.

Killigrew built the first Drury Lane, known as the Theater Royal, in Bridges Street in 1663. It was supposed to be handsome and well-equipped, but the diarist Samuel Pepys complained of catching cold there from a draft and from rain leaking from the glazed cupola over the pit.

In June of 1672, the original building was partly destroyed by fire, and Killigrew housed his company in a deserted theater while Christopher Wren built a new one. This new theater opened in March of 1674, with the king (Charles II) and queen in attendance. Killigrew's mismanagement so weakened the company that the theater was closed in 1676. Thomas Betterton merged two London acting troupes—a troupe he managed for Davenant's

(Richard Leacroft, *The Development of the English Playhouse,* Cornell University Press, Ithaca, N.Y., 1973 By permission of Reed Book Services/Methuen London.)

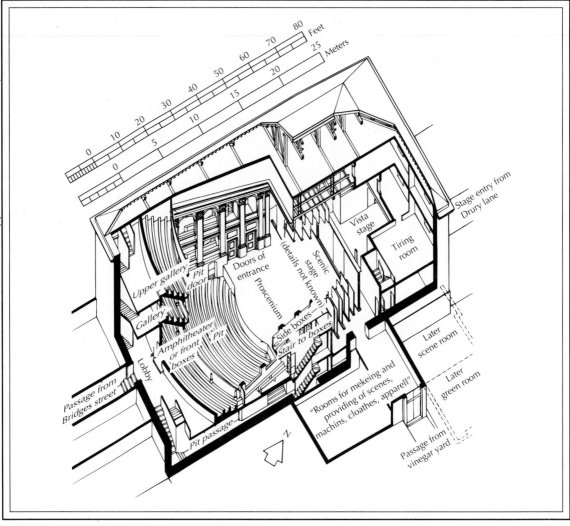

A RECONSTRUCTION OF DRURY LANE.   This reconstruction, of the Restoration period, shows Christopher Wren's design for the Theatre Royal, Drury Lane, 1674. Note the horseshoe-shaped pit for the audience and the two doors on each side of the stage.

heirs, and Killigrew's company—and reopened Drury Lane in 1682. The patent then passed to Christopher Rich, who was interested only in making money. Under his mismanagement the theater again went bankrupt and closed in 1709. Drury Lane reopened later that same year under new management and ran successfully until Charles Fleetwood got control of the patent. Under Fleetwood's regime, there was a riot in 1737 over the abolition of free admission for footmen in the gallery and another in 1741 at the first performance of Charles Macklin's realistic interpretation of Shylock.

When Fleetwood in his turn faced bankruptcy, David Garrick, the company's leading actor, became manager in 1747. Until this time, a few patrons had still been permitted to sit on the stage, but one of Garrick's reforms was to end this practice. Under his careful management, the theater became both prosperous and respected.

Garrick was succeeded in 1776 by the playwright Richard Brinsley Sheridan and Sheridan's father-in-law. They enlarged the building between 1791 and 1794, supposedly making it fireproof. When the actor John Kemble and his sister, the actress Sarah Siddons, left the company, the managers turned to melodrama and spectacle to avoid bankruptcy. Drury Lane burned to the ground in 1809, and for some time there was no money to rebuild it.

Samuel Whitbread, a brewer and a shareholder in the patent, finally raised the money, and the theater was rebuilt in 1812. Drury Lane's history in the nineteenth century included a procession of managers who went into bankruptcy there—though some of them had been successful at other houses—until August Harris took over in the 1880s. Harris's policy was to present spectacular shows and pantomimes, a formula that has worked successfully to this day; Drury Lane has now become the home of musicals.

Drury Lane is said to have a ghost: an eighteenth-century gentleman in cloak and boots who appears in the upper circle at matinees when the house is full.

Theater Architecture in the Restoration

During the Restoration, there were three theaters of note in London: Lincoln Inn Fields (1661), which was a converted tennis court; Dorset Garden (1671); and Drury Lane. Though each of them was distinct, all three had interiors which fused Italianate and Elizabethan features.

By the time of the Restoration, the Elizabethan tradition of open-air public theaters had ended; all theaters were now indoor, proscenium-arch buildings. The area for the audience was divided into pit, boxes, and galleries. The pit in Restoration theaters had backless benches—unlike the pit in French neoclassical theaters, where the spectators stood. Also, the pit in the English houses was raked—slanted downward from back to front—for better sight lines. The total seating capacity was about 650. In size, then, as well as in many other respects, Restoration theaters were similar to Elizabethan private theaters.

The Restoration stage was highly unusual in that it was divided into two distinct, nearly equal halves: the apron—the forestage in front of the proscenium—was very deep, almost as deep as the area behind the proscenium. (In contrast, the apron in a twentieth-century proscenium-arch theater is usually small and inconsequential.) In the seventeenth century, only the English had theater buildings with extended aprons; most historians believe that the extended apron was a vestige of the platform stage of the English Renaissance. The apron was the major area for performance in Restoration theaters; the area behind the proscenium housed the scenery. The entire stage was raked to improve sight lines.

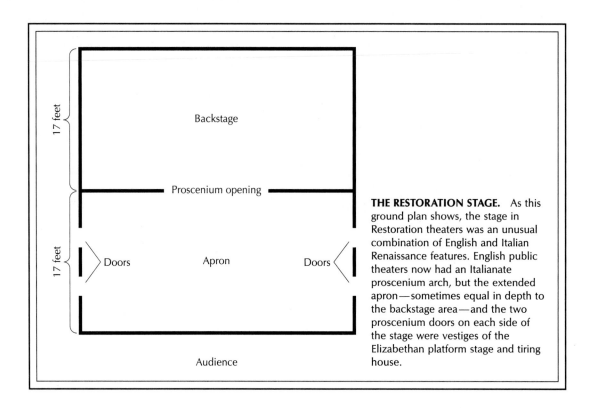

17 feet

Backstage

Proscenium opening

17 feet

Doors

Apron

Doors

Audience

THE RESTORATION STAGE. As this ground plan shows, the stage in Restoration theaters was an unusual combination of English and Italian Renaissance features. English public theaters now had an Italianate proscenium arch, but the extended apron—sometimes equal in depth to the backstage area—and the two proscenium doors on each side of the stage were vestiges of the Elizabethan platform stage and tiring house.

The other unique elements of the Restoration stage were the proscenium doors with balconies above them. Most Restoration theaters had two proscenium doors on each side of the stage—a total of four doors—that led onto the forestage. These doors were used for exits and entrances, and for the concealment scenes popular in Restoration comedy—scenes in which one character listened out of sight of the others. The balconies above these doorways could be used for balcony and window scenes.

As we look at theater history, we often see a thread running through several eras. For instance, the drama of Racine and Molière is a direct outgrowth of neoclassical theater of the Italian Renaissance; and the plays of these two men in turn influenced French theater for the next 300 years. Medieval Spanish theater evolved into the secular dramas of Lope de Vega; traces of English medieval theater appear in the plays of Shakespeare. With the architecture of the Restoration stage, we also find such a process at work: the physical arrangement changes and develops, but elements of the earlier Elizabethan stage remain. Not only is the extended apron of Restoration theaters a vestige of the Elizabethan platform stage; the doors and balconies of the Restoration stage are remnants of the doorways and upper playing areas of the Elizabethan stage. The English were slow to give up familiar features of the Elizabethan stage, and even after the Restoration, eighteenth-century English and American proscenium-arch theaters retained some of these features.

Later, in the 1700s, the stage apron shrank, and the number of doors decreased from two on each side to one. Even so, the continued influence of Elizabethan theater architecture kept the English playhouses from becoming exact duplicates of theaters on the European continent.

Scenery, Lighting, and Costumes

Visual elements—scenery, lighting, costumes—also illustrate the Italianization of the English stage during the Restoration. As noted in Chapter 6, Inigo Jones had designed and painted wing-and-shutter settings for court entertainments during the Caroline and Jacobean periods; and his student, John Webb, used these scenic devices at the close of the commonwealth in his design for *The Siege of Rhodes*. Not surprisingly, then, during the Restoration the basic scenic components were wings, shutters—in which two halves of a stiff backing at the rear of the stage opened or closed—and borders for masking. Sometimes the back shutters were replaced by a single backdrop that was rolled up or lowered. The sets, of course, were painted in perspective.

Debates in Theater History:

THE DORSET GARDEN THEATER

The scanty evidence available about the Dorset Garden Theater, which opened in 1671, has led to a great deal of debate over its appearance. For a number of years, two theater historians—John R. Spring and Robert Hume—argued in scholarly journals about this. Their controversy was set off when Spring questioned an earlier reconstruction of the theater by the historian Edward A. Langhans. According to Spring, Dorset Garden was essentially very similar to another important Restoration playhouse, Drury Lane: the size of the forestage and proscenium opening as well as the four proscenium doors and the scenic machinery at Dorset Garden were almost identical to those at Drury Lane.

Hume's ideas, on the other hand, are closer to Langhans's reconstruction, which had suggested that the two theaters were quite different. Hume argues that the United Company of the Restoration, and later Christopher Rich's company, used Drury Lane for "everyday dramas" but used Dorset Garden for plays that required extensive scenic effects; and that there would have been no reason to use both spaces if they were nearly identical. He con-

cludes: "One of the few things we can say about Dorset Garden is that it surpassed every English theatre of its time in its capacity for scenic splendor. To suggest that its scenic stage was all of 28 ft. 6 in. deep—far less than the space available at Drury Lane—is to suggest an absurdity."[*]

This debate shows how difficult it is to reconstruct a historic playhouse when few substantial sources survive. As Hume himself admits: "What we know with some certainty about the Dorset Garden theater is derived from a few pieces of rather unsatisfactory evidence."[†] The well-known theater historian Richard Leacroft, who has done some remarkable reconstructions of English playhouses—several of which are reproduced in this textbook—has said that he is unable to make an accurate reconstruction of Dorset Garden because the available information is so slight. Very probably, then, this debate will continue.

[*]"The Dorset Garden Theatre: A Review of Facts and Problems," *Theatre Notebook*, 1979, vol. 33, p. 16.
[†]P. 4.

What made the scenic practices of Restoration England distinct from those of Italy and France was that the English rarely used Torelli's pole-and-chariot system for scene changes. Instead, flats were placed in grooves behind the proscenium and on the backstage floor; the flats were pulled off into the wings, revealing new scenery—other flats—directly behind them. With the groove system, each piece of scenery must be removed separately by individual stagehands; therefore, scene changes could not be synchronized as successfully in English theaters as in Italian theaters. In England, shifts were carried out by stagehands stationed at each groove position who moved scenery manually when a whistle was blown by the prompter. (This was a holdover from changes of sails on ships, which were coordinated by blowing a whistle.)

Because the curtain was never closed during the course of a presentation, scene changes were carried out while the audience watched. Even musical entertainments—which were staged between the acts of full-length plays during the Restoration—were presented in front of the scenery already in view. As a result, the audience was always aware of the mechanical aspects of a theater production. All through the nineteenth century, the English, except in their opera houses, used the primitive groove system for changing scenery.

Throughout the Restoration, companies kept collections of perspective settings that were reused frequently. Stock settings were the norm, primarily because of the expense entailed in having scenery painted. For this reason, most Restoration comedies have similar scenic requirements: the drawing room and the park.

Restoration costuming followed the traditions of the English Renaissance and the French neoclassical era: contemporary clothing was standard. Everyday clothes were of course appropriate for Restoration comedy, but not for dramas set in the past. Though traditional costumes and accessories were sometimes worn to indicate historical figures or eras, there was no real attempt to be historically accurate. To take one example, until well into the eighteenth century an actor playing Shakespeare's Roman character Coriolanus would have worn a kind of ballet skirt, breeches, laced boots reaching halfway to the knees, an embroidered jacket, a full wig, and a helmet with plumes—a costume unrelated to the historical setting of the play. This lack of appropriateness and verisimilitude would make the conventions of Restoration costuming—like Restoration scenic practices—jarring to modern theatergoers.

Because Restoration theaters were indoors, lighting was a major concern. Theater performances during the late seventeenth century normally took place in the afternoon, when windows could provide some natural lighting. Inside, candles were the predominant source of lighting, and chandeliers holding them were visible above the stage and the audience. Candles were also placed in brackets attached to the front of the boxes. The stage and the audience area were always lit, and footlights—lights on the floor running along the front of the stage—were also used. In today's theater, footlights are rarely used because they cast unnatural shadows on the performers' faces. During the Restoration, however, theater artists could not be choosy about the quality of lighting; their main concern was simply illumination.

Italian and French influences were fused with English traditions to create the theater of the Restoration. Restoration theater, in turn, prepared the way for eighteenth-century theater in England. We turn to the eighteenth century, in England and elsewhere, in Chapter 10.

SUMMARY

The Restoration brought a strong Italian influence to English stage practices. The proscenium arch, perspective painting, and wing-and-shutter (or backdrop) scenery became indispensable elements of the English stage. A French influence was also present; the neoclassical ideals were introduced into serious English drama.

Nonetheless, English theater maintained its uniqueness. Proscenium-arch doors and balconies, and an extended apron, were significant vestiges of the Elizabethan stage. Comedy of manners, as exemplified in the works of Wycherley and Congreve, borrowed from the French neoclassical playwright Molière but was a unique reflection of English Restoration society. Also popular were the tragedies of John Dryden and the comedies of intrigue of Aphra Behn.

Women appeared on the English stage for the first time during the Restoration; acting companies in London established a contract system; and theatrical entrepreneurs began to emerge.

CHAPTER 10

THEATER IN THE EIGHTEENTH CENTURY

I t is a brisk spring day in May of 1784, and we are in Paris, getting ready to leave for a performance by the Comédie Française at its new theater building, which opened 2 years ago. The Comédie Française is the national theater of France and one of three companies receiving government support.

With great expectations, we depart early so that we can arrive at the theater before the starting time, 5:30. Tonight we are to see Beaumarchais's new play *The Marriage of Figaro;* the Comédie Française is noted not only for traditional neoclassical drama but also for new drama by French authors. There will be dance presentations between the acts and an afterpiece—a short comic play following the full-length production. However, it is *The Marriage of Figaro* itself that we are most interested in seeing.

Not since Molière's *Tartuffe* has there been such controversy over a play. The king, Louis XVI, has refused to give his permission for the production of *The Marriage of Figaro.* Set in Spain, it is about an older man's attempt to seduce a

SHE STOOPS TO CONQUER. Oliver Goldsmith was one of the leading English comic playwrights in the eighteenth century. In *She Stoops to Conquer,* he attempted to replace sentimental comedy with a form that would make audiences laugh at their own eccentricities and absurdities. The plot revolves around mistaken identity, upper-class pretensions, and lovers' intrigues. Shown here is a scene from a production by the Illinois Shakespeare Festival. *(Illinois Shakespeare Festival)*

servant girl, and its key character is a comic servant—but its real point, we have heard, is social and political satire.

Beaumarchais introduced the characters in *The Marriage of Figaro* several years ago, in *The Barber of Seville.* The success of his new play is clear: it has been performed continuously since its opening in April; and some people say that it might run as long as seventy-five performances in a row, an unheard-of accomplishment—most plays run for perhaps three consecutive performances. We have been told by friends who were present on the opening night that the theater was filled hours beforehand and that some of the audience members had brought food with them so that they would not have to risk losing their seats by leaving the theater to eat.

As we enter the theater, we are struck by its beauty and size. Remarkably, there are now seats for everyone. Before this building was constructed, the pit in front of the stage had no seats; in the company's earlier theaters, the spectators in the pit stood during performances. In fact, spectators in the old seatless pits would move about and socialize; and we have heard that the new seats are controversial—Parisians enjoyed the social ambiance of the old pit, and one of our leading playwrights, Louis Sébastien Mercier, has publicly criticized the addition of benches. The audience area is egg-shaped; this configuration, at least, will be welcome, making it easier for all of us to see the action onstage. Like the theaters that preceded it, the new Comédie Française has three rows of boxes and a row of galleries above those. Since we cannot afford the more expensive sections, we take our place in the pit, sitting on the new benches.

When the curtain rises, we are impressed at once by the large stage: it is very deep. However, its apron is smaller than the aprons in the company's previous theaters—the actors must all perform behind the proscenium arch. The scenery is painted and will be changed by wings and shutters.

As the play begins, we are very excited, because we are seeing actors we have heard much about. But we are surprised to find that the great comic actor Préville, who played the title character, Figaro, in *The Barber of Seville,* is not repeating the role; he has chosen instead to play a minor character. (Préville has redefined our perception of comic characters: he is handsome and thin—not the stereotypical overweight, slovenly comic servant.) Tonight, Dazincourt will play Figaro. Count Almaviva—the would-be seducer—is played by the company's great leading actor, François René-Molé, who has been a member of the Comédie Française for almost 25 years. Of course, all the shareholders in this prestigious company are outstanding: not only are they considered the premiere performers of France; they are often acknowledged by actors in England and throughout Europe to be the best in the world.

The plot of *The Marriage of Figaro* is full of intrigue, unexpected twists, and great comic moments. Figaro, the servant, is engaged to marry Suzanne, who is also a servant; but his master, Count Almaviva, wants to sleep with her himself. The count has been unfaithful to his wife, and we watch with great enjoyment the various complications that develop as he tries to conquer another woman but is thwarted. At the end of the play, the count is caught out in his plotting and is humiliated; he pledges fidelity to his wife, and Figaro and Suzanne are brought together.

As we walk home, we relive many of the comic moments in the play. Yet we also understand why this seemingly simple, farcical work has caused such political furor. It is the master who is ridiculed and frustrated: despite his social rank, his machinations are futile—his clever servants outwit him. Clearly, Beaumarchais is questioning the social structure of France. Some people are saying that this play threatens our society with the kind of revolution we have seen in the new world. Are these people right? Was the king right to be concerned about the political implications of this comedy? These questions remain with us long after our evening at the Comédie Française.

BACKGROUND: THE EIGHTEENTH CENTURY

In the textile industry in Berlin, Germany, between 1750 and 1780 the number of looms for making cotton increased from 80 to over 1,000, and the number of silk looms jumped from fewer than 300 to more than 2,000. These changes are typical of what was happening, not only in Germany, but throughout Europe.

The eighteenth century was a time of transition. In textiles, to take one example, there was a move away from wool, which had been the main fabric since the Middle Ages—though manufacturing was still done on handlooms (the machinery of the industrial revolution was yet to come). Transitions like this that marked manufacturing also affected other aspects of life, including theater. Political, philosophical, economic, and cultural changes in the eighteenth century paved the way for even more revolutionary developments in the nineteenth and twentieth centuries.

Beginning with the eighteenth century, the study of history—including theater history—becomes more complex. Homogeneous, self-contained societies began to disappear as the world started to be transformed into a global community. An increase in mercantilism—manufacturing and trade, particularly international trade—affected populations worldwide. Decisions made by the two major eighteenth-century mercantile powers, England and France, directly affected people in North America, India, and Africa. (One effect on Africa, for example, was a marked increase in the slave trade.)

Before the eighteenth century, wars had usually been fought for religious reasons; now they became territorial and economic. There were many wars in the eighteenth century, including the War of the Spanish Succession (1701–1714), the War of the Austrian Succession (1740–1748), and the Seven Years' War (1756–1763). The Seven Years' War, known in America as the French and Indian War, is a clear example of a struggle for mercantile dominance. The opposed powers were England and France, the leading colonists in North America; when France was defeated, England gained control of Canada and all

THE EIGHTEENTH CENTURY

THEATER	YEAR, A.D.	CULTURE AND POLITICS

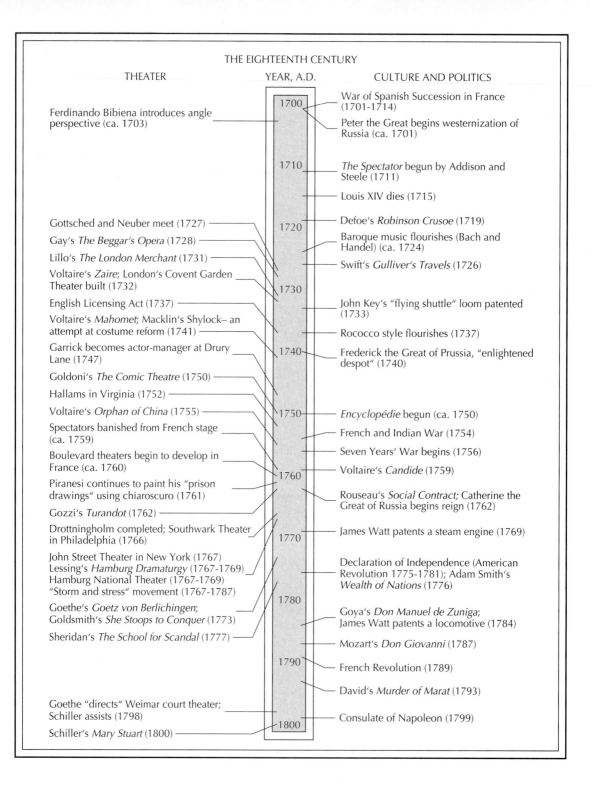

THEATER

Ferdinando Bibiena introduces angle perspective (ca. 1703)

Gottsched and Neuber meet (1727)

Gay's *The Beggar's Opera* (1728)

Lillo's *The London Merchant* (1731)

Voltaire's *Zaire*; London's Covent Garden Theater built (1732)

English Licensing Act (1737)

Voltaire's *Mahomet*; Macklin's Shylock– an attempt at costume reform (1741)

Garrick becomes actor-manager at Drury Lane (1747)

Goldoni's *The Comic Theatre* (1750)

Hallams in Virginia (1752)

Voltaire's *Orphan of China* (1755)

Spectators banished from French stage (ca. 1759)

Boulevard theaters begin to develop in France (ca. 1760)

Piranesi continues to paint his "prison drawings" using chiaroscuro (1761)

Gozzi's *Turandot* (1762)

Drottningholm completed; Southwark Theater in Philadelphia (1766)

John Street Theater in New York (1767)
Lessing's *Hamburg Dramaturgy* (1767-1769)
Hamburg National Theater (1767-1769)
"Storm and stress" movement (1767-1787)

Goethe's *Goetz von Berlichingen*; Goldsmith's *She Stoops to Conquer* (1773)

Sheridan's *The School for Scandal* (1777)

Goethe "directs" Weimar court theater; Schiller assists (1798)

Schiller's *Mary Stuart* (1800)

YEAR, A.D.

1700

1710

1720

1730

1740

1750

1760

1770

1780

1790

1800

CULTURE AND POLITICS

War of Spanish Succession in France (1701-1714)

Peter the Great begins westernization of Russia (ca. 1701)

The Spectator begun by Addison and Steele (1711)

Louis XIV dies (1715)

Defoe's *Robinson Crusoe* (1719)

Baroque music flourishes (Bach and Handel) (ca. 1724)

Swift's *Gulliver's Travels* (1726)

John Key's "flying shuttle" loom patented (1733)

Rococo style flourishes (1737)

Frederick the Great of Prussia, "enlightened despot" (1740)

Encyclopédie begun (ca. 1750)

French and Indian War (1754)

Seven Years' War begins (1756)

Voltaire's *Candide* (1759)

Rouseau's *Social Contract*; Catherine the Great of Russia begins reign (1762)

James Watt patents a steam engine (1769)

Declaration of Independence (American Revolution 1775-1781); Adam Smith's *Wealth of Nations* (1776)

Goya's *Don Manuel de Zuniga*; James Watt patents a locomotive (1784)

Mozart's *Don Giovanni* (1787)

French Revolution (1789)

David's *Murder of Marat* (1793)

Consulate of Napoleon (1799)

the French territory in North America east of the Mississippi. Spain, which had sided with France, had to cede Florida to England, and in compensation was given the French lands west of the Mississippi (the Louisiana Territory).

Western Europe prospered more than ever before because of the growth in trade; ingenious and daring investors of capital became extremely wealthy. Profits from colonial trade filtered down to the emerging middle class, which included merchants and others involved in commerce; in the eighteenth century it became a social as well as a political force. However, the lives of those on the bottom rungs of the economic ladder—such as the eastern European serfs, the French peasants, and the dispossessed English farmers—were not improved by the expansion of trade; some historians suggest that the disparity in wealth between the middle and lower classes became greater during this period.

Because of many new developments in learning and philosophy, the eighteenth century is called the *age of enlightenment* or simply the *enlightenment*. Though France was its center, the enlightenment had international reverberations. The search for knowledge was supported by the educated middle class. Dictionaries and encyclopedias were in great demand; possibly the most famous was the seventeen-volume *Encyclopédie* edited by the French philosopher Denis Diderot between 1751 and 1772.

Besides Diderot, France produced many renowned philosophers in the eighteenth century, including Montesquieu (1689–1755), Voltaire (1694–1778), and Jean-Jacques Rousseau (1712–1778). Montesquieu, in *The Spirit of Laws* (1748), called for a separation and balance of powers in government to end absolute monarchy. Voltaire argued for religious tolerance. Among those who supported Voltaire was the German playwright Gotthold Ephraim Lessing (1729–1781), whose *Nathan the Wise* (1779) dramatized the ideal of religious community. In *The Social Contract* (1762), Rousseau argued that government exists because of an agreement among the people governed—not between a ruler and subjects—and that therefore government officials are representatives, responsible to their constituents. In earlier writings, Rousseau attacked organized society as such, arguing that humanity was better off in a "state of nature."

The political philosophies of Montesquieu, Voltaire, and Rousseau had noticeable effects on eighteenth-century Europe and America. While many rulers were absolutists, believing that their powers were God-given and therefore not to be questioned, some monarchs—known as *enlightened despots* —rejected this concept of "divine right." They believed in religious tolerance and wanted to reform their societies for the good of their subjects. Two major political and social upheavals, the American Revolution (1775–1783) and the French Revolution (1789–1799), were based on the ideals of the enlightenment. Thomas Jefferson's political philosophy, as expressed in the Declaration of Independence, was rooted in enlightenment thought; the American Constitution was a version of Rousseau's social contract. The French revolutionaries' cry for liberty, equality, and fraternity originated in the philosophies of

Montesquieu, Voltaire, and Rousseau. Unfortunately, the ideals of the French Revolution were compromised by the Reign of Terror; and instead of liberty, equality, and fraternity, the French wound up with Napoleon in 1799.

The new knowledge characteristic of the era had practical as well as political applications. Inventions of the late eighteenth century would facilitate the industrial revolution of the nineteenth century: the flying shuttle, the spinning jenny, and the cotton gin revolutionized the textile industry, and James Watt's improved steam engine revolutionized manufacturing and transportation.

In the arts, the seventeenth century and the early eighteenth century were characterized by the baroque style. Baroque painters, such as Peter Paul Rubens (1577–1640) and Rembrandt (1606–1669), emphasized detail, color, and ornamentation to create a total visual illusion. The emerging middle class frequently commissioned realistic baroque landscapes and portraits. The most renowned baroque composers, George Frederick Handel (1685–1759) and Johann Sebastian Bach (1685–1750), achieved unity of mood and continuity of line; but, like baroque paintings, their music was filled with movement and action.

In the late eighteenth century, a new style of art emerged—*rococo*. Rococo art is typified by the paintings of Jean Antoine Watteau (1684–1721); though less ornate and grandiose than baroque art, it was still characterized by careful attention to detail.

In the midst of all these transformations, theater also changed. Although there were some major and many minor revolutions in eighteenth-century theater, few of the theatrical experiments of the 1700s became generally accepted practices. Nevertheless, they served as the foundation for modern theater.

EIGHTEENTH-CENTURY DRAMA

In theater, the eighteenth century—as we will see—was most notably a time when star performers were glorified and people who began to function like the modern director emerged. Still, many first-rate plays were written; and the new dramatic forms that began to appear are evidence of the transitional nature of eighteenth-century drama.

Middle-Class Tragedy

During the early eighteenth century, much of drama in Europe adhered to neoclassicism; but as the century progressed, there were numerous departures from the Renaissance rules. New forms which defied the neoclassical genres were introduced; there were also experiments with the episodic structure that had been used by William Shakespeare and other Elizabethan dramatists, and by dramatists of the Spanish golden age.

Many eighteenth-century dramatic forms deviated from traditional tragedy and comedy. Denis Diderot championed *drame,* a new form which was defined as any serious play that did not fit the neoclassical definition of tragedy. *Bourgeois,* or *middle-class, tragedy* and *domestic tragedy* were eighteenth-century examples of drame: they ignored the neoclassical requirement of royal protagonists and had tragic heroes and heroines from the emerging middle class. Domestic tragedies focused on middle-class family concerns. Bourgeois and domestic tragedies were often dramatizations of eighteenth-century middle-class morality—rewarding the virtuous and punishing the wicked—and they tended to be sentimental and melodramatic; that is, they openly appealed to the emotions as they pitted good against evil. The emergence of middle-class tragic heroes and heroines reflected the rise of the middle class as a political and social force: the new middle-class audiences expected dramas to reflect their problems and points of view.

The London Merchant (1731), by the English playwright George Lillo (1693–1739), is often cited as an example of middle-class tragedy. In this play, an apprentice is seduced by an older woman; he then robs his good-hearted employer and murders his uncle, and he and the woman are eventually apprehended and sentenced to death. Later in the century, Diderot in France and Lessing in Germany wrote middle-class and domestic tragedies, as did many other minor writers. One, Louis Sébastian Mercier (1740–1814), loosely translated *The London Merchant* into French in 1769.

Today, most eighteenth-century bourgeois tragedies seem trite and melodramatic, with their unconvincing last-minute reformations of drunken or evil characters. However, at the time they showed that middle-class characters were appropriate subjects for serious drama. Many critics believe that modern dramas emphasizing family problems and social concerns (such as Arthur Miller's *Death of a Salesman*) grew out of this earlier form. It is also clear that the theories of Denis Diderot were instrumental in changing the way people thought about serious drama and theater in the eighteenth century.

(Culver Pictures)

Denis Diderot

(1713–1784)

"We are slaves of custom," wrote Denis Diderot in an essay on drama; but he hoped to bring about changes: he advocated a rationalist philosophy, based on nature and the intellect, to make things as they should be.

Diderot came from a conservative, middle-class provincial family in Langres, France. He was sent to Paris for his education and received a master of arts degree from the University of Paris in 1732. For a while he studied law, but he was much more interested in mathematics and languages. In 1734, after a quarrel with his family over their middle-class values, he began to lead a bohemian existence in Paris, living on the Left Bank and earning money as a hack writer. It was during this period that he met the philosopher Jean-Jacques Rousseau, who was to influence his theories. (He was reconciled with his family in 1744, after his marriage.)

As his reputation as a writer grew, Diderot was approached by a publisher to plan an encyclopedia. Originally, it was to have been simply a translation of an English work, but Diderot saw it as an opportunity to expand knowledge and to expose reactionary forces in church and state. Work on the *Encyclopédie* began in 1750 and was not completed until 1772.

One of the subjects that Diderot explored in his writing was drama; he published his *Discourse on Dramatic Poetry* in 1758. He advocated the formation of a new genre to supplement the rigidly defined neoclassical genres of tragedy and comedy: *drame bourgeois*. This new genre would seriously examine the problems of ordinary middle-class people and offer moral and philosophical conclusions. To accomplish this goal, he wanted greater realism on the stage, in both scenic elements and acting. Of the plays he wrote to illustrate his theories, the two best-known are *The Natural Son, or The Proofs of Virtue* (1757) and *The Father of the Family* (1758); neither was a great success, but his ideas were influential, particularly in Germany and France, where a new realistic drama was to develop in the next century.

Diderot is also remembered for an important essay, "The Paradox of Acting," written in 1773. He argued in this essay that the best actors invoke emotions in an audience by using calculation and craft, not by experiencing these emotions themselves. Actors who rely on inspiration and "feeling the part" often give mediocre performances, he believed; a studied actor is more consistent. This idea has been debated by many later theorists.

After the completion of the *Encyclopédie*, Diderot no longer had a regular salary. This meant that severe financial problems were added to the harassment he was receiving because of his antigovernment and anticlerical ideas. To help him, Empress Catherine I of Russia bought his library, and then hired him as librarian and gave him the use of the books for his lifetime. For her, the philosopher drew up a plan on how to govern Russia. His books and manuscripts were sent to Russia after his death in 1784.

Diderot's theories about theater were highly influential. His concept of a new genre focusing on the middle class and on domestic situations, and allowing for a combination of serious and comic elements, would influence many nineteenth-century playwrights. His theories of acting continued to be discussed throughout the 1800s; for example, in the late 1800s there was a public debate between the French actor Constant-Benoît Coquelin, who supported Diderot's views, and the English actor Henry Irving, who opposed them. Diderot's concept of the "fourth wall"—the idea that the audience views a play through an invisible wall and that audience and performer should not acknowledge each other's presence—would have a major effect on later realism.

Ballad Opera and Comic Opera

The English also originated new dramatic forms. *Ballad opera,* a parody of Italian opera, was popularized in the 1730s by the success of John Gay's *The Beggar's Opera* (1728). In ballad opera there was no sung dialogue—that is, no recitative. Instead, spoken dialogue alternated with songs set to popular contemporary melodies. Characters in ballad opera were drawn from the lower classes. Frequently, ballad operas were social and political satires poking fun at contemporary issues.

In France, a similar form, known as *comic opera (opéra comique),* developed. It originated at the beginning of the century, when a pantomime-like entertainment was presented at fairground theaters in an attempt to get around the monopoly held by the Comédie Française and the Opera over drama and musical theater. Actors costumed as cupids held signs onstage on which were printed the other characters' speeches (in rhymed couplets). The action was mimed by the performers, and spectators would often sing the dialogue, encouraged by performers positioned throughout the house. The characters were drawn from commedia dell'arte. As some of the legal restrictions were removed, comic opera became more like ballad opera, since it used popular music for its songs, satirized political and social issues or other forms of drama, and had no recitative. By mid-century, however, comic opera became less satirical, less comic in tone, and more sentimental, and it had recognizable French characters. Some historians suggest that French melodrama evolved from comic opera in the 1780s and 1790s.

Sentimental Comedy and Comédie Larmoyante

The sentimental comedies of eighteenth-century England continue to be produced today. *Sentimental comedy* is like Restoration comedy except that it reaffirms middle-class morality: the virtuous are rewarded and the wicked punished. Sentimental comedies, which are comedies of manners, satirize social conventions and norms; they have many of the character types found in Restoration comedy.

In the early and middle eighteenth century, particularly in France, sentimental comedy featured saccharine, overwrought emotions and often dealt with moral characters who were threatened by serious misfortunes but lived happily ever after. The French called this type of drama *comédie larmoyante,* "tearful comedy," because it was meant to bring sentimental tears to the audience's eyes.

Later in the century, however, some playwrights in England and France tried to strike a balance between upholding middle-class virtues and making fun of social pretensions. The major examples of this later form are *The Rivals* and *The School for Scandal* by Richard Brinsley Sheridan. In the emerging American theater, Royall Tyler's *The Contrast* (1787)—the first play by a writer born in America—was patterned after Sheridan's sentimental comedies.

Richard Brinsley Sheridan

(1751–1816)

Richard Brinsley Sheridan, the best-known writer of sentimental comedy, also wrote a noted literary burlesque play, *The Critic*. He is remembered primarily as a playwright, but he was also a successful theatrical manager, and he himself would have preferred to be known as a politician. During his lifetime he combined all three careers, though they sometimes conflicted.

Because his father was an actor, novelist, and playwright, Sheridan was familiar with the stage from childhood. Though born in Ireland, he was raised in London, where his father's acting career had taken the family. His family hoped that he would study law, but he eloped at 21 with the daughter of a prominent singer and composer and turned to the stage for a living. *The Rivals,* which was produced at Covent Garden in 1775, failed at its first performance; but Sheridan's revisions eventually made it a success. He followed this play with *The Duenna,* a ballad opera, which had an unusually long run of seventy-five performances.

These two works and a short farce made Sheridan the most promising new dramatist in London. David Garrick, who was planning to retire as manager of the Drury Lane Theater, was impressed by Sheridan's talent and persuaded him and his father-in-law to become part-owners. Sheridan wrote several plays for Drury Lane, including *The School for Scandal* (1777), considered the best comedy of manners since the Restoration; and *The Critic* (1779), one of the most famous literary burlesques.

As manager of Drury Lane, Sheridan appealed to the public taste for spectacle and pantomime and tried to enforce his monopoly by restricting unlicensed theaters. Politics, however, had become his chief interest after his election to Parliament in 1780. He held several cabinet posts and was an adviser to the prince of Wales, who later became George III. Sheridan was also one of the best political orators of his day.

After 1808—the year Drury Lane burned—Sheridan's career took a downward turn; he lost his seat in Parliament, drank heavily, and was constantly in debt until his death in 1816.

There is an important difference between plays like Sheridan's *The Rivals* and *The School for Scandal* and Wycherley's *The Country Wife,* which was written 100 years earlier. Though all three are comedies of manners, Wycherley's work is far more amoral in its treatment of infidelity and other sexual matters. Sheridan's comedies, with their witty ridicule of the follies of society, can be seen as a link between the Restoration and the later comedies of Wilde and Shaw.

THE SCHOOL FOR SCANDAL. Richard Brinsley Sheridan's play of 1777 has the wit, repartee, and concern with social pretentions of Restoration comedy, but more sense of moral justice. In this scene, Joseph Surface (left, played by William Anton) is exposed as a hypocrite, and Lady Teazle (right, Lynne Griffin) remains with the husband she has been tempted to leave.

Modifications of Sentimentality

Some playwrights modified sentimental comedy; the best-known of these was the English dramatist Oliver Goldsmith (ca. 1730–1774), who wrote two plays: *The Good Natur'd Man* (1761) and *She Stoops to Conquer* (1773). In his "Essay on the Theater," which appeared just before the premiere of *She Stoops to Conquer,* Goldsmith attacked sentimental comedy, calling instead for a "laughing comedy" which would force audiences to laugh at their own eccentricities and absurdities.

In France, the leading writer of this more subtle kind of comedy was Pierre Carlet de Chamblain de Marivaux (1688–1763). Marivaux's plays usually focus on emotional conflicts within young lovers; this focus on characters' psychological makeup makes his comedies seem more modern. Marivaux's best-known works are *The Surprise Love* (1722), *The Game of Love and Chance* (1730), and *The False Confessions* (1737). Another French comic playwright who moved away from sentimentality and focused more on social and political satire was Beaumarchais (Pierre-Augustin Caron, 1732–1799). Beaumarchais's *The Barber of Seville* (1775) and *The Marriage of Figaro* (1783)—which was described at the beginning of this chapter—have many of the same traditional comic characters as sentimental romantic works but also reflect the explosive political, economic, and social issues of the time.

The emphasis on sentimentality and morality in serious and comic drama of the eighteenth century is understandable in light of eighteenth-century philosophy. Thinkers of the enlightenment, influenced by Locke and Hobbes, believed that human beings were rational and perfectible and that societies could learn from history. Sentimental comedies—like middle-class tragedies—expressed the moral optimism of the age.

Storm and Stress

In Germany, many playwrights of the late eighteenth century rebelled against the neoclassical ideals and questioned the clear-cut morality of sentimental comedy and bourgeois tragedy. Lessing, in a critical treatise called *The Hamburg Dramaturgy* (1767–1769), questioned the neoclassical interpretation of Aristotle. Lessing expressed admiration for Shakespeare's dramaturgy, and the Germans' admiration for Shakespeare and the Elizabethans culminated in a movement known as *Sturm und Drang,* "storm and stress."

"Storm and stress" dramatists rejected dramatic rules. They were not uniform in their playwriting techniques; some of them patterned their works after Shakespeare, using episodic structure, mixing genres, and presenting violence onstage. The "storm and stress" movement included such plays as Johann Wolfgang von Goethe's *Goetz von Berlichingen* (1773) and Friedrich Schiller's *The Robbers* (1782). Because "storm and stress" plays were radical in subject matter and style, only a small number were staged; but the movement was the forerunner of nineteenth-century romanticism.

Realism and Antirealism in Commedia dell'Arte

In Italy during the middle of the eighteenth century, there was a struggle between two playwrights—Carlo Goldoni and Carlo Gozzi—over what direction commedia dell'arte should take. Goldoni wanted to make it less artificial; Gozzi wanted to make it more fantastic. For fifteen years, from 1748 to 1762, they carried on a fierce stylistic controversy which foreshadows the nineteenth-century split between realists and antirealists.

Carlo Goldoni (1707–1793)

Carlo Gozzi (1720–1806)

As a former lawyer and the son of a doctor, Goldoni belonged to the rising middle class of Venice, and many of his 212 plays reflect Venetian life. Goldoni moved Italian commedia dell'arte from bare-bones scenarios to fully scripted literary works. He wanted theater to be more realistic and less fanciful, and in his reform of commedia, he discouraged masks and improvisation in order to

Goldoni.

Gozzi.

make the characters more lifelike. Goldoni was part of the eighteenth-century trend toward sentimentality; he softened the traits of the stock characters and made them less vulgar. Goldoni's seemingly endless quarrel with Gozzi was carried out in correspondence and various published articles; in 1762, tired of it, he accepted an invitation from the king of France to write for the Comédie Italienne in Paris. He remained there until his death in 1793.

Gozzi came from a noble but impoverished Venetian family. He began his literary career as a young man and spent much of his life defending Italian culture against what he considered corrupting influences. Gozzi felt that Goldoni's more realistic approach to commedia made it mundane, banal, and meaningless. Instead, he proposed a theater of the fabulous, in which commedia would be transformed through a mixture of prose and poetry and a combination of improvised and planned actions. His ten plays, performed between 1761 and 1765, are fantasies based on popular western and Asian myths.

It is hard to say who won the argument. Goldoni left Venice, but his position at the French court was prestigious. Gozzi's plays were popular in Italy for a while, but they were appreciated more in Germany and France. As one of the first realistic playwrights, Goldoni heralded a movement that was to dominate the modern period. Many of his plays, including *The Fan* (ca. 1763), *The Mistress of the Inn* (ca. 1753), and *The Servant of Two Masters* (ca. 1743), are still performed. Gozzi inspired the romantics of the early nineteenth century and nonrealistic theater of the twentieth century. His *Turandot* (1762) was made into an opera by Puccini; and Prokofiev used his *Love of Three Oranges* (1761) as the basis for a ballet. *The King Stag* (1762), Gozzi's finest play, is still occasionally revived.

Melodrama

By the end of the eighteenth century, melodrama had begun to emerge at the boulevard theaters in Paris. Beginning in the 1790s, the French playwright René Charles Guilbert de Pixérécourt (1773–1844) was immensely popular for plays which presented spectacular effects, violent action, and moral lessons. The German playwright-actor August Wilhelm Iffland (1750–1814) created plays for his own performances; many of them were domestic middle-class melodramas. Another German author, Friedrich von Kotzebue (1761–1819), was—like Pixérécourt—very popular; and many of his plays, including *The Stranger, or Misanthropy and Repentance* (1787), were adapted for audiences in England and America. Kotzebue wrote plays in several different genres; the most successful were visually spectacular and dramatized the battle between good and evil. (Melodrama will be discussed more fully in Chapter 11.)

THEATER PRODUCTION
IN THE EIGHTEENTH CENTURY

Government and Theater

In certain countries—England, France, and the independent German states—
the eighteenth century was marked by governmental attempts to regulate
theater production. In many cases, however, ingenious theatrical entrepreneurs
found ways to outwit these restrictions.

REGULATION OF THEATERS IN ENGLAND

As we have seen, government intervention in English theater can be traced
back to Elizabeth I, who issued proclamations limiting dramatic subject matter
and also designated a Master of Revels as the licenser of theatrical companies
and plays. When Charles II was restored to the throne in 1660, he issued the
first of several licenses—called *patents*—to Davenant and Killigrew, which
resulted in their monopolizing London theater. Later, when the legality of
these patents was questioned, Parliament, in 1737, issued the Licensing Act,
which restricted the presentation of drama to the Drury Lane and Covent
Garden theaters and also made the lord chamberlain responsible for licensing
plays.

Many theatrical figures tried to circumvent the Licensing Act. Some
managers simply opened unlicensed houses, hoping that the act would not be
vigorously enforced. Because—as we noted in Chapter 9—the act applied to
performances of "tragedy, comedy, opera, play, farce, or other entertainment of
the stage, for gain, hire or reward," some entrepreneurs argued that they were
not profiting from their dramatic presentations. The manager of one unlicensed
theater, Henry Giffard (ca. 1695–1772), claimed that his audiences were
paying to hear concerts and that his plays were presented as a free extra.
(Musical entertainments were always part of the extended English theatrical
bill of the eighteenth century.) Another manager, Samuel Foote (1720–1777),
said that he was selling cups of hot chocolate, accompanied by theatrical
presentations at no additional cost. Another way to circumvent the law was to
argue that the type of entertainment presented was not covered by the
Licensing Act, since many highly theatrical popular entertainments were not
regulated by the statute. One such form was the *burletta,* which around 1800
was defined as any three-act play with five or more songs per act; clever theater
managers converted nonmusical dramas, such as Shakespeare's plays, into
burlettas.

Despite all this, and although the Haymarket Theater was licensed as a
summer house in 1766, Drury Lane and Covent Garden dominated London
theater into the nineteenth century. The history of Covent Garden reveals
a great deal about changes in London theater practices in the 1700s and
1800s.

COVENT GARDEN. This famous theater, which opened in 1732, is still in operation today.

Covent Garden

(opened 1732)

When John Rich (ca. 1682–1761), a holder of one of the patents for London theaters, ended the season of 1731, he began a subscription to raise funds for building a new theater in Box Street, Covent Garden. Unlike his father, Christopher Rich—a lawyer who had bought the patent as a business investment and was a poor manager—John Rich was a very able manager; he was also an accomplished performer of pantomime.

Covent Garden Theater, a London playhouse that still exists today, opened on December 7, 1732, with a revival of *The Way of the World*. Under Rich, the theater featured extravagant pantomimes with animals, tumblers, and contortionists, as well as revivals of older plays.

From 1737 to 1843, under the Licensing Act, Covent Garden and Drury Lane were the only two London theaters authorized to present legitimate drama. Thus for a long time, their survival and management were particularly important: these two theaters provided the showcase for British drama.

When Rich died in 1761, his son-in-law managed Covent Garden, concentrating on opera. The Rich family sold the patent in 1767, and from then until 1803, Covent Garden had a series of managers, most notably George Colman the elder from 1767 to 1774. To meet rising costs, the theater was enlarged twice, in 1787 and in 1792; after the second enlargement, it held about 3,000.

John Philip Kemble, an actor, bought a share of the patent in 1803, and he and his sister, Sarah Siddons, performed at Covent Garden until they retired. In 1804, Covent Garden's sensation was Master Betty (1791–1874), a child actor so popular that Parliament adjourned to see him. The theater burned down in 1808, and when it reopened in 1809 Kemble tried to recoup his losses by raising prices. This resulted in the Old Price Riots, which began on opening night and lasted for 67 days until Kemble backed down.

Charles Kemble, who had succeeded his brother in 1817, presented Shakespeare's *King John* in 1824 with the first complete historically accurate scenery and costumes. When he found himself in financial difficulties in 1829, he was rescued by his daughter, Fanny Kemble, whose work as an actress helped him pay his debts. Although she had not intended to pursue an acting career, Fanny Kemble was a popular success as Juliet, Portia, Beatrice, and other heroines.

In the nineteenth century, several other people attempted to manage Covent Garden, with little success. The actor William Charles Macready had a fine company that performed excellent plays, but he refused to keep successes running. Madame Vestris staged several carefully researched Shakespearean revivals, but she also failed. A fire destroyed the theater again in 1856, and it was rebuilt once more in 1858. The theater was then turned over to opera; except for occasional dramatic performances, it has continued to be a home of opera and ballet ever since.

REGULATION OF THEATERS IN FRANCE

In eighteenth-century France, there were government restrictions on what types of plays could be produced. Three major Parisian theaters were subsidized by the government: the Opera; the Comédie Française, the home of nonmusical drama; and after 1716 the Comédie Italienne, the home of commedia dell'arte and later of comic opera.

For most of the eighteenth century, *boulevard theaters*—so called because they were located on Boulevard du Temple—catered to popular tastes. The boulevard theaters invented many types of musical entertainments in order to get around the monopolies granted by the government to other theaters. Boulevard theaters had developed from popular entertainers and companies performing at Parisian fairs; boulevard forms—such as comic opera, pantomime, and melodrama—were so popular that the government-supported houses eventually incorporated them into their own repertoire. All the boulevard theaters were put under the control of the Opera in 1784.

In 1791, during the French Revolution, the government restrictions and monopolies were abolished.

GOVERNMENT AND THEATER IN GERMANY

In Germany, government intervention in theater was of a more positive nature. Eighteenth-century Germany was not unified; it consisted of several independent states. German theater struggled to become established in the early eighteenth century and became an important artistic force during the last quarter of the century.

German theater of the late 1600s and early 1700s consisted mostly of foreign performances, usually of opera and dance at court; educational presentations by the Jesuits; and an early form of popular theater. This popular theater was dominated by performers who had been influenced by English actors appearing in Germany during the first half of the seventeenth century—because of the language barrier, these traveling English actors had emphasized physical action and slapstick in a style similar to commedia dell'arte. One of the German performers was Joseph Anton Stranitzky (1676–1726), who developed a comic peasant character, Hanswurst, and helped establish popular theater in Vienna.

Between 1727 and the 1740s, Caroline Neuber and Johann Gottsched attempted to reform popular theater: they introduced more traditional neoclassical dramatic forms; focused more on rehearsals and carefully stage performances; and, at first, eliminated some of the comic characters who had predominated. Neuber and Gottsched did not succeed in transforming German theater, but they influenced many other significant German actor-managers, including Johann Friedrich Schönemann (1704–1782), Sophie Schroeder (1714–1793), Konrad Ekhof (1720–1778), Heinrich Gottfried Koch (1703–1775), and Konrad Ackermann (1712–1771). Ackermann established Hamburg's first permanent theater; it was there, in 1767, that Johann Friedrich Löwen (1729–1771) established the Hamburg National Theater, for which Lessing was a dramaturg, or literary manager. The Hamburg National Theater was not government-subsidized; it was supported by leading business people. Although it had many of Germany's most important actors, including Ekhof, it failed after only 2 years.

During the last quarter of the eighteenth century, state-subsidized theaters were organized in several German cities and states. Many of the rulers who established these theaters were trying to demonstrate the cultural superiority of their courts; but some of the state theaters received only small subsidies and relied heavily on box-office receipts.

Government subsidization provided stability for German theater artists and resulted in the organization of many excellent theater companies; but it meant that the government could control theatrical presentations by withholding financial support. (Throughout history, this has been true of government support: it can be beneficial to artists, but it can also entail government control of dramatic content. The debate in the United States over whether the National Endowment for the Arts should support certain theatrical presentations with controversial subject matter is only the most recent example.)

THE THEATER AT DROTTNINGHOLM.
Top: This theater in Sweden still has the same sets and stage machinery that were used when it was built as a court playhouse in the eighteenth century. It is an excellent example of an Italianate proscenium theater with the pole-and-chariot system for changing scenery. Each summer, it gives period productions—such as this staging of *Iphigenia at Aulis.*

STAGE MACHINERY AT DROTTNINGHOLM.
Left: Drottningholm still has the machinery of an eighteenth-century Italianate proscenium theater, and productions there today continue to use the same technology. Here, stagehands are using its pole-and-chariot system to execute a scene change.

Theater Buildings

Theater buildings proliferated throughout Europe in the eighteenth century, in such countries as Germany, Russia, and Sweden. These theaters continued the architectural tradition established in the Italian Renaissance. Possibly the most significant theater building surviving from this period is Drottningholm in Sweden, completed in 1766 as part of the royal summer palace outside Stockholm. Drottningholm was boarded up in the 1790s and remained closed until the early twentieth century; but today tourists can take a ferry from Stockholm to the palace grounds and see a perfect working example of an eighteenth-century Italianate proscenium-arch, pole-and-chariot theater—even its wings and shutters, painted in perspective, remain intact.

Although theaters throughout Europe retained Italian Renaissance features, there were some important transformations in the eighteenth-century proscenium-arch theaters. For one thing, playhouses became larger to accommodate the new middle-class audiences, made up of the expanding mercantile class in the growing cities and towns. In London's Drury Lane, for example, the seating capacity increased from about 650 in 1700 to about 3,000 in 1800. Also, the interiors were ovoid (egg-shaped) to improve sight lines. And by the end of the century, the pit—even in France—had backless benches.

By the middle of the century, spectators had been removed from the stage in England and France. This was in keeping with Denis Diderot's "fourth wall" convention: an audience should not disturb a performance, nor should actors acknowledge the presence of spectators; it should be as if an invisible wall separated audience and actors. The "fourth wall" convention did not become an accepted theatrical practice until the nineteenth century, but the removal of spectators from the stage was a step in this direction.

Eighteenth-century English playhouses were significantly different from their counterparts on the continent, and from Restoration theaters. In the eighteenth century, the apron, or forestage, of English theaters shrank; it now extended out only about 12 feet from the proscenium arch, and the backstage area became much deeper. There were two proscenium doors—one on each side of the stage—leading out onto the apron; above each door was a proscenium box. On the European continent, by contrast, the basic configuration of eighteenth-century theaters followed the Italian Renaissance tradition more closely. A typical theater would have a proscenium-arch stage—without doors or an extended apron—as well as pit, boxes, and galleries; it used pole-and-chariot scene-shifting machinery.

Eighteenth-century continental European theaters became very ornate; many were designed by well-known artists and scene designers like the Bibienas (discussed below). Italian opera houses, particularly, had beautifully decorated auditoriums and sometimes luxurious lobbies; one example is La Scala in Milan, which looks much the same today as when it opened in 1778. Many theaters built by German rulers were also ornate and beautiful. In England, on the other hand, decoration of playhouses was much less lavish.

Permanent theaters were also constructed in the new world in the eighteenth century. They had been preceded by touring players. The earliest examples of European theater in America can be traced to the beginning of the 1600s, when there were amateur performances in French Canada and in Spanish Florida. The first English performance probably took place in 1665 in Virginia; presumably because of religious opposition, the actors were promptly arrested. Many popular entertainments are noted in early colonial America, such as tightrope walking and the exhibition of bears, but theatrical performances were rare into the early 1700s.

The first professional entertainer arrived in 1703 and performed in Charleston and New York; in 1714, the first play written in America was published. The first permanent theater was built in Williamsburg, Virginia, in 1716 by William Levingston. Between 1749 and 1752, Walter Murray and Thomas Kean organized the Virginia Company of Comedians, which performed in temporary spaces such as remodeled warehouses in Philadelphia and New York and throughout Virginia and Maryland. In 1752, a company led by Lewis Hallam (1714–1756) and his wife arrived in the British colonies and became quite successful in Williamsburg, Charleston, New York, and Philadelphia. After performing in Jamaica, it merged with a company run by the English actor David Douglass (d. 1786). After Lewis died in 1756, Douglass married Mrs. Hallam and became the leader of this successful company, which continued to perform until the Revolutionary War. Douglass built two permanent theaters: the Southwark Theater (1766) in Philadelphia and the John Street Theater (1767) in New York City. These were modeled after provincial English theaters.

After the American Revolution, theater was revived in New York by Lewis Hallam, Jr. (ca. 1740–1808) and his company, and in Philadelphia by Thomas Wignell (1753–1803), Hallam's leading comedian. The Philadelphia company had the Chestnut Street Theater (1794) constructed along the lines of a small London theater building. Philadelphia was the mercantile center of the new country and was to become its theatrical center in the early nineteenth century; the success of the Chestnut Street theater building and its company was a factor in this development. When Hallam retired from the management of his New York company, William Dunlap (1766–1839), a popular actor and melodramatic playwright, took over, and the Park Theater was opened in 1798 to replace the John Street.

Scenery

In the eighteenth century, the pervasive influence on scene design was Italian. Most continental theaters used Italianate wing-and-shutter settings, painted in perspective, and shifted scenery by Torelli's pole-and-chariot system. (As we have noted, theaters in England, the Netherlands, and America used the groove system for shifting scenery.)

An extremely significant development was the perspective setting with more than one vanishing point, a convention that made settings seem more grandiose and created a stronger sense of reality. There is some debate over when this technique was first used, but traditionally Ferdinando Bibiena is credited with introducing it in the early 1700s. Many other Italian designers—including Filippo Juvarra (1676–1736)—applied it with spectacular results.

Some additional elements were occasionally incorporated into the painted designs: these included borders at the top to mask the fly space; *ground rows*, which were silhouette cutouts along the stage floor; large scenic cutouts, such as painted trees, which could be shifted by the pole-and-chariot system; rolled backdrops which replaced the shutters; and *act drops*, curtains at the front of the stage. Other major changes in scene design during this century had to do with creation of mood, depiction of recognizable locales, attempts at historical accuracy, and more frequent use of three-dimensional properties.

The Italian Gianbattista Piranesi (1720–1778) heightened the atmospheric quality of designs by emphasizing the contrast between light and shadow in painting, a technique known as *chiaroscuro.*

Philippe Jacques de Loutherbourg (1740–1812)—who was hired by the English actor-manager David Garrick for the Drury Lane Theater in 1771 and worked there for a decade—was among the designers who introduced local color into settings and strove to unify all the visual elements. *Local color* refers to the inclusion of places audience members will recognize from their own community; in eighteenth-century London, this would have meant such landmarks as the Tower of London and London Bridge. This interest in recreating recognizable locales was in keeping with the popularity of eighteenth-century landscape painting, and it was a move away from the neoclassical tradition of stock sets. Still, eighteenth-century theater companies (unlike theaters today) could not afford to construct a unique setting for each production.

A developing interest in ancient history in the middle of the century also led some set designers to experiment—albeit usually unsuccessfully—with historical accuracy. But the real explosion in historically accurate designs would occur, as we shall see, in the nineteenth century.

During the 1700s, more three-dimensional, practicable elements were introduced into painted stage settings. For example, the climactic scene in Richard Brinsley Sheridan's sentimental comedy *The School for Scandal* required a screen for concealment.

Increased use of such practicable elements began to transform painted wing-and-shutter settings and would eventually lead to the realism of the *box set,* an arrangement in which flats are cleated together at angles (rather than set up parallel to the audience), to form the three-dimensional walls of a room. Recent research suggests that some type of box set may have been used as early as the late Italian Renaissance. In the last decade of the eighteenth century, the Italian designer Paolo Landriani (1770–1838) used a box set at La Scala, Milan's opera house. The box set was to revolutionize scene design in the nineteenth century and would become an integral element in realistic staging.

Debates in Theater History:

WHEN WAS THE BOX SET INTRODUCED?

The period when the box set was actually introduced into theatrical production has become more and more debatable with recent reevaluations of drawings and writings by scene painters from the seventeenth and eighteenth centuries. As recently as 30 years ago, the nineteenth century was often cited as the time when the box set was first used. However, recent analyses of drawings of operatic productions of the Italian Renaissance and of drawings from the eighteenth century seem to suggest that versions of the box set were used during those earlier periods.

In an article in *The Cambridge Guide to Theatre*, Arnold Aronson writes: "The introduction of the box set is frequently attributed to Mme. Vestris who worked with Planché at the Olympic Theatre in London from 1821 to 1838. However, something like a box set may have been achieved as early as 1642 in Venice by Torelli with the production of *Il Bellerofonte*. Painted perspective borders created an illusion of a ceiling and it is possible that he also placed panels between the wings to achieve continuous walls. And by the early 18th century, the free placement of flats and the enclosure of space downstage practised by the Bibienas created at least the illusion, if not the fact, of a box set."*

*"Theatre Design," in *The Cambridge Guide to Theatre*, Martin Barnham (ed.), Cambridge University Press, New York, 1992, pp. 972–987

In addition, there is a manuscript, entitled *Construction of Theatres and Theatrical Machinery* (1688), by Frabrizio Carini Motta (1627–1699)—a designer who worked at Mantua—that contains a description of scenery which sounds like a box set; and the Italian designer Paolo Landriani is thought to have used a box set at La Scala, the opera house in Milan, at the end of the eighteenth century.

Earlier historians had probably overlooked times when sets with wings and shutters parallel to the audience had been enclosed on the sides by other flats to create the illusion of a room. These box-type sets were still part of the tradition of painted scenery and were therefore seen as closer to the wing-and-shutter system; their historical importance was not recognized. The nineteenth-century box set, on the other hand, began to incorporate more three-dimensional practical objects and so was more like today's settings; it is probably for this reason that theater historians placed the origins of the box set in the nineteenth century. As historians continue to study even earlier drawings of Renaissance and baroque settings, there may be more discoveries regarding when the box set first appeared.

There were also experiments with stage lighting in the late 1700s: attempts to mask lighting sources, to use silk screens for coloring, and to introduce oil lamps and other alternatives to candles. De Loutherbourg was a key innovator in this area. But light sources were still not easily controlled, and the auditorium as well as the stage had to remain lit.

As it had been in the Renaissance, Italy was the birthplace of many of these eighteenth-century scenic innovations. The most influential Italian designers and theater architects of the period belonged to the same remarkable family: Bibiena family.

The Bibiena Family

(from 1690 to 1787)

For nearly 100 years, from 1690 to 1787, the name Bibiena was synonymous with scenic design throughout Europe. Over three generations, seven members of the Bibiena family were designers.

The Bibienas are noted for three innovations: their use of baroque art in scene design; the vast scale and elaborate ornamentation of their settings; and their use of angle perspective. *Angle perspective* is a convention that uses several vanishing points rather than the single vanishing point that had been used since the Renaissance; it gives a scene more complexity and depth than single-point perspective. Italian Renaissance painted sets pull the eye to a central vanishing point; in the Bibienas' designs, the eye is attracted to various vanishing points, and the standard visual pattern is broken. The Bibienas' sets also seem to extend beyond the proscenium arch, whereas Renaissance designs seem totally framed and enclosed by the arch.

The Bibiena family originally came from a town near Florence, Italy, where Giovanni Maria Gialli (1625–1665), an artist and the founder of the family, was born. His two sons, Ferdinando (1657–1743) and Francesco (1659–1739), studied painting in Bologna, Italy, and then studied scene design under an artist called Rivani, who had worked for Louis XIV at Versailles in France. Francesco became ducal architect at Mantua, Italy, and built theaters in Vienna, Rome, Verona, and Nancy. He also assisted his brother Ferdinando with spectacles at the court of Charles VI in Vienna. Before Ferdinando came to Vienna, he had worked in Parma and Barcelona and had published several books.

Ferdinando's sons also became designers. Alessandro (1687–1769) was court painter and architect to the elector of the Palatinate in Germany. Antonio (1700–1774) worked with his father in Vienna and also in Bologna and Mantua. Giovanni Maria (ca. 1704–1769) built a theater near Lisbon. Giuseppe (1696–1757) was the most noted of Ferdinando's sons. He succeeded his father as court designer in Vienna and also worked in Munich, Prague, Dresden, and Bayreuth. Before his death in Berlin, Giuseppe published his designs in three series of engravings.

Giuseppe's son Carlo (1728–1787) was the last to follow the family profession. He also traveled most widely, working in Germany, France, the Netherlands, London, Naples, Stockholm, and Saint Petersburg. The sets he designed for the court theater at Drottningholm in Sweden are still in use today. Some of his designs were also published.

Together, the Bibienas established a style of scene design—on a grandiose scale—that dominated the stage throughout the eighteenth century.

A BIBIENA SET DESIGN. Scene design in eighteenth-century Europe was dominated by one family: the Bibiena family, whose second, third, and fourth generations carried on the tradition begun by Giovanni Bibiena. This engraving shows a typical Bibiena design—vast in scale, ornate, and elegant, with its perspective vista disappearing in several directions.

Costumes

Theatrical costuming remained a primitive art throughout most of the eighteenth century. Actors and actresses, who often provided their own wardrobes, believed that the chief criterion for a costume was showing the performer off to the best advantage. Traditional, conventional costumes for specific characters and eras were common. On the English stage, for example, the Italian Jew Shylock in adaptations of Shakespeare's *The Merchant of Venice* always had red hair and a large nose. Costumes were not unified within a production, nor was there much attempt to make costumes appropriate for characters or time periods. Eighteenth-century experiments with costuming did not make an immediate impact on these practices, though they were seeds that would flower into a theatrical revolution in the nineteenth century.

Daring theater artists throughout Europe experimented with historically accurate costumes. Their attempts were not often exact historical reconstructions, but the experimenters were not totally to blame: accurate historical information was limited, and audiences expected traditional costumes. (In addition, we should bear in mind that completely accurate historical costuming is rare even today: costuming as a production element is usually intended to create an illusion of time and place rather than an accurate reconstruction.) Another factor inhibiting the development of historically accurate costumes in the eighteenth century (and this is also true of settings) was their cost: it was simply too expensive to create new costumes for a show which would have only a short run in repertory. (Not until later, in the nineteenth century—with the extended run and larger audiences in urban centers—would it become economical to develop unique costumes and sets for individual productions.)

Artists who veered from accepted costuming conventions were ridiculed by audiences. Nevertheless, in 1741 the English actor Charles Macklin (ca. 1700–1797) attempted to present a truly Jewish Shylock; and in 1772 he performed Macbeth in Scottish garb. In France, three performers—Marie-Justine Favart (1727–1772), Clairon (1723–1803), and Henri-Louis Lekain (1729–1778)—experimented with costuming that was supposedly appropriate for characters' social position, nationality, and historical era. The German actor-manager Friedrich Ludwig Schroeder (1744–1816) apparently used historically appropriate costumes in a 1774 production of Goethe's *Goetz von Berlichingen*. These first steps were important in setting the stage for greater historical accuracy in later periods.

Acting

The eighteenth century was an era of famous and enormously popular performers. All across Europe, successful actors and actresses developed a dedicated following. Some of these performers worked to improve the social status of the profession, but by and large actors remained suspect members of society.

(The Folger Shakespeare Library)

CHARLES MACKLIN AS SHYLOCK.
Macklin was one of several oustanding eighteenth-century actors who strove for greater reality and authenticity. Macklin caused a sensation with his portrayal of Shylock in *The Merchant of Venice*. Shylock had always been played as a caricature, but through his dress and manner Macklin created a convincing and moving character.

ACTING STYLES

The predominant approach to acting in the eighteenth century is usually described as *bombastic* or *declamatory,* terms that suggest its emphasis on oratorical skills. Standardized patterns of stage movement were necessary because rehearsal time was brief and bills were changed frequently. More often than not, actors would address their lines to the audience, not to the character to whom they were supposed to be speaking. Among the performers who took this "bombastic" approach were the English actors Barton Booth (1681–1733) and James Quin (1693–1766). In Europe and America, actors were often employed by "lines of business," that is, according to type. Normally, actors "possessed" their parts; once they performed a role, it would remain theirs until retirement or death. Performers often fell back on improvisation and relied on the prompter.

In the midst of these conventional practices, there were a few innovators. Some eighteenth-century performers tried to create natural, individualized characterizations, though they were not in the mainstream. Actors and actresses who rejected the bombastic style for a more natural approach include Charles Macklin and David Garrick (both English); Michel Baron (1653–1729), Adrienne Lecouvreur (1692–1730), Clairon, and Henri-Louis Lekain (French); and Friedrich Schroeder (German). They were opposed to formal declamation, stereotypical positioning of performers onstage, and singsong delivery of verse; they wanted to create individual characters, and they wanted to have more careful rehearsal procedures. These performers worked in traditional eighteenth-century companies and were restricted by traditional stage practices; thus they could not attempt to reflect everyday life onstage. Nevertheless, they were the ancestors of modern realistic performers.

Differences in styles of acting in the eighteenth century can be illustrated by the conflicting approaches of two of France's most popular performers: Dumesnil and Clairon.

Dumesnil (1713–1803)

Clairon (1723–1803)

Two of the greatest actresses on the French stage during the eighteenth century, Dumesnil and Clairon, were notorious rivals, and their rivalry was intensified by distinct contrasts in their acting technique and performance style.

Marie-Françoise Dumesnil began her acting career in the provinces and was invited to join the Comédie Française in 1737. An actress of considerable natural ability, Dumesnil was considered excellent in passionate roles. She created characters in several of Voltaire's plays, most notably *Merope* (1743), although Voltaire later preferred the acting of Clairon.

CLAIRON AND DUMESNIL. In this illustration, Dumesnil (left) is shown as Clytemnestra and Clairon (right) as Electra.

Dumesnil's position as the leading tragic actress was challenged in 1743 by Clairon—Claire-Josèphe Hippolyte Léris de la Tude. Clairon had made her stage debut at age 13, playing small parts with the Comédie Italienne in Paris, and had then put in her time in the provinces. She returned to Paris to debut at the Opera in March of 1743, but because she was more talented as an actress than a singer, about 4 months later she applied for admission to the Comédie Française. Clairon was granted a debut with the Comédie Française during which she would be evaluated for membership in the prestigious company. Although she had specialized in soubrette roles (a *soubrette* is a lady's maid), she chose to make her debut in tragedy; even more surprisingly, she insisted on playing Phaedra, a difficult role and one in which Dumesnil excelled. The company agreed, assuming that she would fail and learn a lesson in humility; but Clairon, who had not even rehearsed the play with the company, stunned both actors and the audience with her wonderful performance.

While both Clairon and Dumesnil appeared successfully in leading roles at the Comédie Française for many years, their performance styles were quite dissimilar. Dumesnil was considered to have more natural talent; generally, she relied on the inspiration of the moment to suggest how to play a part. Clairon, on the other hand, became a great actress largely by the force of her own will; she relied on intelligent and industrious preparation—on craft rather than inspiration—and was a much more studied performer than Dumesnil. Clairon's style received praise in Diderot's essay on acting, "The Paradox of Acting." Diderot believed that when a performer relied on flashes of genius, the results would be erratic: the actor would sometimes be brilliant and at other times mediocre. A studied performer like Clairon, he said, would give more consistently excellent performances.

Other differences developed between Clairon and Dumesnil. Around 1752, Clairon began to adopt a less declamatory, more natural speaking style. Clairon also became interested in historical accuracy, using her costumes to reflect different periods and places. Dumesnil, in contrast, continued to wear her expensive, contemporary fashions for every role.

ACTING COMPANIES

Organization of acting companies varied from country to country (often, it varied even within a country). In English companies, for example, plays were rehearsed under the supervision of an actor-manager, who was usually the company's leading performer; rehearsals usually lasted about 3 hours a day and continued for 2 weeks; and actors were contracted for a specific period of time. In France, the sharing plan remained in use in government-supported theater companies in Paris, while the boulevard theaters were managed by business entrepreneurs. The Comédie Française was organized democratically, and the company members voted on such issues as the bill.

The starting time of performances became later and later in the eighteenth century—usually, it was between 5 and 6 P.M. An evening's offering by an English company would be quite varied, with musical performances, a full-length play, entertainments between acts, and an afterpiece. An evening's bill in France would not offer quite so much entertainment, but a French company would also frequently stage a full-length play accompanied by entertainments between acts and an afterpiece. The complexity of the bill led to increases in the size of acting companies during the century.

STATUS OF PERFORMERS

During the eighteenth century, there were attempts to treat the craft and profession of acting seriously. For example, Denis Diderot's *The Paradox of Acting* was a theoretical treatise. (In this work, he suggested that the more emotion a performer actually feels, the less emotion the audience will feel—a view that runs counter to most contemporary theories of realistic acting.) Attempts to establish acting schools in England and France were a further indication of a new, more serious attitude.

However, for the most part performers in the eighteenth century were not held in high esteem socially. (In Rome, to give just one example, women were still not allowed to perform, because of the opposition of the church). Some performers tried to improve the social status of the profession; in the 1730s, for instance, the actress Carolina Neuber—who is well-known for many innovations that she brought to the developing German theater—attempted to accomplish this by policing the morality of her company.

Carolina Neuber

(1697–1760)

Around 1720, as we noted earlier, German theater consisted of traveling troupes who performed farces and improvised comedies at fairgrounds. The literary critic Johann Gottsched wanted to elevate the quality of German theater by improving the repertoire with plays based on French models and by refining the acting style; but it was not until he saw the company headed by Carolina Neuber that he found a troupe to carry out his reforms.

Neuber was born in 1697; her name before she married was Carolina Weissenborn. In 1718, she eloped with Johann Neuber, a young clerk, to escape from her tyrannical father. After serving as apprentices in several companies, the Neubers formed their own troupe in about 1725 and secured a license to perform at the Leipzig Easter fair. Carolina insisted on memorization of lines and careful rehearsals instead of improvisation, and she was responsible for a number of important reforms in German theatrical practice. She attempted to upgrade performances by eliminating the popular clown character Hanswurst, and also tried to improve the social standing of her actors and get better pay for her company. Because she shared Gottsched's desire to improve German theater, she was quite willing to perform his model repertoire; she was also strong-willed and popular enough to impose her views on her company and her public.

The collaboration between Neuber and Gottsched began in 1727 and lasted 12 years, until friction between the independent actress and the dictatorial critic caused a break in 1739. In 1740 the Neubers took their troupe to Russia, introducing modern theater to that country. When they returned to Germany the next year, Gottsched had allied himself with another troupe. The final break came when Carolina Neuber replaced the togas Gottsched had specified for one of his plays with flesh-colored tights. Gottsched attacked the actress in his reviews; she in turn described him as "bat-eared" in one of her prologues.

After the break with Gottsched, the Neubers' company began to decline, but they continued to struggle until they were impoverished by the outbreak of the Seven Years' War in 1756. Carolina died in 1760, a year after her husband. Her alliance with Gottsched—the first in Germany between the literary and performance sides of theater—laid the foundation for late-eighteenth-century and nineteenth-century German theater.

As an actress, Carolina Neuber was most acclaimed for her comic performances. Her staging practices influenced many young German actors—including Henrich Gottfried Koch and Johann Friederich Schönemann—who worked with her and then went on to distinguished careers as actor-managers. She also produced one of Gotthold Ephraim Lessing's earliest plays, which he had written as a student.

The Emergence of the Director

Possibly the most significant development in eighteenth-century theater was the emergence of practitioners who functioned, to some extent, like the modern director. Well into the eighteenth century, as we have noted, playwrights or leading actors normally doubled as directors of stage business. (The medieval pageant master was a distinct exception.) Since playwrights and actors had more pressing primary concerns, their actual directing was minimal; furthermore, the time spent on preparing a production in rehearsal was limited. What was missing in the theater, then, was someone to oversee and unify productions, assist performers, and ensure the appropriateness of the visual elements.

Some of the innovative actor-managers and playwrights we have already mentioned attempted to oversee the quality of productions and thus established a foundation for the development of directing; among these were Voltaire, Neuber and Gottsched, Ekhof, Ackermann, Iffland, and Schroeder. However, the two figures who are said to be the founders of modern stage direction are the English actor David Garrick and the German playwright, poet, and novelist Johann Wolfgang von Goethe.

David Garrick

(1717–1779)

With his reforms in staging, the actor-manager David Garrick revitalized eighteenth-century English theater and won for it the respect of all Europe. Because he oversaw the entire production process, Garrick is often described as an early director.

Garrick's first stage success came in a school play when he was 11 years old. His father, an army officer, gave him a good education, including a term at Dr. Samuel Johnson's academy. A legacy enabled Garrick and his older brother to enter the wine trade; while working at the London branch of a wine company, he became acquainted with prominent actors and producers, including Charles Macklin, with whom he discussed theories of realistic acting.

Resolved to try the stage as a career, Garrick played several roles in amateur productions. On October 18, 1741, he appeared as Richard III at Goodman's Fields, Henry Giffard's unlicensed theater outside London, and his acting swept the city. Garrick was slender and of medium height, with expressive features and dark, piercing eyes. His style was surprisingly natural, compared with the declamatory speech and studied gestures typical of his time. He often based his characters on life, visiting markets and law courts to study people. His repertoire included more than ninety roles, and he was equally good in comedy and tragedy.

DAVID GARRICK IN VENICE PRESERVED. The eighteenth century was an era of great stars. Unlike earlier performers, many of these actors and actresses paid close attention to details of performance and costuming to achieve a greater sense of reality. David Garrick, seen here in a tragedy by Thomas Otway at Drury Lane in 1762, was probably the finest English actor of his day.

In 1747, Garrick became one of the patent holders at the Drury Lane Theater. He took an active part in the management of Drury Lane, where he assembled a distinguished acting company. The reforms he instituted made Drury Lane the dominant London theater until his retirement in 1776.

Garrick was also a fairly accomplished writer. He adapted the works of many earlier playwrights, including Shakespeare, for presentation in his theater. Frequently, he wrote new prologues and epilogues to plays to be spoken by specific members of his company. *Miss in Her Teens* (1774) and *Bon Ton; or, High Life Above Stairs* (1775) were two of the most successful of his original plays. He sometimes collaborated with other writers; for instance, he wrote *The Clandestine Marriage* (1766) with George Colman the elder. *The Clandestine Marriage,* unfortunately, led to a dispute because Garrick would not agree to perform the part of Lord Ogleby; Colman refused to let Garrick act in his later plays, and soon became Garrick's competitor as manager of the Covent Garden Theater.

Though his rivals considered him vain and snobbish, Garrick was a cultured man who enjoyed the company of literary and society figures. When he died in 1779, he was buried in the Poet's Corner of Westminster Abbey. His friend Samuel Johnson wrote, "I am disappointed by that stroke of death that has eclipsed the gaiety of nations, and impoverished the public stock of harmless pleasure."

It was between 1747 and 1776, when David Garrick was a partner in the management of the Drury Lane Theater—and therefore responsible for artistic decisions—that he made his directorial innovations. As the company's leading performer, he championed a more natural style of acting; and he argued for careful development of characters' individual traits, based on meticulous preparation and research. His directorial policies were in keeping with his theories of acting. Garrick's rehearsals could last for weeks—much longer than the usual eighteenth-century practice. Garrick was also a strict disciplinarian: he required his actors to be on time, to know their lines, and to act—not simply recite—during rehearsals; and he established penalties for infractions of these rules. As part of his reformation of theater practices, Garrick banished spectators from the stage.

Garrick was also concerned with the visual elements of his productions. Following the lead of Charles Macklin, Garrick experimented with historically accurate and appropriate costuming, and he is often credited with attempts to "mask," or hide, stage lighting. Garrick was also responsible for hiring the innovative stage designer de Loutherbourg for Drury Lane.

Thus Garrick was a complete theater artist, undertaking many of the responsibilities that are now assigned to the director. However, he was still confined by tradition and by the commercial practices of eighteenth-century English theater—unlike the German Johann Wolfgang von Goethe.

Johann Wolfgang von Goethe

(1749–1832)

Johann Wolfgang von Goethe was responsible for a number of important innovations in German theater, comparable to those of David Garrick in England. Goethe was a man of many talents: in addition to being a theatrical director, he was a playwright, critic, and philosopher; he was also a minister of the court of Weimar, efficiently running everything from court theatricals to mining.

As the son of a wealthy Frankfurt merchant, Goethe had an excellent education. He studied at the University of Leipzig— Leipzig was then the cultural capital of Germany—and in his enthusiasm wanted to learn everything. But mental strain and a whirlwind love affair brought on a physical collapse that forced him to leave school. At home, he became interested in mysticism, alchemy, astrology, and the occult. It was at Strasbourg, where he finished his studies, that he became involved with the "storm and stress" movement in German literature and wrote his first important play, *Goetz von Berlichingen* (1773), in Shakespearean style. ("Storm and stress," which emphasized wide-ranging adventures of independent-minded heroes, was the forerunner of nineteenth-century romanticism.)

During a brief law practice, Goethe continued to write plays, poetry, and a novel; but in 1775 he accepted a post at the court of Weimar as director of theater—a post that soon expanded to the running of almost the entire duchy. Tired of the constant demands on his time, and seeking spiritual renewal, Goethe went to Italy in 1786 and stayed for 2 years. In Italy, he discovered the beauty of Greek and Roman ruins, which inspired a shift to classical themes and forms in his writing. When he returned to Weimar, he shed most of his court duties and devoted himself to writing and scientific research.

A friendship with the dramatist Friedrich Schiller led Goethe to take a renewed interest in the court theater, which he had neglected for several years. Sharing a belief that drama should transcend ordinary experience and reveal ideal truths, the two writers transformed the Weimar theater—Schiller with his plays and Goethe with his staging. After Schiller's death in 1805, Goethe again began to lose interest in the theater and became an increasingly remote figure until his own death in 1832. Goethe's playwriting had culminated in his long dramatic poem *Faust* (Part I, 1808; Part II, 1832).

It was while he worked with Schiller at the Weimar court theater that Goethe made most of the directorial innovations for which he is remembered. Goethe held intensive rehearsals and expected his actors to work as a unified ensemble, and—like Garrick—he penalized those who broke his rehearsal rules. Goethe, however, was not an advocate of a more natural style of acting; he believed that actors should address the audience rather than each other. He also followed routine blocking patterns, though he did emphasize careful stage composition, that is, the pictorial arrangement of performers onstage.

Goethe's approach to acting was reflected in his "Rules for Actors," a set of regulations for acting as well as personal behavior. How closely Goethe monitored his actors' personal behavior—to improve their social status—is apparent in the following rule: "The actor should show no pocket handkerchief onstage; even less should he blow his nose, still less should he spit. It is frightful to be reminded of these natural occasions. One may have with him a small handkerchief, as indeed is now the fashion, as a help in case of need."[1] Not all his regulations were this trivial. Goethe forced his actors to take their craft and profession seriously; he included rules for stage movement and vocal technique as well as deportment in daily life. He also worked on establishing a uniform "stage German" so that his performers would not speak in a variety of dialects.

[1]Johann Wolfgang von Goethe, "Rules for Actors," Arthur Woehl (trans.), in *Actors on Acting*, Toby Cole and Helen Krich Chinoy (eds.), Crown, New York, 1970, p. 274.

Goethe carefully oversaw settings and costumes and believed in historical accuracy. He even trained his audiences by establishing rules for their conduct; the only appropriate reactions, he insisted, were applause and the withholding of applause. Our modern tradition of audience decorum was established by Goethe.

In short, the working methods Goethe employed at the Weimar court theater between 1794 and 1817 influenced many of the nineteenth-century directors who are among the founders of modern theater.

The experimenters of the eighteenth century did not transform theater overnight, but they helped set the stage for modern theater, which would begin to develop in the nineteenth century. In Chapter 11, we turn to the first three-quarters of the nineteenth century, the period from 1800 to 1875.

SUMMARY

The eighteenth century was a time of theatrical experimentation. In drama, many new forms were developed, including ballad opera, comic opera, middle-class tragedy, and sentimental comedy. Innovative playwrights moved away from the neoclassical rules; in Germany, the "storm and stress" movement, which included such authors as Goethe and Schiller, argued against strict dramatic rules. Many plays were episodic in structure.

In scene design, the Bibienas introduced multipoint perspective, and Piranesi used chiaroscuro. Also, local color and three-dimensional properties became more common in sets. Charles Macklin, Marie-Justine Favart, and Friedrich Schroeder were among those who experimented with historical accuracy in costuming. For much of the century, acting was bombastic; but performers such as Macklin and David Garrick attempted to make performing styles more like observed life. In the last half of the century, Garrick and Goethe established practices of modern directing.

CHAPTER 11

THEATER FROM 1800 TO 1875

CHAPTER 11

THEATER FROM 1800 TO 1875

I
t is July 18, 1853, and we are at the National Theater in New York City, where the audience is eagerly awaiting a new stage adaptation of Harriet Beecher Stowe's *Uncle Tom's Cabin*. Adapting a popular story is a favorite way of developing plays in the mid-nineteenth century, and Stowe's abolitionist (antislavery) novel has been a sensational bestseller.

Like many popular melodramas of the day, *Uncle Tom's Cabin* reflects a significant social issue. It is the story of a slave—the title character—who is cruelly mistreated by an overseer, Simon Legree. Uncle Tom is devoted to his white owner's daughter, Little Eva, who dies during the course of the story. Another important figure is Eliza, a mulatto who attempts to escape from slavery. There have been two other attempts to dramatize the novel, but both have failed. This time, however, the signs point to success: this new version has already met with approval in Albany and Troy, two other cities in New York State.

WOYZECK.   One of the most enigmatic plays of the nineteenth century was Georg Büchner's *Woyzeck*. It seems to use romantic techniques but also to foreshadow some elements of realism and expressionism, and it received almost no productions until the twentieth century. Shown here is a scene from Joanne Akalaitis's interpretation at the Public Theater in New York. *(Martha Swope)*

An aspect of this production which reflects a popular custom is that the manager of the theater company, George C. Howard, commissioned the playwright George L. Aiken to write this version specifically for one performer —Howard's daughter Cordelia, who is playing little Eva.

The playhouse where we now find ourselves is a traditional theater of the 1800s: it has benches on the house floor as well as galleries and boxes in the side and back walls. The scenery is shifted by painted flats set in tracks on the stage floor and above; for *Uncle Tom's Cabin*, which is in episodic form, the scenery will be changed often.

The curtain goes up, and we are soon enthralled by a series of spectacular, suspenseful scenes, especially one in which the slave Eliza, fleeing her captors, escapes across the frozen Ohio River. The play also appeals to our emotions by presenting the death of the angelic Little Eva, and the persecution and death of Uncle Tom at the hands of the evil Simon Legree. The black characters are played by white actors and depicted stereotypically.

As we watch the premiere, of course, we cannot know that Aiken's version of *Uncle Tom's Cabin* will set remarkable records. At the National Theater, it will run for 300 performances, sometimes being presented three times a day; in 1879, 49 traveling companies will tour it; in 1899, there will be 500 traveling companies. In fact, *Uncle Tom's Cabin* will remain a popular touring show until the 1930s, when its profitability will finally be curtailed by the depression.

BACKGROUND: THE NINETEENTH CENTURY

Major social changes—the industrial revolution, technological advances, and the rise of nationalism—took place between 1800 and 1875. We should note, however, that the period from 1800 to 1875, like most historical demarcations, is somewhat arbitrary. For example, Johann Wolfgang von Goethe was discussed in Chapter 10 as an eighteenth-century playwright and director; but he was still active in the early 1800s. Thus some of the figures we will discuss in the present chapter had careers that began before 1800, and some had careers that continued long after 1875; and we will make occasional references to events after 1875 that were closely related to preceding events. This should be borne in mind as we consider the changes of this period.

Possibly the most important transformation of the early nineteenth century was the industrial revolution: the replacement of hand tools and human power by machinery, and the development of factories and the factory system. Many inventions were made—including an improved steam engine that transformed textile manufacturing, the leading industry of the time. The foremost textile manufacturing nation, and therefore the leader of the industrial revolution, was Great Britain.

The factory system, which required centralized labor forces, spurred urbanization and eroded traditional European agrarianism. The populations of European and American cities grew, but the way of life created by industrializa-

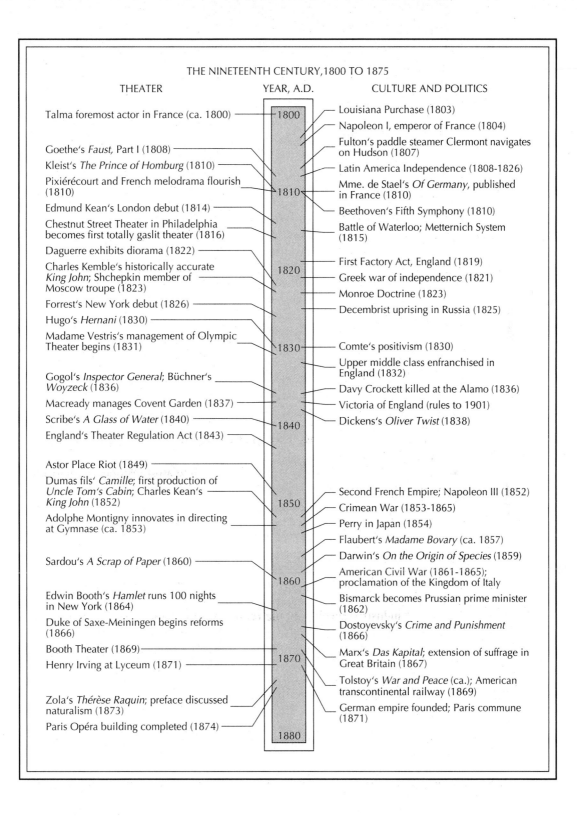

THE NINETEENTH CENTURY, 1800 TO 1875

THEATER	YEAR, A.D.	CULTURE AND POLITICS

Talma foremost actor in France (ca. 1800) —— 1800

Louisiana Purchase (1803)

Napoleon I, emperor of France (1804)

Fulton's paddle steamer Clermont navigates on Hudson (1807)

Goethe's *Faust*, Part I (1808) ——

Kleist's *The Prince of Homburg* (1810) ——

Latin America Independence (1808-1826)

Pixérécourt and French melodrama flourish (1810)

1810

Mme. de Stael's *Of Germany*, published in France (1810)

Edmund Kean's London debut (1814) ——

Beethoven's Fifth Symphony (1810)

Chestnut Street Theater in Philadelphia becomes first totally gaslit theater (1816)

Battle of Waterloo; Metternich System (1815)

Daguerre exhibits diorama (1822) ——

Charles Kemble's historically accurate *King John*; Shchepkin member of Moscow troupe (1823)

1820

First Factory Act, England (1819)

Greek war of independence (1821)

Monroe Doctrine (1823)

Forrest's New York debut (1826) ——

Decembrist uprising in Russia (1825)

Hugo's *Hernani* (1830) ——

Madame Vestris's management of Olympic Theater begins (1831)

1830 —— Comte's positivism (1830)

Upper middle class enfranchised in England (1832)

Gogol's *Inspector General*; Büchner's *Woyzeck* (1836)

Davy Crockett killed at the Alamo (1836)

Macready manages Covent Garden (1837) ——

Victoria of England (rules to 1901)

Scribe's *A Glass of Water* (1840) ——

1840

Dickens's *Oliver Twist* (1838)

England's Theater Regulation Act (1843) ——

Astor Place Riot (1849) ——

Dumas fils' *Camille*; first production of *Uncle Tom's Cabin*; Charles Kean's *King John* (1852)

1850

Second French Empire; Napoleon III (1852)

Crimean War (1853-1865)

Adolphe Montigny innovates in directing at Gymnase (ca. 1853)

Perry in Japan (1854)

Flaubert's *Madame Bovary* (ca. 1857)

Sardou's *A Scrap of Paper* (1860) ——

Darwin's *On the Origin of Species* (1859)

1860

American Civil War (1861-1865); proclamation of the Kingdom of Italy

Edwin Booth's *Hamlet* runs 100 nights in New York (1864)

Bismarck becomes Prussian prime minister (1862)

Duke of Saxe-Meiningen begins reforms (1866)

Dostoyevsky's *Crime and Punishment* (1866)

Booth Theater (1869) ——

Henry Irving at Lyceum (1871) ——

1870

Marx's *Das Kapital*; extension of suffrage in Great Britain (1867)

Tolstoy's *War and Peace* (ca.); American transcontinental railway (1869)

Zola's *Thérèse Raquin*; preface discussed naturalism (1873)

German empire founded; Paris commune (1871)

Paris Opéra building completed (1874) ——

1880

tion was far from pleasant for the working classes. Cities were polluted by coal, and housing was poorly constructed, cramped, and in short supply. Since the factory system required large numbers of unskilled laborers, whole families, including women and children (at first children as young as 6 years old), were employed at minimal wages; a workday was 14 hours long.

The industrial revolution, however, was a boon to the middle class, which was further strengthened financially. In acknowledgment of its new power, legislatures throughout the nineteenth century passed reforms beneficial to the middle class. Among other things, these reforms liberalized the qualifications for voting and for holding elected office. By 1884, three-quarters of all men in Britain could vote, as opposed to only one-eighth in 1832.

Eventually, the plight of the growing working class also began to improve. For example, in 1847 the British parliament passed the Ten Hours Act, which limited the working day for women and children to 10 hours. In the last half of the century, unionization began to develop, and the working class emerged as a social and political force to be reckoned with—as is evident from the numerous workers' uprisings in Europe between 1830 and 1871.

Technological innovations transformed not only industry but transportation and communication. The improved steam engine led to the locomotive, and beginning in the 1840s extensive railroad construction was undertaken in Great Britain and the United States. By 1869, a transcontinental railroad linking the east and west coasts was completed in the United States. Nineteenth-century inventions—including Robert Morse's telegraph (1837), Alexander Graham Bell's telephone (1876), and Thomas Edison's incandescent lamp (1879)— revolutionized daily life.

Nationalism, the desire of peoples to establish unified political states and their belief in the superiority of their own nations, was also a nineteenth-century phenomenon. Many historians suggest that nationalistic fervor was a reaction against Napoleon's attempt to conquer and consolidate most of Europe between 1800 and 1815. Nineteenth-century nationalism resulted in wars of independence in Latin America and Greece, and in the unification of Germany and Italy; but it also resulted in rampant colonialism, with developed countries exploiting the natural resources of underdeveloped areas such as Asia and Africa.

There was ferment on the intellectual front as well; nineteenth-century intellectuals questioned many traditional beliefs. Possibly the two most influential were Karl Marx (1818–1883) and Charles Darwin (1809–1882).

Marx, a German newspaperman who spent most of his productive years in England, outlined a socialist philosophy in *The Communist Manifesto* (1848), which he wrote with Friedrich Engels, and *Das Kapital* (1867). Marxism was a reaction against evils he perceived in the industrial revolution. According to Marx, the working class (the proletariat) is exploited by the owners of private capital (the bourgeoisie); he believed that the workers would unite to overthrow their oppressors and create an egalitarian, classless society in which wealth would be shared. The state and religion—which he saw as bourgeois devices for exploiting workers—would disappear in this utopian socialist society. Thus Marxism questioned dominant nineteenth-century economic, political, social, and religious beliefs.

Darwin's *On the Origin of Species* (1859) outlined his theory of evolution: that animal species evolve through natural selection. Species are constantly changing; these changes are transmitted by heredity; and the fittest individuals and species—those best adapted to the environment—survive and reproduce. Darwin's theory was revolutionary and controversial because it seemed to question traditional religious beliefs about creation, particularly the creation of humanity. Social Darwinism—a distortion of Darwin's theory which he himself never advanced—suggested that some races, nations, and religious groups are fitter than others, an idea that was insidiously exploited in the late nineteenth and early twentieth century.

Darwin and Marx presented a disturbing challenge to long-held beliefs in the supremacy of God and in a social hierarchy established by God. Their ideas and others—notably those of Sigmund Freud, the father of psychoanalysis—were to have a profound effect on the western world.

Theater in the nineteenth century built on the innovations of the eighteenth century and paved the way for modern theater, which began in the years immediately following 1875. As we noted in Chapter 3, there is sometimes a delay before written drama reflects social changes; and the ideas of Marx and Darwin did not surface in drama until the late nineteenth and early twentieth century. However, the theater of the first 75 years of the nineteenth century directly reflected contemporary social and industrial developments. Urbanization and technology, for instance, brought about marked changes in theater architecture and scene design. The concentration of people in cities made larger audiences available for longer runs of popular shows. The changing tastes of a changing audience were mirrored in popular drama; and the increasing diversity of urban populations—particularly in the United States—led to splintered audiences who wanted theater which spoke to their own needs. For example, many foreign-language theaters for immigrant audiences developed in New York City in the middle and late 1800s. Because of its new complexity, theater began to need an artistic overseer—a director.

THEATER IN NINETEENTH-CENTURY LIFE

Before examining specific transformations in nineteenth-century drama and theater production, we should consider the unique place theater held during this era. The dramatic arts exploded during these 75 years: the masses who filled the fast-growing cities demanded theater; for these new audiences it was a fad, a passion, and also a seeming necessity. Nineteenth-century theater, therefore, was a true popular entertainment. It attracted huge numbers of people, and its escapist dramas—though written quickly and often not particularly well—helped them forget the cares and drudgery of their lives.

Popular Entertainments

Nonliterary entertainment also attracted the masses. Americans, for example, supported the minstrel show, burlesque, variety, vaudeville, and the circus.

In the *minstrel show,* white performers were made up as caricatured blacks. White men had performed in burnt cork with exaggerated lips and eyes before minstrelsy—one performer, Daddy Rice, captured the nation's fancy in the early 1830s with a grotesque jump-dance that he called "Jim Crow"—but minstrel shows made performances by whites in blackface a commonplace, beginning in 1843 with a performance by the Virginia Minstrels, a company of four white men.

The recipe for a minstrel show was simple: a group of men, numbering from 6 to 100, dressed in colorful costumes with faces blackened and eyes and mouth enlarged by white and red lines, formed a semicircle on the stage. At one end of this arc sat Tambo, named for his tambourine; at the opposite end sat Bones, named for sheep ribs that he played like castanets; in the center stood Mr. Interlocutor—the straight man and master of ceremonies, and the only performer not in blackface. Unburdened by plot or character development, the show combined comic and sentimental songs, dramatic and farcical skits, and jigs and shuffle dances—all seasoned with a peppering of dialect jokes.

The vast majority of minstrel shows featured white performers, yet by all accounts the greatest minstrel dancer of the period was a black man, William Henry Lane, known as Master Juba, who in 1845 received top billing with a white minstrel troupe. Charles Dickens, who wrote enthusiastically of Juba, called him the "greatest dancer known." It is also true that some blacks founded, operated, and performed in their own minstrel companies; most of these black troupes originated in the 1870s, after the Civil War, when they were able to capitalize on white spectators' interest in seeing "genuine Negroes." To prove that they were not whites in makeup, a few black performers did not use burnt cork; but audiences usually preferred minstrel performers, regardless of race, in blackface. Many talented black performers learned and practiced their art in minstrel shows. Among them was James Bland, the composer of "Carry Me Back to Old Virginny," now the state song of Virginia. W. C. Handy, who composed "Saint Louis Blues," began in minstrelsy, as did Bert Williams and George Walker. This exploitation of black culture by whites changed the character of American music, dance, and theater.

Another extremely popular theatrical form was the *burlesque.* Burlesques were usually parodies of serious plays, such as Shakespeare's works and popular melodramas. (Today, takeoffs of popular films and television shows on *Saturday Night Live* and *In Living Color* are examples of contemporary burlesques.) Later in the nineteenth century, burlesques began to include women dancers; but it was not until the twentieth century that this form became a combination of comedians and strippers.

Throughout the nineteenth century, concert halls, saloons, and playhouses presented collections of entertainments—including songs, dances, acrobatics, and animal acts—on one bill; these developed into the popular *variety* and

Debates in Theater History:

IS POPULAR ENTERTAINMENT WORTHY OF STUDY?

The nineteenth century was an era of highly developed popular entertainments: the circus, minstrelsy, burlesque, melodrama, and variety entertainments presented in saloons and concert halls. Yet only recently have theater historians begun to examine the historical development and impact of these popular forms.

Among historians of past generations, the debate was whether these popular presentations are truly theater and whether they are worthy of study. Should the midget Tom Thumb and the plays written especially for him be studied in the same way that we examine the plays of Goethe and Hugo? (Thumb, whose real name was Charles Stratton, was immensely popular; in 1846 he performed for Queen Victoria in the comedy *Hop o' My Thumb* while on tour in England, and by the 1860s he had amassed a fortune.) Should the careers of actors who performed in minstrel shows and music halls be as carefully recorded and examined as the careers of John Philip Kemble, Sarah Siddons, and Edwin Booth?

A number of contemporary historians argue that popular entertainments were unjustly overlooked by earlier scholars and are most definitely worthy of serious study. These entertainments were the most widely attended theatrical forms of the 1800s; they reflected the interests and concerns of the mass audience, and they frequently contained ideologies and political views that were accepted norms.

It is also argued that we develop an elitist representation of theater history if we focus only on works which we ourselves—with all our own biases—designate as historically significant; and we will never come to understand what types of presentations most people experienced or what theatergoing was most often like. If all we study in nineteenth-century theater is Hugo and Goethe, then we are not getting a complete or accurate sense of that theater or the society which created it. By the same token, future historians who studied only the works of David Mamet and Sam Shepard and ignored hit musical comedies or Neil Simon's popular plays would not be giving their readers an accurate representation of our theater.

An excellent example of a study of contemporary popular and commercial entertainment as a reflection of social values is Alan Woods's "Consuming the Past: Commercial American Theater in the Reagan Era."*

*In *The American Stage: Social and Economic Issues from the Colonial Period to the Present*, Ron Engle and Tice Miller (eds.), Cambridge University Press, New York, 1993, pp. 252–266.

---

vaudeville presentations of the late nineteenth and early twentieth century. (Today, television is the home of variety entertainment.)

The renowned popularizer of the *circus* was P. T. Barnum (1810–1891), who developed spectacular advertising to attract mass audiences. Barnum's earliest successes were at the American Museum in New York City from the 1840s through the 1860s; there he exhibited human curiosities and presented variety acts and plays in a theater especially built for family audiences. Among Barnum's curiosities were Joyce Heth, who he said was 140 years old and had been George Washington's nurse; the "Fiji mermaid," which was actually the head of a monkey sewn onto the body of a fish; and the midget Tom Thumb. Between 1841 and 1865, Barnum sold 37,500,000 admissions to his American Museum. In the 1850s, he became involved with the circus, which was in many ways a touring version of his museum; he advertised the circus as the "greatest show on earth."

Audiences

The increase in numbers of spectators and types of entertainments resulted in the construction of more playhouses throughout the western world. With better rail transportation, dramatic arts were also brought to new areas and audiences; the transcontinental railroad, for example, made it possible for touring theater to reach people living in places like California.

The passion that audiences felt for theater accounts for the immense popularity of the era's star performers, and this intense interest in theater is also reflected in the desire of some of the century's most renowned literary figures to write dramas. Novelists, such as Charles Dickens and Henry James, saw how well drama could reach and affect mass audiences and attempted to write plays. Poets such as Byron, Keats, and Shelley also wrote dramas, though these—because of their unusual style—were rarely produced.

The popularity of theater between 1800 and 1875 has not been equaled in modern times: today, theater no longer holds the same kind of central position. In some ways, movies and television are modern counterparts; they present similar kinds of entertainment, attract mass audiences, and have popular stars. But the intense passion of nineteenth-century audiences has rarely been found in other entertainments; perhaps the closest parallel today is the emotional intensity of audiences at rock concerts.

Theater Riots

The nineteenth-century passion for theater is clearly seen in—and helps to explain—several infamous riots. One of these episodes, the "Old Price Riots," took place when London's Covent Garden Theater was remodeled in 1809 and prices for admission were raised by the actor-manager John Philip Kemble (1757–1823). When the lower-class audiences learned about the higher prices and also discovered that the third-tier gallery had been turned into expensive private boxes rented for the season, they disrupted performances for 67 nights, chanting, sounding noisemakers, and throwing things. Eventually, the management gave in; the old prices for the pit were restored, and the number of boxes was reduced.

Another theater riot took place in Paris in 1830, when *Hernani* by Victor Hugo (1802–1885) premiered at the Comédie Française, the home of French neoclassical drama. As we shall see, Hugo was a romantic and therefore opposed to neoclassicism, and *Hernani* broke all the neoclassical rules. For 55 nights, shouting, rioting, and fights broke out in the theater between supporters of neoclassicism and advocates of romanticism. (At this time, French playwrights often paid some audience members to applaud their works; a paid group like this was called a *claque,* and some of the uproar over *Hernani* may have been set off by rival claques.)

The most violent of the nineteenth-century riots occurred outside New York's Astor Place Theater. This riot grew out of rivalry between an English star, William Charles Macready; and an American star, Edwin Forrest. Forrest,

(The Metropolitan Museum of Art, Bequest of W. C. Arnold, 1954)

ASTOR PLACE RIOT. This riot, which erupted in in New York City in 1849, was a result of nationalistic fervor and the passionate involvement of theater audiences. It was set off when working-class fans of the American star Edwin Forrest attacked a theater in which the English actor William Charles Macready, who had supposedly insulted Forrest, was performing.

who was noted for his portrayal of melodramatic heroes, had made an unsuccessful English tour, and he blamed its failure on Macready, whose style was more subtle and realistic. When Macready appeared at the Astor Place Theater on May 8, 1849, he was prevented from performing by Forrest's working-class fans. Macready's aristocratic admirers persuaded him to perform again on May 10, and a mob of 15,000 attacked the building. The infantry was called out to disperse the rioters, and when the violence finally ended, twenty-two people had been killed and many more wounded.

These events and other audience uprisings illustrate not only the passionate involvement of nineteenth-century audiences but also the social changes of the era. The "Old Price" and Astor Place riots reflected a struggle between the working and upper classes, and the militancy of lower-class audiences foreshadowed later social revolutions. The Astor Place Riot also reflected a growing nationalistic fervor; the violence between Forrest's and Macready's fans was partially a result of anti-British sentiment in the United States.

Theater and Nationalism

In fact, much popular drama itself reflected nationalism. For example, Anna Cora Mowatt, one of America's first significant female playwrights, wrote a comedy of manners, *Fashion* (1845), that depicted the values of hard-working America as more honest than the social pretensions of Europe. The character Adam Trueman in *Fashion* was a descendant of an earlier popular stock figure in American melodramas and comedies—the "stage Yankee," a representative of diligent, unpretentious, rural America.

Anna Cora Mowatt
(1819–1870)

Anna Cora Mowatt is most noted for her popular play *Fashion* (1845), but she also had an active and distinguished career as a writer and actress. She was born in France to American parents, read widely as a child, and participated in her family's amateur theatricals. At age 15 she married James Mowatt—an older, wealthy attorney—and continued her study of literature and history; she also began to write for her own enjoyment. She turned to writing as a career around 1841 (when her husband lost his fortune, as well as his health and most of his eyesight), contributing articles to women's magazines. She also published novels and earned money by giving public recitations of poetry.

Mowatt's first effort as a professional playwright was an astonishing success. *Fashion* premiered at an upscale theater in New York—the Park Theater—on March 24, 1845. It ran for at least eighteen performances, a remarkable achievement at a time when bills usually changed nightly.

One of the very first American social comedies, *Fashion* advocated American sensibility rather than slavish imitation of foreign fashions. It had several different character types—including a Yankee, a French maid, an African American servant, a French count, and an American hero—whose interaction created comic contrasts. The Yankee was an amusing, down-to-earth, homespun New Englander, related to the figure we know today as Uncle Sam; this was a popular, recurring character in American drama.

Fashion was especially important because American drama was not highly esteemed at that time. Many actors and managers in the United States were from England, and they tended to present English plays or adaptations of French or German plays. Because the United States was a young country, with no established dramatic literature, most theatergoers assumed that a play by an American could not be very good. Mowatt's status as a member of the social and literary elite assured *Fashion* more sympathetic attention than was usual for a new American play. (Appropriately, *Fashion* criticized the American tendency to prefer anything European.)

Her success as a playwright, combined with continuing financial pressure, encouraged Mowatt to become an actress: she made her debut on June 13, 1845, and was warmly received. This decision had important implications for the entire profession. Acting was still a low-status occupation, and the morals of actresses were suspect; Mowatt demonstrated that a woman of high social standing could appear onstage without damaging her reputation.

During the next 2 years, she toured the United States in starring roles. She also wrote a romantic drama, *Armand, or The Child of the People* (1847), for herself and E. L. Davenport, the leading man in her company. For the next few years, Mowatt acted in England to great acclaim. She then returned to the United States, making her last stage appearance in Boston in 1854.

NINETEENTH-CENTURY DRAMA

Three major forms of drama came to prominence between 1800 and 1875: romanticism, melodrama, and the well-made play. Romanticism and melodrama, however, were more than just types of plays. Romanticism was a philosophical and literary movement that had a significant impact on theater production; melodrama was also a major style of theater production and continues to exert a significant influence today.

Romanticism

Romanticism, influenced by the German "storm and stress" movement, was a revolutionary philosophical and literary trend of the first half of the nineteenth century. Victor Hugo, the renowned poet, theorist, and novelist, outlined the characteristics of romantic drama in an introduction to his play *Cromwell* (1827). The romantics rejected the neoclassical rules; in fact, they rejected all artistic rules, suggesting that genius creates its own rules. Many romantics used Shakespeare's structural techniques: their plays were episodic and epic in scope. Unlike Shakespeare, however, the romantics were often more interested in creating mood and atmosphere than in developing believable plots or depth of character. Romantic dramatists did not believe in purity of genre; they considered all subject matter—the grotesque as well as the ideal—appropriate for the stage; and they often used supernatural elements. The romantic hero was frequently a social outcast, such as a bandit, who quested for justice, knowledge, and truth. One of the most common romantic themes was the gulf between human beings' spiritual aspirations and their physical limitations.

Romantic drama was often imbued with the independent spirit of the time. This is another excellent example of drama as the mirror of an age: the American and French revolutions had taken place at the end of the eighteenth century, and concepts of freedom and liberty were in the air. Romantic playwrights created heroes who fiercely defended individuality and independence. In addition, these playwrights worked in many other literary forms—novels, poetry, and theoretical essays. Some were also interested in the other arts, including painting. Like later twentieth-century experimental artists, the romantics were stretching the boundaries of art forms and defying rigid artistic categorizations and aesthetic rules.

The most noted romantic dramas of the period were Goethe's *Faust* (Part I, 1808; Part II, 1832) and Victor Hugo's *Hernani* (1830). Besides Goethe, significant romantic German dramatists of the nineteenth century included Ludwig Tieck (1773–1853), who experimented with Shakespearean staging as a director; Heinrich von Kleist, who wrote *The Broken Jug* (1808) and *The Prince of Homburg* (1811); and Georg Büchner, who wrote *Danton's Death* (1835) and *Woyzeck* (1836). As we noted in the Introduction, *Danton's Death* and *Woyzeck* were even more radical and enigmatic than the dramas of Büchner's romantic contemporaries and became popular only in the twentieth century with the advent of naturalism, expressionism, and absurdism. *Woyzeck* (which was left unfinished when Büchner died at age 24) has often been staged in the twentieth century by avant-garde directors who are intrigued by its presentation of the physical and emotional destruction of a lowly soldier. In 1992, for example, a production by the American director Joanne Akalaitis drew parallels to the horrors of the Second World War.

Melodrama

Melodrama means "song drama" or "music drama." The term originally comes from the Greek, but it usually refers to a theatrical form popularized by the French at the end of the eighteenth century and the beginning of the nineteenth. "Music" refers to the background music that accompanied these plays—similar to the music played with silent movies and the music used as a background in later films. In these melodramas, a premium was put on surface effects, especially those evoking suspense, fear, nostalgia, and other strong emotions; the plays were written in a way that would arouse such feelings.

Heroes and heroines of melodrama were clearly delineated and stood in sharp contrast to the villains; the audience sympathized with the good characters and despised the bad ones. In addition to its heroes and villains, melodrama had other easily recognized stock characters: the threatened woman; the sidekick (a comic foil to the hero); and the "fallen woman" who, even after repenting, is punished for her wicked past. The fallen woman suggests the highly moral tone of traditional melodrama; a conflict between good and evil was clearly and firmly established, and virtue was always victorious. Stock characters of melodrama can be compared to those of commedia dell'arte in the Italian Renaissance, and to "lines of business"—the tradition in eighteenth-century theater companies of having actors play specific types of roles. Today, many stock characters appear in situation comedies and soap operas on television, and many popular film and television actors (such as Charles Bronson, Arnold Schwarzenegger, and Sylvester Stallone) play the same type of characters over and over again.

(Martha Swope)

SWEENEY TODD. The story of Sweeney Todd, a barber who cut the throats of his victims and gave the bodies to his colleague Mrs. Lovett to make into meat pies, was dramatized several times in London in the nineteenth century as a stage melodrama. In 1979, it was made into a Broadway musical, starring Len Cariou as Sweeney and Angela Lansbury as Mrs. Lovett.

To hold the audience's interest, melodrama—past and present—has a suspenseful plot, with a climactic moment at the end of each act. In adventure shows on television, for instance—such as detective and cop shows—a climax like a car crash, a sudden confrontation, or the discovery of important evidence will occur just before a break for a commercial. An example from nineteenth-century melodrama is the close of Act I of *The String of Pearls*, written in 1847 by George Dibdin Pitt (1799–1855). This is a play about Sweeney Todd, the "demon barber" of Fleet Street in London—the story on which the Broadway musical *Sweeney Todd* (1979) was based. In Pitt's play, Sweeney has been killing customers in his barbershop and turning the bodies over to Mrs. Lovett, who makes them into meat pies. At the end of Act I, Sweeney decides to get rid of those around him, including Mrs. Lovett; but she overhears his plans. In a few short lines, the action accelerates. She demands half of the profits; he insists that he will deduct money she owes him; she draws a knife and is about to attack him when he pulls out a pistol and shoots her; he then throws her body into a fiery furnace as the curtain falls.

Since melodrama is primarily escapism, it stresses visual spectacle and special effects. Today's science-fiction films, such as the *Terminator* series and *Jurassic Park,* are highly visual melodramas, with no expense spared to create technologically advanced special effects; and the omnipresent car chases in detective dramas on television and in films grow out of nineteenth-century melodramatic spectacle. The nineteenth-century melodramatic playwright Dion Boucicault (1822–1890) had used many special effects (though the available technology was less sophisticated); in *The Poor of New York* (1857), for example, a tenement burned onstage.

Most types of nineteenth-century melodramas have modern-day equivalents. Domestic melodrama became soap opera. Frontier melodrama became the western; in the United States, there were many plays which dealt with life in the west. Frontier melodrama depicted Native Americans in ways that would now be considered stereotyped and racist, though some plays of this era—such as *Metamora* (1829) by John Augustus Stone (1801–1834), which was written especially for Edwin Forrest—tried to present a more positive image. Crime melodrama became the popular mystery or detective show; one of the most famous nineteenth-century crime melodramas was *The Ticket-of-Leave Man* (1863), by the English playwright Tom Taylor (1817–1880), which dealt with a difficult issue: social acceptance of rehabilitated criminals. Nautical melodrama, which dealt with sailors and pirates, was the forerunner of swashbuckler films; one of the most popular nautical melodramas was *Black-Eyed Susan* (1829) by the English dramatist Douglas William Jerrold (1803–1857). Equestrian melodrama—which featured horses performing spectacular tricks—and other popular melodramas with animals as heroic stars were the ancestors of television and film melodramas featuring animals. A popular English equestrian, Andrew Ducrow (1793–1842), appeared in melodramas that featured him on horseback; and Pixérécourt's *The Forest of Bondy, or The Dog of Montargis* (1814), which was translated into English for productions in London and New York, had a canine hero. (One of the twentieth century's great melodramatic filmmakers, Alfred Hitchcock, used birds as villains in *The Birds.)*

Today, however, there has been a major thematic change in much melodrama—a change that is most discernible in films of the 1960s and 1970s. Nineteenth-century audiences did not question social, religious, or moral norms; since the 1960s, by contrast—partly because of the war in Vietnam and recurrent political scandals—audiences have questioned traditional values and no longer believe that good and evil are easily delineated. In films of the 1960s and 1970s like *The Wild Bunch, Bonnie and Clyde,* and *The Godfather,* as well as in more recent films like Clint Eastwood's Oscar-winning *The Unforgiven,* characters who would once have been seen as villains are presented heroically; the forces of law are shown as evil. Also, traditional stereotypes, including racist portrayals of blacks and sexist portrayals of women, have been rejected. These transformations in melodrama mirror our changing beliefs and values. On the other hand, many of today's melodramas—for example, the extraordinarily popular *Star Wars* and *Indiana Jones* films of the 1980s—continue to reflect traditional values.

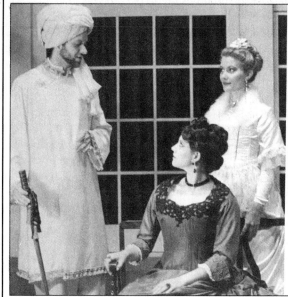

A WELL-MADE PLAY. A nineteenth-century specialty was the well-made play—a tightly constructed drama in which all parts fit neatly together. A number of playwrights perfected this form, and one of the best was the Frenchman Eugène Sardou. A scene from Sardou's *A Scrap of Paper* is shown here.

The Well-Made Play

Many popular melodramas of the nineteenth century had what is called a *well-made-play* structure. In the twentieth century, the term *well-made* has come to describe a play which builds mechanically to its climactic moments and is intended mainly to arouse the audience's interest in these contrived climaxes, not to create truthful emotions or characterizations; when critics today describe a play as "well-made," they are usually being condescending. However, in the nineteenth century the term was complimentary: a "well-made" play was one that showed excellent craftsmanship, and the term itself implied admiration for all the well-crafted goods of the industrial revolution. It is also true that the well-made-play structure was sometimes used creatively by later dramatists.

A well-made play emphasizes careful cause-and-effect development; it is usually a tightly constructed crisis drama. The action often revolves around a secret known to the audience but not to the characters. The opening of the play carefully spells out the needed background information, or exposition. Throughout the play the dramatic action is clearly foreshadowed, and each act builds to a climactic moment. In the major scene, the "obligatory scene," the characters in conflict confront each other in a showdown. The plot is carefully resolved so that there are no loose ends.

One example of a well-made play is *Let's Get a Divorce* (1880) by the French playwright Victorien Sardou (1831–1908). The exposition gives a picture of a bored young housewife and mentions a liberal new divorce law that has been proposed in France. The restless wife flirts with her husband's young cousin. The cousin, hoping to make her his mistress, fakes a report that the proposed divorce law has actually been passed and urges her to become his lover because under the new law she can soon become his wife. The husband encourages this scheme, on the assumption that if it succeeds, he will reverse positions with his cousin and become in his wife's eyes an exotic, out-of-reach lover. The "obligatory" scene takes place in a restaurant, where everything is sorted out and the wife returns to her husband.

Throughout a well-made play, devices such as letters and lost documents seem to motivate the dramatic action. Two of the most famous nineteenth-century well-made plays revolve around such specific dramatic devices: *A Glass of Water* (1840) by Eugène Scribe (1791–1861) and *A Scrap of Paper* (1860) by Sardou. Scribe and Sardou—Scribe, like Sardou, was French—were the most renowned practitioners of the well-made play. Other French playwrights who used this structure were Alexandre Dumas the younger (Dumas fils, 1824–1895), best-known for *The Lady of the Camellias* or *Camille* (1852); Émile Augier (1820–1889); and Eugène Labiche (1815–1888).

A number of nineteenth-century playwrights who used the well-made-play structure focused on more realistic subject matter. For example, domestic melodrama dealt with everyday circumstances and issues, as did the plays of Dumas fils. The English playwright Thomas William Robertson (1829–1871) was noted for *Society* (1865) and *Caste* (1867), which were called "teacup and saucer" and "bread and butter" dramas because they emphasized realistic stage business and dealt with real social concerns—though all of Robertson's plays have contrived "happily ever after" endings. As we will see in Chapter 12, the logical causal structure of the well-made play—coupled with a developing interest in contemporary social issues—was to influence Henrik Ibsen, who has been described as the founder of modern dramatic realism.

NINETEENTH-CENTURY THEATER PRODUCTION

We turn now to theater production in the period from 1800 to 1875: to performers, managers, and directors; and to theater architecture and the visual elements of productions—scenery, lighting, and costumes.

The Acting Profession

THE RISE OF THE STAR

The nineteenth century was an era of star actors and actresses, performers who were idolized by the audiences that flocked to see them. Many of these actors were not simply national stars but became international figures; for instance, the Italian stars Adelaide Ristori (1822–1906) and Tommaso Salvini (1829–1915) toured Europe, the United States, and South America. Some of these performers amassed—and frequently lost—fortunes. Major changes in the art and business of acting were caused in part by the rise of the star.

Two of the most famous stars of the nineteenth century were Sarah Bernhardt and Eleanora Duse.

Bernhardt.

Duse.

Sarah Bernhardt (1845–1923)

Eleanora Duse (1859–1924)

Two stars, Sarah Bernhardt and Eleanora Duse, dominated the international stage for part of the nineteenth century. They played many of the same roles, though they had different acting styles.

Bernhardt—"Madame Sarah"—was the more flamboyant of the two, and her eccentricities and temperament are legendary (among other things, she demanded her salary in gold and supposedly slept in a coffin). Bernhardt was the daughter of a French father and a Dutch Jewish mother. She originally wanted to become a nun; but her family opposed that choice, and instead she attended the Conservatoire to train as a classical actress. In 1862, she made her debut at the Comédie Française, and she continued an intermittent, stormy relationship with that company until 1880. Slim, with large dark eyes, Bernhardt was a master of stage technique, but her chief asset was her voice, which was often compared to a golden bell. Twice she managed theaters in Paris, and she was also a sculptor and a writer of poetry and plays. She toured the United States many times.

Bernhardt was noted for her performances in *Phaedra, Hernani,* and *The Lady of the Camellias.* She also starred in works by Sardou and Edmond Rostand (1868–1918); and she performed the title role—a male part—in a version of Shakespeare's *Hamlet.* Her own personality always shaped her characterizations; she was strong-willed and continued to perform even after one of her legs was amputated.

While Bernhardt looked backward to the "grand style" of the nineteenth century, Eleanora Duse foreshadowed the sincere realism of the twentieth century. Duse was as quiet and reclusive as Bernhardt was flamboyant. Her parents were both actors, and she made her own stage debut at age 4; at 14, she was playing Juliet. After her parents died, she had to struggle for several years, until she appeared in Naples in 1879 as the title character in Émile Zola's *Thérèse Raquin* and astonished the critics with the anguish she conveyed. After touring as leading lady to the popular actor Ernesto Rossi (1827–1896), she formed her own company.

Duse's repertoire included the poetic dramas of her lover Gabriele D'Annunzio (1863–1938), the melodramas of Dumas fils and Sardou, and the more modern plays of Ibsen. Her style was greatly admired by critics, such as George Bernard Shaw, who advocated realism. Slender and attractive, she wore no makeup but used her expressive face, eyes, and gestures to convey the thoughts of a character. She was apparently the epitome of a natural, totally believable actress who projected sincerity and inner fire rather than outward flamboyance. She retired in 1909 because of ill health, but financial reverses forced her to return to the stage after World War I. She died while on tour, in Pittsburgh.

Touring—which developed because of the exploding populations in urban centers—allowed star performers to bring their talents to people throughout the world and build international reputations. Early in the century, touring stars performed with local repertory companies. Later, as transportation improved, not only stars but complete productions known as *combination companies* began to tour; these included supporting players, scenery, and costumes. (Combination companies were a factor in the decline of local repertory companies, discussed later.)

Star actors toured to make money, of course, but they sometimes had other reasons as well. For example, George Frederick Cooke (1756–1812), the first significant English actor to tour the United States (where he performed for the 2 years preceding his death), came to America because his alcoholism was destroying his reputation in England. On the other hand, in 1825 a significant American actor, Ira Aldridge, became a touring star in Europe because, as an African American, he could not gain acceptance in the United States.

Ira Aldridge

(ca. 1806–1867)

Before the 1960s, theater historians paid little attention to early African American theater artists. More recently, scholars have begun to redress this, and in particular they have focused on the career of Ira Aldridge.

One of the leading Shakespearean actors of the nineteenth century, Aldridge performed for 40 years, mostly in Europe, where he won wide recognition. The son of a pastor of a Presbyterian chapel in New York City, he was born around 1806 or 1807 in either Manhattan or Bel Air, Maryland. He attended the African Free School in New York until age 16, when he began acting with the African Grove Theater in New York City.

The African Grove, the first formal black theater company in America, was founded in the season of 1820–1821 by William Brown (an African American) and James Hewlett (a West Indian actor). On its stage, *King Shotaway* (1823)—believed to be the first play both written and performed by African-Americans—was presented, and Hewlett became the first black man to play Othello. Its repertoire consisted mainly of Shakespearean drama and popular plays of the day.

When racial tensions led the police to close the African Grove, Aldridge took a backstage job at the Chatham Theater, but he continued to act in amateur productions, playing a few minor roles. His first lead was in Sheridan's *Pizarro.*

At age 17, Aldridge found employment as a steward on a ship bound for England. After studying briefly at the University of Glasgow in Scotland, he went to London and appeared in many plays there, including the melodrama *Surinam, or A Slave's Revenge.* For the next 8 years he toured the British

IRA ALDRIDGE. Aldridge, one of the leading nineteenth-century Shakespearean actors, is shown here as Othello.

provinces, playing a number of roles and earning the reputation of one of the finest tragedians in England.

He returned to London in April 1833 as Othello at the Royal Theater, Covent Garden. The critical praise was overwhelming; one account proclaimed the production the "greatest theatrical presentation London has ever witnessed." Aldridge also appeared as King Lear and Richard II and revived *Titus Andronicus*, which had not been staged in England for almost two centuries.

For the next three decades, Aldridge toured Europe, appearing before royalty and winning praise from such figures as the composer Richard Wagner and the tragedian Edmund Kean. He was sometimes billed as the "African Roscius." (Roscius, as noted in Chapter 2, was a famous actor in ancient Rome, and his name was often used to honor major performers.) The king of Sweden invited Aldridge to appear in Stockholm. In 1852, Aldridge went to Germany; he stayed for 3 years and was awarded the Gold Medal of the First Class of Art and Science and the Medal of the Order of Chavalier.

Aldridge also visited Russia, where the czar granted him the Cross of Leopold, and the students of Moscow University accorded him their highest honor by unhitching the horses of his carriage and pulling it through the streets themselves. His performance as a slave in a farce delighted Russian audiences, though it offended some people because his pitifully comic portrayal aroused comparisons with the Russian serfs. When he performed in *The Merchant of Venice,* a procession of Jews came to thank him for his very human interpretation of Shylock.

Aldridge died on August 7, 1867, while on tour in Lodz, Poland. Today he is honored by a tablet in the New Memorial Theater in Stratford-on-Avon. In 1979 he was inducted posthumously into the New York Theater Hall of Fame; this honor in his native land conferred on him the well-deserved respectability he could never achieve there during his lifetime.

THE LONG RUN AND THE DECLINE OF REPERTORY COMPANIES

At about the same time that touring stars and combination companies were becoming prevalent, the long run became more common: a popular play might run for 100 consecutive performances (as the American Edwin Booth's *Hamlet* did in New York in 1864) or even more. This too was occurring because of expanding audiences in major cities, and also because of the proliferation of smaller theaters which began to cater to specific segments of the public.

During the nineteenth century, the traditional repertory company—a troupe performing together for a set period of time in a number of plays—gradually disappeared, because the long run made hiring a repertory company impractical. By the close of the century—as in today's commercial Broadway theater—a cast would be hired to perform a single play for the length of its run.

This movement away from repertory companies was a significant change for actors. Today, performers in commercial theater are usually free-lancers; they are hired for individual shows. If a production is unsuccessful, they must audition for something else. Many critics suggest that the demise of the repertory company made the lives of actors and actresses more unstable because they were no longer hired for a set time. Furthermore, in a repertory company young performers could be trained by actually performing, since beginners were hired to play minor roles. Today's performers have more difficulty finding opportunities to learn through actual stage experience.

The shortening of the typical evening's bill also diminished the need for repertory companies. The bill had previously included a full-length play, a curtain-raiser or an afterpiece, and entr'acte entertainments. (A curtain-raiser preceded the main play; an afterpiece was a short play following the main play; entr'acte entertainments were variety acts—such as songs, dances, and acrobatics—presented during breaks in the main play.) By 1900, however, the bill consisted only of the full-length drama.

The number of repertory companies was, therefore, diminishing by 1875. Not all repertory troupes disbanded, and in many countries such troupes still play a significant role; but in commercial theater they became the exception rather than the rule.

ACTING STYLES

Most historians agree that classical, romantic, and melodramatic performance styles dominated the nineteenth-century stage.

In the early nineteenth century, the most renowned classical actors were the English stars John Philip Kemble and his sister Sarah Siddons (1755–1831), who were both noted for their dignified, carefully planned, and detailed performances.

The romantic stars, by contrast, were noted for emotional outbursts; they punctuated dramatic moments with strong physical gestures, made "vocal points" (that is, they emphasized specific speeches and lines), and they relied on inspiration. Among the great British romantic actors was Edmund Kean (1787–1833), of whom the poet Samuel Taylor Coleridge wrote, "To see Kean was to read Shakespeare by flashes of lightning." The first native-born American star, Edwin Forrest (1806–1872), whose performances stressed his physical prowess, is often characterized as a romantic actor, as are the major French stars of the century, François Joseph Talma (1763–1826), Sarah Bernhardt, and Constant-Benoît Coquelin (1841–1909).

There were many popular melodramatic and comic performers, who portrayed specific character types and emphasized physical and emotional display. In American theater, for example, many actors played a comic "Yankee," a country bumpkin with noble values who would eventually outwit a city slicker. Two actors who became very successful playing this kind of character were James H. Hackett (1800–1871) and George Handel Hill (1809–1849).

EDWIN FORREST. Forrest is considered the first native-born American star. He was known for his physical acting style, which he used in many melodramas written especially for him. Forrest's fans were instigators of the Astor Place Riot; they felt that he had been insulted by the English actor William Charles Macready.

TALMA IN HAMLET. François-Joseph Talma was the greatest French actor of the late eighteenth and early nineteenth centuries and the leading member of the Comèdie Française. Noted for his emotional, romantic presentations, Talma strove for consistency in costuming and carefully developed characterizations. Here, as Hamlet, he confronts Gertrude, played by Catherine-Joséphine Rafuin Duchesnois (1777–1835).

Actors who specialized in specific types of roles throughout their careers were very popular in England and the United States. Some of these stars could never transcend their popular image and continued to play the same role over and over again. Two examples are the American actors Francis Chanfrau (1824–1884), who popularized "Mose the Bowery Fireboy"; and Frank Mayo (1839–1896), who made his debut in Shakespeare but became known for his portrayal of Davy Crockett—they spent most of their careers acting in plays written especially for them and their characters.

Some actors, however, prepared the way for a style of performing which has become more the norm in modern theater. They used stage movements, vocal patterns, and characterizations that were based on everyday life. Performers who worked in this new style included the English actors William Charles Macready, Marie Wilton Bancroft (1839–1921), and her husband, Squire Bancroft (1841–1926); the American Edwin Booth; the Italian Eleanora Duse; and the Russian Mikhail Shchepkin (1788–1863), a serf who began acting in a theater established by his master and was released from his indenture through the efforts of Russia's leading literary figures. Macready's career has been closely examined by scholars because of his innovations in many areas of production.

William Charles Macready

(1793–1873)

Williams Charles Macready was an important figure in nineteenth-century English theater as both an actor and a director. Many of his innovations were built on the foundation laid by David Garrick a century earlier.

As the son of an actor and provincial manager, Macready grew up with the theater, but he entered Rugby School to prepare for a career in law. In 1810, after his father's death, he went onstage—temporarily, as he thought—to support the family. After 6 years in the provinces, he made his London debut at Covent Garden as Orestes in *The Disturbed Mother.* He then played villains in several melodramas, winning acceptance as an actor but developing a growing loathing for the profession. He was finally allowed to play Richard III in 1819 and began to excel in tragic roles.

Macready was a dignified, studious actor who thoroughly researched and rehearsed each role. He was a pioneer in stage realism and introduced the "Macready pause"—he would stop momentarily during the delivery of his lines to give the impression that he was thinking.

Hoping to apply his principles to the acting of others, Macready directed the companies at Covent Garden and Drury Lane from 1837 to 1843. He was one of the first actor-managers to impose blocking—planned stage movement—on his actors; he also made them act during rehearsals rather than go through the motions lifelessly. The scenic elements of his productions were united by an image or theme from the play and were carefully researched and elaborately executed.

Besides his improvements in staging, Macready sought to improve the repertoire. He convinced some leading literary figures to write for the stage and produced plays by Browning and Byron; Charles Dickens—his friend and a supporter of his efforts—tried several times to write a stageworthy comedy. Macready was also one of the first to begin restoring Shakespearean texts to something closer to the original version.

Macready's management at Covent Garden and Drury Lane was not a financial success, partly because of his policy of presenting no drama more than four times a week. After he left management, he toured England and played twice in the United States. His rivalry with the American actor Edwin Forrest—sharpened by a quick temper on each side, and by anti-British sentiment—led to the Astor Place riot describe earlier in the chapter.

In 1851, Macready retired from the stage, devoting the rest of his life to his family and his literary friends. His work had paved the way for the realistic acting and staging of the late nineteenth century.

ACTING THEORY: DELSARTE

Much acting between 1800 and 1875 was based on stereotypical physical gestures and vocal patterns—as can be seen in the work of François Delsarte (1811–1871), the era's major acting theorist and teacher. Delsarte believed that actors could convey emotions and inner thoughts through specific, preestablished gestures and body movements. His system was rejected by modern realists because it assumed that all human beings have the same physical reactions and thus did not allow for individual characterizations. Delsarte's method, however, did require that actors' physicalizations be based on observations of everyday life, and later realistic systems also stressed this as a source of artistic inspiration.

Directing

The first steps toward the art of directing had been taken in the eighteenth century by David Garrick and Johann Wolfgang von Goethe. In the nineteenth century, further steps were taken by some actor-managers and playwright-managers, and there were two people who functioned as early directors—Richard Wagner and the duke of Saxe-Meiningen.

ACTOR-MANAGERS AND PLAYWRIGHT-MANAGERS

The goal of innovative nineteenth-century actor-managers and playwright-managers was to create a unified stage picture, particularly through increased rehearsal time and more careful attention to production details. Many of them experimented with historical accuracy in scenery and costuming, and some expected a more realistic acting style.

Nineteenth-century actor-managers were responsible for choosing scripts, casting, overseeing rehearsals, working with scene painters, selecting costumes, and dealing with finances—in addition, an actor- or actress-manager was usually the company's star performer. Numerous actor-managers took greater interest and care in creating stage productions; almost all these innovators oversaw the visual elements, required careful rehearsals, and experimented with blocking patterns, and they are often credited with moving theater toward greater realism. In England, they included Macready, who managed Covent Garden from 1837 to 1838 and Drury Lane from 1841 to 1843; and Madame Vestris, who managed the Olympic Theater from 1831 to 1838. In the United States, they included Edwin Booth, who managed several theaters in New York.

Some innovators in directorial practices were not primarily actors; these included some playwrights. In France, Pixérécourt oversaw all the details of staging his spectacular and immensely popular melodramas; Adolphe Montigny (1805–1880) ran the Gymnase, a Parisian boulevard theater, and strove for more realistic settings and acting in popular well-made plays; and the romantic novelist and playwright Victor Hugo staged his own dramas. In Germany, Ludwig Tieck and Karl Immermann (1796–1840) experimented with unlocalized staging for Shakespearean productions. The American playwright-manager Augustin Daly (1836–1899)—whose melodrama *Under the Gaslight* (1867) is often cited as the first play in which a character was tied to a railroad track—oversaw all elements of staging and wanted completely unified productions. Daly's acting company had many young stars whom he had discovered.

A number of the innovative theatrical managers were women—despite the fact that theater management, like many other occupations in the nineteenth century, was unusual for a woman. In England, as we noted above, there was Madame Vestris (who will also be discussed later). In the United States, the major actress-managers were Anne Brunton Merry (1769–1808), Charlotte Cushman (1816–1876), Catherine Sinclair (1817–1891), Matilda Viney Wood (1821–1915), Louise Lane Drew (1820–1897), and Laura Keene, who was one of the most famous.

Laura Keene

(ca. 1826–1873)

The actress Laura Keene was one of the most successful women to enter the competitive business of theater management during the nineteenth century in the United States.

Keene had been born in England, and—interestingly—she acted briefly in the company of Madame Vestris, the prominent London actress-manager. Little else is known of Keene's early life, however: even the year of her birth and her real name are uncertain. She was married at a young age to a man who was apparently exiled to Australia as a convict. When she arrived in America, her two small daughters from this marriage were introduced as her nieces.

James Wallack (ca. 1795–1864) hired Keene as the leading lady at his new theater, which opened in New York City in 1852. She was then relatively inexperienced, but, coached by Wallack, she added many new roles to her repertory and quickly became a favorite with New York audiences.

Early in the 1853–1854 season, Keene surprised the theatrical world by suddenly leaving Wallack's company to accept an offer from several businessmen in Baltimore to manage her own theater there. Keene's management of the Charles Street Theater in Baltimore lasted only a few months. From there she traveled to California, where she acted and also had brief stints as a manager. These experiences helped prepare her to launch her management of a theater in New York City.

When she opened Laura Keene's Varieties in December 1855, she became the first woman to run a large, first-class New York theater. In the competitive world of commercial theater, she was not welcomed by established male managers. In fact, Keene faced strong opposition during her first season, including libelous newspaper reports, the destruction of her scenery by a vandal on opening night, and the loss of her lease to a rival manager.

Still, she prevailed. She had a new theater built, which she managed profitably until 1863. Laura Keene's Theater gained a reputation for its scenic splendor; and she herself became known as a strict and resourceful manager who popularized such innovations as regular matinee performances and long runs of successful plays. One of the biggest hits of the nineteenth century, Tom Taylor's *Our American Cousin* (1858), was first produced by Keene.

In 1863, Keene decided to give up her theater and tour as the head of a company. This gave her the variety of several roles in succession, in contrast to the monotony of a long run. She toured for the next several years and also briefly managed the Chestnut Street Theater in Philadelphia.

Unfortunately, Keene is probably most often remembered as a footnote to a national tragedy: she was onstage performing in *Our American Cousin* at Ford's Theater in Washington the night Abraham Lincoln was assassinated there.

Eventually forced into retirement by ill health, Keene died in 1873. By then, her prominence as a manager had already encouraged several other women to enter the field.

TWO EARLY DIRECTORS

Possibly the most important directorial innovators at the close of this period were Richard Wagner and Georg II, the duke of Saxe-Meiningen. Neither of them was a performer in his company, and thus they are closer to our modern conception of the director.

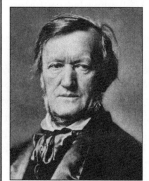

(Victoria and Albert Museum, London)

Richard Wagner
(1813–1883)

Wilhelm Richard Wagner, who is of course best-known as an opera composer, was also important as a stage theorist. One of his theories was that a production, whether opera or theater, should be a *Gesamtkunstwerk*, a "masterwork" in which all elements—music, words, action, scenery, and lighting—are integrated as "total theater." Wagner also argued that one person should serve as writer, composer, and director.

Throughout the many reversals in his life, Richard Wagner held fast to his vision of opera. He was egocentric, forceful, and convinced of the superiority of his own ideas; and though his personality was sometimes his greatest hindrance, it eventually helped him achieve his goal of creating a new kind of opera.

Wagner's stepfather was a painter, singer, and actor; as a result, Wagner was acquainted with opera and theater from his earliest years. Even as a child, growing up in Leipzig, Germany, he was impulsive and self-willed, neglecting all his studies except music. At age 17, he had an overture performed in the Leipzig Theater. He spent a short (but wild) time at the University of Leipzig, and for the next several years he worked as the conductor of a series of third-rate provincial orchestras and composed his earliest operas. Shortly thereafter, he was forced to flee his creditors and went to Paris, hoping to dazzle its operatic establishment.

In 1842, after 3 poverty-stricken years in Paris, Wagner gladly returned to Dresden, where his opera *Rienzi* was a resounding success. He then received a post at the court opera. The works that followed—*The Flying Dutchman* (1843), *Tannhaüser* (1845), and *Lohengrin* (1848)—were popular with audiences, though the critics disapproved of Wagner's "total theater" and some of his other techniques. In 1849, Wagner was forced to flee again, this time to avoid arrest for having taken part in the Revolution of 1848.

During his 12 years in exile, Wagner developed his theories and began composing the works that form his great operatic cycle, *The Ring of the Nibelung.* For these operas, he chose a national myth that he hoped would serve as a unifying force for Germany. (Because of Wagner's interest in Germanic myths, his belief in the superiority of the German people, and his anti-Semitism, he was Adolf Hitler's favorite composer. That, of course, took place long after his death; but his political and social ideas still make him controversial today.)

Wagner first tested his theories in 1876, when he staged the *Ring* cycle at his new theater in Bayreuth, built with the help of his patron, Ludwig II of Bavaria. Several times during his years of struggle, he had nearly been ruined because of debts or adulterous affairs, but he persisted until he had overwhelmed his critics with his music. After his death in 1883, his second wife, Cosima Liszt Wagner—and then his sons and grandsons—carried on his work.

Wagner's concept of a totally unified artwork—the *Gesamtkunstwerk*—controlled by one person influenced twentieth-century theories of "total theater" and has also been a major influence on modern directing theory. He believed that an opera, which is made up of many musical and theatrical elements, needs a controlling figure to unify it. He insisted that this figure must have dictatorial control; at his Bayreuth Festspielhaus, he put this theory into practice, becoming its *régisseur*—the French term for "director."

Wagner's innovations for increasing stage illusion are particularly important. Musicians were forbidden to tune their instruments in the orchestra pit; and audience members were not supposed to applaud during the course of a presentation. Wagner is also often credited with being the first director to extinguish the house lights in order to focus the audience's attention on the stage.

Georg II, Duke of Saxe-Meiningen

(1826–1914)

The other crucial nineteenth-century innovator in stage direction was Georg II of Saxe-Meiningen, a small German duchy. If he had been able to choose his own profession, he would have pursued a military career in Berlin, where he was a lieutenant in the Royal Guards. When the Revolution of 1848 broke out in Germany, however, his father, Duke Bernhard II, ordered him to return to Saxe-Meiningen; once home, he became involved in theater.

As the only son of Duke Bernhard, he was given an education which prepared him to rule the duchy. But two of his childhood tutors—one a theologian and the other an artist—instilled in him a love of nature and of art; and art remained a part of his education during his years at the University of Bonn and while he was in the Royal Guards. Though he painted in oils, his talent was mainly for drawing and sketching.

When he was called home in 1848, Georg became active at court, where he found a competent but uninspired theater company. In 1850 he married Princess Charlotte of Prussia, with whom he had three children. When she died 5 years later, he turned for consolation to art and music, traveling to Italy for a year of study. In 1858, he married a German princess, who died in 1872.

During the 1850s and 1860s, Prussia was becoming the dominant force in Germany. Duke Bernhard opposed the Prussian influence; but Georg was in favor of Prussian-German unification, and in 1866 a Prussian army occupied Saxe-Meiningen and forced Bernhard to abdicate in favor of his son. As duke, Georg was an enlightened monarch, liberalizing land ownership, promoting trade agreements and tariff reforms, and providing health and welfare benefits for his subjects. He also served in the Franco-Prussian War of 1870.

In the evenings, he supervised the court theater, planning and directing productions and providing sketches for scenery and costumes. Ludwig Chronegk, an actor in the company and its régisseur, was responsible for its daily operations. The third person involved in the company's artistic management was the duke's third wife, Ellen Franz, baroness von Heldburg, with whom he had eloped after the death of his second wife. She was responsible for the selection of plays and for the actors' stage diction.

The productions of the Meiningen players were quite stunning visually. To create appropriate scenic illusions, Georg insisted on historical accuracy and spent lavish sums on rich fabrics and authentic decor. He even extended his attention to the traditionally bare stage floor, decorating it with carpets, steps, shrubbery, and the like. The stage picture was further enhanced by carefully worked-out crowd scenes.

The Meiningen company astounded the world with its acting ensemble and its unified, historically accurate productions. Georg, Chronegk, and Ellen Franz continued to direct it until it was disbanded in 1890. The years before Georg's death in 1914 were tranquil, and his third marriage was happy.

The theatrical innovations that the duke supported made the Meiningen players the most renowned company in the world between 1874 and 1890; because of them, he is considered one of the first modern directors: as the director of many Shakespearean and romantic dramas, he revolutionized stage production. A major reason for his ability to organize such a successful theatrical venture was his enormous wealth. He rehearsed his actors with scenery and costumes for extensive periods of time, refusing to open a show until he believed that all the elements were completely unified. His intricately planned crowd scenes used company actors rather than amateurs or paid extras. (However, as an opponent of the star system, he employed mostly young performers.) His productions were admired for their historically accurate and practical settings; their costumes, which helped to establish character and period; their lighting; and their sound effects. Moreover, all these theatrical innovations became well-known throughout Europe because his company toured frequently, giving over 2,500 performances in 38 European cities. His influence on future directors of realistic drama is often noted.

Theater Architecture

There were several developments in theater architecture between 1800 and 1875 which led to the building of playhouses much like those in today's commercial centers.

Early in the nineteenth century, as we have already noted, playhouses were enlarged to accommodate expanding lower-class urban audiences. (For a while in England, this influx of working-class audiences caused the social elite to abandon theaters for opera houses.) The Bowery Theater in New York City—nicknamed "The Slaughterhouse" because it offered sentimental "blood and guts" melodrama—is an example of a huge nineteenth-century theater for lower-class audiences. (The regular audience at the Bowery included the "Bowery B'hoys," street toughs who drank, ate, and threw the remnants of their food into the pit from the gallery.) In its first year of operation, 1826, the Bowery held 2,500 spectators and was the largest playhouse in New York; 19 years later, it was enlarged to hold 4,000. Quite late in the century, large theater spaces were still being built in Europe; one of these was the Paris Opera, which had a huge stage area and held over 2,000 spectators.

By the 1860s, however, there was generally a shift away from the construction of huge theaters. This shift can be explained by the proliferation of playhouses in European and American urban centers for specific segments of society. In London, for example, the number of theaters staging various types of dramas that were not covered by the Licensing Act of 1737 increased significantly during the early 1800s; in 1843, the Theater Regulation Act finally abolished the unenforceable monopoly that was supposed to have been in effect.

(Richard Leacroft, The Development of the English Playhouse, Cornell University Press, Ithaca, N.Y., 1973. By permission of Reed Book Services/Methuen London.)

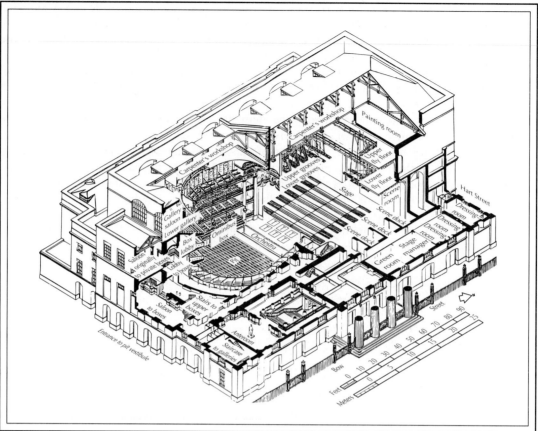

COVENT GARDEN IN THE NINETEENTH CENTURY. This plan shows Covent Garden as it appeared in the 1800s. While it still had pit, boxes, and galleries, the proscenium doors and the large apron were disappearing. The theater itself had also been enlarged.

The traditional proscenium arch and pit, box, and gallery dominated theater buildings in the nineteenth century. English and American theaters became more like continental theaters: the proscenium doors began to disappear and the apron continued to diminish.

Many theater buildings, however, broke away from the traditional architectural pattern established during the Italian Renaissance. In London, the boxes in the Adelphi Theater were raised so that the pit could be extended to the side walls, making the tiers more like balconies; late in the century, the English architect C. J. Phipps (1835–1897) popularized the balcony and orchestra configuration in many London theaters. By the late 1800s, advances in engineering and new materials like structural steel allowed balconies to be constructed without supporting columns; these technological advances also led to the construction of many new buildings because remodeling older playhouses became less cost-effective.

The comfort of the audience became a greater concern. The French architect Émile Trélat recommended mechanical ways to improve ventilation in the galleries; and even early in the century a few innovative theaters had comfortable individual seats instead of backless benches in the pit, so that it became the equivalent of the modern orchestra. Marie and Squire Bancroft, for instance, removed the benches and installed seats in London's Haymarket Theater. (The Bancrofts' reforms also included changes intended to increase illusionism in all aspects of theater: they used box sets; they worked with the playwright Thomas William Robertson, who dealt with real social concerns; and their acting was more realistic.) Individual seats allowed for reserved seating, which had become more necessary with long runs and the need to know how much advance sale a show might have.

BOOTH'S THEATER

The Booth Theater, completed in 1869 for the American Shakespearean actor Edwin Booth, is often said to have been the first modern theater in New York City. Instead of a pit and galleries, it had a modern orchestra area and balconies. The seats were individual armchairs, although there were boxes in the proscenium arch. The stage was also revolutionary: it was not raked and was not designed for traditional wing-and-shutter scenery. Scenery could be raised from the basement by elevators or lowered ("flown in") from above, and scenic pieces were often supported by braces. The fly space was high enough to accommodate scenic drops without their being rolled up. By 1875, with theaters like Booth's, the modern proscenium-arch theater had been established.

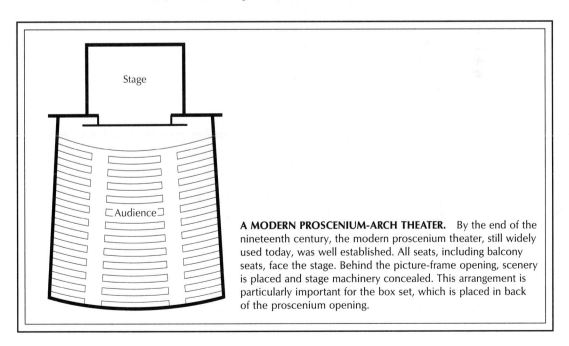

A MODERN PROSCENIUM-ARCH THEATER. By the end of the nineteenth century, the modern proscenium theater, still widely used today, was well established. All seats, including balcony seats, face the stage. Behind the picture-frame opening, scenery is placed and stage machinery concealed. This arrangement is particularly important for the box set, which is placed in back of the proscenium opening.

Edwin Booth

(1833–1893)

Edwin Booth's reputation as America's finest actor has survived for over 100 years, and his name will always be linked with Hamlet, his greatest role. His innovations in staging are not as well known, but he anticipated modern scenic developments.

Though Booth's father was a famous actor, Junius Brutus Booth (1796–1852), Edwin was not encouraged in his stage career; his family felt that it was his younger brother, John Wilkes Booth (1839–1865), who had inherited their father's fiery acting ability. However, Edwin began accompanying his father on tours at the age of 13, having proved adept at calming his father's mad moods and restraining his drinking. Edwin made his own dramatic debut in 1849 in a bit role, to relieve an overworked prompter, and then continued to play small parts in his father's company. When the two toured the west, Edwin decided to remain there and played several seasons in repertory.

Edwin Booth's New York debut in 1857 established him as the most promising young actor in the United States. He was short and slight, with piercing eyes and a rich, melodious voice. His acting, particularly his portrayal of Hamlet, was remarkable for its depth of character, grace, and freedom from mannerisms. (As we noted earlier, in 1864 he played Hamlet for 100 consecutive nights in New York, a record that was not surpassed until 1923).

Booth believed that art, including theater, should inspire and ennoble. To carry out his ideas, in 1869 he built his own theater, where for 5 years he presented a series of magnificent Shakespearean productions. Abandoning the wing-and-groove method of scene shifting, he used heavy set pieces and freestanding scenery to create historically accurate settings. He also used uncorrupted texts of Shakespeare's plays many years before English theater had returned to them.

Poor financial management forced Booth's theater into bankruptcy in 1874, and for the rest of his life he was a touring star. His touring took him to England, where he alternated the roles of Iago and Othello with Henry Irving, and to Germany. He was one of the first American actors to achieve international fame.

In private life, Booth was quiet, almost melancholy. He experienced three major personal tragedies: his beloved first wife died after 2½ years of marriage; his second wife went mad after the loss of their infant son; and his brother assassinated Abraham Lincoln.

Edwin Booth had the respect and friendship of the leading literary and cultural figures of his day. He felt that acting was an honorable profession, and he endowed the Player's Club in New York in 1888 as a place where actors and other gentlemen could meet. Booth presented the club with his house on Gramercy Park in New York City, where he lived until his death in 1893.

WAGNER'S FESTSPIELHAUS

Another innovative nineteenth-century theater building was the Bayreuth Festspielhaus, built for Richard Wagner. It opened in 1876, after 4 years of construction.

This theater also broke with the earlier tradition of pit, boxes, and gallery; Wagner wanted a theater in which seating would not emphasize class distinctions. There were 1,300 individual seats in thirty raked rows, forming a fan-shaped auditorium; the rows became longer the farther away they were from the stage; and audiences entered and exited at the ends of rows: this arrangement is now known as *continental seating*. There was a single line of boxes at the rear of the house, and a 300-seat balcony above them. The price was the same for every seat in this opera house.

The stage of the Bayreuth Festspielhaus, modeled along traditional Italianate lines, was not as revolutionary as the auditorium, though it did have a few innovations. There was a double proscenium arch, and a sunken orchestra pit separated the audience from the stage; Wagner referred to the orchestra pit as his "mystic gulf." For special effects, steam jets were built into the fore-stage.

WAGNER'S FESTSPEILHAUS. Richard Wagner's Festspeilehaus at Bayreuth in Germany, completed in 1876 and designed to be the ideal home for his operas, was one of the first modern theaters. Its "continental" seating and balcony set the pattern for modern auditoriums, and its sunken orchestra pit became an integral part of the modern musical playhouse.

(The Bettmann Archive)

Scenery, Costumes, and Lighting

Eighteenth-century experiments with realistic devices and conventions in scenery and costuming were carried further in the nineteenth century.

HISTORICAL ACCURACY

Historical accuracy in sets and costumes became more common with the increasing availability of works of historical research, such as *The History of British Costume* (1834) by J. R. Planché (1795–1880). This new knowledge of the past, combined with the nineteenth-century fascination with antiquity, led a number of theater artists to mount historically accurate productions; they included the English actor-managers Charles Kemble (1775–1854), William Charles Macready, and Charles Kean (1811–1868); the American actor-manager Edwin Booth; and the duke of Saxe-Meiningen. In the Saxe-Meiningen productions, as we have seen, costumes were carefully researched and authentic materials were used regardless of the cost or difficulty of obtaining them, and performers were not allowed to alter their costumes. The same careful attention was given to the settings the duke designed.

THE BOX SET

In scene design, the gradual replacement of painted wing-and-shutter settings shifted by a pole-and-chariot or groove system was even more important than the trend toward historical accuracy. The wing-and-shutter arrangement did not suddenly disappear, and it continued to be used for some time. Nonetheless, alternatives were introduced throughout the first 75 years of the nineteenth century.

We have already mentioned experiments in Germany by Tieck and Immermann, who staged Shakespeare in a way they believed came closer to the Elizabethan playhouse. In the United States, as noted above, Edwin Booth broke with the traditional wing-and-shutter set by placing scenic pieces wherever he wished on the stage floor (in his theater, the stage was not raked) and supporting them with braces. Also, many English and American theater artists of the late 1800s began to stage all the action behind the proscenium; this reinforced the illusion of a "fourth wall."

Another significant alternative was the box set. A *box set* consists of flats hinged together to represent a room; it often has practicable elements, such as doors and windows, which can be used during the course of a presentation. Between 1800 and 1875, many theater artists began to use box sets; Edwin Booth is credited with popularizing them in the United States.

Madame Vestris, an English actress-manager, was often said to have introduced the box set, during her management of London's Olympic Theater in the 1830s. We now know that Vestris was not the first to use the box set; as we noted in Chapter 10, some historians believe that it may have begun in the eighteenth century, or even as early as the Italian Renaissance. However, she was undoubtedly a key innovator, who popularized the box set and filled her settings with many realistic accouterments.

Madame Vestris

(Lucia Elizabetta Bartolozzi; 1797–1856)

Theater management—as we noted earlier—was an unusual profession for a woman in 1830 and, given the disorder and chaos of the London stage, a financially unstable profession for anyone. In spite of these difficulties, Madame Vestris not only was able to make major innovations in staging but also made a profit as proprietor of the Olympic Theater.

By the time she opened her theater, Madame Vestris had 15 years of theatrical experience. The daughter of a London engraver, she married Auguste Armand Vestris—a dancer and a member of a famous family of ballet performers—when she was 16. Two years later, she made her stage debut. After her husband left her in 1820, she continued acting, playing in Paris for several years and then at the Drury Lane and Covent Garden theaters in London. She had an excellent singing voice and might have made a career in opera but instead played in burlesques, extravaganzas, and comedies. She was much admired for her beautiful figure, sparkling eyes, and dark hair. Breeches roles—roles in which a woman played a young man and thus had an opportunity to show off her legs—were one of her specialties.

Madame Vestris opened her Olympic Theater with *Olympic Revels,* an extravaganza written by J. R. Planché, the best writer of burlesques, extravaganzas, and farces in England at that time. Planché was to be her resident dramatist at the Olympic and later at the Lyceum Theater. (Planché, as we mentioned earlier, also wrote a history of costumes.)

Though she presented only light entertainment at the Olympic, Madame Vestris produced it with a degree of care that was usually reserved for the classics, paying close attention to every aspect of a production and coordinating all the elements as a unified whole. She is credited with introducing the box set—complete with ceiling—to England around 1832. She dressed all her settings with real properties—doorknobs, dishes, rugs, tables, chairs, curtains —instead of painting them on the set as was usually done. Her care extended to costuming; she replaced the exaggerated costumes of extravaganza and burlesque with clothes from everyday life. To achieve the effects she wanted onstage, she also maintained strict control over her acting company.

In 1838, Madame Vestris married Charles Mathews (1803–1878), a light comedian in her company. After an American tour, they managed Covent Garden for 3 years. There they presented legitimate dramas, with the same staging practices she had used earlier at the Olympic. Though their production of *London Assurance* (1841), Dion Boucicault's first play, was a success, this managerial venture ended in financial failure in 1842. They then took over the Lyceum Theater in 1847, but their insistence on quality led to another failure. Madame Vestris died in 1856, in the midst of the Lyceum's bankruptcy proceedings.

NEW TECHNOLOGY

During the nineteenth century, the technology of the industrial revolution was applied to theater. Many historians believe that the popularity of melodrama, with its emphasis on stage spectacle and special effects, accelerated these technological innovations. For example, Dion Boucicault was responsible for the introduction of fireproofing in the theater when one of his melodramatic plays called for an onstage fire.

The *moving panorama*—painted settings on a long cloth which could be unrolled across the stage by turning spools—created an illusion of movement and changing locales. A popular American play, William Dunlap's *A Trip to Niagara* (1828), used this device to show a voyage from New York City to Niagara Falls. The emphasis on re-creating natural environments onstage was probably influenced by romanticism, which called for a "return to nature." (Today, in film, a similar technique, known as *rear projection,* is used to create an illusion of movement. Behind a stationary object—such as the interior of a car—a film of changing backgrounds and locales is projected; the stationary object and the projected material are then filmed.)

New means of scene shifting were needed for the new types of settings. The French architect Trélat proposed hydraulic lifts for scene shifting in a book published in 1860. We have already noted that elevators and equipment for flying scenery were used at the Edwin Booth Theater. By the close of the century, the elevator stage and the revolving stage were perfected. An *elevator stage* allows sections of a stage floor, or even the entire floor, to be raised or lowered. A *revolving stage* is a large turntable on which scenery is placed; as it moves, one set is brought into view as another turns out of sight. One innovative theater technologist was Steele Mackaye (1842–1894). (Mackaye was a noted playwright whose melodramas focused on more realistic circumstances. He was also interested in the teaching of acting, and particularly in Delsarte's methods; and he founded the American Academy of Dramatic Art, which is still functioning today.) In 1880, at the Madison Square Theater in New York, Mackaye used two stages, one above the other, which could be raised and lowered; while one stage was in view of the audience, the scenery on the other, which was either in the basement or in the fly area, could be changed.

Nineteenth-century technology revolutionized stage lighting, which until then had been primitive. The introduction of *gas lighting* was the first step. In 1816, Philadelphia's Chestnut Street Theater was the earliest gaslit playhouse in the world. By the middle of the century, the *gas table*—the equivalent of a modern dimmer board—allowed a single stagehand to alter the intensity of lighting throughout a theater. This new control of lighting allowed significant changes in architecture and staging. In the 1860s, two Parisian theaters were built without obtrusive chandeliers hanging over the audience; gas lighting also allowed Richard Wagner to extinguish the lights in the auditorium of the Bayreuth Festspielhaus.

Thomas Edison's electric *incandescent lamp,* invented in 1879, was the next step. By 1881, the Savoy Theater in London was using incandescent lighting, though some other playhouse may actually have been the first to introduce it. Electricity, of course, is the most flexible, most controllable, and safest form of lighting; in the twentieth century, it would make stage lighting design a true art.

ASIAN THEATER IN THE NINETEENTH CENTURY: PEKING OPERA

During the nineteenth century, the western world came into closer contact with Asia. As western nations began to establish "spheres of influence," or imperialistic control, over Asian countries, there was a great deal of cross-cultural influence. Late in the 1800s and then in the twentieth century, western theater would adopt many practices of traditional Asian theaters, and Asian theater would be influenced by western practices.

The best-known Asian theater to develop during the nineteenth century was Peking (or Beijing) opera in China. Elements of folk drama and other genres close to the ordinary people formed the basis for this truly popular theater, which is one of the most colorful and most striking theatrical forms now practiced in Asia.

Though it is called *opera,* Peking opera combines music, theater, and dance in its own unique way. Because of its origins in popular entertainment, it has little to offer in terms of high literary merit or philosophical speculation. But it preserves long traditions of popular singing, acrobatics, and acting and thus provides insights into the high development of performance techniques in traditional Chinese theater. Its plays or skits involve elaborate and colorful conventions of makeup, movement, and voice production.

In staging, Peking opera stresses symbolism. The furniture onstage usually consists only of a table and several chairs, but these few items are used with imagination. Depending on how they are arranged or referred to, they may represent a dining hall, a court of justice, or a throne room. The table may stand for a cloud, a mountain, or any other high place. A tripod on a table, holding incense, indicates a palace. When the script calls for a long journey, the performers walk in a circle about the stage. Later, this creative use of the stage impressed many western dramatists, among them the German playwright Bertolt Brecht and the American playwright Thornton Wilder, author of *Our Town.*

Well before the turn of the century, the vitality of Peking opera had made it the most popular form of traditional theater in China, and later its stars—including the great twentieth-century actor Mei Lanfang (who is discussed below)—became performers of enormous reputation not only in China but also in the west.

PEKING OPERA. A highly formalized type of theater, Peking opera was developed in China in the nineteenth century. It is not like western grand opera; rather, it is popular entertainment filled with song, dance, and acrobatics. It makes wide use of symbols—a table, for instance, may stand for a mountain—and its performers wear ornate costumes and makeup, as in the scene shown here.

Mei Lanfang

(1894–1961)

Mei Lanfang, the most renowned modern performer of Peking opera, preserved and expanded its traditions. He was acclaimed throughout the world for his portrayal of female characters and was one of the first Asian theater artists to influence the development of western theater.

Like most actors in Peking opera, Mei came from a family of performers; both his father and his grandfather had specialized in *tan*, or female roles. Mei began his training at age 8 and made his stage debut when he was 10. Through his technical perfection and precise characterizations, he enhanced the importance of the female roles, which had been considered secondary. Mei worked with the playwright and theater scholar Qi Rushan to expand and revise the traditional repertoire and to introduce historical accuracy in costumes and dances.

In 1919 and 1925, Mei toured Japan, where his performances and innovations were greatly admired. When he performed in the United States in 1930, he was the guest of Douglas Fairbanks and Mary Pickford in Hollywood. He also met Charlie Chaplin, whom he enthusiastically admired. During his tour of the Soviet Union in 1935, Mei met both Konstantin Stanislavski and Bertolt Brecht; Mei's work was one of the most important influences on Brecht's theories of acting.

After the Japanese invasion of China in 1937, Mei refused to act; in fact, he grew a mustache so that it would be impossible for him to play female roles. Though it meant financial hardship, he continued his retirement until the Japanese surrendered in 1945. After the war, when he returned to performing, he made several films, including *Bitter Life and Death* (1947). Throughout his career, he trained many performers, including some of the first actresses to appear in Peking opera. Mei continued to perform until 1959, 2 years before he died.

(Eastfoto/Sovfoto)

MEI LANFANG. Stars of Peking opera—like Mei Lanfang, shown here, have achieved international fame.

By 1875, the elements that would form the foundation for a realistic revolution were in place, including the emergence of the director, more realistic acting, and the box set. What was missing was serious realistic drama, and that began to emerge in the 1870s, as we will see in Chapter 12.

SUMMARY

Transformations in theater between 1800 and 1875 prepared the way for modern theater. In drama, the romantics broke away from the neoclassical rules and argued that all subject matter—the grotesque as well as the ideal—was appropriate for the stage. Melodrama was the most popular nineteenth-century genre and is still popular in modern films and on television. The well-made play, refined by the French writers Scribe and Sardou, still exists in twentieth-century drama.

Acting was transformed in the nineteenth century by the star system, the long run, and the decline of the repertory company. While classical, romantic, and melodramatic acting styles were predominant, many performers—including William Charles Macready, the Bancrofts, Mikhail Shchepkin, and Eleanora Duse—based their acting more on observable life. Steps were taken toward the figure of the director as an overseer of the production process; Richard Wagner and the duke of Saxe-Meiningen were notable in this development.

The modern, comfortable proscenium-arch theater became a reality. Two of the most innovative playhouses were Booth's Theater in New York City and Richard Wagner's Festspielhaus in Bayreuth. Historical accuracy became more commonplace in scenery and costuming, and the box set began to replace painted scenery. Gas and then electricity provided a controllable source of light.

In China, Peking opera developed as an important popular theatrical form. Interaction between east and west created significant cross-cultural trends in their theaters.

PART FOUR

MODERN THEATER

PART FOUR

MODERN
THEATER

T he period beginning in 1875 and continuing to the present is called *modern*, not just because it is close to us in time but because it has characteristics and a shape all its own.

Forces that began to emerge in the nineteenth century had surfaced at its end. Charles Darwin's theory of evolution was a direct challenge to the centuries-old biblical concept that all living things, including human beings, are created by God; and the German philosopher Friedrich Nietzsche (1844–1900) went so far as to declare that God was dead. Just as Darwin's theory challenged traditional religious beliefs, so the theories of Karl Marx challenged traditional political beliefs, especially theories of capitalism. Sigmund Freud (1856–1939) declared that people are ruled as much by subconscious thoughts and desires as by conscious ones. In the early twentieth century, Albert Einstein (1879–1955) developed his theory of relativity, and certain aspects of the universe that had been considered fixed were now seen as changeable.

All this added up to a drastic shift in the way people regarded themselves and the world around them. This upheaval of long-held beliefs is one mark of the modern period. Another has to do with advances in technology and communications.

The past hundred years have seen the invention of radio, films, and television; of computers and telecommunications; and of propeller airplanes, jet planes, and space rockets. These inventions have brought the world closer together: news travels around the globe instantaneously, and people can travel from continent to continent in a matter of hours. This has brought advantages to people everywhere, but it has also increased the possibility of horror. Twentieth-century wars have often been world wars, and mass murder—of Armenians in Turkey, of Jews by the Nazis, of political prisoners in Soviet Russia, and of Muslims in Bosnia—has occurred on a scale never known before. Turmoil in the modern world has included not only the two world wars but the Russian Revolution, the great depression, the war in Vietnam, terrorism, the fall of communism in the former Soviet Union and eastern Europe, and wars in the Falkland Islands and the middle east—including a war between Iraq and Kuwait in which the United Nations, and especially the United States, took part. There was frequent unrest and continual tension between Israel and its neighbors, though 1993 finally brought the signing of a peace accord by Israel and the Palestine Liberation Organization.

Worldwide upheavals have been reflected in modern theater, which has been fragmented by numerous movements and trends, particularly avant-garde movements. Some historians divide twentieth-century theater into two camps: realists and antirealists. Realists include Henrik Ibsen, August Strindberg, George Bernard Shaw, Anton Chekhov, the Moscow Art Theater, and the Group Theater; among the antirealists are symbolists, expressionists, futurists, dadaists, surrealists, absurdists, Vsevelod Meyerhold, Antonin Artaud, Bertolt Brecht, and Jerzy Grotowski. Other analysts make a sharp distinction between commercial artists—such as those who work in New York's Broadway theater—and noncommercial artists who initiate idealistic ventures like "little theaters," off-Broadway, and off-off-Broadway.

Which twentieth-century theatrical trends will prove to be historically significant is difficult to predict. What is certain is that modern theater will be remembered for spawning a great many revolutionary movements.

CHAPTER 12

THEATER FROM 1875 TO 1915

I t is the evening of December 17, 1898, and the Moscow Art Theater is about to give its first performance of *The Sea Gull* by the Russian playwright Anton Chekhov. We have joined a friend in the company backstage. We notice that the performers are nervous—so nervous that, now, just before the curtain is to rise, most of them have taken valerian drops, a popular tranquilizer. Konstantin Stanislavski, the director—who is also playing the role of Trigorin, a bored commercial writer—finds it difficult to control a twitch in his leg.

Our friend has explained why there is so much anxiety over this production of *The Sea Gull*. The author, Anton Chekhov, is one of the best-known short-story writers in Russia; but so far, his plays have not met with the same approval. In fact, when *The Sea Gull* was first performed 2 years ago in Saint Petersburg, it was a fiasco. The company there did not understand Chekhov's innovative dramatic techniques and had barely rehearsed the play. To make matters worse, the audience had come to the theater that night hoping to see a favorite actress, a large woman who performed broad comic parts. When they discovered that she was not in the play, they began to hiss and yell, drowning out the dialogue. Chekhov had disappeared during the last act, and when the play was over he left the theater in despair to walk the streets of Saint Petersburg most of the night. He was so devastated by the whole experience that he swore never again to write for the theater or let his plays be performed.

PEER GYNT. The Norwegian playwright Henrik Ibsen was a giant of modern theater who wrote plays in many different styles. His early dramas were based on historical and mythological subject matter, but his best-known works are his realistic plays, and late in his career he turned to symbolism. Shown here is a scene from one of his earlier works, *Peer Gynt,* which uses many elements of fantasy. The production is by Ingmar Bergman at the Royal Dramatic Theater in Stockholm. *(Bengt Wanselius/Royal Dramatic Theater, Stockholm, Sweden)*

One reason why the production in Saint Petersburg failed so badly is that *The Sea Gull* was very different from any of the plays the actors were accustomed to performing. The play takes place on a country estate in Russia and tells the story of two generations of actresses and writers. One of the main characters is Madame Akardina, a vain, self-absorbed actress. Her son Treplev is an idealistic young writer in love with Nina, a young woman who aspires to be an actress. But Nina falls in love with Arkardina's lover, Trigorin (the part Stanislavski is playing now in Moscow), a successful writer dissatisfied with his life. A number of other people are involved with these four main characters, and one of the unusual features of the play is the way their lives are all closely intertwined. Another unusual feature is that the play has no melodramatic developments or confrontations. Sudden plot twists such as murders, suicides, and reversals of fortune have been staples of nineteenth-century drama, but in Chekhov's play the action and the characters are understated and carefully modulated. This makes the characters much more lifelike, but it also calls for understanding and flexibility on the part of the actors—demands that are not made by traditional, stereotypical roles.

The same qualities that confused the Saint Petersburg company, however, attracted the playwright and producer Vladimir Nemirovich-Danchenko—a cofounder with Stanislavski of the Moscow Art Theater. These two wanted their theater to be different from any other, and Nemirovich-Danchenko felt that *The Sea Gull* was just the kind of play to set it apart. At first, Chekhov refused to let the Moscow Art Theater present *The Sea Gull* because of the debacle in Saint Petersburg; it has taken all of Nemirovich-Danchenko's powers of persuasion to win Chekhov over.

We can understand, then, how much is at stake tonight in Moscow as the curtain is about to go up on *The Sea Gull*. Chekhov himself is so uneasy about the outcome that he is not even here; he is far away in Yalta—partly because of ill health it is true, but also because of his nervousness.

Now the curtain rises on Act I: the time has come for the performers and director to face the audience and take their chances on the outcome of the production.

Halfway through Act I, the actors cannot tell how the audience is responding; when the act ends, they are greeted by a monumental silence. The actress Olga Knipper (who will later become Chekhov's wife) fights desperately to keep from breaking into hysterical sobs. Then, all of a sudden, the silence is broken—there is thunderous, tumultuous applause. One member of the audience will later write: "Like the bursting of a dam, like an exploding bomb, a sudden deafening eruption of applause broke out." The applause goes on and on, and Stanislavski dances a jig.

The same reaction greets the next three acts; both Chekhov and the Moscow Art Theater have triumphed, and a new chapter in modern theater has begun. So significant is this event that a century later the symbol on the curtain of the Moscow Art Theater will still be a sea gull.

BACKGROUND: THE TURN OF THE CENTURY

Possibly the most significant social development of the late nineteenth century was the rise of the working class. As we saw in Chapter 11, industrialization resulted in urbanization; and throughout the nineteenth century the working class grew in size. It also grew in power: politicians, social scientists, and artists focused on its concerns. One indication of the increased political power of the working class was a trend, throughout Europe, to allow more people to vote. The growing suffragist movement, which sought voting rights for women, was tied to this political transformation. Workers also gained economic and political power by unionizing; some of the early American theatrical unions, for example, were founded during this era.

Scientific advances continued to alter western lifestyles radically. Advances in medicine increased life expectancy. The work of Freud, Einstein, and Nietzsche, following the writings of Darwin and Marx earlier in the century, were an assault on accepted religious, scientific, and political beliefs. In psychology, Sigmund Freud established a new approach: psychoanalysis. Psychological motivations, Freud maintained, could be discovered; and seemingly illogical subconscious processes, such as dreams, could be analyzed and explained. In physics, the work of people like Einstein altered our understanding of the universe. Many philosophers observe that the growth of modern scientific knowledge resulted in western society's becoming more atheistic; God and religion became less important in daily life.

Einstein's term *relativity* is, in a sense, a key to these developments: things that were thought to be absolute or fixed became relative. Not only was religion questioned; the supposed "natural order" of the universe and even the workings of human beings—their conscious control of their actions—were also challenged. It was a time characterized by both intellectual and moral upheaval.

There were also radical technological changes. Inventions—including Alexander Graham Bell's telephone, Thomas Edison's electric light, Wilbur and Orville Wright's flying machine, and the early automobile—made daily life easier. Some of the inventions of this period—such as recording devices, film, and radio—resulted in new electronic art forms.

In addition, trends of the first part of the nineteenth century, such as nationalism, imperialism, and urbanization, continued to transform European and American society. This radical transformation of western society between 1875 and the outbreak of World War I in 1914 was mirrored in theater. To give one specific example, the further development of industrialization resulted in huge monopolies controlling certain businesses, and this had its counterpart in theater. In 1896, for instance, American theater became dominated by six producers who banded together to form the Theatrical Syndicate, which controlled the best playhouses throughout the nation and produced the most noteworthy touring shows.

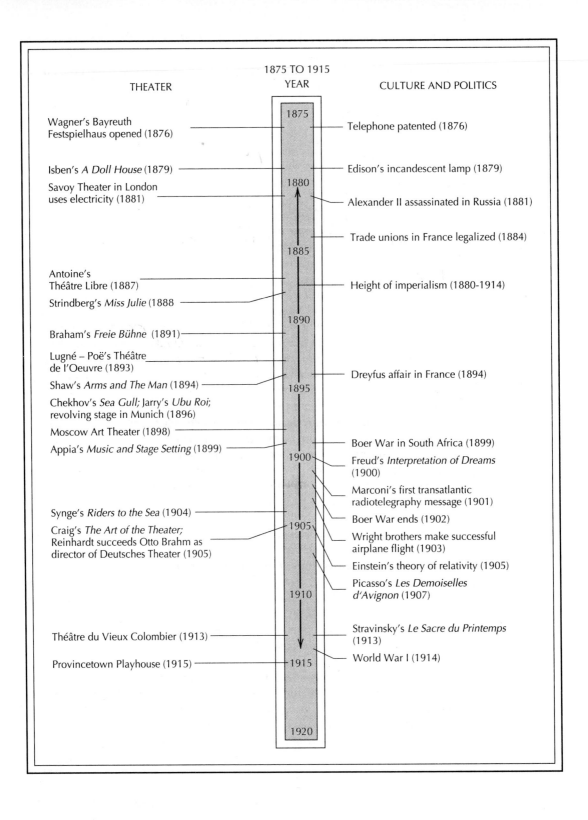

1875 TO 1915
YEAR

THEATER

CULTURE AND POLITICS

Wagner's Bayreuth
Festspielhaus opened (1876)

1875

Telephone patented (1876)

Isben's *A Doll House* (1879)

Edison's incandescent lamp (1879)

Savoy Theater in London
uses electricity (1881)

1880

Alexander II assassinated in Russia (1881)

Trade unions in France legalized (1884)

1885

Antoine's
Théâtre Libre (1887)

Height of imperialism (1880-1914)

Strindberg's *Miss Julie* (1888

Braham's *Freie Bühne* (1891)

1890

Lugné – Poë's Théâtre
de l'Oeuvre (1893)

Shaw's *Arms and The Man* (1894)

Dreyfus affair in France (1894)

1895

Chekhov's *Sea Gull;* Jarry's *Ubu Roi;*
revolving stage in Munich (1896)

Moscow Art Theater (1898)

Appia's *Music and Stage Setting* (1899)

Boer War in South Africa (1899)

1900

Freud's *Interpretation of Dreams*
(1900)

Marconi's first transatlantic
radiotelegraphy message (1901)

Boer War ends (1902)

Synge's *Riders to the Sea* (1904)

Wright brothers make successful
airplane flight (1903)

1905

Craig's *The Art of the Theater;*
Reinhardt succeeds Otto Brahm as
director of Deutsches Theater (1905)

Einstein's theory of relativity (1905)

Picasso's *Les Demoiselles
d'Avignon* (1907)

1910

Théâtre du Vieux Colombier (1913)

Stravinsky's *Le Sacre du Printemps*
(1913)

World War I (1914)

Provincetown Playhouse (1915)

1915

1920

More broadly, in theater between 1875 and 1915 we can see the emergence of two artistic impulses that have stood in sharp contrast throughout the twentieth century. On one hand, realistic artists attempted to create an illusion of everyday life onstage. On the other hand, abstractionist theater artists created seemingly illogical stage pictures that were rooted in the subconscious or in a dream world.

THE EMERGENCE OF REALISM

Here, we consider the first of the two contrasting twentieth-century approaches to theater: *realism,* and a closely related movement called *naturalism.* Later in this chapter, we will turn to the second approach, which took various forms that collectively can be called *departures from realism.*

Realistic Drama

WHAT IS REALISM?

Realism ushered in modern theater. Realists sought to convince their audiences that stage action represented everyday life. Unlike drama that featured larger-than-life characters, was written in verse, and had supernatural figures such as witches and ghosts, realistic drama mirrored life. The action onstage resembled what people could observe around them: characters behaved, spoke, and dressed like ordinary people.

This is not, of course, a revolutionary concept for today's audiences, but in the late nineteenth century many theatergoers and critics were scandalized by realism in the theater. One reason is that realism touched a raw nerve. In the attempt to portray daily life, realists argued, no subject matter should be excluded from the stage. Among the taboo subjects dramatized by realists were economic injustice, the sexual double standard, unhappy marriages, venereal disease, and religious hypocrisy. In fact, many realists believed that the purpose of drama was to call the audience's attention to social problems in order to bring about change.

Furthermore, realists refused to make simple moral judgments or to resolve dramatic action neatly. Unlike popular melodramas, realistic plays frequently implied that morality and immorality were relative—not easy to distinguish or define.

Instead of stock characters, realists created complicated personalities who would seem to have been molded—as real people are—by heredity and environment. The language of these characters was colloquial and conversational. (In today's realistic drama, the dialogue often includes obscenities; though contemporary audiences are used to realism in general, they are sometimes still shocked by this aspect of it.)

For all these reasons, then, it is not surprising that realists faced a great deal of opposition and were constantly plagued by censorship.

The Norwegian playwright Henrik Ibsen is often said to be the founder of realism. As we will see later in this chapter, though, he was not a realistic dramatist throughout his career: as a young man, he wrote romantic dramas, and near the end of his career he experimented with abstract symboiist drama. (Another prominent realist, the Swedish dramatist August Strindberg, later turned to highly surreal, dreamlike works.)

Henrik Ibsen
(1828–1906)

As a playwright, Henrik Ibsen is known for his mastery of dramatic technique, his psychological insights into human nature, and his poetic symbolism.

For much of his life, Ibsen was an outcast from the society that he dramatized. When he was born in Skien, Norway, in 1828, his father was a prosperous businessman; but in 1834 the business failed, and the family was forced to move outside of town. At 15, Ibsen left home to work as a pharmacist's apprentice; later he tried to qualify for the university. In 1852, at age 24, he became producer at the theater in Bergen and was commissioned to write one play a year for the theater's anniversary. While he was a producer at Bergen, he took a study tour of German and Danish theaters.

He moved to Christiania in 1857 to become artistic director of the Norwegian Theater there. When it went bankrupt, he secured a small government grant and, in 1864, left Norway. For the next 27 years, he would live in Rome, Dresden, and Munich. He returned to Norway in 1891, continuing to work in his careful, methodical way (he allowed himself 2 years to write and polish a play).

Ibsen was incapacitated by a stroke in 1900; after another stroke the following year, he remained an invalid, nearly helpless, until his death in 1906.

Ibsen's earliest plays, based on Norwegian history and mythology, are romantic verse dramas examining the extremes of the Norwegian national character. They include *Lady of Ostraat* (1855), *The Vikings of Helgeland* (1858), *The Pretenders* (1863), *Brand* (1866), and *Peer Gynt* (1867). The plays of his middle period—the realistic social dramas for which he is best-known—explore the interaction of people with society, dealing with such problems as unhappy marriages, the sexual double standard, infidelity, and the position of women. Among these realistic plays are *A Doll's House* (1879), *Ghosts* (1881), *An Enemy of the People* (1882), and *Hedda Gabler* (1891). Because of their frank treatment of controversial subject matter, they often provoked angry debate when they were first presented.

While still working in a realistic Norwegian setting, Ibsen moved toward symbolism and mysticism in his last plays. The dramas in this group include *The Wild Duck* (1884), *Rosmersholm* (1886), *The Lady from the Sea* (1888), *The Master Builder* (1892), *John Gabriel Borkman* (1896), and *When We Dead Awaken* (1899). Regardless of their period or style, Ibsen's plays all have a common theme: the individual amidst conflicting social pressures.

IBSEN'S REALISM: GHOSTS

One of Ibsen's realistic plays that created a furor was *Ghosts*. The negative commentary that followed its initial London presentation in 1891 (a decade after it was written) was typical of the criticism it received. William Archer, an English critic who admired and translated Ibsen, published a summary of this criticism; here is a sampling of what was said: "An open drain; a loathsome sore unbandaged; a dirty act done publicly. . . . Candid foulness. . . . Revoltingly suggestive and blasphemous. . . . If any repetition of this outrage be attempted the authorities will doubtless wake from their lethargy. . . . As foul and filthy a concoction as has ever been allowed to disgrace the boards of an English theater."[1]

The subject matter of Ibsen's *Ghosts* must indeed have been startling to Victorian audiences. The action revolves around the character of Mrs. Alving. Many years before the time when the play begins, she had wanted to leave her philandering husband and sought the advice of her minister, Pastor Manders. She was attracted to Manders, but he persuaded her to remain with her husband.

As the action starts, Mrs. Alving's husband is dead, and she and Manders are preparing to dedicate an orphanage to his memory. She reveals to Manders that her husband did not change his ways when she returned to him and that he died from the ravages of venereal disease; she also reveals that her servant Regina is Alving's illegitimate daughter.

The dramatic action is complicated by the fact that Mrs. Alving's son Oswald, who has recently returned home, is unaware that Regina is his half-sister and in fact wants to marry her. Before Manders and Mrs. Alving can reveal the truth to him, the orphanage—which has not been insured because Manders fears that insuring it would imply a weakening of his belief in God—burns down. Manders is convinced by Engstrand, a drunken carpenter and Regina's supposed father, that he, Manders, is responsible for the fire. To avoid scandal, Manders agrees to use the funds remaining in Alving's estate to help Engstrand establish a home for sailors, though it is obvious that the home will actually be a brothel.

[1]Henrik Ibsen, *Ghosts and Other Plays,* Michael Meyer (trans.), Doubleday-Anchor, New York, 1966, pp. 115–116.

MODERN REALISM. Henrik Ibsen addressed serious themes in the format of the well-made play. *Ghosts* is a powerful drama of family relationships shaped by past actions—adultery, deceit, hypocrisy. Here, we see Mrs. Alving, a victim of hypocrisy (played by Patricia Conolly); and Pastor Manders, who is himself something of a hypocrite (played by Richard Easton). The scene is from a production at the Old Globe Theatre in San Diego.

In the final act, Oswald confesses that he too has a venereal disease. Mrs. Alving then reveals to him and Regina the truth about their father. Oswald begs his mother to promise to help him commit suicide when the venereal disease has destroyed his mind. At the close of the play, Oswald deteriorates completely; at daybreak, as he goes blind, he calls for his mother to give him "the sun." When the curtain falls, Ibsen has not revealed whether or not Mrs. Alving will carry out the mercy killing.

Ghosts touches on many subjects which were, and might still be, considered offensive. The sexual double standard, for instance, is questioned when Mrs. Alving asks Manders why only women must be virgins on the wedding night. Ibsen also suggests that the women of his era have been forced to sublimate their sexuality; Mrs. Alving, for example, recognizes that she brought "no joy of life" into her marriage. Furthermore, the institution of marriage is derided. Oswald tells Manders that while he was in Paris he knew couples who lived together and had children but because of financial hardships were unmarried, arguing that these relationships are more honest than most conventional marriages. Ibsen also satirizes religious hypocrisy. Pastor Manders's foolishness is illustrated by his refusal to insure the orphanage, his inability to see through Engstrand, and his attacks on books he has not read. The references to venereal disease, incest, and euthanasia were, of course, all controversial. Still, as Ibsen frequently pointed out, *Ghosts* is not a play about syphilis; it is about people who are haunted by the past.

The realistic qualities of Ibsen's *Ghosts* are typical of realistic drama. The characters are not stereotypes, and there are no heroes or villains. The audience is made to understand each character's psychological, social, and economic motivations: each personality has been shaped by environment and heredity. Just as there is moral deformity in this universe, there is also physical deformity. Engstrand's "left leg is slightly crooked; under the sole of his boot is fixed a block of wood." The language is colloquial. The setting is a box set representing a "spacious garden room."[2]

To make the dramatic action believable and logical, Ibsen uses the crisis structure of the well-made play. Like a Greek tragedy, *Ghosts* observes the unities of time, place, and action, and much of its action has occurred before the beginning of the play. This dramatic structure is well-suited to a play in which the characters are haunted by ghosts of the past. The technique by which the past is slowly revealed is reminiscent of Sophocles' *King Oedipus*. The influence of the well-made-play form perfected by Scribe and Sardou in France earlier in the nineteenth century is also apparent. Each of the three acts concludes with a climax: Oswald chasing Regina at the end of Act I, the burning of the orphanage at the end of Act II, and Oswald's mental deterioration at end of Act III. All the action is carefully prepared for and foreshadowed. In the first act, for instance, Mrs. Alving casually remarks that a fire has been extinguished in the orphanage, preparing the audience for the later catastrophic fire. The plot revolves around two central secrets: the identity of Regina's father and the origin of Oswald's disease.

Despite his use of well-made-play devices, however, Ibsen breaks one of the fundamental rules of Scribe's formula: *Ghosts* does not resolve neatly; the audience does not know whether or not Mrs. Alving will assist in her son's suicide. This departure from a formula is part of Ibsen's creativity and gives more substance and meaning to his plays.

As we have noted, Ibsen later turned from realism to a more abstract form, symbolism. His realistic plays also illustrate his dramatic use of symbols. The orphanage, symbolizing Alving's reputation, burns down, and Engstrand's brothel is a more fitting memorial for the dissolute husband. Gloomy weather symbolizes the pall hanging over the Alving household. Eventually, Ibsen would shift his focus from creating a realistic world to drawing a universe in which such symbolic elements predominated.

---

[2]*Ghosts and Other Plays*, p. 131.

THE LOWER DEPTHS. Shown here is a scene from the Moscow Art Theater's original production of Gorki's famous naturalistic drama. In the center is Konstantin Stanislavski, the renowned actor, director, and theorist of realistic acting. *The Lower Depths,* set in a turn-of-the-century Russian flophouse, is an example of naturalism as defined by the French theorist Émile Zola.

Naturalistic Drama

Naturalism, a movement that began in France in the nineteenth century and spread to other European countries, is closely related to realism. Naturalism can be seen as a subdivision of realism—an extreme form. As a pure movement it did not last long, but some of its ideas appeared frequently in later dramas as well as in films and on television.

The French writer Émile Zola (1849–1902) is probably the most famous proponent of naturalism. Zola espoused the concept of "scientific objectivity," the idea that an artist should present a picture of the real world without making his or her own presence felt. The best-known naturalistic dramas from this era are *The Weavers* (Germany, 1892) by Gerhart Hauptmann (1862–1946) and *The Lower Depths* (Russia, 1902) by Maxim Gorki (1868–1936).

The naturalists argued that what should be presented onstage is a "slice of life": events should be shown as if they were sliced from a time continuum, without the selection, editing, and rearrangement that ordinarily occurs in playwriting. Because the naturalists wanted the controlling hand of the artist to remain unseen, they argued against stage contrivances. Instead, the artist should function as an objective scientist; everything onstage—characters, language, properties, settings, costumes—should seem to have been lifted directly from everyday life. Authenticity was the basic requirement.

Many naturalists believed that the most appropriate subject matter for drama was the lower class. The naturalists frequently focused on sordid and seamy aspects of society, to call attention to social problems and initiate reforms. Gorki's *The Lower Depths,* for example, presents characters who have sunk to the bottom of Russian society. Most naturalistic dramas present a series of episodes demonstrating the control that environment and our own animal desires have over us. For this reason, naturalistic works seem more loosely structured than realistic works. A modern parallel to this kind of naturalism is found in film documentaries, sometimes called *cinema verité,* of people who live wretched lives in squalid conditions: a film about a homeless man, for example, who sleeps in doorways and exists on scraps of food, or a film about people in a desert country suffering the effects of drought and famine.

Naturalism is a more stringent form than realism. One reason is its insistence on showing the stark side of life; the other is its attempt to be like a documentary, which means that its action cannot be shaped by same kind of artistic techniques used in realism. Realism can use symbols and can structure events in a way that is often more aesthetically satisfying. In fact, the naturalists' extreme position ultimately prevented their movement from being more influential; realism was seen as a more viable theatrical form. Nonetheless, the naturalist movement helped further the development of theater dedicated to reproducing life onstage, and its influence can be seen in plays like Eugene O'Neill's *The Iceman Cometh* (United States, 1939) and David Storey's *The Changing Room* (England, 1971).

Producers of Realism and Naturalism

There were both legal and commercial barriers to the production of realistic and naturalistic drama. In countries where theater was censored, realists often could not get their dramas staged at all; in England, for example, the lord chamberlain refused to license many of these works. Even in countries with no official censorship, such as the United States, legal problems could still arise: a 1905 production in Brooklyn of George Bernard Shaw's realistic play *Mrs. Warren's Profession* led to the arrest of the entire cast. Moreover, because realistic drama was so controversial, the theater establishment did not consider it commercially viable.

In order to produce realistic and naturalistic drama, then, a number of independent theaters were established throughout Europe. These theaters were exempt from government censorship because they were organized as subscription companies, regarding their audiences almost like members of a private club. Also, the independent theaters were not striving for commercial success—rather, their objective was to present new dramatic forms to the small audiences who were interested in them. Some of these theaters also used realistic production techniques. The four major independent theaters were the Théâtre Libre in France, the Freie Bühne in Germany, the Independent Theater in England, and the Moscow Art Theater in Russia.

THE THÉÂTRE LIBRE

The Théâtre Libre, or "Free Theater," was founded in 1887 by André Antoine (1858–1943). At that time, Antoine was a clerk with a gas company and a member of an amateur theater group in Paris. When he suggested that the group produce a one-act adaptation of a short story by Zola, the other members refused. Undaunted, Antoine rented a theater and organized another company to present the work. From this modest beginning, the Théâtre Libre would go on to revolutionize French theater, introducing Parisian audiences to major realistic and naturalistic playwrights like Zola, Ibsen, and Henri Becque (1837–1899).

By applying many of the illusionistic stage practices previously used by Madame Vestris and the duke of Saxe-Meiningen, Antoine popularized theatrical realism. Antoine strove to create the illusion of a "fourth wall" so that audiences would seem to be peeking in on everyday life. His stage settings, individually designed for each production, were box sets filled with practicable elements. As part of his concern with illusionism, he used *motivated lighting*—illumination of the stage picture which seems to come from actual onstage sources, such as a table lamp. Like Richard Wagner in the Bayreuth Festspielhaus, Antoine extinguished the house lights to focus attention on the stage. (We should note, however, that Antoine also produced—though unsuccessfully—some plays which departed from realistic dramatic techniques.)

Antoine also transformed French stage acting. Arguing against the star system, as typified by Sarah Bernhardt and Constant-Benoît Coquelin, Antoine organized a company of amateur actors who worked to create ensemble performances. Ensemble acting requires balanced casting and integration of all performances, and it never allows a star to overshadow supporting players. In striving for an ensemble, he was following the example of the duke of Saxe-Meiningen. Antoine also believed that an actor should appear to be living—not acting—onstage, and accordingly he was opposed to conventional gestures, vocal patterns, and blocking.

Antoine transformed business practices by selling subscriptions to develop loyal audiences and financial support. His impact on modern French theater can be seen in his later career. He left the financially troubled Théâter Libre in 1894 and 3 years later founded the Théâtre Antoine. More significantly, in 1906 he was appointed head of the Odéon, France's second national theater. Obviously, then, by the first decade of the new century realism had become an accepted movement in France. Antoine's influence could also be seen in German and English independent theaters.

THE FREIE BÜHNE

Two years after Antoine's Théâtre Libre was founded, the Freie Bühne, or "Free Stage," began in Berlin. Like Antoine's company, it was a subscription theater dedicated to introducing realism and naturalism. The Freie Bühne was noted for its productions of the plays of Ibsen and the German naturalist Gerhart Hauptmann.

Though both were noncommercial, there were differences between the Théâtre Libre and the Freie Bühne. For one thing, the Freie Bühne was operated by a board of directors, with Otto Brahm (1856–1912) as its chairman. Antoine, by contrast, was the sole director of his company. Also, the Freie Bühne employed professional actors and therefore could perform only on Sundays, when its performers were not otherwise engaged; for this reason, it paid less attention to production details. In addition, the Théâtre Libre rented small, out-of-the-way Parisian theaters whereas the Freie Bühne rented professional houses.

The Freie Bühne ceased regular operations in 1891 but continued to produce occasional noteworthy dramas to which the German government had denied permission. For example, in 1892 the Freie Bühne was revived to produce Hauptmann's *The Weavers*. Brahm's success with the Freie Bühne was reflected in his appointment, in 1894, as director of Berlin's Deutsches Theater.

THE INDEPENDENT THEATER

The English Independent Theater, which was founded in 1891 by the Dutch-born critic Jacob Thomas Grein (1862–1935) and operated in London for 6 years, was organized as a subscription company to circumvent censorship by the lord chamberlain. The Independent Theater was run much like the Freie Bühne: it hired professional actors, leased professional theaters, and performed on Sundays. Grein's goal was to introduce realists and naturalists, including Ibsen and Zola, to the English public. The first production by the Independent Theater was Ibsen's *Ghosts,* which received the disparaging reviews quoted earlier.

In 1892, the Independent Theater introduced the Irish-born George Bernard Shaw to the London public by producing his first play, *Widowers' Houses*. As a theater critic, Shaw defended the realists and naturalists, and he believed that drama should inspire social reform. Unlike the works of other realists, however, many of Shaw's socially conscious dramas are comedies. In Shaw's hands, subjects that most realists saw as gloomy and tragic became objects of satirical ridicule. When the Independent Theater ceased operating in 1897, Shaw's works were staged by other independently organized English companies, including the Incorporated Stage Society and the Royal Court Theater, which was run by John Vedrenne (1863–1930) and Harley Granville Barker (1877–1945), himself an actor and playwright.

(Theatre Collection,
Museum of the City of New York)

George Bernard Shaw

(1856–1950)

If George Bernard Shaw had died before his fortieth birthday, he would have been remembered—if at all—as a somewhat eccentric ne'er-do-well who let his mother support him, published five unsuccessful novels, and was a vegetarian and a Fabian socialist. It was only after a friend, the critic William Archer, got him jobs as a book reviewer and an art critic that Shaw was able to make effective use of his abilities as a writer.

Shaw spent his years of unemployment developing his intellect and his writing style. He had been born in Dublin, Ireland, of English parents, and had been an indifferent student who wanted to pursue his own interests in art, music, and literature. At age 16, he was working as a clerk in a land agent's office. His mother had left his father—an alcoholic—and was living in London, teaching music. Shaw joined her in 1876. He read widely, wrote extensively on political issues for the Fabian Society (a socialist organization), and became a noted political speaker.

In 1895, Shaw became the theater critic for the magazine *Saturday Review.* His commentaries, later published in book form as *Our Theater in the Nineties,* set a new standard of excellence in dramatic criticism. He championed the new realistic theater, particularly the plays of Ibsen, and condemned the stale commercial theater of the time. Finding no English drama that reflected his views, he began writing his own plays to convey his ideas on political and social reform.

Shaw's first plays were produced privately for small, selected audiences to circumvent the censor, but in 1898 he published them as *Plays Pleasant and Unpleasant.* With this collection, Shaw began his practice of writing long prefaces discussing issues raised in his plays. He also provided stage directions to help readers visualize the plays.

Though most of Shaw's plays took up social problems and philosophical concepts, they were also witty, engaging comedies with lively dialogue and unusual, well-drawn characters. They could be characterized as realistic comedies of manners. Among the best-known are *Candida* (1895), *Caesar and Cleopatra* (1899), *Man and Superman* (1903), *Major Barbara* (1905), *Pygmalion* (1914), and *Saint Joan* (1923).

Shaw was awarded the Nobel Prize for literature in 1925. In his later years, his plays became more philosophical and less interesting dramatically. He was also in disfavor socially and politically because of his attitude toward war—he considered it a useless enterprise—and his occasional praise of Mussolini and Hitler. (However, in 1938 he did write a play attacking all twentieth-century totalitarianism, *Geneva.)* Greatly saddened by the death of his wife in 1943, he himself lived 7 more years. On October 31, 1950, he announced "I am going to die," and 3 days later he did.

Possibly the most influential of the late-nineteenth-century theaters dedicated to realism was the Moscow Art Theater, which was founded in 1898 by Konstantin Stanislavski and Vladimir Nemirovich-Danchenko (1858–1943) and continues to produce drama today.

The production style of the Moscow Art Theater was originally influenced by the duke of Saxe-Meiningen, but a turning point came as early as its first season, with the production of *The Sea Gull* described at the opening of this chapter. Chekhovian drama, with Stanislavski's carefully realized realistic productions, would establish the company's reputation.

(The Bettmann Archive)

Anton Pavlovich Chekhov

(1860–1904)

When he first arrived in Saint Petersburg in 1885 to finish his medical studies, Anton Chekhov was astonished to discover that he was already a famous writer—the short stories that he had been writing casually to support his family and pay for his education had been highly acclaimed. As a result, he resolved to improve his work habits and concentrate on literature as a career.

As a schoolboy in Taganrog, Russia, Chekhov had acted and written for the local theater. During his last years in school, his father, a grocer, went bankrupt, and the family fled to Moscow to escape its creditors. Chekhov's literary sketches, written for magazines in Moscow and Saint Petersburg, helped him support the family and continue his medical studies. He did finish medical school, but because of his literary career he never entered active practice.

In 1887, Chekhov's first successful play, *Ivanov,* was produced in Moscow. (An earlier drama, *Platonov,* written while he was a student, had been rejected by the Moscow theaters.) Two one-act comedies, *The Bear* (1888) and *The Marriage Proposal* (1888), were produced successfully; but his play *The Wood Demon,* influenced by Tolstoy's philosophy, was a failure in 1889. Chekhov also wrote several short farces—or "jokes," as he called them—in his late twenties. These early works are very different from his later dramas in structure and action, but they show his interest in ordinary incidents of middle-class provincial life and in the outside forces that change people's lives. Particularly in the farces, he was able to draw characters swiftly and insightfully and to intertwine comedy and tragedy.

It was 7 years before Chekhov's next play, *The Sea Gull,* was produced. During this time, he perfected his dramatic technique, relying on indirect action and character development to create tension. Like complex music, his

UNCLE VANYA. The Moscow Art Theater, famous for realism, is also known as the home of Chekhov's plays. *Uncle Vanya,* one of Chekhov's realistic tragicomedies, was first produced by the Moscow Art Theater in 1899; it was directed by Stanislavski. This production photo of *Uncle Vanya* was taken for the company's fiftieth anniversary in 1948.

plays have a variety of themes, and these themes are developed through many characters and images.

As we have seen, the first production of *The Sea Gull* was hardly a success, but the production by the Moscow Art Theater was acclaimed. The Moscow Art Theater also produced Chekhov's next three plays, *Uncle Vanya* (1899), *The Three Sisters* (1900), and *The Cherry Orchard* (1904). These too were successful, though Chekhov berated Stanislavski—who had directed all four—for neglecting the humor in them.

Chekhov's plays are significant not only as realism but also as perfect examples of modern tragicomedy. We have already seen that in some earlier periods of theater history, such as Elizabethan England, comic scenes—like the gravediggers' scene in *Hamlet*—might occur in tragic plays, but they would be separated from the serious scenes. In modern tragicomedy, the tragic and the comic are blended; these plays are bittersweet. Comedy does not provide a contrast but rather increases our awareness of the tragic circumstances.

Sharpening the sense of tragedy in Chekhov's plays is the fact that his tragicomic characters are unable to fulfill their deepest desires. In *The Cherry*

Orchard, Madame Ranevsky and her family lose their beloved country home, with its orchard, to Lopakhin, whose father was a serf—the play reflects the changing class structure of turn-of-the-century Russia. The members of the aristocratic family are often comic in their inability to save the orchard. For example, Varya—Madame Ranevsky's eldest daughter—and Lopakhin seem destined to marry, and their marriage would keep the orchard in the family. In the final act, Varya and Lopakhin are left alone so that he can propose. Instead, they are unable to discuss their feelings. The "nonproposal scene" is quite funny, because she is fumbling with luggage while he is discussing the weather, but after it is over we realize that the last chance to save the beloved orchard has been lost. Part of Chekhov's genius is his ability to make us see that underneath comedy there is often tragedy.

Chekhov had contracted tuberculosis when he was 23, and in the last years of his life was forced to leave his estate outside Moscow and move south to Yalta for the sake of his health. In 1901, he married Olga Knipper (1870–1959), an actress with the Moscow Art Theater. He was elected to the Russian Academy of Science, but resigned when his friend the writer Maxim Gorki was expelled. He died in 1904 at Badenweiler, Germany, where he had gone in another attempt to regain his health.

Realistic Acting

STANISLAVSKI: THE PIONEER

The most famous system for training performers to act realistically—that is, to be believable—was developed by Konstantin Stanislavski, the cofounder of the Moscow Art Theater and the director of Chekhov's major plays. Recollecting his early career, Stanislavski wrote: "Herein lies the problem, to bring life itself upon the stage."

(The New York Times)

Konstantin Sergeivich Stanislavski

(1863–1938)

Konstantin Stanislavski's father was an industrialist, but his grandmother (who was French) had been an actress, and at 15 Stanislavski founded the Alekseev Circle, an amateur group consisting of many members of his family. (Alekseev was his family's surname; Stanislavski was his stage name.) He attended a theatrical school and observed contemporary actors before studying with F. P. Komissarzhevsky, a dramatist and producer.

In 1888, he and Komissarzhevsky founded another amateur group, the Society of Art and Literature, which became noted for its productions of works by Tolstoy and Dostoyevsky. When the Meiningen players visited Russia, Stanislavski was fascinated by their realistic staging and modeled his own productions after theirs, but he sought to substitute realism in acting for their declamatory, or oratorical, style.

In 1898, the playwright V. I. Nemirovich-Danchenko, director of the drama school of the Moscow Philharmonic Society, invited Stanislavski to form a new theater, which they called the Moscow Art Theater. Nemirovich-Danchenko was responsible for literary and administrative duties while Stanislavski handled staging and production. With the Moscow Art Theater, Stanislavski was able to refine his system of realistic acting.

The Moscow Art Theater had early successes with productions of Tolstoy, but as we have seen, it became famous for its productions of Chekhov's plays. Stanislavski created many of the leading roles in these plays, including Trigorin in *The Sea Gull,* Doctor Astrov in *Uncle Vanya,* and Gaev in *The Cherry Orchard.*

Though most of his work was with realistic drama, Stanislavski also staged the symbolist plays of Maeterlinck and Leonid Andreyev (1871–1919) and encouraged the work of other antirealist theater artists. He worked with the designer Edward Gordon Craig (who will be discussed later in this chapter) on an experimental production of *Hamlet.* The leaders of Russian avant-garde theater of the 1920s—Meyerhold, Vakhtangov, and Tairov—all worked with the Moscow Art Theater early in their careers.

After the Russian Revolution, the Moscow Art Theater confined itself to realism. Stanislavski himself was no longer acting, because of poor health, but he continued to develop his acting system until his death in 1938. Stanislavski's books explaining his system have been published in English as *An Actor Prepares, Building a Character,* and *Creating a Role.* He also wrote an informative memoir, *My Life in Art.*

THE STANISLAVSKIAN TECHNIQUE

Stanislavski developed his system of acting as a response to the problem of making characters "live" onstage, particularly in the realistic drama of the late nineteenth century. He worked very intensively with his actors and spent a long time on rehearsals. He focused on internally based—that is, psychological—methods. However, it should be remembered that Stanislavski took for granted traditional training in vocal techniques and body movements—a fact often overlooked by his twentieth-century imitators.

According to Stanislavski, an actor must do a great deal of script analysis. The performer must be aware of the character's background, environment, and relationships, as well as any additional information the dramatist provides; these are the *given circumstances* of the play.

To place himself or herself in a character's situation, the performer uses the *magic if*, asking, "What would I do *if* I were confronted by similar circumstances?" The performer must ascertain what motivates a character. The *super-objective*, also referred to as the *spine* or *through line*, is the "active verb" that expresses a character's overall goal. For each scene, the performer must be able to identify the character's specific objective.

A key element in Stanislavski's approach is *relaxation*. Stanislavski had noted that well-known performers of his day seemed to be in a state of complete freedom and relaxation, allowing the behavior of their characters to come through effortlessly.

Concentration also is central to Stanislavski's system: the actor must listen to and observe the stage action as if it had never occurred before. In an essay written in 1915, the American actor-playwright William Gillette (1855–1937), who also attempted to define the characteristics of realistic performance, referred to this technique as the "illusion of the first time."

To help performers portray emotions realistically, Stanislavski devised an exercise known as *emotional recall* or *affective memory:* the performer is called on to remember an event in his or her own life that parallels the emotional situation in the play. However, Stanislavski cautioned against excessive use of emotional recall. He believed that if a performer was immersed in the "given circumstances" of a drama, the desired emotions would develop out of the dramatic action. Emotional recall was to be used only for particularly difficult situations.

Stanislavski's influence on modern theater cannot be overstated. Most actors in the United States today are trained with some variation of the Stanislavskian system. There have been alterations and adaptations of his system, but through it all his work remains pervasive.

Visual Elements in Realistic Theater

For visual elements in realistic theater, the goal was the same as for scripts and acting: to make every feature as much like everyday life as possible. To this end, costumes, lighting, and sets—the rooms the characters lived in—were to correspond to what audiences observed in their own lives. Characters' clothing duplicated that of real people from the same social station or occupation; and the lighting in a room would not seem to come from arbitrary spotlights or floodlights, but would be made to appear to come from a lamp on a table, say, or from sunshine coming through a window.

In his preface to *Miss Julie,* Strindberg insisted that the pots and pans in the kitchen where the play takes place should be real, not painted on a piece of canvas as traditionally they would have been. Not surprisingly, the scenery in late-nineteenth-century realistic drama most often took the form of a box set, an arrangement that closely simulates a room in a home. This was closed in on three sides—sometimes with a ceiling—and was meant to be as lifelike as possible.

MISS JULIE. One of Strindberg's controversial realistic plays is *Miss Julie,* in which Julie and her servant Jean seduce each other, and Julie—disturbed about her reputation—commits suicide. Today, some critics find the representation of Julie sexist. This scene is from a production at the McCarter Theatre in New Jersey.

EARLY DEPARTURES FROM REALISM

As we have noted earlier in this chapter, it can be said that the two basic theatrical trends of the last hundred years are realism and departures from realism. Between 1875 and 1915, there were many antirealistic experimenters opposed to the concept of showing a "slice of life" onstage. Among dramatists, these experimenters included the symbolists and others—like Ibsen and Strindberg—who are not easily categorized. There were also antirealist approaches to theater production.

Symbolism

The leading antirealistic movement between 1880 and 1910 was symbolism. While its major proponents were French, symbolism influenced playwrights and other theater artists throughout the world.

The symbolists believed that drama should present, not mundane day-to-day activities, but the mystery of being and the cosmos—the infinite qualities of the human spirit. They called for a poetic theater in which symbolic images rather than concrete actions would be the basic means of communicating with the audience. Frequently, symbolist plays appear to take place in a dream world, and their major dramatic goal is evoking atmosphere and mood instead of telling a story. The symbolists, unlike realists, were not interested in creating individualized characters; they wanted their characters to be figures representative of the human condition. The symbolists also argued against realistic scenic detail, believing that a stage picture should have only the bare essentials necessary to evoke the dramatic universe.

Probably the most renowned symbolist dramas were *Pelléas and Melisande* (1892) by Maurice Maeterlinck (1862–1949) and *The Tidings Brought to Mary* (1921) by Paul Claudel (1868–1955).

Wedekind, Ibsen, and Strindberg as Antirealists

It is difficult to categorize many of the authors who wrote antirealistic dramas between 1880 and 1910. Even the symbolists tended to be highly individual in style, and some playwrights wrote both realistic and antirealistic drama or even mixed the two.

One turn-of-the-century German playwright who is not easy to classify was Benjamin Franklin Wedekind (1864–1918). Wedekind's plays, such as *Spring's Awakening* (1891), combine symbolist and grotesque elements with realistic—sometimes controversial—subject matter. *Spring's Awakening,* for instance, deals with adolescent sexuality, and even today there have been protests when it is produced. Wedekind himself was a controversial figure who created and performed cabaret acts which were attacked as sexually provocative and obscene.

Two important playwrights who were influenced by symbolism but whose antirealistic works defy facile categorization are Henrik Ibsen and August Strindberg: both are remembered for their realistic plays, but late in their careers they moved away from realism. As we have seen, in *The Master Builder, Little Eyolf, John Gabriel Borkman,* and *When We Dead Awaken,* Ibsen followed many symbolist tenets. August Strindberg's later antirealistic dramas have been more influential than Ibsen's. The two best-known are *A Dream Play* (1902) and *The Ghost Sonata* (1907).

As its title indicates, *A Dream Play* evokes the world of a dream. We see a Christ-like goddess, the Daughter of Indra, journeying through a variety of human situations and experiencing continual suffering. The scenes are not always causally related but rather are a series of stages or—to emphasize the Christian imagery—"stations" in the journey. Time, place, and characters are transformed suddenly and unexpectedly. Characters such as the Officer, the Attorney, the Poet, He, She, and the Dean of Philosophy are representatives, not individuals, and are referred to by titles rather than names. Symbols abound: a castle grows out of a dung hill, a shawl holds all human suffering; two lands are referred to as Foulgut and Fairhaven; an Attorney's face has become hideously lined by the torment of those who have engaged him. In *A Dream Play*, Strindberg deals with many of the concerns found in his realistic dramas—the destructiveness of marriage, materialism, and the class struggle —but he dramatizes these concerns, as he says in the preface, in "the disconnected but apparently logical form of a dream. Anything can happen; everything is possible and probable."[3]

August Strindberg

(1849–1912)

August Strindberg was the son of a steamship agent and a former waitress and servant. He had an unhappy, insecure childhood, and his youthful unhappiness was a prelude to a troubled adulthood that included frequent episodes of mental illness; but he was able to use these experiences as a basis for his writings.

After some intermittent study at the University of Uppsala in Sweden, Strindberg returned to Stockholm and worked as a teacher, librarian, and journalist while revising *Master Olaf* (1872), his first play. In 1875, when he was 26, he met Siri von Essen, whom he married in 1877. Their stormy marriage, which lasted until 1891, provided many situations for his novels and plays, especially the dramas *The Father* (1887) and *Miss Julie* (1888). In 1884 Strindberg was prosecuted for blasphemy because of the publication of *Married*, a collection of his stories. This increased his paranoia and his dislike for Sweden, and as a result he spent much time abroad, particularly in Paris, until 1897. When his second marriage failed in 1894, he went through a period of severe stress and mental instability—often referred to as his "inferno crisis" after *Inferno*, his autobiography of this time in his life. He then underwent a conversion to religious mysticism. His plays written after 1897—such as *To Damascus* (1898) and *A Dream Play* (1902)—were expressionistic, using symbolism and unrealistic shifts in action, and were steeped in his new beliefs. The plays from this period would be influential on the surrealist movement and later on theater of the absurd.

Several of Strindberg's late plays deal with events in Swedish history—a possible reflection of his return to Stockholm in 1899. In Stockholm, Strindberg, who was again embracing the radical ideas of his youth, wrote many social and political treatises for the press. In 1902 he married Harriet Bosse, a young actress, but the marriage failed in 1904.

[3]August Strindberg, *Six Plays of Strindberg* (trans. Elizabeth Sprigg), Doubleday-Anchor, New York, 1955, p. 193.

Some of Strindberg's most experimental and influential plays were written for the Intimate Theater in Stockholm, which he and August Falck ran for a time. His chamber plays, like *The Ghost Sonata* (1907), reflected his interest in music, particularly Beethoven, and showed a preoccupation with removing facades to reveal grotesque elements beneath the surface. *(Chamber plays* are analogous to chamber music: they are smaller-scaled and more intimate in terms of production and presentation.)

When Strindberg died in 1912, the Swedish Academy ignored him, as it had always done, but the Swedish people mourned him as their greatest writer.

Producing Antirealism

THEATER COMPANIES

Like the realists, the symbolists needed independently organized theater companies. In France, two independent theater companies were dedicated to antirealistic drama and production style. In 1890, Paul Fort (1872–1960) organized the Théâtre d'Art, which is remembered for producing Maeterlinck's one-act plays *The Intruder* and *The Blind.* When this theater closed 3 years later, Aurélien-Marie Lugné-Poë (1869–1940)—who had acted for Fort, and for André Antoine at the Théâtre Libre—established the Théâtre de l'Oeuvre. Fort and Lugné-Poë both followed symbolist theories of stage production. They deemphasized scenery, experimented with stylized vocal and physical techniques, and presented avant-garde antirealistic drama.

Possibly the most notorious of Lugné-Poë's presentations was *Ubu the King* (1896) by Alfred Jarry (1873–1907), a comic-book-style takeoff on Shakespeare's *Julius Caesar* and *Macbeth* and the history plays, in which the bungling, gluttonous Ubu conspires to take over as ruler of Poland and is later dethroned by the assassinated king's only surviving son. The play's opening line, "Merdre"—from French slang for feces—created an immediate furor, as did its other scatological references. In light of twentieth-century history, Jarry's cynical, absurdist view of political leaders seems shockingly prophetic.

Ireland's Abbey Theater is often associated with early symbolist drama. Its founders, in the first decade of the twentieth century, wanted to establish a company to deal with the concerns and myths of the Irish people. The playwrights initially associated with the Abbey were William Butler Yeats (1865–1939), Augusta Gregory (1863–1935), and John Millington Synge (1871–1909). Yeats, who was opposed to realism, created symbolist plays based on Irish myth. Later, he experimented with the stylized conventions of Japanese noh drama. The works of Gregory and Synge were more realistic; Synge—for instance, in *Riders to the Sea* (1904)—created poetic drama in realistic form. The Abbey also introduced the works of Sean O'Casey (1884–1964) in the 1920s. Today, it is the national theater of Ireland.

There were also many individual theater artists other than playwrights and directors whose style and theories of production departed from realism. Two of the most famous were the designers Appia and Craig.

Appia.

Craig.

Adolphe Appia (1862–1928)

Edward Gordon Craig (1872–1966)

Modern stage design begins with two men: Adolphe Appia, who was born in Switzerland; and Edward Gordon Craig, who was English. Among other innovations, they saw the tremendous possibilities of using light for scene changes and striking effects, and of moving away from the realistic box set.

Adolphe Appia was the first to develop a theory of antirealistic staging. Trained in music, he admired Wagner's operas but felt that realistic staging detracted from their effect. In 1891, he proposed simple, symbolic sets that would work with the actor. He also advocated multidirectional colored lighting to paint the stage and move in harmony with the production.

Appia had only a few opportunities to demonstrate his ideas. For some years he worked at a theater school in Hellerau, Germany, run by Émile-Jaques Dalcroze (1865–1950), where he designed experimental and dance productions. He also designed sets for Wagner's operas at La Scala and in Basel, Switzerland. He wrote two significant books: *Music and the Art of Theater* (1892) and *The Work of Living Art* (1921). A simple, shy man, he shunned publicity, preferring to let his work speak for itself.

Craig, by contrast, delighted in the limelight and sometimes was deliberately provocative in order to make his theories known. The son of the actress Ellen Terry and Edwin Godwin—an architect and scene designer—Craig had been an actor in Henry Irving's company before turning to design. Though he designed several productions for the Purcell Operatic Company and for his mother's theater, he could not find financial support for his ideas in England.

In 1904, Craig was invited to go to Germany, and there he published his book *The Art of the Theater.* Craig wanted to free theater from dependence on realism, literature, and the actor, and to create a unified art work—with light as a key element—under the control of one person. His magazine *The Mask* (1908–1928) was influential in avant-garde theater. For a few years before

A DESIGN BY APPIA. Adolphe Appia's ideas about lighting and scenery were revolutionary. He moved away from realistic settings to the use of shapes and levels which would serve as acting areas; one example is this design for *Iphigenia at Aulis*. Appia was also among the first to recognize the vast possibilities of modern lighting techniques.

World War I, Craig ran a theater school in Italy. After the war, he lived in both Italy and France, writing steadily, wittily, and sometimes acidly about his theories until his death in 1966.

While these two designers worked independently of each other, they arrived at many similar conclusions. Both attacked realistic theater, arguing against photographic reproduction as a basis for scene design. Appia disregarded the realistic "fourth wall" convention and designed a theater building at Dalcroze's school which was the first in the modern era without a proscenium arch. Both men believed that settings should suggest, not reproduce, locale. Both used levels and platforms, designing spaces that were functional for performers. Moreover, both of them took full advantage of the introduction of electricity—which made it possible for stage lighting to develop as an art—and both used light as an integral visual element. Most of their designs are extremely atmospheric, stressing contrasts between light and dark.

A DESIGN BY CRAIG. Edward Gordon Craig's ideas were ahead of his time, and most of them remained unrealized. Shown here is one of his designs, for a scene in *Electra.*

However, Appia and Craig were not in total agreement. Craig believed that theater needed a master artist who could create all the production elements. Appia believed that the régisseur, or "master" director, fused the theatrical elements and that the designer was an interpretive artist, bringing an author's work to life and providing a functional environment for the performers. Craig felt that the star system had made acting the weakest element of theater and argued that the best performer would be an *Übermarionette,* a "superpuppet," who would allow the director to control the performance totally. Craig's designs were frequently conceived on a more grandiose scale than Appia's. Appia's designs usually required a set change for each locale; but Craig, on the other hand, established the modern *unit setting*—one basic setting that can represent various locales through movement of its elements along with slight additions of properties. Craig was also especially noted for his experiments with movable screens.

Appia and Craig influenced many leading twentieth-century American designers, including Robert Edmond Jones (1887–1954), Lee Simonson (1888–1967), Norman Bel Geddes (1893–1958), Donald Oenslager (1902–1975), Boris Aronson (1900–1980), and Jo Mielziner (1901–1976). These designers, working between the world wars, proved the practicality of Appia's and Craig's theories.

The reaction against realism also influenced directors. In Russia, a number of artists rejected the artistic principles of Stanislavski and the Moscow Art Theater. Possibly the most influential of these was Vsevolod Meyerhold.

(R. Gorelov/Sovfoto)

Vsevelod Emilievich Meyerhold
(1874–1940)

If Stanislavski was the most significant twentieth-century theorist of psychologically based realistic acting, Vsevolod Emilievich Meyerhold was his counterpart in the external, antirealistic movement.

Meyerhold was born near Moscow in 1874. In the second year of his law studies, he was admitted to the drama school of the Moscow Philharmonic Society, where he studied with Nemirovich-Danchenko. As one of the original members of the Moscow Art Theater, Meyerhold played the role of Treplev, the frustrated young writer, in its production of *The Sea Gull*. However, during the next 4 years Meyerhold's position in the Moscow Art Theater became less prominent. In 1902, he left Stanislavski's company to work as a director.

Between 1902 and the outbreak of the Russian Revolution in 1917, Meyerhold experimented with antirealism, staging a number of symbolist dramas. In 1905, he was invited to direct at an experimental studio in the Moscow Art Theater, but this association did not last out the year. Meyerhold was then invited to direct the Russian actress Vera Komissarzhevskaya's company; again, however, after two seasons he was forced to leave because of his contention that the director, not the star performer, was the primary theater artist. During the next 10 years, when he worked at the Imperial Theater in Saint Petersburg, his productions became increasingly stylized and theatrical. He also staged studio productions using techniques of commedia dell'arte, vaudeville, and the circus.

Meyerhold's importance for Russian theater became apparent after the Russian Revolution. Between 1919 and the mid-1930s, he would become the leading Russian "theatricalist." In 1920, he was appointed deputy commissar of the theater department of the Commissariat for Education, and for 3 years he was involved in the government's organization of theatrical arts.

During the 1920s, Meyerhold undertook his renowned antirealistic experiments, in such productions as *The Magnificent Cuckold* (1922) and *The Inspector General* (1926). In the early 1930s, he was attacked by the Soviet government for failing to produce "socialist realism." Ironically, after his theater was taken from him he was invited to work in the Opera Studio of the Moscow Art Theater, where he staged *Rigoletto* in 1938. In June of 1939, he was invited to address the All-Union Conference of Stage Directors. It was expected that he would recant his stylistic experimentation, but instead he attacked Soviet-controlled theater art and was arrested. Meyerhold was tortured in a Soviet labor camp and executed in 1940. His wife, Zinaida Raikh (1894–1939), who was his leading actress, was found brutally murdered in their apartment.

MEYERHOLD'S THEATRICALIST EXPERIMENTS

Much of what would be called *avant-garde* in the theater of the 1960s and later can be traced back to Meyerhold's experiments in the early twentieth century. Meyerhold's theater was a director's theater; as director, he was also literally the author of his productions, frequently restructuring or even rewriting classic works. He searched for suitable environments for his presentations, arguing for the use of found spaces—that is, spaces not originally meant for theater, such as streets, factories, and schools. Meyerhold wanted to shatter the "fourth wall" convention. On occasion he would leave the house lights on, extend the stage apron into the audience, or station performers in the house. He experimented with, and theorized about, multimedia in stage productions. He attempted to train his actors physically by using techniques from commedia dell'arte, the circus, and vaudeville. He frequently experimented with theatricalism. *Theatri-calists* expose the devices of theater, such as the way stage machinery works, to make audiences aware of watching a performance; they also borrow techniques from the circus, music halls, and similar popular entertainments.

Meyerhold's best-remembered experiments were undertaken in the 1920s, immediately after the Russian Revolution. He devised an acting system known as *biomechanics,* which emphasized external physical training and performance style, and suggested that the actor's body could be trained to operate like a machine. Furthermore, he argued that through physical actions performers could evoke desired internal responses in themselves and their audiences. In his early biomechanical experiments, Meyerhold had his performers create outlandish physicalizations to represent emotional states, though later he moved to more natural physicalizations.

Meyerhold's settings, known as *constructivist* sets, provided machines for his performers to work on. These settings frequently looked like huge tinker toys, consisting of skeletal frames, ramps, stairways, and platforms. Constructivist sets were highly theatrical; they were not meant to indicate a specific locale, such as a room in a house, but were rather a practical apparatus for the actors.

Meyerhold used a constructivist design for his production of *The Magnificent Cuckold* in 1922. This setting, according to his biographer, Edward Braun,

> consisted of the frames of conventional theater flats and platforms joined by steps, chutes, and catwalks; there were two wheels, a large disc bearing the letters "CR-ML-NCK," and vestigial windmill sails, which all revolved at varying speeds as a kinetic accompaniment to the fluctuating passions of the characters. Blank panels hinged to the framework served as doors and windows."[4]

[4]Edward Braun, *The Theatre of Meyerhold*, Eyre, Methuen, London, 1979, p. 170.

MEYERHOLD: A DIRECTING GENIUS. One of the giants of twentieth-century theater was the Russian director Vsevelod Meyerhold, who carried out many antirealistic experiments. He used commedia and circus techniques, created "constructivist" stage sets, and reinterpreted the classics. In this scene from *The Inspector General,* he crowds the stage with a wild assemblage of character types.

A description of the opening scene indicates how the set worked:

> You heard an exultant voice ring out offstage, full of joyful strength and happiness; and then up the side ladder to the very top of the construction flew—and "flew" is the word—[Igor] Ilinsky [Meyerhold's leading actor] as Bruno [the "magnificent cuckold"]. His wife Stella . . . ran to meet him and stood, indescribably youthful, lithe, and athletic, with her straight legs apart like a pair of compasses. Without pausing, Bruno hoisted her onto his shoulder, then slid down the highly-polished chute and gently lowered his weightless load to the ground."[5]

Meyerhold, as we have noted, was not the only Russian antirealist. Alexander Tairov, for example, also experimented with various nonrealistic techniques at his Kamerny (Chamber) Theater between 1914 and 1950. After the revolution, he too was harassed by the Soviet regime.

[5]Ibid., pp. 172–173.

Debates in Theater History:
ARE WOMEN'S CONTRIBUTIONS TO THEATER HISTORY OVERLOOKED?

As we have seen in several earlier chapters, feminist historians argue that significant female innovators in theater history are frequently overlooked.

One case in point could be made with regard to the innovations in Russian theater between 1875 and 1915. While the work of Stanislavski and Chekhov at the Moscow Art Theater has received major attention, for instance, little notice has been paid to the acting career of Olga Knipper. Knipper was Chekhov's wife, but—more important—she was also the leading actress in this realistic theater. What was her theory of acting? How did she further the realistic innovations made at the Moscow Art Theater? Similarly, the leading actress in Meyerhold's company was his wife Zinaida Raikh, but her theoretical viewpoints and how they relate to Meyerhold's innovations are rarely mentioned. Again, Tairov's wife, the dancer Alice Koonen (1889–1974), must have been a major influence on his early theatricalism, yet there is little mention of her contributions to the work at the Kamerny Theater.

As we examine the history of many of the major twentieth-century theater companies, it is clear that the contributions of their women members receive less detailed examination than those of the men. (As a matter of fact, in the present chapter, Henry Irving's contributions to the Lyceum Theater are given more attention than those of Ellen Terry. Is our own representation of history unbalanced here?) Later examples might also be cited, including the Group Theater in the United States: in discussions of the Group Theater, the contributions of Cheryl Crawford and Stella Adler are almost always overshadowed by the directorial innovations of Lee Strasberg and Harold Clurman.

Are feminist historians right? Have women's contributions been excluded from theater history by a male-dominated perspective? How can we address this issue? We tend to think that this question and the debate over it apply only to the remote past, but actually they cross all chronological boundaries. The issue will confront theater historians as they consider how our historical perspective on all periods should be revised.

ECLECTICS

Some early-twentieth-century theater artists tried to bridge the gap between realism and antirealism. These *eclectics,* as they were known, were not doctrinaire in their practices, arguing instead that each play should define its own form. Eclectic directors included the Austrian Max Reinhardt (1873–1943) and the Russian Yevgeny Vakhtangov (1883–1922).

Max Reinhardt began his career as an actor with the Freie Bühne. He was a major director in Austrian and German theater from 1905 until 1933, when, as a Jew, he was forced to leave Hitler's Germany. Reinhardt's productions were particularly noteworthy because of his innovative use of theater spaces. He staged *King Oedipus* and *Lysistrata* in a converted 3,000-seat circus building and directed a modern adaptation of the medieval morality play *Everyman* outside the cathedral at Salzburg. He experimented with adaptations of the Elizabethan stage for Shakespearean drama; and for his productions of a drama called *The Miracle* he had theaters remodeled to look like the interior of a cathedral.

Reinhardt also experimented with Asian theatrical conventions and conventions from earlier periods of western theater. Throughout his career, he was a total régisseur, or director-designer, overseeing all aspects of his productions. He produced a wide variety of plays, and during his career he staged over 500 productions and managed more than thirty playhouses and companies.

Another eclectic, Yevgeny Vakhtangov, staged most of his significant works for studios of the Moscow Art Theater. Vakhtangov believed that every production had its own inherent style, derived from the text, the performers, and the intended audience. He directed his four best-known productions in 2 years: Maeterlinck's *The Miracle of Saint Anthony* (1921), Strindberg's *Erik XIV* (1921), S. Anski's *The Dybbuk* (1922), and Carlo Gozzi's *Turandot* (1922). Vakhtangov was able to synthesize Stanislavski's psychological realism with Meyerhold's theatricalism.

THE MIRACLE. A twentieth-century director who liked to present plays on a vast scale was the Austrian Max Reinhardt. Reinhardt used a circus building for some plays and the outside of a cathedral for an adaptation of *Everyman*; for *The Miracle*, shown here, he converted the inside of a theater to look like a cathedral.

A leading performer with Vakhtangov was Mikhail Chekhov (1891–1955), Anton Chekhov's nephew, who developed a system of acting based on what he called the *psychological gesture*. He maintained that a performer could create a realistic stage portrayal by finding physical characteristics for a role that would then trigger internal responses. Again, one can see the influence of Stanislavski and Meyerhold. Mikhail Chekhov left Russia in the 1920s and taught acting in England and the United States.

COMMERCIAL AND POPULAR THEATER

So far, we have been focusing on significant experimenters who worked between 1875 and 1915. However, mainstream theater of this period remained highly commercial in orientation, and popular dramas and theatrical entertainments predominated. This can be seen, for example, in both American and English theater.

In the United States, melodrama remained extremely popular. Successful playwrights, such as Clyde Fitch (1865–1909), emphasized melodramatic plot lines and devices to excite their audiences. Many producers, such as David Belasco (1853–1931), used highly realistic techniques to create sensational stagings of these melodramas, and many actors built successful careers performing in them. James O'Neill (1847–1920)—the father of Eugene O'Neill—spent most of his career performing in a stage adaptation of *The Count of Monte Cristo*.

American theater production was dominated by business people who tried to monopolize it. One group of producers, nicknamed the "Syndicate," did exercise a monopoly over commercial American theater by producing major shows with leading stars and allowing theaters across the country to book these shows only if the theater owners did all their booking with the Syndicate. In addition, Syndicate members controlled many of the major theaters throughout the United States and would not book other producers' shows. Star actors who would not work with the Syndicate found their opportunities severely limited. One actress who opposed the Syndicate was Minnie Maddern Fiske (1865–1932), who became well-known for her performances in plays by Ibsen, Shaw, and Wilde. The Syndicate's stranglehold was broken by the Shubert brothers, whose organization then went on to monopolize American theater until 1956, when it lost an antitrust suit and had to relinquish a number of its playhouses.

In England, there were many experimenters: the playwrights included Shaw and Oscar Wilde (1856–1900), the author of the popular comedies of manners *The Importance of Being Earnest* (1895) and *An Ideal Husband* (1895); and the directors included William Poel (1852–1914) of the Elizabethan Stage Society, who tried to revive unlocalized staging for Elizabethan plays. However, most productions in England during this period were staged in a conventional, illusionistic way; and most of the famous actor-managers chose plays by Shakespeare or by popular melodramatic authors. Among the most best-known and most commercially successful actor-managers of the time were Herbert Beerbohm Tree (1853–1917) and Henry Irving.

Henry Irving
(1838–1905)

Henry Irving was the most acclaimed actor on the English stage during the last part of the nineteenth century and one of the last great English actor-managers.

Irving was—like Edwin Booth, Richard Wagner, and the duke of Saxe-Meiningen—one of the first modern theater artists to insist on a total effect in his productions and was responsible for innovations in staging and lighting. He employed the best stage designers of the day, rehearsed his large corps of stagehands so that scene changes would be smooth and precise, and experimented with control of stage lighting. In 1895, Irving became the first English actor to be knighted—in recognition of his work and his high professional standards.

Irving's real name was John Henry Brodribb; he spent 4 years as a clerk in London before changing it and becoming an actor. By 1871, when he had his first London success as Mathias in Leopold Lewis's melodrama *The Bells,* Irving had spent 15 years on the stage, playing over 500 roles with provincial and London companies. He followed his success as Mathias with other leading roles in melodrama, and in 1874 he played Hamlet for a record-breaking 200 nights.

Though he was criticized for such physical flaws as an unmelodious voice and a shambling gait, as well as for unusual characterizations, Irving was a master at using gesture and pantomime to communicate a character's feelings and thoughts. He was not a romantic leading man but excelled in melodrama and in roles like Iago, in which he could portray scorn, malice, horror, and fear.

Irving became manager of the Lyceum Theater in 1878 and for 21 years staged productions there that were known for scenic splendor and totality of effect. His leading lady, Ellen Terry (1847–1928), brought beauty, freshness, and vitality to her roles. Together, they became one of the most renowned stage duos of the century.

Irving gave up management of the Lyceum in 1898, after several unprofitable seasons. His farewell London performance was at Drury Lane in 1905. Irving died while on tour and was buried in Westminster Abbey. Describing him, Ellen Terry wrote, "He was quiet, patient, tolerant, impersonal, gentle, close, crafty, incapable of caring for anything outside of his work."

ABYSSINIA. Bert Williams and his partner George Walker were among the early twentieth-century African American artists who helped create Broadway musicals and operettas that starred black performers. Shown here is a scene from a revival of *Abyssinia,* with Williams and his wife, Lottie Thompson (Cole) Williams (1866–1929).

AFRICAN-AMERICAN THEATER

In the United States just before and after the turn of the century, most theater was a continuation of earlier nineteenth-century practices—European developments in realism and experimentation would not have their full effect on American theater until after World War II. There were, however, several noteworthy developments in African American theater.

The 1890s, called the "gay nineties" (at that time, the word *gay* meant simply "lighthearted" or "blithe"), was ironically also a decade which saw widespread lynchings, and in which the Supreme Court—in *Plessy* v. *Ferguson*—made Jim Crow principles the law of the land by permitting "separate but equal" schools for white and black children. In this decade, too, the Reverend Thomas Dixon adapted his novel in praise of the Ku Klux Klan for the stage, and later into the film *Birth of a Nation.* In theater, though, the same period encompassed a series of vibrant musical shows written, acted, and produced by African Americans.

Ragtime

Rising prices, worn-out jokes, the incipient motion picture industry, and the introduction of women into revues all contributed to the decline of the minstrel show. By 1895, musical theater had developed a new form, the *revue*, which had more plot than vaudeville and a new kind of music—the vigorous, infectious ragtime.

The syncopated rhythms of ragtime had originated in saloons, sawmill camps, and houses of prostitution from the spontaneous talent of unknown African American composers and piano players. American youngsters, who had been plunked down on piano stools to practice "Whispering Hope," discovered suddenly that it was more fun to play "Maple Leaf Rag" by Scott Joplin (1868–1917). (Sixty years later, Joplin's music would become a hit again in the musical *Pippin* and the movie *The Sting*. Joplin, who died in poverty, was buried in an unmarked grave, and his ragtime opera *Treemonisha*, published at his own expense, remained unproduced until 1972.)

As ragtime spread across the nation, it served as a bridge to legitimate musical comedy for a number of talented African Americans. In 1891, *The Creole Show* introduced sixteen beautiful "colored" women into minstrelsy. Bob Cole (1864–1912) and William Johnson (1873–1954) conceived, wrote, produced, and directed the first black musical comedy, *A Trip to Coontown* (1898).

In the same year, Will Marion Cook (1869–1944) and Paul Lawrence Dunbar (1872–1906) wrote "Clorindy: The Origin of the Cakewalk." This high-stepping ragtime dance was an instantaneous success and the first of many black dances—such as the turkey trot, the Charleston, the lindy hop, the jitterbug, and the twist—to become popular in the United States.

Among the great cakewalkers, the comedians Bert Williams (1874–1922) and George Walker (1873–1911) and their wives joined composers and writers to produce musicals and operettas that put black performers on Broadway. Their most successful shows, *In Dahomey* (1902) and *Abyssinia* (1906), reflect two different but important interests of the time: operetta, with its aristocratic characters involved in romantic plots; and Africa and things African. For the first time Americans saw blacks onstage without burnt cork, without dialect, and costumed in high fashion.

African American Stock Companies: The Lafayette Players

The success of black writers and producers encouraged the formation of African American stock companies. The first of these was founded in 1904 by Robert Motts (died 1911) on Chicago's South Side. At his Pekin Theater, a new show opened every 2 weeks. In 1914, a second important stock company was founded in New York by Anita Bush (1894–1938), who had played in Williams's and Walker's shows. Her stock company opened at the Lincoln Theater in Harlem, but a year later she moved the troupe to the Lafayette Theater and dubbed it the Lafayette Players.

The Lafayette Players produced a new play every week. By 1932, when the company finally closed in the face of the depression, it had presented over 250 productions and employed a host of black stars, including Charles Gilpin (1878–1930), Evelyn Preer, and Clarence Muse.

The company's repertoire consisted entirely of "white" plays—that is, it brought Broadway to African American audiences. One of the great delights for these audiences was to watch Clarence Muse, a very dark-skinned man, play *Doctor Jekyll and Mister Hyde* in white makeup and wig. Muse later moved to Hollywood and starred in *Hearts in Dixie* (1929), the second talking picture with an all-black cast.

The Lafayette Players proved to white audiences that black actors were capable of serious drama and that a black company could sustain itself financially over a long period. Certainly the African American dramatic groups that followed—the Negro Art Theater, the Gilpin Players, and the Ethiopian Players—owed their inspiration to Anita Bush's pioneer work.

African Americans in Popular Theater

Most African American performers in this era, and later, made a living not on the legitimate stage but in vaudeville. While a few white circuits like Keith-Albee and Columbia would book blacks, most black vaudeville acts depended on the Negro circuit, which extended from New York to Texas and from Chicago to Birmingham. Bookings were handled by the Theater Owners Booking Association, TOBA—an acronym which the performers translated as "Tough on Black Actors." The Negro circuit, founded by blacks in 1920, was eventually able to book acts in over eighty theaters, however; and it is estimated that between the years 1910 and 1930 blacks owned and operated seventeen theaters.

Black vaudeville acts, like white acts, included song-and-dance teams, stunt dancing, cakewalk artists, blues singers, comics, specialty acts, and even dramatic skits. Among the hundreds of black vaudeville performers were Pigmeat Markham, the Nicholas Brothers, Nipsey Russell, Bessie Smith, Butterbeans and Susie, and Sweet Mama Stringbean (Ethel Waters). This lucrative circuit collapsed with the great depression of the 1930s.

ASIAN THEATER

The period at the end of the nineteenth century and the beginning of the twentieth saw increasing interchange between Asian and western theaters. Particularly, western theater had a growing influence on the modern theaters of India, China, and Japan. In all three countries, traditional theater continued: kathakali in India, Peking opera in China, and noh and kabuki in Japan. But awareness of western theater was widening.

Theater in India

By the turn of the century, Ibsen and Chekhov began to influence intellectuals in India (as they also would in China and Japan). Perhaps the greatest of the Indian writers influenced by both modern European theater and traditional Indian theater was Rabindranath Tagore, whose fifty plays, some in modern style and some in a more traditional mode, formed the basis and inspiration for much of the best work that has followed. Tagore is regarded as a classic writer in India, where his plays are frequently produced. Attempts to stage his elusive and poetic dramas, however, have met with great difficulty in the west.

Rabindranath Tagore

(1861–1941)

Rabindranath Tagore was the youngest of fourteen children of Debendranath Tagore, a prominent philosopher and social reformer. He received an excellent education, particularly in Hindu philosophy, and began writing verses while still at home; his first important collection of poetry, *Manasi,* was published in 1890. In 1891, Tagore became the manager of his father's estates in Shileida and Sayadupur. Through close contact with the villagers, he learned about their lives and problems and also became familiar with traditional Bengali folk drama.

Tagore's plays, written in Bengali, cover a wide variety of styles and subjects. *Nature's Revenge* (1884) uses the nature imagery of Sanskrit poetry. *The King of the Dark Chamber* and *Rakta Karaui* (1924) are allegories. In *Vis Barjan* (1890), Tagore invents a myth to focus on the issue of nonviolence. In *Last Cause* (1904) and *The Bachelor's Club* (1904), he writes realistic comedy and satire. Many of Tagore's later works, such as *Chitrangada* (1936), are dance dramas, a form he came to favor late in life. His works include song, mime, dance, and lyrical verse and are tinged with mysticism. Because of these elements, English translations of his plays, even those Tagore did himself, seem stilted and unnatural.

Tagore received the Nobel Prize for literature in 1913 and was knighted in 1915, but he relinquished his title in 1919 to protest the Amritsar massacre, in which British troops had killed nearly 400 Indians during an outbreak of rioting and mass demonstrations. In 1924, he founded the Visva-Bharati University in Santiniketan as a center for Indian and international culture. At his school in Santiniketan, he directed and acted in his own plays. Since his death in 1941, Tagore's reputation in India as a dramatist has grown. Much of his international reputation comes from his numerous collections of poetry and short stories and his lectures in Europe, America, and Asia.

Theater in China and Japan

At the turn of the century, increased contact with the west by Chinese scholars and intellectuals led to great curiosity concerning western drama. Students in urban centers were excited to realize that theater could deal with ideas as well as sentiment, and they began to translate and stage plays by Ibsen, Chekhov, and Shaw as a way of educating the public about social and political problems. Many of the writers and actors who became interested in this *spoken drama,* as they called it, had been impressed by its possibilities while living in Japan, where interest in European theater had developed even earlier. With the help of Japanese colleagues, Chinese students living in Tokyo staged versions in modern Chinese of *La Dame aux Camelias* and *Uncle Tom's Cabin.*

In 1868 the Japanese ruling family—the house of Tokugawa—was overthrown, and this led to contact with the west, which had long been forbidden. When young Japanese intellectuals began to travel abroad, western influence spread in Japan. Among the Japanese intellectuals drawn to the west were a number of gifted men who developed a strong interest in theater and saw it as a way to express social concerns. The work of Ibsen became a particularly strong force for these men. Feeling that traditional kabuki had nothing to contribute to such a movement, they decided to create a means of performing spoken drama in the western manner.

In 1909, Osanai Kaoru (1881–1928) presented the first professional production in Japan of a modern play, with specially trained actors. A remarkable pioneer in the development of western-style theater, Osanai continued his experiments until 1923. Then, with the help of a wealthy colleague, Hijikata Yoshi, he was able to build the Tsukiji Little Theater, which served as the center for the development of modern Japanese drama until its destruction in the bombing of Tokyo during World War II.

As we now turn, in Chapter 13, to the revolutionary theatrical developments from 1915 to 1945, the strong influence of trends and innovators of the turn of the century will be apparent.

SUMMARY

The beginning of modern theater was marked by the advent of realism and naturalism. The most noted realistic playwrights were Henrik Ibsen, August Strindberg, George Bernard Shaw, and Anton Chekhov; among the naturalists were Émile Zola, Gerhart Hauptmann, and Maxim Gorki. The controversial works of these playwrights were produced by independent theaters, which included André Antoine's Théâtre Libre, Otto Brahm's Freie Bühne, J. T. Grein's Independent Theater, and Konstantin Stanislavski's Moscow Art Theater.

One of the earliest reactions against realism was symbolism, and theaters like the Théâtre d'Art and the Théâtre de l'Oeuvre were independent producers of symbolist plays. Among designers who broke with the conventions of realistic theater were Adolphe Appia and Edward Gordon Craig; directors who experimented with antirealistic staging included Vsevolod Meyerhold and Alexander Tairov.

Eclectics, such as Yevgeny Vakhtangov and Max Reinhardt, strove to reconcile the contrasting styles which were emerging in early modern theater. Some writers, like Ibsen and Strindberg, created both realistic and nonrealistic drama.

American and English theater, though primarily commercial in orientation, did have some experimenters. African Americans had a significant impact in the United States as members of stock companies and in popular theater.

Increased contact between Asia and the western world led to cross-cultural influences in theater.

CHAPTER 13

THEATER FROM 1915 TO 1945

T he date is August 28, 1928, and we are at the Theater am Schiffbauer-
damm in Berlin, Germany. The theater, an ornate nineteenth-century
building in the center of the city, has been taken over by Ernst Josef
Aufricht, a 27-year-old actor with a rich father. Aufricht wants to become a
producer, and we have been following the story of his first venture.

He began by looking for a play to present as the first offering in his newly
acquired theater. A few months ago, he met a 29-year-old German poet and
playwright, Bertolt Brecht. Brecht was then writing a play and tried to persuade
him to produce it, but Aufricht was not interested. The young producer was
struck, however, by one of Brecht's ideas—an adaptation of an eighteenth-
century British ballad opera called *The Beggar's Opera*. Brecht agreed to work on
the adaptation but insisted that his musical collaborator would have to be the
German composer Kurt Weill. Aufricht did not like that; in fact, he secretly
hired someone else to work on orchestrations of the original version. Nevertheless, Brecht and Weill went to work.

THE THREEPENNY OPERA. This musical play is one of Brecht's most popular works, both
because it is based on the well-known *Beggars' Opera* and because of Kurt Weill's music.
It is also an example of what Brecht called *epic drama*: it has a number of episodic scenes,
and songs interrupt the action to teach a lesson. Shown here is a recent avant-garde
production by Richard Foreman, a director we will be discussing in our final chapter.
(Richard Feldman/Williamstown Theatre Festival)

By then, it was late spring, and Aufricht wanted rehearsals to begin early in August so that the production could open on his birthday, August 28. Brecht and Weill worked furiously and were nearly finished when rehearsals began. They changed their minds several times about what to call their musical play but finally decided on *Die Dreigroschenoper*—in English, *The Threepenny Opera.*

We have some theatrical acquaintances who tell us that the rehearsals have been frantic and plagued by mishaps. Shortly after rehearsals began, the leading actress left to care for her sick husband. He died 2 weeks ago, and she returned; but her part had been cut down so much that she refused to play it, and so Brecht and the director—Erich Engel—searched desperately for a replacement. Just a week ago, Engel himself quit, and Brecht had to take over the rehearsals. Brecht has let some of his friends attend rehearsals, and word has spread around Berlin that the production will be a disaster. Aufricht has been advised by *his* friends to find a new play which can be moved quickly into the theater as soon as *The Threepenny Opera* fails.

Now, opening night has arrived. The plot, we discover, has to do with a group of low-life figures in Victorian England. One of them is Peachum, the boss of a gang of underworld beggars who pose as disabled people; another major figure is Macheath, a swashbuckling burglar who marries Peachum's daughter Polly; another is Tiger Brown, the chief of police.

During the first act, the audience is wary and unresponsive. A song about "Mack the Knife" is greeted with an uncertain silence; the same thing happens when Peachum sings a number explaining his business. A song by Polly Peachum about "Pirate Jenny" also gets a cool reception. To make matters worse, the two most important theater critics in Berlin—Alfred Kerr and Herbert Ihering—are furious because the management, although well aware that they despise each other, has seated them together.

But then, as the opening-night performance continues to unfold, we come to a duet by Macheath and Tiger Brown about their army days in India. Suddenly, the theater explodes. We all applaud, stamp our feet, and shout for an encore—and from then on, everything seems to go right.

Kerr and Ihering, the critics, are so impressed with the show that afterwards they will put aside their indignation and write highly laudatory reviews. The leading lady who dropped out will ask when she can return. And the careers of Bertolt Brecht and Kurt Weill will reach a new level of importance.

BACKGROUND: A TIME OF UNREST—
THE WORLD WARS

The period from 1915 to 1945—from the year after the start of World War I to the end of World War II—was a time of unusual unrest for the western world. On the one hand, the world was being brought closer together by radio, telephone, and motion pictures. On the other hand, some nations were jealously guarding their independence and sovereignty as other nations tried to take them over. Drastic political and economic changes led to instability.

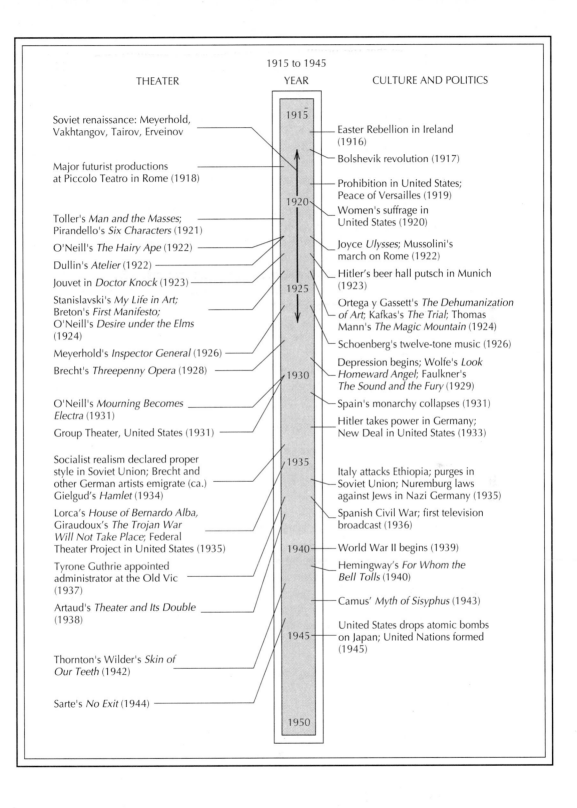

1915 to 1945

THEATER   YEAR   CULTURE AND POLITICS

Soviet renaissance: Meyerhold,
Vakhtangov, Tairov, Erveinov

Major futurist productions
at Piccolo Teatro in Rome (1918)

Toller's *Man and the Masses*;
Pirandello's *Six Characters* (1921)

O'Neill's *The Hairy Ape* (1922)

Dullin's *Atelier* (1922)

Jouvet in *Doctor Knock* (1923)

Stanislavski's *My Life in Art*;
Breton's *First Manifesto*;
O'Neill's *Desire under the Elms*
(1924)

Meyerhold's *Inspector General* (1926)

Brecht's *Threepenny Opera* (1928)

O'Neill's *Mourning Becomes
Electra* (1931)

Group Theater, United States (1931)

Socialist realism declared proper
style in Soviet Union; Brecht and
other German artists emigrate (ca.)
Gielgud's *Hamlet* (1934)

Lorca's *House of Bernardo Alba,*
Giraudoux's *The Trojan War
Will Not Take Place*; Federal
Theater Project in United States (1935)

Tyrone Guthrie appointed
administrator at the Old Vic
(1937)

Artaud's *Theater and Its Double*
(1938)

Thornton's Wilder's *Skin of
Our Teeth* (1942)

Sarte's *No Exit* (1944)

1915

1920

1925

1930

1935

1940

1945

1950

Easter Rebellion in Ireland
(1916)

Bolshevik revolution (1917)

Prohibition in United States;
Peace of Versailles (1919)

Women's suffrage in
United States (1920)

Joyce *Ulysses*; Mussolini's
march on Rome (1922)

Hitler's beer hall putsch in Munich
(1923)

Ortega y Gassett's *The Dehumanization
of Art*; Kafkas's *The Trial*; Thomas
Mann's *The Magic Mountain* (1924)

Schoenberg's twelve-tone music (1926)

Depression begins; Wolfe's *Look
Homeward Angel*; Faulkner's
The Sound and the Fury (1929)

Spain's monarchy collapses (1931)

Hitler takes power in Germany;
New Deal in United States (1933)

Italy attacks Ethiopia; purges in
Soviet Union; Nuremburg laws
against Jews in Nazi Germany (1935)

Spanish Civil War; first television
broadcast (1936)

World War II begins (1939)

Hemingway's *For Whom the
Bell Tolls* (1940)

Camus' *Myth of Sisyphus* (1943)

United States drops atomic bombs
on Japan; United Nations formed
(1945)

This era of unrest was ushered in by the First World War, which resulted in nearly 8.5 million deaths. The ultimate cost of the conflict—which the American president Woodrow Wilson had called the "war to make the world safe for democracy"—was not, however, immediately apparent. When the war ended in 1918, most people believed President Wilson's idealistic pronouncements, and attempts were made to organize a workable League of Nations and World Court. Unfortunately, a policy of isolationism—that is, determination to stay out of foreign affairs—prevented the United States from becoming a member of the League, and thus the organization could never become a viable international force. Furthermore, because of fervent nationalism, many countries refused to give the League of Nations any real power.

Unrest in Europe also contributed to the Russian Revolution, which began in 1917 and led to the establishment of the Soviet government. Before it took control, the new communist regime had to fight a costly civil war.

Throughout Europe and America, economic problems developed. In the 1920s, rampant inflation was followed by a depression—another cost of the previous political turmoil. The economies of many nations were destroyed, and monetary systems were devalued. A famous photograph of the period shows a German citizen pushing a wheelbarrow full of paper money to buy a loaf of bread.

Many historians believe that this political and economic unrest set the stage for the rise of totalitarianism in Europe. Totalitarianism is a form of government under which the individual is totally subservient to the state; most totalitarian states are controlled by dictators. Between the world wars, there were fascist totalitarian dictatorships in Italy and Germany, nationalist dictatorships in several other countries, and a communist totalitarian dictatorship in the Soviet Union. The fascists believed in dictatorial government and forcible suppression of opposition; they argued that nation and race were more important than the individual and established extreme economic and social regimentation. The leading fascist dictators were Adolf Hitler, whose Nazis dominated Germany beginning in 1933; Benito Mussolini, who took control of Italy in 1922; and Francisco Franco, who ruled Spain from 1939 until his death in 1975.

The extremes of fascism were horribly illustrated in Nazi Germany, known as the Third Reich. Political opposition and individual liberties were totally suppressed, and dissenters were imprisoned in concentration camps. The Nazis also imprisoned Jews, Gypsies, homosexuals, and pacifist Jehovah's Witnesses. The "Aryan race"—an unscientific concept grouping non-Jewish, Nordic Europeans—was exalted, and "non-Aryans" were persecuted as racially inferior.

Hitler used nationalistic arguments as a pretext for the takeover of Austria and the dismemberment of Czechoslovakia; his invasion of Poland on September 1, 1939, began World War II. During the war, the Nazis turned some of their concentration camps, such as Auschwitz in Poland, into extermination centers. All together, the Third Reich murdered 6 million Jews and 1 million Gypsies.

Similar atrocities took place in the other fascist regimes, and in the Soviet Union under the communist dictatorship of Josef Stalin, who was in power from 1928 until his death in 1951. Stalin suppressed individual freedom and imprisoned his political opponents, dispatching several million people to slave-labor camps in Siberia—the infamous Gulag Archipelago—where many of them died. (As we saw in Chapter 12, one of Stalin's victims was the director Vsevolod Meyerhold, who was executed in a prison camp.)

In 1940, the prime minister of Japan, General Hideki Tojo, allied himself with the fascist dictators in Europe. A Japanese attack on Pearl Harbor on December 7, 1941, brought the United States into World War II, which was then fought in the Pacific as well as in Europe.

Given the nationalistic fervor of the totalitarian dictators, the chaotic economic situation, and the widespread political instability, many historians believe that the Second World War was inevitable. It lasted 6 years and was even more horrible than any of its predecessors: over 35 million people died. The Nazi concentration camps became mechanized death factories, where innocent victims of anti-Semitism and of the war were exterminated. The atomic bomb, which finally ended the war, proved that humanity was now capable of annihilating itself.

World War II has confronted us with unanswerable questions: How could civilized, rational societies wreak such irrational destruction? Were individuals responsible for societal actions? How could genocide be explained?

A THEATER OF UNREST: DRAMATIC MOVEMENTS

Not surprisingly, the years from 1915 to 1945 were also turbulent ones for theater. During the era of the world wars, theater mirrored the general unrest, and many of the theatrical movements we will examine were defined by their relationship to emerging political, social, or economic ideologies.

Some innovators were reacting to popular commercial theater as well as to the tumultuous world situation. Artists who rebelled against commercial theater—particularly in France, Great Britain, and the United States—did not equate artistic accomplishment with financial success. As the cost of productions increased because of inflation, depression, unionization, and other factors, innovative artists searched for noncommercial outlets.

Many theatrical innovators between the wars also rebelled against realism. Realism had by then become the most popular form of theater, but for a number of avant-garde artists and theorists, it seemed too simplistic and too limited. Several antirealist practitioners discussed in Chapter 12, like the Russians Meyerhold and Tairov, continued to be productive; and the eclectics —people like Vakhtangov in Russia and Reinhardt in Germany, who worked in more than one form of theater—introduced new antirealistic production techniques. In the early years of the twentieth century, many new antirealistic movements developed in continental Europe: they included expressionism, futurism, dada, and surrealism. Several of them began primarily as movements in the visual arts and subsequently became important in avant-garde theater.

Still, most of the movements and artists we will consider were reacting to the chaotic world scene. Some movements, such as expressionism and epic theater, supported socialism. Others, such as futurism, supported fascism. Many playwrights—including Ernst Toller, Stanisław Ignacy Witkiewicz, Karel Čapek (Czechoslovakia, 1890–1938), Jean Giraudoux, and Bertolt Brecht—dealt with specific political concerns.

Expressionism

The term *expressionism* was first used in France just after the turn of the century to describe a style of painting. Expressionism developed in Germany around 1905 as a movement in art and literature in which the representation of reality is distorted to communicate inner feelings. In a painting of a man, for example, the lines in his face might be twisted to indicate his inner turmoil.

EXPRESSIONIST DRAMA

Expressionism in drama was a first cousin to symbolism (which we discussed in Chapter 12), and it had well-defined characteristics. Expressionist plays are often highly subjective: the dramatic action is seen through the eyes of the protagonist and therefore frequently seems distorted or dreamlike. Expressionist drama is often opposed to society and the family. The protagonist in a typical expressionist play journeys through a series of incidents that are often not causally related. These dramas are therefore said to be structured as *station plays*, a term that refers to the stations of the cross and thus emphasizes parallels between the protagonist and Christ. The characters are representative types who are often given titles (such as Man, Woman, or Clerk) rather than names. The language is telegraphic, with most speeches consisting of one or two lines, though these sections of short speeches alternate with long lyrical passages. Many of the expressionist playwrights were politically motivated, supporting socialist and pacifist causes, though some were apolitical.

One of the first German expressionist playwrights was Walter Hasenclever (1890–1940). Hasenclever's play *The Son* (1914) depicts an angry young man who threatens to kill his father, feeling that his parents' rigidly restrictive, hypocritical attitude has inhibited his own ability to experience life to the fullest. During World War I, expressionistic writers began to move from such highly personal issues to a concern with social oppression. For example, Hasenclever's *Antigone* (1916)—written 2 years after *The Son*—put forward the idea that love offers the only way to achieve happiness but cannot flourish until immoral, authoritarian rulers are deposed. World War I presented a stark example of evils abroad in the modern world—evils which the expressionists and other serious dramatists had been proclaiming.

Two other German expressionists were Georg Kaiser (1878–1945) and Ernst Toller (1893–1939). Kaiser's *From Morn to Midnight* (1916) is a typical

EXPRESSIONISM IN THEATER. One major departure from realism in the years between the world wars was expressionism. The expressionists presented dramatic action as seen through the eyes of the protagonist, and thus it is often distorted or dreamlike. Among the significant expressionist playwrights was the German Ernst Toller. Shown here is a scene from a New York production of Toller's *Man and the Masses* in the 1920s.

expressionist play: in a single day, an Everyman character moves through a series of episodes, seeking the meaning of life but finding only cruelty and greed; he ends as a defeated martyr. In a trilogy of plays by Kaiser—*The Coral* (1917), *Gas I* (1918), and *Gas II* (1920)—the main characters, successive generations of a wealthy industrialist family, move from optimism to pessimism. *Gas II* concludes with a cataclysmic showdown between the forces of capitalism and socialism.

Toller also depicted the descent from optimism to disillusionment. His play *Transfiguration* (1918) has a protagonist who begins as an innocent, patriotic soldier and ends as a militant antiwar activist. Toller's most important work, *Man and the Masses* (1921), is noteworthy—among other reasons—because its main character is a woman. Toller's heroine struggles to aid oppressed workers but is caught in the crossfire between those who uphold humanitarian ideals and zealous ideologues who believe that any means, including violence, is justified in attaining the workers' aims. Again, *Man and the Masses* ends on a note of despair.

EXPRESSIONISTIC DIRECTORS

Several directors developed expressionistic production techniques. Jurgen Fehling (1885–1968), for example, directed *Man and the Masses* at Berlin's Volksbühne Theater, using devices that underscored the play's expressionistic style: for a scene in a stock exchange, the furniture was extremely exaggerated and distorted; for an episode in a prison, the protagonist was in a small, cramped birdcage.

Another expressionist director, Leopold Jessner (1878–1945), worked on both classic and contemporary plays. He became well-known for using platforms and flights of stairs, and for changing the lighting and costumes to reflect emotions. In his version of Shakespeare's *Richard III,* for instance, he used blood-red costumes for the scene of Richard's coronation and white costumes for the army of Richard's opponent Richmond, and Richard dies under an intense red spotlight.

In its pure form, expressionism was short-lived, lasting only about 15 years. Many expressionistic techniques, however, found their way into later experimental and traditional theater, and today's dramatists still use nonrealistic devices that can be called expressionistic.

Futurism and Dada

Two other nonrealistic movements that emerged around the time of World War I, futurism and dada, had less impact on theater than expressionism. Later, however, the aesthetic principles of these movements influenced avant-garde theater artists in the 1960s.

Futurism originated in Italy in 1909; its leading exponent was Filippo Marinetti (1876–1944). The futurists, unlike the expressionists, idealized war and the developing machine age. In the first decade of the twentieth century, Italy was the least industrialized nation in western Europe, and this may explain the futurists' fascination with machinery and war. The futurists attacked artistic ideals of the past, ridiculing "museum art" and arguing that new forms had to be created for this new era. They advocated a "synthetic" theater of short, seemingly illogical dramatic pieces: one example is Marinetti's *They're Coming* (1915), in which actors playing servants do little more than rearrange furniture onstage. They also believed that audiences should be confronted and antagonized, and they argued against the separation of performers and audience. The futurists also wanted to incorporate new electronic media, puppetry, and visual arts into theater.

Dada, which originated in Switzerland in 1916 with a series of manifestos written by Tristan Tzara (1896–1963), was a short-lived movement that never really caught on, though (like futurism) it did influence other, later avant-garde movements. Dada was a reaction to the insanity of World War I, and its proponents argued that it mirrored the madness of the world. Like the futurists, the dadaists railed against traditional "museum" art and tried to confuse and antagonize their audiences. Unlike the futurists, however, the dadaists did not glorify war—on the contrary, they were pacifists. They concentrated on nonsense and the irrational and questioned conventional definitions of art, suggesting that almost anything could be art. Along with other types of radical artistic expression, they presented short plays that defied rational explanation —attempting to reflect in this way the irrationality of the world they saw around them.

Both futurism and dada emphasized a mixture of arts and used techniques of popular entertainment; in this, they foreshadowed today's performance art (discussed in Chapter 15).

Surrealism

In 1924, *surrealism* developed out of the dada movement. The major exponent of surrealism was the French writer André Breton (1896–1966), but the term itself had been used earlier: in 1917, the French playwright Guillaume Apollinaire (1880–1918) described his play *The Breasts of Tiresias* and the ballet *Parade* as surrealistic. The surrealists argued that the subconscious was the highest plane of reality and attempted to recreate its workings dramatically. Many of their plays seem to be set in a dream world, mixing recognizable events with fantastic happenings.

France was the center of surrealism, and one French playwright influenced by surrealism was Jean Cocteau (1889–1963), who worked on the ballet *Parade*. Cocteau's best plays—*Antigone* (1922), *Orpheus* (1926), and *The Infernal Machine* (1934), a reworking of the Oedipus story—were based on Greek myths and contrasted modern ideas with these traditional stories.

The surrealist movement also had an international impact. Stanisław Ignacy Witkiewicz (1885–1935), for example, was a noted Polish surrealist; his dramas include *The Water Hen* (1921), *Gyubal Wahazar* (1921), and *The Cuttlefish* (1922).

Theater of Cruelty

Antonin Artaud, who had originally been associated with the surrealists, theorized about *theater of cruelty* in a series of essays and manifestos written in the 1930s. He believed that western theater needed to be totally transformed, that its literary tradition—which emphasized language—was antithetical to its ritualistic origins, and that western theater artists should study the stylized Asian theaters. Renouncing literary tradition, Artaud asserted that there were "no more masterpieces." By this he meant that classics should be produced not for the sake of their historical significance but only if they were still relevant to contemporary audiences. Furthermore, he did not believe that the text was sacred; he felt that a script could and should be reworked in order to point up its relevance.

If theater, for Artaud, was not a literary event, it was a sensory experience. His emphasis on the sensory is what characterizes theater of cruelty. Artaud did not use the term *cruelty* to mean that theater artists should literally assault or maul their audiences—although some avant-garde theater artists in the 1960s did think of cruelty as actual physical confrontation with spectators. Rather, he meant that the viewers' *senses* should be bombarded. Today's multimedia presentations are designed to create such sensory involvement.

Artaud, like many of the antirealists who preceded him, called for a restructuring of the theatrical event. He wanted, for example, to reorganize the theater space to make the audience the center of attention. He argued that productions could be staged in "found spaces"—spaces such as warehouses or airplane hangars that had not originally been intended for theater. He also attacked Stanislavski's acting technique, arguing instead for stylized, ritualized performances.

Artaud believed that humanity's natural inclination toward violence and aggression—manifested in Europe in the mid-1930s by the rise of fascism and Stalinism—could be purged in theater of cruelty. For Artaud, theater could act (as he put it) like a "plague," cleansing modern society of all that was ugly.

Artaud was the most radical and innovative theorist in France during this period. Like the designers Adolphe Appia and Edward Gordon Craig (discussed in Chapter 12), he had few opportunities during his lifetime to put his theories into practice, but his ideas were extremely influential in the decades that followed. Artaud's own life reflected much of the anguish and pain his theories dealt with.

(Roget-Viollet)

Antonin Artaud

(1896–1948)

Antonin Artaud was born in Marseilles, France. He went to Paris in 1920 and became an actor, working with several important directors: Lugné-Poë, Charles Dullin, George Pitoëff, and Louis Jouvet. He also acted in films, where his most notable role was the monk in Carl Dreyer's *The Passion of Joan of Arc*. For Dullin, he directed and designed Calderón's *Life Is a Dream*. Some of his poems were also published.

From 1924 to 1926, Artaud was heavily involved with the surrealist movement in theater and wrote the play *Spurt of Blood* (1924). Later, however, because of his interest in the occult, Asian religions, and mysticism, he was expelled from the movement by its leader, André Breton. Artaud, who suffered from physical as well as mental disorders all his life, also experimented with drugs, chiefly morphine. In 1926, together with Roger Vitrac and Robert Aran,

Artaud founded the Théâtre Alfred Jarry, which produced four programs between 1927 and 1929, including Strindberg's *A Dream Play*.

Artaud was greatly influenced by a Balinese dance group he saw in Paris in 1931; he was impressed by their use of song, dance, and pantomime in a physical, nonverbal form. Artaud went to Mexico in 1936 to search for an authentic primitive culture. He lived among the Tarahumara Indians and experimented with peyote. Convinced that unidentified forces were seeking to destroy him, he returned to France the following year and spent the next 9 years in mental institutions. He was released in 1945, through the efforts of his theatrical associates, but died of cancer 2 years later.

Most of Artaud's books and theories were written in the 1930s. Though overlooked in his time, they became a major influence on the experimental theater of the 1960s. Jerzy Grotowski, Peter Brook, and the Living Theater were, in part, inspired by Artaud's theater of cruelty.

Epic Theater

Germany was the birthplace not only of expressionism but also of *epic theater*. Though epic theater is often associated with Bertolt Brecht, who appropriated the term in his writings, the director Erwin Piscator (1893–1966) could more justifiably claim to have originated the concept.

PISCATOR AND THE GOOD SOLDIER SCHWEIK

Piscator was greatly influenced by the communist revolution in Russia and wanted to develop what he called "proletarian theater." After working in other theaters in the early 1920s, Piscator became director of the Volksbühne Theater in Berlin from 1924 to 1927. In his productions there, and in later productions, he introduced a number of elements that would become hallmarks of epic theater.

Piscator's epic theater was first and foremost political and was meant to instigate social change. To underline his political concerns, Piscator often used documentary materials—that is, dramatizations of or interpolations from current events—and he believed that a director could make whatever changes seemed necessary in a text. His productions had heightened theatrical and staging effects, such as multimedia. He also explored ways of changing the traditional actor-audience relationship, and the architect Walter Gropius (1883–1969) designed a playhouse for him which could change from proscenium to thrust to arena, though it was never actually built. (Gropius was a cofounder, in 1919, of the Dessau Bauhaus, a school of fine arts which experimented with performance techniques, the interrelationship of visual and performance arts, and the incorporation of art into everyday life; the Bauhaus lasted until 1932.)

Piscator's most famous production was probably *The Good Soldier Schweik* (1928), a dramatic adaptation of a novel by the Czechoslovakian writer Jaroslav Hasek in which a lowly soldier in World War I, Schweik, continually exposes the foolishness and cruelty of people in authority—often unintentionally. Piscator used a conveyer belt (reminiscent of an impersonal, mechanized factory) on which the "antihero" Schweik walked through the many phases of his life. The production also included film sequences, caricatures, marionettes, and other theatrical devices. He described the play as *epic* because of its epic sweep, because Schweik's journey is a kind of modern epic, and because the audience—like people reading an epic—saw many dimensions of Schweik's saga.

BRECHT'S EPIC THEATER

Bertolt Brecht is one of the few dramatists who are as well-known for their theories as for their plays. Brecht's theories—most of which were formulated in the 1930s but were frequently revised—have influenced many later playwrights and directors. Brecht had worked with Piscator during the 1920s and used many of Piscator's techniques in his own plays. Because Brecht was also a dramatist, however, his epic theater was more text-centered that Piscator's.

Developing his own form of epic theater, Brecht wrote plays that are episodic in structure. They usually deal with history or foreign lands, cover a long time, shift locale frequently, have intricate plots, and include many characters. The goal of epic theater, according to Brecht, is to instruct. An ardent socialist, he believed that theater could create an intellectual climate for social change. In the early 1930s he wrote short dramas he called *Lehrstücke*—"learning pieces"—and he attacked theatrical works created purely for mass consumption and entertainment, referring to them as "culinary art."

Brecht felt that if theater was to succeed at teaching, the audience should be involved not emotionally but intellectually. (Here too he differed from Piscator, who believed in emotional engagement.) He argued that a production should actually force the audience to remain emotionally detached—or "alienated," as he put it—from the dramatic action. (The German term he used, *Verfremdung,* literally means "alienation" or "distancing.") To achieve this effect, he held, epic theater had to abandon Wagner's goal of a *Gesamtkunstwerk,* a unified work of art. Instead, each production element should independently convey the political message.

To lessen emotional involvement, Brecht's works are highly theatrical. Narrators are frequently used to comment on the dramatic action, and audiences are always made aware that they are in a theater. Lighting instruments, for example, are not hidden but are clearly visible to the audience, and multimedia are often used. Brecht also warned actors against Stanislavski's techniques; he believed that the audience should be aware of watching an actor play a character.

THE CAUCASIAN CHALK CIRCLE. Since Brecht believed that theater should be highly theatrical, he was greatly influenced by Asian theater, and *The Caucasian Chalk Circle* is based on a Chinese play. Brecht used the Chinese drama to create a modern play which attacked capitalism. Here is a scene from a production at the Berliner Ensemble, the theater Brecht founded after World War II.

To alienate or distance the audience, Brecht also used a technique he called "historification." Though many of his plays, such as *Galileo* (1938–1939), are set in the past, it is apparent that he is really concerned with contemporary issues paralleling the historic ones. Placing the events of the play in the past is simply a way of distancing the audience from the dramatic action. Similarly, Brecht often set his plays in fictitious foreign lands.

Brecht used many other epic techniques in his plays and productions. As another way of preventing the audience from becoming too involved in the dramatic action, scenes in his plays sometimes have opening titles which indicate what is to happen. The songs, rather than revealing more about plot or character, usually underline the political message.

Brecht's life was as dramatic as many of his plays and was greatly affected by the political unrest of his time.

Bertolt Brecht

(1898–1956)

Bertolt Brecht, who was educated in his native Bavaria, was bored by regular schooling but loved to write. While still in high school, he began to write both prose and poetry, and his work from these years shows remarkable talent. When he graduated from high school in 1917, he began to study medicine in Munich, but he was drafted as an orderly in 1918.

Brecht's father offered to publish his first play, *Baal* (1918), but only if the Brecht family name was not mentioned—a condition the playwright refused. In 1920, he moved to Munich, where he began to write plays which were produced. It was at this time, too, that Brecht married his first wife, Marianne, and had his fiirst child, Hanne. In 1922, Brecht's *Drums in the Night* was awarded the Kleist Prize, one of Germany's highest literary honors. Both of these early plays were expressionistic. Shortly thereafter, he wrote *Jungles of the Cities* (1923) and *Edward II* (1924).

Brecht settled in Berlin in 1924, where he worked for a time with the directors Max Reinhardt and Erwin Piscator, but mostly with smaller experimental groups. One of Brecht's friends was the composer Kurt Weill (1900–1950), with whom he wrote *The Threepenny Opera,* the modern version of *The Beggar's Opera* described at the beginning of the chapter. While he was in Berlin, he became a Marxist and at this same time began to develop his theories of theater: his concepts of epic drama and alienation. Forced by the Nazis to flee Germany in 1933, he lived in Denmark, Sweden, and the United States, where he did some filmwriting in Hollywood.

During his years in exile, Brecht had time to refine his ideas on epic theater and wrote several important plays, including *Mother Courage and Her Children* (1938), *Galileo* (1938–1939), *The Good Person of Setzuan* (1938–1940), *The Resistible Rise of Arturo Ui* (1941), and *The Caucasian Chalk Circle* (1944–1945). In 1947, Brecht was called before the House Committee on Un-American Activities because of his leftist ideas, and he left the United States shortly thereafter.

He settled in East Berlin, where the government gave him his own theater, the Berliner Ensemble, which opened in 1949 with *Mother Courage.* For the next 7 years, he and his wife, the actress Helene Weigel (1900–1971), worked to develop epic theater. When Brecht died in 1956, his wife took over the company, which had developed into one of the foremost acting troupes in the world; it continues to produce today.

MOTHER COURAGE AND HER CHILDREN

The play with which Brecht opened the Berliner Ensemble, *Mother Courage and Her Children,* is probably his most famous work, and it reflects many of his ideas about epic theater.

Mother Courage is set in Europe between 1624 and 1636, during the Thirty Years' War. An episodic play, consisting of twelve scenes with many shifts in locale, it chronicles the losses of Anna Fierling, known as Mother Courage, who operates a traveling canteen from which she sells supplies to soldiers. During the course of the action—sometimes because of her own greed and opportunism—Mother Courage loses her two sons and her deaf-mute daughter.

Mother Courage teaches a political lesson. "Courage" is an ironic name for the protagonist. As is noted by Eric Bentley, a leading critic and translator of Brecht,

> Valor is conspicuously absent at those times when Mother Courage however unwittingly seals the fate of her children. At moments when, in heroic melodrama, the protagonist would be riding to the rescue, come hell or high water, Mother Courage is in the back room concluding a little deal.[1]

Ultimately, Brecht shows a protagonist and a war which are both created and controlled by the profit motive, and he is arguing for a change in the capitalist economic system.

Many techniques of epic theater are used in *Mother Courage and Her Children.* One, obviously, is historification. Though the play is set during the Thirty Years' War—which has been described as a seventeenth-century world war—contemporary parallels can be drawn: the play was written in 1938 and revised by Brecht in the early 1940s, and its premiere took place in 1941; the reverberations of World War II are apparent.

Another epic technique is Brecht's use of titles preceding each scene, revealing the coming action and forcing the audience to think about its political and economic implications. Scene 1, for example, opens with a title that reads: "Spring 1624. In Dalarna, the Swedish Commander Oxenstierna is recruiting for the campaign in Poland. The canteen woman Anna Fierling, commonly known as Mother Courage, loses a son."[2] There are a number of songs which comment on the thematic implications of the dramatic action. The most famous is "The Song of the Great Capitulation," in Scene 4, which describes a person who begins life with high ideals but quickly learns to compromise. The representative nature of Brecht's characters is also clear, since they are frequently referred to by titles rather than names (e.g., Chaplain, Cook, Recruiting Officer.)

[1]Bertolt Brecht, *Mother Courage and Her Children,* Eric Bentley (trans.), Grove, New York, 1966, p. 10. Reprinted by permission of Grove Press, Inc. Translated from the German by Eric Bentley. Copyright © 1955, 1959, 1961, 1963, 1966 by Eric Bentley.
[2]Ibid., p. 23.

EUROPEAN THEATER DURING THE WAR YEARS

We turn now to some other European developments in theater from 1915 to 1945, on the continent and in England. We will also note briefly what became of theater under the totalitarian regimes.

France

COPEAU AND TEXT-ORIENTED THEATER

Text-oriented theater in France was served after World War I by Jacques Copeau, who insisted on high standards in production and whose theoretical concepts were to influence a generation of French theater directors.

Jacques Copeau
(1879–1949)

Working as a theater critic in Paris in the early years of the twentieth century, Jacques Copeau became convinced that drama as an art had reached a low point, and that the time had come for new, practical research into European theatrical methods. While he applauded French directors such as André Antoine for bringing the works of Ibsen, Hauptmann, and others of the new "naturalist" school to the attention of the public, Copeau felt that naturalism denied the "essential theatricality" of theater. He was appalled by the growing reliance on stage "tricks" like moving walls and excessively detailed and realistic sets, and he argued that theater ought to focus on the play rather than on its trappings.

With this end in mind, Copeau, at the age of 34, founded a new theater company, the Théâtre du Vieux Colombier. The new company made a somewhat hesitant start but soon had a tremendous success with Copeau's production of Shakespeare's *Twelfth Night*.

The outbreak of the First World War closed Copeau's theater, Copeau joined the army, and the company dispersed. However, Copeau was discharged from military service in 1915 because of injuries and then spent his time preparing for the rebirth of the Vieux Colombier. He studied constantly, corresponded with members of the company who were at the front, and managed to visit Edward Gordon Craig in Italy and Adolphe Appia in Switzerland. Georges Clemenceau, the head of the French government, had been a great fan of the Vieux Colombier in its first season, and it may have been his influence that allowed Copeau to take a company to New York in 1917. The company mounted two seasons of performances there, and Copeau gave many lectures on his theories of drama which influenced postwar American theater.

Copeau focused on training the actor. His contributions to modern training include emphasis on the text, improvisation as a tool for exploring a text, drama games, ensemble acting, mask work, and theater as communion. He rejected the naturalists' idea of theater as presenting a scientifically objective view of the world, and he sought ways to break down the barrier between audience and actor. He designed his theater as a bare stage with no proscenium arch, and he used simple screens and lighting effects to establish locale.

In his later years, Copeau distanced himself from the company he had founded and left Paris for nearly 15 years before returning to head the Comédie Française from 1939 until he was forced to leave during World War II.

As was true of many of his contemporaries, some of Copeau's fondest aspirations for a new theater were never realized. His greatest contribution to modern drama may be his belief that theater is an ongoing process rather than a finished work. Two important directors influenced by Copeau were Louis Jouvet (1887–1915) and Charles Dullin (1885–1949). He also influenced his nephew Michel Saint-Denis (1897–1971), who worked with leading companies and theater schools in France, Great Britain, and the United States.

GIRAUDOUX AND ANOUILH

Two significant French playwrights of the period between World War I and World War II were Jean Giraudoux (1882–1944) and Jean Anouilh (1910–1987). Giraudoux, whose plays were frequently directed by Jouvet, believed in the primacy of the word, and his language was usually eloquent as well as witty. He also stressed contradictions, ironies, and antitheses in working out the themes of his plays. Among his better-known works are *Amphitryon 38* (1929), *Judith* (1931), *The Trojan War Will Not Take Place* (1935), and *Ondine* (1939). As can be seen from their titles, many of his plays were based on classic themes or plots. Jean Anouilh also used a classic source for his best-known play, *Antigone* (1943), a reworking of the Greek classic which spoke to the situation in Nazi-occupied France.

Spain

In 1913, one of Spain's most esteemed philosophers, Miguel de Unamuno (1864–1936), wrote a treatise about theater—*The Tragic Sense of Life*—which was to have considerable influence, especially on the existential playwrights who emerged just after World War II. In this work, Unamuno juxtaposes the human desire for immortality and the serious doubt that it can be achieved. From the conflict of these two notions arises tragedy.

Because of the political climate in Spain, Unamuno's plays—such as *Fedra* (1917) and *Dream Shadows* (1931)—were given few productions before the end of World War II. The same was true of the plays of another Spanish dramatist, Ramón del Valle-Inclán (1866–1936). Inclán's works had grotesque elements, and he sometimes used devices such as puppets.

Perhaps the most significant Spanish dramatist of this period was Federico García Lorca, a poet as well as a playwright. García Lorcas's plays, in language of exquisite lyricism, dealt with the unfortunate effects of the strictures of Spanish society, and with the dark side of the Spanish character.

Federico García Lorca

(1898–1936)

Spain's best-known modern poet and playwright, Federico García Lorca, was killed in the Spanish civil war. His death at the hands of the fascists ended a productive career but enhanced his reputation. His plays, banned in Spain until the death of Franco in 1975, were seen as protests against the oppression of the Spanish people.

Born into a wealthy family, García Lorca was presenting elaborate theatricals at home by the age of 8. When he was 16, his family moved to Granada, and he began to study philosophy, literature, and law at the university there. His first book of prose was published in 1918.

Later, García Lorca studied in Madrid, where his first play, *The Butterfly's Crime,* was produced in 1920. Three books of poems followed, along with other plays—*Mariana Pineda* (1927), based on a historical character from the nineteenth century; and *The Love of Don Perlimplin and Belisa in the Garden* (not published until 1931). In June 1929 García Lorca left Spain to spend a year in North America. His many writing projects from that year included *Poet in New York* (a collection of poems published in 1940) and the completion of his comic play *The Shoemaker's Prodigious Wife.*

On his return to Spain, García Lorca was appointed director of La Barraca, a traveling theater company—sponsored by the government and composed mainly of university students—that performed classic Spanish plays for remote, rural audiences. This inspired him to develop his own plays based on traditional Spanish stories, themes, and characters and intended for a popular audience. Of these folk plays, his most successful were a tragic trilogy: *Blood Wedding* (1933), *Yerma* (1934), and *The House of Bernarda Alba* (1936).

All three folk tragedies have strong female protagonists whose desires are thwarted by the oppressive circumstances of their lives. In *The House of Bernarda Alba* (completed shortly before Lorca's death and produced posthumously) a recently widowed woman, Bernarda Alba, determines to keep her five unmarried, grown daughters locked in her house and away from all men. Imprisoned, the daughters oppose their mother and jealously compete with each other for the chance to marry Pepe el Romano (an offstage character). The play ends tragically when the youngest daughter hangs herself. Bernarda is not moved to repent—in fact, she takes pride in the fact that her daughter died a virgin. The play is often interpreted as a criticism of the self-destructive course of Spain under Franco in oppressing its own people.

THE HOUSE OF BERNARDA ALBA.   García Lorca, a Spanish playwright and poet, wrote about repression in Spain and opposed the political party later headed by Franco; he was killed by Franco's supporters during the Spanish civil war. In *The House of Bernarda Alba,* a mother keeps her four daughters completely under her domination. Her youngest daughter opposes her and ends by committing suicide. Shown here is a scene from a production by Repertorio Español.

Italy

In Italy, by far the most original dramatist between the two world wars was Luigi Pirandello. Pirandello's plays often questioned the relationship between appearance and reality, and they used highly theatrical devices. In an unusually imaginative way, Pirandello broke the bounds of traditional dramatic construction to call attention to the work itself. In his *Six Characters in Search of an Author* (1921), for instance, six fictional characters, created and then abandoned by a writer, appear at the rehearsal of a play and demand that their story be presented. The juxtaposition of real actors and imaginary characters gives rise to many philosophical and aesthetic issues, including appearance versus reality, the relativity of truth, and the role of fiction.

Pirandello's life and career, like his plays, reflected theoretical, social, and political upheavals in Italy and Europe.

Luigi Pirandello

(1867–1936)

The Italian dramatist Luigi Pirandello experimented boldly with theatrical techniques to dramatize ideas that fascinated him. "My art is full of bitter compassion for all those who deceive themselves," he wrote, "but this compassion cannot fail to be followed by the ferocious decision of destiny which condemns man to deception." Deception, illusion, and the subjectivity of truth were concepts Pirandello explored in his plays, novels, and short stories.

As the son of a sulfur merchant, Pirandello received private tutoring at home in Agrigento, Sicily, before attending universities in Palermo, Rome, and Bonn. He received his doctorate in Bonn in 1888. His father had wanted him to become a businessman, but Pirandello chose literature as a career and by 1893, when he was 26, he had settled in Rome. He was married the following year to a woman he barely knew—an arranged marriage to unite two families of sulfur merchants. When the sulfur mines were flooded in 1904, the family fortune was lost, and his wife became mentally ill for the rest of her life. This economic and personal disaster forced Pirandello to supplement his earnings from writing by teaching at a girls' school.

By the beginning of World War I, Pirandello had become a respected novelist and short-story writer but had done little playwriting. After the success of his play *Right You Are If You Think You Are* in 1916, he began to concentrate on

LUIGI PIRANDELLO. A significant dramatist just before and after World War I, Pirandello combined intellectual probing with dramatic form in a way that has rarely been equalled. He raised intriguing questions about the differences between appearance and reality and about truth in relation to art.

drama. In *Right You Are,* as in his other famous plays—*Six Characters in Search of an Author* (1921) and *Henry IV* (1922)—Pirandello explores illusion versus reality, truth versus fiction, and madness versus sanity.

Pirandello ran his own theater, the Teatro d'Arte, from 1925 to 1928, touring its productions in Europe and America. In 1924 he had joined the fascist party, possibly partly because theater needed state subsidies. But it is also true that Pirandello's political views were conservative, and he often praised Mussolini in his newspaper articles; he even donated his Nobel Prize for literature (which he won in 1934) to the Italian government during its invasion of Ethiopia.

Pirandello's private life was brightened by his love for Marta Alba (1906–1988), the leading actress in the Teatro d'Arte, to whom he willed nine of his plays. He died in Rome in 1936, requesting that his death be ignored and his body burned.

Great Britain

British theater between the world wars was, unlike much of the theater on the continent, highly commercial. However, in reaction to this growing commercialization, some small, independent theaters arose. There were also individual actors and directors, most of them renowned for their work with Shakespeare, whose focus was on the artistic rather than the business side of theater.

Britain's most noteworthy directors during this era were Harley Granville Barker (1877–1946) and Tyrone Guthrie (1901–1971). Granville Barker, who was also a playwright and critic, is best remembered for his approach to staging Shakespeare. He focused on remaining faithful to the spirit of the plays and making their poetry come alive. He considered acting the central element in his productions, and so his settings were simple and suggestive and his costumes not lavishly detailed.

Tyrone Guthrie is remembered in North America for founding two theaters: the Stratford Theatre in Ontario, Canada, in 1953; and the Guthrie Theater in Minneapolis in 1963. However, he had made his reputation at the Old Vic in London between the wars. The Old Vic was the home of Shakespearean productions, and Guthrie broke with traditional staging by interpreting classic dramas imaginatively and developing unique production concepts. He often presented Shakespeare in modern dress. Guthrie's influence is still felt by directors who attempt to direct Shakespeare's works in ways that will make them more accessible to today's audiences. Many of the productions staged for the summer Shakespeare festival in New York's Central Park—such as the musical version of *Two Gentlemen of Verona* and A. J. Antoon's *Much Ado about Nothing,* with its use of Mack Sennett's comic silent-film techniques—are descendants of Guthrie's experiments.

Only a few of the British playwrights who were considered significant during this era continue to be admired. Noël Coward (1899–1973), in such witty works as *Private Lives* (1930) and *Blithe Spirit* (1941), continued the tradition

(AP/Wide World Photo) *(AP/Wide World Photo)*

EDITH EVANS. *Above left:* One of England's leading actresses of the twentieth century, Edith Evans was noted for her roles in Shakespearean drama, Restoration and eighteenth-century comedies, and the works of Wilde, Shaw, and Chekhov. Her most renowned performance was as Lady Bracknell in Wilde's *The Importance of Being Earnest.*

PEGGY ASHCROFT. *Right:* One of the most versatile English actresses was Peggy Ashcroft, who performed in plays by authors as diverse as Shakespeare, Sheridan, Ibsen, Shaw, Brecht, Beckett, and Pinter. She costarred with many of England's leading actors, including Michael Redgrave and John Gielgud.

of comedy of manners, satirizing the social pretensions of theater people and the English upper class. The poet T. S. Eliot (1888–1965)—an American by birth who spent most of his life in England—attempted to revive verse drama in such works as *Murder in the Cathedral* (1935) and *The Family Reunion* (1939). While British drama between the wars was less avant-garde than continental drama, British experimentation with traditional forms and classic plays foreshadowed similar undertakings in the decades that followed.

British theater between the wars introduced many stars who developed international reputations. Most were noted for their Shakespearean work, but they were amazingly versatile; many of them, for example, also had successful careers in film. Their technique is often contrasted with that of American realistic performers. Among the most important are Edith Evans (1888–1976), Peggy Ashcroft (1907–1993), Michael Redgrave (1908–1985), Alec Guinness (1914–), Laurence Olivier, Ralph Richardson, and John Gielgud.

Laurence Olivier (1907–1989)

Ralph Richardson (1902–1983)

John Gielgud (1904–)

Considered by many to be the greatest English-speaking actor of recent times, Laurence Olivier was equally acclaimed in Shakespearean and modern roles. A handsome man, able to effect dramatic changes in his appearance, Olivier had tremendous range as an actor, from deep passion to comedy. Besides his versatility, he was noted for his intelligence and discipline.

Born in 1907, Laurence Kerr Olivier first attracted attention in 1922, as Katherine in a school production of *The Taming of the Shrew*. During his first years as a professional, he was a member of the Birmingham Repertory Theater. By 1935, he was appearing at the New Theater in London, alternating the roles of Romeo and Mercutio with John Gielgud.

Olivier rose to real fame after joining the Old Vic company in 1937. His uncut production of *Hamlet* was especially notable. In 1944, Olivier became codirector of the Old Vic with Ralph Richardson; later, he was the first artistic director of Britain's National Theater. While continuing his acting career, he also made a name as a stage and film director. His film versions of *Hamlet, Henry V,* and *Richard III,* starring himself, brought Shakespeare to a wide audience. Olivier was knighted in 1947, and in 1970 he became the first actor to be made a life peer.

Laurence Olivier (left), early in his career; Ralph Richardson (center), shown in character in a role; and John Gielgud (right), a recent photo.

(The Bettmann Archive)

(Donald Cooper/Photostage)

(AP/Wide World Photo)

In 1974, ill health forced Olivier to retire from the physical demands of the stage, but he continued to appear in movie roles. He published an autobiography, *Confessions of an Actor,* in 1982; and another book, *On Acting,* in 1986. Olivier was married three times, to the actresses Jill Esmon, Vivien Leigh, and Joan Plowright.

Though Olivier may have been England's greatest twentieth-century actor, he was closely rivaled by John Gielgud and Ralph Richardson. Richardson began his career in 1921 and first became known to audiences in the United States during a tour in 1935. His ability to reveal the strong, somewhat hidden passions of rather ordinary men—especially the frightening or baffling emotions that can suddenly surface—was one of his trademarks. He was knighted in 1941.

John Gielgud—the grandnephew of Ellen Terry—made his debut at the Old Vic in 1921, achieved popular success as an actor in the 1930s, and was knighted in 1953. Especially noted for his excellent speaking voice, Gielgud also directed plays, managed theater companies—including the Queen's Theater (1937–1938) and the Haymarket (1944–1945)—and acted in many films. He continued to perform both onstage and in films into the 1980s. He has written several volumes of autobiography, including *Early Stages* and *Stage Directions.*

Theater under Totalitarianism

As might be expected, totalitarianism curtailed the development of European theater and drama. This is not to suggest, however, that theatrical activity ceased to exist under totalitarianism. In the totalitarian societies, particularly the Soviet Union under Stalin and Germany under Hitler, there were government-supported theaters, used as instruments of propaganda. There were also some daring theater artists who attempted to attack these regimes, though for the most part expression and experimentation were suppressed.

The Soviet government immediately recognized the value of theater as propaganda. After the revolution, mass spectacles—usually elaborate outdoor events with casts made up partly of amateurs—were organized. In the 1930s, the Soviet Union established "socialist realism" as the only acceptable theatrical form: plays were to be written in realistic style and were to convey a clear socialist message. In Nazi Germany, analogous theatrical forms were supported, and numerous melodramas exalting Nazism were staged. Early in Hitler's regime, mass spectacles called *Thingspielen* were presented. One example of this form was Richard Euringer's *Deutsche Passion: 1933,* which presented Hitler as a Christ figure, wearing a "crown of thorns" made of barbed wire, and gathering apostles and converts to save Germany from the evil Weimar Republic; after rescuing the fatherland, the Nazi dictator is crucified and ascends to heaven amid organ music and a chorus of angels.

Debates in Theater History:
EVALUATING TOTALITARIAN ART

How can we evaluate works created by artists who support dictatorial regimes? We have noted that there were many playwrights who wrote "socialist realism" during the Stalin era. There were also many actors, directors, and designers who served Hitler by creating theatrical propaganda. How can we assess such works aesthetically? Can anything be classified as great or even good art if it is politically horrendous? Can we distinguish between an artist's politics and the aesthetic qualities of his or her works?

One debate of this nature is over the films of Leni Riefenstahl (1902–), a German director greatly admired by Adolf Hitler. Riefenstahl's films are documentaries which are formally beautiful and were significant advances in the art of documentary filmmaking. However, her films *The Triumph of the Will* (1935) and *Olympia* (1936–1938) glorify Nazism and paint a glowing picture of Hitler's Germany in the mid-1930s. Can we divorce the aesthetic qualities of these works from their poli-

tics? How should we discuss Riefenstahl's contributions to filmmaking?

Similar questions can be asked about the theater artists who wrote and produced plays in Hitler's Germany, Mussolini's Italy, Franco's Spain, and Stalin's Soviet Union. For example, the playwright Maxim Gorki became a proponent of socialist realism. How can we evaluate his later works, in light of the terror that was inflicted on artists who resisted the aesthetic control imposed in the name of socialist realism? How can we deal with Luigi Pirandello, who was an avid supporter of fascism and Mussolini and donated his Nobel Prize to the fascist Italian government? Does Pirandello's support of a fascist regime decrease the significance of his plays? How can we reconcile his politics with his aesthetics?

Such questions do not seem difficult when an artist's work, aesthetically, is simply not very good; but they become extremely difficult when the work is aesthetically accomplished.

Obviously, theater artists who opposed totalitarian regimes were suppressed. In Spain, as we have seen, the playwright Federico García Lorca was killed by Franco's forces during the Spanish civil war, and productions of Lorca's works—which dramatized the oppression of Spanish women—were prohibited (this ban remained in effect until Franco's death in 1975).

In the Soviet Union, the works of playwrights considered politically dangerous were censored and were not allowed to be staged. About 50 years later, one of these dramas—Nikolai Erdman's *The Suicide* (1928), which presents suicide as an act of political resistance—was produced in London, Chicago, and New York. We have already noted that the director Vsevolod Meyerhold, who attempted unsuccessfully to stage *The Suicide* in 1929, was imprisoned and executed for his opposition to "socialist realism."

Numerous German theater artists, because of their religion or their politics, were forced to flee Germany after Hitler came to power in 1933. They included the directors Max Reinhardt and Erwin Piscator as well as the playwrights Bertolt Brecht and Ernst Toller. Many artists who opposed the Third Reich but did not leave Germany were interred in Nazi concentration camps.

Nonetheless, some theater artists did resist the rise of totalitarianism. During the 1940s, for example, the exiled Bertolt Brecht wrote *The Resistible Rise of Arturo Ui,* which characterized Hitler as a Chicago gangster.

Theater as a form of resistance to totalitarianism—and to the horrors of World War II—is most vividly illustrated by the theatrical activities organized by inmates of the Nazi concentration camps. In the mid-1930s, the Nazi guards at Oranienburg and Dachau forced internees to stage productions. Surviving accounts reveal that these presentations satirized the camps, yet the artists were not punished. During the war, in the concentration camps in Nazi-occupied territories such as Auschwitz, there were surreptitious, improvised entertainments in the barracks. These presentations consisted of literature and drama recited from memory, satirical skits, and traditional songs. In the camp at Theresienstadt, in Czechoslovakia, satirical plays, operas, and cabaret entertainments were written and staged. Such entertainments were possible there because the Nazis were using Theresienstadt as a "model" camp: they showed it to Red Cross officials and foreign visitors to discredit rumors of atrocities. Most of the artists at Theresienstadt were later sent to extermination centers.

AMERICAN THEATER

In the period between the two world wars, theater in the United States finally began turning to the experiments in realism and nonrealism that had started in Europe several decades earlier. This kind of experimentation still did not develop rapidly, however, because the grip of commercial theater was very strong.

Commercial Theater in the United States

At the beginning of the twentieth century, realistic production techniques had been appropriated by American commercial theater and had become so popular and so commonplace that audiences expected detailed, authentic settings for even the tritest melodrama. The turn-of-the-century American producer David Belasco was one of the popularizers of authentic settings and lighting; in a melodrama of 1912, for example, he recreated an actual restaurant onstage.

Still holding onto the past, American theater between the world wars remained probably the most commercially oriented in the world. The Theatrical Syndicate, a group of business people who had controlled theater in the United States, was toppled in 1915 by Lee Shubert (1875–1954) and his brother Jacob J. Shubert (1880–1963); but the Shuberts developed their own monopoly, owning or controlling almost 75 percent of all theater buildings in the country. The Shubert heirs, now organized as a foundation, still control 50 percent of the Broadway theaters in New York.

Possibly the most commercially successful form of this period was the musical. In the 1920s and 1930s, *revues*—productions consisting of dramatic sketches and musical numbers—were extremely popular. The Broadway producer Florenz Ziegfeld (1869–1932) made his reputation with annual productions of the spectacular *Ziegfeld Follies*. More important, the modern American musical comedy was born during this era. In the 1920s and 1930s, a generation of composers and lyricists created for Broadway musicals songs that are still performed around the world. Outstanding composers included Jerome Kern (1885–1945), Irving Berlin (1888–1989), George Gershwin (1898–1937), Cole Porter (1893–1964), and Richard Rodgers (1902–1979). Among the important lyricists were Ira Gershwin (1896–1983), who teamed up with his brother George; and Lorenz Hart (1895–1943), who collaborated with Richard Rodgers.

The stories of musical comedies were usually inconsequential. However, beginning with *Showboat* (1928)—by Oscar Hammerstein II (1895–1960) and Jerome Kern—music, song, and dance were more carefully integrated with plot and character development. *Oklahoma!* (1943)—by Richard Rodgers and Oscar Hammerstein, with choreography by Agnes DeMille (1905–1993)—is often considered a landmark in this integration of story, songs, and dance.

Despite its successes, American commercial theater was facing troubles. Economic unrest in the 1920s, as well as higher production costs, decreased the number of commercial shows produced annually. Another factor hurting commercial theater was the growing popularity of movies, especially after the introduction of sound in 1929.

Serious American Drama

Commercial theater held sway in the United States through the 1920s and 1930s, but beginning at the time of World War I, playwrights, actors, directors, and producers began to develop the kind of serious theater that had become established in Europe, including both realism and nonrealism. One example of an actress-director committed to producing serious drama in repertory was Eva Le Gallienne (1889–1991), who ran the Civic Repertory Theater in New York from 1926 to 1933.

There were many important dramatists in the United States between the world wars. In *The Adding Machine* (1923), Elmer Rice (1892–1967) used expressionism to explore the depersonalization and mechanization of American life. In *Our Town* (1938), Thornton Wilder (1897–1975) used a narrator to paint a picture of small-town life and set it against larger issues. Maxwell Anderson (1888–1959) attempted a return to dramatic poetry in *Winterset* (1935). A new, vigorous realism emerged in the plays of Clifford Odets (1906–1963), and in such works as *The Little Foxes* (1938) by Lillian Hellman (1905–1984). There were also notable comedies by Philip Barry (1896–1949), George S. Kaufman (1889–1961), and Moss Hart (1904–1961).

One playwright, Eugene O'Neill, is frequently cited as having paved the way for meaningful drama in the United States. O'Neill saw theater not just as entertainment or a way to make money, but as a high calling. He considered theater not a commercial enterprise but art. O'Neill—like many European experimental theater artists—had much pain and sorrow in his own life, and his later drama was often autobiographical.

Eugene O'Neill

(1888–1953)

The reputation of Eugene Gladstone O'Neill as a leading American playwright rests in part on his ambition and persistence. He wrote almost every form of drama—realism, expressionism, modern versions of Greek tragedy—in an attempt to bring American theater to maturity. In large measure, he succeeded.

As the son of James O'Neill—an actor famous for playing the Count of Monte Cristo—Eugene O'Neill spent his childhood in hotels and on trains before being sent to a series of boarding schools. His mother, Ella, was recurrently addicted to drugs, and his older brother James was an alcoholic who introduced the young Eugene to a loose, bohemian lifestyle. After being expelled from Princeton for a prank, O'Neill spent 6 years leading a haphazard, alcoholic existence, often working as a sailor. After a suicide attempt, he pulled himself together and worked as a newspaper reporter for 6 months. He had to leave the newspaper when he contracted tuberculosis; confined to a sanitarium, he became an avid reader and began to work seriously on his writing.

He spent a year at Harvard in George Pierce Baker's playwriting course. In 1916, an experimental theater group in Provincetown, Massachusetts, produced his one-act play, *Bound East for Cardiff.* The Provincetown Players reappeared that fall in Greenwich Village, New York, where O'Neill then lived. Several of his early plays were produced there before moving to Broadway. In 1920 he won his first Pulitzer Prize for *Beyond the Horizon.*

O'Neill experimented with a variety of forms and styles throughout his career. His early plays, like *Anna Christie* (1921), are realistic, and many of them deal in some way with the sea. He experimented with expressionism in *The Hairy Ape* (1922), with characters who speak their subconscious thoughts in *Strange Interlude* (1928), and with masks in *The Great God Brown* (1926).

The Hairy Ape, which has many expressionistic elements, is an excellent example of how O'Neill experimented with avant-garde dramaturgical techniques. The protagonist, Yank, a stoker on a ship, is ridiculed by a wealthy woman and begins to see himself as an impotent, hairy ape. Later, Yank punches a wealthy man who is strolling on Fifth Avenue, but the man shows no effect: he is unharmed. When Yank is imprisoned for this attack, he acts like a

ANNA CHRISTIE. Eugene O'Neill experimented with many different styles throughout his career as a playwright: some of his dramas were expressionistic, others highly realistic. One of his early works, *Anna Christie,* was a controversial realistic play. The scene here is from a production at the Roundabout Theater in New York, starring Natasha Richardson and Liam Neeson.

caged animal. The play has eight scenes, which present the action from the highly personal viewpoint of the protagonist. Most of the characters are representative types, and the play is an attack on the depersonalization of twentieth-century society.

A later three-part drama, *Mourning Becomes Electra* (1931), combines Greek myth (the *Oresteia* of Aeschylus) with Freudian psychology. Though O'Neill planned an eleven-part saga covering one family's life in America, he finished only a portion of it. His last plays are tied closely to his own experiences, especially the powerful realistic drama *Long Day's Journey into Night* (published and produced posthumously in 1956), in which he finally comes to an understanding of his family.

In 1936, O'Neill became the first American dramatist to win the Nobel Prize for literature. After that, however, he wrote less, though the plays he did write are among his finest. In his final years, he became depressed and was hampered by a nerve disorder that eventually made him an invalid. His first two marriages ended in divorce, and his third, to Carlotta Monteray, was often stormy. At the time of his death—in a Boston hotel in 1953—his plays were considered outmoded, but he is now recognized as the finest dramatist the United States has produced.

Noncommercial American Theater

THE "LITTLE THEATER" MOVEMENT

In a development paralleling the emergence of serious playwrights, a number of small independent producing theaters also appeared at the time of World War I. In one sense, these noncommercial "little theaters" were the spiritual heirs of late-nineteenth-century independent theaters in Europe and Great Britain. Many historians believe that "little theaters" inspired the off-Broadway movement that began after World War II.

The "little theater" movement flourished in the second decade of the twentieth century. Among the "little theaters" were the Provincetown Playhouse and the Washington Square Players, both founded in 1915 as an alternative to commercial theater.

The Provincetown Playhouse provides a good example of the development of the "little theater" movement. The company was organized in 1915 in Provincetown, Massachusetts, by vacationing artists. Its two founding members were George Cram Cook (1873–1924) and his wife, the playwright Susan Glaspell (1882–1948). After presenting a series of plays in Massachusetts, the playhouse moved, the following year, to a small Greenwich Village theater in New York City, outside the Broadway district. In 1923, the company split into two separate producing agencies, and in 1929 the depression brought the venture to an end.

The Provincetown was an extremely influential theater. In its earlier years, it was dedicated to new American drama; and as the first to produce the works of Eugene O'Neill, it helped establish him as an important playwright. The Provincetown also introduced new production styles, particularly the designs of Robert Edmond Jones, a leading figure in the "new stagecraft" movement in the United States. This design movement put into practice many of the theories of Adolphe Appia and Edward Gordon Craig, especially their emphasis on lighting. The "new stagecraft" designers also strove for "simplified realism," using detail only to suggest specific locales and to reinforce characterization and dramatic action.

Another "little theater," the Washington Square Players, operated in Greenwich Village from 1915 through 1918 and later evolved into the Theater Guild. The Guild, a subscription-based professional organization which eventually built its own theater in the Broadway district, introduced in the 1920s many leading experimental European and American playwrights, including O'Neill, as well as new production techniques. The Guild also attempted to establish a permanent acting company. The Guild was so badly hurt by the depression— and by its own attempts to expand into other American cities—that it eventually became simply another commercial producing entity. During its most active period, the Theater Guild supported the early efforts of the Group Theater.

THE GROUP THEATER'S AWAKE AND SING.   Clifford Odets's *Awake and Sing,* produced in 1935, is an example of a realistic social drama: it deals with American concerns of the 1930s. The play—an intense family drama set in a Bronx apartment during the depression —required the realistic ensemble acting for which the Group Theater was noted. This original production was directed by Harold Clurman.

THE GROUP THEATER

The Group Theater—often referred to as America's Moscow Art Theater— was a noncommercial company which produced plays in the Broadway district. It was dedicated to introducing Stanislavski's system to the United States and to producing socially relevant drama. Politically, the company leaned toward the left wing, and its members hoped to motivate political and social action through theater. The founding members of the Group Theater were Lee Strasberg (1901–1982), Cheryl Crawford (1902–1986), and Harold Clurman (1901–1980), and its actors included Franchot Tone, Morris Carnovsky, Stella Adler, Luther Adler, and John Garfield. The company's resident playwright was Clifford Odets. Its productions of Odets's *Awake and Sing* (1935) and *Golden Boy* (1937) set a standard for realistic writing and performance that was to last for several decades.

Dissension over the correct interpretation of Stanislavski's system developed in the Group Theater in the mid-1930s, and Lee Strasberg left the Group after Harold Clurman and Stella Adler had criticized him for overemphasizing emotional recall—the technique of calling on past experiences to create present emotions. (Adler called for greater emphasis on analysis of a script's "given circumstances.")

The Group Theater disbanded in 1941, but its influence on American theater continued to be strong. Harold Clurman was a leading director and critic until his death in 1980; and Lee Strasberg, beginning in the late 1940s at the Actors Studio, trained many well-known actors, including Marlon Brando (1924–   ). Two other members of the Group Theater, Elia Kazan (1909–   ) and Robert Lewis (1909–   ), are leading directors today. Stella Adler remained a leading acting teacher until her death in 1992.

(UPI/Bettmann Newsphotos)

Stella Adler

(1902–1992)

Konstantin Stanislavski's theory of acting did not reach the United States until the 1920s, when some members of the Moscow Art Theater emigrated to New York and began teaching it. In 1931, however, the Group Theater was founded, in part to explore the Stanislavskian system. One of its founding members was Stella Adler, an actress with 25 years of stage experience.

In Yiddish theater, an important part of theater in New York City at the turn of the century, the name Adler was synonymous with excellence in acting. Stella's father, Jacob Adler, was the premier actor of the Yiddish stage, famous for his portrayal of King Lear. She made her own stage debut in 1906 as a member of her father's Yiddish company, in which she performed for several years. In 1919, she made her London debut; and in 1922, her Broadway debut. Her three sisters and two brothers were also actors.

Stella Adler and her brother Luther studied Stanislavski's system under Maria Ouspenskaya (1876–1949) and Richard Boleslavsky (1889–1937), who had come to the United States after distinguished theatrical careers in Europe. Stella and Luther Adler became original members of the Group Theater, and in 1934, Stella and Harold Clurman—who was one of the Group's directors and later became her husband—went to France to study with Stanislavski himself. When they returned, they reported that Stanislavski emphasized the study of text and character more than the actor's emotional memory. As we have seen, this led to dissension with Lee Strasberg, who left the company.

Though Stella Adler had an active career as an actress and director, she was primarily interested in teaching acting. After teaching in the Dramatic Workshop of the New School for Social Research, she opened the Stella Adler Theater Studio in New York City in 1949. Following her own interpretation of Stanislavski's method, she emphasized the text of the play and encouraged students to explore the possibilities of their characters. Many leading American film actors studied with her throughout her illustrious career.

A PRODUCTION BY THE FEDERAL THEATER PROJECT. A theater funded by Congress during the depression to give work to theater professionals, the Federal Theater Project nurtured a great deal of talent and achieved some important productions. One was the all-black version of *Macbeth* shown here; set in Haiti, it was conceived and directed by Orson Welles.

THE FEDERAL THEATER PROJECT

One additional experiment in noncommercial American theater between the wars should be noted. During the depression, President Franklin Delano Roosevelt established the Works Progress Administration (WPA), which organized government-subsidized agencies to put the unemployed back to work. The Federal Theater Project, headed by Hallie Flanagan Davis (1890–1969), a college professor, was one of these agencies. For 4 years, the Federal Theater Project supported theatrical ventures throughout the United States and helped to revitalize interest in theater outside New York City. One of the most popular forms developed by the project was the *living newspaper*—dramatizations of current events, such as bread lines and rising unemployment.

For political reasons, the government discontinued funding for the Federal Theater Project in 1939—many legislators had said that the project was sympathetic to communism. Today, federal, state, and local governments provide some support to theater companies, but the Federal Theater Project is the closest the United States has ever come to establishing a national theater.

COLLEGE AND UNIVERSITY THEATERS

Another noteworthy development in noncommercial American theater at this time was the emergence of theater departments in colleges and universities across the country. George Pierce Baker (1866–1935) at Harvard and Yale, Thomas Wood Stevens (1880–1942) at the Carnegie Institute of Technology (now Carnegie Mellon) in Pittsburgh, and Frederick Koch (1877–1944) at the University of North Carolina inaugurated the study of theater at academic institutions. This unprecedented movement was to become important in preparing playwrights, performers, directors, designers, and technicians for both professional and nonprofessional theater.

African American Theater

During World War I, thousands upon thousands of rural southern blacks in the United States went north to find work in the war industries. With them, they brought their folk customs, music, religion, and dreams of a better life. When the war ended in 1918, a spirit of unity and hope prevailed.

AFRICAN AMERICAN THEATER IN THE 1920s

The early twentieth century saw the formation of African American stock companies. The most significant of these was the Lafayette Players, discussed in Chapter 12: by the time it closed in 1932, it had employed many black stars and presented over 250 productions. African American performers and writers were also making inroads in commercial theater during the 1920s. Twenty plays with black themes were presented on Broadway in this decade, five of them written by African Americans. These included *Shuffle Along* (1921), with music and lyrics by Noble Sissle (1889–1975) and Eubie Blake (1883–1983). The decade also saw some black performers achieve recognition in serious drama, including Charles Gilpin (1879–1930) and Ethel Waters.

Ethel Waters

(1896–1977)

The Broadway and motion picture actress and singer Ethel Waters made famous such songs as "Taking a Chance on Love," "Cabin in the Sky," and "Am I Blue." At the height of her popularity she was reported to be worth several million dollars, but when she died in 1977 she was close to poverty.

Ethel Waters was born on October 13, 1896, in Chester, Pennsylvania. Her early years were hard. As she revealed in her autobiography, *His Eye Is on the Sparrow* (1951), her first job was as a chambermaid at a small hotel in Philadelphia, earning $4.75 a week. She sometimes stole food to keep from going hungry.

Her luck began to change when, at the age of 17, she won a talent contest at a local theater. This led to a job singing and dancing at the Lincoln Theater in Baltimore, Maryland. From there Waters began working the TOBA circuit (the booking organization mentioned in Chapter 12), playing mainly to black audiences in the south. She was known to her fans as "Sweet Mama Stringbean."

Waters began to taste real success with her rendition of W.C. Handy's classic "Saint Louis Blues." By the time she moved to New York in the early 1920s, she was already a star in the south, known for the class and innocence she brought to her repertoire of mostly "blue" material.

In 1924, she substituted for the singing sensation Florence Mills in *The Plantation Revue of 1924.* From that point on, Waters became one of New York's brightest stars. Irving Berlin, after hearing her rendition of "Cabin in the Sky," wrote several songs for her, such as "Harlem on My Mind," "Heat Wave," and the poignant lament "Supper Time." Waters introduced these songs in the Broadway revue *As Thousands Cheer* (1933). She also appeared in several other revues on Broadway: *Africana* (1929), *Blackbirds* (1930), *Rhapsody in Black* (1933), and *At Home Abroad* (1935).

In 1938, Waters received critical acclaim for her first dramatic performance on Broadway, in Dorothy and DuBose Heyward's play *Mamba's Daughter.* She returned to the musical stage in 1940 in *Cabin in the Sky.* For this performance, the *Herald Tribune* praised Waters as "one of the great musical comedy stars of her time." In 1943, Waters appeared in a movie version of *Cabin in the Sky,* which also featured such notables as Lena Horne, Louis Armstrong, Eddie "Rochester" Anderson, Rex Ingram, and Butterfly McQueen.

Waters appeared in nine motion pictures, starred in several radio and television shows, and performed all over Europe, but her most remarkable performance was in Carson McCullers's *A Member of the Wedding,* at first on Broadway in 1950, and then in a film version in 1952.

Waters died in Chatsworth, California, of kidney and heart failure. In her final years, she had devoted her life to religion, singing in revivals all over the world.

AFRICAN AMERICAN THEATER IN THE 1930s AND 1940s

The depression curtailed the advances that were being made by African American theater and theater artists, forcing performers to turn to other careers or to devise ingenious ways of creating their own theater. The 1930s did see two popular shows written by whites for black performers: *The Green Pastures* (1930) and *Porgy and Bess.* There were also a few Broadway productions of plays by African Americans: the folk musical *Run Little Children* (1933) was one, and another was *Mulatto* (1935) by Langston Hughes (1902–1967).

Possibly the most significant development of the 1930s for African American theater was the Federal Theater Project, discussed above, which was meant to help theater artists through the depression. The project formed separate black units in twenty-two cities. These units mounted plays by African American and white authors and employed thousands of African American actors, dancers, vaudevillians, technicians, writers, and scholars. The Federal Theater Project created a new generation of African American theater artists who would develop the theater of the 1940s and 1950s.

The 1940s saw, in 1941, a stage adaptation of the controversial novel *Native Son* by Richard Wright (1915–1985). Directed by Orson Welles (1915–1985) and presented by Welles's Mercury Theater, it featured Canada Lee (1907–1952) in the lead role and was unanimously praised. Other important Broadway ventures included *Tropical Revue* (1943) by the choreographer Katherine Dunham (1910–   ), which consolidated her dance company and her influence on American dance; and *Our Lan'* (1946), a historical drama about the struggle of freed slaves to hold property. The longest-running venture was *Anna Lucasta* (1944), adapted by Abram Hill (1911–   ), which played for 3 years. *Anna Lucasta* originated with the American Negro Theater (ANT), which was founded in 1940 and created training workshops for actors, playwrights, and technicians.

The 1940s introduced many new African American stars, but the leading actor of the 1940s was a man who had been struggling for almost two decades to earn his rightful place on the American stage—Paul Robeson.

(Culver Pictures)

Paul Robeson

(1898–1976)

Internationally known as an actor, singer, athlete, scholar, and political activist, Paul Robeson had a controversial and luminous career that spanned 50 years.

Born on April 9, 1898, in Princeton, New Jersey, Robeson was the son of a runaway slave who had become a Presbyterian minister. He attended Rutgers University on an academic scholarship but rose to national prominence as a college athlete, winning a total of twelve athletic letters in four different sports and being named an All-American in football in 1917 and 1918. After graduating Phi Beta Kappa, Robeson attended Columbia University and earned a law degree in 1923.

Eugene O'Neill saw Robeson perform in an amateur production and offered him the lead in *The Emperor Jones*. Robeson initially turned it down because of other commitments, but later he played Brutus Jones onstage in 1924 and in the film version in 1933. Robeson also appeared in O'Neill's controversial *All God's Chillun Got Wings*.

It was in *The Emperor Jones* that Robeson launched his career as a concert singer. Asked by the director to whistle in one scene, Robeson sang instead, and the response was overwhelming. In 1926, following a series of successful performances the year before at the Greenwich Theater, Robeson presented a program of spirituals and work songs at Town Hall in New York City. This was the first solo program of all-black music ever sung on the New York stage.

From 1927 to 1939, while living in England, Robeson appeared in many productions, including *The Hairy Ape, Stevedore,* and *Show Boat,* in which he introduced "Ol' Man River," the song that was to become his trademark. But his greatest achievement in England was *Othello,* in which he headed a cast that included Peggy Ashcroft, Sybil Thorndike, and Ralph Richardson. Robeson repeated this success on Broadway in 1945 with Uta Hagen as Desdemona and Jose Ferrer as Iago. The play ran for 296 performances, a record for any Shakespearean play on Broadway.

In Europe, Robeson had become very outspoken about the racial situation in the United States. Because of this, and because of his strong affection for the Soviet Union, the State Department took away his passport in 1950, effectively denying him the right to leave the country. He was blacklisted and denied the use of recording studios and concert halls, and his annual income fell from $104,000 to $16,000.

In 1958, after an 8-year worldwide campaign by his supporters, Robeson regained his passport. He gave a triumphant concert at Carnegie Hall and then left the country. In 1959, he appeared as Othello in Stratford-on-Avon and went to the Soviet Union to receive the Stalin Peace Prize. In 1963, Robeson returned to the United States. He spent the remainder of his life in seclusion, making only a few public appearances, and died on January 26, 1976.

ASIAN THEATER

Many of the leading experimental theater artists of this era, especially Artaud and Brecht, were greatly influenced by Asian theater. By the same token, Asian theater artists borrowed extensively from western theater.

Chinese Theater

After the revolution of 1911, when the Qing Dynasty was overthrown, Shanghai—the most westernized of the large cities in China—became the focal point for a growing interest in modern spoken Chinese drama. Many of the Chinese playwrights were leftist in their political orientation and wrote on social themes. The greatest playwright of this period was Cao Yu (1910–   ), whose works were written before the Second World War. His *Thunderstorm* (1934) and *Peking Man* (1938) show both a grasp of modern dramaturgy and a burning sense of social injustice. Novelists and other writers, among them Mao Dun and Lao She (1899–1966), also began to create plays.

Japanese Theater

By the 1930s, two kinds of modern drama were important in Japan. One was leftist political drama, usually based on German and Russian models; the other was a drama, strongly literary in flavor, that took French plays and Chekhov as models. Probably the finest literary dramatist of the period was Kishida Kunio (1890–1954), who had studied with Jacques Copeau in Paris and whose work as a critic, playwright, and producer did much to incorporate western influences in the theater of his time.

As a critic, Kishida was convinced that Japanese writers must learn western dramatic principles by producing foreign plays and then, after absorbing these ideas, use them to create modern Japanese drama. In his own plays, such as *Autumn in the Tyrol* (1925), and *A Space of Time* (1935), Kishida used poetic dialogue and a central organizing symbol to describe Japanese attitudes. To develop his ideas, Kishida helped found the Literary Theater in 1937.

The Literary Theater was the only modern Japanese company permitted to perform during the Second World War and became a major theatrical force after the war. During the war years, the government suppressed most theatrical activity, particularly the work of artists of socialist or communist leanings.

Theater during the era of the world wars illustrates the significance of drama in western culture. Drama and theater of this period offered an escape from harsh realities, reflected social upheavals, and became instruments for both propaganda and political resistance. Theater between 1915 and 1945, in many ways, suggests why the dramatic arts survive the transformations and ravages of history.

SUMMARY

Theater between 1915 and 1945—the era of the world wars—mirrored the social upheavals of these three decades.

In Europe, many antirealistic movements developed, including expressionism, futurism, dada, and surrealism. Possibly the two most influential European theorists were Antonin Artaud and Bertolt Brecht. Artaud had few opportunities to realize his theater of cruelty, but Brecht developed his epic style in his own plays and later in plays he directed at the Berliner Ensemble after World War II.

The rise of totalitarianism affected theater in the Soviet Union, Germany, Spain, and elsewhere. Theater was used for propaganda by totalitarian regimes, and courageous artists also used it as a means of resistance.

In the United States, "little theaters," such as the Provincetown Playhouse and the Washington Square Players, reacted against commercial Broadway fare and introduced new playwrights such as Eugene O'Neill. The Theater Guild and the Group Theater also produced new dramas using innovative production styles. During the depression, the Federal Theater Project was an experiment with government-subsidized theater.

CHAPTER 14

THEATER FROM 1945 TO 1970

T he date is November 19, 1957, and we are at San Quentin prison in California. We have come here with members of the Actors' Workshop, a theater troupe that performs new work, both American and European. In the North Dining Hall, a stage has been set up where the actors are going to perform Samuel Beckett's *Waiting for Godot*—the first theatrical performance at San Quentin in over 40 years.

The actors are nervous, not only because they are performing in a penitentiary but also because of the play itself. For one thing, *Waiting for Godot* has little action. It is about two tramps who meet each day on a barren plain, hoping that an unknown figure named Godot will come. They have a vague expectation that somehow Godot—if he ever comes—will be able to help them; and while they wait for him, they try to break up the painful monotony of their lives with bickering and occasional vaudeville routines. Furthermore, the play is filled with literary and religious references, and it has baffled intellectuals in Europe and the United States. How, the actors wonder, will a group of restless prisoners react to it? Will they be impatient because there is no story to follow, no conflict, no suspense such as they would find in a mystery or an adventure story? Will they be confused by the philosophical questions?

CAT ON A HOT TIN ROOF. The American playwright Tennessee Williams's *Cat on a Hot Tin Roof* is one of his most famous works and deals with many of the themes for which he is best-known, including hypocrisy within a family structure. Shown here is a scene between Maggie—who is called "the cat"—played by JoBeth Williams, and her husband Brick, played by James Morrison, in a production at the McCarter Theatre.
(T. Charles Erickson/McCarter Theatre)

Shortly after the performance begins, the actors have part of the answer. The audience grows quiet, and we notice that several men sitting on some steps, who had planned to leave early, become engrossed and stay. Then, as the play unfolds, we can see that the audience is following it closely from beginning to end.

After the performance is over, it is clear that the audience has understood a great deal, perhaps more than other, more sophisticated audiences might. One reason is that the prisoners—waiting out their sentences in boredom and frustration—intuitively connect with the men onstage as they wait for the unknown Godot, who never comes.

BACKGROUND: THE POSTWAR WORLD— A TIME OF SOCIAL UPHEAVAL

World War II, as we noted in Chapter 13, left many haunting questions. How could the civilized world have engaged in a war that resulted in over 35 million deaths? How could rational societies undertake genocide? Would the atomic bomb lead to annihilation of the human race? Questions like these led to other questions, forcing western society to reevaluate its most cherished beliefs. Is humanity as rational and civilized as the eighteenth- and nineteenth-century philosophers proclaimed? Could God exist and allow the destruction of so many innocent human beings? Are individuals responsible for group actions? This questioning formed the basis of new philosophies, such as existentialism, which rejected traditional beliefs.

The end of World War II did not mean the end of conflict. Possibly, the most destructive struggle was psychological. In the 1950s, the superpowers—the United States and the Soviet Union—began a "cold war," each trying to establish military superiority and extend its sphere of influence. The toll of this cold war was high, and both feared a nuclear holocaust. A climax was reached in 1962, when the American president, John F. Kennedy, threatened to blockade communist Cuba if the Soviet Union did not remove nuclear missiles it had set up there. The situation was defused, and later—in the 1970s, during the administration of Richard Nixon—a policy of détente and disarmament was undertaken; but détente was threatened by events like the Soviet intervention in Afghanistan in 1980 and the suppression of the Polish labor union Solidarity at the close of 1981.

The United States was also involved in several military conflicts during the 25 years from 1945 to 1970. In the early 1950s, the Korean war was an attempt to prevent communist North Korea from invading South Korea; and in the late 1960s and early 1970s, the United States fought a controversial war in Vietnam. This war in Vietnam aroused enormous opposition: antiwar activities included draft resistance as well as sit-ins and were often violent. Many Americans felt that the United States was protecting a corrupt regime in South

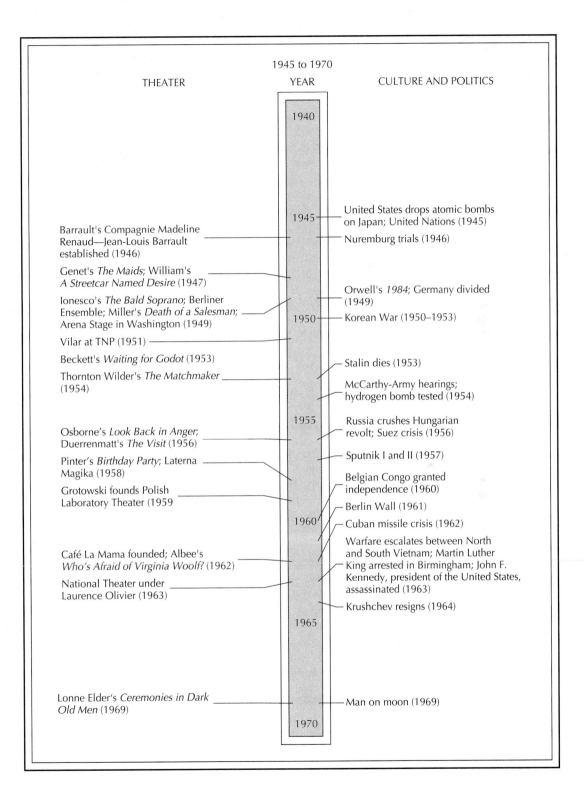

1945 to 1970

THEATER   YEAR   CULTURE AND POLITICS

1940

1945 — United States drops atomic bombs on Japan; United Nations (1945)

Barrault's Compagnie Madeline Renaud—Jean-Louis Barrault established (1946) — Nuremburg trials (1946)

Genet's *The Maids*; William's *A Streetcar Named Desire* (1947)

Orwell's *1984*; Germany divided (1949)

Ionesco's *The Bald Soprano*; Berliner Ensemble; Miller's *Death of a Salesman*; Arena Stage in Washington (1949) — 1950 — Korean War (1950–1953)

Vilar at TNP (1951)

Beckett's *Waiting for Godot* (1953) — Stalin dies (1953)

Thornton Wilder's *The Matchmaker* (1954) — McCarthy-Army hearings; hydrogen bomb tested (1954)

1955 — Russia crushes Hungarian revolt; Suez crisis (1956)

Osborne's *Look Back in Anger*; Duerrenmatt's *The Visit* (1956)

Pinter's *Birthday Party*; Laterna Magika (1958) — Sputnik I and II (1957)

Grotowski founds Polish Laboratory Theater (1959) — Belgian Congo granted independence (1960)

— Berlin Wall (1961)

1960 — Cuban missile crisis (1962)

Café La Mama founded; Albee's *Who's Afraid of Virginia Woolf?* (1962) — Warfare escalates between North and South Vietnam; Martin Luther King arrested in Birmingham; John F. Kennedy, president of the United States, assassinated (1963)

National Theater under Laurence Olivier (1963)

— Krushchev resigns (1964)

1965

Lonne Elder's *Ceremonies in Dark Old Men* (1969) — Man on moon (1969)

1970

Vietnam and should not have become involved in a civil war. In 1972, the United States pulled out of Vietnam, which eventually became entirely communist. Reverberations of this war are still apparent, and the ambivalence of the American conscience is reflected in such plays as *Streamers* (1976) by David Rabe (1940–), *Still Life* (1983) by Emily Mann (1952–), and *Redwood Curtain* (1993) by Lanford Wilson (1934–). Today, continued political turmoil throughout southeast Asia precludes any final analysis of American involvement in Vietnam.

During this period there were also a series of wars in the middle east, following the founding of the state of Israel. These wars were a product of Israeli and Arab nationalism, complicated by geography, oil resources, and competition between the superpowers.

The desire for worldwide peace was strong, however. The institution that represented this idealistic goal was the United Nations, founded immediately after World War II; but peace proved elusive, and nationalistic fervor often prevented the United Nations from resolving international conflicts.

Nationalism was a factor in the rise of third world nations. African nations, for example, broke from colonial rule and asserted their independence. While many of the third world nations in Africa and Asia have valuable natural resources, they are still struggling to develop self-sustaining economies. The third world nations which prospered most were the oil-rich middle eastern countries. Unfortunately, many third world nations were wracked by political turmoil: two examples are Uganda, which deposed its dictator Idi Amin but was then unable to establish a stable government; and Iran, which deposed its shah but was then controlled by the unstable Islamic regime of Ayatollah Khomeini.

This 25-year period was a time of general social unrest. In the United States, a series of assassinations claimed the lives of John F. Kennedy, Robert Kennedy, Martin Luther King, Jr., and—12 years later—John Lennon. Throughout the western world, terrorist organizations used violence as a means of publicizing political discontent.

Radical social transformations took place between 1945 and 1970. The civil rights, gay rights, and feminist movements led people to reevaluate their perceptions of minorities and oppressed groups. The sexual revolution brought a reevaluation of traditional morality, including such institutions as marriage and the family. Twentieth-century society continued to be technologically innovative: television joined film as a major competitor of theater; medical advances resulted in the eradication of polio and in genetic experimentation; nuclear energy became a controversial source of power; and space exploration culminated in Americans' walking on the moon.

Theater reflected the social upheaval of these tumultuous decades. Though it is still difficult to assess the relative importance of the theatrical innovations of this era, there is no question that many theater artists led us to question long-held beliefs about life and about theater itself.

POSTWAR EXPERIMENTAL THEATER

The 25 years from 1945 to 1970 were turbulent for theater. There was an explosion of experimentation, with new avant-garde trends springing up one after another. These movements are so close to our own time that we cannot evaluate their historical significance conclusively. It is clear, however, that established theatrical and dramatic forms were questioned and restructured, and that movements such as absurdism and environmental theater led to new perceptions and new definitions of drama and theater.

Existentialism

Existentialism is a philosophy most clearly articulated by two Frenchmen, Jean-Paul Sartre (1905–1980) and Albert Camus (1913–1960). Existentialists believe that there is little meaning to existence, that God does not exist, and that humanity is therefore alone in an irrational universe. The only significant action an individual can take is to accept responsibility for his or her own actions. Most historians see an obvious impact of World War II on the existentialists.

Camus and Sartre both wrote existentialist plays. The best-known are Sartre's *The Flies* (1943), an adaptation of the Greek *Oresteia;* and *No Exit* (1944), in which hell is represented as other people. While the philosophy of these dramas is revolutionary, their dramatic form is fairly conventional: the plots are based on traditional cause-and-effect logic, and the characters are recognizable, fully developed human beings.

Theater of the Absurd

After World War II, a theatrical approach emerged which combined existential philosophy with revolutionary, avant-garde dramatic form. Although it was not a movement, it was called *theater of the absurd* (in a 1961 book of the same title) by the English critic Martin Esslin (1918–   ).

ABSURDIST DRAMA

Absurdist playwrights differ markedly from one another, but there are certain qualities that they have in common. One is their belief that much of what happens in life cannot be logically explained; it is ridiculous or absurd. Another is their attempt to reflect this ridiculousness or absurdity in the dramatic action of their plays.

Absurdist drama presents human existence, including relationships and language, as futile or absurd. In order to reinforce this thematic statement, it also uses seemingly illogical dramatic techniques. Plots do not have either traditional crisis structure or episodic structure. Frequently, nothing seems to happen, because the plot moves in a circle, concluding the same way it began. The characters are not realistic, and little expository information is provided about them. The setting is frequently a strange, unrecognizable locale or an ostensibly realistic world that suddenly becomes topsy-turvy. The language is often telegraphic and sparse; the dialogue seems to make little sense, and the characters fail to communicate.

An example of absurdist dialogue is the following exchange from Ionesco's play *The Bald Soprano:*

MR. SMITH: Take a circle, caress it, and it will turn vicious.

MRS. SMITH: A schoolmaster teaches his pupils to read, but the cat suckles her young when they are small.

MRS. MARTIN: Nevertheless, it was the cow that gave us tails.[1]

Recently, critics have asked whether all the presumably absurdist playwrights truly fit into a category that can be labeled *theater of the absurd,* since their work is highly individualistic and not all the characteristics we have just mentioned appear in all of it. Nonetheless, many playwrights have been categorized as absurdists, including the Frenchman Jean Genet (1910–   ) and the American Edward Albee (1928–   ). Albee's work, however, is a perfect example of the problem of categorization. Some of his plays—such as *The Sandbox* (1959), *American Dream* (1960), and *Seascape* (1974)—seem to be absurdist in theme and style; but his best-known work, *Who's Afraid of Virginia Woolf* (1962), is much more realistic.

The playwrights who are most often categorized as absurdists are Samuel Beckett, Eugène Ionesco, and Harold Pinter. These three are also among the most influential dramatists of their generation.

Samuel Beckett
(1906–1989)

Samuel Beckett is the most renowned of the absurdist playwrights. His dramas deal with the dullness of routine, the futility of human action, and the inability of humans to communicate; and the plots, language, and characters themselves seem absurd. Thus, his dramatic style underlines his thematic statements: he captures and reflects the ridiculous aspects of life in dramatic form.

[1]Eugène Ionesco, *Four Plays,* Donald M. Allen (trans.), Grove, New York, 1958, p. 38. Reprinted by permission of Grove Press, Inc. Translated from the French by Donald Allen. Copyright © 1958 by Grove Press.

SAMUEL BECKETT DIRECTS WAITING FOR GODOT. One play that typifies the spirit of alienation and loneliness in drama after World War II is *Waiting for Godot*. Here, the playwright, Samuel Beckett (at right), is seen at a rehearsal for a production which he directed.

Beckett was born on April 13, 1906. The day of his birth happened to be not only Friday the thirteenth but Good Friday, and the sense of sorrow, isolation, and ill luck associated with these dates was an important concept to him. However, for someone so obsessed with the futility of existence, Beckett had a very normal childhood in a cultured, affectionate, upper-middle-class Irish family. At prep school, he was not only a brilliant scholar but an extremely popular student and an excellent athlete, particularly at cricket. He received his M.A. in modern languages from the University of Dublin in Ireland. He then taught at schools in Paris and Dublin, wandered around Europe for a while, and finally settled in Paris in 1937.

It was during his first visit to Paris, in 1929, that Beckett became acquainted with the writer James Joyce. Joyce encouraged Beckett to write and arranged to have some of his early essays published; in turn, Beckett sometimes assisted Joyce with *Finnegan's Wake*. They were drawn together by their shared Irish background, literary tastes, and tendency to depression. According to one account, they conversed mainly in silences.

Beckett wrote and published essays, short stories, poetry, and novels during the 1930s and the 1940s, but his work was known only to a very small part of the avant-garde. A French translation of his novel *Murphy* sold ninety-five copies in 4 years. It was not until the early 1950s, with the publication of three novels and the play *Waiting for Godot* (1953), that he came to be considered one of the major writers of the postwar generation.

In *Waiting for Godot*, Beckett used many themes and dramatic techniques that would recur in his later plays. The futility of action reappears as a theme in *Act without Words* I (1957) and II (1960). Two people who need each other but cannot get along are seen again in *Endgame* (1957). *Happy Days* (1961) and *Krapp's Last Tape* (1958) dramatize failure to communicate. One of Beckett's last short plays, *Catastrophe* (1982), uses the setting of theater to reflect on totalitarian control of the artist and ideas. He dedicated this drama to the Czech playwright Vaclav Havel (1936–   ), who at the time was under attack by the communist regime (after the fall of communism, Havel became president of Czechoslovakia).

Besides writing for the theater, Beckett wrote for television and radio and also wrote a short film that starred Buster Keaton. After a spurt of writing in the late 1950s and early 1960s, his output diminished, but his short plays of the 1960s, 1970s, and 1980s—including *Come and Go* (1966), *Not I* (1971), and *Rockaby* (1981)—showed that neither his concerns nor his dramatic powers had changed. Beckett received the Nobel Prize in 1969 but did not attend the ceremony.

Waiting for Godot: An important absurdist drama   Samuel Beckett's *Waiting for Godot* is probably the most famous of the enigmatic, nontraditional absurdist dramas. (This is the play, described at the beginning of the chapter, that was presented at San Quentin prison.) The setting is "A country road. A tree." The tree is leafless in Act I, but in Act II four or five leaves appear on it. The two central characters, Vladimir and Estragon—also known as Didi and Gogo—are tramplike clowns. They are waiting for Godot, but Godot's identity is never revealed, nor does he ever appear. Instead, a young messenger promises that he will arrive tomorrow. Godot may be God, or he may not even exist. Two additional characters, Lucky and Pozzo, switch roles as master and slave in their two appearances.

Waiting for Godot epitomizes the absurdist form. The characters are absurd, clownlike figures who have problems communicating and dealing with their environment. They contemplate suicide, for example, as a means of relieving their perpetual boredom. The setting represents everywhere and nowhere. Some critics have remarked that this barren, sterile world conjures up an image of the aftermath of a nuclear holocaust. The language is stichomythic—that is, written in brief, alternating lines—and frequently ludicrous. Lucky, in Act II, gives a three-page speech of seemingly unrelated ideas. As in many absurdist dramas, the plot is cyclical: the action appears to start over with nothing having changed. The closing lines and stage direction suggest the absurdity of the universe:

VLADIMIR: Well? Shall we go?

ESTRAGON: Yes, let's go. *(They do not move.)*[2]

This final moment of *Waiting for Godot* underlines its absurdist philosophy of futility. Vladimir and Estragon have spent their time waiting; they accomplish nothing, showing only their inability to take control of their existence. Lucky and Pozzo have no control over their destiny; fate reverses their roles, transforming one from master into servant and the other from servant into master.

Some critics consider *Waiting for Godot* a modern allegory, much like the medieval *Everyman*. The playwright suggests that we spend our lives waiting for the unknowable. Godot may represent God; more generally, though, Godot is anything and everything that human beings wait for during their lives—and our lives are thus defined by absurd waiting rather than by our actions. Beckett himself described *Waiting for Godot* as a "tragicomedy in two acts," revealing his own view of the human condition: human inaction is comical but has tragic consequences.

Eugène Ionesco

(1912–   )

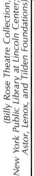

Eugène Ionesco is one of the most productive of the playwrights who have been grouped together as absurdists. He often turns his characters into caricatures and pushes dramatic action to the point of the ridiculous. Since he is particularly concerned with the futility of communication, the language of his plays frequently seems nonsensical. He dramatizes the absurdity of the human condition by presenting comic characters who lose control of their own existence.

As a child, Ionesco was enchanted by Punch and Judy puppet shows and enjoyed performing in plays. He was born in Romania, but as a boy he lived with his mother in Paris for 13 years; when he returned to Romania, he had to learn his native language. At the University of Bucharest, he studied French and occasionally wrote poetry. When he graduated, he taught French in high school. He married in 1936, and in 1938 he returned to France on a government grant, supposedly to write a thesis on Baudelaire. He has not yet written a word of the thesis.

[2]From the book *Waiting for Godot* by Samuel Beckett. Copyright © 1954 by Grove Press; renewed copyright © 1982 by Samuel Beckett. Used with the permission of Grove/Atlantic, Inc.

Ionesco became a playwright by accident. As a reader in a legal publishing firm, he decided to learn English and began by using a simple primer. He took the empty and illogical phrases he was learning in the primer and turned them into dialogue for his first play, the one-act drama *The Bald Soprano* (1949). That he wrote a play at all is somewhat ironic, because at the time he claimed to dislike theater—he felt that the reality of living performers clashed with the fictionalized world of the stage.

Ionesco followed his first play with several other one-act dramas, including *The Lesson* (1951) and *The Chairs* (1952). His full-length plays include *Amedée* (1954), *Rhinoceros* (1959), *Exit the King* (1962), *Hunger and Thirst* (1966), and *Journeys to the Homes of the Dead* (1981). He has also written sharp, sometimes argumentative criticism and some political works. He remains adamantly opposed to the concept of didactic drama, feeling that the purpose of theater is not to teach a lesson but to present a vision of life that is enlightening, entertaining, or both. Ionesco's election to the French Academy in 1970 was a clear indication that absurdism had been accepted by the mainstream.

Harold Pinter

(1930–   )

Harold Pinter is now the leading English-language absurdist playwright. In his dramas, he feels no need to explain why something happens or who a character is; existence within the world of the play is sufficient. Characteristics of Pinter's works include a lack of explanation of backgrounds or motives, introduction of menacing outside forces which upset a seemingly stable environment, and dialogue which captures the pauses, evasions, and incoherence of modern speech. Pinter acknowledges Franz Kafka, Samuel Beckett, and American gangster films as the strongest influences on his work. Unlike Beckett or Ionesco, he creates a dramatic world that seems somewhat realistic.

Though he began writing poetry while still at school in London's East End, Pinter's first choice of a career was acting. He attended the Royal Academy of Dramatic Art for a time, completed his studies at the Central School of Speech and Drama, and acted professionally under the name of David Baron.

Pinter's debut as a playwright was accidental. He had mentioned an idea for a play to a friend in the drama department of Bristol University. The friend wrote that he was interested in the play but needed the script within a week if the school was to produce it. Pinter wrote back "no," but he finished the play anyway—in 4 days. It was called *The Room* and was performed in May 1957. Two of his other plays, *The Dumbwaiter* and *The Birthday Party*, were also produced in 1957.

The term *comedy of menace* is sometimes applied to such plays as *The Birthday Party, A Slight Ache* (1958), and *The Homecoming* (1965) because they frighten and entertain at the same time. The term is not as applicable to Pinter's later plays, such as *Old Times* (1971), which, though uncomfortably funny, deal more realistically with failed human relationships and do not have unexplained menacing forces. In a later work, *Betrayal* (1978), he experiments with form, reversing time in order to trace a relationship from its end back to its beginning. For some time, Pinter did not do much playwriting, except for some short plays, including *A Kind of Alaska* (1982), *One for the Road* (1984), and *Mountain Language* (1988); but a new longer play, *Moonlight*, was well received in 1993.

Pinter also writes for television, radio, and film, adapting his own plays and the works of others as well as writing original scripts. Occasionally, he also directs for the theater, and he is noted especially for staging plays of the British dramatist Simon Gray (1936–   ). In late 1992 and early 1993, Pinter returned to acting, appearing in a revival of his own play *No Man's Land* (originally produced in 1975).

Pinter's creativity and adaptability in several media have made him one of the most vital forces in English theater.

DIRECTORS OF ABSURDIST DRAMA

Although many absurdist dramatists—including Beckett, Pinter, and Albee—have directed their own plays, some directors who are not playwrights have become renowned for their staging of dramas that reflect absurdity, ridiculousness, or the enigmatic. In France, for instance, Roger Blin (1907–1984) was noted for his productions of Samuel Beckett's dramas in the early 1950s.

The reputation of the American director Alan Schneider (1917–1984) was based on his productions of plays by Beckett, Albee, and Pinter. Schneider was especially known for productions which carefully illuminated these enigmatic texts. When he was directing *Waiting for Godot*, he wrote to Beckett and asked point-blank, "Who is Godot?" Beckett answered that if he had wanted anyone to know, he would have revealed the answer in the text.

The English director Peter Hall (1930–   ), who served as the artistic director of the Royal Shakespeare Company in the 1960s and the National Theater in the 1970s and 1980s, established his early reputation with productions of Beckett's and Pinter's works. (The Royal Shakespeare Company, which grew out of the Stratford Memorial Theater in 1961, is noted for significant productions of new plays and revivals by important directors. The National Theater is best-known for revivals with major British and international directors and significant actors. It was founded as a government-subsidized theater in 1963, after the Old Vic had closed; Laurence Olivier was its first artistic director, followed by Hall in 1973.)

Hall, who is a truly eclectic director, left the National Theater in the late 1980s and established his own production company, dedicated to reviving difficult texts by historically significant authors as well as producing new plays and touring them in the United States and throughout Europe. His productions of Tennessee Williams's *Orpheus Descending* featuring Vanessa Redgrave in 1988, *The Merchant of Venice* with Dustin Hoffman in 1989, and Oscar Wilde's *An Ideal Husband* in 1992 were all well received. (The first two were transferred from London to New York.)

During the 1960s and into the 1970s there were further attempts to break away from traditional theater practices. Some of these experiments built on the work of Artaud and Brecht, and they went in many directions—a reflection, no doubt, of the fragmentation of modern life. This experimentation included happenings, multimedia, and environmental theater.

Happenings and Multimedia

Two developments of the 1960s and 1970s were happenings and experiments with multimedia. *Happenings* were what the term suggests: nonstructured events that occurred with a minimum of planning and organization. The idea, which was quite popular in the 1960s, was that art should not be restricted to museums, galleries, or concert halls but can happen anywhere—on a street corner, in a grocery store, at a bus stop. Happenings were closely analogous to the work of abstract painters, and they usually took place only once. The originator, with a few colleagues, would set up a situation and then act it out in an improvisatory fashion.

Multimedia is a joining of theater with other arts, especially dance, film, and television. Work of this sort, in which live performers interact with sequences on film or television, still goes on. The idea is to fuse the art forms or to incorporate new technology into a theatrical event.

Environmental Theater

The term *environmental theater* was coined in the 1960s by the American director and teacher Richard Schechner (1934–   ), but many characteristics of environmental theater had developed out of the work and theories of earlier twentieth-century avant-garde artists, including Vsevelod Meyerhold and Antonin Artaud. Environmental theater is based on the idea that the entire theater space is performance space—a concept which implies that the division between performers and spectators is artificial. For every production, the spatial arrangements are transformed. Schechner does not consider the script sacred, or even essential, and he allows both improvisation and reworking of the text. The major influence on Schechner's theories was the Polish director Jerzy Grotowski.

Jerzy Grotowski

(1933–   )

The son of a painter-sculptor and a schoolteacher, Grotowski was born in Rzeszow, Poland. His family was well-educated, and both of his parents were interested in Asia, an interest that he shares. Grotowski became gravely ill at the age of 16 and spent an entire year in the hospital, much of it in a ward for terminal patients; but instead of following his doctor's advice and remaining indefinitely under care, he returned home and began to lead a normal life. He also began to meditate and to read extensively.

Despite his family's opposition, Grotowski entered the Advanced School of Dramatic Art in Cracow in 1951, first to study acting and then to study directing. He became interested in Stanislavski's work, which he admired because he felt that Stanislavski had asked the right questions about acting. The work of another Russian, Meyerhold, was also an important influence on him. During a trip abroad, Grotowski was impressed by the Berliner Ensemble's production of Brecht's *Mother Courage*. Between 1956 and 1959, Grotowski staged his earliest professional productions, including Ionesco's *The Chairs* (1957) and several radio plays, one of which was a version of the Indian classic *Shakuntala*. In 1959, he became director of a theater in Opole in Poland, where he began his Polish Laboratory Theater. In 1965, the Laboratory Theater, now the Institute for Research in Acting, moved to Wroclaw.

Grotowski's productions for the Polish Laboratory Theater, particularly *Akropolis* (1962–1967), *The Constant Prince* (1965–1968), and *Apocalypsis cum Figuris* (1968), attracted worldwide attention. The group performed in New York in 1969 to small, select audiences and transformed the way in which many theater artists thought about theater. In the 1970s, the Polish Laboratory Theater undertook a series of paratheatrical experiments, including *Holiday* (also known as *Special Project,* ca. 1970–1973) and *Mountain Project* (ca. 1975–1978), in which the company and outside participants organized communal events lasting for extended periods of time. As is true of Artaud and Brecht, many historians believe that Grotowski's theories, rather than his practical work, have exerted the most influence on modern theater. However, Grotowski—unlike Artaud or Brecht—was sometimes criticized for being more interested in the nature and form of theater as an art than in theater as a social or political instrument.

In the 1980s, Grotowski came to the United States and worked at the University of California at Irvine. The Polish Laboratory Theater ceased to function in 1984. In recent years, Grotowski has continued his activities in Italy.

Grotowski's Poor Theater and Paratheatrical Experiments

Jerzy Grotowski's concept of *poor theater*, which he developed while working with his Polish Laboratory Theater, is an attempt to answer the endlessly debated question, "What is theater?" It stems from his belief that there are only two essentials for theater: the actor and the audience. Script, scenery, and other elements are considered less important—hence the term *poor*. To intensify the actor-audience relationship, Grotowski experimented with various spatial arrangements that would intertwine performers and spectators, though he did not advocate eliminating the barrier that separates them. The plays he produced were reduced to their essential ideas, and they were cut, rearranged, or rewritten to serve his purposes. The actor—the core of his productions— was trained so that nearly every muscle of the body would be under complete control and could be moved at will.

Grotowski's theories and the works he staged with the Polish Laboratory Theater from its founding in 1959 until 1970 presented the guiding principles of environmental theater. For each production, the theater space and the actor-audience relationship were arranged to conform to the play. In his production of *Kordian* (1962), the space resembled a mental institution, with audience members scattered among beds and patients (the actors). In his version of *Doctor Faustus* (1963), the theater space was filled with two large dining tables at which audience members sat as if attending a banquet given by Faustus. And in *The Constant Prince*, a small fence was built around the playing area and the audience sat around it as if watching a bullfight.

For most of Grotowski's productions, existing scripts were radically modified by the actors and director; the classic turn-of-the-century Polish play *Akropolis*, for example, was placed in a Nazi concentration camp, and Grotowski turned the script into a scenario. The acting style for this production—as for all his works—was externally based, with the emphasis on control of body and voice rather than on inner emotions; and there was no attempt to create a realistic representation of a concentration camp. Grotowski was attempting, through such productions, to identify the essential elements of theater. He concluded, as we have noted, that the essence of theater is interaction between performers and audiences, and his emphasis on reorganizing the spatial arrangements followed from this. (His stress on the theatrical environment and on non-verbal aspects of performance has a strong affinity with the ideas of Antonin Artaud.)

After about 1970, Grotowski stopped producing and became involved in *paratheatrical* experiments. In these experiments, the members of his company, and some other people, took part together in rituals of daily life to rediscover the origins of theater. Many critics felt that this was closer to therapy— sociodrama or psychodrama—than to theater.

Debates in Theater History:
WILL EXPERIMENTAL THEATER HAVE A LASTING INFLUENCE?

Will the experiments of groups like the Polish Laboratory Theater, the Performance Group, the Living Theater, and the Open Theater have a lasting impact on theater practices? These experiments were closely aligned to the political and social turmoil of the 1960s. All political and social institutions were questioned, and so were traditional techniques and conventions of theater—resulting in environmental staging, participatory techniques, deemphasis of the text, and radical forms of drama.

Some historians argue that the return to a focus on commercial and traditional drama in the 1980s and 1990s indicates that the experiments of the 1960s were short-lived and will have little lasting impact. Others, however, note that similar assessments were made for earlier twentieth-century movements, such as dada and surrealism, and that—although these avant-garde experiments did not initially seem to affect theater significantly—a good deal of later experimentation was clearly influenced by them.

Some critics note that many avant-garde techniques are now included in commercial productions and consider this proof that these experiments have transformed how we think about all theater. For example, Peter Shaffer's *Equus* required some of the physical acting techniques found in Grotowski's productions. Harold Prince, in his revival of the musical *Candide* in the 1970s, used environmental staging techniques and remodeled a Broadway theater with ramps throughout.

The recent interest in performance art, which—as we shall see—breaks down the boundaries between arts, is also cited as proof that the 1960s have had an impact on today's theater. The fact that performance artists like the Blue Man Group and Bill Irwin have had successful runs on and off-Broadway is also evidence that avant-garde ideas of 30 years ago affect even current commercial theater.

Given the proximity of the 1960s to our own time, it is difficult for us to assess how important the experiments of that period will be for future theater practitioners. Only a significant passage of time will tell.

POSTWAR REALISTIC DRAMA

Although realism was constantly questioned in the years from 1945 to 1970, its hold on theater remained apparent. One good indication is the fact that most of the plays which won the Pulitzer Prize in the United States in those years were realistic. These included *The Subject Was Roses* (1965) by Frank D. Gilroy (1925–), *That Championship Season* (1973) by Jason Miller (1939–), and *The Gin Game* (1978) by D. L. Coburn (1938–).

Selective Realism

The leading postwar American playwrights, Arthur Miller and Tennessee Williams, wrote realistic works but were also successful with *selective realism*, a type of realism that heightens certain details of action, scenery, and dialogue while omitting others.

SELECTIVE REALISM. Arthur Miller's *Death of a Salesman* is the story of Willy Loman, an unsuccessful salesman, shown here with his wife on the left, and his two sons on the right. The play mixes realistic scenes with antirealistic devices such as flashbacks and fantasized scenes from Willy's imagination.

For example, in *Death of a Salesman*, Miller highlights selected physical elements of the world of Willy Loman—the salesman of the title—which symbolize his downfall: a refrigerator in need of repair, a tape-recorder in his boss's office. Rarely is the setting completely naturalistic; frequently, scenes from the past are presented from Willy's point of view. However, the play is set in a recognizable, realistic world. Williams uses a similar stylistic technique in such plays as *The Glass Menagerie* (which has a narrator) and *A Streetcar Named Desire:* elements of a realistic world are carefully selected to underline thematic concerns.

Arthur Miller and Tennessee Williams have had a strong impact on the development of American drama; along with Eugene O'Neill, they are now considered perhaps the most important playwrights in the history of American theater.

Arthur Miller

(1915–   )

Focusing on failure, guilt, responsibility for one's own actions, and the effects of society on the individual, Arthur Miller repeatedly tries to make us examine our own lives. His most successful dramas are reminiscent of Ibsen's well-made problem plays, and in fact he wrote an adaptation of Ibsen's *An Enemy of the People* in the early 1950s.

Miller was born and raised in New York City. As the son of a garment manufacturer who lost his business in the depression, Miller understands failure. After high school, Miller worked as a shipping clerk in a warehouse before attending the University of Michigan. There he won a Hopwood Award for playwriting. Until he became a successful dramatist, he worked for 10 years at a variety of jobs, including one at the Brooklyn Navy Yard, and wrote at night.

Though his first Broadway play, *The Man Who Had All the Luck* (1944), was a failure, *All My Sons* (1947), the story of a wartime manufacturer, established Miller as a promising new dramatist. With the Pulitzer Prize-winning *Death of a Salesman* (1949)—often characterized as a modern "tragedy of the common man"—he became one of the most renowned American playwrights. His next play, *The Crucible* (1953), was about witch-hunting in seventeenth-century Massachusetts and was also a commentary on the anticommunist investigations of the McCarthy era. In 1956, Miller appeared before the House Un-American Activities Committee (HUAC), and though he admitted to sympathy for leftist organizations, he denied being a communist; he also refused to give information about others.

Miller returned to contemporary America in his next two plays, *A View from the Bridge* (1955) and *A Memory of Two Mondays* (1955). In his play *After the Fall* (1964), he gives a thinly disguised account of his marriage to Marilyn Monroe. Another play, *Incident at Vichy* (1964) deals with the issue of guilt during the Nazi Holocaust.

Except for *The Price* (1968), Miller's later dramas were not as well received by American critics as his earlier works. His two plays of the 1970s, *The Creation of the World and Other Business* (1972) and *The Archbishop's Ceiling* (1979), were failures, though *The American Clock*, which opened in 1980, and the New York production of *The Last Yankee* (1993) did better. Several of his early plays have recently been revived successfully, particularly in England; and a recent work, *The Ride Down Mount Morgan*, premiered successfully in London in 1991.

Miller's television adaptation of a musician's account of life in a concentration camp, *Playing for Time* (1980), was critically acclaimed. He has also written short stories and screenplays, as well as his memoir *Timebends* (1988).

Tennessee Williams

(Thomas Lanier Williams; 1911–1983)

Tennessee Williams was one of the foremost twentieth-century playwrights in the United States. He had a series of critical and popular successes from the 1940s through the 1960s, including *The Glass Menagerie* (1945), *A Streetcar Named Desire* (1947), *Summer and Smoke* (1948), *The Rose Tattoo* (1950), *Cat on a Hot Tin Roof* (1954), *Sweet Bird of Youth* (1959), and *The Night of the Iguana* (1961). Both *A Streetcar Named Desire* and *Cat on a Hot Tin Roof* won the Pulitzer Prize.

A common theme running through these works is the plight of society's outcasts, outsiders trapped in a hostile environment. These characters are usually victims who are unable to comprehend their world, and Williams creates compassion for them through the use of lyrical and poetic language as well as symbolism. His most popular plays are fairly realistic, but in his later dramas—such as *The Seven Descents of Myrtle* (1968)—he increasingly used nonrealistic techniques.

Williams had a long wait for his critical and commercial success. The son of a traveling shoe salesman, he was born in Columbus, Mississippi, and grew up in Saint Louis. He entered the University of Missouri in 1929, but financial difficulties forced him to leave school. After several years and many jobs, he received his B.A. from the University of Iowa in 1938.

In 1939, Williams received a citation from the Group Theater for his collection of one-act plays, *American Blues.* The Theater Guild production of his full-length drama *Battle of Angels* closed in Boston in 1940 after a brief run. He spent 6 months as a contract writer for Metro-Goldwyn-Mayer in 1943, and it was while he was in Hollywood that he wrote the first draft of *The Glass Menagerie.*

In his later years, Williams himself became somewhat of an outsider, at least to theater. His late full-length plays were failures, though some of his shorter plays like *Small Craft Warnings* (1973) had extended runs off-Broadway. His work continues to be performed frequently and to influence other American playwrights.

Angry Young Playwrights

In England in the 1950s, a group of antiestablishment playwrights known collectively as the *angry young men* dealt with the dissolving British empire, class conflict, and political disillusionment. Most of the dramas by the "angry young men" are in traditional realistic form, slightly modified. The most famous of these plays was *Look Back in Anger* (1956) by John Osborne (1929–   ).

Two theater companies in the 1950s were extremely well-known for introducing "angry young" playwrights to English audiences: the English Stage Company and the Theater Workshop. At the time of its founding in 1956, the artistic director of the English Stage Company was George Devine (1910–1966); the company performed at the Royal Court Theater and became best-known for giving the first performances of Osborne's *Look Back in Anger* and *Saved* (1963) by Edward Bond (1935–). Under succeeding artistic directors—including its recent director, Max Stafford-Clark (1941–)—the Royal Court has continued to introduce new playwrights whose works are often controversial in style and content.

The other company which developed a reputation for staging the works of angry young playwrights was the Theater Workshop, particularly under the direction of Joan Littlewood (1914–). Two important playwrights—Brendan Behan (1923–1965), author of *The Hostage* (1958); and Shelagh Delaney (1939–), author of *A Taste of Honey* (1958)—were nurtured there.

Some critics say that today's most successful English playwright, Peter Shaffer (1926–), was influenced by the "angry young men" movement in such works as *The Royal Hunt of the Sun* (1964), *Equus* (1973), *Amadeus* (1980) and *The Gift of the Gorgon* (1992). Shaffer's plays, particularly *Equus*, combine realistic characteristics and causally related plots with highly theatrical devices. In *Equus*, for example, actors wear metallic kothornoi (platform shoes) and head coverings to represent horses.

Documentary Drama

A German movement of the 1960s called *documentary drama* has also been influential. Documentary dramas, by playwrights like Peter Weiss (1916–1982), Rolf Hochhuth (1931–), and Heinar Kipphardt (1922–), are based on historical documents which give an air of authenticity. The goal of documentary drama was to convince audiences that they were watching history unfold. These dramatists, however, did modify documents for dramatic effect.

Peter Weiss's *The Investigation* (1965) dramatizes the Frankfurt war-crimes tribunal, which tried people who had been guards at the Nazi extermination camps. While Weiss's play is based on transcripts of the proceedings, he has made specific changes and has used Brechtian epic techniques. His witnesses are given numbers, not names; this symbolizes the way camp inmates were stripped of their identity. His stage directions require the actors to deliver testimony unemotionally so that the audience will focus on the facts. The victims are not referred to as Jews, nor is the camp specifically identified, since Weiss's intention is to universalize the Holocaust so that it will represent all kinds of barbarity.

We should note that during the 1950s and 1960s a number of other important German-language playwrights dealt with themes similar to those of Hochhuth and Weiss, but not in documentary form. These playwrights focused on the issue of responsibility in a society that asks people to act inhumanely.

Two of the most famous examples of fictional drama dealing with this issue are *Biedermann and the Firebugs* (1958) by Max Frisch (1911–) and *The Visit* (1956) by the Swiss playwright Friedrich Duerrenmatt (1921–1992).

Documentary dramas were also written in the United States during the 1960s. Many of them reflected social upheavals, including the civil rights movement and the war in Vietnam. Among these plays were *The Trial of the Catonsville Nine* (1970) by Daniel J. Berrigan (1921–) and *Are You Now or Have You Ever Been* (1972), a play about the McCarthy era by Eric Bentley (1916–). Documentary dramas are still being written; one example is Emily Mann's *Execution of Justice* (1984).

POSTWAR ECLECTICS

In the period from 1945 to 1970, there were many theater artists around the world who experimented with a wide variety of techniques and whose artistic output defies easy categorization. These artists can be described as *eclectics*.

Among the postwar European theatrical innovators were numerous directors whose productions borrowed from the theatrical experiments discussed above —eclectics who used varied avant-garde techniques. It would be impossible to cite all of them, but we can mention a few.

The French director Jean-Louis Barrault (1910–), who worked with the director Charles Dullin and Antonin Artaud between the wars, has used many Artaudian and environmental staging techniques. These influences were particularly prominent in his production of *Rabelais* in 1968. Barrault was also noted for his productions of Ionesco's plays, and for his outstanding abilities as an actor.

Two Italian directors had an impact on the international theater scene: Giorgio Strehler (1921–) and Franco Zeffirelli (1923–). Strehler has directed important productions of classical and contemporary plays at the Piccolo Teatro, which he founded in Milan in 1947; and at the Théâtre de l'Europe, which was founded in 1983 as a showcase for major productions from the countries of the European Common Market. (The Common Market is an ongoing attempt to unify Europe economically; one of its goals, for example, is a single currency.) Strehler was director of the Théâtre de l'Europe until 1990 and directed many historically important plays for it. All together, he has directed over 200 productions, including dramas, comedies, and operas; but his most famous was *The Tempest* in 1983, which he brought to the United States.

Zeffirelli, who first worked in theater as an actor and designer, is best-known for his Shakespearean productions—*Romeo and Juliet* (1960), *Othello* (1961), and *Hamlet* (1964)—and his opera productions. He has also done film versions of *Romeo and Juliet* (1965) and *Hamlet* (1991), the latter starring Mel Gibson.

The English director Peter Brook is, however, possibly the most renowned of the contemporary eclectics.

Peter Brook

(1925–   )

Peter Brook is an English producer-director whose daring work has contributed significantly to the development of twentieth-century theater. He was born in London in 1925 and educated at Oxford, where he founded the Oxford University Film Society. As a young man, he had already attained the status of one of the foremost British directors. He introduced the plays of Jean Cocteau and Jean-Paul Sartre to England. In the 1950s and early 1960s, he directed productions of Shakespeare's *Titus Andronicus, The Winter's Tale,* and *King Lear* and worked with some of England's leading actors, including Laurence Olivier. Influenced by Artaud's theater of cruelty, he produced Jean Genet's *The Screens* and, in 1964, Peter Weiss's sensational play *The Persecution and Assassination of Jean-Paul Marat as Performed by the Inmates of the Asylum of Charenton under the Direction of the Marquis de Sade* (usually referred to as *Marat/Sade).* The unconventional style and staging of *Marat/Sade* shocked the theater world and won Brook international fame. Brook's production of Shakespeare's *A Midsummer Night's Dream* (1970) was clearly influenced by Meyerhold's experiments with biomechanics and circus arts; for example, the fairies appeared on trapezes.

Brook has staged plays at the Birmingham Repertory Theater, at Stratford-on-Avon, and at many theaters in London, in New York, and on the European continent. In the early 1960s, he was part of the artistic team which managed the Royal Shakespeare Company. In 1971, he founded the International Theater Research Center in Paris, where he continues to create experimental productions. Brook's eclecticism is also illustrated by several productions of the 1980s: a stripped-down version of the opera *Carmen,* an adaptation of the Indian epic *Mahabharata,* and a production of *The Cherry Orchard* played without intermissions. His films include *Lord of the Flies, Marat/Sade,* and *King Lear.* In 1993, he staged *L'Homme Qui,* an adaptation of a book about thirteen hospital patients with serious neurological disorders.

Brook's work reflects the influence of Grotowski's innovations. Like Grotowski, Brook has become more concerned with the *process* of theater—that is, how things are done—than with the product or end result. As he indicates in his theoretical work *The Empty Space* (1968), he tries to avoid "deadly" commercial theater, which does not allow for experimentation. In 1988, Brook published his autobiography, *The Shifting Point: Forty Years of Theatrical Exploration, 1946–1987.*

NEW TECHNOLOGY

Any discussion of postwar theater must take into account the introduction of new technology into scene and lighting design. Computer technology, for example, has been incorporated into many modern theater buildings, and lighting can now be controlled by computer. Some critics, however, argue that the human factor—the performer—is the basic element of theater and that this fact will limit computerization.

The Czechoslovakian designer Josef Svoboda has experimented with such technological elements as projections, multimedia, movable platforms, and new materials, including plastics.

Josef Svoboda

(1920–   )

Josef Svoboda was born on May 10, 1920, in Caslav, Czechoslovakia, a small city some 50 miles east of Prague. Even in his early years, Svoboda demonstrated the multiplicity of talents and interests which would mark his work throughout his life. His father was a cabinetmaker and carpenter who taught Svoboda the fundamentals of these trades at an early age. He attended a local gymnasium—an academically oriented high school—where he showed talent as a painter and scene designer. In 1939, he was admitted to Prague's Charles University, apparently destined for an academic career in the fine arts and classical studies. The German occupation of Bohemia closed down the universities, however, and Svoboda entered a 2-year advanced vocational school for master carpentry.

During the war years, Svoboda continued his technical training, but he also pursued his interest in painting and—more important—an active participation in theater. He established ties with the intensely dedicated young theater artists in Prague and was a principal organizer of the semiprofessional New Group theater housed in Prague's Smetana Museum.

After the war, several members of the New Group became the principal organizers of a new major theater ensemble, the Grand Opera of the Fifth of May, which moved into Prague's largest theater. While working for a university degree in architecture, Svoboda became its chief designer and technical director.

Svoboda's work was greatly influenced by the multimedia experiments of Czechoslovakian theater artists before the Second World War. He became internationally known when his designs, which combined live performers with projected images on multiple screens, were presented at the Brussels World's Fair in 1958. In spite of varying degrees of government censorship during the 1950s and 1960s, when Czechoslovakia was under Soviet domination, Svoboda became one of the leading influences on design worldwide.

JOSEF SVOBODA: SCENIC INNOVATOR Many technical wonders of today's theater are offshoots of Svoboda's experiments. This scene is from his production of *The Snow Queen*.

Svoboda's work centers on the concept of *kinetics*. He believes that because a play exists only in performance, its setting must be dynamic, changing throughout the performance according to the demands of the text. Toward this end, he has experimented with complex integrations of performers and projected images, a technique he calls *laterna magika*. Svoboda is also interested in finding ways to change settings easily and fluidly, and (as we have noted) he has experimented with a wide variety of new materials, such as plastics.

In the past three decades, Svoboda designed in many of the major cities in Europe and the United States, and he is credited with having worked on over 500 productions. From 1969 to 1990 he was a professor of architecture at the School of Applied and Industrial Arts in Prague. Since 1970, he has been the chief scenographer at the National Theater in Prague; and from 1973 on, the artistic head of a branch of the National Theater in Prague dedicated to experiments with the media techniques for which he is famous—this branch is called, appropriately, Laterna Magika. He has received many awards, including one for outstanding achievement from the United States Institute for Theatre Technology (USITT) in 1986 and the Gold Medal for Scenography in Czechoslovakia in 1988. In 1992, an English-language edition of Svoboda's writings, *The Secret of Theatrical Space*, was published.

POSTWAR DEVELOPMENTS IN AMERICAN THEATER

We will now look specifically at the United States in the period 1945–1970, since many of the international developments we have been examining can also be found in American theater, despite the fact that at the close of World War II there were limited outlets for experimentation in the United States.

One reason for this limitation was (and still is) the high cost of commercial productions. Commercial Broadway theater, on the west side of midtown Manhattan in New York City, has always been traditionally oriented, with large proscenium-arch playhouses and plays that usually appeal to popular tastes. For example, among the most popular productions since World War II have been musicals and the comedies of Neil Simon (1927–), including *The Odd Couple* (1965), *The Sunshine Boys* (1972), *California Suite* (1976), *Brighton Beach Memoirs* (1982), *Biloxi Blues* (1984), and *Lost in Yonkers* (1991). Though significant serious drama has also been produced on Broadway—including Arthur Miller's and Tennessee Williams's major works as well as more recent plays— the commercial nature of Broadway leads primarily to popular entertainments.

Musical Theater

As we saw in Chapter 13, *Oklahoma!*—which brought the team of Rodgers and Hammerstein together for the first time—was produced in 1943. It heralded a golden age of the American book musical. *Oklahoma!* seamlessly fitted together story, music, lyrics, and dances so that the production combined tone, mood, and intention in a unified whole. Its choreography, by Agnes DeMille, included a famous ballet sequence and influenced many later choreographers in musical theater, including Jerome Robbins (1918–) and Bob Fosse (1927–1987). Rodgers and Hammerstein went on to create other significant musicals such as *Carousel* (1945), which was revived very successfully at the National Theater in London in 1992; *South Pacific* (1949); *The King and I* (1951); and *The Sound of Music* (1959).

Among other notable musicals during the 1940s and 1950s were Irving Berlin's *Annie Get Your Gun* (1946), based on the life of Annie Oakley; Cole Porter's musical version of *The Taming of the Shrew*, called *Kiss Me Kate* (1948); *Guys and Dolls* (1950) by Frank Loesser (1910–1969), successfully revived on Broadway in 1992; *My Fair Lady* (1956) by the librettist and lyricist Alan Jay Lerner (1918–1986) and the composer Frederick Lowe (1904–1988), based on George Bernard Shaw's *Pygmalion;* and *West Side Story* (1957), a modernization of *Romeo and Juliet* which was created by the composer Leonard Bernstein (1918–1990), the lyricist Stephen Sondheim (1930–), and the librettist Arthur Laurents (1918–).

The 1940s and 1950s were remarkable not only for the number of outstanding musicals produced but also for the range and depth of those musicals. A wide variety of subjects were covered, and the quality was impressive. Not only composers and writers, but performers, directors, designers, and choreographers were all working at the top of their form.

MUSICAL COMEDY FLOURISHES. One of the great American "golden age" musicals is *Guys and Dolls* by Frank Loesser, which presents lovable underworld New York figures in a traditional romantic story line (it also became a successful film). Shown here is the famous number "Sit Down, You're Rocking the Boat" in the Tony Award-winning revival.

Fiddler on the Roof (1964)—with music by Jerry Bock (1928–), lyrics by Sheldon Harnick (1924–), and book by Joseph Stein (1912–)—is often said to mark the end of this golden era of book musicals. *Fiddler on the Roof,* which tells of a Jewish family whose father attempts to uphold tradition in a Russian village where the Jewish community faces persecution, was directed and choreographed by Jerome Robbins.

Off-Broadway and Off-Off-Broadway

The off-Broadway movement developed in the late 1940s as a reaction to Broadway commercialism. Its primary goal was to provide an outlet for experimental and innovative works, unhindered by commercial concerns. Off-Broadway was dedicated to introducing new playwrights and reviving significant plays that had initially been unsuccessful on Broadway. For example, one noted off-Broadway playhouse, the Circle in the Square, revived Tennessee Williams's *Summer and Smoke* in 1952 and Eugene O'Neill's *The Iceman Cometh* in 1956; both plays had failed in their original runs on Broadway. In the 1960s, plays of several young Americans, including Israel Horowitz (1939–), John Guare (1938–), and Lanford Wilson, were produced off-Broadway.

CIRCLE IN THE SQUARE. Off-Broadway came to the attention of the theatergoing public with revivals of significant American plays which had failed in their initial productions. The Circle in the Square made its reputation with a successful revival of Tennessee Williams's *Summer and Smoke* in 1952. This scene is from its 1957 production of the same play.

This movement also introduced new actors, directors, and designers. Among the performers who made debuts off-Broadway were Jason Robards, Colleen Dewhurst, Dustin Hoffman, and Al Pacino—all later recognized as significant professionals. The director José Quintero (1924–   ) established his reputation as the leading interpreter of Eugene O'Neill at the Circle in the Square theater.

Off-Broadway also popularized intimate playhouses that were not in traditional proscenium-arch form. Off-Broadway theaters typically seat only about 200 spectators, and many of them have thrust or arena stages. Even those with proscenium-arch stages are much more intimate than their Broadway counterparts, because of their smaller size. Such theaters had been found earlier in the United States, but off-Broadway playhouses—along with many regional theaters—proved the viability of alternative spaces.

In the 1960s and 1970s, off-Broadway itself became more commercial and therefore less experimental. As production costs rose, more conventional productions were staged off-Broadway. In the last two decades, many off-Broadway productions—such as the enormously popular musical *Grease* (1972)—have later moved to Broadway, indicating that the distinction between the two has been blurred.

Beginning in the 1960s, and increasingly in recent years, off-off-Broadway has replaced off-Broadway as the center for experimentation in New York. Off-off-Broadway is—as off-Broadway originally was—dedicated to introducing and showcasing new talent, experimenting with new styles of production, and

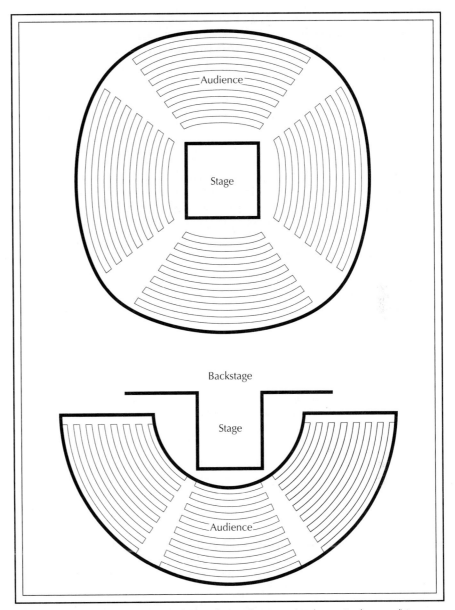

ARENA STAGE. *Top:* As this ground plan shows, the arena (or *theater-in-the-round*) is square or round and has the stage in the center with the audience surrounding it. This audience-performer relationship—one of the most ancient—became popular again after World War II. It provides intimacy and is economical because it precludes elaborate scenery.

THRUST STAGE. *Bottom:* The thrust stage is one of the most popular configurations in all of theater history. As this ground plan shows, a thrust stage juts into the audience, which surrounds it on three sides. It was used by the Greeks, Romans, and Elizabethans and has been revived in recent years. It allows a focus for the players and a scenic background, but it also creates intimacy, since spectators partly surround the action.

avoiding the limitations of commercialism. Many off-off-Broadway groups perform in *found spaces,* that is, spaces (such as factory lofts, churches, and warehouses) not originally intended for theater. American experiments with environmental theater have frequently been undertaken off-off-Broadway, as have some of the experiments with participatory theater—theater in which audience members are asked to take an active part.

The number of experimental off-Broadway and off-off-Broadway groups which tried to transform accepted theatrical conventions is impressive. Many of these companies flourished in the turbulent 1960s and were highly political, attacking capitalism, traditional values, and American involvement in Vietnam. Three such groups that deserve mention are the Living Theater, founded in 1946 by Julian Beck and Judith Malina; the Open Theater, founded in 1963 by Joseph Chaikin (1935–); and the Performance Group, founded by Richard Schechner in 1968. Each of these groups went through several phases, and the three were distinct in style, but they all experimented with improvisation, restructuring of texts, environmental staging, and acting based on externals.

The turbulent career of the Living Theater is in many ways representative of the many political companies which developed in the 1960s. Two significant individuals are Ellen Stewart and Joseph Papp.

The Living Theater

(founded 1946)

The Living Theater, founded in 1946 by Julian Beck (1925–1985) and Judith Malina (1926–), was a particularly influential avant-garde company of the late 1950s and the 1960s. Its transformations reflected changes in American society and experimental theater.

Initially, the Living Theater performed poetic dramas and plays by earlier avant-garde dramatists. Among the authors it staged were Bertolt Brecht, Federico García Lorca, Gertrude Stein (1874–1936), W. H. Auden (1907–1973), August Strindberg, Jean Cocteau, and Jean Racine. The group also experimented with production styles, using masks, stylized gestures and vocalizations, and theatrical conventions from the past. In the late 1950s, the Living Theater also became interested in the theories of Antonin Artaud.

The two productions that established the Living Theater's reputation were *The Connection* (1959) by Jack Gelber (1932–) and Kenneth Brown's *The Brig* (1963). *The Connection* presents dope addicts waiting to make a connection for a fix. *The Brig* dramatizes the daily routine in a Marine Corps prison. Both productions tried to make the spectators feel as if they were watching actual occurrences.

In the 1960s, because of tax problems, the Living Theater became nomadic, presenting many of its productions in Europe. (These problems were related to

JUDITH MALINA AND JULIAN BECK.
Beck and Malina founded the Living Theater
in 1946.

the political activism of its members, particularly their opposition to the war in Vietnam and to capitalism, and their anarchism. In 1971, members of the company were arrested in Brazil for political activities.) During this period, the group also developed the production style for which it became noted. Many of the works it staged were created by improvisation. Rather than play characters, the members portrayed themselves confronting social institutions and norms. Their best-known work of this period, *Paradise Now* (1968), included audience participation and confrontation in order to arouse spectators to the call for social revolution. Two other noteworthy works by the Living Theater in the mid-1960s were *Frankenstein* and *Mysteries and Smaller Pieces.*

The Living Theater has undergone numerous personnel changes. One early member, Joseph Chaikin, left the group and organized the Open Theater. Before the Brazilian tour, the company broke up into three groups.

Beck, Malina, and the Living Theater were not highly visible in the 1970s, but they continued to produce. In their production of *Prometheus* in London in 1979, audience members were invited to help enact the communist revolution and, after the performance, to join the company in a march outside a nearby prison. This production was a continuation of the Living Theater's experiments of the 1960s.

A revival of the 1960s productions in 1984 at New York's James Joyce Theater was unsuccessful. In the late 1980s, after Julian Beck's death, Judith Malina reorganized the Living Theater in a small storefront space on the lower east side of New York. The company dedicated itself to contemporary political and social issues; for example, it created a production employing homeless people who lived in the neighborhood. In 1993, the Living Theater once again had problems with the authorities when the city condemned the space in which it was working.

Ellen Stewart (ca. 1920–)

Joseph Papp (1921–1991)

Another influential off-off-Broadway figure, Ellen Stewart—who is of Cajun extraction—began as a fashion and millinery designer. Stewart founded the Cafe La Mama in 1961 and has been instrumental in introducing new playwrights and directors. She helped establish the careers of such authors as Lanford Wilson, Sam Shepard, Rochelle Owens (1936–), and Megan Terry (1932–). Stewart continues to work in New York at an East Village space known as La Mama Experimental Theater Club, into which she moved in 1969; however, she almost lost her theater in 1992 for lack of funding.

Joseph Papp (his name was originally Papirofsky) was an off-off-Broadway producer who had a strong impact on American theater. (He was also a director, but he was more successful as a producer.) In 1954, he opened the New York Shakespeare Festival, which gives free productions every summer in New York's Central Park. Beginning in 1967, he also operated the Public Theater—known simply as the Public—a series of theater spaces in a converted library. The Public is noted (among other things) for casting roles without regard to race.

At the Public and for the Shakespeare festival, Papp produced a number of successful shows which he moved to Broadway to help underwrite the production costs of his off-off-Broadway spaces. These included *Hair* (1968), *Two Gentlemen of Verona* (1971), *That Championship Season* (1973), and *A Chorus Line* (1975). Papp introduced a number of significant young playwrights, among them David Rabe, the author of three dramas of the war in Vietnam: *The Basic Training of Pavlo Hummel* (1971), *Sticks and Bones* (1971), and *Streamers* (1976, mentioned above). In the summer of 1980, he presented Gilbert and Sullivan's operetta *The Pirates of Penzance* in Central Park, with the pop star Linda Ronstadt—another show that moved successfully to Broadway.

Because Papp was so effective at the Public, he was asked in 1973 to run the theater at Lincoln Center, the major performing arts complex in New York City; but despite some artistically interesting productions, he was not successful there.

In the 1980s, Papp began staging Shakespeare's plays at the Public and the summer festival with famous film stars. As his health deteriorated, he appointed associate artistic directors at the Public, among them Joanne Akalaitis and the African American director-playwright George C. Wolfe. When Papp died, Akalaitis was appointed to head the Public, but after a tumultuous 18 months she was replaced by Wolfe. (Akalaitis and Wolfe will be discussed in Chapter 15.)

Regional Theater

American theater was transformed by the professional regional theater movement, which began in the late 1940s. A *regional theater company* is a permanent company operating in one community; among the most notable regional companies today are the Alley Theater in Houston (founded in 1949), the Arena Stage in Washington, D.C. (1949), the Tyrone Guthrie Theater in Minneapolis (1963), the Actors Theater of Louisville (1964), the Long Wharf in New Haven (1965), and the Mark Taper Forum in Los Angeles (1967).

These regional companies presented theater relevant to their communities. They offered classics and also discovered new talent. A few were resident companies, that is, acting troupes which remained together for an extended period of time. Their playhouses were often architecturally innovative; many of them were thrust or arena spaces.

One indication of the success of the regional movement is the number of dramas that originated in regional theater and were then transferred to Broadway in the 1960s and 1970s; they included Howard Sackler's *The Great White Hope*, Preston Jones's *The Texas Trilogy*, Michael Cristofer's *The Shadow Box*, G. L. Coburn's *The Gin Game*, and Mark Medoff's *Children of a Lesser God*.

The impact of large regional theaters remains strong today. The Mark Taper Forum, for example, was an early producer of *Angels in America: The Millennium Approaches* (1993) by Tony Kushner, which won both a Pulitzer Prize and a Tony Award. However, as we shall see in Chapter 15, regional theaters became financially pressed in the 1970s and 1980s, and in many instances could not be considered experimental or innovative. As a result, a new generation of alternative theaters would be established outside New York City.

African American Theater

As we mentioned at the opening of this chapter, the era from 1945 to 1970 saw many major social changes in the United States. One of the most significant was the civil rights movement, which included the landmark Supreme Court decision ordering integration of public schools; the ascendancy of the African American leaders Martin Luther King, Jr., and Malcolm X; and both violent and nonviolent activism. African American theater reflected this ongoing struggle.

AFRICAN AMERICAN THEATER IN THE 1950s

The 1950s saw the first phases of an explosion of African American theater that would occur over the next three decades. *Take a Giant Step* by Louis Patterson (1922–), a play about growing up in an integrated neighborhood, premiered in 1953. In 1954, the playwright-director Owen Dodson (1914–1983)—a significant figure in black theater since the 1930s—staged *Amen Corner* by James Baldwin (1924–1987) at Howard University.

At this time, too, the Greenwich Mews Theater, an off-Broadway house, began casting plays without regard to race. Two history dramas were staged there: *In Splendid Error* (1954) by William Branch (1927–   ), about the conflict between John Brown and Frederick Douglass; and *Land beyond the River* (1957) by Loften Mitchell (1919–   ), about a black minister's efforts to end school segregation. The Greenwich Mews also produced *Trouble in Mind* by Alice Childress (1920–   ). Although by this time there had been approximately 125 plays written by African American women, *Trouble in Mind* was the first to receive a professional staging. Three years later, Lorraine Hansberry became the first black woman to have a play on Broadway.

(UPI/Bettmann Newsphotos)

Lorraine Hansberry

(1930–1965)

Lorraine Hansberry's first play, *A Raisin in the Sun,* is considered by many critics to have been a turning point in American theater. To quote James Baldwin: "Never before in the entire history of the American theater has so much of the truth of Black people's lives been seen on the stage."

Hansberry was born on May 19, 1930, into an upper-middle-class family in Chicago. She first wanted to be a painter and studied at the Chicago Art Institute, at the University of Wisconsin, and in Guadalajara, Mexico. At Wisconsin, however, she saw a production of Sean O'Casey's *Juno and the Paycock.* Inspired by O'Casey's ability to universalize a specific people and their culture—in this case, the Irish—she decided to become a playwright.

In 1952, Hansberry went to New York and joined the staff of *Freedom,* a Harlem-based journal founded by Paul Robeson. Reacting against what she called a "whole body of material about Negroes. Cardboard characters. Cute dialect bits. Or hipswinging musicals from exotic scores," Hansberry set out to write a "social drama about Negroes that will be good art." That play was *A Raisin in the Sun.*

A Raisin in the Sun takes its title from a poem by Langston Hughes which asks, "What happens to a dream deferred?" It is set in the apartment of the Younger family on Chicago's South Side, and by including several generations within this one household, Hansberry is able to present an across-the-board picture of the changing and conflicting ideologies, dreams, and frustrations of black Americans in the 1950s.

When *A Raisin in the Sun* opened on Broadway on March 11, 1959, it marked several firsts: Hansberry was the first black female writer—as well as the youngest American playwright to that date and only the fifth woman—to win the New York Drama Critics Circle Award for Best Play of the Year; and Lloyd Richards (1922–   ) was the first African American director on Broadway.

(Richards later became head of the Yale School of Drama, a post he held until his retirement in 1992; at Yale, he nurtured the talents of the African American playwright August Wilson in the 1980s.)

A Raisin in the Sun also began an explosion of black theater in New York in the 1960s and 1970s. Hansberry's second play to be produced, *The Sign in Sidney Brustein's Window* (1964), was—in her words—about "the Western intellectual poised in hesitation before the flames of involvement." It had the passionate support of the artistic community, but it ran for only 101 performances, closing on the day of her death, January 22, 1965.

Hansberry's other completed works include *The Drinking Gourd, What Use Are Flowers,* and *Les Blancs,* which had a short run on Broadway in 1970. *To Be Young, Gifted, and Black,* a theatrical collage based on Hansberry's writings, was the longest-running drama of the 1968–1969 off-Broadway season. Though Hansberry's reputation suffered somewhat in the 1970s, in recent years there has been renewed interest in her work, partly because it has been praised by such authors as Amiri Baraka and August Wilson, and partly because of successful revivals of *A Raisin in the Sun* in theaters and on television.

CIVIL RIGHTS AND AFRICAN AMERICAN MILITANCY: 1960–1970

In the 1960s, African American theater was strongly influenced by the civil rights movement. Theater aimed at improving the rights and opportunities of minorities became especially important to black Americans.

The actor-playwright Ossie Davis (1917–   ) wrote *Purlie Victorious* (1961), a comedy satirizing the traditional racial stereotypes of the south, and 9 years later it returned to Broadway as a musical. A drama of southern racism by James Baldwin (1924–1987), *Blues for Mister Charlie* (1964), was also produced, though it closed quickly.

Perhaps the outstanding example of theater inspired by civil rights at the grassroots level was the Free Southern Theater, established in 1963 by Tom Dent, Gilbert Moses, and Richard Schechner (Schechner would later champion environmental theater). Based in New Orleans, the company toured Louisiana's rural communities with plays and skits about freedom.

By the middle to late 1960s, it was clear that African American playwrights had found their voice in both realism and departures from realism. Playwrights like Adrienne Kennedy (1931–   ) in *Funnyhouse of a Negro* (1964), Lonne Elder III (1932–   ) in *Ceremonies in Dark Old Men* (1969), and Charles Gordone (1925–   ) in *No Place to Be Somebody* (1969) proved themselves masters at placing characters in true-to-life settings and using dialogue to make accurate observations about life. Many other African American playwrights used highly imaginative techniques which broke with realistic tradition. Douglas Turner Ward (1930–   ), for example, had black men play in whiteface—a reversal of the minstrel show—in his play *Day of Absence* (1970). Possibly the most controversial African American playwright of the 1960s, both for his subject matter and for his theatrical techniques, was Amiri Baraka.

(UPI/Bettmann Newsphotos)

Amiri Baraka

(1934–   )

A prolific and provocative dramatist, Amiri Baraka has well over thirty plays to his credit. Before Baraka, black protest drama had been largely realistic; by infusing allegory and lyricism into his vivid depictions of racially torn America, Baraka changed the shape of this protest drama and inspired a whole school of writing.

Baraka was born on October 7, 1934, in Newark, New Jersey; his original name was Everett LeRoi Jones. He attended Rutgers University and then Howard University. After serving briefly in the Air Force, he moved to New York, where he attended Columbia University and earned an M.A. in German literature from the New School of Social Research. During this time, he became associated with the "beat" poets of the 1950s.

Two of Baraka's earlier plays—*A Good Girl Is Hard to Find* (1958) and *Dante* (1961)—had been produced, but it was *Dutchman* (1964) that brought him to the forefront of American theater. Set in a steamy subway car in New York City, *Dutchman* is a verbal and sexual showdown between a middle-class assimilated black man and a white temptress. Their conflict becomes a metaphor for political, sociological, and psychological dilemmas confronting African Americans. *Dutchman* earned Baraka a Guggenheim Fellowship and an Obie Award for the Best American Play of 1963–1964. It is also credited with beginning a renaissance of African American theater in the 1960s and 1970s and with demonstrating a need for a new aesthetic for contemporary black works.

Baraka's *The Slave* and *The Toilet*, a double bill of one-act plays, opened off-Broadway in 1965. *The Slave* is a domestic battle involving an interracial couple, set against the background of a race war; *The Toilet*, set in a washroom in an inner-city high school, is an impassioned work in which teenage gang members pummel a boy to death. These plays foreshadowed the urban violence that was soon to engulf the United States. Baraka's next notable work, *Slave Ship* (1970), used a number of ritualistic devices.

After Baraka rose to success in New York theater, he left to form his own performing company in the black community. The Black Arts Repertory Theater and School in Harlem was his first endeavor. He then returned to Newark, where he became founder and director of the Spirit House Movers and Players.

In addition to being a dramatist, Baraka is also a poet, novelist, musicologist, essayist, critic, and editor. In the 1980s, he returned to Marxist philosophy and published a controversial autobiography. He continues to write plays; his most recent drama, *Meeting Lillie,* was produced off-off-Broadway in 1993.

By 1970, the Black Theater Alliance listed over 125 producing groups in the United States. Only a few of these survived the decade, but many had a significant impact. For example, the New Lafayette Theater, founded in 1966, operated until 1972; it introduced the playwright Ed Bullins (1935–), experimented with black ritual, and published the journal *Black Theater.*

Among production organizations, the Negro Ensemble Company (NEC) is the oldest professional African American company in continuous production. It was conceived and administered by Douglas Turner Ward, originally with assistance from Robert Hooks and Gerald Krone. Beginning in 1967, it produced many significant original plays, including some which moved to Broadway, among them *The River Niger* (1973) by Joseph Walker (1935–), *The First Breeze of Summer* (1975) by Leslie Lee (1935–), and *A Soldier's Play* (1981) by Charles Fuller (1939–), which won the Pulitzer Prize. In the 1990s, the Negro Ensemble Company has had serious financial difficulties and has at least once nearly ceased operating. In 1993, it produced in a theater at LaGuardia Community College in the borough of Queens, since it could not afford either Broadway or off-Broadway houses.

ASIAN THEATER

Since the end of the Second World War, contemporary theater in Japan has been in a healthy state. A number of truly gifted playwrights have emerged, chief among them Kinoshita Junji (1914–), whose work combines social concerns with humor and, when appropriate, elements from Japanese folk tradition.

During the 1960s, avant-garde theater also developed in Japan. Some actors and directors felt that spoken theater—though originally a nontraditional movement—had become "establishment." They decided to strike out toward other kinds of theater experiences, and some of them drew on the kind of abstraction and exaggeration that had long been a part of kabuki and noh. Thus arose an unusual situation: the old became a way of radicalizing the new. A key figure in this movement is Tadashi Suzuki (1939–).

In China, after the civil war and Mao Zedong's rise to power, spoken drama continued to be written, but additional emphasis was given to traditional forms of popular theater. These traditional forms were familiar in the countryside and became a medium for carrying messages of the government to remote corners of the nation. During the cultural revolution, which began in 1966, theatrical activity—particularly spoken drama—was more restricted; increasing emphasis was placed on a few dance-dramas, elaborately staged and danced, that had a very heavy ideological or propagandistic content. For the most part, theater artists, along with intellectuals, were seen as subversive and suffered greatly during this era in Chinese history.

Movements in theater between 1945 and 1970 both continued traditions from the past and forced audiences and artists to reevaluate earlier forms of drama and earlier staging practices. In the years that followed, these experiments would have an impact on commercial as well as avant-garde theater.

SUMMARY

A number of theatrical movements were in evidence between 1945 and 1970. The absurdist dramas of Samuel Beckett, Eugène Ionesco, and Harold Pinter have had a profound influence on contemporary playwriting. Other movements included the "angry young men" in England and documentary drama. The two leading American dramatists, Arthur Miller and Tennessee Williams, continued to work in a more conventional realistic style but also used "selective realism."

Happenings, multimedia, environmental theater, and poor theater—as in the productions of Jerzy Grotowski's Polish Laboratory Theater—forced theatergoers to reevaluate their traditional expectations about the actor-audience relationship and other aspects of drama. Many significant eclectic directors, including Peter Brook, had an international impact.

In the United States, off-Broadway, off-off-Broadway, and regional theater attempted to break away from commercialism. Producers such as Joseph Papp and Ellen Stewart introduced new playwrights and practitioners. Regional professional theaters became firmly established in many American cities. African American theater artists wrote plays and organized production companies which focused on civil rights issues of the 1950s and 1960s.

In Japan, some avant-garde theater artists incorporated traditional elements from noh and kabuki. In China, the cultural revolution suppressed spoken drama, though traditional popular theater was used for ideological purposes.

CONTEMPORARY THEATER: 1970 TO THE PRESENT

....

CONTEMPORARY THEATER: 1970 TO THE PRESENT

I t is a beautiful May evening in New York City in 1993, and we are about to attend a new production on Broadway. Given the high cost of a ticket— anywhere from about $45 to $65—we have carefully considered all the shows that are running before deciding which one we want to see, and we are amazed by the diversity of the offerings. We also realize that these shows reflect recent changes in American theater.

Among the shows we could have seen are two hit musicals that opened recently: *The Who's Tommy* and *Kiss of the Spider Woman*. *Tommy* was originally presented at the La Jolla Playhouse in San Diego by Des McAnuff, a director who made his reputation in alternative theater. *Kiss of the Spider Woman*, directed by Harold Prince, has lyrics and music by John Kander and Fred Ebb, who also wrote the hit musical *Cabaret*; and a book by Terence McNally, who made his reputation off-Broadway in the 1960s and 1970s. It was showcased a few years ago at the State University of New York at Purchase and was presented in London before its Broadway run.

FOOL MOON. Bill Irwin is a leading postmodern artist who relies on traditions of commedia dell'arte, mime, Charlie Chaplin, and vaudeville. In *Fool Moon* Irwin (left) created a series of vaudevillian mime sketches with another clown, David Shiner (right). These pieces, while highly comic, also touched on the difficulties of human interaction in our contemporary society. *(Joan Marcus)*

Wendy Wasserstein's latest hit, *The Sisters Rosensweig,* with an all-star cast, moved to Broadway after a sold-out run at Lincoln Center. *The Song of Jacob Zulu,* a play about apartheid in South Africa which has the Ladysmith Black Mambazo Singers as a chorus, was transferred from Chicago's Steppenwolf Theater. The show receiving the greatest acclaim is Tony Kushner's *Angels in America: Millennium Approaches,* a 3½-hour epic play which is the first half of a 7-hour work. It deals with gay life in the United States and the impact of AIDS; its subtitle is *A Gay Fantasia on National Themes. Angels* had earlier performances at the Eureka Theater in San Francisco, the National Theater in London, and the Mark Taper Forum in Los Angeles.

All these choices available to us show how much the Broadway scene has changed in the last 30 years. The productions come from regional theaters, off-Broadway, and London. Many of the artists began their careers in alternative theater. The subject matter is as diverse as American society and has often been shaped by social upheavals involving gender roles as well as sexual and racial relations.

The show we finally choose, *Fool Moon,* is a perfect example of the changing commercial theater in New York. *Fool Moon* was created by two performance artists, Bill Irwin and David Shiner. Irwin, who is highly regarded, has created many of his own works, including *The Regard of Flight* in 1982. His performance style is very physical, relies heavily on mime, and is reminiscent of silent films and vaudeville. With all its physicality, however, Irwin's work also has a strong cerebral quality. Shiner was the lead comic of the critically acclaimed Cirque du Soleil, a highly theatrical circus from Montreal, Canada, and his performance style is also based on the great tradition of clowning. The two worked together last summer at "Serious Fun!"—a festival of performance artists at Lincoln Center—and decided to create a full-length production.

As we enter the Richard Rodgers Theater on 46th Street between Broadway and Eighth Avenue, we are struck by the oddness of seeing performance artists—who are more likely to use alternative spaces—in this commercial setting: a handsome proscenium-arch playhouse.

The opening moments of *Fool Moon* sets the tone for the evening. Irwin gets tangled in the theater's rigging for flying and is pulled up into the fly space. Shiner, trying to find a seat, fights with several audience members here and there in the theater. The show is almost 2 hours long, but there is no dialogue—just a series of slapstick moments which frequently involve audience participation. Irwin's clown is more lovable; Shiner's is more aggressive. In one of the comic skits, Shiner stages a silent film melodrama using audience members as the cast. In another, Shiner takes a woman—again an audience member—out on a date, and after a hilarious car ride, they stop at a restaurant where Irwin is the maitre d'. The production ends with Irwin and Shiner flying off on a crescent moon with a beautiful star-filled background behind them. We have spent the evening unable to control our laughter.

As we leave, we realize how well *Fool Moon* represents both the past and the present of American theater. Irwin and Shiner are stars of contemporary performance art. People who frequent avant-garde theater love them for their physical performances and their cynical insights into human nature. On the other hand, their current production also appeals to audiences who remember the great Broadway vaudevillians of the past.

BACKGROUND: WORLDWIDE CHANGES SINCE 1970

It is difficult to assess the social, political, and economic upheavals of the past 25 years; we are too close to these developments to evaluate or predict their eventual significance for western society. We can, however, look at certain key events.

These 25 years have seen continued turmoil around the world. Although the war in Vietnam ended in the early 1970s, there were many conflicts during the 1980s and 1990s, including a war in Afghanistan initiated by the Soviets, interventions by the United States in Granada and Panama, and a war in the Persian Gulf in which United Nations forces expelled Iraqi troops from Kuwait.

There were early hopes for peace in the middle east, after Israel and Egypt signed a nonaggression agreement at Camp David in 1977, but then these hopes were dimmed by turmoil over Israel's occupation of the West Bank, by the Islamic fundamentalist movement, and by continued episodes of terrorism. The release of long-held American hostages in Lebanon and the alliance formed by the United States and several Arab nations during the Gulf War later revived optimism again, and in September of 1993 Israel and the Palestine Liberation Organization signed an agreement respecting each other's right to exist.

There were radical changes in what had been the communist world in both Europe and Asia. By 1990, eastern Europe was being democratized as the communist regimes collapsed. One of the most vivid images of that year was the demolishing of the Berlin Wall, which had symbolized the cold war. In Czechoslovakia, the playwright Vaclav Havel—who had been attacked and even imprisoned by the communist regime and whose politically charged works had been banned in his own country—was elected president in 1989. However, the democratization of communist Europe has not been tranquil. In Russia, Poland, and Czechoslovakia, the new governments proved unstable. In what was once Yugoslavia, there has been an ongoing civil war between Muslims and Christians, in which the attacks on Muslims are reminiscent of the genocide directed against Jews under Nazisim. The reunification of Germany weakened its economy and also brought a neo-Nazi movement and terrorist attacks on immigrants.

In China, there was a remarkable change in economic policies in the 1980s. With the opening of relations with the west a few years earlier, the Chinese communist government allowed more capitalist ventures and the introduction of western businesses. However, the Chinese government viciously crushed democratic demonstrations in 1989, in scenes which were televised across the world. It is still not clear how soon the Chinese government will allow liberalization.

There has also been worldwide economic turmoil, though some European and Asian economies have flourished. In the late 1970s and again in the late 1980s, recessions had a significant impact on the American economy, which has at best been sluggish. Fiscal uncertainty was one reason why Bill Clinton was elected president in 1992, defeating the incumbent, George Bush, and ending a 12-year reign by the Republicans which had begun with Ronald Reagan in 1980.

Throughout these years, there have been conservative movements which attempted to counter the advances made by gays, feminists, and other minorities. Gay groups, for instance, had become more vocal politically, partly because of AIDS, which was killing many homosexuals. (AIDS is a disease which destroys the body's natural immune system. It began to reach epidemic proportions in the 1980s, and a significant number of theater figures have died of it, including the Broadway musical director Michael Bennett and the founder of the Ridiculous Theater Company, Charles Ludlam.) Conservative politicians worldwide also questioned government support of the arts.

Technological innovations have continued to change the way we live, and particularly the way we communicate. Microcomputers, introduced in the late 1970s, have become more and more advanced: laptops and powerbooks—portable computers—are now as powerful as some of the early mainframes. "Faxes" allow documents to be sent around the world instantaneously over telephone lines; and telephone lines themselves may eventually be replaced by wireless communication.

What is the state of theater in the 1990s? Where is it headed? We cannot be certain about the answer to the second question, but we can draw some reasonable conclusions about the first. A good way to consider theater in the 1990s is to look at some key examples from the past two decades. We cannot cover all of Europe or the United States, of course, but in this final chapter we will look at a variety of American and international developments which will serve to indicate what has been happening in theater throughout the western world.

CONTEMPORARY PLAYWRIGHTS

During the past two decades, a significant number of playwrights throughout the world have attacked what they see as oppressive social and political institutions and have used unique theatrical techniques.

Some of these playwrights are described as *postmodernist* in style. This term suggests that "modernist" interest in antirealism is no longer central, and that art has moved beyond abstraction. Contemporary playwrights—and other theater artists—combine abstraction and realism, so that their work cannot be easily classified. Also, the distinction between "high" art and popular art is no longer entirely clear: postmodernists use both "artistic" and popular concerns and techniques.

American Playwrights

GENDER DIVERSITY

In the United States, many female playwrights have questioned traditional gender roles and the place of women in American society. Representative works include *'night, Mother* (1983) by Marsha Norman (1947–), *Crimes of the Heart* (1977) by Beth Henley (1952–), and *The Heidi Chronicles* (1988) and *The Sisters Rosensweig* (1992) by Wendy Wasserstein (1950–). Feminist theater companies have also forced audiences to reexamine gender biases. Some scholars estimate that more than 100 feminist companies have been founded in the United States; these companies include At the Foot of the Mountain, Women's Experimental Theatre, and the Omaha Magic Theater. One company, Split Britches, became well-known for its production of *Belle Reprieve* (1991), which made satiric references to Tennessee Williams's *A Streetcar Named Desire*.

One of the most political and most prolific of women playwrights is Maria Irene Fornes, whose long and distinguished career goes back to the off-off-Broadway movement of the 1960s.

(Anne Cusak/Chicago Tribune)

Maria Irene Fornes

(1930–)

Maria Irene Fornes is among the avant-garde dramatists who began the off-off-Broadway movement. Unlike many of her contemporaries, she has continued to work off-off-Broadway and shows no sign of wanting to leave noncommercial theater.

Fornes was born in Havana, Cuba, in 1930 and came to the United States in 1945 with her mother and one sister. After becoming a naturalized citizen in 1951, she went to Europe for 3 years and pursued her original goal of becoming a painter. In 1954, in Paris, she saw Roger Blin's production of *Waiting for Godot*. Even though she spoke no French, she was so moved by the experience that she decided to devote her life to playwriting.

She returned to New York in 1957 and worked as a textile designer. In 1960 she started to write plays, and in 1964 she had her first important production, *Tango Palace*. In 1965 she won two Obie awards, one for *The Successful Life of 3: A Skit for Vaudeville* and one for the musical *Promenade* (written in collaboration with Al Carmines), perhaps the best-known of her early works.

Fornes's plays are unconventional in structure, dialogue, and staging. They are fundamentally symbolic and often contain both brutality and slapstick humor. Her work of the 1960s showed a strong absurdist influence and was full of linguistic tricks and deliberately fanciful incongruities of time, space, and character. In the 1970s, Fornes continued to search for her own unique voice, and many critics believe she found it in *Fefu and Her Friends* (1977), which took a more realistic approach. In the 1980s, she wrote a number of plays, including *Mud* (1983, revised 1985), *The Conduct of Life* (1985), and *Abingdon Square* (1984). In 1992, her epic opera *Terra Incognita*, a revisionist treatment of Columbus, had its premiere in Italy. Since 1968, Fornes has directed many of the productions of her plays.

Because of the unique nature of her work, Fornes has not achieved the kind of national recognition typically associated with success in American theater. Her plays embody the ethic of off-off-Broadway and strike a balance between concern with human relationships and social and political consciousness.

CULTURAL DIVERSITY

Maria Irene Fornes is not only a significant female playwright but also a significant Hispanic playwright: her work often reflects her cultural background as well as her concerns with issues of gender. In American theater since 1970, many playwrights—and many theater companies—have focused on multicultural concerns: the special concerns of racial and ethnic groups and other subcultures within American society.

Influential playwrights and performers as well as important issues have been brought to the attention of the theatergoing public by Hispanic companies, such as Teatro Campesino, INTAR, and the Puerto Rican Traveling Company; and by Asian groups, including the Pan Asian Repertory Theater. The earliest works by David Henry Hwang (1957–   ), for example, were staged by the Pan Asian Repertory Theater. Hwang went on to write *M. Butterfly*, which won most of the major "best play" awards in 1988.

Gay theater companies have forced audiences to consider their own attitudes toward homosexuality. For instance, the Ridiculous Theater Company, which was founded in 1967 by Charles Ludlam (1943–1987), burlesques historic literature by presenting it in drag.

African American theater and drama continue to be a vital force, not only in New York but in all the major cities of the United States. One of today's most significant playwrights, August Wilson, is an African American.

August Wilson

(1945–)

The critical and popular success of August Wilson's plays make it clear that he is one of the major American dramatists of the twentieth century. Wilson evokes the African American experience at various times in history through richly poetic texts.

The son of a white father and a black mother, Wilson grew up in a two-room apartment behind a grocery store on Bedford Avenue in Pittsburgh. He attended Catholic schools until, at the age of 15, he left school when a teacher wrongly accused him of plagiarism. To keep his mother from worrying, Wilson spent his afternoons in the public library, completing his education on his own. During his hours in the library, he developed a love of poetry, in particular the works of Dylan Thomas. Following a brief enlistment in the army, Wilson moved into a boardinghouse, resolved to become a poet.

In 1968, Wilson helped found the Black Horizons Theater Company in Pittsburgh. In the late 1970s and early 1980s, he struggled to establish himself as a poet and held various odd jobs in Minneapolis. At the same time, he became interested in playwriting and wrote a number of dramas, including *The Homecoming* (1979), *The Coldest Day of the Year* (1979), *Fullerton Street* (1980), *Black Bart and the Sacred Hills* (1981), and *Jitney* (1982).

It was when Wilson submitted a draft of *Ma Rainey's Black Bottom* to the Eugene O'Neill Center in Waterford, Connecticut—a workshop devoted to new plays—that his work came to the attention of Lloyd Richards, the artistic director. Richards had directed the original production of *A Raisin in the Sun* and was also the head of the Yale Drama School and the Yale Repertory Theater. With Richards directing, *Ma Rainey's Black Bottom* opened at the Yale Rep in April 1984 and 6 months later moved to Broadway. (Wilson had to borrow a tuxedo for the Broadway opening.) Since *Ma Rainey's Black Bottom*, Richards has been Wilson's mentor, directing all his plays at the Yale Rep or at other regional theaters before bringing them to New York.

Wilson's play *Fences*, a family drama set in the 1950s, was produced in New Haven in 1985; in 1987, it opened in New York, where it received rave notices and went on to win the Pulitzer Prize. *Joe Turner's Come and Gone*, which deals with a turn-of-the-century African American searching for his lost wife, also opened in New York in 1987, while *Fences* was still running. In *Joe Turner*— more than his two preceding plays—Wilson uses a heavily poetic style of realism. *The Piano Lesson* won Wilson his second Pulitzer Prize in 1990. *Two Trains Running* (1992), a play which deals with the turmoil of the 1960s, was more comedic than his earlier works but was received less enthusiastically by the New York critics when it opened on Broadway in 1992.

THE PIANO LESSON.   August Wilson's Pulitzer Prize-winning play *The Piano Lesson* was presented at a number of major regional theaters, including the Yale Repertory Theater in New Haven and the Goodman Theater in Chicago, before its Broadway premiere. It deals with an African American family in the early twentieth century trying to come to grips with its past. Shown here is a scene from a production at the Seattle Repertory Theatre.

Wilson's major plays to date are part of a proposed cycle of ten dramas—one for each decade of the twentieth century—tracing the African American experience. Wilson's work is not political in the usual rhetorical sense: it remains poetic rather than polemical. Wilson argues that in order to know who you are now, you must know who you were in the past. His characters are universal figures, standing for everyone who has ever struggled with himself or herself and with social forces. He has said, "I write about the black experience in America and try to explore in terms of the life I know best those things which are common to all cultures."

OTHER AMERICAN DRAMATISTS

Many of the young off-Broadway and off-off-Broadway playwrights of the 1960s have made major contributions to American theater during the past two decades. Examples are *Talley's Folly* (1979), *The Fifth of July* (1980), *Burn This* (1987), and *Redwood Curtain* (1993) by Lanford Wilson (1937–   ); and *Six Degrees of Separation* (1991) by John Guare (1938–   ). Possibly the two most important American dramatists of the past 25 years have been Sam Shepard and David Mamet.

Sam Shepard

(1943–   )

Sam Shepard, whose dramas adroitly blend images of the American west, pop motifs, science fiction, and other elements of popular and youth culture, is one of the most inventive American playwrights. He has won dozens of awards, including Obies for eleven plays (more than any other author). Many critics consider him the dominant American playwright of his generation. Having written forty-two plays in just about 22 years, he is surely among the most prolific.

Shepard's father was in the army, and Shepard spent his childhood on military bases. His original ambition to become a veterinarian came to an end after a single year in college, and in 1963 he arrived in New York at the age of 19 determined to become an actor. Two years later, the *New York Times* called him the "acknowledged 'genius' of the off-off-Broadway circuit"—not as an actor, however, but as a playwright. In 1966 Shepard became the first dramatist to receive three Obies in one year, winning awards for *Chicago, Icarus's Mother,* and *Red Cross.*

Shepard lived in England from 1971 to 1974. Two notable plays of this period—*The Tooth of Crime* (1972) and *Geography of a Horse Dreamer* (1974)—premiered in London. In late 1974, he became playwright in residence at the Magic Theater in San Francisco, where most of his subsequent plays of the 1970s were first produced.

TRUE WEST. Sam Shepard exemplifies modern dramatists who combine the realistic and nonrealistic, theatricality, and recognizable characters in a way that is particularly emblematic of today's theater. His play *True West* deals with a love-hate relationship between two brothers. In this production by the Steppenwolf company in Chicago, Jeff Perry (left) and John Malkovich (right) play the brothers.

Shepard's characters are storytellers, and his plays are characterized by lengthy monologues. While his characters tell many stories, though, the truth of any particular story is never verified. The audience is invited to speculate, to form opinions about the dynamics of a person or family. Shepard's best-known works belong to what he calls his "family trilogy": *Curse of the Starving Class* (1977), *Buried Child* (1978), and *True West* (1980). *Fool for Love* (1983), which Shepard also directed, and *A Lie of the Mind* (1985) explored many of the same themes as the trilogy, including the death of traditional family structure, inability to establish lasting relationships, the violence of American society, and a longing for a simpler time.

In the last decade, Shepard has done less dramatic writing. His play *States of Shock* (1991), which deals allegorically with the Persian Gulf war, was not well received. Shepard has also turned his attention to screenwriting, film directing, and acting, appearing in many films, including *The Right Stuff, Crimes of the Heart, Voyager,* and *Thunderheart.* Most recently, he has led a reclusive life with his wife, the film star Jessica Lange.

(Gerry Goodstein)

David Mamet

(1947–)

Although relatively young, David Mamet has established himself as a mainstay of American theater. He has written twenty full-length plays, a number of short plays, and several original and adapted screenplays. He has won numerous awards, including three Chicago Jefferson Awards for best new play of the season, two Obies, two New York Drama Critics Circle Awards, and the Pulitzer Prize for *Glengarry Glen Ross* (1984).

Mamet was born in Chicago on November 30, 1947, and was brought up in the Jewish area of the South Side. His mother was a teacher and his father a labor lawyer and amateur semanticist. After his parents divorced, Mamet lived with his mother and attended a private school in a Chicago suburb, Olympia Fields. Mamet's uncle was the Director of Broadcasting for the Chicago Board of Rabbis, and for a time Mamet appeared on television playing Jewish children with various religious problems.

Mamet attended Goddard College in Vermont, majoring in literature and theater. From 1968 to 1969, he took an 18-month break from formal studies to work at the Neighborhood Playhouse, a Stanislavski-oriented program under the direction of Sanford Meisner, who had been an actor with the Group Theater in the 1930s. Mamet completed his degree in 1969. For a short time, he tried to work as an actor, but his ambition diminished after he worked for one season in a summer stock theater. After a succession of jobs, he returned to

(Gerry Goodstein)

OLEANNA. David Mamet is a leading American playwright. His works—with their sparse use of language and their enigmatic plotlines—have been compared to Harold Pinter's. Shown here is a scene from Mamet's highly controversial *Oleanna,* a play about sexual harrassment.

Goddard College as an instructor and began writing plays for use in his drama classes.

In 1972, he returned to Chicago, where his one-act play *Sexual Perversity in Chicago* won a Jefferson Award as best new play of the year. In 1975, *Sexual Perversity* and another one-act play, *Duck Variations,* opened in New York as a double bill and won the Obie for best play. In 1977, *American Buffalo* opened on Broadway and was voted best new play by the New York Drama Critics Circle. *Glengarry Glen Ross* (1983), which opened at the National Theater in London and was dedicated to Harold Pinter, brought Mamet international attention and in 1992 was adapted as a film. The Broadway production of *Speed-the-Plow* (1988) featured the rock star Madonna. In 1992, *Oleanna,* which Mamet also directed, stirred up a controversy because of its handling of the subject of sexual harassment—it involves charges made by a woman student against a college professor.

Mamet's plays are very reminiscent of Pinter. They have naturalistic language and settings and down-and-out characters whose struggles are clearly recognizable, but they do not provide the clear-cut exposition or dramatic resolutions of traditional realism. Mamet's plays question the ability of humans to communicate and interact honestly.

International Playwrights

Many playwrights throughout the world have questioned the traditional values of western society. For instance, the Brazilian director-playwright Augusto Boal (1931–), whose theories are discussed in *Theatre of the Oppressed* (1975), has written dramas reflecting his revolutionary Marxist ideas.

Three Germans who have received significant attention in the United States are Peter Handke (1942–), Franz Xaver Kroetz (1946–), and Heiner Müller (1929–). Handke's plays—including *Offending the Audience* (1966), *Self-Accusation* (1966), *Kaspar* (1968), *Ride across Lake Constance* (1970), *They Are Dying Out* (1973), and *Slow Homecoming* (1982)—focus on the shortcomings of language as a tool for communication and are surreal and symbolic in style.

Kroetz's plays, with their stichomythic language and grotesque relationships, are reminiscent of Mamet and Shepard. Kroetz's best-known works include *Farm Yard* (1972) and *Mensch Meier* (1978). Two of his most poignant works are *Request Concert* (1971), a short play with only one character and no dialogue which carefully details the last night of a lonely woman's life before her suicide; and *Extended Forecast*, which deals with a woman preparing to enter an old age home. *Extended Forecast* had its New York premiere in 1993 at Cafe La Mama.

Müller, who began his career in communist East Germany in the 1950s, became known for the short plays he wrote in the late 1970s and 1980s—explosions of images ridiculing traditional values and institutions. His most famous play is *Hamletmachine* (1977), an Artaud-like scenario. Müller has directed many of his own works.

The Italian playwright Dario Fo (1926–) is known for his satirical political comedies, which attack capitalist institutions and are reminiscent of Aristophanes. Among his best-known works are *The Accidental Death of an Anarchist* (1970) and *We Won't Pay, We Won't Pay* (1974). Fo—with his wife, the actress Franca Rame (1929–)—has run his own theater companies, directing and acting in his plays.

Concern for political and social equality is at the heart of the works of the South African playwright Athol Fugard (1932–) and the Nigerian playwright Wole Soyinka (1934–). Fugard, who is white, has attacked apartheid in such plays as *The Blood Knot* (1964), *Sizwe Banzi Is Dead* (1973), *Master Harold . . . and the Boys* (1982), *A Lesson from Aloes* (1987), and *Playland* (1992). He sometimes stages and acts in his own works.

Soyinka—who is also a poet, essayist, and novelist—began his career with the Royal Court Theater in London in the late 1950s. His politically charged works led to his arrest in Nigeria in 1967, and to 2 years' imprisonment. In 1973, he adapted Euripides' *The Bacchae* for the National Theater in England. Soyinka gained international recognition in 1986, when he received the Nobel Prize in Literature. Among his best-known dramas are *The Swamp Dwellers* (1957), *The Road* (1965), *Death and the King's Horsemen* (1975), and *A Play of Giants* (1985).

British Playwrights

In English theater, Tom Stoppard (1937–) has written plays emphasizing wordplay and intellectual concerns. A significant number of "angry" playwrights have attacked traditional political, social, and economic institutions. Among the best-known of these authors are David Hare (1947–) and Howard Brenton (1942–); but it is probably Caryl Churchill who has achieved the greatest recognition worldwide for politically charged plays.

Caryl Churchill
(1938–)

Caryl Churchill was born in London on September 3, 1938. From 1948 through 1955, her family lived in Montreal, Canada; in 1957, she returned to England to study at Oxford University, where she completed her B.A. in English language and literature in 1960. While at Oxford, she wrote her first play, *Downstairs,* which was produced there and at the National Union of Students/*Sunday Times* Student Drama Festival. During the 1960s, she married, had three sons, and spent a long apprenticeship writing radio plays.

As the women's movement began to gather momentum in the 1970s, Churchill had her first major success with *Owners* (1973). Since then she has become famous for her plays *Cloud Nine* (1979), *Top Girls* (1982), *Fen* (1983), *Serious Money* (1985), and *Mad Forest* (1990). Most of her plays have been created with the Joint Stock Company or the English Stage Company; frequently, she has developed these dramas by working closely with the actors, who make suggestions for changes, additions, and deletions.

Churchill's work is characterized by a unique fluidity of structure. She often mixes chronological and anachronistic events. She also double-casts roles in many of her plays, and she reverses gender roles, forcing audiences to explore generally accepted sexual stereotypes. (In *Cloud Nine,* for example, she has men play some of the female roles and women play some of the male roles.) She is brilliant at mixing theatricality with reality to create a unique postmodernist blend in plays that are extremely political. For instance, *Top Girls* opens with a party given by a modern-day professional woman who has just been promoted; attending this celebration are historical and mythological figures who are used to suggest that women who try to emulate men's superficial successes are not true feminists. *A Mouthful of Birds* (1986) and *Lives of the Great Poisoners* (1991) combine dramatic text, music, and dance.

Churchill has received wide recognition and numerous awards, including the Susan Smith Blackburn Prize, which she won twice.

MUSICAL THEATER

We should bear in mind that in all the world's major cities, commercial theater continues to be prominent. A good example is the sustained popularity of musical theater. Though the musical has undergone significant changes, it remains primarily a commercial enterprise.

As we noted in Chapter 14, *Fiddler on the Roof* (1964) is often considered the end of a "golden era" of traditional American musicals. The rock musical *Hair* (1967)—by Galt McDermott (1928–), Gerome Ragni (1942–), and James Rado—marked a significant change: it had no real story line and was a celebration of the antiestablishment lifestyle of the 1960s.

After *Hair,* the musical scene became increasingly fragmented. Fewer and fewer book musicals were written; instead, there were other approaches. One new approach was the *concept musical,* in which a production is built around an idea rather than a story. Two examples, both composed by Stephen Sondheim and directed by Harold Prince (1928–), are *Company* (1970) and *Follies* (1971). Three of Sondheim's more recent works, *Sunday in the Park with George* (1985), *Into the Woods* (1988), and *Assassins* (1991) can also be considered concept musicals.

Another significant trend, which started in the 1960s and then began to dominate musical theater in the 1970s and 1980s, was the choreographer-turned-director as the artist who provides the vision for a musical. Two significant director-choreographers were Gower Champion (1920–1980), who was responsible for *Hello Dolly!* (1964) and *42nd Street* (1980); and Bob Fosse (1927–1989), who directed *Sweet Charity* (1966) and *Pippin* (1972). Jerome Robbins is generally recognized as the leading American director-choreographer, and a retrospective revue of his major work—*Jerome Robbins' Broadway*—was the only successful musical of the 1988–1989 season. *A Chorus Line* (1975), which is so far the longest-running musical in American theater history, was developed by the director-choreographer Michael Bennett (1943–1987).

Another recent development in musical theater has been the emergence of British composers and lyricists. The leading figure in this trend is the composer Andrew Lloyd Webber (1948–), who wrote *Jesus Christ Superstar* (1971) and *Evita* (1979) with the lyricist Tim Rice (1944–). Webber, working with others, has also written the immensely popular *Cats* (1982) and *The Phantom of the Opera* (1987). His musical adaptation of the film *Sunset Boulevard* opened in London in 1993. Two other lavish musicals originating in Britain are *Les Misérables* (1987) and *Miss Saigon* (1989).

There has also been a trend toward revivals of earlier musicals—an indication that the output of new work has diminished but also an indication that these earlier works form part of an important heritage and have lasting value.

ALTERNATIVE THEATER

In the past two decades, many theater artists have explored new ways of breaking away from mainstream theater. This is evident in the United States, where theater artists have tried to find outlets for their work outside commercial Broadway theater, and even outside the larger regional theaters, which have become more reliant on commercial successes for their own financial survival. (The trend has also been international: a number of significant avant-garde theater companies have been established in European cities—in Germany and France, for example. Possibly the best-known is the Théâtre du Soleil, a French company founded by Ariane Mnouchkine, who is discussed later in this chapter.)

Alternative Theater Groups

Among the most significant groups which have developed off-off-Broadway since 1970 are the Performance Group, the Wooster Group, and Mabou Mines. All have experimented with striking theatrical images, physical performance techniques, improvisation, texts created by performers and directors, and environmental staging.

RICHARD SCHECHNER AND THE PERFORMANCE GROUP

The Performance Group was founded in 1968 by Richard Schechner and used a remodeled garage known as the Performing Garage. The company was known for its environmental stagings of *Dionysus in '69* (1969), *The Tooth of Crime* (1973), *Mother Courage* (1975), and *The Balcony* (1979). In directing *Mother Courage,* Schechner had the audience members move from time to time and reconfigure themselves so that their relationship to the stage action continually changed.

After the Performance Group disbanded in 1980, Schechner continued to be a significant theorist, educator, and practitioner. In the 1980s, he wrote about the relationship between anthropology and theater and was a leading teacher and theorist of performance. In 1993, he directed *Faust Gastronome,* a reworking of the Faust story, loosely based on Marlowe and Goethe, in which Faust was presented as obsessed with and surrounded by images of food. For this production, Schechner worked with a new company, East Coast Artists. In Schechner's version, Hitler and other anachronistic figures inhabit Faust's world. Schechner used outrageous and grotesque devices: Mephistopheles—the Devil—had a tail shaped like a phallus, and the piece closed with a naked Faust being covered with Chinese food and boiled in a large vat. Schechner also commented on gender stereotypes by casting women as men and vice-versa.

THE WOOSTER GROUP AND MABOU MINES

Out of the Performance Group grew the Wooster Group, under the artistic direction of Elizabeth LeCompte (1944–). The Wooster Group, which gained international renown in the 1980s, is noted for "deconstructing" well-known texts—that is, taking them apart and commenting on them—in performance pieces which tackle controversial social issues. (Arthur Miller sued the company to keep them from using parts of his play *The Crucible.*) The Wooster Group's best-known productions are *Route 1 & 9* (1981), which used sections of *Our Town; L.S.D.* (1983); and *Brace Up* (1991), a performance adaptation of *The Three Sisters,* which commented on the text through narration and video.

Mabou Mines was organized in 1970, originally under the artistic direction of Lee Breuer (1937–), and is well-known for staging the plays of Samuel Beckett. This company has a highly visual style and has developed many theater pieces using imagery and techniques from popular culture, including cartoons. One of its early works, *The B. Beaver Animation* (1974), brought the audience into a world of cartoon-like beavers constructing a dam; it was part of a series of works Breuer referred to as "animations." Like the Greek Old Comedy *The Birds* by Aristophanes, *B. Beaver* used the animal kingdom to reflect comically on the human condition. Breuer's most controversial production was *Lear* (1990), which reversed the gender of the characters in Shakespeare's play: thus Lear was played by a woman. Breuer has also directed a number of works on his own, including *Gospel at Colonus* (1983), an adaptation of Sophocles' tragedy using African American music.

Another significant director with Mabou Mines was Joanne Akalaitis (1937–). Akalaitis not only directed for Mabou Mines but also created many intriguing Shakespearean productions with the Public Theater, including *Cymbeline* (1989) and *Henry IV,* Parts I and II (1991). She has directed works for many other theaters as well, including *Endgame* (1984) at the American Repertory Theater in Boston, Genet's *The Screens* (1989) at the Guthrie Theater, *Tis Pity She's a Whore* (1990) by John Ford (1586–1640) at the Goodman Theatre in Chicago, and *In the Summer House* (1993) by Jane Bowles (1917–1973) at Lincoln Center in New York.

NEW OFF-BROADWAY AND OFF-OFF-BROADWAY COMPANIES

A number of newer off-Broadway companies became noted for introducing dramatists and plays. Two of the most significant were the Circle Repertory Company (founded in 1969), which introduced many of Lanford Wilson's plays of the 1970s and 1980s; and the Manhattan Theater Club (founded in 1970), which presented new works by American and European playwrights.

Newer off-off-Broadway companies in the middle to late 1980s developed a reputation for staging alternative works. Among them were the Cucaracha Theater, under the artistic direction of Richard Caliban, who also directs at

'TIS PITY SHE'S A WHORE. Joanne Akalaitis is a leading American postmodern director, known for taking classical scripts and developing unique production concepts to highlight her point of view. The scene here is from her updating of the Jacobean drama *'Tis Pity She's a Whore* at the off-Broadway Public Theater in New York. Akalaitis was artistic director at the Public for a brief time after the death of its founder, Joseph Papp.

many other off-off-Broadway venues; and En Garde Arts, organized by Anne Hamburger, which has authors write plays for specific sites, such as an abandoned warehouse or a vacant automobile showroom. Maria Irene Fornes wrote her short play *Hunger* (1988) for En Garde Arts, as part of an evening of works entitled *Three Pieces for a Warehouse*. One of the more successful productions by En Garde Arts was *Crowbar* (1990) by Mac Wellman (1945–   ), set in a rundown theater where ghosts of the theatrical past confront socioeconomic realities of the present. Richard Caliban was the director of *Crowbar*, and an actual theater scheduled for demolition on 42nd Street was chosen as the environment. (Wellman is one of a number of young American playwrights whose work is gaining significant critical attention through productions by alternative theaters.)

Alternative Directors

A number of directors continue to experiment with alternative styles of production. Many base their work on the theories of avant-garde artists of the early twentieth century, such as Meyerhold, Brecht, and Artaud. Others create a highly individual and personal aesthetic, in work that is often autobiographical.

AMERICAN DIRECTORS: RICHARD FOREMAN AND ROBERT WILSON

Two experimental directors in the United States whose works were initially seen off-off-Broadway are Richard Foreman (1937–) and Robert Wilson (1944–). Their work is usually unified by a theme or point of view which they determine, and the material is often organized as units analogous to the frames of television or film. Often, stunning theatrical images are a key to, and contain the essence of, the ideas that interest them.

Richard Foreman's work is autobiographical and self-reflexive—that is, it always makes the audience aware of watching a theatrical work which is commenting on itself. Foreman has staged most of his productions with the Ontological-Hysteric Theater, which he founded in 1968. As the name of his company suggests, his theatrical pieces focus on inability to communicate

(Paula Court)

EDDIE GOES TO POETRY CITY. The director Richard Foreman is known for productions with striking visual images. Foreman writes, directs, and designs his own works, which frequently deal with the inability of human beings to communicate meaningfully. Shown here is a scene from *Eddie Goes to Poetry City,* whose protagonist cannot make honest contact with other people. Notice the surrealistic properties, costumes, and acting style.

DANTON'S DEATH. Robert Wilson is a director known for his epic works, which emphasize strong visual imagery rather than the text. In recent years, Wilson has brought his style to historically significant dramas. Shown here is his production of Georg Büchner's *Danton's Death* (a play which received no productions when it was first written), staged at the Alley Theater in Houston and starring Richard Thomas.

through language. His works use a number of repeated theatrical devices, including voiceovers to comment on the stage action, exaggerated physical and vocal techniques, and visual elements such as clotheslines strung across a setting. Among Foreman's most recent pieces are *Film Is Evil, Radio Is Good* (1987), *Lava* (1990), and *Eddie Goes to Poetry City* (1991). In 1988, the Ontological-Hysteric and the Wooster Group coproduced his *Symphony of Rats*. The company moved into a new home in Saint Mark's Church in New York City in 1992.

Robert Wilson creates huge, extremely long epic productions which revolve around intensely theatrical images and are frequently accompanied by music in an operatic style. Among his best-known works are *Deafman Glance* (1970), *The Life and Times of Joseph Stalin* (1972), *A Letter to Queen Victoria* (1974), *The $ Value of Man* (1975), *Einstein on the Beach* (1976), *Death Destruction & Detroit* (1979), *The Man in the Raincoat* (1981), *The Golden Windows* (1982), *CiVil warS* (1983–1984), and *Death Destruction & Detroit II* (1987). Theatrical images woven into *Death Destruction & Detroit II* underscored Wilson's thematic interests: these images included ancient Chinese warriors, a mythological monster, a fat dwarf, a woman who cuts her baby open and eats salad from its belly, terrorists, a black panther, and giant rats.

In the late 1980s and 1990s, Wilson has also brought his technique of striking images to productions of existing texts. He staged Euripides' *Alcestis* (1986) in Europe; Ibsen's *When We Dead Awaken* (1991) for the American Repertory Theater; and Büchner's *Danton's Death* (1993), starring the well-known television and theater actor Richard Thomas, for the Alley Theater in Houston.

Wilson's work has found more support, critically and financially, in Europe than in the United States. For example, his *The Black Rider,* an extremely visual piece based on a German folk tale, premiered in Germany in 1992 and ran there for over a year; it was presented at the Brooklyn Academy of Music in 1993.

EUROPEAN DIRECTORS

In Europe, many directors have radically reinterpreted classical plays to make these texts speak more directly to contemporary audiences. These directors are postmodernist in their outlook: they believe that they can find unique "readings" of plays, and they use techniques of both "high" and "low" art. Often, their works are condemned by critics and audiences who believe that these directors are perverting classical texts. Among the directors who do this type of experimentation are Peter Zadek (1926–), Andrei Serban (1943–), Peter Stein (1937–), and Yuri Lyubimov (1917–).

The German director Peter Zadek staged controversial readings of Shakespeare in the 1970s and 1980s. Zadek's productions, which he developed out of improvisations with his company, included a vaudeville *King Lear* and an *Othello* performed in blackface.

Andrei Serban was born in Romania and emigrated to the United States in 1969; Ellen Stewart introduced him to American audiences at Cafe La Mama in 1970. Among his best-known productions in the United States are *The Cherry Orchard* (1977) at Lincoln Center, a postmodernist *Marriage of Figaro* (1982) at the Guthrie Theatre, *Uncle Vanya* (1983) at La Mama with Joseph Chaikin in the cast, and *The King Stag* (1984) at the American Repertory Theatre in Boston. Serban has also directed a number of highly theatrical operas. His work, like that of Wilson and Foreman, uses striking visuals to help convey his viewpoint on the text he is staging. For Serban, image and mood are frequently more important than the spoken word. For example, his postmodern production of *The Marriage of Figaro* featured characters dressed in trenchcoats and sunglasses who were pushed around the shiny, mirrorlike stage in a shopping cart; another character rode a skateboard wherever he went; and Figaro himself flew over the heads of the audience on a huge swing while making his most famous speech.

PETER STEIN. Stein, one of Germany's leading directors, is also renowned internationally. Stein began his career by reworking texts to reflect his own political and social viewpoints. In recent years, he has also directed productions with strong, realistic ensemble performances.

Peter Stein became known in the 1970s for postmodernist productions in which he reworked classical texts to heighten the ideological statements he felt were inherent in them and to express his own political viewpoints. He often used techniques of Brecht, Artaud, and naturalism. Among Stein's early productions were Edward Bond's *Saved* (1967), Weiss's *Vietnam Discourse* (1968), Brecht's *The Mother* (1970), Ibsen's *Peer Gynt* (1971) and Aeschylus's *The Oresteia* (1980). From 1970 to 1985, Stein was the artistic director of Berlin's Schaubühne Theater; the German government recognized his stature as a theatrical innovator by building the new Schaubühne am Lehniner Platz in Berlin in 1981. In the mid-1980s Stein departed from his earlier experimentation and began to stage more traditional productions, including *The Three Sisters* (1984), *Phaedra* (1987), and *The Cherry Orchard* (1989). In 1987, he directed an expressionistic production of *The Hairy Ape* at London's National Theater. He still directs at the Schaubühne and often stages operas at European theaters.

Yuri Lyubimov took over the artistic direction of the Taganka Theater in the Soviet Union in 1964. The Taganka was considered a home of experimentation, and its productions were reminiscent of Meyerhold's antirealistic work. Because of its experiments with form, however, the theater and Lyubimov were constantly under attack by the Soviet government. Eventually, the government took away Lyubimov's control of the Taganka, and he was not allowed to return from a western tour in 1984. Lyubimov then directed in Europe, the United States, and Israel, receiving a great deal of attention for his experiments with theatrical style. His best-known works are his adaptations of Dostoyevsky's novels *Crime and Punishment* and *The Possessed*. In 1989, after the democratization of what was then still the Soviet Union, Lyubimov was reinstalled as artistic director of the Taganka. In the early 1990s, he directed Ibsen's *The Wild Duck* at the Arena Theater in Washington, D.C.

Another eastern European, the Polish director Tadeusz Kantor, became noted in the United States in the 1980s for his avant-garde productions; and Ariane Mnouchkine, a French director of Russian extraction, is also widely admired.

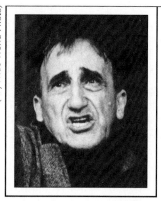

Tadeusz Kantor

(1915–1990)

Tadeusz Kantor was a Polish director who also worked as a scene designer and visual artist. He was born in Wielopole, Poland, on April 6, 1915. After studying painting and stage design, he graduated from the Cracow School of Fine Arts in 1939. During the Nazi occupation he founded the experimental Independent Theater, which had to produce its plays secretly in private homes. After the war, he became known as an avant-garde stage designer, creating designs for such productions as *Saint Joan* (1954), *Measure for Measure* (1956), and *Hamlet* (1956).

Kantor became disenchanted with the increasing artistic rigidity of the avant-garde and formed his own company, Cricot 2, in 1955 with a group of visual artists. In the 1960s he became widely known for staging happenings, and he traveled abroad with his company. He also became particularly interested in the work of the absurdists and the Polish surrealist Stanisław Ignacy Witkiewicz. His best-known productions of this period included *The Cuttlefish* (1956) and *The Water Hen* (1968).

In the 1970s, he began creating his own theater pieces; the most famous of these was *Dead Class* (1970), in which a teacher (played by Kantor himself) presided over a seance-like world in which seemingly dead characters confronted their younger selves, represented by mannequins. The use of mannequins with live actors was a technique he had begun to experiment with as early as the 1950s.

During the next two decades, Kantor toured the world with his company and his productions, among them *Wielopole, Wielopole* (1980), *Where Are the Snows of Yesteryear* (1982), *Let the Artists Die* (1985), *I Shall Never Return* (1988), and *Today Is My Birthday* (1990). These later works have been described as very personal reflections in which Kantor reveals his deepest, inmost thoughts through stunning theatrical imagery. In some of these works, as in *Dead Class*, he represented himself onstage. Kantor's work became well-known in the United States through presentations at Ellen Stewart's Cafe La Mama in the 1980s.

Ariane Mnouchkine

(1940–)

Since her founding of the avant-garde Théâtre du Soleil in Paris in 1964, Ariane Mnouchkine has become one of the most widely admired directors in Europe. Although strongly influenced by Copeau, Brecht, Artaud, and Meyerhold, she is also known for her effective use of nonwestern dramatic techniques, especially those of Japan and India.

Ariane Mnouchkine was born in Boulogne-sur-Seine, near Paris, in 1940. She was the eldest daughter of Alexandre Mnouchkine, a well-known film producer who came originally from Russia. As a child, Mnouchkine was fascinated by film work and often visited her father on his sets. While studying psychology at Oxford University, she became involved with the Oxford University Drama Society. On returning to Paris in 1959, she joined with a group of like-minded students at the Sorbonne to form the Association Théâtrale des Étudiantes de Paris and was elected its first president. In the

ARIANE MNOUCHKINE. Here, we see Mnouchkine (left) directing Juliana Carneiro de Cunha in the role of Clytemnestra in a production of *Iphigenia at Aulis* by the Théâtre du Soleil.

early 1960s, Mnouchkine scraped together enough money to realize a lifelong dream of traveling to the far east. In Japan, Cambodia, and other parts of Asia, she found a beauty of form and a sense of ritual which she considered indispensable to theater.

When she returned to Paris in 1963, Mnouchkine and several of her friends established a "theatrical community" which was to become the Théâtre du Soleil. The company has produced everything from loose collections of improvised materials to acclaimed versions of Shakespeare's works to a powerful 10-hour staging of the *Oresteia,* the cycle of Greek tragedies about the house of Atreus.

Among the best-known collectively created productions of the Théâtre du Soleil are *The Clowns* (1969); *1789* (1970), which environmentally dramatized the historical background of the French Revolution; *The Age of Gold* (1975); and *Les Atrides* (1991), the adaptation of the *Oresteia.* Among its text-based productions were a stage version of the novel *Mephisto* (1979); Shakespeare's *Richard II* (1981), *Twelfth Night* (1982), and *Henry IV,* Part I (1984); and two plays by a leading French feminist theorist, Helène Cixous.

Mnouchkine gained significant attention in the United States through presentations by the Théâtre du Soleil at the Olympics Art Festival in Los Angeles in 1984 and at the Brooklyn Academy of Music in 1992. Her presentation of *Les Atrides* by the Brooklyn Academy of Music at an armory won a special Obie award in 1993.

Performance Art

Performance art is an alternative form of theater which is difficult to define. In this type of theater, story, character, and text are minimized or even eliminated. The emphasis is not on a narrative or recognizable characters but rather is on the visual and ritualistic aspects of theater. The overall effect is sometimes like a constantly transforming collage. As might be expected from this description, performance art—focusing on the visual picture formed onstage—has an affinity with painting.

Stage movement in performance art is often closely related to dance. One leading performance artist is Martha Clarke (1944–), who began her career in dance and has continued to stage dance performances. Clarke's presentations combine dance, popular entertainment, and stunning visual effects. Among her best-known productions are *Garden of Earthly Delights* (1984), *Vienna Lusthaus* (1986), *Miracolo d'Amore* (1988), and *Endangered Species* (1990). She directed two Mozart operas, *The Magic Flute* and *Cosi Fan Tutte,* in 1992 and 1993 at Glimmerglass Opera in upstate New York, incorporating many of the techniques of her visual style.

Another strain of performance art is referred to as *new vaudeville.* New vaudevillians combine popular techniques such as mime, clowning, and stand-up comedy with serious subject matter, creating performances which are not easy to categorize.

(William Gibson/Martha Swope Associates)

PERFORMANCE ART. In contemporary theater, *performance art* is an enigmatic term. Some performance artists mix visual art and performance to create highly conceptual pieces. Others present monologues which deal with their own lives. Shown here is a scene from Anna Deavere Smith's *Fires in the Mirror,* a one-person performance piece Smith developed out of her own interviews with people affected by racial unrest between Chasidic Jews and African Americans in the Crown Heights neighborhood in New York City.

Two artists who began performing solo pieces in alternative spaces but have since received commercial productions are Spalding Gray (1941–   ) and Bill Irwin (1950–   ). Gray, who began as a member of the Performance Group and the Wooster Group, is a monologuist who discusses issues ranging from world politics to his own personal concerns and personal relationships, and his art is reminiscent of ancient storytellers who created a theatrical environment singlehanded. His works include *Swimming to Cambodia* (1984), *Monster in the Box* (1991), and *Gray's Anatomy* (1993). Irwin, who appeared on Broadway in 1989 in *Largely New York* and in 1993 in *Fool Moon*—the production described at the opening of this chapter—presents mimelike performances in which he uses popular slapstick techniques to reflect on the contemporary human condition.

Many performance artists focus on political issues, such as feminism, gay rights, and multiculturalism. Among these artists are Rachel Rosenthal, Laurie Anderson, Karen Finley, Holly Hughes, Tim Miller, and Ann Magnuson. In the early 1990s, Miller, Hughes, and Finley were embroiled with the National Endowment for the Arts in a battle over the funding of controversial art works. (The National Endowment is a federal agency which provides support for artists in the United States.) John Leguizamo received popular acclaim—also in the early 1990s—for his performance pieces, including *Spic-o-rama,* which deal with Hispanic life in the United States. Several spaces in New York have become known for presenting performance artists, including P.S. 122 and the Kitchen.

Anna Deavere Smith (1952–   ), an African American performance artist, won considerable acclaim for pieces dealing with racial unrest in the early

1990s. A teacher and actress, Smith developed a series of one-woman works entitled *On the Road: A Search for American Character*. In this series, she portrays many real people she has met and interviewed. Two of her works focus on recent racial explosions: *Fires in the Mirror,* which was critically acclaimed when it was presented at the Public Theater in New York in 1992; and *Twilight: Los Angeles 1992,* which premiered at the Mark Taper Forum in 1993 and was then presented at the Public Theater in New York. In *Fires in the Mirror,* she portrayed individuals involved in the racial conflict between Hasidic Jews and African Americans in Crown Heights, Brooklyn; in *Twilight: Los Angeles 1992,* she presented people affected by the Los Angeles uprising that followed the acquittals in the first trial of the police officers charged with brutalizing Rodney King.

There are significant performance artists in most major cities around the world. For example, Issei Ogata (1952–   ) is a solo artist who creates many characters based on urban life in Japan.

ESTABLISHED THEATER COMPANIES

Since 1970, many theaters that had become historically important institutions found themselves confronting the same questions as alternative theaters. In the face of dwindling audiences; competition from commercial theater, film, and television; and, in many cases, diminished government support, these established theaters began to ask what their mission was and what artistic direction they should take in order to survive into the twenty-first century. Some of these companies turned to alternative artists to regain the sense of experimentation which had originally been important to them. At the same time, however, these theaters had economic problems which limited their ability to experiment and often threatened their very existence.

American Regional Theaters: Traditional and New

An important development in American theater is that an equivalent of off-off-Broadway emerged in other major cities across the country—Washington, Chicago, Minneapolis, Los Angeles, San Francisco, Seattle. Small groups performed as alternatives to the larger regional theaters which had been established in the 1940s, 1950s, and 1960s.

In Chicago, for example, a number of smaller theaters, including Wisdom Bridge, Victory Gardens, Body Politic, and Steppenwolf, were founded in the 1970s. Steppenwolf has brought many productions to New York, including *The Grapes of Wrath,* which won the 1990 Tony Award; and, in 1993, *The Song of Jacob Zulu.* The La Jolla Playhouse in San Diego, under the artistic direction of Des McAnuff, has had many commercial successes, including its 1993 adaptation of The Who's rock musical *Tommy,* which moved to Broadway. The Actors Theater of Louisville became known for introducing new plays and

THE SONG OF JACOB ZULU. Many theaters outside New York City are having a major impact on American theater. In the 1970s, a number of new alternative regional theaters sprang up in many cities and developed new actors, directors, and playwrights. The Steppenwolf Theater was established in Chicago as an "off-Loop" company—that is, outside Chicago's commercial theater center. Many well-known film and television actors came out of Steppenwolf, including John Malkovich, Laurie Metcalf, Gary Cole, and John Mahoney. Steppenwolf's production of *The Song of Jacob Zulu,* shown here, later moved to Broadway.

playwrights. A number of Actors Theater productions were transferred to Broadway in the late 1970s. The American Repertory Theater, founded in 1979 by Robert Brustein in conjunction with Harvard University, became noted for productions of classical plays by avant-garde directors.

Transformations in Established American Theater Companies

Some of the established theaters in the United States have undergone significant changes in the last three decades. Many of these theaters made changes by hiring new artistic directors, often replacing figures who had been instrumental in founding them. Two examples are the Guthrie Theater in Minneapolis and the Public Theater in New York.

The Guthrie Theater hired the Romanian Liviu Ciulei (1923–) as artistic director in 1981. Ciulei brought an approach that included practices of many alternative directors; under his artistic direction and that of Garland Wright (1945–), who followed him in 1986, the Guthrie became known for developing a strong acting ensemble and for controversial stagings of historic plays. In 1993, for example, Wright staged a nineteenth-century Russian comedy, *Too Clever by Half* (1858) by Aleksandr Nikolaevich Ostrovsky (1823–1886), in a highly expressionistic style.

The Public Theater in New York experienced a tumultuous period after the death of its founder, Joseph Papp. Joanne Akalaitis, who succeeded Papp, brought in avant-garde companies and performance artists; however, the theater's board said that she had been unable to generate audiences or to give enough productions, and in 1993 (as we noted in Chapter 14) replaced her with George C. Wolfe (1955–   ). Wolfe, an African American, was the author-director of *The Colored Museum* and *Spunk*—critically acclaimed productions that had been presented at the Public in the late 1980s—and of the hit Broadway musical *Jelly's Last Jam* (1992). At the time of his appointment, Wolfe was directing Tony Kushner's *Angels in America: Millennium Approaches,* for which he won the Tony award for Best Direction in 1993. Later in the same year, Wolfe directed the second half of this epic work, *Angels in America: Perestroika;* the two halves were then running in repertory on Broadway. He also directed a public television production of Anna Deavere Smith's *Fires in the Mirror.*

Transformations in Government-Subsidized European Theaters

Some of the national theaters of Europe have also incorporated avant-garde techniques and artists, though others have been forced to become more commercial to avert financial crises. The Comédie Française, the Royal Shakespeare Company, and the National Theater are representative of the kinds of changes that occurred in many government-subsidized theaters throughout Europe.

Antoine Vitez (1930–1990) ran the Comédie Française from 1988 until his death in 1990. Under his brief direction, this 300-year-old theater began to present radical reinterpretations of many historically important French writers. Vitez was greatly influenced by Grotowski's "poor theater," by Marxism, by Brecht's theories, by his own background in mime, and by unique postmodernist readings of texts. Vitez's early work was in Marseilles in the 1960s; later, in the 1970s, he brought productions to the meeting halls and schools of working-class Paris. In 1968, he was appointed director and leading teacher of the Conservatoire, the renowned acting school affiliated with the Comédie Française. From 1972 to 1974, he was a coartistic director of the Théâtre National de Chaillot, and he took over complete artistic direction of this theater in 1981. Many French critics believe that his early death robbed the Comédie Française, France's oldest government-supported theater, of an artistic director who could have transformed it.

In England, the Royal Shakespeare Company and the National Theater suffered from increased costs—incurred partly by new buildings—and from reduced government support. In the 1980s, under the artistic direction of Trevor Nunn (1940–   ) and Terry Hands (1941–   ), and after it had moved into a new facility, the Royal Shakespeare Company experienced financial and artistic crises. Nunn was criticized for staging productions which were as

Debates in Theater History:

CAN THEATER SURVIVE?

A recurrent contemporary debate is whether live theater can survive into the twenty-first century. The cost of producing theater—even for alternative groups—declining audiences, and competition from film and television lead some analysts to argue that theater will not be as vital an art form in the next century as it has been in the past, and that it will probably become an art appealing only to a very specialized audience, much like opera today.

Others, however, argue that theater is a unique art form, that it has been and still is able to incorporate other arts into its aesthetic makeup, and that these factors will keep it alive and healthy. These analysts point out that a significant number of alternative theaters continue to spring up in major cities throughout the world. They also argue that theater will survive and be vigorous despite challenges from electronic media, because in the future modern technology will play an important role in theater. There will be continuing experiments with multimedia, fusing theater with film, television, and dance.

With all these innovations, though, the people who believe that theater will remain vital argue that in certain ways the theater of the future will be an extension of the theater of the past. Theater will be enacted by women and men, in person, before an audience. The works these performers present will deal primarily with the hopes, fears, agonies, and joys of human beings. Even the most radical alternative artists deal with the same human issues that have always been part of theater.

A television critic in a popular national newspaper, reviewing a Public Broadcasting System special on the Broadway production of *Angels in America*, remarked, "What this demonstrates is how the theater can seize a moment with immediacy, with a bolder impact than the more dominant, yet less visionary, entertainment media of films and TV."*

*Matt Roush, "*Angels* and the '80s: Tony Winner Soars in Its Social Context," *USA Today*, June 11, 1993, section D, p. 3.

---

commercial as those of the West End—London's equivalent of Broadway. These attacks were fiercest following the company's highly successful musical *Les Misérables*. Among the productions that were best received, artistically and commercially, during this period was an epic adaptation of Charles Dickens's novel *Nicholas Nickelby* (1980).

The National Theater also ran into controversy under the artistic direction of Peter Hall and his successor Richard Eyre (1943–   ). Much of this controversy developed because a huge amount of governmental support was required to operate its new facility. The National Theater, however, maintained its reputation for employing England's most important actors and for reviving historically significant but forgotten dramas. During the London season of 1992–1993, one of the most successful productions—artistically and commercially—was the National's revival of the Rodgers and Hammerstein musical *Carousel*, directed by Nicholas Hytner. This was a revival of a neglected work, with a new interpretation that underscored an inherent theme—the dark side of the class struggle.

The complexity of contemporary theater makes it difficult to draw conclusions about its eventual significance. Future historians, however, will undoubtedly consider theater from 1970 to the 1990s as a clear reflection of concerns which confronted our world.

SUMMARY

The period since 1970 has seen continued upheaval throughout the world, and in theater. Postmodernist theater artists and companies develop unique readings of historical texts and create controversial productions based on radical reinterpretations. Playwrights have dealt with the tumultuous social and political scene by using a wide variety of techniques, including many borrowed from the popular arts.

Theater since 1970 reflects the fragmentation of contemporary society. Some playwrights and companies treat issues of sexual identity, gender, and race; frequently, their work appeals to specific racial, ethnic, and other subcultures.

New forms of theater have developed, often defying categorization. Performance art, combining popular elements and techniques from the visual arts and dance, became a significant alternative form. A number of artists known as *new vaudevillians* have used popular comic techniques to comment on the world around them.

Throughout the world, many new companies and established theaters confronted new aesthetic issues by engaging directors who were part of alternative theater; all these companies have had to deal with financial problems and declining audiences. Despite such issues, however, both mainstream theater and alternative theater continue to thrive in widely dispersed areas.

THEATRICAL TERMS

Afterpiece In eighteenth- and nineteenth-century theater, an entertainment staged after the main play.

Agon In Greek Old Comedy, a scene with a debate between the two opposing forces in the play, each representing one side of a social or political issue.

Agonthetes In Hellenistic Greece, the government official responsible for producing plays for festivals.

Alienation An aspect of Bertolt Brecht's theory of epic theater: the concept that audiences' emotional involvement should be minimized so that they will instead be involved intellectually with the political message.

Allegory Representation of an abstract theme or themes through symbolic use of character, action, and other concrete elements of a play. In its most direct form—for example, the medieval morality play—allegory uses personification to present characters representing abstract qualities, such as virtues and vices, in action which spells out a moral or intellectual lesson.

Alojero In corrales of the Spanish golden age, a box from which refreshments—food and drinks—were sold.

Amphitheater (1) Large oval, circular, or semicircular outdoor theater with rising tiers of seats around an open playing area; *also,* an exceptionally large indoor auditorium. (2) In French neoclassical theater, an undivided gallery at the rear with inexpensive, bleacher-like seating.

Angle perspective Use of two or more vanishing points, frequently at the sides of a painted design. Ferdinando Bibiena is usually credited with introducing angle perspective early in the eighteenth century.

Angry young men Group of antiestablishment English playwrights of the 1950s who dealt with the dissolving British empire, class conflict, and political disillusionment.

Antagonist Character who is the chief opponent of the main character (the protagonist) in a drama. In some cases there may be several antagonists.

Aposentos In the Spanish golden age, the boxes in a corral.

Apprentice In Elizabethan England, a young performer in an acting company who was taught the art of acting through actual experience and who received room and board from a key member of the troupe.

Apron Stage space in front of the curtain line or proscenium; also called the *forestage*.

Archon Athenian government official appointed to

oversee the staging of drama at the City Dionysia festival.

Arena Type of stage which is surrounded by the audience on all four sides; also called *theater-in-the-round.*

Aside In a play, thoughts spoken aloud by one character without being noticed by others onstage.

Atellan farce Form of Roman theater: improvised comedic pieces dealing with exaggerated family situations or satirizing historical or mythological figures.

Auleum In Roman theater, a front curtain which was raised and lowered on telescoping poles.

Autos sacramentales In the Spanish golden age, religious dramas combining characteristics of mystery and morality plays.

Avant-garde Term applied to plays of an experimental or unorthodox nature which attempt to go beyond standard usage in either form or content.

Backdrop Large drapery or painted canvas which provides the rear or upstage masking of a set.

Backstage Stage area behind the front curtain; *also,* the areas beyond the setting, including wings and dressing rooms.

Ballad opera Eighteenth-century English form which burlesqued opera: there was no recitative, songs were set to popular tunes, and characters were drawn from the lower classes. John Gay's *The Beggar's Opera* is the most famous example.

Benefit Tradition begun in eighteenth-century theater whereby the profits from an evening's performance were given to a performer, a group of performers, or a playwright.

Biomechanics An aspect of Vsevelod Meyerhold's theory of acting: the idea that an actor's body should be machinelike and that emotion can be represented externally.

Blocking Arrangement of actors' movements onstage with respect to each other and the stage space.

Bookholder In Elizabethan theater, the prompter who gave actors their lines.

Border Strip of drapery or painted canvas hung across the top of the stage from a batten to mask the area above the stage; *also,* a row of lights hung from a batten.

Boulevard theaters In eighteenth-century France, theaters located on Boulevard du Temple in Paris, catering to popular tastes.

Box Small, private compartment for a group of spectators, built into the walls of a traditional proscenium-arch theater.

Box set Interior setting using flats to form the back and side walls and often the ceiling of a room.

Breeches roles Male roles played by females, particularly popular in Restoration and eighteenth-century English theater.

Bunraku Japanese puppet theater. The puppets are two-thirds life-size and are manipulated by men in black robes who are conventionally regarded as invisible by the audience.

Burlesque Ludicrous imitation of a dramatic form or a specific play. Closely related to satire, but usually lacking the moral or intellectual purposes of reform typical of satire.

Burletta Eighteenth-century English dramatic form resembling comic opera and defined by the lord chamberlain as a play with no more than three acts, each of which had to include at least five songs.

Business Obvious and detailed physical movement of actors to reveal character, aid action, or establish mood; e.g., pouring drinks at a bar, opening a gun case.

Canon Set of literary works believed to be universally accepted as important and historically significant. Today, many critics argue that certain groups are underrepresented in the canon, and that it therefore does not adequately reflect human accomplishments.

Capa y espada Literally, "cape and sword": full-length Spanish play which revolved around intrigue and duels over honor.

Carros In the Spanish golden age, pageant wagons on which autos sacramentales were staged.

Cavea In Roman theater, the seating area.

Cazuela In the Spanish golden age, the gallery located above the alojero in the back wall of a theater; the area in which unescorted women were segregated.

Chiaroscuro In painting, emphasis of contrasts between light and shadow, associated with Gianbattista Piranesi and others.

Choral odes In classical Greek drama, songs chanted by the chorus between the episodes.

Choregus In ancient Greece, a wealthy person who underwrote most of the expenses for the production of an individual playwright's works at a dramatic festival.

Chorodidaskalos In ancient Greek theater, the person who trained and rehearsed the chorus.

Chorus (1) In ancient Greek drama, a group of performers who sang and danced, sometimes participating in the action but usually simply commenting on it. (2) Performers in a musical play who sing and dance as a group rather than individually.

City Dionysia   The most important Greek festival in honor of the god Dionysus; it was staged in Athens in the spring and was the first to include dramatic activities.

Claque   People in the audience who are hired to applaud; the tradition of the claque began in Roman theater.

Combination company   In the nineteenth century, a complete touring production, including supporting players, scenery, and costumes.

Comedia   In the Spanish golden age, a three-act full-length nonreligious play.

Comedy   Category of drama that is generally light in tone; it is concerned with issues that are not serious, has a happy ending, and is designed to amuse and provoke laughter. (*See also* Old Comedy, New Comedy, Comedy of humors, Comedy of manners, Farce, Satire, Slapstick.)

Comédie larmoyante   "Tearful comedy": in eighteenth-century France, a form of drama meant to evoke sentimental tears.

Comedy of humors   Form of comedy developed by Ben Jonson in the early seventeenth century. It is based on Roman comedy and stresses ridicule directed at characters who are dominated by a single trait (or "humor") to the point of obsession.

Comedy of manners   Form of comic drama that became popular in the latter half of the seventeenth century in France and among English playwrights during the Restoration. It emphasizes a cultivated or sophisticated atmosphere, witty dialogue, and characters whose concern with social polish is charming, ridiculous, or both.

Comic opera (opéra comique)   In eighteenth-century France, an entertainment in which action was mimed by the performers and dialogue was often sung by the audience. Later, French comic opera became more like ballad opera.

Commedia dell'arte   Form of comic theater, originating in Italy in the sixteenth century, in which dialogue was improvised around a loose scenario involving a set of stock characters, each with a distinctive costume and a traditional name.

Compañias de partes   In the Spanish golden age, acting troupes organized according to the sharing system.

Complication   Introduction in a play of a new force which creates a new balance of power and makes a delay in reaching the climax necessary and progressive. It is one way of creating conflict and precipitating a crisis.

Confidant (confidante)   Minor character in whom the protagonist confides.

Conflict   Tension between two or more characters, leading to a crisis or a climax. The basic conflict is the fundamental struggle or imbalance underlying the play. May also be a conflict of ideologies, actions, etc.

Constructivism   Following World War I, a movement in scene design in which sets were created to provide greater opportunities for physical action. The sets, which were frequently composed of ramps, platforms, and levels, were nonrealistic. The Russian director Vsevelod Meyerhold used many constructivist settings.

Continental seating   Auditorium arrangement in which audience members enter and exit at the ends of rows; there is no center aisle.

Contract system   System under which performers are hired for a specific period of time and paid a set salary.

Corral   In the Spanish golden age, a theater usually located in the courtyard of a series of adjoining buildings.

Crisis drama   Dramatic structure, developed in classical Greece and popular with modern realists, in which the action begins near a climax, with the characters in the midst of their struggles. Usually, crisis drama has few characters, much exposition, only one main action, few locales, and a short passage of time.

Curtain-raiser   In nineteenth-century theater, a short play staged before a full-length drama.

Cycle plays   *See* Mystery plays.

Cyclorama   Large curved drop used to mask the rear and sides of the stage, painted a neutral color or blue, representing sky or open space. It may also be a permanent stage fixture made of plaster or a similar durable material.

Dada   Movement in art between the world wars which was based on deliberate presentation of the irrational and on attacks against traditional artistic values.

Deconstructionism   In theater history, an approach based on the concept that history is written and taught by people in power and should be analyzed in terms of who is and is not empowered.

Decorum Neoclassical rule, developed in the Italian Renaissance, that dramatic characters must behave in set ways based on their social class and background.

Denouement The moment when suspense is finally satisfied and the "knot is untied." The term is from the French and was used to refer to the working out of the resolution in a well-made play.

Desvánes "Attics": in the Spanish golden age, cramped, low-ceilinged boxes located on the fourth floor of corrales.

Deus ex machina Literally, "god from a machine." In ancient Greek theater, the convention of bringing in gods on a mechane. The term now refers to any unjustified or arbitrary dramatic device used to resolve a plot, usually in the final moments.

Director In American usage, the person who is responsible for the overall unity of a production, coordinating the efforts of the contributing artists. The director is in charge of rehearsals and supervises the actors in the preparation of their parts. The American *director* is the equivalent of the British producer and the French *metteur en scène*.

Dithyramb In ancient Greece, a choral song describing the adventures of a god or heroic figure.

Documentary drama Term encompassing different types of twentieth-century drama that present material in the fashion of journalism or reporting. *Living newspaper* drama of the 1930s used signs and slide projections to deal with broad social problems; other documentary dramas use a more realistic approach.

Domestic drama Also known as *bourgeois drama*. Domestic drama deals with problems of the middle and lower classes, particularly problems of the family and home.

Dominus Leader of a Roman acting troupe.

Double-entendre Word or phrase in comedy that has a double meaning, the second often sexual.

Doubling Having an actor play more than one role in a play. Doubling was common in Greek and Elizabethan theater.

Downstage Front of the stage toward the audience.

Doyen In the Comédie Française, the head of the company and the actor with the longest service.

Drame Eighteenth-century French term usually denoting a serious drama that dealt with middle-class characters. Some critics suggest that drame included such eighteenth-century forms as domestic tragedy, middle-class tragedy, and tearful comedy (comédie larmoyante).

Drolls In seventeenth-century England, short dramas that were either excerpts from or condensations of longer plays. Drolls were presented during the commonwealth and at the beginning of the Restoration.

Drop Large piece of fabric, generally painted canvas, hung from a batten to the stage floor, usually to serve as backing.

Eclectic Theater artist who works in a variety of modes and does not identify with one particular artistic movement.

Ekkyklema In ancient Greek theater, a wagon used to bring characters onstage—often to reveal the results of offstage violence.

Elevator stage Stage which allows the entire floor or sections of the floor to be raised and lowered automatically.

Emotional recall Stanislavski's exercise to assist the actor in presenting realistic emotions. The performer thinks of an event in his or her own life which led to an emotion similar to that which the character is supposed to feel in the play. By mentally recreating these circumstances, the performer will feel the emotion.

Ensemble playing Acting which stresses the total artistic unity of a performance rather than the individual performances of specific actors.

Entremeses In the Spanish golden age, interludes during the intermissions of comedias; these could be comic sketches, songs, and dances.

Environmental theater A type of theater production in which the total theater environment—the stage space and the audience arrangement—is emphasized. A form of environmental theater came to the forefront in experimental theater of the 1960s. Among its aims are elimination of the distinction between audience space and acting space, a more flexible approach to interactions between performers and audience, and substitution of a multiple focus for the traditional single focus.

Epic theater Form of presentation associated with the German dramatist Bertolt Brecht, its chief advocate and theorist. Epic theater is aimed at the intellect rather than the emotions, seeking to present evidence regarding social questions in such a way that they may be considered objectively and an intelligent conclusion may be reached.

Epilogue Speech addressed to the audience after the conclusion of a play and spoken by one of the performers.

Episkenion In Hellenistic Greece, the second story of the skene.

Episodic drama Dramatic structure, developed during the Middle Ages and extremely popular in the English Renaissance and the Spanish golden age, in which the dramatic action begins early in the story. Episodic drama has little exposition, many characters, frequent changes of time and place, and subplots.

Existentialism Set of philosophical ideas whose principal modern advocate was Jean-Paul Sartre. The term *existentialist* is applied to plays by Sartre and others which illustrate these views. Sartre's central thesis was that there are no longer any fixed standards or values by which one can live, and that each individual must create his or her own code of conduct regardless of conventions imposed by society.

Exodos In classical Greek drama, the final scene, in which all the characters exit from the stage.

Exposition Imparting of information that is necessary for an understanding of the story but will not be covered by the action onstage: events or knowledge from the past, or occurring outside the play, which must be introduced if the audience is to understand the characters or the plot. Exposition is always a problem in drama because relating or conveying information is static; the dramatist must find ways to make expository scenes dynamic.

Expressionism Movement which developed and flourished in Germany during the period immediately preceding and following World War I. Expressionism in drama was characterized by an attempt to depict subjective states through distortion; striking, often grotesque, images; and lyric, unrealistic dialogue.

Farce One of the major genres of drama, sometimes regarded as a subclass of comedy. It aims to entertain and to provoke laughter, and its humor is the result primarily of physical activity and visual effects.

Feminism In theater history, an approach based on the belief that women's place in theater has not been sufficiently explored.

Flat Single piece of scenery, usually of standard size, combined with similar units to create a set. Formerly made of canvas stretched over a wooden frame, but now frequently made of a hard substance such as Luan; a hard flat is sometimes called a *Hollywood* or *movie* flat.

Fly loft or flies Space above the stage where scenery may be lifted out of sight by means of ropes and pulleys when it is not needed.

Footlights Row of lights in the floor along the edge of the stage or apron; once a principal source of stage light but now used only rarely.

Forestage *See* Apron.

Found space Space not originally intended for theater which is converted for productions. Avant-garde artists of the 1960s often produced in found spaces.

Fourth-wall convention Pretense that in a proscenium-arch theater the audience is looking into a room through an invisible fourth wall. The term is often attributed to the eighteenth-century French philosopher Denis Diderot.

Futurism Art movement begun in Italy about 1905 which idealized mechanization and machinery.

Gallery In traditional proscenium-arch theaters, the undivided seating area cut into the walls of the building.

Gesamtkunstwerk Richard Wagner's term for a unified operatic work of art, in which all elements—music, words, story, scenery, costumes, orchestra, etc.—form a total piece.

Glories In the Italian Renaissance, flying machines used for special effects.

Gradas In the Spanish golden age, bleacher-like seating along the side walls of the patio in a corral.

Groove system System in which there were tracks on the stage floor and above the stage which allowed for the smooth movement of flat wings on and off the stage; usually there were a series of grooves at each stage position. The system was developed during the Italian Renaissance and was used through the nineteenth century in England, the United States, and the Netherlands.

Groundlings In Elizabethan theater, audience members who stood in the yard.

Hamartia Ancient Greek term usually translated as "tragic flaw." The literal translation, however, is "missing the mark," and this suggests to some scholars that hamartia is not so much a flaw in character as an error in judgment made by the protagonist.

Hanamichi In kabuki theater, the bridge from behind the audience (toward the left side of the audience) on which actors can enter to the stage. Important scenes are also played on the hanamichi.

Happenings Form of theatrical event developed out of the experimentation of certain American abstract artists in the 1960s. Happenings are nonliterary, replacing the script with a scenario which provides for chance occurrences, and are performed (often only once) in such places as parks and street corners.

Hashigakari In noh theater, the bridge on which actors make their entrance from the dressing area to the platform stage.

Heavens Also called *shadows*. In the English Renaissance, a roof protecting the stage of a public theater, often painted on the underside to represent heavens literally. (For French neoclassical usage, *see* Paradis.)

Hireling A member of an Elizabethan acting company who was paid a set salary.

History play In the broadest sense, a play set in a historical milieu which deals with historical personages; but the term is usually applied only to plays which deal with vital issues of public welfare and are nationalistic in tone.

Householders In Elizabethan England, star members of an acting company who were given part-ownership of its playhouse; *also,* people who owned buildings and rented them to acting companies.

Hubris Ancient Greek term usually translated as "excessive pride"; hubris is a common tragic flaw.

Hypokrite Greek term for "actor."

Innamorata In commedia dell'arte, the stock female lover.

Innamorato In commedia dell'arte, the stock male lover.

Inner stage Area at the rear of the stage which is hidden by curtains, doors, or scenery.

Interludes In medieval England, short dramatic pieces, usually presented between courses of a banquet.

Intermezzi In the Italian Renaissance, entertainments performed between the acts of operas and full-length plays.

Irony Condition that is the reverse of what we have expected; *also,* a verbal expression whose intended implication is the opposite of its literal sense. Irony is a device particularly suited to theater and found in virtually all drama.

Joruri In Japanese puppet theater, chanted texts.

Kabuki The most eclectic and theatrical of the major forms of Japanese theater. Roles of both sexes are performed by men in a highly theatrical, nonrealistic style. Kabuki combines music, dance, and dramatic scenes with an emphasis on color and movement. The plays are long and episodic, consisting of loosely connected dramatic scenes which are often performed independently.

Kathakali In southwestern India, a form of dance drama presented by torchlight, dealing with clashes of good and evil.

Katharsis Greek word, usually translated as "purgation," which Aristotle used in his definition of tragedy. It refers to the vicarious cleansing of certain emotions in the audience through their representation onstage.

Kothornus In Hellenistic Greek theater, the platform boot worn by actors.

Kyōgen In noh theater, farcical entertainment presented between plays.

Lazzi In commedia dell'arte, comic pieces of business repeatedly used by characters.

Lehrstücke "Learning pieces": short dramas written by Bertolt Brecht in the early 1930s.

Liturgical drama Any religious drama, usually sung or chanted, that relates to the Bible and is presented in Latin inside a church sanctuary. The form was highly developed in the medieval period.

Living newspapers The Federal Theater Project's dramatizations of newsworthy events in the 1930s.

Local color Inclusion in scenery of locations that audience members will recognize from their own community. Use of local color in settings became more common in the eighteenth century.

Loges In French neoclassical theater, boxes.

Long run In commercial theater, presentation of a drama for as long a period of time as it is popular. In nineteenth-century American and English theater, the long run replaced repertory.

Lords' rooms In English Renaissance theater, boxes frequented by wealthy patrons.

Ludi Romani Roman festival in honor of Jupiter into which drama was first introduced.

Luñetas In the late Spanish golden age, semicircular benches located in the front of the patio.

Magic if Stanislavski's acting exercise which requires the actor to ask, "How would I react *if* I were in this character's position?"

Mansion Medieval scenic unit, often presented as an individual house or locale.

Masking Scenery or drapes used to hide or cover.

Masque Lavish, spectacular form of private theatrical entertainment which developed in Renaissance

Italy and spread rapidly to the courts of France and England. The masque combined poetry, music, elaborate costumes, and spectacular effects of stage machinery.

Mechane In ancient Greek theater, a crane used for flying characters into the playing area.

Medieval drama Range of plays that make up the religious and folk drama developed during the Middle Ages. (*See* Liturgical drama, Mystery plays, Miracle play, Morality play.)

Melodrama Historically, a distinct form of drama popular throughout the nineteenth century which emphasized action and spectacular effects and used music to heighten the dramatic mood. Melodrama had stock characters and clearly defined villains and heroes, and it presented unambiguous confrontations between good and evil.

Mime In ancient Greece and Rome, a form of theatrical entertainment which consisted of short sketches characterized by risqué subjects and slapstick.

Minstrelsy Type of nineteenth-century production featuring white performers made up in blackface.

Miracle play Medieval drama based on the life of a saint.

Mise-en-scène Arrangement of all the elements in a stage picture, either at a given moment or dynamically throughout a performance.

Morality play Medieval drama designed to teach a lesson. The characters were often allegorical and represented virtues or faults, such as good deeds, friendship, or avarice. The most famous example is *Everyman*.

Mosqueteros Literally, "mosquitos": in the Spanish golden age, the noisy groundlings in the corrales.

Moving panorama In the nineteenth century, a setting painted on a cloth which was unrolled by spools to create an illusion of movement and changing locales.

Multiculturalism In theater history, an approach focusing on groups that have traditionally been underrepresented.

Multimedia Use of electronic media, such as slides, film, and videotape, in live theater.

Multiple setting Form of stage setting, common in the Middle Ages, in which several locations are represented at the same time; also called *simultaneous setting*. Used also in various forms of contemporary theater.

Musical theater Broad category which includes opera, operetta, musical comedy, and other musical plays (the term *lyric theater* is sometimes used to distinguish it from pure dance). It includes any dramatic entertainment in which music and lyrics (and sometimes dance) are integral and necessary.

Musicians' gallery In English Renaissance theater, the third level of the tiring house, where the accompanying musicians were located.

Mystery plays Also called *cycle plays*. Short medieval dramas presented in western Europe and England, based on events of the Old and New Testaments. Many such plays were organized into historical cycles which told the story of human history from the creation to doomsday.

National theater A theater which is dedicated to the drama of a specific country and usually is subsidized by the government.

Naturalism Special form of realism. The theory of naturalism came to prominence in France and elsewhere in Europe in the latter half of the nineteenth century. The French playwright Émile Zola advocated theater that would follow the scientific principles of the age: drama should look for the causes of "disease" in society the way a doctor looks at disease in an individual, and theater should expose social "infection" in all its ugliness. Naturalism attempts to achieve the verisimilitude of a documentary film, conveying the impression that everything about the play—the setting and the way the characters dress, speak, and act—is exactly like everyday life.

Naumachia In ancient Rome, sea battles staged in a flooded amphitheater or on a lake.

Neutral platform stage Unlocalized stage which allows for easy shifts of locale through the use of properties, entrances, and exits. It was used first in the Middle Ages and later in the English Renaissance.

New Comedy Hellenistic Greek and Roman comedies which deal with romantic and domestic situations.

Noh Also spelled *nō* and *no*. Rigidly traditional Japanese drama which in its present form dates back to the fourteenth century. Noh plays are short dramas combining music, dance, and lyrics with a highly stylized and ritualistic presentation. Virtually every aspect of a production—including costumes, masks, and a highly symbolic setting—is prescribed by tradition.

Objective Stanislavski's term for that which is urgently desired and sought by a character, the desired goal which propels a character to action.

Obstacle   That which delays or prevents the achieving of a goal by a character. An obstacle creates complication and conflict.

Off-Broadway   Movement developed in the late 1940s as a reaction to Broadway commercialism; its primary goal was to provide an outlet for experimental and innovative works, unhindered by commercial considerations. Off-Broadway theater spaces are small (usually holding about 200 spectators), and many have thrust or arena stages. Many American actors and directors began their careers off-Broadway.

Off-off-Broadway   Center for experimentation in New York theater that developed when off-Broadway became commercialized in the 1960s. Off-off-Broadway is dedicated to introducing and showcasing new talent, experimenting with new styles of production, and avoiding the limitations of commercial theater.

Offstage   Areas of the stage, usually in the wings, which are not in view of the audience.

Old Comedy   Classical Greek comedy which pokes fun at social, political, or cultural conditions and at individuals. The only surviving examples are by Aristophanes.

Onkos   In Hellenistic Greece, the high headdress of a mask.

Onnagata   In Japanese kabuki, women's roles played by male actors.

Orchestra   (1) Ground-floor seating in an auditorium. (2) In ancient Greek theater, the circular playing space.

Pageant master   In the Middle Ages, a professional stage manager who oversaw the production of a cycle of mystery plays.

Pantomime   Originally, a Roman entertainment in which a narrative was sung by a chorus while the story was acted out by dancers. Now used loosely to cover any form of presentation which relies on dance, gesture, and physical movement.

Parabasis   In Greek Old Comedy, a scene in which the chorus directly addressed the audience members and made fun of them.

Paradis   "Heavens": in French neoclassical theater, the third tier of galleries along the side walls.

Parados   In classical Greek drama, the scene in which the chorus enters. *Also,* the entranceway for the chorus in Greek theater.

Parasite   In Roman New Comedy, a stock character who is motivated purely by sensual needs, e.g., gluttony.

Paraskenia   In ancient Greek theater, the wings of the skene.

Parterre   In French neoclassical theater, the pit where audience members stood.

Pastoral   Idealized dramatization of rural life, often including mythological creatures, popular during the Italian Renaissance.

Patio   In the Spanish golden age, the pit area for the audience.

Peking opera   Popular theater of China which developed in the nineteenth century.

Pensionnaire   Hireling in a French acting troupe.

Performance art   Alternative form of theater, difficult to define, in which story, character, and text are minimized or eliminated. Performance art uses elements of the visual arts, dance, and popular entertainment in unique configurations.

Periaktoi   In ancient Greek theater, a three-sided scenic piece which could be revolved to show the audience three different scenes.

Perspective   Illusion of depth in painting; introduced into scene design during the Italian Renaissance.

Pinakes   In ancient Greek theater, painted flats.

Pit   Floor of the house in a traditional proscenium-arch theater. The pit was originally a standing area; later, backless benches were added.

Platea   In medieval theater, an unlocalized playing area.

Plot   (1) As distinct from *story,* a patterned arrangement of events and characters for a drama. The incidents are selected and arranged for maximum dramatic impact. A plot may begin long after the beginning of the story and refer to information regarding the past in flashbacks or exposition. (2) In Elizabethan theater, an outline of the dramatic action which was posted backstage so that actors could refresh their memory during a performance.

Point of attack   The moment in a story when a play actually begins. The dramatist chooses a point in time along the continuum of events which he or she judges will best start the action and propel it forward.

Pole-and-chariot system   Giacomo Torelli's mechanized means of changing sets made up of flat wings.

Poor theater   Term coined by Jerzy Grotowski to describe his ideal of theater stripped to its barest essentials. According to Grotowski, the lavish sets, lights, and costumes usually associated with theater reflect only base, materialistic values and must be eliminated.

Positivism   In theater history, the idea that history

can be chronicled objectively and explained logically.

Postmodernism Theory that division of art works into modernist categories, such as realism and departures from realism, is artificial. Postmodernist works mix realistic and nonrealistic elements as well as techniques from both "high" and "low" art.

Preparation (1) Previous arranging of circumstances, pointing of character, and placing of properties in a production so that the ensuing actions will seem reasonable. (2) Actions taken by a performer getting ready for a performance.

Private theaters In Elizabethan England, indoor theaters.

Proagon In classical Greece, an initial event of a festival; performers and playwrights appeared in presentations intended to announce and advertise the coming plays.

Processional staging In the Middle Ages, a form of staging popular in England and Spain. Though there is much debate about how it actually worked, apparently each mystery play was set up on a wagon which moved from locale to locale within a town, so that the play would be presented separately at each stop—each audience area—along its route.

Producer In American usage, the person responsible for the business side of a production, including raising money. In British usage, a *producer* is the equivalent of an American *director.*

Proedria In ancient Greek theaters, front-row seats reserved for political and religious dignitaries.

Prologos In classical Greek drama, the opening scene which sets the action and provides the necessary background information.

Prologue Introductory speech delivered to the audience by a performer before a play begins.

Props *Properties;* objects that are used by performers onstage or are necessary to complete a set.

Proscenium Arch or frame surrounding the stage opening, like a picture frame; developed during the Italian Renaissance.

Proskenion In Hellenistic Greece, the bottom level of the skene, or stage house.

Protagonist Principal character in a play, the one whom the drama is about.

Psychological gesture According to the twentieth-century Russian acting theorist Mikhail Chekhov, a characteristic movement or activity which would sum up a character's motives and preoccupations.

Public theaters In Elizabethan England, outdoor theaters.

Pulpitum In Roman theater, a raised platform stage.

Rake To position scenery on a slant or angle other than parallel or perpendicular to the curtain line; *also,* an upward slope of the stage floor away from the audience.

Raked stage Stage which slopes upward away from the audience toward the back of the set.

Realism Broadly speaking, the attempt to present onstage people and events corresponding to those observable in everyday life.

Regional theater (1) Theater whose subject matter is specific to a particular geographic region. (2) Theaters situated outside major theatrical centers.

Régisseur Continental term for *theater director;* it usually denotes a dictatorial director.

Rejas In the Spanish golden age, windows, protected by grills and overlooking a corral, from which the play could be seen.

Repertory or repertoire Acting company which at any given time has a number of plays it can perform alternately; *also,* the plays themselves.

Restoration drama English drama after the restoration of the monarchy, from 1660 to 1700. Presented for an audience primarily of aristocrats who gathered about the court of Charles II, Restoration drama consisted largely of heroic tragedies in neoclassical style and comedies of manners which took a cynical view of human nature.

Reversal Sudden switch or turnaround of circumstances or knowledge which leads to a result contrary to expectations. Called *peripeteia* or *peripety* in Greek drama.

Revisionism In theater history, an approach based on the belief that history is usually told from the viewpoint of a social, political, or cultural elite; that it is therefore usually distorted; and that in consequence it needs to be rewritten.

Revolving stage Large turntable on which scenery is placed so that as it moves, one set turns out of sight while a new one is brought into view.

Ritual Specifically ordered, ceremonial religious event.

Romanticism Nineteenth-century literary and dramatic movement which developed as a reaction to the strictures of neoclassicism. Imitating the loose, episodic structure of Shakespeare's plays, the romantics sought to free the writer from all rules and considered the unfettered inspiration of artistic genius the source of all creativity. They laid more stress on mood and atmosphere than on content, but one of their favorite themes was the gulf between human beings' spiritual aspirations and physical limitations.

Sacra rappresentazioni "Sacred representations": in the late Middle Ages and early Renaissance, Italian religious dramas in medieval style, based on biblical stories and lives of saints.

Satire In theater, drama that uses techniques of comedy—such as wit, irony, and exaggeration—to expose and attack folly and vice.

Satyr play One of the three types of classical Greek drama. A satyr play was usually a ribald takeoff on Greek mythology and history and included a chorus of satyrs, mythological creatures who were half-man and half-goat.

Scaena In Roman theater, the stage house.

Scaena frons In Roman theater, the ornate three-dimensional facade of the stage house.

Scene (1) Stage setting. (2) One of the structural units into which a play or an act of a play is divided. (3) Location of a play's action.

School drama In the English Renaissance, plays written at the universities and presented at schools rather than to the general public.

Script Written or printed text of a play or some other theatrical representation; a script consists of dialogue, stage directions, descriptions of characters, and the like.

Secrets In medieval theater, special effects.

Semiotics In theater history, an approach based on the argument that historians need to focus on audiences' responses to elements of a production which function as signs and have a specific meaning for viewers.

Sentimental comedy In eighteenth-century England, comedy that reaffirmed middle-class morality: the virtuous characters were rewarded and the wicked punished.

Set Scenery, taken as a whole, for a scene or an entire production.

Set piece Piece of scenery which stands independently in a scene.

Shadow play Play in which the audience sees shadows of puppets or actors on a screen; developed most fully in southeast Asia.

Shareholders In Elizabethan acting troupes, members who received part of the profits as payment.

Shite In noh theater, the leading actor.

Shutters Two large flat wings that close off a perspective setting in back.

Sides An actor's own lines and cues. Elizabethan actors learned their roles from sides.

Simultaneous setting (*See* Multiple setting.)

Siparium In Roman theater, a backdrop curtain at the rear of the stage.

Skene In ancient Greek theater, the scene house behind the orchestra.

Slapstick Type of comedy or comic business which relies on ridiculous—often violent—physical activity for its humor.

Sociétaire Shareholder in a French acting troupe.

Soliloquy Speech in which a character who is alone onstage utters inner thoughts.

Sottie In the Middle Ages, a short, satirical French farce.

Spine In the Stanislavski method, the dominant desire or motivation of a character; usually thought of as an action and expressed as a verb.

Stage convention An understanding, established through custom or usage, that certain devices will be accepted or assigned specific meaning or significance on an arbitrary basis, that is, without requiring that they be natural or realistic.

Stanislavski method Set of techniques for and theories about acting which promotes a naturalistic style stressing "inner truth" as opposed to conventional theatricality.

Stationary staging In the Middle Ages, a form of staging popular on the European continent. A series of small scenic mansions were set up side by side, usually in conjunction with a large platform stage, so that all the plays of a cycle could be presented in one location.

Stock characters Stereotypical characters, usually not fully developed as unique individuals. In the Italian Renaissance, commedia dell'arte had many popular stock characters, including servants, masters, and young lovers. Modern melodrama has stock characters such as heroes and villains.

Stock set Standard setting for a locale used in every play which requires that environment.

Storm and stress An antineoclassical movement in eighteenth-century Germany which was a forerunner of romanticism.

Street theater Generic term for groups that perform in the open and attempt to relate to the needs of a specific community or neighborhood; *also*, their presentations.

Subtext Meaning and movement of a play below its surface; that which is implied but never stated. Often more important than surface activity.

Surrealism Movement attacking formalism in the arts which developed in Europe after World War I. Seeking a deeper and more profound reality than the rational or the conscious, the surrealists replaced realistic action with the strange logic of dreams and cultivated such techniques as automatic writing and free association of ideas.

Symbolism In drama, a movement of the late nineteenth and early twentieth century which sought to replace realistic representation of life with the expression of inner truth. Symbolist drama used myths, legends, and symbols in an attempt to reach beyond everyday reality; it was closely linked to symbolist poetry.

Taburetes In the Spanish golden age, a row of stools or a few benches at the front of the patio (pit) of a corral, near the stage.

Tan In Peking opera, a female role.

Tetralogy In classical Greek theater, three tragedies and one satyr play written by a single author for a festival.

Theater of cruelty Antonin Artaud's visionary concept of theater based on magic and ritual which would liberate deep, violent, erotic impulses. He wanted to reveal the cruelty which he saw as existing beneath all human action—the pervasiveness of evil and violent sexuality.

Theater of the absurd Term first used by Martin Esslin to describe the works of certain playwrights of the 1950s and 1960s who expressed a similar point of view regarding the absurdity of the human condition. In theater of the absurd, rational language is debased and replaced by clichés and trite or irrelevant remarks. Realistic psychological motivation is replaced by automatic behavior which is often absurdly inappropriate to the situation. Although the subject matter is serious, the tone of these plays is usually comic and ironic.

Theatricalism Style of production and playwriting which emphasizes theatricality for its own sake. Less a coherent movement than a quality found in the work of many artists rebelling against realism, it frankly admits the artifice of the stage and borrows freely from the circus, the music hall, and similar entertainments.

Theatron In ancient Greek theater, the seating area, carved into a hillside.

Theme Central thought of a play; the idea or ideas with which the play deals and which it expounds.

Thespian Synonym for "actor"; the term is derived from Thespis, who is said to have been the first actor in ancient Greek theater.

Thingspielen In Nazi Germany, massive propagandistic theatrical spectacles staged outdoors.

Thrust stage Platform stage surrounded on three sides by the audience.

Thymele In ancient Greek theater, the altar in the center of the orchestra.

Thyromata In Hellenistic Greece, large openings into the second story of the skene.

Tiring house In English Renaissance theater, a three-story stage house behind the platform stage.

Total theater In Asia, a synthesis or complete integration of all elements—acting, mime, music, dance, and text. Some twentieth-century avant-garde theater artists have also called for the creation of total theater.

Tragedy One of the most fundamental forms of western drama. Tragedy involves a serious action of universal significance and has important moral and philosophical implications. Following Aristotle, most critics agree that a tragic hero or heroine should be an essentially admirable person whose downfall elicits our sympathy while leaving us with a feeling that there has in some way been a triumph of the moral and cosmic order which transcends the fate of any individual. The disastrous outcome of a tragedy should be seen as the inevitable result of the character and his or her situation, including forces beyond the character's control. Traditionally, tragedy was about the lives and fortunes of people of stature—kings, queens, and the nobility—and there has been a great deal of debate about whether or not modern tragedy, tragedy about ordinary people, is possible.

Tragic flaw The factor which is a character's chief weakness and makes him or her most vulnerable; it often intensifies in time of stress. An abused and often incorrectly applied theory from Greek drama.

Tragicomedy In the Renaissance, plays that had tragic themes and noble characters yet ended happily. Modern tragicomedy combines serious and comic elements. Many plays of this type involve comic or ironic treatment of a serious theme.

Trap Opening in the stage floor, normally covered, which can be used for special effects, such as having scenery or performers rise from below, or which permits the construction of a staircase which ostensibly leads to a lower floor or cellar.

Trilogy   In classical Greece, three tragedies written by the same playwright and presented on one day; they were connected by story or thematic concerns.

Tropes   In the Early Middle Ages, lyrics added to musical passages in religious services; these interpolations were often structured like playlets and evolved into liturgical drama.

Tsure   In noh theater, a minor role.

Übermarionette   "Superpuppet": term coined by Edward Gordon Craig to describe what he considered the ideal performer—one who would allow the director to control the performance totally.

Unities   Term referring to the rule that a play should occur within one day (unity of time), in one place (unity of place), and with no action irrelevant to the plot (unity of action). Contrary to widespread opinion, Aristotle insisted only on unity of action. Certain neoclassical critics of the Renaissance insisted on all three unities.

Unit setting   Single setting, developed by Edward Gordon Craig, that can be made to represent various locales by moving basic elements and adding properties.

University wits   In the English Renaissance, university graduates and professional dramatists who wrote plays based on Roman models but incorporating some medieval elements.

Vomitoria   In Roman theater, covered-over exits.

Waki   "Explainer": in Japanese noh, the second most important character.

Well-made play   Type of play popular in the nineteenth and early twentieth century which combined apparent plausibility of incident and surface realism with a tightly constructed and contrived plot.

Wings   (1) Left and right offstage areas. (2) Narrow standing pieces of scenery, or "legs," more or less parallel to the proscenium, which form the sides of a setting.

Yard   In Elizabethan public theaters, the pit, or standing area

Zanni   In commedia dell'arte, comic male servants.

Zarzuela   In the Spanish golden age, a court entertainment; usually, a short, stylized musical drama based on mythology and with ornate scenic effects, influenced by Italian opera and intermezzi.

Zibaldoni   In the Italian Renaissance, manuscripts compiled by actors in commedia dell'arte, containing jokes, comic business, and repeated scenes and speeches; some of these manuscripts survive today.

SELECTED

BIBLIOGRAPHY

GENERAL THEATER HISTORIES

Banham, Martin (ed.), *The Cambridge Guide to the Theatre*, Updated Version, Cambridge University Press, New York, 1992.

Berthold, Margot, *A History of World Theater*, Felicia Londre (trans.), Ungar, New York, 1972.

Brandon, James R. (ed.), *Cambridge Guide to Asian Theatre*, Cambridge University Press, New York, 1993.

Brockett, Oscar, *History of the Theatre*, 6th ed., Allyn and Bacon, Boston, 1991.

———, and Robert Findlay, *Century of Innovation: A History of European and American Theatre and Drama since the Late Nineteenth Century*, 2d ed., Allyn and Bacon, Boston, 1991.

Carlson, Marvin, *Theories of the Theatre: A Historical and Critical Survey from the Greeks to the Present*, Expanded Edition, Cornell University Press, Ithaca, N.Y., 1993.

Cole, Toby, and Helen K. Chinoy (eds.), *Actors on Acting*, rev. ed., Crown, New York, 1980.

———, *Directors on Directing: A Source Book of the Modern Theatre*, Bobbs-Merrill, Indianapolis, 1976.

Gillespie, Patti P., and Kenneth M. Cameron, *Western Theatre: Revolution and Revival*, Macmillan, New York, 1984.

Hartnoll, Phyllis, and Peter Found (eds.), *The Concise Oxford Companion to the Theatre*, new ed., Oxford University Press, New York, 1993.

Leacroft, Richard, *The Development of the English Playhouse*, Cornell University Press, Ithaca, N.Y., 1973.

Londre, Felicia, *The History of World Theater: From the English Restoration to the Present*, Continuum, New York, 1991.

Nagler, Alois M., *Sources of Theatrical History*, Theatre Annual, New York, 1952.

Postlewait, Thomas, and Bruce McConachie (eds.), *Interpreting the Theatrical Past: Essays in the Historiography of Performance*, University of Iowa Press, Iowa City, 1989.

Note: This bibliography of key historical works has been selected from the many writings available in English. There is a general list, followed by a specific list for each chapter in the text; a work may be listed under more than one chapter.

Roberts, Vera M., *On Stage: A History of the Theatre*, 2d ed., Harper and Row, New York, 1974.

Watson, Jack, and Grant F. McKernie, *A Cultural History of Theatre*, Longman, New York, 1993.

Wickham, Glynne, *A History of the Theatre*, Cambridge University Press, Cambridge, 1992.

Wilmeth, Don B., and Tice L. Miller (eds.), *Cambridge Guide to American Theatre*, New York, Cambridge University Press, 1993.

INTRODUCTION

Brown, Ivor, *The First Player: The Origin of Drama*, Morrow, New York, 1928.

Hunningher, Ben, *The Origin of the Theater*, Hill and Wang, New York, 1961.

Kirby, E. T., *Ur-Drama: The Origins of Theatre*, New York University Press, New York, 1975.

Ridgeway, William, *The Drama and Dramatic Dances of Non-European Races*, Cambridge University Press, Cambridge, 1915.

Turner, Victor, *From Ritual to Theatre*, Performing Arts Journal, New York, 1982.

Wilson, Edwin, *The Theater Experience*, 6th ed., McGraw-Hill, New York, 1994.

CHAPTER 1: GREEK THEATER

Arnott, Peter D., *The Ancient Greek and Roman Theatre*, Random House, New York, 1971.

———, *Public and Performance in the Greek Theatre*, Routledge, New York, 1991.

Aylen, Leo, *The Greek Theater*, Associated University Presses, London, 1985.

Bieber, Margarete, *The History of Greek and Roman Theatre*, 2d ed., Princeton University Press, Princeton, N.J., 1961.

Butler, James H., *The Theatre and Drama of Greece and Rome*, Chandler, San Francisco, 1972.

Dearden, C. W., *The Stage of Aristophanes*, Athlone, London, 1976.

Flickinger, Roy C., *The Greek Theatre and Its Drama*, 4th ed., University of Chicago Press, Chicago, 1936.

Pickard-Cambridge, A. W., *The Dramatic Festivals of Athens*, 2d ed., John Gould and D. M. Lewis (rev.), Clarendon, Oxford, 1968.

Rehm, Rush, *Greek Tragic Theatre*, Routledge, New York, 1992.

Stone, Laura, *Costume in Aristophanic Comedy*, Arno, New York, 1981.

Vince, Ronald W., *Ancient and Medieval Theatre: A Historiographical Handbook*, Greenwood, Westport, Conn., 1984.

Walton, J. Michael, *Greek Theatre Practice*, Greenwood, Westport, Conn., 1980.

———, *Living Greek Theatre: A Handbook of Classical Performance and Modern Production*, Greenwood, Westport, Conn., 1987.

Webster, T. B. L., *Greek Theatre Production*, 2d ed., Methuen, London, 1970.

CHAPTER 2: ROMAN THEATER

Allen, James T., *Stage Antiquities of the Greeks and Romans and Their Influence*, McKay, New York, 1927.

Arnott, Peter D., *The Ancient Greek and Roman Theatre*, Random House, New York, 1971.

Beare, William, *The Roman Stage: A Short History of Latin Drama in the Time of the Republic*, Methuen, London, 1968.

Bieber, Margarete, *The History of Greek and Roman Theatre*, 2d ed., Princeton University Press, Princeton, N.J., 1961.

Butler, James H., *The Theatre and Drama of Greece and Rome*, Chandler, San Francisco, 1972.

Duckworth, George E., *The Nature of Roman Comedy*, Princeton University Press, Princeton, N.J., 1952.

Forehand, Walter E., *Terence*, Twayne, Boston, 1985.

Vince, Ronald W., *Ancient and Medieval Theatre: A Historiographical Handbook*, Greenwood, Westport, Conn., 1984.

CHAPTER 3: MEDIEVAL THEATER

Case, Sue-Ellen, "Re-Viewing Hrotsvit," *Theatre Journal,* vol. 35, December 1983, pp. 533–542.

Chambers, E. K., *The Medieval Stage,* 2 vols., Clarendon, Oxford, 1903.

Hardison, O. B., *Christian Rite and Christian Drama in the Middle Ages,* Johns Hopkins Press, Baltimore, Md., 1965.

Nagler, Alois M., *Medieval Religious Stage: Shapes and Phantoms,* Yale University Press, New Haven, 1976.

Nelson, Alan H., *The Medieval English Stage: Corpus Christi Pageants and Plays,* University of Chicago Press, Chicago, 1974.

Tyedeman, William, *English Medieval Theatre, 1400–1500,* Routledge and Kegan Paul, London, 1986.

Vince, Ronald W., *Ancient and Medieval Theatre: A Historiographical Handbook,* Greenwood, Westport, Conn., 1984.

———, *A Companion to the Medieval Theatre,* Greenwood, New York, 1989.

Wickham, Glynne, *The Medieval Theatre,* Weidenfeld and Nicolson, London, 1974.

Young, Karl, *The Drama of the Medieval Church,* 2 vols., Clarendon, Oxford, 1933.

CHAPTER 4: EARLY ASIAN THEATER

Arnott, Peter, *The Theatres of Japan,* Macmillan, New York, 1969.

Bowers, Faubion, *Theatre in the East: A Survey of Asian Dance and Drama,* Grove, New York, 1969.

Dolby, William, *A History of the Chinese Drama,* Harper and Row, New York, 1976.

Ernst, Earle, *The Kabuki Theatre,* Oxford University Press, New York, 1957.

Gargi, Balwant, *Theatre in India,* Theatre Arts, New York, 1962.

Howard, Roger, *Contemporary Chinese Theatre,* Heinemann Educational, London, 1978.

Jain, Nemi Chandra, *Indian Theatre: Tradition, Continuity, and Change,* Vikas, New Delhi, 1992.

Keene, Donald, and Kaneko Hiroshi, *No and Bunraku: Two Forms of Japanese Theatre,* Columbia University Press, New York, 1990.

Leiter, Samuel L., *The Art of Kabuki: Famous Plays in Performance,* University of California Press, Berkeley, 1979.

Ortolani, Benito, *The Japanese Theatre: From Shamanistic Ritual to Contemporary Pluralism,* E. J. Brill, New York, 1990.

Scott, A. C., *The Classical Theatre of China,* Allen and Unwin, London, 1957.

Waley, Arthur, *The No Plays of Japan,* Knopf, New York, 1922.

CHAPTER 5: THE THEATER OF THE ITALIAN RENAISSANCE

Bjurstrom, Per, *Giacomo Torelli and Baroque Stage Design,* Nationalmuseum, Stockholm, 1961.

Ducharte, Pierre, *The Italian Comedy,* R. T. Weaver (trans.), Dover, New York, 1966.

Gordon, Mel (ed. and trans.), *Lazzi: The Comic Routines of the Commedia dell'Arte,* Performing Arts Journal, New York, 1992.

Hewitt, Barnard (ed.), *The Renaissance Stage: Documents of Serlio, Sabbatini, and Furttenbach,* University of Miami Press, Coral Gables, Fla., 1958.

Mullin, Daniel C., *The Development of the Playhouse: A Survey of Architecture from the Renaissance to the Present,* University of California Press, Berkeley, 1970.

Oosting, J. Thomas, *Andrea Palladio's Teatro Olimpico,* UMI Research Press, Ann Arbor, Mich., 1981.

Richards, Kenneth, and Laura Richards, *The Commedia dell'Arte: A Documentary History,* Blackwell, New York, 1990.

Vince, Ronald W., *Renaissance Theatre: A Historiographical Handbook,* Greenwood, Westport, Conn., 1984.

CHAPTER 6: THE THEATER OF THE ENGLISH RENAISSANCE

Adams, John C., *The Globe Playhouse: Its Design and Equipment*, Barnes and Noble, New York, 1966.

Beckerman, Bernard, *Shakespeare at the Globe, 1599–1602*, Macmillan, New York, 1962.

Bentley, Gerald E., *The Profession of Player in Shakespeare's Time, 1590–1642*, Princeton University Press, Princeton, N.J., 1984.

Chambers, E. K., *The Elizabethan Stage*, 4 vols., Clarendon, Oxford, 1965.

Eccles, Christine, *The Rose Theatre*, Routledge, New York, 1990.

Gurr, Andrew, *Playgoing in Shakespeare's London*, Cambridge University Press, Cambridge, 1987.

———, *The Shakespearean Stage, 1574–1642*, Cambridge University Press, Cambridge, 1970.

———, and John Orrell, *Rebuilding Shakespeare's Globe*, Routledge, New York, 1989.

Hildy, Franklin J. (ed.), *New Issues in the Reconstruction of Shakespeare's Theatre: Proceedings of the Conference Held at the University of Georgia, February 16–18,* 1990, vol. 1., *Artists and Issues in the Theatre*, Lang, New York, 1990.

Hodges, C. W., *The Globe Restored: A Study of the Elizabethan Theatre*, Coward, McCann, and Geoghegan, New York, 1953.

Leggatt, Alexander, *Jacobean Public Theatre*, Routledge, New York, 1992.

Nagler, Alois M., *Shakespeare's Stage*, Yale University Press, New Haven, 1958.

Orrell, John, *The Human Stage: English Theatre Design, 1567–1640*, Cambridge University Press, New York, 1988.

Smith, Irwin, *Shakespeare's Blackfriar's Playhouse: Its History and Its Design*, New York University Press, New York, 1964.

Thomson, Peter, *Shakespeare's Theatre*, Routledge, New York, 1992.

Vince, Ronald W., *Renaissance Theatre: A Historiographical Handbook*, Greenwood, Westport, Conn., 1984.

CHAPTER 7: THE THEATER OF THE SPANISH GOLDEN AGE

Allen, John J., *The Reconstruction of a Spanish Golden Age Playhouse: El Corral del Principe, 1583–1744*, University Presses of Florida, Gainesville, 1983.

Crawford, J. P. W., *Spanish Drama before Lope de Vega*, Lippincott, Philadelphia, 1937.

McKendrick, Melveena, *Theatre in Spain, 1490–1700*, Cambridge University Press, Cambridge, 1989.

Shergold, N. D., *A History of the Spanish Stage from Medieval Times until the End of the Seventeenth Century*, Clarendon, Oxford, 1967.

Stoll, Anita K., and Dawn L. Smith, *The Perception of Women in Spanish Theater of the Golden Age*, Associated University Presses, Cranbury, N.J., 1991.

Vince, Ronald W., *Renaissance Theatre: A Historiographical Handbook*, Greenwood, Westport, Conn., 1984.

CHAPTER 8: FRENCH NEOCLASSICAL THEATER

Arnott, Peter D., *An Introduction to the French Theatre*, Rowman and Littlefield, Totowa, N.J., 1977.

Lawrenson, T. E., *The French Stage in the Seventeenth Century: A Study in the Advent of the Italian Order*, rev. ed., AMS, New York, 1986.

Lough, John, *Paris Theatre Audiences in the Seventeenth and Eighteenth Centuries*, Oxford University Press, Oxford, 1957.

Turnell, Martin, *The Classical Moment: Studies in Corneille, Molière, and Racine*, New Directions, New York, 1963.

Vince, Ronald W., *Renaissance Theatre: A Historiographical Handbook*, Greenwood, Westport, Conn., 1984.

Wiley, W. L., *The Early Public Theatre in France*, Harvard University Press, Cambridge, Mass., 1960.

CHAPTER 9: THE THEATER OF THE ENGLISH RESTORATION

Hotson, Leslie, *The Commonwealth and Restoration Stage*, Russell and Russell, New York, 1962.

Hume, Robert D. (ed.), *The London Theatre World, 1660–1800*, Southern Illinois University Press, Carbondale, 1980.

Kenny, Shirley Strum (ed.), *British Theatre and the Other Arts, 1660–1800*, Folger, Washington, D.C., 1984.

The London Stage, 1660–1800, 11 vols., Southern Illinois University Press, Carbondale, 1960–1968.

McCollum, John I. (ed.), *The Restoration Stage*, Houghton Mifflin, Boston, 1961.

Milhous, Judith, and Robert D. Hume, *Producible Interpretation: Eight English Plays, 1675–1707*, Southern Illinois University Press, Carbondale, 1985.

Southern, Richard, *Changeable Scenery: Its Origin and Development in the British Theatre*, Faber and Faber, London, 1952.

Summers, Montague, *The Restoration Theatre*, Macmillan, New York, 1934.

Vince, Ronald W., *Neoclassical Theatre: A Historiographical Handbook*, Greenwood, Westport, Conn., 1988.

CHAPTER 10: THEATER IN THE EIGHTEENTH CENTURY

Baur-Heinhold, Margarete, *The Baroque Theatre: A Cultural History of the Seventeenth and Eighteenth Centuries*, McGraw-Hill, New York, 1967.

Brown, Frederick, *Theater and Revolution: The Culture of the French Stage*, Viking, New York, 1980.

Bruford, W. H., *Theatre, Drama, and Audience in Goethe's Germany*, Greenwood, Westport, Conn., 1974.

Carlson, Marvin, *Goethe and the Weimar Theatre*, Cornell University Press, Ithaca, N. Y., 1978.

———, *The Italian Stage: From Goldoni to D'Annunzio*, McFarland, Jefferson, N.C., 1981.

Hughes, Leo, *The Drama's Patrons: A Study of the Eighteenth-Century London Audience*, University of Texas Press, Austin, 1971.

Nicoll, Allardyce, *The Garrick Stage*, University of Georgia Press, Athens, Ga., 1980.

Pedicord, Harry W., *The Theatrical Public in the Time of Garrick*, King's Crown, New York, 1954.

Price, Cecil, *Theatre in the Age of Garrick*, Rowman and Littlefield, Totowa, N.J., 1973.

Prudhoe, John, *The Theatre of Goethe and Schiller*, Blackwell, Oxford, 1973.

Stone, George Winchester, Jr. (ed.), *The Stage and the Page: London's "Whole Show" in the Eighteenth-Century Theatre*, University of California Press, Berkeley, 1981.

Vince, Ronald W., *Neoclassical Theatre: A Historiographical Handbook*, Greenwood, Westport, Conn., 1988.

CHAPTER 11: THEATER FROM 1800 TO 1875

Booth, Michael, *English Melodrama*, Jenkins, London, 1965.

Brown, Frederick, *Theater and Revolution: The Culture of the French Stage*, Viking, New York, 1980.

Carlson, Marvin, *The French Stage in the Nineteenth Century*, Scarecrow, Metuchen, N.J., 1972.

———, *The German Stage in the Nineteenth Century*, Scarecrow, Metuchen, N.J., 1972.

———, *The Italian Stage: From Goldoni to D'Annunzio*, McFarland, Jefferson, N.C., 1981.

Durham, Weldon B. (ed.), *American Theatre Companies, 1749–1887*, Greenwood, Westport, Conn., 1986.

Engle, Ron, and Tice L. Miller (eds.), *The American Stage: Social and Economic Issues from the Colonial Period to the Present*, Cambridge University Press, New York, 1993.

Grimstead, David, *Melodrama Unveiled: American Theatre and Culture, 1800–1850*, University of Chicago Press, Chicago, 1968.

Marshall, Herbert, and Mildred Stock, *Ira Aldridge, the Negro Tragedian*, Southern Illinois University Press, Carbondale, 1968

McConachie, Bruce, *Melodramatic Formations: American Theatre and Society, 1820–1870*, University of Iowa Press, Iowa City, 1992.

Rowell, George, *The Victorian Theatre: A Survey*, Oxford University Press, London, New York, 1956.

Vardac, A. Nicholas, *Stage to Screen: Theatrical Methods from Garrick to Griffith*, Harvard University Press, Cambridge, Mass., 1949.

CHAPTER 12: THEATER FROM 1875 TO 1915

Appia, Adolphe, *Essays, Scenarios, and Designs,* Walther R. Volbach (trans.), Richard C. Beacham (ed.), UMI Research Press, Ann Arbor, Mich., 1989.

Bentley, Eric, *The Playwright as Thinker: A Study of Drama in Modern Times,* Reynal and Hitchcock, New York, 1946.

Brown, Frederick, *Theater and Revolution: The Culture of the French Stage,* Viking, New York, 1980.

Garten, Hugh, *Modern German Drama,* Grove, New York, 1962.

Hatch, James V., and Ted Shine, *Black Theater, U.S.A.,* Free Press, New York, 1974.

Innes, Christopher, *Edward Gordon Craig,* Cambridge University Press, New York, 1983.

Isaacs, Edith J., *The Negro in the American Theatre,* Theatre Arts, New York, 1947.

Koller, Ann Marie, *The Theatre Duke: Georg II of Saxe-Meiningen and the German Stage,* Stanford University Press, Stanford, Calif., 1984.

Miller, Anna Irene, *The Independent Theatre in Europe 1887 to the Present,* Long and Smith, New York, 1931.

Mitchell, Loften, *Black Drama: The Story of the American Negro in the Theatre,* Hawthorn, New York, 1967.

Patterson, Michael, *The Revolution in the German Theatre, 1900–1933,* Routledge and Kegan Paul, London, 1981.

Roose-Evans, James, *Experimental Theatre: From Stanislavsky to Peter Brook,* Routledge and Kegan Paul, London, 1984.

Shattuck, Roger, *The Banquet Years: The Arts in France, 1885–1918,* Harcourt, Brace, New York, 1961.

Slonim, Marc, *Russian Theatre from the Empire to the Soviets,* Collier, Cleveland, 1962.

Styan, J. L., *Max Reinhardt,* Cambridge University Press, New York, 1982.

Valency, Maurice, *The Flower and the Castle: An Introduction to Modern Drama,* Macmillan, New York, 1963.

Volbach, Walther R., *Adolphe Appia, Prophet of the Modern Theatre,* Wesleyan University Press, Middletown, Conn., 1968.

Whitton, David, *Stage Directors in Modern France: Antoine to Mnouchkine,* Manchester University Press, Manchester, 1987.

CHAPTER 13: THEATER FROM 1915 TO 1945

Abramson, Doris, *Negro Playwrights in the American Theatre, 1925–1959,* Columbia University Press, New York, 1969.

Artaud, Antonin, *The Theatre and Its Double,* M. C. Richards (trans.), Grove, New York, 1958.

Brecht, Bertolt, *Brecht on Theatre,* John Willett (trans.), Hill and Wang, New York, 1964.

Carter, Huntly, *The New Spirit in the European Theatre, 1914–1924,* Doran, New York, 1926.

Clunes, Alec, *The British Theatre,* Cassell, London, 1964.

Goldberg, RoseLee, *Performance Art: From Futurism to the Present,* Abrams, New York, 1988.

Hatch, James V., and Ted Shine, *Black Theater, U.S.A.,* Free Press, New York, 1974.

Houghton, Norris, *Moscow Rehearsals,* Harcourt, Brace, New York, 1936.

Isaacs, Edith J., *The Negro in the American Theatre,* Theatre Arts, New York, 1947.

Mitchell, Loften, *Black Drama: The Story of the American Negro in the Theatre,* Hawthorn, New York, 1967.

Patterson, Michael, *The Revolution in the German Theatre, 1900–1933,* Routledge and Kegan Paul, London, 1981.

Rabkin, Gerald, *Drama and Commitment: Politics in the American Theatre of the Thirties,* Indiana University Press, Bloomington, 1964.

Roose-Evans, James, *Experimental Theatre: From Stanislavsky to Peter Brook,* Routledge and Kegan Paul, London, 1984.

Rudlin, John, *Jacques Copeau,* Cambridge University Press, New York, 1986.

Whitton, David, *Stage Directors in Modern France: Antoine to Mnouchkine,* Manchester University Press, Manchester, 1987.

Willett, John, *Expressionism,* McGraw-Hill, New York, 1970.

CHAPTER 14: THEATER FROM 1945 TO 1970

Abramson, Doris, *Negro Playwrights in the American Theatre, 1925–1959*, Columbia University Press, New York, 1969.

Bigsby, C. W. E., *Modern American Drama, 1945–1990*, Cambridge University Press, New York, 1992.

Brook, Peter, *The Empty Space*, Atheneum, New York, 1982.

Cohn, Ruby, *Currents in Contemporary Drama*, Indiana University Press, Bloomington, 1969.

Esslin, Martin, *The Theatre of the Absurd*, Anchor, Garden City, New York, 1969.

Grotowski, Jerzy, *Towards a Poor Theatre*, Simon and Schuster, New York, 1969.

Hatch, James V., and Ted Shine, *Black Theater, U.S.A.*, Free Press, New York, 1974.

Kolin, Philip C. (ed.), *American Playwrights since 1945: A Guide to Scholarship, Criticism, and Performance*, Greenwood, Westport, Conn., 1989.

Mitchell, Loften, *Black Drama: The Story of the American Negro in the Theatre*, Hawthorn, New York, 1967.

Poggi, Jack, *Theater in America: The Impact of Economic Forces, 1870–1967*, Cornell University Press, Ithaca, N.Y., 1968.

Schechner, Richard, *Public Domain: Essays on the Theatre*, Discus, New York, 1970.

Svoboda, Josef, *The Secret of Theatrical Space: The Memoirs of Josef Svoboda*, Jarka Burian (trans.), Applause, New York, 1993.

Weales, Gerald, *American Drama since World War II*, Harcourt, Brace, and World, New York, 1962.

Whitton, David, *Stage Directors in Modern France: Antoine to Mnouchkine*, Manchester University Press, Manchester, 1987.

CHAPTER 15: CONTEMPORARY THEATER: 1970 TO THE PRESENT

Bigsby, C. W. E., *Modern American Drama, 1945–1990*, Cambridge University Press, New York, 1992.

Calandra, Denis, *New German Dramatists: A Study of Peter Handke, Rainer Werner Fassbinder, Heiner Müller, Thomas Bernhard*, Macmillan, New York, 1983.

Goldberg, RoseLee, *Performance Art: From Futurism to the Present*, Abrams, New York, 1988.

Kantor, Tadeusz, *A Journey through Other Spaces: Essays and Manifestos, 1944–1990*, Michal Kobialka (trans.), University of California Press, Berkeley, 1993.

Kolin, Philip C. (ed.), *American Playwrights since 1945: A Guide to Scholarship, Criticism, and Performance*, Greenwood, Westport, Conn., 1989.

Marranca, Bonnie, *The Theatre of Images*, Drama Book Specialists, New York, 1977.

Mottram, Ron, *Inner Landscapes: The Theatre of Sam Shepard*, University of Missouri Press, Columbia, 1984.

Patterson, Michael, *Peter Stein: Germany's Leading Theatre Director*, Cambridge University Press, New York, 1981.

Savran, David, *The Wooster Group, 1975–1985: Breaking the Rules*, UMI Research Press, Ann Arbor, Mich., 1986.

Shyer, Laurence, *Robert Wilson and His Collaborators*, Theatre Communications Group, New York, 1989.

Whitton, David, *Stage Directors in Modern France: Antoine to Mnouchkine*, Manchester University Press, Manchester, 1987.

Williams, Mance, *Black Theatre in the 1960s and 1970s*, Greenwood, Westport, Conn., 1985.

INDEX

Note: (illus.) indicates an illustration; (n.) indicates a note.

Spanish theater during world wars, 413–415, 421
Spanish Tragedy, The (Kyd), 172, 177
Special effects, 49, 100–101, 140, 151, 164, 168, 214, 240–241, 326, 345, 348
Spectacles, 271, 286, 326, 347–348, 420
Spectateurs sur le Théâtre, Les (Jullien), 240 (illus.)
Speed-the-Plow (Mamet), 485
Spic-o-rama (Leguizamo), 499
Spine, 375, 514
Spirit House Movers and Players (Newark, N.J.), 470
Spirit of Laws, The (Montesquieu), 281
Split Britches, 479
Spoken decor, 220
Spoken drama, 395
Spring, John R., 273
Spring's Awakening (Wedekind), 377
Spunk (Wolfe), 502
Spurt of Blood (Artaud), 406
Stafford-Clark, Max, 455
Stage convention, 514
Stage Directions (Gielgud), 420
Stage house, 57, 74 (illus.)–75 (illus.)
Stagecraft, 98, 100–101, 126, 133, 220, 232, 241, 249, 294 (illus.), 307 (illus.), 370, 386, 406, 413, 451, 498
Stalin, Josef, 255, 401, 406, 420–421
Stalin Peace Prize, 433
Stallone, Sylvester, 324
Stanislavski, Konstantin Sergeivich, 351, 357–358, 366 (illus.), 371–375, 386
Stanislavski method, 374–375, 383, 387, 406, 408, 427–428, 449, 484, 514
Star system, 249, 282, 320, 328, 330, 341, 382–383
Star Wars, 326
States of Shock (Shepard), 484
Station plays, 102, 402
Stationary staging, 98, 100–101, 514
Steele, Richard, 262
Stein, Gertrude, 464
Stein, Joseph, 461, 488
Stein, Peter, 494–495
Stella Adler Theater Studio (New York), 428
Steppenwolf Theater (Chicago), 476, 483, 500–501 (illus.)
Stereotypes, 149, 326, 333–334
Stevedore, 433
Stevens, Thomas Wood, 430
Stewart, Ellen, 464, 466, 494, 496
Stichomythic language, 444, 486
Sticks and Bones (Rabe), 466

Still Life (Mann), 440
Sting, The, 391
Stock characters, 51, 65, 67, 73, 139 (illus.)–140, 150, 153–155, 237, 260, 263, 322, 324, 514
Stock companies, 391–392, 430
Stock set, 514
Stone, John Augustus, 326
Stoppard, Tom, 2, 487
Storey, David, 367
Storm and stress (Sturm und Drang), 288, 309, 323, 514
Story of the Lime Pen, The, 118
Storytelling, 2–3, 29, 499
Stowe, Harriet Beecher, 17, 147, 313–314, 394
Strange Interlude (O'Neill), 424
Stranger, The (Pixérécourt), 289
Stranitzky, Joseph Anton, 293
Strasberg, Lee, 386, 427–428
Stratford Memorial Theater, 447
Stratford Shakespeare Festival (Canada), 251 (illus.)
Stratford Theater (Ontario, Canada), 417
Stratton, Charles, 319
Streamers (Rabe), 440, 466
Street pageant, 106
Street theater, 514
Streetcar Named Desire, A (Williams), 452, 454, 479
Strehler, Giorgio, 456
Strindberg, August, 39, 355, 362, 375–379, 387, 407, 464
String of Pearls, The (Pitt), 325
Stuart, Mary (Mary, queen of Scots), 175
Sturm und Drang (storm and stress), 288, 309, 323, 514
Styan, J. L., 197
Subject matter, human, 12
Subject Was Roses, The (Gilroy), 451
Subscription companies, 367, 369
Subtext, 515
Successful Life of 3, The: A Skit for Vaudeville (Fornes), 480
Suetonius, 66
Suffragist movement, 359
Suicide, The (Erdman), 421
Sullivan, Arthur, 466
Sullivan Street Playhouse (New York), 1
Summer and Smoke (Williams), 454, 461–462 (illus.)
Sunday in the Park with George (Sondheim), 488
Sunset Boulevard (Webber), 488
Sunshine Boys, The (Simon), 460
Supernatural characters, 69, 176–177, 182, 216, 232, 323

Superobjective, 375
"Supper Time," 431
Suppliants, The (Aeschylus), 33
Suppliants, The (Euripides), 35
Suppositi, I (The Counterfeits) (Ariosto), 144
Surinam, or A Slave's Revenge, 331
Surprise Love, The (Marivaux), 287
Surrealism, 355, 362, 378, 402, 405, 451, 492 (illus.), 515
Susan Smith Blackburn Prize, 487
Suzuki, Tadashi, 471
Svoboda, Josef, 458–459
Swamp Dwellers, The (Soyinka), 486
Swan Theater (London), 185 (illus.)–186, 190–192
Swashbuckler films, 326
Swedish Academy, 379
Sweeney Todd (Sondheim and Wheeler), 148, 325
Sweet Bird of Youth (Williams), 454
Sweet Charity, 488
Sweet Mama Stringbean (Ethel Waters), 392, 430–431
Swift, Jonathan, 262
Swimming to Cambodia (Gray), 499
Symbolism, 111, 113, 349–350 (illus.), 355, 357 (illus.), 362–364, 376–379, 383, 402, 480, 515
Symphony of Rats (Foreman), 493
Symposium (Plato), 44
Syndicate, 388
Synge, John Millington, 379
Synthetic theater, 404

Taburetes (benches), 209, 217, 515
Taganka Theater (Soviet Union), 495
Tagore, Debendranath, 393
Tagore, Rabindranath, 393
Tairov, Alexander, 374, 385–386, 401
Take a Giant Step (Patterson), 467
"Taking a Chance on Love," 430
Tale of Genji, The (Murasaki), 125
Tale of the Heike, The, 125–126
Talley's Folly (Wilson), 482
Talma, François Joseph, 242, 333–334 (illus.)
Tambo (in minstrel show), 318
Tamburlaine the Great, Parts I and II (Marlowe), 179
Taming of the Shrew (Shakespeare), 199, 419, 460
Tan (female roles), 350–351, 515
Tang dynasty, 117, 123
Tango Palace (Fornes), 481
Tannhäuser (Wagner), 339
Tarahumara Indians, 407
Tartuffe (Molière), 227–228, 237–238, 246, 277